CORRECTION CODE AND SYMBOLS

S0-ARK-652

The Little, Brown Handbook

Instructor's Annotated Edition

The Little, Brown Handbook

Fifth Edition

Instructor's Annotated Edition

H. Ramsey Fowler   *Memphis State University*

Jane E. Aaron   *Parsons School of Design/*
The New School for Social Research

Kay Limburg   *Montgomery College at Rockville*

HarperCollins*Publishers*

Acknowledgments

In the sections on working with and documenting sources for the research paper, the majority of the resources and ideas are drawn from James E. Ford et al., "Research Paper Instruction: Comprehensive Bibliography of Periodical Sources, 1923–1980," *Bulletin of Bibliography* 39 (1982): 84–98. Throughout the text, resources and ideas have been adapted from the Educational Research Information Center (ERIC) database.

Sponsoring Editor: Patricia Rossi
Development Editor: Marisa L. L'Heureux
Project Editor: Robert Ginsberg
Design Supervisor: Jaye Zimet
Text and Cover Design: Brand X Studios/Robin Hessel Hoffmann
Production Administrator: Beth Maglione/Kathleen Donnelly
Compositor: The Clarinda Company
Printer and Binder: R. R. Donnelley & Sons Company
Cover Printer: The Lehigh Press, Inc.

Instructor's Annotated Edition/The Little, Brown Handbook, Fifth Edition
Copyright © 1992 by HarperCollins Publishers Inc.

ISBN 0-673-52132-X (student edition)
ISBN 0-673-52203-2 (teacher edition)

91 92 93 94 9 8 7 6 5 4 3 2 1

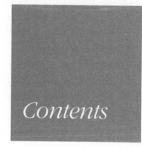

Contents

Designing and Teaching Composition Courses

These chapters appear only in this *Instructor's Annotated Edition.*

Brief Contents of the Student Edition

The complete student edition of *The Little, Brown Handbook,* Fifth Edition, with its detailed table of contents, follows the four chapters appearing only in this instructor's edition.

The annotations in the margins of this instructor's edition—which include answers to the exercises and tips for presenting the material—do not appear in the student edition.

v

The Little, Brown Handbook

Instructor's Annotated Edition

Designing and Teaching Composition Courses

Chapter 1

*Teaching Writing:
Process
and Beyond*

Writing: A process

Drawing on the results of two decades of careful research on the composing process of novice and professional writers, most writing instructors emphasize the *how* of writing. Instructors are helping their students become aware of the various stages of the writing process:

- strategies for discovering
- planning
- drafting
- revising

This approach is a reaction against teaching that places inordinate attention on the form of the essay. Rather, it emphasizes ideas, audience, self-discovery, and self-expression.

A difficulty for students and instructors in process-oriented instruction is keeping the focus on process while adapting form for varying audiences and purposes. Fortunately, studies of the social contexts for writing and programs of writing across the curriculum have both contributed to a renewed interest in forms of expression and led to greater understanding of readers' expectations and needs.

Most composition instructors who accept the key assumptions of the process approach emphasize flexibility in the composing process, particularly as they attend to the forms of writing. As the introductory chapters and the handbook make plain, *The Little, Brown Handbook,* Fifth Edition, is designed to alert students to the processes and also to the forms of written expression. The blending of flexibility with firm, concrete advice that characterizes the handbook is highlighted in the *Annotated Instructor's Edition* to enable beginning and experienced instructors to draw on the text's resources in designing and teaching a composition course.

 ## Assumptions about the process paradigm

It would be foolish to suggest that all composition instructors who emphasize the composing process are in agreement over specific teaching strategies—or that they ought to be. Two teachers who share a belief in the importance of revision or who encourage students to discover ideas and information through freewriting may also disagree strongly about the purposes for writing:

- Personal focus: Personal discovery
  Self-expression
- Social focus: Argument
  Academic discourse

Yet it is possible to identify some generally agreed-upon elements of a process paradigm. Eminent researchers and theorists have brought to our attention skilled and unskilled writers (Emig, *Composing;* Perl; Sommers, "Revision"); cognitive models of the composing process (Flower and Hayes); arguments about primacy of personal discourse and its relationship to expository and persuasive discourse (Britton; Moffett); and process-oriented teaching strategies (Murray; Sommers, "Responding").

 ## Assumptions shaping *The Little, Brown Handbook*

The process paradigm of *The Little, Brown Handbook* is based on the following assumptions:

- Writing consists of a variety of activities including developing (exploring, gathering, focusing, organizing); drafting (finding and expressing meaning, establishing relationships); and revising (rethinking, rewriting, editing, proofreading).
- The activities that make up the writing process are recursive, not fixed in order. For example, revising often includes the discovery of fresh insights, and the drafting of one part of a paper may occur at the same time the writer is gathering materials for another part.
- Writing often is a process of discovering ideas, arriving at knowledge of the self, and selecting effective ways to present concepts and information.
- Knowledge of the conventions of expression and of stylistic options is an important part of the writer's repertoire, but a premature striving for correctness and for grace and clarity often can impede the free flow of ideas and the discovery of appropriate form. Thus, activities like editing and proofreading, which pay con-

siderable attention to style, grammar, and mechanics, are generally best left until relatively late in the composing of an essay.

- Skilled writers (in contrast to unskilled writers) are characterized by the range of strategies they know and employ in developing, drafting, and revising—strategies that can be both taught and learned.
- Effective writing is the product of interaction among the three elements of the writing situation: author, subject, and audience.

These assumptions shape the advice offered throughout *The Little, Brown Handbook,* not only in discussions of the writing process and the whole paper (Part I), but also in treatments of the research paper and writing in the disciplines (Part VIII) and in the treatment of strategies for clear and effective sentences (Parts III and IV). Even the discussions of grammatical sentences (Part II), punctuation (Part V), and mechanics (Part VI) mix firm and relatively conservative advice with an awareness of the demands of various audiences and of the difference between an early draft and a final, carefully edited draft.

At the same time, however, discussions in the handbook point out that different writing situations may call for different composing processes and that the knowledge of forms for expression—the *what* of writing—is an important companion to an awareness of the *how*. In this, the handbook agrees with the work of such theorists and teachers as Maxine Hairston, James Reither, Patricia Bizzell, Richard Coe, and Arthur Applebee. These writers share a belief that the process paradigm needs to be augmented by

- An awareness of the ways the writing process varies according to the writer's purpose and the social context
- A recognition of the important roles knowledge of form and convention can play in guiding the composing process
- An acknowledgment of the extent to which communities of readers and writers are bound together by specific expectations governing the form and content of discourse

 ## The post-process approach to writing instruction

While the outlines of a post-process approach to writing instruction are still a matter of considerable debate, several areas of broad agreement have emerged, and these are reflected in the current edition of *The Little, Brown Handbook.*

As Maxine Hairston points out in "Different Products, Different Processes: A Theory About Writing," writing situations may call for contrasting composing processes and varying sorts of knowledge. Some tasks such as technical reports or routine memoranda may be conventional in form and draw on knowledge the writer has already mastered, but at the same time they may pose stylistic challenges in adapting to the needs and attitudes of a particular audience. Other kinds of prose, such as much scholarly writing and nonroutine professional or personal writing, may require originality in content and expression and require extensive discovery and revision.

The handbook recognizes that the processes of composing are "strategies that writers employ for particular purposes" (Applebee 106) and emphasizes this perspective in

- The initial treatment of composing (Chapters 1 and 2)
- The discussions of commonly used rhetorical patterns and specialized forms of writing:
  — Paragraphing (Chapter 3)
  — Critical thinking and writing (Chapter 4)
  — Argument (Chapter 4)
  — The research paper (Chapters 35–38)
  — Writing in the academic disciplines (Chapter 39)
  — Writing essay exams (Chapter 40)
  — Writing business letters and memoranda (Chapter 41)

The emphasis throughout is on (1) seeing the forms as the shared expectations of readers and writers and (2) using these expectations to guide the discovery and expression of ideas so as not to constrain creativity.

The treatment of conventions of thought and expression in Chapter 39 may be particularly interesting and useful for both instructors and students because of what it reveals about the social and generative roles of rhetorical form in academic settings.

Ultimately, however, the roles that form plays in composing will depend on the willingness of instructors and students to regard rhetorical patterns as flexible frameworks rather than as rigid formulas—as essential parts of a creative composing process.

 Resources for teaching writing

Applebee, Arthur N. "Problems in Process Approaches: Toward a Reconceptualization of Process Instruction." In *The Teaching of Writing*. Chicago: National Society for the Study of Education, 1986. 95–113.

Beach, Richard, and Lillian S. Bridwell, eds. *New Directions in Composition Research*. New York: Guilford, 1984.

Bizzell, Patricia. "Beyond Anti-Foundationalism to Rhetorical Authority: Problems Defining 'Cultural Literacy.'" *College English* 52 (1990): 661–75.

---. "College Composition: Initiation into the Academic Discourse Community." *Curriculum Inquiry* 12 (1982): 191–207.

Britton, James, et al. *The Development of Writing Abilities* (11–18). London: Macmillan, 1975.

Coe, Richard M. "An Apology for Form; or, Who Took the Form Out of the Process?" *College English* 49 (1987): 13–28.

Cooper, Charles R., and Lee Odell, eds. *Research on Composing: Points of Departure*. Urbana: NCTE, 1978.

D'Angelo, Frank J. *A Conceptual Theory of Rhetoric.* Cambridge, MA: Winthrop, 1975.

Elbow, Peter. "Reflections on Academic Discourse: How It Relates to Freshmen and Colleagues." *College English* 53 (1991): 135–55.

Emig, Janet. *The Composing Processes of Twelfth Graders.* Urbana: NCTE, 1971.

---. *The Web of Meaning.* Upper Montclair: Boynton/Cook, 1983.

Faigley, Lester. "Competing Theories of Process: A Critique and a Proposal." *College English* 48 (1986): 527–42.

Flower, Linda, and John R. Hayes. "A Cognitive Process Theory of Writing." *College Composition and Communication* 32 (1981): 365–87.

---. "The Construction of Purpose in Writing and Reading." *College English* 50 (1988): 528–50.

Hairston, Maxine. "Different Products, Different Processes: A Theory About Writing," *College Composition and Communication* 37 (1986): 442–52.

Knoblauch, C. H., and Lil Brannon. *Rhetorical Traditions and the Teaching of Writing.* Upper Montclair: Boynton/Cook, 1984.

Moffett, James. *Teaching the Universe of Discourse.* Boston: Houghton Mifflin, 1968.

Murray, Donald M. *A Writer Teaches Writing.* 2nd ed. Boston: Houghton Mifflin, 1985.

Perl, Sondra. "The Composing Process of Unskilled College Writers." *College Composition and Communication* 31 (1980): 389–401.

Perelman, Les. "The Context of Classroom Writing." *College English* 48 (1986): 471–79.

Reither, James A. "Writing and Knowing: Toward Redefining the Writing Process." *College English* 47 (1985): 620–28.

Rose, Mike. "Rigid Rules, Inflexible Plans, and the Stifling of Language: A Cognitivist Analysis of Writer's Block." *College Composition and Communication* 31 (1980): 389–401.

Sommers, Nancy. "Responding to Student Writing." *College Composition and Communication* (1982): 148–56.

---. "Revision Strategies of Student Writers and Experienced Adult Writers." *College Composition and Communication* 31 (1980): 378–88.

Tirrell, Mary Kay, et al. "Re-Presenting James Britton: A Symposium." *College Composition and Communication* 41 (1990): 166–86.

Chapter 2

The Handbook in Composition Courses

The students and their work are at the center of the process-oriented composition course. The majority of their time spent together involves

- Exploring and discovering topics
- Drafting their own essays
- Responding to each other's writing
- Revising their own essays
- Editing

Instructors and textbooks are aids in process-oriented composition courses and do not dominate.

Because of its flexibility, *The Little, Brown Handbook* can be a valuable resource in organizing the composition course. Almost as many ways to organize a composition course exist as there are processes involved in the many different kinds of reading and writing tasks expected of students.

The complex act of writing involves the abilities

- To discover and organize ideas
- To reach a compromise between the aims of personal expression and the needs of an audience
- To produce readable sentences and paragraphs

In their reading, students are generally expected to be familiar with texts likewise complex and diverse, whether persuasive, informative, expressive, or academic. The students' complex tasks of writing and reading present the composition instructor with a wide range of options in deciding how to structure a course and what to emphasize. This section suggests possible uses of *The Little, Brown Handbook* with a variety of organizations and emphases.

 ## Organizing a composition course

Organizing a composition course means choosing to emphasize those aspects of writing or kinds of texts that the instructor or the department considers most important and that meet the students' needs. In recent years, composition teaching has followed several general patterns for organizing a course, including emphasis on

- Patterns of expression and thought
- The writing process
- Content and ideas
- Genres of nonfiction
- Academic writing (writing across the curriculum)

Each approach can be successful if it meets the needs of a particular group of students and if the instructor pays some attention to all aspects of composing.

 ## Emphasis on patterns of expression and thought

Many instructors believe that a composition course ought to give students a chance to understand and practice basic patterns of expression and thought. Such courses may vary widely in the patterns they emphasize:

- Rhetorical and logical patterns, such as classification, comparison-contrast, and deduction
- General essay structures, such as thesis and support or general to specific
- Types of essays, such as informative and argumentative
- Patterns of paragraph development
- Sentence patterns

Basic writing courses

Assumption and focus

By understanding and mastering the elements of a finished essay, students will be able to improve their writing.

Instructors who choose this approach generally argue that the basic sentence pattern of subject + assertion and the standard paragraph pattern of subject + assertion + support are simply smaller versions of the thesis + support pattern of whole essays and the assertion + support pattern of thought characteristic of much expository writing, particularly in academic settings. Thus, skills courses not only try to break the task of academic writing into manageable units but also help introduce patterns of thought essential to success in college courses. The course begins with sentence and paragraph construction, moving to the whole essay only after students have mastered different kinds of paragraphs.

Organizing the course

In organizing a skills course, you might begin with a unit on sentence structure, drawing on Chapters 5–9 of the handbook ("Grammatical Sentences"), and you might stress an understanding of phrases, clauses, basic sentence types, and verb forms and tenses. Along with this, or beginning later in the semester if appropriate, you might require paragraph-length writing and make use of the extensive discussion in Chapter 3 ("Composing Paragraphs"). Paragraph-length writing can continue through the semester, accompanied by work in Chapters 10–15 ("Clear Sentences") and 16–19 ("Effective Sentences"). Chapters on punctuation, mechanics, diction, and usage can be assigned whenever they meet the needs of the class or of individual students.

Teaching suggestions

Start paragraphs as early in the semester as possible to give students a sense of accomplishment and a chance to put into practice what they are learning in the sentence units. Also early on, you can incorporate essay-length writings into the course by requiring students to keep a writing journal with a specific number of pages to be devoted to a single topic at least once a week. You can integrate the journals into the class work by having them serve as topics for the students' paragraph and sentence constructions.

Other considerations

Although an effective basic course, often planned for developmental students, can focus on sentence, paragraph, and essay patterns, it also needs to pay attention to the writing process and to audience (see Chapters 1, 2, and 4 in the handbook). Students who have trouble mastering the basic forms of expression are also likely to underestimate the importance of planning and revising and to have difficulty shaping their writing to the needs of an audience. These matters need to be covered and reinforced throughout the course through assignments that require planning, drafting, and revising and also create realistic audiences and situations for students to address in their writing.

Rhetorically oriented courses

Assumption and focus

Patterns of expression can also be ways of viewing experience.
The course is rhetorically oriented:

- Basic essay types (narration, description, exposition, argument)
- Patterns of development (classification, analysis, comparison-contrast, and so on)
- Specific essay types (forms of argument, forms of exposition)

Patterns of development may be introduced as a means of probing subjects and developing and organizing essays. Regardless of their focus, instructors who use a rhetorical approach share the belief that students who have understood these patterns and practiced them in their writing will be able to make use of them in a variety of writing tasks. Most of these instructors would also agree that each pattern of development directs attention to a different aspect of a subject and thus the patterns can be seen as shaping the way we think about a subject and as affecting a reader's attitudes. Instructors of rhetorically oriented courses often rely on a reader or rhetoric to provide examples of essay types and patterns of development.

Organizing the course

If you wish to give your course a rhetorical orientation, you may want to begin with Chapters 1–4 of the handbook ("The Whole Paper and Paragraphs") as a way of showing students how to develop, write, revise, and edit an essay and to adapt it to an audience. Later in the course, you may want to return to this material to remind students how important are the stages of the writing process, particularly planning and revising. You can also point out that Chapters 1 and 3 treat the rhetorical patterns as answers to questions about aspects of a topic, as well as ways of organizing and developing essays and paragraphs. The main portion of the course might consist of a review of essay types or patterns of essay and paragraph development (Chapters 1–3) with assignments that give students a chance to use the forms. The chapters on coordination and subordination, parallelism, sentence emphasis, and variety (Chapters 16–19, "Effective Sentences") can be introduced later in the course to add variety and style to students' writing. The chapters on common sentence errors, punctuation, mechanics, diction, and usage can be assigned according to the needs of individuals or of the class and may also be used for reference. The course might culminate in a research paper (Chapters 35–38) or essay questions and business writing (Chapters 40–41).

Teaching suggestions

The risk in a rhetorically oriented course is that students will come to regard the various forms as ends in themselves and ignore the role they play in viewing experience and in shaping communication to an audience or situation. For this reason, many instructors emphasize throughout the course the process of exploring subjects and revising the plan for an essay, and they try to create specific audiences and situations for students to address in their writing.

 Emphasis on the writing process

Assumption and focus

Process-oriented writing enables students to respond effectively to future writing tasks.

In the course,

- Students are taught to respond to writing situations with a full awareness of the importance of each activity in the writing process: discovering, focusing, planning, drafting, revising, and editing.
- Students are given the opportunity to adapt the process to the demands of different kinds of writing.

- Forms of expression are presented as strategies best learned in the context of a particular writing task.
- Grammar, punctuation, and mechanics are learned most readily when necessary for effective communication in an essay.

Organizing the course

In organizing a course that emphasizes the writing process, you might begin by having students look over the discussion of the process in the handbook (Chapters 1 and 2, "Developing an Essay" and "Drafting and Revising the Essay"). You will have to briefly review the writing process as part of each assignment, both to remind students that each of the elements of composing is important and to show how the kinds of planning and revising a writer must do will vary slightly depending on the subject, the aim of the writing task, and the audience for the essay. You may wish to start the course with personal writing because it turns attention inward and often makes students aware of how their minds operate as they write. When you move to more public kinds of writing, however, Chapter 4 (section g, "Reaching Your Readers") will help alert students to the need to take their readers into account as they shape what they have to say and decide how to say it.

Teaching suggestions

Assignments in a process-oriented course should stress planning and revising in all writing tasks and also suggest writing strategies that students can use to deal with a subject and meet the needs of a reader.

If the assigned essay requires particular attention to paragraphing—a persuasive paper, for example—then students might be required to look at Chapter 3 ("Composing Paragraphs"). Chapters 16–19 ("Effective Sentences") will also help introduce students to useful strategies, and Chapters 35–39 ("Research Writing") and Chapters 40–41 ("Practical Writing") can be good resources when students are asked to write academic papers or memos directed at a business or professional audience. Coverage of matters of grammar, punctuation, diction, and usage will depend on the needs of the class and of individual students.

Since many problems in student writing can be traced to a lack of effective planning or revising, a composition course that emphasizes process can have a significant effect on student writing. But students need to be aware that word choice, sentence structure, paragraph development, and essay organization also contribute to the effectiveness of writing. Therefore a course that emphasizes the writing process needs to introduce students to the options and to their usefulness in communicating the writer's purpose to an audience.

 Emphasis on content and ideas (thematic courses)

Assumption and focus

The best kind of writing grows out of a strong need to communicate, and students are most likely to desire to communicate when they are exposed to significant ideas and issues.

The course focuses on ideas and issues, whether personal (family life, education, social relationships) or public policy (the environment, pornography, the American legal system). The source for content may be an anthology, a lecture series, films, or the students' own research and experience.

Organizing the course

Since instructors who teach such courses generally consider a piece of writing important for what the writer has to say, they cover the forms of writing and the writing process primarily to help students communicate ideas and feelings clearly and effectively. If you choose to emphasize the content of essays in your composition course, you may wish to begin by introducing students to the writing process and the basic forms of the essay with Chapters 1–4 ("The Whole Paper and Paragraphs"). These chapters suggest ways students can develop their ideas and organize them into paragraphs and whole essays.

Teaching suggestions

As students struggle to express their ideas, you may wish to assign Chapters 31–34 ("Effective Words") to help them communicate more precisely and Chapters 16–19 ("Effective Sentences") to help them add variety, clarity, and style to their writing. Chapters on punctuation, mechanics, grammar, and usage can be assigned to the class or to individual students according to need. If students are required to use research in their writing, Chapters 35–38 ("Research Writing") will be helpful.

 ## Emphasis on genres of nonfiction

Assumptions and focus

Some instructors may take a dim view of patterns like comparison and contrast and cause and effect as strategies for whole essays because the patterns do not represent widely used types of writing and because most good writing combines patterns to suit its purposes. Many of these instructors would point out that while writers employ comparison and contrast in evaluating a product or performance and use cause and effect in analyzing a problem, the patterns that actually guide their composing are genres of nonfiction.

The course focuses on nonfiction genres—evaluation, autobiography, problem-solution, explanation, issue analysis, the proposal, the position paper—which grow out of the practices of many writers and the demands of common writing situations. These nonfiction genres represent, moreover, the expectations that readers use as guides when they encounter a text. The genres of nonfiction are not fixed forms any more than the genres of literature are. Yet they are a valuable part of any writer's knowledge and can offer students fresh perspectives on a topic or a social situation, particularly one that requires students to take the role of knower or persuader.

Organizing the course

Courses emphasizing the genres of nonfiction generally provide students with examples in the form of readings or ask students to locate and identify different kinds of writing on their own. Chapter 4 of the handbook ("Critical Thinking and Argument"), particularly 4a ("Thinking and Reading Critically") and 4c ("Reading Arguments Critically"), can help students develop analytical skills important for examining and constructing different kinds of writing. The attention paid to audience and the needs of readers in Chapters 1 and 2 should also be of help in developing the skills and awareness necessary to understanding the range and uses of different kinds of nonfiction. Much nonfiction is based on research, and the extensive treatment of research papers in the handbook (Chapters 35–38) introduces students to some of the many different kinds of writing with sources. In addition, Chapter 39 ("Writing in the Disciplines") looks at the many forms of academic writing.

Teaching suggestions

The attention to form in courses of this kind needs to be balanced with an attention to process, particularly to revision. The advice given on using the handbook in process-oriented courses (pp. IAE 10–11) is appropriate here, as are the many resources the handbook offers for achieving correctness and variety in writing.

 Emphasis on academic writing

Writing across the curriculum in a writing course

Chapter 39 of the handbook, "Writing in the Disciplines," covers much of the territory appropriate for a course emphasizing *writing across the curriculum*. Such a course may ask students to write papers in each of the areas covered by the chapter—the humanities, the social sciences, and the natural and applied sciences—and may ask students to become acquainted with the research tools in each area (also discussed in detail in Chapter 39). The treatment of the writing process in Chapters 1 and 2, of paragraphing in Chapter 3, of critical thinking and writing in Chapter 4, and of the varieties of sentence structure in Chapters 16–19 can also be important elements of a course built around the varieties of academic writing.

Writing across the curriculum in the disciplines

In many writing-across-the-curriculum programs, writing instruction is part of content courses, employed both as a tool for learning and as a way of sharing knowledge in forms appropriate to a discipline. Because it is designed as a reference tool and therefore does not impose a particular design on a course, the handbook can be a useful resource for content courses emphasizing writing. It provides discussions of the writing process and of research and documentation in specific disciplines as well as resources for editing style, grammar, and mechanics. Whatever the particular uses of writing in a course, the handbook's advice about the process of writing (Chapters 1 and 2) is likely to prove valuable.

 Using the handbook with other texts

Although the handbook can be used as the only text in a course, many instructors also adopt a reader, a rhetoric, or a workbook like *The Little, Brown Workbook*. Each kind of text enables you to emphasize different elements of the course and also provides activities to help students develop their writing.

 Readers

Readers are generally of three kinds: rhetorical, thematic, or cross-curricular.

Rhetorical readers

Rhetorical readers illustrate the different aims and patterns of writing with selections by professional authors and sometimes by students. Readers of this type frequently begin with writing patterns that students find most accessible—narration, description, exemplification—and move on to patterns that students find more difficult to use—classification, comparison-contrast, inductive and deductive argument. Many readers provide extensive introductions to the rhetorical patterns, discussing their uses in writing and the aspects of a subject that they focus on. Some recent rhetorical readers go beyond the basic rhetorical patterns to discuss common forms of nonfiction writing—such as the problem-solution report, the personal essay, the evaluation, and the proposal—that combine the basic patterns in a number of ways. Rhetorical readers, as well as some thematic readers with rhetorical indices, can be sources for model essays that illustrate, among other things, patterns of development, essay and paragraph strategies, variety in tone, and sentence emphasis and variety. The questions accompanying the essays in most rhetorical readers direct students' attention to the most important features of the models and suggest ways students can incorporate such features in their own writing.

Thematic readers

Thematic readers present writings that illustrate and explore a number of themes, such as the stages of personal growth or family relationships, or topics of general interest, such as capital punishment or the impact of technology. The writings may include fiction or poetry as well as essays. If the main purpose for using the reader is to provide subject matter for essays, a thematic reader may be preferable because, as a rule, readers of this type provide several perspectives on a subject and more background information to get class discussion started and give students material to use in their writing.

Some readers are both rhetorical and thematic in organization and coverage, providing a table of contents for each emphasis. Both types of readers can be used to generate class discussion and topics for student writing. Some readers even provide questions to stimulate discussion and include lists of possible topics for papers.

Cross-curricular readers

Cross-curricular readers typically provide examples of writing in a variety of disciplines and cover a range of topics. Some include essays directed to general readers as well as specialists. Others focus on the kinds of writing expected from students or professionals in a discipline. While the primary aim of readers of this type is to provide models of academic and professional prose, some also arrange readings in thematic clusters designed to encourage discussion and suggest subjects for students to pursue in their own writing. It is important for an instructor to choose a reader whose essays are intrinsically interesting to students or are arranged in intriguing clusters, because a purely formal approach to models of academic writing is likely to prove boring to most students, even those planning to study one or more of the disciplines represented in the sections.

Integrating *The Little, Brown Handbook* with a reader

Instructors who adopt a reader typically make discussion of its essays a major activity in the course, yet they also tend to make significant use of a handbook. If the reader chosen for a course does not provide a rhetorical framework for students' essays or a thorough coverage of writing and reasoning processes, instructors using *The Little, Brown Handbook* may wish to direct students to the coverage of these matters in Chapters 1, 2, and 4. The handbook provides explanations and examples of other matters frequently not covered in readers, such as paragraphing (Chapter 3); sentence structure, grammar, and style (Chapters 5–19); diction and usage (Chapter 31 and Glossary of Usage); the research paper (Chapters 35–38); and writing in the disciplines (Chapter 39). In addition, the handbook can be used as a reference guide for punctuation and mechanics, as an aid in marking student papers, and as a guide for revision. Some instructors who use a reader like to devote one period each week to subjects covered in the handbook; others like to set aside part of each day.

 Rhetorics

Rhetorics and handbooks

Rhetorics cover many of the same topics as handbooks—discovering, planning, drafting, revising, rhetorical patterns, and paragraphing—but do so in greater depth, at the same time giving much less coverage to grammar, punctuation, mechanics, and usage. A rhetoric usually embodies a particular perspective toward writing and the teaching of writing—a theoretical bias, perhaps, or an emphasis on thesis-and-support essays, personal writing, academic writing, argumentation, critical thinking, or tone and style. Since a rhetoric thus helps determine the emphasis within a course, it provides less flexibility for the teacher than the handbook does, especially if the rhetoric has been chosen by a department rather than by the instructor.

Integrating *The Little, Brown Handbook* with a rhetoric

Because rhetorics provide full coverage in some areas at the expense of others, instructors frequently adopt a handbook as a supplement. Used in this way, *The Little, Brown Handbook* can provide treatment of sentence style (Chapters 16–19), the research paper (Chapter 35–38), and writing in the disciplines (Chapter 39) for rhetorics that give only brief attention to these matters. It can also provide discussion and exercises for sentence structure and grammar (Chapters 5–15), punctuation and mechanics (Chapters 20–30), and diction and usage (Chapter 31 and Glossary of Usage). The discussions of paragraphs, the essay, and the writing process (Chapters 1–3) can supplement the material in a rhetoric and provide useful exercises.

When the handbook is used with a rhetoric, instructors often assign its chapters and exercises along with those in the rhetoric, and they devote class time to discussing both texts and reviewing the exercises. They also use the handbook as a reference for students, as an aid to grading papers, and as a guide for revision.

 ## The handbook's ancillary publications

When combined with its ancillary publications—*The Little, Brown Workbook,* Fifth Edition; *The Little, Brown ESL Workbook,* First Edition; Competency, Diagnostic, Sample CLAST, and Sample TASP Tests; an on-line handbook and word processor (*The 53rd Street Writer*); a portable correction chart; transparency masters; and several other learning aids, including a short video which shows how to use a handbook—the handbook is the center of an instructional package that will meet the needs of many classes.

The Little, Brown Workbook is designed to give students more extensive practice with fundamentals than the handbook alone can provide. Since each section of the workbook includes a brief, simplified version of the discussion in the handbook, the workbook can be used on its own. Yet because each section corresponds to the treatment of the same subject in the handbook, the workbook can be a source of individual and class activities to complement the primary text. Answers for exercises in the handbook and the workbook are published as separate booklets that instructors can order, free, for their students.

The Little, Brown ESL Workbook, First Edition, is designed, like *The Little, Brown Workbook,* to give students more extensive practice with fundamentals that are particularly difficult for non-native speakers; it includes whole chapters on articles and different verb tenses.

The diagnostic tests provide a way for instructors to determine their students' needs at the beginning of a course and to design the course accordingly. Because the tests are keyed to the sections of the handbook, instructors can decide what chapters in the text need most emphasis. (The tests can also be used to place students in different courses or levels within a composition program.)

The 53rd Street Writer, a word-processing software program designed by the Daedalus Group, allows students to spend just a few minutes learning how to use the program and the rest of their class and lab time learning how to write. The on-line handbook included with *The 53rd Street Writer* encourages students to consult the handbook because they can do so without leaving their computers.

The marginal notes in this *Instructor's Annotated Edition* describe many activities for class discussion, small-group work, and individual preparation, each keyed to a particular section of the handbook. The chapter "Using Collaborative Learning with the Handbook" on pages IAE-42–IAE-60 of the *Instructor's Annotated Edition* discusses how the handbook may be used in courses emphasizing collaborative learning and includes advice on adapting particular handbook exercises for small-group work.

Sentence combining with the handbook

During the past decade, extensive research has shown that having students work with the elements of sentences—manipulating, combining, and altering—leads not only to a greater understanding of sentence structure but also to a greater command of options for expression. Best of all, students who practice sentence combining develop a willingness to use the structures emphasized in the exercises, and their writing begins to display the flexible, expressive syntax characteristic of mature writing.

The handbook contains several kinds of sentence-combining exercises. Some ask students to combine two short (kernel) sentences so that the new sentence displays the grammatical or stylistic feature being emphasized in a chapter. Others ask students to combine sentences to produce a longer sentence following the pattern illustrated by a model sentence. And still others ask students to combine sentences to form a paragraph.

Sentence-combining exercises can be assigned at any point in the semester; however, they are most likely to have a positive effect on students' writing when they are part of an ongoing program of sentence combining. Regular work on sentence combining each week for an entire semester can be even more effective than an intense two- to three-week session of sentence combining.

Students can begin a sentence-combining program by working with simple exercises like those in Chapter 5 ("Understanding Sentence Grammar"). Though some of the exercises in that chapter may seem a bit basic for many classes, the ones dealing with appositives and absolutes will acquaint students with features they have probably used little in past writing. From the basic exercises, students can move on to those which introduce relatively complex sentence strategies, and they can conclude their work with paragraph-length exercises. The list below suggests a sequence for a sentence-combining program and identifies chapters in the handbook that contain appropriate exercises. If you decide to make sentence combining a substantial part of your composition course, you may want to supplement the exercises in the text by making up your own. Doing so will undoubtedly be necessary if your students discover that they like discussing and comparing the results of the exercises in class and want to spend a good deal of time on the activity.

A sequence for sentence combining

Chapter 5, "Understanding Sentence Grammar," Exercises 9, 11, 13, 14, 16, 17, 18, 22

Chapter 6, "Case of Nouns and Pronouns," Exercise 4

Chapter 11, "Comma Splices and Fused Sentences," Exercise 3

Chapter 14, "Misplaced and Dangling Modifiers," Exercise 6

Chapter 21, "The Comma," Exercises 2, 4, 6

Chapter 22, "The Semicolon," Exercises 2, 4, 7

Chapter 16, "Using Coordination and Subordination," Exercises 1, 3, 4, 7

Chapter 17, "Using Parallelism," Exercise 3

Chapter 18, "Emphasizing Main Ideas," Exercises 2 and 4

Chapter 19, "Achieving Variety," Exercises 1, 2, 3

Chapter 3, "Composing Paragraphs," Exercises 3 and 10

Chapter 5 introduces students to basic sentence structures, and Chapters 14 and 21 introduce modifying clauses and phrases along with their primary focus on grammar and punctuation. Chapters 21 and 22 present strategies of coordination as well as of punctuation, and Chapters 16 and 17 introduce progressively more sophisticated sentence strategies. In Chapters 18 and 19 students encounter sentence patterns characteristic of mature writing, and in Chapter 3 they get a chance to combine all the strategies in paragraphs.

 ## Tutoring with the handbook

Writing centers and tutoring programs can make good use of the handbook and its entire package. The handbook provides explanations and exercises for students but it can also perform several other valuable functions. It can help resolve conflicts over points of grammar and usage by being a primary reference, the final arbiter in debates. It can be a training manual for new tutors, providing simple and clear explanations of problems they will encounter every day. And it can be a reference for students who are working on a paper in the writing center without direct supervision by a tutor.

The *Diagnostic Tests of Standard Written English to Accompany The Little, Brown Handbook* can be used to screen students as they come to the center, identifying their writing problems and helping the tutor choose appropriate instructional materials. *The Little, Brown Workbook* and *The Little, Brown ESL Workbook* can provide the "raw material" of tutoring—sample sentences, exercises, and brief explanations—to be used in discussion with the student or for independent work. The workbooks can be particularly effective for tutoring if students are taking composition courses that use the handbook, because the language, rules, and exercises encountered in tutoring will be consistent with those encountered in the classroom.

Chapter 3

Evaluating and Responding to Student Writing

Nothing we do as composition teachers—not lecturing, setting up peer critique groups, leading discussions, or preparing activities—has as much potential for helping students improve their writing as do our efforts to respond as sensitive and thorough readers. Moreover, as readers we can play several roles, some of them simultaneously. We can respond to a work in progress, acting as editors and critics with suggestions for revision or as ordinary readers whose reactions students can take into account as they shape the final product. Or we can be judges of a finished work, justifying a grade (as evaluators) or pointing out strengths and weaknesses (as teachers), encouraging students to build on one and avoid the other.

Yet evaluating student papers can be time-consuming: Instructors often report spending fifteen to twenty minutes on each paper, making marginal notes, writing summary comments, and deciding on a grade. Many set aside hours of office time for individual conferences. To help make the job of marking papers somewhat easier and quicker, *The Little, Brown Handbook* provides a number of aids:

- A list of correction symbols keyed to discussions in the text
- A number-and-letter correction code that refers students to appropriate sections of the handbook
- A thorough index and glossary of terms directing students to explanations of grammatical and rhetorical terms used in an instructor's written comments

The roles of response

It takes more than an efficient correction system to bring about improvement in writing. How we respond and when are most important. In addition, the correction system we choose needs to be consistent with our purposes for responding and the roles we play as readers.

 ## Responses to papers in progress

Responses directed toward a paper in progress often need to pay as much attention to the way the writer approaches the task as to the evolving text. On the one hand, it makes little sense to comment on detailed matters of punctuation in a draft full of helter-skelter ideas, thereby drawing attention away from advice about strategies the writer can employ to develop focus and discover purpose. On the other hand, helpful comments on agreement or mechanics coming at later stages in the writing of an essay can enable students to understand the importance of editing and can provide knowledge for later use.

Responses to a paper in progress ought to focus to a considerable extent on the writer's behaviors. Novice writers generally need to pay as much attention to learning how to discover ideas or draft an entire paper as to using topic sentences and effective patterns of paragraph development. Much of the advice in the handbook, especially in Chapters 1 and 2, is directed toward strategies for writing. Other discussions, such as the treatment of paragraphs in Chapter 3, pay more attention to the specific features of essays, though they do not ignore the process of composition.

In commenting on drafts of an essay, we can assume the role of a general reader, noting points of interest or confusion, expressing an interest in more information or requesting stronger support, sharing feelings of pleasure and surprise—but always recognizing that at this point a paper belongs primarily to the writer, not yet to the reader. When a draft of an essay has a clear purpose and structure, however, we can read as editors or critics, identifying particular options for paragraphing or expression the writer might consider during revision or suggesting areas of grammar and style that need attention.

 ## Responses to final drafts

Response to a final draft ought to provide a clear evaluation and the justification for it yet at the same time look toward future efforts. Student writers need to recognize and consolidate their successes; they need as well to understand what steps they can take in later essays. The essentially supportive tone of explanations in the handbook can help create this kind of understanding even when comments or the number-and-letter codes are used to identify outright errors.

When as evaluators we comment on a graded final draft, we need to provide a clear justification for the judgment on one or more of the following grounds:

- The paper's success in achieving its goals
- The requirements set by the assignment
- The standards established for the course

At the same time, our comments can convey our responses as teachers, helping students develop images of themselves as writers, with an understanding both of their strengths and of the skills they need to develop. Comments that refer students to a particular section of the handbook, perhaps to specific sets of exercises, can provide a bridge to future writing efforts.

Three methods for commenting on papers

Composition instructors have developed innovative and useful ways of evaluating student writing, including conferences, tape-recorded commentary, and peer evaluation. The handbook can be a useful aid for all these approaches, particularly peer evaluation (see "Using Collaborative Learning with the Handbook," pp. IAE-47–IAE-60). Many teachers, however, still prefer to respond to student essays through marginal and summary comments. These responses take three general forms: a correction code, correction symbols, and written comments. Each method has advantages and disadvantages, and most teachers choose to combine them to draw on the strengths of each.

Using the correction code

To use the correction code, an instructor simply writes in the margin of a paper the number and letter of the section of the handbook a student should consult for help with a particular problem or error, for example, 8b (pronoun and antecedent agreement), 11a (comma splice), or 1d (problem with thesis). The code for each section of the handbook is listed inside the back cover; after a short time, most instructors find they have memorized the codes for common problems and seldom have to consult the list.

Here is a section of a student paper marked using the correction code:

```
    watching a special show or a favorite series.  In some ways,

    parents are using the television as a substitute for personal

    communication with the child.  The days, then, remain a never   ②1c
                                                                      34d
    ending chain of program after program.
```

When students get their graded papers back, they need only turn to the back of the handbook to understand what the instructor's notations mean and then refer to the appropriate section of the text for a full explanation (the code for each section appears in colored boxes at the sides of the pages). Students, too, quickly learn to recognize the notations for common errors and problems.

Using the correction symbols

Correction symbols work in much the same way as the number-and-letter code. An instructor locates the appropriate symbol in the list inside the front cover of the handbook (e.g., *dev, log, agr, coh*) and writes it in the margin of the essay, often drawing a line to indicate the location and extent of the problem. Students reverse the procedure, looking up symbols on the list, which also gives the name of the problem and a reference to the appropriate section of the text: for example, *dm*—Dangling modifier, 14f. Here is the passage from above marked in this way:

```
    Parents have become more lenient with regard to television

    watching.  For example, allowing their children to watch car-   frag
            s
    toon, in the early morning before school.  As soon as they come  rep
                                                                      sp
P   home from school, they sit before the set again, completely   in-
          ww
    grossed with a soap opera or a talk show.  Some parents ac-

    tually allow their children to watch television while they are  ref

    at the supper table.  Of course, the latter part of the eve-

    ning, the prime time, is solely set aside for the purpose of  mm

    watching a special show or a favorite series.  In some ways,

    parents are using the television as a substitute for personal

P   communication with the child.  The days, then, remain a never  ○-hyph

    ending chain of program after program.
```

Because correction symbols are easier to remember than the number-and-letter code, both students and teachers can spend less time turning away from a paper to consult the list of symbols than they might do with the code. Yet symbols are less specific than the code; *shift,* for instance, covers a variety of problems—13a (person and number), 13b (tense and mood), 13c (subject and voice), and 13d (indirect and direct quotation). Moreover, instead of being able to turn directly from the paper to a discussion in the handbook, students may need to consult the list of symbols to find the appropriate section of the text. The symbols, however, also appear in the colored boxes in the margins of the pages.

Using written comments

Although using a correction code or correction symbols can be an efficient way to grade papers, most instructors prefer to give their comments a more personal touch than numbers and letters or symbols alone can offer. Moreover, while the need to have the handbook at hand to understand the instructor's comments may be an advantage for some students, others—perhaps those who need help the most—may put off reviewing their papers or ignore the job entirely because of the effort involved. If you choose to use the code or symbols, you should remember also that there is nothing in either system to let students know they have done a good job on a passage or to encourage them to do a thorough job of looking up explanations in the handbook. To praise good work and make sure students turn to the handbook for help, you will have to rely on written or oral comments. You may also wish to require students to do exercises in the text and hand them in.

Although written comments take a good deal more time than symbols or the correction code, they allow the instructor to address specific problems in an essay, not just indicate a general type of problem. For example, even though the symbol *mng* ("meaning unclear") may be an accurate response, the following written comment tells the student writer a good deal more about the need to communicate clearly with an audience: "I've read this several times and I still can't figure out which side you agree with on this issue—or if you are just trying to avoid taking a stand." In addition, written comments give the teacher a chance to praise successful passages and respond to interesting ideas.

Combining the three methods of grading

Written comments can be specific and helpful, but they are seldom as detailed as explanations in the handbook. Most instructors therefore combine grading systems by using written comments to praise a paper's strengths and including references to relevant sections of the handbook in their notations on serious problems—for example, "This passage is hard to follow because of the loose way you use *that* and *which.* See 12c." Without such a reference, the student who wants more help than the comment gives may have to look elsewhere, a procedure that will work only if the student already knows something about the problem or if the instructor has used a term that also appears in the Glossary of Terms or the index. By combining the correction code with written comments, however, an instructor can provide the necessary guidance.

Another reason for combining methods of grading is that a system may be better suited to some kinds of problems than to others. For example, most instructors prefer writing *21a* in the margin rather than "You need a comma before *and* connecting main clauses"—particularly if the error occurs again and again in an essay. And ‖ is more direct and can be just as effective as the comment "You need to make the elements in this sentence parallel." Yet when brevity is less important, when a symbol doesn't say enough, or when the problem is peculiar to an essay and no reference to the handbook is possible or desirable, a written comment is appropriate.

Terry Perez's final essay in Chapter 2 of the handbook (pp. 61–64) illustrates how an instructor may combine code, symbols, and written comments. Here, in addition, is a selection from a student paper showing all three methods:

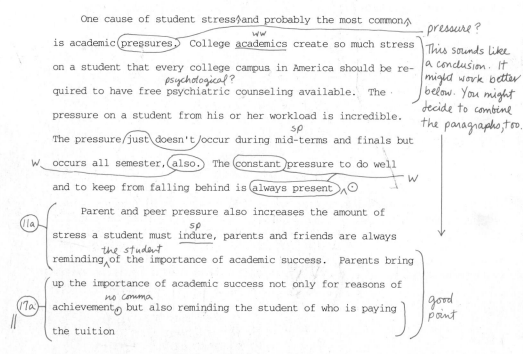

Whether you rely on a single method or a combination of methods to mark students' papers, it is usually important to provide students with a comment at the end of their papers to explain the grade and to tie together the marginal commentary, emphasizing the key points. This is also a good place to assign exercises in the handbook and to remind students what they need to do in future essays. The discussion "Evaluating Essays for a Grade" later in this chapter contains several examples of summary comments.

Making sure students understand your comments

Dealing with codes and symbols

Having chosen a method for commenting on papers, you need to make sure that your students understand the system; unless they do, the time you spend grading papers will be largely wasted. Perhaps the most common reason students fail to understand our comments is that they do not understand the symbols or terms we use. If you were to ask a class what a fused sentence is, some students might answer in this vein: "a sentence where everything seems to run together and gets confused or awkward." Terms like *reference, development,* and *parallelism* are also likely to draw puzzled or incorrect responses, though a few students might be able to give general explanations. Asking students the meaning of common symbols like *pass, cs, dm,* and ‖ will produce similar results.

Telling students to look up correction marks on the front or back endpapers of the handbook can help, as can alerting them to the Glossary of Grammatical Terms or handing out a list of terms you plan to use in written comments. A lot of students, however, are likely to put off learning the symbols or terms until they absolutely have to, perhaps several papers into the semester, when they realize how much help they need to improve their writing.

Quizzing the students

A more effective way to alert students to the need to understand your correction system and at the same time to find out how much they already know is to quiz them on the terms or symbols you will be using. Here are some sample questions:

What is parallelism? Give an example.

Define "fused sentence" and give an example.

What does each of these symbols mean: *frag, dm, ww, t,* and ‖?

The misconceptions that surface from such a quiz can be an aid to instruction. For example, students who think fused sentences are "long sentences where everything seems to run together" are likely to respond to criticism of fused sentences in their work by writing short, choppy sentences. The teacher who has spotted the potential misunderstanding can point out in class discussion that fused sentences are caused by a failure to recognize sentence boundaries and to punctuate them correctly, not by the length or complexity of sentences. Comments on papers can also be expanded in an appropriate manner: "There are a lot of fused sentences in this paper. Make sure you know what a fused sentence is by reading section 11c in the handbook and by doing Exercises 2 and 3."

Discussing a graded paper

Another good way to help students understand your comments is to discuss a graded paper with them. As noted earlier, Chapter 2 of the handbook (pp. 61–64) contains an example of a marked paper that you may wish to use as the basis of class discussion. In addition, the paragraphs presented earlier in this chapter contain many errors of the kind likely to turn up on student papers. The paragraphs can be distributed in class with either or both of the marking systems or with some other system you prefer. If you choose to distribute the paragraphs without markings, you can ask the students to work with you in identifying errors and choosing appropriate symbols or comments.

 ## Focused, positive commentary

 ## Being selective

Two ways to avoid the problem of unfocused commentary are to make selective comments and to make comments that establish priorities for future writing. Selective commentary assumes that errors vary in importance depending on the particular assignment, the goals of the course, or the student's progress. On a narrative or descriptive paper, for example, selective commentary might focus on the presence or absence of vivid, concrete detail. In grading an argumentative essay, however, an instructor might pay primary attention to thesis, adequate support, and transitions. If class discussion has placed considerable emphasis on avoiding fragments and comma splices and has paid relatively little attention to reference problems, the instructor's commentary might take note only of the most serious reference problems, those which are particularly confusing or irritating. Of course, after the class has discussed pronoun reference, the instructor would begin paying considerable attention to it when marking papers.

Other assumptions behind selective commentary are that it is difficult for students (and the rest of us) to pay attention to more than one major job at a time and that students who are having the most trouble with their writing may also have trouble understanding elements that have not been reviewed in class. A or B students with only a few minor marks on their papers—*ref, sp, ww*—can be expected to profit from looking up all the problem areas on their own in the handbook. But weaker students with ten or fifteen serious errors—*frag, agr, log, shift, coh, dev*—need the combined assistance of lecture, small-group discussion, and readings and exercises in the handbook. They will need time to come to grips with the many different problems in their writing.

In addition, students who see a host of grammar, punctuation, and usage errors marked on a paper may assume that these are the most important problems in their writing and may pay less attention to matters such as thesis, development, and organization. Or, having corrected sentence-level problems, they may be unwilling to undertake large-scale revision that would require throwing out the very sentences they have just worked so hard to fix.

Yet one might argue that students have to learn to pay attention to all the problems in their writing and that to ignore some errors in a student's paper, whatever the reason, may be to send a misleading signal. Even instructors who find selective commentary useful may find it hard to refrain from making numerous notations on some papers, feeling that it is their responsibility to alert students to serious problems in communication. For these instructors the solution may be to establish priorities for the way students are to understand and respond to the comments. A system of priorities allows the instructor to point out all the different problem areas in a paper while at the same time directing a student's attention to the most important kinds of problems.

 ## Establishing priorities for the students

Perhaps the easiest way to establish priorities is to use the summary comment to identify the most serious problems (and strengths, too) and to suggest concrete steps for solving the problems through revision or in future papers. Here are two examples of such comments:

> . . . The most serious problem in this essay is the lack of development in the paragraphs. You need many more extended examples to support your point about the role of computers at all levels of education. But the many comma splices in the paper are also an important problem because they are so distracting to a reader. I have taken note of comma splices in determining the grade; work on avoiding them in your next paper because they will count even more heavily in the grade. The other problems noted in the margins—14f, etc.—occur less consistently and do not interfere as much with the reader's perception of your meaning and enjoyment of your essay. Look them up in the handbook, however, and watch for them as you proofread your next essay.

> Your topic and your point of view on it are very intriguing. But the lack of concrete detail at the places I have noted weakens the essay. Work to add detail as you revise. The problems in logic in the fourth paragraph are significant and need to be dealt with if you decide to retain the preceding paragraph (see 4f in the handbook). After you have completed these more substantial revisions, look for problems in pronoun reference, which make many of your sentences confusing. (Do Exercises 1 and 2 in Chapter 12 of the handbook.) Check on the other problems pointed out in the body of the paper, and be sure to correct the spelling errors before you hand in the revised essay for a final grade.

Many instructors read student essays twice, the first time to identify general strengths and weaknesses, the second time to make comments praising successful passages and indicating areas that need more work. Other instructors decide ahead of time which elements of the assignment or course are most important and try to restrict their comments to these. But though the latter procedure saves a bit of time, it will not be successful unless both the instructor and the students understand the aims for the assignment and the grading standards in the course. Making the goals of the course clear is a good procedure because it provides a firm basis for evaluation.

Evaluating essays for a grade

A grade can carry several messages: it can describe the overall quality of a paper; it can indicate how close the essay comes to achieving the goals for writing set forth in the course; and it can help tell a student writer what elements to work on in the next assignment. But unless grading standards are clear, the grades we assign will have little value for teaching beyond establishing a final grade for the course.

To help establish clear evaluation standards, many instructors discuss grading criteria with students and distribute sample papers, either already graded or to be graded in class. Another method is to attach to each paper a comment sheet reflecting the goals for the assignment. Preparing a comment sheet for each assignment can be taxing, however, and so many instructors prepare a sheet that can be used for all assignments. Here are two samples, each of which uses different grading criteria:

These are the areas in which your paper is

strong   weak

	thesis	
	development	
	paragraphs	
	sentences	
	grammar	
	word choice	
	punctuation	
	style	

Comment/grade:

Thesis:

Organization:

Development:

Grammar and
punctuation:

Style:

Comment/grade:

If you do not like to use comment sheets, you may prefer to hand out grading criteria at the beginning of the course. Sometimes a department or program provides its own set of criteria for grading papers; if yours does not, you may wish to adapt for your own use the following set that reflects the major areas of emphasis in the handbook:

- *A* (superior). An *A* paper meets the standards in all these areas and excels in one or more of them:

  The *paper as a whole* presents a fresh subject or main idea or treats it in an interesting or original manner, displaying unusual insight. The paper has a clear pattern appropriate to the audience. The *paragraphs* are fully developed with detail that supports the main idea; sentences within the paragraphs are clearly linked, forming an appropriate pattern; transitions are effective. *Sentences* are varied and imaginative in style, concise and creative in wording. The paper contains few errors in *grammar and punctuation* or errors only in sophisticated matters, and few *spelling* errors.

- *B* (strong). A *B* paper meets the standards in all these areas:

  The *paper as a whole* presents an interesting subject or main idea and approaches it in a consistent and careful manner, displaying good insight, though without the freshness or originality characteristic of the *A* paper. The pattern of the essay is appropriate to its purpose, and the writing makes use of consistent rhetorical strategies and a tone appropriate to the audience. *Paragraphs* are, with only a few exceptions, adequately developed and generally successful in supporting the main idea; transitions are clear, and sentences within the paragraphs are, for the most part, clearly related. *Sentences* are clear and correct in structure and style and are not excessively wordy. Word choice is usually appropriate. *Grammar, punctuation, and spelling* follow accepted conventions, except for a few minor errors.

● *C* (adequate). A *C* paper is seriously deficient in one of these areas:

The *paper as a whole* presents a clearly defined subject or main idea, but the treatment may be trivial, uninteresting, or too general and the insight adequate but not marked by independent thought. The plan and purpose are clear but inconsistently or incompletely carried out; tone may be inconsistent. Some *paragraphs* may lack adequate supporting detail or may be only loosely linked to the main idea. Sentences within paragraphs may be only loosely related, and some transitions may be missing. *Sentences* are generally correct in structure but may be excessively wordy, vague, or, at times, even incorrect. Style and word choice may be flat, inconsistent, or not entirely appropriate to the audience. The paper may display isolated serious errors in *grammar and punctuation* or frequent minor errors that do not interfere substantially with meaning or that do not greatly distract the reader; the paper may contain occasional *misspellings*.

● *D* (weak). A *D* paper is seriously deficient in any one of these areas:

The *paper as a whole* presents a poorly defined or inconsistently treated subject or central idea and displays little insight. The plan and purpose are not treated consistently. The tone is inappropriate to the audience. *Paragraphs* contain little supporting detail. Sentences within paragraphs are often unrelated to the main idea, and transitions are lacking. *Sentences* are frequently incorrect in structure, vague, wordy, and distracting. Style and word choice are inappropriate, incorrect, or inconsistent. The paper may contain serious and distracting errors in *grammar and punctuation* as well as numerous irritating minor errors and frequent *misspellings*.

● *F* (unacceptable/no credit). An *F* paper is unacceptable in any one of these areas:

The *paper as a whole* does not have a clear subject or main idea and has no apparent purpose or plan; *or* the subject and main idea are defined and treated in a way that clearly does not meet the requirements of the assignment. *Paragraphs* are not related to the main idea; sentences within paragraphs are unrelated, and transitions are missing. *Sentences* are so faulty in structure and style that the essay is not readable. Frequent serious errors in *grammar, punctuation, and spelling* indicate an inability to handle the written conventions; there are excessive minor errors or misspellings.

These criteria need to be adapted to the level of students in a particular course or institution and to the goals set for the course. For example, admirable organization or style may differ markedly for a student in a two-year technical program and a student in a four-year school that stresses the arts and humanities. The following samples of graded papers attempt to put into practice the grading techniques suggested in this section. (The papers are preceded by the instructors' assignments.) Because of the wide variations one can expect between schools and courses, ranges of quality rather than specific grades are suggested: good, average, and weak. Keep in mind that these are merely samples and that the best grading procedures are those which reflect the personality of the teacher as a sensitive and thorough reader.

Good

[Assignment: Write an essay in which you try to give your readers a fresh look at a subject, perhaps by choosing one they probably have not paid much attention to in the past. You may wish to present examples, look at causes and effects, classify, or compare and contrast. Remember that the detail you use to develop your essay and make your point will help determine the essay's effectiveness.]

Winter in New England

So you were raised in Miami and now you are moving to New England. You say you are excited about the move, but do you know how your life will change here? Living in a cold climate like New England's influences how you spend your money, what you do with your time, and how you feel about yourself and others.

good opening paragraph

The most obvious effect of the winter cold is financial, as you'll quickly learn. Even though you wear only casual clothes, you'll need a new wardrobe: a collection of sweaters and flannel shirts; a very warm coat; and a pair of boots suitable for deep snow, glassy ice, messy slush, and rain. You have probably heard enough about our heating bills up here, so I won't go into that financial effect of the cold. But you may not know what this climate will do to your car. You'll have to "winterize" it, which means putting antifreeze in the radiator and who knows what else. Inevitably, more than once your winterized car will refuse to start in the cold weather, so you'll have to fork over money for road service or towing. But that inconvenience and cost does not compare to the agony of watching your car disintegrate over a few years from the salt laid down on the roads to melt ice.

Explaining this a bit more would make your point even more effective.

Yes, this really is agony.

Even if you are prepared for the financial costs of
living in the North, you will probably be startled by how
the cold climate affects your activities. Winter here is
hibernating time. The outdoors is something to be passed
through as quickly as possible on your way from one heated
place to another. In winter you resign yourself to hud-
dling around the radiator (if you have paid the heating
bill). With all your money going toward self-defense from
the cold, boredom can be a problem, so you may find yourself cooking soups, playing games, or imprinting on the

This is an interesting use of the word.

television. Actually, you may end up relishing your free
time, no matter how boring or frustrating, when you experience the great winter activity--battling ice and snow.
If it's a wet winter, count on spending a few hours minimum every week shoveling snow from driveways and sidewalks, scraping ice and snow off your car, and (most fun
of all) pushing your car or someone else's out of icy
snowbanks.

Ugh! (but these are good details)

The strangest effect of life in the cold is the way
it influences your attitudes. After a hot, humid summer
the crisp, dry air of autumn at first fills you with energy and cheerfulness. But, as the air becomes downright
chilly and the tree branches become bare, you will sense
yourself and others dying a little each day. Gradually
you find it necessary to don heavy, constricting clothing;
you avoid any contact with the depressing out-of-doors;
you begin to shiver inside your own home, for turning on
the heat for the first time since last winter is an admis-

true — good insight into human nature

good phrase

sion of death that everyone puts off. But inevitably win-

ter comes, in full force. Your face feels tight, and you

see your expression mirrored in the thin-lipped scowls of

the people you pass quickly on the street. Your posture

is hunched, elbows squeezed to the waist, and your mood is

similarly withdrawn. Except for the Christmas/Chanukah

frenzy, you will spend the next four months in a gray mood

that matches the dominant color of the sky.

excellent detail

So you won't be discouraged from coming north at all,

I've held the saving grace of winter for last. It ends.

And when the punishment finally stops, you understand that

you had to go through it to experience the sheer elation

of spring. So come ahead and do not fear. Bad as it is,

winter is worth the intense joy of its leaving.

Fine paper. Your thesis is clear and you develop each part of it with effective detail. The third set of effects you discuss, the effect on feelings, is particularly insightful. And the last paragraph ties the whole essay together nicely.

Average

[Assignment: Write an essay in which you use classification to help readers understand a complicated topic or to highlight the characteristics of groups of people, ideas, objects, or events in such a way that you shed fresh light on the subject. Remember that the details you use to develop your essay will help determine its effectiveness.]

The Second Half of Sleeping: Waking

The human being, it is estimated, sleeps away one

third of his or her life. Much research on this topic   21j

has been done in sleep clinics throughout the world. A

sp

more fasinating aspect of the sleeping process has been
virtually ignored: waking up. The ways in which people
wake up can, however, be narrowed down and described in
four main groups.

the thesis is clear, but not very interesting

The Last-Minute Riser is often seen stumbling through
the quad, five minutes into class time, with wet hair and
still wearing pajamas. The actual waking process is an
extremely painful one. The last minute riser has mathe-
matically calculated the number of minutes it takes to get
ready in the morning. He is awakened by the piercing
screech of the alarm clock at the predetermined moment,
and again five minutes later, and five minutes after that.
Alarm clock manufacturers have installed "snooze buttons"
on alarm clocks for people falling into this category.

17a

hyph

good

hyph

The last minute riser realizes with a mixture of shock
and teror that he has slept well into the alloted getting-
ready time. He begins an emotional display of a person in
panic as he rushes to and fro throughout the room in an
effort to make up for lost time. This person never has
time for breakfast and must deal with an array of stomach
gurgling noises that last through his first three classes.
Persons fitting this description have been known to
change in and out of majors so as to avoid required morning classes.

sp *sp*

no comma *w* *w*

hyph

true!

The Early Birds are in direct contrast to the last
minute riser. Early birds are easy to spot, they are the
people who look bright-eyed, and cheerfully well-rested,
the people who eagerly answer questions during an eight
o'clock class. They make a point to skip to the cafeteria

hyph

cs

22e

¶ dev

every morning to eat an elaborate meal. Then the early

bird is fully alert and anxious to begin the day.

¶
dev

    The Zombie is a living testimonial to the theory that

we are fully alert only one minute of each hour. The zom-

bie is not aware of her alarm clock when it buzzes, but

she manages to shut it off anyway. A zombie usually awak-

ens halfway through lunch. Although this is a daily oc-

curence, she is nonetheless always bewildered at finding

that she is not asleep in bed as she imagined.

true

    The Complainer does not enjoy waking up, as is well

known by anyone he lives with. He finds it soothing to

know that although he is unhappily awake, so, too, is any-

one within listening range. The complainer allows his

alarm clock to beep continuously for twenty minutes. He

does not hear this; everyone else in his dorm does. When

he does respond, the alarm clock is hurled across his   dm

room. It lands with a blood-curdling crash. The com-

plainer is ready to get up. He shocks the room to life by

turning on every light and blaring his stereo. When at-   ww (while?)

tempting to get ready, the complainer is unable to find

any of his belongings. He finds it necessary to awaken

                 no commas necessary

his roommate several times and make him aware of the di-

lemma. After slamming shut any drawer within reach, he

stomps to the cafeteria. The cafeteria is often visited   good

by complainers, as it supplies an inexhaustible supply of   phrase

subjects to grieve over. It is best to avoid the com-

plainer until noontime.

    In college life, a person is forced to deal with oth-

ers every hour of the day: the hours when others are

asleep, awake, and especially the hours in between.

Awareness of the ways different people wake up is neces-

sary if one is to survive the first half of every day.

This essay is often quite funny, but the paragraphs on "The Early Birds" and "The Zombie" need more development. You might add details like these in the paragraphs describing the other categories. The thesis is clear, but it is not very interesting. You might try to indicate what the readers will learn from your essay -- you do this effectively in the last paragraph. Watch out for the sentence and punctuation problems. Look up the appropriate sections in the Handbook.

Weak

[Assignment: Write a narrative about an event in your life that had an important impact on you or that you remember vividly because of the insight it gave you into yourself and other people. Remember to choose details carefully because they will make your narrative vivid and effective.]

The First Day

It was a beautiful day in late August, kind of warm

and very nervewracking for me. Because I was embarking on

the most important day in my life, the beginning of my   10a

college experience. The day began with its normal rituals

and everything appeared to be fine until I arrived at the

college. Suddenly I found myself asking, what am I doing

here? Am I really ready for this. I wanted to cry, but I   24a

pushed back the tears and plunged onward. Before I knew

sp

it, I was pushed amoungst the hustle and bustle of the

first day.

good *whose*

I must have looked like a child whoe teddy bear was

taken from him.

sp   *sp*   (3c)

Being as how I was truely frightened I desparately

sp

tried to find my first class and with the aide of a few

older students I successfully found my place.

sp

After that things got easier, but not to. The hard-

est part was yet to come. The adjustment to new and dif- (10d)

ferent people. The biggest difficulty was starting a con-

versation. Most of the time you say nothing for the fear (13a)

of sounding dumb. The first time beginning to talk to

good detail   *t*

someone, my voice cracks and I must have turned scarlet   *dm*

find out what?

red, but I never stuck around to find out. I ducked out

sp   *ladies'*

quicly and found the nearest (lady's) room. *(ladies is plural)*

The strange thing about college is its proffessors. *sp*

a professor is a "he" or a "she"

Each has (its) own technique but the same basics. On the *use the*

one s   *he or she   s*   *singular*

first day they each tell you what they expect during the   *here*

s   *too much exaggeration here*

semester and then they hand you a forty page syllabus of

work to be done in fifteen weeks. I had (another) who when

This ¶   *31c*   *one professor*

doesn't   (every time) she spoke sounded like she was having her hand *!!*

fit with

the thesis.   for dinner.

People asked me what I thought about my first year in *You didn't*

really cover

school. My response is simply, "It was different".   *this much*

territory in

This is a good topic for an essay, but you need to spend more   *the essay.*

time describing specific incidents so that your readers can

share and understand your experience. The second and third

paragraphs, for example, are far too short. They ought to
be combined and developed with concrete details.
The fourth paragraph also needs to contain specific
incidents -- you would be better off concentrating on the
first day and describing the events in detail. The
paragraph about professors doesn't seem to fit in
with the rest of the essay because it covers a
different topic.
   When you revise, try to focus the essay more clearly on
the first day and pay attention to the marginal comments.

Evaluating for revision

Revision in composition teaching

In recent years the process of revision has come to be viewed as increasingly important in composition instruction. Instructors who make revision a regular part of their composition classes argue that writers should be judged not (or not only) on the early version of an essay but on what they are able to make of the essay after they have had a chance to revise it and, perhaps, to take into account the comments of readers.

Composition instructors have long viewed revision as an important process for student writers to learn. What is new is the extent to which revision is being made a regular part of instruction, an emphasis reflected in the extensive treatment of both revision and editing in Chapter 2 of the handbook. Furthermore, many instructors have begun structuring their classes around collaborative learning groups that provide audiences for papers in progress and advice for revision. This method is reinforced in the handbook's Chapter 2, which contains checklists for students' giving and receiving criticism. The chapter "Using Collaborative Learning with the Handbook," which follows this discussion, contains suggestions for handouts to help students analyze their peers' work.

Commenting on drafts for revision

The distinction made in Chapter 2 of the handbook between revision and editing is important for instructors to keep in mind when responding to a student paper in progress. For essays whose perspective, form, and content are well enough developed to require only editing, your role may be simply to call attention to errors or to suggest ways to polish sentences and paragraphs. Many of the techniques already discussed for commenting on papers can be used to aid editing, particularly those which refer students to sections of the handbook for advice on improving a passage or correcting a problem. In addition, you may wish to refer students to the editing checklist in Chapter 2 (p. 59).

Evaluation for revision, however, is more likely to suggest extensive changes in a paper, often encouraging the writer to adopt a different perspective on a topic. An instructor commenting on a draft might suggest, for example, that the essay could be more interesting or useful if the writer shifted from arguing about recent government regulations controlling the disposal of dangerous substances to examining the effects of toxic wastes or discussing the costs to industry of completely safe disposal procedures. Since revision may and often should involve substantial changes in the direction of an essay, you should be wary, however, of comments that impose your view of what a paper should do or how it should be accomplished. Instead, try to identify a problem clearly and offer some possible solutions but at the same time leave the student writers free to make their own choices. Comments like "your thesis statement needs to focus more sharply on the specific government toxic-waste regulations to which you object" may be helpful in cases where the student's intentions and the direction of a paper are quite clear. But when a writer is still struggling with subject and intention, such statements may limit the process of revision rather than encourage it. A comment like the following, however, leaves the eventual direction of the essay up to the student:

> I'm not sure which specific regulations you object to most. Is this a place in the essay where you want to focus your concerns sharply for readers? From the detailed evidence you present later about the struggles of small businesses to pay for state-of-the-art pollution equipment, I suspect that one of your main purposes is to have readers understand the hard times these ordinary people are facing. What do you care most about in this subject, and what do you most want your audience to understand and feel?

In commenting on papers for revision, you should call attention to any serious errors. At the same time, however, keep in mind this maxim: "Don't spend time improving a sentence that ought to be dropped from the paper." Remember, too, that awkward and confused sentences are often signs of confusion about the overall direction of an essay, and problems at the sentence level may disappear as the writer resolves the larger problems. Thus comments on errors are most effective when they place the errors in a larger context, as in this comment:

> You shift pronouns often in this passage, sometimes addressing the reader as "you," sometimes using "one" or "we." I think the root of the problem is that you are not sure of your relation to your readers. Since you are talking about a situation that you face along with most readers, you might choose "we" and stick to it.

In addition, most students need more than advice about what sections of a paper need to be revised; they need advice about the process of revision itself. By focusing your comments on how to go about revising rather than solely on the direction of possible changes, you can avoid doing the students' work for them and can instead help them develop an effective writing/revising process. Instead of simply telling a student to add more detail to an essay discussing the social effects of unemployment, you might say:

> Imagine that you are the father of five children and that your wife is a homemaker. You have just lost your job. Write for five minutes about how your being home all day, depressed because you are out of work, might upset the normal life of your family. When you are done, look over what you have written for details and examples you can use in your paper.

Advice of this sort not only helps a student revise the paper at hand but also shows the student ways to revise future papers.

Conferences

Conferences are worthwhile alternatives to written responses. While some instructors choose to rely solely on them, others use them as supplements to provide a fresh perspective for student writers. They give an instructor a chance to respond to essays as a sensitive reader, with opinions and feelings, words of encouragement, and suggested corrections—all of which are generally hard to convey in the margins of papers. Conferences also require students to contribute by commenting on their own papers, explaining why they made certain choices, and indicating how they want to revise an essay or how they plan to change their approach in the next assignment. In a conference you may find that your judgment of a paper or of the source and seriousness of a writing problem changes when you hear what the student writer was trying to accomplish.

Remember, however, that conferences ought to provide an opportunity for students to talk about their papers. Try to resist the temptation to use the conference as a lecture period. Whenever possible, make your advice come in response to a student's questions or comments. And make your comments direct and relatively personal so that the student can understand better how a reader reacts to an essay, not just how a teacher grades a student paper.

Resources for evaluation and response

Brannon, Lil, and C. H. Knoblauch. "On Students' Rights to Their Own Texts: A Model of Teacher Response." *College Composition and Communication* 33 (1982): 157–66.

Cooper, Charles R., and Lee Odell, eds. *Evaluating Writing: Describing, Measuring, Judging.* Urbana: NCTE, 1977.

Dietrich, Julia C. "Explaining One's Rhetorical Choices." *College Composition and Communication* 29 (1978): 195–96.

Faigley, Lester. "Judging Writing, Judging Selves." *College Composition and Communication* 40 (1989): 395–412.

Ford, James E., and Gregory Larkin. "The Portfolio System: An End to Backsliding Writing Standards." *College English* 39 (1978): 950–55.

Freedman, Sarah Warshauer. *Response to Student Writing*. Urbana: NCTE, 1987.

---, and Melanie Sperling. "Teacher Student Interaction in the Writing Conference: Response and Teaching." In *The Aquisition of Written Language: Response and Revision*. Ed. Sarah Warshauer Freedman. Norwood: Ablex, 1985.

Gere, Ann Ruggles, and Robert Stevens. "The Language of Writing Groups: How Oral Response Shapes Revision." In *The Acquisition of Written Language: Response and Revision*. Ed. Sarah Warshauer Freedman. Norwood: Ablex, 1985. 85–105.

Hillocks, George. "The Interaction of Instruction, Teacher Comment, and Revision in Teaching the Composing Process." *Research in the Teaching of English* 16 (1982): 261–78.

Johnston, Brian. "Non-Judgmental Responses to Students' Writing." *English Journal* 71 (1982): 50–53.

Knoblauch, C. H., and Lil Brannon. "Teacher Commentary on Student Writing: The State of the Art." *Freshman English News* 10 (1981): 1–4.

McDonald, W. U. Jr., "The Revising Process and the Marking of Student Papers." *College Composition and Communication* 29 (1978): 167–70.

Miller, Linda P. "A Conference Methodology for Freshman Composition." *Teaching English in the Two-Year College* 7 (1980): 23–26.

Olsen, Gary A. "Beyond Evaluation: The Recorded Response to Essays." *Teaching English in the Two-Year College* 8 (1982): 121–23.

Purves, Alan. "The Teacher as Reader: An Anatomy." *College English* 46 (1984): 259–65.

Schiff, Peter. "Responding to Writing: Peer Critiques, Teacher-Student Conferences, and Essay Evaluations." In *Language Connections: Writing and Reading Across the Curriculum*. Urbana: NCTE, 1982. 153–65.

Shaw, Margaret L. "What Students Don't Say: An Approach to the Student Text." *College Composition and Communication* 42 (1991): 45–54.

Sommers, Nancy. "Responding to Student Writing." *College Composition and Communication* 33 (1982): 148–56.

Stanford, Gene, Ed. *How to Handle the Paper Load*. Urbana: NCTE, 1978. (Includes Neil Ellman, "Structuring Peer Evaluation for Greater Student Independence"; David A. England, "Objectives for Our Own Composing Processes—When We Respond to Students"; Mary Louise Foster and Patricia Markey Naranjo, "Peer Evaluation: One Approach"; Isabel Hawley, "Critique Groups for Composition Classes"; Muriel Harris, "The Overgraded Paper: Another Case of More Is Less"; Sheila Ann Lisman, "The Best of All Possible Worlds: Where X Replaces AWK"; Thomas Newkirk, "Read the Papers in Class"; Audrey J. Roth, "Editorial Groups"; Linda Shadiow, "Eureka! Moments and Reflection Questions"; and R. Baird Shuman, "How to Grade Student Writing" and "Writing Roulette: Taking a Chance on Not Grading.")

Chapter 4

*Using
Collaborative
Learning with the
Handbook*

Within the past few years, writing instructors have been rediscovering the value of collaborative learning, in which students work together to solve problems, do exercises, and evaluate one another's work. Some instructors ask students to work in groups only occasionally, and others design their entire writing courses around group work. Whether you use collaborative learning and peer criticism regularly or would like to try just a few collaborative exercises in your course, you will find that it is easy to use this teaching method with *The Little, Brown Handbook*. This discussion will define collaborative learning, offer suggestions for designing collaborative exercises, and suggest ways to guide students in peer criticism.

 What collaborative learning is

Collaborative learning is a general phrase used to describe any of a number of different kinds of activities in which students work together as active colaborers rather than passive learners.

Most exercises can be completed in small groups. Possibilities include analyzing essays, correcting flawed sentences, identifying parts of speech, identifying rhetorical strategies, and revising prose. There are several advantages to having students work on exercises together:

- All students have a chance to participate.
- Students are exposed to each other's opinions.
- Students negotiate among themselves to reach an answer that they all can accept.

Another form of collaborative learning is peer criticism, in which students comment on each other's writing. Students can exchange papers in small groups of three or four, or they can work in pairs; they can summarize a classmate's essay; they can provide feedback on another student's thesis, organization, style, or grammar; they can provide counterarguments; or they can provide additional support for their classmates' essays.

The instructor plays an important role in both collaborative classroom exercises and peer criticism. Even though these are student-centered activities, the instructor must shape them carefully by designing a sheet of questions or instructions to guide the students' work. In this way, the instructor controls the learning activity, even though the students carry it out. (There are sample instruction sheets at the end of this chapter.)

The benefits of collaborative learning

The advantages of collaborative learning—either work on exercises or peer criticism—are substantial:

- Students take an active role in their own education.
- In small groups they can participate and hear reactions to their ideas.
- They get individualized attention rare in these times of increasing class size.
- Students learn to cooperate with as opposed to compete against one another for the best grades or the instructor's approval.
- Collaborative learning mirrors the real world of work outside of school. Students develop interaction skills they will need for working on projects with colleagues, and they learn to accept criticism of their work.
- Collaborating reminds students that language and writing are social products. Students experience firsthand how groups of people develop standards for writing and experience how these standards are enforced. Through negotiation they learn to exercise independent judgment. They see how others make decisions; they practice defending their ideas; and they learn to compromise or shift their positions as necessary.
- Peer criticism provides students with valuable feedback during the writing process, a time when few instructors have time to do so. Students consider and question suggestions made by peers, whereas they too often respond slavishly to instructors' comments. Furthermore, students are exposed to a variety of points of view on their writing. Peer comments are not dismissed as quickly as those made by instructors, whom students perceive as representing a set of standards not shared by the rest of the world. Peers comprise a more believable audience.
- Students see the importance of writing to communicate an idea, not just to demonstrate competence.

Using the handbook to design collaborative activities

The wide variety of types of exercises and levels of difficulty in *The Little, Brown Handbook* will make it fairly easy for you to select exercises that will not bore your students or be too difficult for them. The exercises are well suited for use during class time.

- Exercises are usually focused on one aspect of writing and thus will not take long for a group to complete.
- Groups can complete exercises and compare their answers with those of other groups during the same class period.
- The exercises give students the freedom to consider alternatives, but most do not ask students to write from scratch—a very difficult task for a group to accomplish.
- During class time, groups can be asked to revise short passages of prose or to create sentences and paragraphs from ideas, phrases, and sentences given them.

To write whole compositions as a group, students need to spend large amounts of time working together outside of class, a useful exercise for students in technical and scientific fields.

To avoid limiting the ways in which students and instructors use the handbook, none of the exercise instructions in the students' edition specifies that the work should be completed in groups. In this *Instructor's Annotated Edition,* however, the exercises thought most useful for collaborative work are labeled immediately above their answers:

COLLABORATIVE LEARNING

In the students' edition, the instructions for each exercise are explicit but can easily be adapted for group work. In many cases, you simply need to direct students to complete the exercise in groups. Just be sure that one student in the group takes notes as its members work so that the group can reconstruct its discussion if necessary.

In some cases an exercise will be more suitable for collaborative learning if you make one of the following changes:

- If the exercise asks students to choose among alternatives, then add the requirement that students defend their choice.
- If an exercise informs students that there is more than one correct answer, ask students working in groups to find as many correct answers as possible.
- If an exercise directs students to revise their own work, ask them to exchange papers and provide each other with peer criticism.

Although almost any exercise in the book could be adapted for collaborative work, some are more suitable than others. Those kinds of exercises throughout the handbook which will work best in groups are the following:

- Exercises requiring students to use judgment
- Exercises in critical reading
- Difficult exercises in identification
- Exercises in sentence combining
- Exercises in revision

- Exercises that invite group invention or brainstorming
- Exercises in controlled composition

Exercises that are not appropriate for group work include

- Private kinds of writing (such as the journal in Chapter 1, Exercise 1)
- Exercises designed to lead an individual writer through an extended writing assignment (as often appear in Chapters 1–2 and 35–37)
- Exercises with only one correct answer (identifying parts of speech or choosing from a pair of possible answers)

Although you will probably mix group work with individual exercises and work with the entire class, you can see that you have many opportunities to use the handbook as the basis for collaborative learning. To identify quickly those exercises easily adapted for group work, refer to the index below or to the highlighting throughout this *Instructor's Annotated Edition*.

Chapter 1: Exercises 5, 6, 7, 8, 9, 11, 14, 15, 17, 18, 19

Chapter 2: Exercises 1, 3, 4, 5, 6, 7, 8

Chapter 3: Exercises 1, 2, 3, 5, 6, 7, 8, 10, 12, 13, 15, 17, 18, 19

Chapter 4: Exercises 1, 2, 3, 4, 5, 6, 8, 9, 10, 12, 13, 14, 15, 16, 17, 18, 19, 20, 21

Chapter 5: Exercises 3, 9, 11, 13, 14, 16, 17, 18, 22

Chapter 6: Exercises 4, 5

Chapter 7: Exercises 5, 6, 8, 9

Chapter 8: Exercises 1, 2, 3, 4

Chapter 9: Exercises 2, 4, 5

Exercise on Chapters 5–9 (following Chapter 9)

Chapter 10: Exercises 1, 2, 3, 4, 5

Chapter 11: Exercises 1, 2, 3, 4

Chapter 12: Exercises 1, 2, 3

Chapter 13: Exercises 1, 2, 3, 4, 5

Chapter 14: Exercises 1, 4, 5, 6, 7

Chapter 15: Exercises 1, 2

Exercise on Chapters 10–15 (following Chapter 15)

Chapter 16: Exercises 1, 2, 3, 4, 5, 6, 7

Chapter 17: Exercises 1, 3, 4

Chapter 18: Exercises 2, 3, 4, 5, 6

Chapter 19: Exercises 1, 3, 5

Exercise on Chapters 16–19 (following Chapter 19)

Chapter 20: Exercise 4

Chapter 21: Exercises 3, 4, 5, 6, 12, 13, 14

Chapter 22: Exercises 2, 4, 7, 8, 9

Chapter 23: Exercise 6

Chapter 24: Exercises 4, 5

Chapter 25: Exercise 5

Exercise on Chapters 20–25 (following Chapter 25)

Exercise on Chapters 26–30 (following Chapter 30)

Chapter 31: Exercises 1, 3, 4, 5, 7, 8, 9, 10, 11, 12, 13

Chapter 35: Exercise 1

Chapter 36: Exercises 1, 3, 4, 5, 8

Chapter 37: Exercise 2

 ## Preparing students to work in groups

You may be hesitant to use collaborative learning because it seems unstructured. This is not the case. Collaborative learning is just as structured as traditional methods of learning—but it is structured in a different way. You direct the students' learning not by controlling discussion but by carefully preparing students to work collaboratively as they confront questions and problems in writing.

 ## Designing instructions for group work

The instructions that you give students should explain both the tasks they must accomplish and the reasons for doing the exercise. If students cannot understand the goal of an exercise, they will be less able to tell when they are on the right track. In these written instructions, you may also want to remind students that their task is to cooperate, not compete. Students are so accustomed to battling with each other to speak and to gain the instructor's attention that they need to be reminded constantly how to work together as allies rather than rivals. Here are a few additional tips for instructions:

- If you have made significant changes in an exercise, you should probably write revised instructions for the students.
- Make sure each student has a copy of the instructions.
- Be clear about how much time students should spend on the exercise or, if it is a long exercise, how much time on each part of it.
- Allow enough time for groups to report to the entire class.
- It is preferable for groups to discuss an exercise and report during the same class period to sustain interest and involvement.

 ## Helping students learn to work in groups

The following suggestions may ease your students (and you) into group work:

- Groups of three to five work best.
- In general, do not worry about whether students in a given group are at the same or at different levels.
- Vary the ways in which students are grouped in order to expose them to as many points of view as possible during the semester.
- Groups should decide upon a note taker and spokesperson; these positions should rotate so all students can participate in these different kinds of group responsibility.
- You should expect a higher-than-normal noise level, a byproduct of collaborative learning.
- You may float from group to group, but will find that students will be more independent if left to themselves. Once you are comfortable with collaborative learning, you can do your own work while the students collaborate.
- If a group arrives at a wrong answer or prefers slang to standard English, explain to the class why users of standard written English have agreed upon a different convention. Explain that if students want to be considered proficient writers by the users of standard written English, they must conform to the standards set by that community. In this way, you can teach students the conventions of good writing and also reinforce the idea that these are, after all, just conventions.

Preparing students to provide peer criticism

You need to prepare students to comment on each other's writing just as carefully as you prepare them to do collaborative exercises in groups. Sometimes students may comment directly on a photocopy of a writer's paper; at other times, they will write on a reader response sheet like those at the end of this chapter. You will probably be designing a set of instructions for each peer criticism exercise, but you will also need to let students practice this new way of responding to each other's work. Students rarely receive careful peer criticism of their work. Some may ask their friends or roommates to read over a paper and give them a general response, but this kind of evaluation usually amounts to simple proofreading or is not very detailed (after all, the students want to remain friends). Because students do not know what serious peer evaluation is, they need to study several models and to practice on sample essays before they go to work on each other's papers.

Coaching students

The following are basic steps in teaching students how to be peer critics:

- Thoroughly discuss with students what they will be doing.
- Practice the peer response process with a sample paper written by a student.
- Explain how the students' role as peer readers differs from the instructor's role when assigning a grade to the paper: in short, they are assisting in the writing process as opposed to judging the final draft.

- Collect and respond to students' written responses to the practice session paper and to each other's papers as the semester progresses; your feedback can encourage their helpful evaluation and criticism.

It is essential also to give students guidance on appropriate versus inappropriate responses:

- Students are not acting as proofreaders looking for errors.
- Students are most helpful when they give specific suggestions rather than make vague generalizations about the writing.
- Students need to focus their responses—to deal with the most important elements of the paper first. The questions on the peer response sheets at the end of this chapter can be helpful in focusing.
- Students should move from large to small, from the overall scope of the paper to paragraphs to sentences to grammar and mechanics, so their comments on each aspect will be logical in terms of the paper's purpose and intended audience.
- Chapter 2 of the handbook distinguishes between revising and editing and will help the students respond to each others' writing. The "Checklist for Revision" (p. 53), "Guidelines for Criticizing Others' Work" (p. 65), and "Guidelines for Benefiting from Criticism" (p. 66) delineate the interactive peer response process.
- Remind students that they are responding to and not revising their peers' papers; the papers remain the property of the writers, who make the final decisions about what revisions should be made.
- Because students find it easier to be negative than positive, teach them how to make positive comments by focusing on a paper's strengths. For example, if a paper is boring because it is too general throughout, the student can look for a concrete example and suggest that kind of writing should be interspersed throughout the paper.

Setting up and overseeing groups

Once students have a good introduction to peer criticism, they are ready to comment on each other's work. This activity can take place during class time or as homework. You may ask students to exchange papers within groups of three so that each student reads the work of the other two in the group. With this arrangement, students will get more than one set of responses and will be able to practice evaluating two different papers in the same exercise. What they see in one paper may help them comment on the other. But, of course, commenting on two papers takes more time than commenting on just one.

For this reason, the most common arrangement is for students to exchange papers in pairs. As with collaborative classroom exercises, you need not worry much about assigning students in pairs. Whomever they work with, students will learn from their peers' comments. You will want to be sure, however, that students group themselves in different pairs as the semester proceeds so that they benefit from a variety of readers' opinions.

In addition to commenting in writing on each other's essays, students should talk together about their papers. The written comments are a record that will help the author remember the reader's comments and allow the instructor to evaluate the work of the peer evaluators. But the oral comments may actually be the most valuable kind of feedback for the writer. When writer and reader talk together, they can question each other's responses and judgments. In this way, they learn not only how each reacted to the other's paper, but also why each responded that way. These conversations will also help students learn which of their comments are most helpful to the writer. Face-to-face conferences remind students that writing is communicating. It is not an act like competitive diving, in which you perform, someone responds by judging you, and it's over. In writing, one person performs, another responds, the first reacts to that response, the other responds, and so on.

Another form of oral conferencing is the group critique wherein a writer reads aloud and then readers respond while the writer listens. In such a forum it is important that the writer listen carefully to the listeners' responses before "answering" them. If writers interrupt or appear defensive, they may discourage their listeners from commenting fully. Like any other kind of peer evaluation, these group conferences need to be carefully directed by the instructor, who should create a sheet of directions to focus the peers' discussion.

After students have received their peer evaluation(s), they should be required to revise their essays. Peer criticism should be part of the writing process, not an evaluation of the final product. As they revise the papers, writers will need to study readers' comments carefully and find a way to respond to them. Be sure students understand that after considering a reader's responses, they may accept or reject them. Although many people may become involved in the production of a single writer's essay, the final responsibility for that essay belongs solely to the writer.

Preparing guidelines

For each peer evaluation exercise, you will want to provide written guidelines for the reader. (The sample forms referred to below appear at the end of this chapter.) Although some of the same questions may appear on every instruction sheet (requests for positive comments, for example), you can tailor the directions so that peer critics focus their attention either on particular aspects of the essay assignment or on a certain feature of writing. (See Forms F and G.) Although students may want to refer to the handbook if they are concentrating on a skill like paragraphing, they should avoid using the symbols or error correction codes, since those imply the strong voice of the judge, not the helpful suggestions of a peer reader.

The peer evaluation forms are arranged in order of increasing specificity and sophistication. Here are some suggestions for their use:

● You can use Form A to provide some very general guidelines. These procedures could be focused to suit any given class and its specific needs.

- Over the course of the semester, move from relatively straightforward critiques to more sophisticated kinds of responses. At first, direct the students just to describe the writer's paper: What is its main idea? What evidence is offered in support of that idea? This kind of student response requires little training beyond the ability to distinguish between description and evaluation, but it is frequently the most useful way for writers to find out whether their messages are being received loud and clear. Writers and readers must reach a fundamental understanding about what an essay says (or intends to say) before they can evaluate its success in fulfilling its objective. For this reason, every peer evaluation should begin with a summary of the paper's content. (See Form B.)
- Later in the semester, your reader response sheets can direct students to evaluate the writer's paper as well as summarize it. Students at this level can comment on the organization, logic, paragraphing, style, diction, or grammar of the paper, but they should not take sides or argue with the writer about the content of the essay. At this stage, students need to know how to respond as careful peer critics, but they do not need to entangle themselves in the writer's argument. (See Form C.)
- By the end of the semester, your students may be ready to comment on the content as well as the expression of a writer's work. To construct this kind of criticism, students need to be comfortable in their role as readers rather than judges, and they need to be proficient at limiting the number of their comments and focusing them. In this type of peer critique, students respond as "real" readers who argue with the writer's statements, question his or her evidence, provide additional support, or raise counterarguments, as well as noticing the quality of the writer's organization and style. (See Form D.)
- Because this kind of peer critique may lead the reader and writer to debate an issue, you may want to allow writers to respond formally to their readers. In fact, some instructors suggest that this kind of sophisticated peer evaluation be done in two rounds: the writer writes and the reader responds; then the writer answers and the reader responds again before the writer revises the paper for the last time. Students undertaking this kind of critical reading should be reminded that their first job as a peer evaluator is to summarize the writer's argument. Only when the writer and reader understand how each views the essay can they begin to discuss the merits of the essay's content. (See Form E.)

Some students may not be able to reach the last stage, but even those who practice only descriptive responses to their peers' work will be providing valuable feedback to the writer and learning valuable critical-reading processes themselves. When students practice this kind of peer criticism regularly, they learn from one another and they come to internalize their "editor," the voice inside their heads that tells them when an idea is irrelevant or a sentence incomplete.

 Combining self-evaluation and peer criticism

Sometimes you may want to give writers a chance to direct some of the peer critics' comments. Allowing writers to construct part of the reader response sheet for a given assignment may make the process of peer criticism more efficient. (See Form C, for example.) This extension of the conversation between writer and reader will also help emphasize that writing is an act of communication.

Another way of involving writers early in the process of peer evaluation is to have them fill out self-evaluation sheets, which can then be used either by peer readers or by an instructor. Knowing what strengths and weaknesses the writers see in their essays can help readers respond more efficiently. They do not have to waste time telling writers what those writers already know—that their transitions are rough, for example. Instead, readers can acknowledge where they agree with the writers' assessments and then spend more time discussing areas where the reader and writer disagree. If the two agree completely about the strengths and weaknesses of an essay, then they can move immediately to considering how to revise it.

Constructing a self-evaluation sheet is much like creating a reader response form. Be sure writers discuss the strengths as well as the weak points in the essay, and help them focus first on large elements and then on smaller elements of writing. Form H provides a sample self-evaluation sheet.

Students will also need some guidance in responding to criticism. You can refer them first to Chapter 2 of the handbook, but you will also want to discuss this valuable skill with the class as a whole. It is important for writers to share with one another the joys and frustrations of having their work evaluated. Writers must learn how to curb their anger if a reader disagrees with them, and they should practice separating themselves from their writing.

Give writers as many practical tips as possible. You will want to help students learn to question readers carefully in order to understand all the readers' comments. If writers are extremely sensitive about their prose, you can suggest that they pretend to be discussing and revising someone else's work instead of their own. You can also suggest that when writers want to experiment with following or rejecting readers' comments as they revise, they can photocopy their papers in order to retain the original version while they cut and paste or scratch out and scribble in words on the photocopy. Sometimes it is easier to accept a reader's suggestions if the writer feels that the pristine, original version still exists. It is always difficult to accept a reader's criticism of our writing—whether we are professional writers or novices. But if our students play the role of writer and reader simultaneously, they will be more apt to remember that the reader is simply trying to help them.

When you first experiment with collaborative learning, you may be surprised to find that some students do not want to participate. They may find it difficult to adjust to this new method of learning. Usually, though, it does not take long for these students to overcome their initial fears about exposing themselves to peer criticism, and they soon discover that while students' comments may differ from yours, they are equally valuable.

 ### Sample reader response forms

On the following pages are some samples of the instruction sheets used to guide peer critiques. You can use these samples as models when you create your own forms to suit your particular course objectives, or you can simply duplicate the forms and use them intact.

Form A
General Guidelines for Peer Readers
Commenting Directly on a Writer's Work

Author: Reader:

As a reader, you are going to comment directly on a photocopy of a classmate's paper. Read the paper through carefully before making any comments. Then follow the guidelines below. If the writer has submitted a self-evaluation sheet, read it *after* answering question 1.

1.   Consider the thesis, purpose, and audience for the paper. Are they indicated clearly? Are they consistent? If not, ask the writer questions to help clarify these essential elements of writing.

2.   Skim the paper to see how it is organized. Are there any breaks in the organization? If so, try to explain why you feel that a gap exists. Whenever possible, phrase your comments as questions, not judgments. If you think that the organization needs to be revised significantly, skip to question 7 after answering this question.

3.   Now go back and look at each paragraph. Is it unified, coherent, and developed? If not, ask the writer a question to help focus or complete the paragraph.

4.   Are the paragraphs connected to one another smoothly and logically? If there are any logical gaps between the paragraphs, ask the writer how one paragraph is linked to the next. If you think that most of the paragraphs need to be revised significantly, skip to question 7 after answering this question.

5.   Now look at sentences. Do any sentences confuse you? If so, try to describe your confusion or ask the writer a question about the sentence.

6.   Are there any mechanical or grammatical problems in the paper? If so, point them out to the writer, but do not correct them.

7.   Decide what the paper's two most important strengths are. Point these out to the writer.

Form B
Reader Response Sheet for a
Descriptive Critique

Author: Reader:

Answer the questions below, being as specific as possible.

1.   Read the first paragraph and then pause. Write down what you expect will be the topic, purpose, and audience of the paper.

2.   Now finish reading the paper. Were your expectations for the paper's topic, purpose, and audience fulfilled? If not, what do you now think the topic, purpose, and audience are?

3.   What do you think the main idea, or thesis, of the paper is?

4.   What sort of evidence is used to develop or support this main idea?

5.   Summarize the paper, devoting one sentence to each paragraph.

Form C
Reader Response Sheet for an
Evaluative Critique

Author: Reader:

Answer the questions below, being as specific as possible. If the author has included a self-evaluation sheet, do not read it until you have answered questions 1 through 6.

1. Read the first paragraph and then pause. Write down what you expect will be the topic, purpose, and audience of the paper.

2. Now finish reading the paper. Were your expectations for the paper's topic, purpose, and audience fulfilled? If not, what do you now think the topic, purpose, and audience are?

3. What do you think the main idea, or thesis, of the paper is?

4. What sort of evidence is used to develop or support this main idea?

5. Summarize the paper, devoting one sentence to each paragraph.

6. What did you like best about the paper?

7. Did anything in the paper surprise you?

8. What two features of the paper most need improvement?

9. Please respond to the author's questions on the back of this sheet.

———————————————————————————————

 To the author: Before giving this sheet to your reader, list below the three questions that you would like your reader to answer about this paper.

Form D
Reader Response Sheet for a
Thorough Critique

Author: Reader:

Answer the questions below, being as specific as possible. If the author has included a self-evaluation sheet, do not read it until you have answered questions 1 through 3.

1. Read the first paragraph and then pause. Write down what you expect will be the topic, purpose, and audience of the paper.

2. Now finish reading the paper. Were your expectations for the paper's topic, purpose, and audience fulfilled? If not, what do you now think the topic, purpose, and audience are?

3. Summarize the paper, devoting one sentence to each paragraph.

4. What do you think the main idea, or thesis, of the paper is? Do you agree with this thesis? Why or why not? What is your position on this topic?

5. What sort of evidence is used to develop or support this main idea? Is this evidence appropriate? Is there sufficient evidence? If not, what sort of evidence should the writer consider?

6. Does the author take into account different points of view about the thesis of the paper? Does the author consider counterarguments?

7. Are there any counterarguments that the author does not consider, but should?

8. What did you like best about this paper?

9. What two features of the paper most need improvement?

10. Please respond to the author's questions on the back of this sheet.

To the author: Before giving this sheet to your reader, list below the three questions that you would like your reader to answer about this paper.

Form E
Author's and Reader's Responses in
the Second Round of a Thorough Critique

Author: Reader:

Author's section. Please attach a revision of your original paper to this form and answer the following questions.

1. What do you think is your reader's point of view on this subject? Do you share that point of view?

2. What assumptions does your reader make about the topic? Do you agree with these assumptions? Why or why not?

3. What two comments by the reader were the most useful? Why were they helpful?

4. What are the two most important changes that you have made in this revision?

5. What do you like best about the essay?

6. What two questions would you like your reader to answer about this revision?

Reader's section. Please respond to the questions below.

1. Please summarize the author's revision, devoting one sentence to each paragraph.

2. How do you think that the author has improved the essay?

3. Has the author changed your feeling about the topic?

4. What is the strongest argument against the revised essay?

5. What two features most need improvement?

6. Respond to the author's questions.

Form F
Reader Response Sheet for an Essay Assignment
Stressing Paragraphing (Handbook, Chapter 3)

Author: Reader:

Answer the questions below, being as specific as possible. If the author has included a
self-evaluation sheet, do not read it until you have answered questions 1 through 6.

1.   Read the first paragraph and then pause. Write down what you expect will be the
topic, purpose, and audience of the paper.

2.   Now finish reading the paper. Were your expectations for the paper's topic, purpose, and audience fulfilled? If not, what do you now think the topic, purpose, and
audience are?

3.   What do you think the main idea, or thesis, of the paper is?

4.   What sort of evidence is used to develop or support this main idea?

5.   Next, number the paragraphs. Are the author's paragraphs unified, coherent, and
developed? If so, note them. Also indicate any that confuse you, and explain why.

6.   Do the paragraphs follow a logical order? Describe how the argument does or
does not flow from the first to the second, from the second to the third, and so on.

7.   What did you like best about the paper?

8.   What two features of the paper most need improvement?

Form G
Reader Response Sheet for an Essay Assignment
Stressing Clear and Effective Sentences
(Handbook, Parts III and IV)

Author:　　　　　　　　　　　　　　Reader:

Answer the questions below, being as specific as possible. If the author has included a self-evaluation sheet, do not read it until you have answered questions 1 through 4.

1.　Read the first paragraph and then pause. Write down what you expect will be the topic, purpose, and audience of the paper.

2.　Now finish reading the paper. Were your expectations for the paper's topic, purpose, and audience fulfilled? If not, what do you now think the topic, purpose, and audience are?

3.　What do you think the main idea, or thesis, of the paper is?

4.　What sort of evidence is used to develop or support this main idea?

5.　Were the author's sentences easy to read? Number the sentences and indicate below any that you thought were confusing. Next to the sentence numbers, try to explain why the sentences were confusing.
　　Sentence number　　　Problem

6.　Did you notice any grammatical problems in the author's sentences? If so, list the sentence number and the grammatical problem below.
　　Sentence number　　　Problem

7.　Describe the most common sentence structure found in the author's paper. Does the author vary sentence structure? If so, describe two instances in which sentence variety was especially effective. If not, suggest places where sentences need to be varied.

8.　What did you like best about the paper?

9.　What two features of the paper most need improvement?

Form H
Self-Evaluation Sheet to Accompany an
Essay for Peer Response or Instructor's Evaluation

Author:

In order to help your instructor or peer reader evaluate this essay, you should explain where you are in the writing process. Be as specific as possible in answering the following questions.

1. What are you trying to say in this paper? What is your main idea?

2. Who might be interested in reading this paper?

3. What do you like best in the paper?

4. What do you like least in the paper?

5. What would you work on if you had twenty-four hours more to spend on the project?

6. What three questions would you like to ask your reader? How can your reader help you develop the paper further?

Resources for collaborative learning and peer criticism

Bruffee, Kenneth. "Collaborative Learning and the 'Conversation of Mankind.' " *College English* 46 (1984): 635–52.

---. *A Short Course in Writing*. 3rd ed. Boston: Little, 1985.

Clark, Beverly Lyon. *Talking About Writing: A Guide for Tutor and Teacher Conferences*. Ann Arbor: U of Michigan P, 1985.

Fox, Len. "What to Do When Grammar Exercises No Longer Help: Group Proofreading." *College Composition and Communication* 32 (1981): 332–33.

Fraser, Scott C., et al. "Two, Three, or Four Heads Are Better Than One: Modification of College Performance by Peer Monitoring." *Journal of Educational Psychology* 69 (1977–78): 101–08.

Gebhardt, Richard. "Team Work and Feedback: Broadening the Base of Collaborative Writing." *College English* 42 (1980): 69–74.

George, Diana. "Working with Peer Groups in the Composition Classroom." *College Composition and Communication* 35 (1984): 320–26.

Gere, Anne Ruggles. *Writing Groups: History, Theory, and Implications*. Carbondale: Southern Illinois UP, 1987.

Gere, Anne Ruggles, and Robert D. Abbott. "Talking About Writing: The Language of Writing Groups." *Research in the Teaching of English* 19 (1985): 362–86.

Gere, Anne Ruggles, and Ralph Stevens. "The Language of Writing Groups: How Oral Response Shapes Revision." In *The Acquisition of Written Language: Response and Revision*. Ed. Sarah Warshauer Freedman. Norwood: Ablex, 1985. 85–105.

Hawkins, Thom. *Group Inquiry Techniques for Teaching Writing*. Urbana: NCTE, 1976.

Kail, Harvey. "Collaborative Learning in Context: The Problem with Peer Tutoring." *College English* 45 (1983): 817–23.

Knox-Zuinn, Carolyn. "Collaboration in the Writing Classroom: An Interview with Ken Kesey." *College Composition and Communication* 41 (1990): 309–17.

Reither, James A., and Douglas Vipond. "Writing as Collaboration." *College English* 51 (1989): 855–67.

Salmon, Phillida, and Hilary Claire. *Classroom Collaboration*. London: Routledge, 1984.

Schuster, Charles. "The Un-Assignment: Writing Groups for Advanced Expository Writers." *Freshman English News* 13 (Winter 1984): 433–46.

Spear, Karen. *Sharing Writing: Peer Response Groups in English Classes*. Portsmouth: Heinemann, 1988.

Trimbur, John. "Collaborative Learning and Teaching Writing." In *Perspectives on Research and Scholarship in Composition*. Ed. Ben W. McClelland and Timothy R. Donovan. New York: MLA, 1985. 87–109.

---. "Consensus and Difference in Collaborative Learning." *College English* 51 (1989): 602–16.

*The
Little,
Brown
Handbook*

The Little, Brown Handbook

Fifth
Edition

H. Ramsey Fowler   *Memphis State University*

Jane E. Aaron   *Parsons School of Design/*
                       The New School for Social Research

HarperCollins*Publishers*

Sponsoring Editor: Patricia Rossi
Development Editor: Marisa L. L'Heureux
Project Editor: Robert Ginsberg
Design Supervisor: Jaye Zimet
Text and Cover Design: Brand X Studios/Robin Hessel Hoffmann
Production Administrator: Beth Maglione/Kathleen Donnelly
Compositor: The Clarinda Company
Printer and Binder: R. R. Donnelley and Sons Company
Cover Printer: The Lehigh Press, Inc.

The Little, Brown Handbook, Fifth Edition
Copyright © 1992 by HarperCollins Publishers Inc.

Library of Congress Cataloging-in-Publication Data

Fowler, H. Ramsey (Henry Ramsey)
    The Little, Brown handbook / H. Ramsey Fowler, Jane E. Aaron.—
5th ed.
      p.   cm.
    Includes index.
    ISBN 0-673-52132-X.— ISBN 0-673-52203-2 (instructor's ed.)
    1. English language—Grammar—1950-   2. English language—
Rhetoric.   I. Aaron, Jane E. II. Little, Brown and Company.
III. Title.
PE1112.F64 1992
808'.042—dc20   91-15903
                                                                        CIP

91 92 93 94 9 8 7 6 5 4 3 2 1

*We thank the following authors and publishers for permission to quote from their
works.*

The American Heritage Dictionary. Synonym study for *real.* Copyright © 1985 by Houghton
    Mifflin Company. Reprinted by permission from *The American Heritage Dictionary, Second
    College Edition.*
Bonnie Angelo. Excerpt from "Those Good Ole Boys," *Time,* 27 September 1976. Copyright ©
    1976 Time Warner Inc. Reprinted by permission.
Peter Bogdanovich. Excerpted from "Bogie in Excelsis" in *Pieces of Time.* © 1973 by Peter
    Bogdanovich. Used by permission of Arbor House Publishing Company and the author.
Daniel J. Boorstin. Excerpt from *The Discoverers* by Daniel J. Boorstin. Copyright © 1983 by
    Daniel J. Boorstin. Reprinted by permission of Random House, Inc.
Suzanne Britt. Excerpt from "That Lean and Hungry Look," *Newsweek,* 9 October 1978. Copy-
    right © 1978, 1988 by Suzanne Britt. Reprinted by permission.
Lynn M. Buller. Excerpt from "The Encyclopedia Game" in Saul D. Feldman and Gerald W.
    Thielbar, eds., *Life Style: Diversity in American Society.* Copyright © 1977 by Little, Brown
    and Company (Inc.). Reprinted by permission.

(Credits continue on page 789)

Preface for Instructors

Beginning this fifth edition of *The Little, Brown Handbook,* we expected to have plenty to change. A hard-used text like this one collects myriad suggestions for improvement from the instructors and students who rely on it. And changes would also be needed, we knew, to keep pace with the vigorous and challenging field of composition instruction. We were right. The book you're holding is in many important ways the same: it remains a comprehensive guide to the possibilities and conventions of writing, with clear, accessible information on the writing process and the research paper as well as on grammar and rhetoric. But scores of significant alterations and expansions have made this new edition, we think, a more effective classroom text and reference for writers than ever before.

Features of the fifth edition

Our revisions have concentrated on improving ease of use and tone and on revamping or expanding text, examples, and exercises to make them more current, useful, and interesting.

Ease of use

- The **new design** is brighter and more open, with a larger typeface, different colors for main and secondary headings, and more white space.

- Nearly twice as many **boxes** highlight important information and speed reference time.
- **Lists** replace paragraphs of text for practical tips, guidelines, and the like.
- **Running heads** at the tops of pages have been reduced to key words for quicker reference. Positioned as before on the outsides of pages, they are visible to anyone thumbing the book.
- The students' preface, "Using This Book," features a **visual guide to the handbook** (p. xiii).
- The **glossary of terms** includes more than a hundred new entries for rhetoric and composition as well as grammar—for instance, *critical thinking, paraphrase, transition.*

Tone

- Pruning has produced a more **streamlined text** emphasizing essential skills and stategies.
- The **writing** is fresher and more immediate, addressing students more directly and informally.
- Consistently **positive wording of headings** stresses what *to* do, eliminating "avoid" and "don't."

Expanded and updated text

- In the material on the **writing process** (Chapters 1–2), highlights of this edition include new advice on understanding and responding to writing assignments (pp. 5–7); a more detailed discussion of audience, placed closer to the start of the process (11–17); new tips to help students gain distance from their work for revision and editing (51, 58, 61); and coaching for students involved in collaborative learning (65, 66). A new student essay-in-progress, on cultural diversity in the media, illustrates the writing process from initial freewriting through four drafts.
- Chapter 4, **"Critical Thinking and Argument,"** is almost wholly new. It emphasizes strategies of critical reading (pp. 120–32), how to read an argument critically (132–50), and how to write arguments that stand up to critical reading (143–68). Among many other features, the chapter includes a sample text that has been read and annotated by a student, practical advice for analysis, and tips for organizing and revising an argument.
- Chapter 31 on **diction,** now titled "Choosing and Using Words," contains new material on double talk (p. 481) and a more detailed discussion of writing concisely—or, as we used to say, avoiding wordiness (494–501).
- Many changes have improved the chapters on **research writ-**

ing (35–38). The chapters still outline a process of research writing, with two student essays-in-progress to illustrate the stages. But the stages themselves have been streamlined, and documentation now has its own easy-to-find chapter (37) covering the MLA system. As before, the documentation pages are edged in color for quick reference. The models—including many new ones—are numbered and indexed in boxes. New text and illustrations on computerized databases introduce students to these contemporary resources (560–62). The discussion of evaluating sources is expanded (568–70). And the vexing problem of introducing quotations and other borrowed material receives its own heading along with more advice and illustrations (590–93). By request, we have retained the annotated student research papers on women in business management and the editing of the Declaration of Independence.

- The well-received chapter on **writing in the disciplines** (now 39) retains the literary analysis based wholly on the student's reading but includes a new literary analysis using secondary sources (pp. 686–89). In the discussion of social sciences writing, the APA documentation system has received close attention: boxed indexes direct students to numbered models, including half a dozen new ones, and all the models receive clear explanation (693–703).

Examples and exercises

- We have overhauled the **content** of the handbook's examples and exercises to reflect more closely the kind of writing expected of students in college and at work, to broaden the range of cultural experiences and concerns represented, and to enliven the book with interesting and significant writing. Topics range from business ethics to the search for extraterrestrial life, from AIDS to music to soccer.
- **End-of-part revision exercises** conclude all the parts of the book concerned with sentences, punctuation, and mechanics. In each exercise, students are asked to revise a brief essay containing a range of the errors or usages covered in the preceding group of chapters. The exercise concluding Part II, for instance, includes errors in case, verb form, agreement, and adjectives and adverbs. (See pp. 270, 326, 372, 450, 474.)
- New **titles for all exercises** clearly indicate what is expected—for instance, "Revising: Case" or "Sentence combining: *Who* versus *whom*." As the titles make clear, the handbook's exercises stress revision.
- All exercises now consist of **connected discourse** rather than isolated sentences on unrelated topics.

Supplements

- The **Instructor's Annotated Edition,** prepared by Kay Limburg of Montgomery College, combines material for teachers and the students' edition in one convenient volume. Besides answers to all the handbook's exercises (adjacent to the exercises themselves), the instructor's edition contains essays on approaches to composition teaching, using the handbook, evaluating and responding to student writing, and using collaborative learning in the classroom. In addition, it features extensive reading suggestions and scores of classroom discussion topics and activities—all positioned next to the relevant text in the student version. In this edition, exercises especially suited for collaborative learning and material available on transparency masters are marked for easy reference.
- **The Little, Brown Workbook,** Fifth Edition, by Donna Gorrell of St. Cloud State University, parallels the handbook's organization but provides briefer text and many more exercises for students who need extra work with the writing process, grammar, or usage. The fifth edition also covers the short research paper.
- **The Little, Brown ESL Workbook,** by Joseph K. Dowling of Nassau Community College, is also geared to the handbook but specifically addresses students using English as a second language, emphasizing the issues most challenging to them.
- **53rd Street Writer,** word-processing software developed by the Daedalus Group, provides students with an easy-to-learn, writing-oriented tool for drafting and revision. It includes *Documenter,* which helps students put their citations in correct MLA or APA form.
- An **on-line version of the handbook** is available both with *53rd Street Writer* and as stand-alone software.
- **PFS: First Choice,** integrated software with printed documentation, combines word processing, a dictionary and thesaurus, file management, spreadsheet analysis, graphics, and electronic communications.
- **MacWrite,** a word processor created by Claris, is accompanied by *MacWrite and the Writing Process,* a guide for writers, by Mark Coleman of SUNY–Potsdam.
- **Collins Gem Thesaurus** and **Webster's Dictionary** are available at a discount when purchased with *The Little, Brown Handbook.*
- A **comprehensive assessment package** includes *Competency Profile Test Bank,* objective tests covering ten areas of English competency; diagnostic tests in several forms (two keyed to *The Little, Brown Handbook*); and samples of the Florida and Texas state exams (CLAST and TASP). The test

bank and diagnostic tests are available on-line for use in computer labs.

- **Other supplements** are a book of seventy-five transparency masters reproduced from the handbook; an answer key to the handbook, available to students at an instructor's option; a student manual to guide peer evaluation; a correction chart for easy reference; *Teaching Writing: Theories and Practices; Model Research Papers from Across the Disciplines; 80 Readings,* a collection of student and professional essays; *80 Practices,* supplementary exercises; and *Writing, Teaching, and Learning,* a video and printed supplement for teachers of writing across the curriculum.

All the supplements are available from your local Harper-Collins representative.

Acknowledgments

If *The Little, Brown Handbook* stays fresh and useful, it is because hundreds of generous and thoughtful instructors have talked with sales representatives, phoned the publisher, answered questionnaires, participated in focus groups, and written reviews—all to let us know what's right with the book and what's wrong. This time around, we are especially grateful to more than two dozen instructors who wrote us in detail about their impressions of teaching, textbooks, and *The Little, Brown Handbook:* Barbara Arthur, University of Houston; Kathleen L. Bell, Old Dominion University; Barbara Fahey Blakey, Scottsdale Community College; Patricia Bridges, Grand Valley State University; Robert P. Burke, Joliet Junior College; David L. Elliott, Keystone Junior College; R. Scott Evans, University of the Pacific; Kim Flachman, California State University, Bakersfield; M. Kip Hartvigsen and Ralph W. Thompson, Ricks College; Milton Hawkins, Del Mar College; Rebecca Wagner Hite, Southeastern Louisiana University; Maureen Hoag, Wichita State University; Marjorie C. Horton, Framingham State College; Paul Hunter, North Lake College; Edward A. Kline, University of Notre Dame; Faye J. Maclaga, Wilson Technical Community College; Daniel McGavin, Davenport College of Business; Thomas Pribek, University of Wisconsin, La Crosse; William O. Shakespeare, Brigham Young University; Judy Shank, Valencia Community College; Ann C. Spurlock, Mississippi State University; Claudia Thomas, Wake Forest University; Merle O'R. Thompson, Northern Virginia Community College; P. Eugene Violette, Southern Illinois University, Edwardsville; and Karen W. Willingham, Pensacola Junior College. In addition to these teachers, we owe special debts to Mary Sue Ply, Southeastern Louisiana University, who not only reviewed the manuscript but also contributed many new exercises, and to Kay Limburg, Montgomery College, who read the fifth edition in its several drafts and prepared the estimable *Instructor's Annotated Edition*.

At or surrounding HarperCollins, a number of very talented and genial people have made it their business to see this edition into instructors' and students' hands. Patricia Rossi, Marisa L'Heureux, and David Munger gave unstinting editorial support. Debora A. Person helped update the library section. Ann Stypuloski contributed a sharp marketing sense. Robin Hoffman invented a stunning new design under the creative direction of Jaye Zimet. Robert Ginsberg shepherded the book (and its authors) through production without a blink. Merilyn Yee made normally plagued steps in the process seem easy, even fun.

There might be no fifth edition of *The Little, Brown Handbook* if not for the earlier contributions of the late Richard S. Beal, professor emeritus at Boston University. We are among the lucky to have known and learned from this man of great wisdom, pragmatism, and humanity.

The Little, Brown Handbook is a basic resource that will answer almost any question you have about writing. Here you can find out how to get ideas, overcome writer's block, punctuate quotations, use capital letters, cite sources, or write a résumé. All this information and more is written and arranged to help you locate what you need.

Using this book will not by itself make you a good writer; for that, you need to care about your work at every level, from finding a subject to spelling words. But learning how to use the handbook and mastering the information in it can give you the means to write *what* you want in the *way* you want.

Organization and content

An overview of the handbook appears inside the front cover. Briefly, the book divides into the following sections:

- Chapters 1–4 deal with the big picture: the goals and strategies of writing, the construction of paragraphs, and the essential skills of critical thinking and argument.
- Chapters 5–19 cover sentence basics: the system of English grammar and its conventions, errors that affect clarity, and techniques of effective sentences.
- Chapters 20–30 treat two technical elements of sentences and

words, punctuation and mechanics (meaning capital letters, underlining, and the like).

- Chapters 31–34 move to words—how to choose them, look them up, learn them, spell them.
- Chapters 35–39 cover research writing from planning through revising, with a complete guide to documenting sources and a special chapter on writing in various academic disciplines.
- Chapters 40 and 41 and Appendixes A and B contain very practical information on taking essay exams, writing business letters and job applications, preparing a manuscript, and writing with a word processor.
- Two glossaries—one of problem words and expressions, the other of terms—and a detailed index finish the book.

Finding information

How you use the handbook will depend on your instructor's wishes and your own inclinations. Your instructor may assign whole sections of the book and discuss them in class or may use comments on your papers to direct you to particular sections. He or she will certainly encourage you to look things up on your own whenever you have a question. To help you do that, the handbook provides many ways of finding information quickly. Some of these surround the main text:

- The **Plan of the Book,** inside the front cover, displays the book's entire contents in abbreviated form. This plan also shows the system of coded headings (explained below).
- The **Contents,** immediately after this preface, gives a more detailed version of the book's plan.
- The list titled **Useful Lists and Summaries,** inside the back cover, indexes topics that students frequently ask about.
- The list titled **Correction Symbols,** also inside the back cover, gives the abbreviations often used to mark papers (explained below).
- The **Index,** on the last pages of the book, lists every term and concept and every problem word or expression mentioned in the book. It is very detailed so that you can locate the precise point you seek and the page number where the point is discussed.

Many of the handbook's reference and learning aids appear on the text pages themselves, as illustrated by the reduced samples on the facing page.

Running head (header) in orange: topic discussed on this page

Vertical line in yellow: exercise

Marginal box in blue-green: symbol for topic being discussed (agr) and code of nearest section heading (8b)

Section heading, in blue-green, with heading code in box: chapter number (8), section letter (b)

Text in black: explanation

Box in gray with yellow circle: summary or checklist

Cross-reference to further discussion: here, to section 8b, subsection 3

Subsection heading in orange, with heading number in triangle

Indented text: examples, often in labeled pairs showing revisions

Bold type in text: term being defined

Pronoun and antecedent / 255

13. When someone who has seemed too easily distracted is entrusted with updating the cartoons, his or her concentration often improves.
14. In the face of levity, the former sourpuss becomes one of those who hides bad temper.
15. Every one of the consultants caution, however, that humor has no place in life-affecting corporate situations such as employee layoffs.

agr
8b

8b **Make pronouns and their antecedents agree in person and number.**

The **antecedent** of a pronoun is the noun or other pronoun it refers to.

Home owners fret over *their* tax bills. [*Home owners* is the antecedent of *their.*]

Its constant increases make the *tax bill* a dreaded document. [*Tax bill* is the antecedent of *its.*]

As these examples show, a pronoun agrees with its antecedent in gender (masculine, feminine, neuter), person (first, second, third), and number (singular, plural). (See p. 247 for an explanation of these terms.) Since pronouns derive their meaning

Summary of pronoun-antecedent agreement

- Basic pronoun-antecedent agreement:
  Old Faithful spews *its* columns of water, each of *them* over 115 feet high.
- Antecedents joined by *and* (8b-1):
  Old Faithful and Giant are geysers known for *their* height.
- Antecedents joined by *or* or *nor* (8b-2):
  Either Giant or Giantess ejects *its* column the highest.
- Indefinite pronouns as antecedents (8b-3):
  Each of the geysers has *its* own personality. Anyone who visits has *his or her* memories.
- Collective nouns as antecedents (8b-4):
  A crowd amuses *itself* watching Old Faithful. The crowd go *their* separate ways.

2 **When parts of an antecedent are joined by *or* or *nor*, the pronoun agrees with the nearer part.**

When the parts of an antecedent are connected by *or* or *nor*, the pronoun should agree with the part closer to it.

Tenants or owners must present *their* grievances.
Either the tenant or the owner will have *her* way.

When one subject is plural and the other singular, the sentence will be awkward unless you put the plural subject second.

Awkward Neither the tenants nor the owner has yet made *her* case.

Revised Neither the owner nor the tenants have yet made *their* case.

3 **Generally, use a singular pronoun when the antecedent is an indefinite pronoun.**

Indefinite pronouns such as *anybody* and *something* refer to persons or things in general rather than to a specific person or thing. (See p. 251 for a list.) Most indefinite pronouns are singular in meaning. When these indefinite pronouns serve as antecedents to other pronouns, the other pronouns are singular.

Notice especially two features of the text page: the heading code in both blue-green boxes (**8b** on the samples) and the symbol in the marginal box (**agr** in the samples). You can use these abbreviations in two ways:

- In the plan of the book, you can find the topic you want, note its heading code or symbol, and thumb the book until you locate the matching code or symbol in the marginal box.
- Your instructor may use heading codes or correction symbols to mark specific weaknesses in your papers—for instance, either **8b** or **agr** on your paper would indicate an agreement problem. To discover just what the problem is and how to revise it, you can consult the plan of the book or the list of correction symbols, or you can thumb the book. (A sample student paper marked by an instructor with some codes and symbols appears on pp. 61–64.)

The handbook's reference aids are meant to speed your work, but you need not use any or all of them. You may of course browse or read this book like any other, with no particular goal in mind but seeing what you can learn.

Recommended usage

The conventions described and illustrated in this handbook are those of standard written English—the label given the language of business and the professions. Written English is more conservative than spoken English in matters of grammar and usage, and a great many words and constructions that are widely spoken remain unaccepted in careful writing.

When clear distinctions exist between the language of conversation and that of careful writing, the handbook provides examples of each and labels them *spoken* and *written*. When usage in writing itself varies with the level of formality intended, the handbook labels examples *formal* and *informal*. When usage is mixed or currently changing, the handbook recommends that you choose the more conservative usage because it will be acceptable to all readers.

If you follow the advice in this handbook, your writing will be clearer and more compelling than it might have been. Remember, though, that adhering to established conventions is but a means to the real achievement and reward of writing: effectively communicating your message.

Contents

Part II
Grammatical Sentences   169

Part III
Clear Sentences   *271*

Part IV
Effective Sentences   327

Part V
Punctuation   373

Part VI
Mechanics   *451*

Part VIII

Research Writing   539

Part IX
Practical Writing   719

Appendixes

Part I

The Whole Paper and Paragraphs

Why write? Many students are likely to have this question in mind when they first open *The Little, Brown Handbook* or even when they first register for a composition course or sit listening to the instructor on the first day of the class.

This chapter begins by addressing the question directly and recognizing the difficulties faced by all writers—experienced or inexperienced. Next, the chapter alerts students to the various elements of the writing situation and the writing process and discusses ways to discover subjects and purposes for writing. The concluding sections explore flexible strategies for considering audience, developing and grouping ideas, focusing on a thesis, and creating a plan for the initial draft.

Exploratory strategies discussed are journal writing, observing, freewriting, listing, clustering, reading, questioning, and using patterns of development. Strategies for developing and planning include using thesis sentences, tree diagrams, and outlines. Two special features of this chapter are the attention paid to the role of audience throughout the composing process and the list of "Questions About Audience" (page 13).

Though Chapter 1 looks at activities typical of the early stages of composing and Chapter 2 treats drafting and revising, the text does not endorse a strictly linear view of the composing process. Instead, both chapters emphasize the writer's many options and the flexibility of the composing process. They point out that writing is a way of thinking and discovering: that in the middle of drafting an essay a writer may recognize the need to develop new supporting ideas, to make major changes in the organization, or to shift the purpose of the essay and modify the thesis.

AT EASE

Students often bring their apprehensions about writing (and writing instructors) with them to class. To create a positive atmosphere for your course, you may wish to establish a setting in which students feel at ease about acknowledging and sharing their apprehensions. One way to do this is to ask them to *list* what they dislike (and like) about writing without worrying about the form or correctness of entries in their lists. Voluntary sharing of the entries can help reduce the

Chapter 1

Developing an Essay

"Writing is easy," said the late sportswriter Red Smith. "All you have to do is sit down at the typewriter and open a vein." Clearly, Smith found writing demanding. But if it hurt, why did he bother to write? Why should you?

- Writing will help you explore the world and yourself. Through writing, you can share your discoveries with others.
- Writing is a powerful tool for thinking and learning. It can help you understand ideas, manage information, and demonstrate your abilities.
- Writing will help you get through college and into a good job. The better writer you are, the better student and worker you'll be.
- Writing will increase your power by helping you to express yourself and persuade others to agree with you.

Part of gaining these rewards as a writer is learning the skills to express yourself clearly and interestingly, skills covered throughout this book. But you can also learn from other writers— from the comments of classmates and teachers on your work, from the reading you do for information and stimulation, and (a particular concern of Chapters 1 and 2) from an understanding of how other writers work. You'll know you're really working at writing if now and then you experience some of Red Smith's pain; but the insight and control you earn in exchange will more than make up for it.

1a   The writing situation and the writing process

All writing occurs in a context that simultaneously limits and clarifies the writer's choices. Most obviously, context includes the nature of the assignment, the assigned length, and the deadline. But context can also be seen as the **writing situation,** in which the writer aims to communicate something about a subject to a particular audience of readers. For each writing task, considering the following questions can help you define and make choices:

- What is your subject?
- Who is your audience?
- How can you present yourself and your subject to that audience?

Sometimes the writing situation is clearly defined from the start. Imagine that you are assigned a report on an experiment in your physics course, a report expected to show your instructor that you have mastered scientific observation and the principles studied in the course. In this case, your subject, your audience, and the way you should present yourself are predefined for you by the assignment. For other writing tasks, however, the writing situation may be left to you to define. If your composition instructor asks you to write an essay relating a significant learning experience, you will have to determine what experience to relate as well as how you want to present yourself and your experience, and you may need to select your audience.

Understanding the writing situation is an important part of the **writing process**—the term for all the activities, mental and physical, that go into writing what eventually becomes a finished piece of work. Even for experienced writers the process is usually messy, which is one reason that it is sometimes difficult. Though we may get a sense of ease and orderliness from a well-crafted magazine article, we can safely assume that the writer had to work hard to achieve it, suffering frustration when ideas would not come, struggling to express half-formed thoughts, shaping and reshaping the same paragraph to make a point convincingly.

There is no *one* writing process: no two writers proceed in the same way, and even an individual writer adapts his or her process to the task at hand. Still, most experienced writers pass through certain stages that overlap and circle back on each other.

isolation many students feel and help you (and them) set priorities for instruction.

RESOURCES AND IDEAS

Laura Brady, "Overcoming Resistance: Computers in the Writing Classroom," *Computers and Composition* 7.2 (1990): 21–33. Brady found that word processing in the freshman composition classroom increased the volume of student writing, prompted new ways of thinking about topics, encouraged collaboration, and fostered a positive workshop atmosphere.

Kathleen G. Dixon, "Intellectual Development and the Place of Narrative in 'Basic' and Freshman Composition," *Journal of Basic Writing* 8 (1989): 3–20. Dixon discusses the effect of developmental models, such as those developed by Piaget and Vygotsky, on theories of composition and the consequent role of narrative in the freshman writing program.

R. Baird Shuman, "Basics in Composition: Fluency First," *Teaching the Basics—Really!* ed. Ouida Clapp (Urbana: NCTE, 1977) 43–46. Shuman presents activities to overcome students' fears of writing and to help them get started.

RESOURCES AND IDEAS
The Writing Situation

Linda S. Flower and John R. Hayes, "The Cognition of Discovery: Defining a Rhetorical Problem," *College Composition and Communication* 31 (1980): 21–32. This article reports on a detailed study of how good writers and poor writers conceive of writing tasks as they begin to compose.

Ken David, "The Circle Game: A Heuristic for Discovering Rhetorical Situations," *College Composition and Communication* 29 (1978): 285–87. David suggests giving students roles to play in social situations and challenging them to develop writing tasks appropriate to the situations.

David Tedlock, "The Case Approach to Composition," *College Composition and Communication* 32 (1981): 253–62. Tedlock argues for the use of cases—detailed, self-contained descriptions of a writing situation—as a basis for assignments and instructions.

dev
1a

dev
1a

The Writing Process

Linda Flower and John R. Hayes, "A Cognitive Process Theory of Writing," *College Composition and Communication* 32 (1981): 365–87. This article contains what is probably the best known and most widely accepted discussion of the elements and goals of the writing process, though the model it presents is admittedly theoretical rather than practical.

Nancy MacKenzie, "Teaching the Composing Process: A Three-Part Project," *The Writing Instructor* 1 (1982): 103–11. MacKenzie describes an in-class exercise, a diary assignment, and a process paper designed to direct "students' attention to the strengths and weaknesses of their own composing processes."

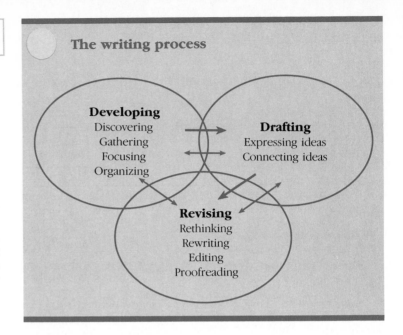

1. *Developing* or *planning*: discovering a subject, gathering information, focusing on a central theme, and organizing material.
2. *Drafting*: expressing and connecting ideas.
3. *Revising*: rethinking and improving structure, content, style, and presentation.

You, too, will experience these stages as you write. At various points, you will need to take stock of these elements:

Your topic (section 1b)
Your purpose (1c)
Your audience (1d)

And you will probably find it helpful to experiment with some techniques that have worked for experienced writers:

Developing a topic (1e)   Revising (2b)
Developing a thesis (1f)   Editing (2c)
Organizing (1g)   Proofreading (2d)
Drafting (2a)   Receiving criticism (2e)

With experience, as you complete varied assignments and try varied techniques, you will develop your own basic writing process.

Periodically in this chapter and the next you will see examples of how one student worked from an assignment to a finished essay by drawing on some of the procedures discussed. Occasionally, examples of other students' work will also be introduced to illustrate other approaches. These students' writing situations are not yours, and their solutions to writing problems may not work for you. But following their progress should supplement what you learn on your own about the difficulties and the rewards of writing.

Exercise 1
Starting a writing journal

Recall several writing experiences that you have had—a letter you had difficulty with, an essay you enjoyed, an allnighter spent happily or miserably on a term paper, and so on. What do these experiences reveal to you about writing, particularly your successes and problems with it? For instance:

> Do you like to experiment with language?
> Do you prefer writing in response to specific assignments rather than general ones?
> Are some kinds of writing easier than others?
> Do you have trouble getting ideas or expressing them?
> Do you worry about grammar and spelling?
> Do your readers usually understand what you mean?

Write these thoughts down as the first entry in a continuing journal or log in which you track your new experiences as a writer. As you complete writing assignments for your composition course and other courses, keep adding to the journal, noting especially which procedures seem most helpful to you. Your aim is to discover your feelings about writing so that you can develop a dependable writing process of your own.

ANSWERS: EXERCISE 1

Individual response.

1b Discovering and limiting a subject

For most college and business writing, you will write in response to an assignment. The assignment may specify your subject, or it may leave the choice to you. (If you're stuck, you can use the discovery techniques in section 1e to think of subjects.) Whether the subject is assigned or not, it will probably need some thought if it is to achieve these aims:

- The subject should be suitable for the assignment.
- It should be neither too general nor too limited for the length of paper and deadline assigned.
- As much as possible, it should be something you care about.

RESOURCES AND IDEAS

Susan Guiher-Huff, "Involvement in a Current Problem as a Basis for Writing," *Teaching English in the Two-Year College* 17 (1990): 187–88. Guiher-Huff describes how students used a range of essay formats, made a cause-and-effect oral presentation, and wrote persuasive letters around the topic of pollution. The sustained topic seemed to make the writing meaningful for the students.

Peter H. Schreffler, " 'Where All the Children Are Above Average': Garrison Keillor as a Model for Personal Narrative Assignments," *College Composition and Communication* 40 (1989): 82–85. Schreffler discusses the de-

dev
1b

lightful experience personal narrative writing can be as students delve into themselves as well as into the world around them.

D. Gordon Rohman, "Pre-writing: The State of Discovery in the Writing Process," *College Composition and Communication* 16 (1965): 106–12. Rohman describes a program of invention based on techniques of self-analysis and meditation.

Raymond J. Rodrigues, "Folklife: An Unlimited Writing Source," *On Righting Writing,* ed. Ouida H. Clapp (Urbana: NCTE, 1975) 37–39. This selection offers a list of family and community traditions that students can explore as sources for essays.

TRANSPARENCY MASTER
AVAILABLE

RESOURCES AND IDEAS

Marcia Bundy Seabury, "The Abstraction Ladder in Freshman Composition," *College Composition and Communication* 40 (1989): 89–92. Seabury has found that teaching S. I. Hayakawa's abstraction ladder can benefit freshmen composition students in their thinking through and writing about their topics.

TRANSPARENCY MASTER
AVAILABLE

 Pursuing your interests and experiences

Some assignments, such as a physics lab report or a business case study, leave you little room to express yourself. But even these assignments provide some leeway—for instance, in how you conduct and write your research. And many other subjects that may seem inflexible actually allow you considerable freedom. If you are assigned a comparison-and-contrast essay on two people you know, the choice of people and the way you compare them could make the difference for you between simply enduring the writing process or enjoying and learning from it. An assigned history essay on Abraham Lincoln as President offers you the chance to look at Lincoln from your own unique angle—perhaps the President as economist, or the weaknesses of such a heroic President.

When no subject is assigned, find one in your experiences, interests, or curiosities.

- What subject do you already know something about or have you been wondering about? Athletic scholarships? Unemployment in your town?
- Have you recently participated in a lively discussion about a controversial topic? About an event in your family's history? About a change in relations between men and women?
- What have you read or seen at the movies or on television? A shocking book? A violent or funny movie? An effective television commercial?
- What topic in the reading or class discussion for a course has intrigued you or seemed especially relevant to your own experiences? A social issue such as homelessness? A psychological problem such as depression?
- What makes you especially happy or especially angry? A hobby? The behavior of your neighbors?
- Which of your own or others' dislikes and preferences would you like to understand better? A demand for gas-guzzling cars? A taste for raw fish?

 Matching subject and assignment

When you receive an assignment, consider the following questions to guide your choice of subject.

- What's wanted from you? Many writing assignments contain words such as *describe, analyze, report, interpret, explain, define, argue,* or *evaluate.* These words specify the way you are to approach your subject and what your broad purpose is (see 1c).

- For whom are you writing? Some assignments will specify your readers, but usually you will have to figure out for yourself whether your audience is the general reading public, your classmates, your boss, the college community, your instructor, or some other group or individual. For more on analyzing your audience, see section 1d.
- What kind of research is required? Sometimes an assignment specifies the kinds of sources you are expected to consult, and you can use such information to choose your subject. (If you are unsure whether research is required, check with your instructor.)
- What is the length of the paper? The deadline? Having a week to write three pages or three weeks to write six pages can make a big difference in the subject you select (see below).

 3   Limiting the subject

Because most assignments leave some room for you to shape the subject, they are usually quite general. The same may be true of your first attempts to make the assigned subject your own or to invent a subject. Lincoln's weaknesses as President, federal aid to college students, corporate support for the arts, summer jobs—all these cover broad areas that whole books might be written about. For a brief paper, you'd need a topic much narrower, much more specific, so that you could provide the facts, examples, and other details that make writing significant and interesting. Instead of corporate support for the arts, for instance, you could focus on why Apex, Inc., supports the arts. Instead of Lincoln's weaknesses, you could focus on a specific weakness.

The examples below illustrate how broad subjects can be scaled down to one of several manageable **topics**—limited, specific essay subjects.

Broad subjects	Specific topics
Lincoln's weaknesses as President	Lincoln's most significant error as commander-in-chief of the Union army
	Lincoln's delay in emancipating the slaves
	Lincoln's difficulties in controlling his cabinet
Summer jobs	Kinds of summer jobs for unskilled workers

RESOURCES AND IDEAS

Richard M. Coe, "If Not to Narrow, Then How to Focus: Two Techniques for Focusing," *College Composition and Communication* 31 (1981): 272–77. Coe describes ways to get students to focus on a particular aspect of a topic as an alternative to the usual approach of narrowing a topic.

Terry Dean, "Multicultural Classrooms, Monocultural Teachers," *College Composition and Communication* 40 (1989): 23–37. Topics and assignments can be used that help students maintain their individual cultures while learning the language of academia and that help instructors further understand the interaction of home and university cultures.

Broad subjects	Specific topics
	How to find a summer job
	What a summer job can teach
Federal aid to college students	Which students should be entitled to federal aid
	Kinds of federal aid available to college students
	Why the federal government should (or should not) aid college students
Two friends	How _____ and _____ are alike despite their differences
	Why _____ and _____ don't like each other
	The different roles of _____ and _____ as friends

Here are some guidelines for narrowing subjects to topics:

1. Again, pursue your interests, and consider what the assignment tells you about purpose, audience, sources, length, and deadline (see pp. 6–7).
2. Break your subject into as many topics as you can think of. Make a list.
3. For each topic that interests you and fits the assignment, roughly sketch out the main ideas and consider how many paragraphs or pages of specific facts, examples, and other details you would need to pin those ideas down. This thinking should give you at least a vague idea of how much work you'd have to do and how long the resulting paper might be.
4. If an interesting and appropriate topic is still too broad, break it down further and repeat step 3.

You may find that you need to do some planning and writing, exploring different facets of the general subject and pursuing your specific interests, before you hit on the best topic. And the topic you select may require further narrowing or may shift subtly or even dramatically as you move through the writing process. Still, the earlier you can narrow your subject to a specific topic, the more focused your subsequent work will be.

Exercise 2
Pursuing your interests

For each of the following general subjects, provide at least one specific topic that interests you and that you think you could cover well in a brief essay of two or three pages.

1. Music, dance, painting, drama, or some other art form
2. Automobile safety
3. Relations between parents and children
4. Relations between the sexes
5. Travel

Exercise 3
Working with assignments

Following are some general writing assignments. Use the given information and your own interests to find specific topics for three of these assignments.

1. For a letter to the editor of the town newspaper, describe the effects of immigration on your community. Length: two pages. Deadline: unspecified.
2. For a course in environmental science, research and evaluate the federal government's policies for an environmental hazard. Length: five pages. Deadline: three weeks.
3. For a writing course, explain some aspect of campus employment. Length: three pages. Deadline: one week.
4. For the school newspaper, report on an issue in sports. Length: four pages. Deadline: two weeks.
5. For a course in sociology, research and analyze the dynamics of a particular group of people. Length: unspecified. Deadline: four weeks.
6. For a writing course, read and respond to an essay in a text you are using. Length: three pages. Deadline: two weeks.
7. For a writing course, relate a significant learning experience you have had. Length: three pages. Deadline: one week.

ANSWERS: EXERCISE 3

Possible Answers

1. The positive effects of immigration on food choices.
2. The policy for ocean dumping of shipboard waste.
3. How to get a campus job.
4. The gambling rules in professional ice hockey.
5. How slang binds members of the college community.
6. How X's point about math anxiety applies to me.
7. Learning from my great-aunt what the elderly have to give.

Exercise 4
Finding a topic for your essay

As the first step in developing a two- to three-page essay for your writing course, choose one of the topics you arrived at in Exercises 2 and 3 or some other topic you like. Use the guidelines in the previous section to come up with a topic that is suitably interesting, appropriate, and narrow.

ANSWERS: EXERCISE 4

Individual response.

1c   Defining your purpose

As a writer, your **purpose** is your chief reason for communicating something about a topic to a particular audience. Purpose thus includes all three elements of the writing situation: you the writer, your topic, and your audience. It ties together both the specific context in which you are working and the goal you hope to achieve.

IDENTIFYING PURPOSE

Use paragraphs drawn from magazine articles, essays in a reader, or student papers as the basis for class discussion of the purposes of writing. You may ask students to compare the aims of individual paragraphs with the overall purpose of the essay from which they are taken and to decide what role the paragraphs play within the essay.

dev
1c

RESOURCES AND IDEAS

James L. Kinneavy, *A Theory of Discourse* (Englewood Cliffs: Prentice, 1971). Kinneavy classifies discourse according to purpose and emphasis. Expressive discourse emphasizes the writer or speaker; persuasive discourse focuses on the audience; referential discourse focuses on the object and may be informative, scientific, or exploratory; and literary discourse emphasizes the text.

C. H. Knoblauch, "Intentionality in the Writing Process: A Case Study," *College Composition and Communication* 31 (1980): 153–59. Knoblauch argues that (1) the purposes used to classify finished works differ from "operational" purposes that guide the act of writing and (2) the teaching of composition needs to pay attention to the shifting, tentative purposes that guide writing.

COLLABORATIVE LEARNING

ANSWERS: EXERCISE 5
Possible Answers

1. Effects of immigration: explanation.
2. Government policies for an environmental hazard: explanation or persuasion.
3. Campus employment: explanation.
4. An issue in sports: explanation.
5. Dynamics of a group of people: explanation.
6. Response to an essay: self-expression or persuasion.
7. Significant learning experience: self-expression.

The purposes for writing

- To entertain readers
- To express your feelings or ideas
- To explain something to readers (exposition)
- To persuade readers to accept or act on your opinion (argument)

Most writing you do will have one of four main purposes. Occasionally, you will *entertain* readers or *express yourself*—your feelings or ideas—to readers. More often you will *explain* something to readers or *persuade* readers to respect and accept, and sometimes even act on, your well-supported opinion. These purposes often overlap in a single essay, but usually one predominates.

Most college and business writing has the primary purpose of explaining or persuading. Writing that is mainly explanatory is often called **exposition** (from a Latin word meaning "to explain or set forth"). Almost any topic is suitable for exposition, from how to pitch a knuckle ball to why you want to major in business to the implications of a new discovery in computer science. It is the kind of writing encountered most often in newspapers, magazines, and textbooks; and it is the kind of writing this book concentrates on. (Expository essays appear on pp. 67–69.) Writing that is primarily persuasive is often called **argument.** A newspaper editorial favoring city council reform, a magazine article urging mandatory seatbelt use, student papers recommending more required courses or disputing legalized abortion—all these are arguments. (Chapter 4 discusses argument in some detail and provides an illustrative essay.)

Often a writing assignment will specify or imply your purpose: when assigned a report on a physics experiment, for instance, you know the purpose is to explain; when assigned an editorial presenting a case for or against expanding your school's health facilities, you know the purpose is to persuade. If the assignment leaves your purpose up to you, then try to define it soon after you have your topic, to give yourself some direction. You may not be successful: sometimes writers do not discover their purpose until they begin drafting. Or you may find that your initial sense of purpose changes as you move through the writing process. Nonetheless, if you are able to define a purpose early, it can set a preliminary course for you to follow and help you recognize changes in your thinking when they occur.

Exercise 5
Finding purpose in assignments

For each assignment in Exercise 3 (p. 9), suggest a likely purpose for an essay on the topic (entertainment, self-expression, explanation, persuasion).

Exercise 6
Matching topic and purpose

For each of the following general subjects, write down four specific topics, each one suitable for a brief essay written with a different purpose (entertainment, self-expression, explanation, persuasion). For each topic and purpose, also give an audience that might be interested in such an essay.

Example:

General subject: sports
Topics: (1) Football training as torture (entertainment; students who don't play football). (2) Learning by losing (self-expression; composition classmates). (3) How to avoid injury during weight training (explanation; fellow weight trainers). (4) Why the school should build a new athletic facility (persuasion; college administrators).

1. Music
2. Saturday night
3. Work
4. Television
5. Driving

Exercise 7
Defining a purpose for your essay

To begin developing a brief essay of your own, select a topic that has particular interest for you. (The topic may come from your answers to Exercise 4 on p. 9 or to Exercise 6.) Define a purpose for your essay and a likely audience.

1d Considering your audience

Who are your readers? Why are they reading your writing? What do they need and expect from you? These questions are central to the writing process and will crop up again and again, for the audience completes the transaction of writing. Your audience may influence your choice of topic and your definition of purpose. It will certainly influence what you say about your topic and how you shape your ideas.

Like purpose, audience is often specified or implied in a writing assignment. When you write an editorial for the student news-

---

dev 1d

ANSWERS: EXERCISE 6
Possible Answers

1. The joys of playing guitar (self-expression; busy people looking for a hobby). A klutz tries to master the guitar (entertainment; people without musical training).
   How to buy a guitar (explanation; teenagers).
   Guitar music should be outlawed (persuasion; parents).
2. A lonely Saturday night on campus (self-expression; college students).
   Saturday night at Lupo's Club (entertainment; lonely college students).
   What's wrong with Saturday-night television (explanation; *TV Guide* readers).
   Why the school should sponsor Saturday-night dances (persuasion; school teachers and administrators).
3. What working does for me besides pay the bills (self-expression; fellow students or workers).
   Baby-sitting for a monster (entertainment; parents of young children).
   How to prepare for a job interview (explanation; college students).
   Why working students should not have to pay income tax (persuasion; legislators).
4. My favorite situation-comedy character (self-expression; TV viewers).
   A ludicrous soap-opera subplot (entertainment; people who seldom watch daytime TV).
   The differences between two popular crime dramas (explanation; avid TV viewers).
   Why the federal government should support cultural programming on television (persuasion; voting public).
5. A seat belt saved my life (self-expression; people with children).
   Riding shotgun in a demolition derby (entertainment; drivers).
   Road safety for the tractor-trailer driver (explanation; people who do much highway driving).
   Why the 55 mph speed limit should be abolished (persuasion; legislators).

ANSWERS: EXERCISE 7

Individual response.

dev
1d

RESOURCES AND IDEAS

Dean R. Baldwin, "Introducing Rhetoric in Remedial Writing Courses," *College Composition and Communication* 29 (1978): 392–94. Baldwin suggests that prewriting sheets can help students identify an occasion, audience, and purpose for their writing.

Russell C. Long, "Writer-Audience Relationships: Analysis or Invention?" *College Composition and Communication* 31 (1980): 221–26. Long describes the kinds of strategies student writers must develop to create in their minds the potential audiences for their writing.

R. J. Willey, "Audience Awareness: Methods and Madness," *Freshman English News* 18.2 (1990): 20–25. Willey found that when rhetorical, informational, and social perspectives on audience awareness were considered in the composition classroom, the social perspective was the most productive because of its transactional nature.

> TRANSPARENCY MASTER
> AVAILABLE

paper favoring expansion of the college health facilities, your audience is fellow students, who will be reading the paper for information of general and personal interest. When you write a report on a physics experiment, your audience is your physics instructor, who will be reading to evaluate your competence and see if you need help. If no particular audience is specified or implied, then, as with purpose, you are free to decide whom you want to address: your classmates? your boss? those who drive cars?

This sense of your readers tells you something about how you need to treat your topic: for example, your fellow students will expect you to treat the subject of health facilities nontechnically, listing the benefits of the proposed expansion for them. A sense of audience can also help you discover ideas about your topic by making your purpose more concrete. The realization that you want to address an essay on bicycle riding to car drivers could direct you to a persuasive purpose and ideas about drivers' carelessness toward riders.

Knowing what readers need

As a reader yourself, you know what readers need:

- *Context:* a link between what they read and their own knowledge and experiences.
- *Predictability:* an understanding of the writer's purpose and how it is being achieved.
- *Information:* the specific facts, examples, and other details that make the subject clear, concrete, interesting, and convincing.
- *Respect:* a sense that the writer respects their values and beliefs, their background, and their intelligence.
- *Voice:* a sense that the writer is a real person.
- *Clarity and correctness:* writing free of unnecessary stumbling blocks and mistakes.

For much academic and business writing, the needs and expectations of readers are specifically prescribed; thus Chapters 39 and 41 discuss the special concerns of writing in various disciplines and in business, respectively. But even in these areas, you must make many choices based on audience. In other areas where the conventions of structure and presentation are vaguer, the choices are even more numerous. The box opposite contains questions that can help you define and make these choices.

dev
1d

Questions about audience

- Why are readers going to read my writing? Will they expect information, opinion, entertainment, self-expression, or some combination?
- What do I want readers to know or do after reading my work, and how should I make that clear to them?
- What characteristic(s) do readers share? For instance:

  Age or sex
  Occupation: students, professional colleagues, etc.
  Social or economic role: adult children, car buyers, potential employers, etc.
  Economic or educational background
  Ethnic background
  Political, religious, or moral beliefs and values
  Hobbies or activities

- How will the characteristic(s) of readers influence their attitudes toward my topic?
- What do readers already know and *not* know about my topic? How much do I have to tell them?
- If my topic involves specialized language, how much should I use and define?
- What ideas, arguments, or information might surprise readers? excite them? offend them? How should I handle these points?
- What misconceptions might readers have of my topic and or my approach to the topic? How can I dispel these misconceptions?
- What is my relationship to my readers? What role and tone should I assume? What role do I want readers to play?

2 Matching specific information to audience

When you write, you use specific information to gain and keep the attention of your readers and to guide them to accept your conclusions or opinions. This information may be concrete details, facts, examples, or any other evidence that makes your ideas clear or supports your assertions. And your selection of information must suit what you know of the background of your audience: its familiarity with your topic, its biases, and its special interests.

RESOURCES AND IDEAS

Fred R. Pfister and Joan Petrick, "A Heuristic Model for Creating a Writer's Audience," *College Composition and Communication* 31 (1980): 213–20. The authors describe questions writers can ask to probe the nature of a potential audience and the relationship among the audience, the subject, the writer, and possible forms of expression.

Walter J. Ong, S. J., "The Writer's Audience Is Always a Fiction," *PMLA* 90 (1975): 9–21. Ong argues that writers must construct audiences in their imaginations as an essential part of the act of writing and that readers must play the role defined for them by the writer's act of imagination.

dev

1d

AUDIENCE INVENTORY

Ask students to choose a possible topic for an essay and to list the kinds of people who might be interested in the topic. Tell students that if they wish they may employ the "Questions About Audience" on page 13. (In theory, the lists might be very long. In practice, students soon run out of ideas, but not until they have begun to visualize the audience for their essays.) To extend the exercise, ask students what part of the potential audience they would most like to address or what kinds of people would be most interested in the topic. Then ask them to list either (1) what the restricted audience probably already knows about the topic and what it needs to know or (2) what its attitudes are and what kinds of arguments will be needed to change them.

RESOURCES AND IDEAS

Shirley K. Rose, "The Voice of Authority: Developing a Fully Rhetorical Definition of Voice in Writing," *Writing Instructor* 8 (1989): 111–18. Rose argues that voice, or authority, over one's texts is a measure of effective writing and shows how this quality can be developed in students' writing in a fifteen-week time period.

Consider the student who works part-time in a small company and wants to get her coworkers to conserve paper. She writes two memos, the first to other clerical workers:

> Ever notice how much paper collects in your trash basket every day? Well, most of it can be recycled with little effort, I promise. Basically, all you need to do is set a bag or box near your desk and deposit wastepaper in it. I know, space is cramped in these little cubicles. But what's a little more crowding when the earth's at stake? . . .

The second memo goes to the president of the company:

> In my four months here, I have observed that all of us throw out baskets of potentially recyclable paper every day. Considering both the drain on our forest resources and the pressure on landfills that paper causes, we could make a valuable contribution to the environmental movement by helping to recycle the paper we use. At the company where I worked before, the employees separate clean wastepaper from other trash at their desks. The maintenance staff collects trash in two receptacles, and the trash hauler (the same one we use here) makes separate pickups. I do not know what the hauler charges for handling recyclable material . . .

Notice the markedly different information contained in these two memos. In the first the student concentrates on how the individual employee could handle recycling, and she doesn't mention cost. In the second she focuses on how the company as a whole could recycle, and she addresses cost. In the first memo the student is vague about the reasons for recycling (*the earth's at stake*). In the second she spells out the reasons (*the drain on our forest resources and the pressure on landfills*). In the first she serves as her own authority. In the second she cites successful recycling at another company. And all the differences are attributable to the different audiences.

 Deciding on an appropriate role and tone

Besides deciding what information your audience needs, you should also consider how you want to present yourself and your topic to readers—that is, how you want them to perceive both you and your attitude toward your topic. One way to make this decision is to think of yourself, as writer, playing a role in relation to the reader. The possible roles are many and varied—for instance, storyteller, portrait painter, lecturer, guide, reporter, advocate, inspirer. The choice of a role for yourself will depend partly on your purpose and partly on how you feel about your topic and expect your readers to feel about it. As you write your essay, the role you choose will help determine *what* you say and also the *way* you say it—your **tone.** Tone in writing is like tone of voice in speaking: words and sentence structures on the page convey some of the same information about attitude as pitch and volume in the voice.

Conceived broadly, tone may be informal or formal, as illustrated by the two memos opposite. In the first, the student's tone is informal, personal. Her sentences are typical of conversation: fragmented, loose, full of the second-person pronoun *you,* contractions (*what's, earth's*), and casual expressions such as *Well* and *all you need to do.* She is sympathetic (*I promise; I know, space is cramped*). She plays the role of the chatty, cheerful, equally harried colleague. In contrast, the second memo is written in a much more formal tone. The student's words are formal and serious (*forest resources, valuable contribution*). She avoids *you* and contractions. Her carefully constructed sentences would sound stiff in most conversation (*Considering the drain . . .*). Her purpose is strictly to persuade the president to begin a recycling program, and she assumes the role—serious, thoughtful, responsible—that she believes the president expects.

As these examples suggest, different roles and tones are appropriate for different topics, purposes, and audiences. You have the widest range of choice when your purpose is entertainment or self-expression and when you can assume your audience is sympathetic. Then your attitude toward your topic may lead you to play any role from comedian to tragic figure, adopting any tone from teasing to solemn. For other purposes, one or more elements of the writing situation, in addition to your own attitude, are likely to narrow your choices. In business reports and memos, for instance, clarity and conciseness take precedence over self-expression, and formality of tone tends to increase with the rank and number of readers being addressed.

Most writing you do for your college courses will demand an academic role and tone. You will be expected to present yourself as a serious and competent student of the subject you are writing in, one who possesses at least a basic understanding of the discipline's research methods, vocabulary, and principles and who can write clearly. Befitting such a role, the tone of most academic writing is somewhat formal and impersonal. Here, for instance, is a passage from a student's psychology paper:

> One technique for heightening the emotional appeal of advertisements is "color engineering." Adding color to a product or the surrounding advertisement can increase sales despite the fact that the color serves no practical purpose. For example, until the

DISCOVERING SOMEONE ELSE'S AUDIENCE

Distribute to your class an article from a special-interest magazine, a newspaper feature or editorial, or another brief essay whose appeal to a particular audience students will be able to recognize fairly easily. Ask students to read the essay and then to write down the characteristics and attitudes of the intended audience as they think the author viewed it. Ask them also to identify the tone of the essay and to decide whether or not it is appropriate to the subject, the intended audience, and the publication in which the essay appeared. Tell them to be ready to point out what evidence in the essay they used to identify the intended audience and the tone.

1920s fountain pens were made of hard black rubber. When colorful pens were suddenly introduced, sales rose dramatically.

Such straightforward writing allows considerable room for you to express your attitudes by your choice of words and sentence structures. Consider the different effect of this version:

> "Color engineering" can intensify the emotional appeal of advertisements. New color in a product or the surrounding ad can boost sales even when the color serves no other use. In the 1920s, for example, fountain pens that had been hard black rubber suddenly became colorful, and sales shot up.

The brisker tone and the idea of the writer it conveys still fall within the range of academic writing. As you gain experience with such writing, you will develop the flexibility to write in your own voice while also respecting the conventions of the various disciplines.

 Writing for a general audience—or for your instructor

What do you do when you are not writing exclusively for your coworkers or your boss—when, in other words, you don't know much about your audience? From a composition assigned to be written "for your classmates" to a pamphlet on campus employment, much of the writing you do will be for a **general audience**—"general" because it includes people of diverse backgrounds and interests. A general audience has these characteristics and needs:

- Its members read newspapers and magazines such as *Time* and *Newsweek*. They watch television news and entertainment.
- They are skeptical and easily distracted, but they are also curious and thoughtful.
- They may not share all your interests, but they can understand and appreciate anything you write, as long as it is specific, clear, honest, and fresh.
- They will expect you to explain any specialized terms you use and to support any position you take with ample details, examples, and reasons.
- They will expect you to present yourself as thoughtful and competent, in control of your information and a careful writer.
- They will appreciate almost any tone from lighthearted to

grave, as long as it is appropriate for the topic and the writing situation. A moderate and assured tone midway between extreme informality and formality will usually be effective.

Of course, much of your college writing may have only one reader besides you: the instructor of the course you are writing for. In a composition course your instructor is likely to read your work as a representative of a general audience and respond to it in the additional role of helpful critic (see 2e). That means you should not assume specialized interest in or knowledge of your topic, nor should you expect the patience of a doting parent who fills in what his or her child can't (or won't) express. If something about your topic would need to be said to a classmate or a reader of your local newspaper, say it clearly and carefully.

As discussed earlier, most writing for the academic disciplines such as literature, psychology, management, and chemistry is not really addressed to a general audience but to a specialized audience of practitioners of the discipline, represented by your instructor. If you are writing a paper on the economic background of the War of 1812 for an American history course, you may assume your instructor's familiarity with the key events, players, and published interpretations. Your job is to show your own command of them and their relevance to your topic while assuming an appropriate academic role and tone and, as you would for any reader, being specific, clear, and concise.

Exercise 8
Analyzing content and tone

Analyze the content and tone of each paragraph below. What do the writer's choice of information and selection of words and sentence structures indicate about his or her role, attitude toward the subject, and intended audience?

1.   It is Friday night at any of ten thousand watering holes of the small towns and crossroads hamlets of the South. The room is a cacophony of the ping-pong-dingdingding of the pinball machine, the pop-fizz of another round of Pabst, the refrain of *Red Necks, White Socks, and Blue Ribbon Beer* on the juke box, the insolent roar of a souped-up engine outside and, above it all, the sound of easy laughter. The good ole boys have gathered for their fraternal ritual—the aimless diversion that they have elevated into a life-style.   —BONNIE ANGELO, "Those Good Ole Boys"

2.   All air bags [in automobiles] work in essentially the same way. First, a sensor detects a sudden decrease in speed and triggers the device. The sensitivity of the sensor is such that no nor-

ANSWERS: EXERCISE 8
Possible Answers

1. Author's role: humorous guide. Attitude toward subject: disparaging yet indulgent. Intended audience: readers who share the same attitude (i.e., not the "good ole boys" being discussed).

2. Author's role: educator. Attitude toward subject: objective. Intended audience: readers interested in the details of how air bags work.

COLLABORATIVE LEARNING

ANSWERS: EXERCISE 9
Possible Answers

1. *For elementary school students:* physical effects in simple terms; statistics in simple figures; difficulty of quitting once addicted; importance of resisting peer pressure.
Role: combined teacher and parent. Tone: warm, slightly admonitory.
For adult smokers: graphic depiction of physical effects; detailed statistics; influence on children; effect on smoker's appearance, odor, breath.
Role: combined friend and lecturer. Tone: no-nonsense.

2. *For someone who is on welfare:* help for children; possibility that government support will lead to self-support; need for bureaucracy to manage system; need for periodic checks to protect against cheating by a few recipients.
Role: caring observer. Tone: sympathetic.
For someone who opposes welfare: need to provide for people who can't work; need to provide for children; low cost relative to other budget expenditures; low incidence of cheating.
Role: fellow citizen. Tone: reasonable, appealing to shared values.

3. *For the camper:* chance to get out of the dirty city; opportunity to swim and hike; chance to meet other children; chance to get away from parents.
Role: guide and conspirator. Tone: light, cheerful.
For the parents: low cost; expert staff; constructive experience; opportunity to be free of the child.
Role: salesperson. Tone: sincere, responsible.

4. *For your neighbors:* angry feelings of neighborhood residents; dangers to children and pets; lowered property values; threat of petition to zoning board.
Role: peer. Tone: direct, a bit angry.
For the zoning board: violation of zoning regulations; length of time the wrecked truck has been present; number of unsuc-

mal driving situation, such as abruptly slamming on the brakes at highway speeds or hitting another car while parking, will trigger it: an impact equivalent to hitting a wall at a speed of at least 12 miles an hour is required to set it off. Then a powdered chemical, sodium azide, is electrically ignited, and produces a quick burst of nitrogen gas to inflate a fabric bag. Nitrogen is a harmless gas that constitutes 78 percent of the air we breathe, but sodium azide can be poisonous and is therefore carefully sealed in the air-bag cannister until used. The bag can inflate fully within 1/25th of a second, then deflates again within seconds.

—David L. Chandler, "Air Bags"

Exercise 9
Considering audience

Choose one of the following topics and, for each audience specified, ask the questions on page 13. Decide on four points you would make, the role you would assume, and the tone you would adopt for each audience. Then write a paragraph for each based on your decisions.

1. The effects of smoking: for elementary school students and for adult smokers
2. Your opinion of welfare: for someone who is on welfare and for someone who is not and who opposes it
3. The advantages of a summer camp: for a prospective camper and for his or her parents
4. Why your neighbors should remove the wrecked truck from their yard: for your neighbors and for your town zoning board
5. The beauty of a snowfall: for someone who has never experienced snow and for someone who hates it

Exercise 10
Analyzing the audience for your essay

Use the questions on page 13 to determine as much as you can about the probable readers of your essay-in-progress. What does your analysis reveal about the specific information your readers need? What role do you want to assume, and what tone will best convey your attitude toward your topic?

1e Developing your topic

To develop your topic means to generate the ideas and information that will help you achieve your purpose. Sometimes ideas will tumble forth on paper, especially if your topic is very familiar or personal. But when they do not, you may need a technique for freeing them. Anything that gets your mind working is appropriate: if you like to make drawings or take pictures, for instance, then try it. The following pages describe varied strategies that writers find helpful. *Whatever strategy or strategies you use, do your work in writing, not just in your head.* Not only will your ideas be retrievable, but the act of writing will aid your concentration and lead you to fresh, sometimes surprising, insights.

Techniques for developing a topic

- Keep a journal (1e-1).
- Observe your surroundings (1e-2).
- Freewrite (1e-3).
- Make a list or brainstorm (1e-4).
- Cluster (1e-5).
- Read (1e-6).
- Ask the journalist's questions (1e-7).
- Use the patterns of development (1e-8).

---

 1   **Keeping a journal**

Many writers record their thoughts and observations in a **journal,** a diary that is concerned more with ideas than with day-to-day events. *Journal* comes from the Latin for "daily," and many journal keepers do write faithfully every day; others make entries less regularly, when the mood strikes or an insight occurs or they have a problem to work out. Journal keepers often become dependent on the process for the writing practice it gives them and the concentrated thought it encourages. Usually for the same reasons, teachers of writing and other subjects sometimes require students to keep journals.

A journal gives you a place to record your reactions to movies, books, television, and concerts. It gives you an outlet when you need some relief from the pressures of family, friends, studies, and work. It gives you a private place to confide your dreams. In the following sample, a student responds to the day's news.

11/21/91
The paper today was full of bad news. Does it only seem this way, or do newspapers and TV really play up conflicts between racial and ethnic groups? Here at school there are some conflicts,

cessful appeals to neighbors; dangers to children and pets.
Role: plaintiff. Tone: serious, reasonable.
5. *For someone who has never experienced snow:* the air during snowfall; how snow accumulates on the ground; appearance after snowfall of trees, buildings, and so on; muffled sounds after snowfall.
Role: landscape painter. Tone: serene.
For someone who hates snow: interruption by heavy snow of boring routine; cheering effect of snowfall on children; peace and quiet of city during and after snowfall; snow's protection of plants against cold.
Role: friend. Tone: cheerful.

ANSWERS: EXERCISE 10

Individual response.

RESOURCES AND IDEAS

Linda S. Flower and John R. Hayes, "Problem-Solving Strategies and the Writing Process," *College English* 39 (1977): 442–48. Flower and Hayes describe techniques for discovering and developing ideas, including cue words, nutshelling, idea trees, role playing, and brainstorming.

Susan Hunter, "Oral Negotiations in a Textual Community: A Case for Pedagogy and Theory," *Writing Instructor* 8 (1989): 105–10. Hunter states that validating oral communication during the composing process is theoretically sound and helpful in generalizing successful oral communication to successful written communication.

JOURNALS

Ask students to keep a journal for ten days to two weeks, writing for ten to fifteen minutes a day. Encourage them to record past or present experiences and feelings or to explore ideas and opinions. To make sure the journals contain different kinds of writing, ask students to devote a certain number of entries to specific tasks, such as describing a scene, exploring feelings about a controversial topic, or creating a character sketch of a friend. The journal entries can later be developed into formal essays. Journals can also be

dev
1e

used to record responses to essays and literary works or to develop reactions to newspaper articles and television programs. When used in this way, journals can be a preparation for critical, argumentative, or expository essays.

This activity can be combined with Exercise 1, which asks students to record their experiences as writers.

RESOURCES AND IDEAS

Toby Fulwiler, ed., *The Journal Book* (Portsmouth: Boynton/Cook Heinemann, 1987). The essays in this collection describe the uses of journals for discovering and exploring ideas and as an important strategy for writing and learning in various subject areas.

Fred D. White, "Releasing the Self: Teaching Journal-Writing to Freshmen," *The Writing Instructor* 1 (1982): 147–54. White offers practical advice on the use of journals: kinds of journals and entries, professional samples, exercises, and a summary of supporting research.

Sharon Whitehill, "Using the Journal for Discovery: Two Devices," *College Composition and Communication* 38 (1987): 472–74. Whitehill argues that journal assignments calling for lists and for imaginary dialogues can help generate ideas and alleviate writing blocks, and she provides detailed examples of each strategy.

ACTIVITIES THAT SUGGEST TOPICS AND IDEAS

1. Ask students to take a notebook with them to some place likely to be filled with activity and vivid sense impressions—a laundromat, the center of the campus, a busy restaurant. They can record their impressions of the scene in the notebook, later turning those impressions into a structured description or using the material in some other form of writing.

2. Ask students to look at a variety of magazines and to bring in a list of the topics covered in the articles. These topics may in turn suggest topics for student essays. The exercise can be extended by asking students to summarize the contents of one or more of the articles and to indi-

sure. But it's more interesting how many different types of people from different backgrounds manage to live together and learn from each other. Isn't that true elsewhere?

If you write in a journal every day, even for just a few minutes, the routine will loosen up your writing muscles and improve your confidence. And the writing you produce can supply ideas when you are seeking an essay topic or developing an essay. With your assignment or topic in mind, scan your journal entries for relevant ideas. A thought you recorded months ago about a chemistry lab may provide direction for a research paper. Two distant entries about arguments with your brother may suggest what you need to anchor a psychology paper on sibling relations.

2   Observing your surroundings

Sometimes you can find a good subject or good ideas by looking around you, not in the half-conscious way most of us move from place to place in our daily lives but deliberately, all senses alert. On a bus, for instance, are there certain types of passengers? What seems to be on the driver's mind? On campus, which buildings stand out? Are bicycle riders and pedestrians at peace with each other? At a movie, do the viewers seem well suited to the film? Does one type of viewer eat popcorn?

To get the most from observation, you should have a tablet and pen or pencil handy for notes and sketches. If you have a camera, you may find that the lens sees things your unaided eyes do not notice. (When observing or photographing people, though, keep some distance, take photographs quickly, and avoid staring. Otherwise, your subjects will feel uneasy.) Back at your desk, study your notes, sketches, or photographs for oddities or patterns that you'd like to explore further.

3   Freewriting

Another way to find a subject is to write your way into it: write without stopping for a certain amount of time (say, ten minutes) or to a certain length (say, one page). The goal of this **freewriting** is to generate ideas and information from *within* yourself by going around the part of your mind that doesn't want to write or can't think of anything to write. You let words themselves suggest other words. *What* you write is not important; that you *keep* writing is. Don't stop, even if that means repeating the same words until new words come. Don't go back to reread, don't censor ideas that seem dumb or repetitious, and above all don't stop to edit: grammar, punctuation, spelling, and the like are irrelevant at this stage.

In the physical act of freewriting, you may gain access to ideas you were unaware of. Here is an example of freewriting done to come up with a subject for writing.

> Write to write. Seems pretty obvious, also weird. What to gain by writing? never anything before. Writing seems always—always— Getting corrected for trying too hard to please the teacher, getting corrected for not trying hard enuf. Frustration, nail biting, sometimes getting carried away making sentences to tell stories, not even true stories, *esp.* not true stories, *that* feels like creating something. Writing just pulls the story out of me. The story lets me be someone else, gives me a disguise.

In this rough sample the student has broken through his resistance to writing to realize that he enjoys fiction writing for the sense of creation and disguise it gives him. He seems to have learned something about himself and to have given himself a general subject at the same time.

Focused freewriting is more concentrated: you start with your topic and write about it without stopping for, say, fifteen minutes or one full page. As in all freewriting, you push to bypass mental blocks and self-consciousness, not debating what to say or editing what you've written. With focused freewriting, though, you let the physical act of writing take you into and around your subject.

An example of focused freewriting can be found in the work of a student, Terry Perez. An entry from Perez's journal appeared on pages 19–20, and we will follow her writing process in this chapter and the next. In a composition course, Perez and her classmates read and discussed an essay titled "America: The Multinational Society," by Ishmael Reed. Their instructor then gave them the following assignment.

> Respond to Reed's essay with a limited and well-supported opinion of your own about cultural diversity in the United States. Your paper should be 500–750 words. The first draft is due Friday for discussion in class.

Reed's essay argues that the United States is a "multinational society," consisting of many different cultural groups with their own customs, beliefs, and languages, and that the country is stronger

cate how the content might appeal to a particular audience.

3. Check with your audiovisual center on a film rental service for short films that deal with values or controversies. The films or the ensuing discussions can become the basis of student papers.

4. Set up class presentations or debates on an issue in order to provide information and sharpen the focus for papers dealing with the issue or related topics.

RESOURCES AND IDEAS

Kris Lackey, "Amongst the Awful Subtexts: Scholes, the *Daily Planet,* and Freshman Composition," *College Composition and Communication* 38 (1987): 88–93. In this thought-provoking piece, Lackey suggests encouraging and enabling students to tease out the binary oppositions in texts as a way of discovering various subtexts that suggest topics for students' own writing.

PLACES TO WRITE

To help students discover interesting topics and ideas through freewriting, you might give them some places to begin. For essays focusing on events:

> sports, contests, camping, accidents, storms, childhood experiences, giving a speech, getting lost in a department store, robberies, fires

For writing about a scene or character:
> outdoors—woods, seashore, mountains, fields, city streets, parks
> indoors—dorm rooms, laundromats
> scenes—family gatherings, football games, funerals, a snowy morning
> people—parents, grandparents, uncles, aunts, childhood friends, people in a public place, teachers, unpleasant people, cartoon characters

For informative or explanatory writing:

> hobbies, jobs, investments, fields of study, recent scientific discoveries, places to visit, ways to save money, fishing, gardening, study hab-

its, car repairing, canoeing, audio equipment, magazines

For persuasive writing:

campus issues, environmental concerns, automobile or airline safety, support for education, cost of medical care, regulation of new drugs, specialized education versus liberal arts education, rights of minorities and women, gun control, divorce and child rearing, school prayer, censorship, proposals to improve campus or local services, ways of dealing with a social problem

RESOURCES AND IDEAS

Mark Reynolds, "Make Free Writing More Productive," *College Composition and Communication* 39 (1988): 81–82. Reynolds offers twenty "questions, activities, and guidelines" for drawing useful ideas and promising topics from the often jumbled material provided by freewriting.

Gayle B. Price, "A Case for a Modern Commonplace Book," *College Composition and Communication* 31 (1980): 175–82. This article reviews freewriting and other techniques for helping students generate ideas and tells how students can use a notebook to record ideas.

Peter Elbow, *Writing Without Teachers* (New York: Oxford UP, 1973). Elbow discusses freewriting and other techniques for tapping imagination and creativity during the writing process.

Michael G. Southwell, "Free Writing in Composition Classes," *College English* 38 (1977): 676–81. This article shows how freewriting can be used to encourage fluent writing and to provide material that can be used for working on basic skills or as a preparation for more formal papers.

for its diversity. Perez agreed with Reed but saw little point in just saying so. She reread Reed's essay for passages that might spark ideas of her own. Several did, but one especially struck Perez: at one point Reed notes that conflict among different people "is played up and often encouraged by the media." It was a thought Perez herself had recorded in her journal, and it prompted the following freewriting.

> Cultural diversity in the media? The media has a one track mind, cultural diversity is bad. Like Reed says the media makes a big deal of conflict between racial and ethnic groups, it's almost constant in the papers, on TV. TV especially—the news vs. all the white bread programs, the sitcoms and ads. That's a whole other view—*no* conflict, *no* tension. No diversity. So we have all people the same except when they're not, then they're at war. Two unreal pictures.

With this freewriting, Perez discovered some interesting complexity in her topic that she had originally missed: the media do overplay cultural conflict, she thought, but they also downplay cultural diversity by portraying people as basically similar. Explaining these two distortions would be her purpose and topic, Perez decided.

   Making a list

Like focused freewriting, list making requires opening yourself to everything that seems even remotely connected to your topic, without concern for order or repetition or form of expression. You can let your topic percolate for a day or more, recording thoughts on it whenever they occur. (For this approach to work, you need to keep a notebook and pen or pencil with you at all times.) Or, in a method more akin to freewriting, you can **brainstorm** about the topic—that is, focus intently on the topic for a fixed amount of time (say, fifteen minutes), pushing yourself to list every idea and detail that comes to mind.

Like freewriting, brainstorming requires turning off your internal editor so that you keep moving ahead instead of looping back over what you have already written to correct it. It makes no difference whether the ideas and details are expressed in phrases or complete sentences. It makes no difference if they seem silly or irrelevant. Just keep pushing.

A list of ideas and details made while brainstorming might look something like the one following. The student's topic is what a summer job can teach—one of the specific topics derived earlier from the general subject of summer jobs.

> summer work teaches—
> > how to look busy while doing nothing
> > how to avoid the sun in summer
> > seriously: discipline, budgeting money, value of money
> which job? Burger King cashier? baby sitter? mail-room clerk?
> mail room: how to sort mail into boxes: this is learning??
> how to survive getting fired—humiliation, outrage
> Mrs. King! the mail-room queen as learning experience
> the shock of getting fired: what to tell parents, friends?
> Mrs. K was so rigid—dumb procedures
> initials instead of names on the mail boxes—confusion!
> Mrs. K's anger, resentment: the disadvantages of being smarter
> > than your boss
> The odd thing about working in an office: a world with its own
> > rules for how to act
> what Mr. D said about the pecking order—big chick (Mrs. K)
> > pecks on little chick (me)
> probably lots of Mrs. Ks in offices all over—offices are all barn-
> > yards
> Mrs. K a sad person, really—just trying to hold on to her job,
> > preserve her self-esteem
> a job can beat you down—destroy self-esteem, make you desper-
> > ate enough to be mean to other people
> how to preserve/gain self-esteem from work??
> Mrs. K had to call me names to protect herself—I forced her into
> > a corner
> if I'd known about the pecking order, I would have been less
> > show-offy, not so arrogant

This informal list jumps around quite a bit, but toward the end the student focuses on what she learned about office politics from working as a mail-room clerk. Thus list making helps her both refine her topic and discover what she thinks about it.

 5   Clustering

Like freewriting and list making, **clustering** also draws on free association and rapid, unedited work, but it combines writing and nonlinear drawing. When clustering, you radiate outward from a center point—your topic. When an idea occurs, you pursue its implications in a branching structure until they seem exhausted. Then you do the same with other ideas, staying open to

RESOURCES AND IDEAS

Gabriele Lusser Rico, *Writing the Natural Way* (Los Angeles: Tarcher, 1983). Rico draws on research about brain functions as the basis for advice about strategies—especially clustering—that encourage creativity in expression.

dev

1e

possibilities and connections, continuously branching out or drawing arrows.

The example of clustering below shows how a student used the technique for ten minutes to expand on the topic of creative writing as a means of disguise, an idea he arrived at through free-writing (see p. 21). Though the student ventured into several dead ends, he also came to the interesting possibility (lower right) that the fiction writer is like a god who forgives himself by creating characters that represent his good and bad qualities. With such a start, the student next began a draft of his paper. If he had felt the need to develop ideas further, he could have tried another diagram or another strategy such as focused freewriting.

6 Reading

Some assignments require reading. To respond to Ishmael Reed's essay on cultural diversity, for instance, Terry Perez had to digest Reed's work. And essays on literary works as well as research papers demand reading. But even when reading is not required by an assignment, it can help you locate or develop your topic by introducing you to ideas you didn't know or expanding on what you do know. (See 35c for techniques of library research that you can use to locate readings on a topic.)

People often read passively, absorbing content like blotters, not interacting with it. To read for ideas, you need to be more active, probing text and illustrations with your mind, nurturing any sparks they set off. Read with a pen or pencil in your hand and (unless the material is yours to mark up) with a pad of paper by your side. Then you will be able to keep notes on what you read and—more important—on what the reading makes you *think*. (For more on the reading process, see 4b, p. 120.)

Caution: Whenever you use the information or ideas of others in your writing, you must acknowledge your sources in order to avoid the serious offense of plagiarism. (See 36c.) If a writer's ideas merely suggest a direction for you, you need not acknowledge the source. But if you actually present any of those ideas in your final paper, then you must also acknowledge where they came from. (See Chapter 37 for how to acknowledge sources.)

7 Using the journalist's questions

Asking yourself a set of questions about your topic—and writing out the answers—can help you look at the topic objectively and see fresh possibilities in it. Asking questions can also provide some structure to the development of ideas.

One such set of questions is that posed by a journalist with a story to report:

Who was involved?
What happened and what were the results?
When did it happen?
Where did it happen?
Why did it happen?
How did it happen?

These questions can also be useful in probing an essay topic, especially if your purpose is to entertain or to explain by telling a

RESOURCES AND IDEAS

Robert A. Schwegler, *Patterns in Action,* 2nd ed. (New York: HarperCollins, 1988). In the opening chapter the author describes four processes in the act of reading—responding, understanding, analyzing, and evaluating—and discusses the use of reading logs as a bridge between reading and writing.

Bob Frye, "Artful Compositions, Corder's 'Laws of Composition,' and the Weekly Letter: Two Approaches to Teaching Invention and Arrangement in Freshman English," *Journal of Teaching Writing* 8 (1989): 1–14. Frye argues that having students write replies to the instructor's weekly letters allows them to experience genuine rhetorical invention rather than experiencing closure, often the product of structure.

RESOURCES AND IDEAS

Charles W. Kneupper, "Revising the Tagmemic Heuristic: Theoretical and Pedagogical Considerations," *College Composition and Communication* 31 (1980): 160–68. Kneupper offers a simplified version of the powerful question system introduced by Young, Becker, and Pike in their text *Rhetoric: Discovery and Change* (New York: Harcourt, 1970).

Eugene Washington, "WH-Questions in Teaching Composition," *College Composition and Communication* 28 (1977): 54–56. Washington suggests using what, why, where, and how questions to increase density of information in essays and clarify structure.

dev
1e

USING QUESTIONS AND PATTERNS

To help students discover the power of sets of questions or the patterns of development for exploring topics, begin by giving them a list of general subjects—music, sports, guns, the environment—and then ask them to explore each, looking for limited aspects that might make good topics for essays. Do not encourage students to use either the questions or the patterns in probing the topics. Class discussion can focus on how to limit the topics and can indicate how an audience might respond to them.

Following the discussion, ask students to explore the same topics using either the journalist's questions (1e7) or the patterns of development as described in 1e8. Ask students to direct their attention to as many different aspects of the topic as they can and at the same time to suggest ways of developing it and organizing an essay around it. Discussion should focus on differences between the "guided" and "unguided" approaches to developing a topic.

RESOURCES AND IDEAS

Frank J. D'Angelo, *A Conceptual Theory of Rhetoric* (Cambridge: Winthrop, 1975). D'Angelo argues that rhetorical patterns of organization (e.g., analysis, classification, and description) are also patterns of thought and invention and can be used to probe experience as part of the composing process. See also D'Angelo's "Topoi and Form in Composition," *The Territory of Language,* ed. Donald A. McQuade (Carbondale: Southern Illinois UP, 1986) 114–22.

Lance Wilcox, "Time Lines in the Composing of Narratives: A Graphic Aid to Organization," *The Writing Instructor* 6 (1987): 162–73. Wilcox describes in detail the use of time lines to help develop and organize narrative essays.

Neil Berman, "Language, Process, and Tinkertoys," *College Composition and Communication* 26 (1975): 390–92. Berman offers concrete exercises to teach process analysis as a form of writing.

Terry Dean, "Causal, Not Casual: An Advance Organizer for Cause-and-Effect Compositions," *Structuring for Success in the English Classroom,* ed. Candy Carter (Urbana: NCTE,

story from your experience or from history or by examining causes and effects. (See also p. 27.) For instance, the student writing about a summer job as a mail-room clerk could use the journalist's questions to isolate the important people involved, the main events and their order, and the possible causes of the events.

 8   Using the patterns of development

The **patterns of development**—such as narration, definition, and comparison and contrast—are ways we think about and understand a vast range of subjects, from our own daily experiences to the most complex scientific theories. They also serve as strategies for writing about these subjects. Asking questions based on the patterns can help you view your topic from many angles. Not all these questions will be productive, but at least a few should open up new possibilities.

How did it happen?

In **narration** you develop the topic as a story, with important events usually arranged chronologically (as they occurred in time): for instance, an exciting hockey game or the steps leading to a war. (A student's narrative essay appears on pp. 67–68.)

How does it look, sound, feel, smell, taste?

In **description** you use sensory details to give a clear impression of a person, place, thing, or feeling, such as a friend, a favorite room, a building, or the experience of riding a skateboard.

What are examples of it or reasons for it?

The pattern of **illustration** or **support** suggests development with one or more examples of the topic (one couple's efforts to adopt a child, say, or three television soap operas) or with the reasons for believing or doing something (three reasons for majoring in English, four reasons for driving defensively).

What is it? What does it encompass, and what does it exclude?

These questions lead to **definition:** specifying what the topic is and is not to give a precise sense of its meaning. Abstract terms —such as *justice, friendship,* and *art*—especially need defining. (See 4c-1.)

What are its parts or characteristics?

Using the pattern of **division** or **analysis,** you break a subject into its elements and examine the relations between elements. You might analyze a short story, for instance, by dividing it into characters, setting, plot, and so on. (Analysis is key to critical thinking, so it comes up again in Chapter 4, p. 126.)

What groups or categories can it be sorted into?

Classification involves separating a large group (such as cars) into smaller groups (subcompact, compact, and so on) based on the characteristics of the individual items (the sizes of the cars). Another example: academic, business, personal, literary, and other types of writing.

How is it like, or different from, other things?

With **comparison and contrast** you point out the similarities and differences between ideas, objects, people, places, and so on: the differences between two similar computer systems, for instance, or the similarities between two opposing political candidates. (A student's comparison-and-contrast essay appears on pp. 68–69.)

Is it comparable to something that is in a different class but more familiar to readers?

This question leads to **analogy,** an extended comparison of unlike subjects. Analogy is often used to explain a topic that may be unfamiliar to readers (for instance, the structure of a government) by reference to a familiar topic (the structure of a family).

What are its causes or its effects?

With **cause-and-effect analysis,** you explain why something happened or what its consequences were or will be, or both: the causes of cerebral palsy, the effects of a Supreme Court decision, the causes *and* effects of a gradual change in the climate.

How do you do it, or how does it work?

In **process analysis** you explain how the topic is accomplished (how to write an essay) or how it happens (how a plant grows, how a robot works).

More than one of these questions are likely to seem promising, and several may in fact play a role in the development of a single essay. Even when you are assigned an essay in a specific pattern, other patterns will almost inevitably prove useful to develop certain ideas.

As you will see later, the patterns of development also provide a means of introducing information in paragraphs (pp. 95–105, with paragraph-length examples). Further discussion of how the patterns may combine in an essay appears on pages 115–17.

Exercise 11
Using freewriting, brainstorming, or clustering

Experiment with freewriting (p. 20), brainstorming (p. 22), or clustering (p. 23) on the topic you worked with in Exercises 7 (p. 11) and 10 (p. 18), or start anew with one of the following topics.

1982) 92–97. Dean describes exercises to make students aware of causal relationships and to provide a basis for writing.

George D. Haich, "If the Reader Never Saw One, How Would You Describe It?" *College Composition and Communication* 26 (1975): 298–300. The author suggests having students describe an object the class has not seen so that the class can begin to understand what information and strategies are necessary for effective description.

Richard L. Larson, "Towards a Linear Rhetoric of the Essay," *College Composition and Communication* 22 (1971): 140–46. Larson proposes teaching students to shape their essays by planning a linear sequence of moves or stages rather than a hierarchical structure.

Leonard A. Podis, "Teaching Arrangement: Defining a More Practical Approach," *College Composition and Communication* 31 (1980): 197–204. Podis describes a teaching sequence designed to make students aware of the basic principles of organization, and he reviews some standard patterns of arrangement useful for academic and professional writing.

Judith G. Stitzel, "Is There a Box on the Board? An Exercise in Classification," *On Righting Writing,* ed. Ouida H. Clapp (Urbana: NCTE, 1975) 87–93. The author outlines classroom activities providing an awareness of how the mind organizes perceptions, ideas, and experience.

COLLABORATIVE LEARNING

ANSWERS: EXERCISE 11

Individual response.

Write or draw for at least ten minutes without stopping to edit. When you finish, examine what you have written for ideas and relationships that could help you develop the topic.

1. A shopping mall or other center or building
2. A restaurant
3. Borrowing (or lending) money
4. Prejudice in my hometown
5. The college grading system
6. Pigeons
7. A country music singer
8. A television show
9. A brother or a sister
10. An awkward or embarrassing moment
11. A radio personality
12. Basketball strategies
13. Shyness
14. Parties
15. Patriotism

ANSWERS: EXERCISE 12

Individual response.

Exercise 12
Using the patterns of development

Continuing from the preceding exercise, generate further ideas on the topic by writing answers to each of the questions derived from the patterns of development (pp. 26–27). Give the closest consideration to the questions that seem most promising. Which pattern might you use for the overall development of your essay, and which other patterns might you use to introduce or organize ideas within the overall pattern?

ANSWERS: EXERCISE 13

Individual response.

Exercise 13
Reading, or using the journalist's questions

If you feel that the topic from Exercises 11 and 12 should be developed further, try reading about it or asking the journalist's questions (p. 25). Subsequent exercises for your essay-in-progress will be based on the ideas you generate in Exercises 11–13.

1f Developing your thesis

Most essays are focused on and controlled by a single main idea that the writer wants to communicate to readers—a central point to which all the essay's paragraphs, all its general statements and specific information, relate. This main idea, called the **thesis,** encompasses the writer's attitude toward the topic and purpose in writing.

Sometimes your thesis may be apparent to you very early in the writing process: you may have chosen your topic in the first place because you had an idea about it that you wanted to communicate. At other times you may need to organize your ideas or write and rewrite before a central, controlling idea emerges. Still, it's wise to try to pin down your thesis once you have a sense of your purpose, your audience, your attitude, and the information you will use. Then the thesis can help you start drafting, help keep you focused, or serve as a point of reference when changes occur in intention or direction.

1 Conceiving your thesis sentence

A good way to develop your thesis is to frame it in a **thesis sentence.** The thesis sentence gives you a vehicle for expressing your thesis at an early stage, and eventually it or a revised version may be placed in the introduction of your final essay as a signal to your readers.

As an expression of the thesis, the thesis sentence serves two crucial functions and one optional one:

Functions of the thesis sentence

- It narrows the topic to a single idea that you want readers to gain from your essay.
- It asserts something about the topic, conveying your purpose, your opinion, and your attitude.
- It *may* provide a concise preview of how you will arrange your ideas in the essay.

Here are some examples of topics and corresponding thesis sentences that fulfill the first two and, in one case, the third of these functions.

Topic	Thesis sentence
1. Why the federal government should aid college students	If it hopes to win the technological race, the United States must make higher education possible for any student who qualifies academically.
2. The effects of strip-mining	Strip-mining should be tightly controlled in this region to reduce its pollution of water resources, its permanent destruction of the

RESOURCES AND IDEAS

Thomas R. Liszka, "Formulating a Thesis for Essays Employing Comparison," *College Composition and Communication* 38 (1987): 474–77. Liszka offers a method that helps students to generate theses and guides them in organizing and developing their essays; the method appears to be adaptable to various kinds of essays.

TRANSPARENCY MASTER
AVAILABLE

ORAL PROGRESS REPORTS

Have students report orally to the class or to their peer writing groups on topics and thesis statements for a coming paper. Giving an oral presentation forces students to focus their ideas and adopt a stance. As they speak, moreover, students may sense difficulties with the topic or thesis. Comments from classmates can help identify strengths and weaknesses and suggest an appropriate tone for the essay.

Topic	Thesis sentence
	land, and its devastating effects on people's lives.
3. A terrible moving experience	The surest way to lose good friends is to enlist their help in a move from one fourth-floor walkup to another.
4. My city neighborhood	The main street of my neighborhood contains enough variety to make almost any city dweller feel at home.
5. Abraham Lincoln's delay in emancipating the slaves	Lincoln delayed emancipating any slaves until 1863 because his primary goal was to restore and preserve the Union, with or without slavery.
6. The dynamics of single-parent families	In families consisting of a single parent and a single child, the boundaries between parent and child often disappear so that the two interact as siblings or as a married couple.
7. What public relations is	Although most of us are unaware of the public relations campaigns directed at us, they can significantly affect the way we think and live.

All of these thesis sentences serve the first two functions listed above: they state a single idea about the topic, and the assertion conveys information about the writer's stand on the topic. (Sentence 2 also serves the third function of previewing the main supporting ideas and their order.) We know from these sentences what each writer's primary purpose is: persuasion in 1 and 2, entertainment in 3, and explanation in 4 through 7. In addition, these sentences not only state opinions but also reveal something of the writers' attitudes, including strong feelings and a sense of urgency (1 and 2), a groaning good humor (3), pride (4), objectivity (5 and 6), and caution (7).

2   **Writing and revising your thesis sentence**

To draft a thesis sentence, ask yourself what central idea emerges from the work you have done so far, how you can frame that idea as an assertion about your topic, and how you can convey your purpose and attitude in that assertion. Answering all these questions in a sentence usually requires more than one attempt, sometimes over one or more drafts of the essay. But the thinking required can help you discover potentially serious problems, such as that you're trying to write about three ideas, not one.

Terry Perez went through a common procedure in writing and revising her thesis sentence on cultural diversity in the media. First she turned her topic into an assertion, a statement about the topic.

> Television, newspapers, and magazines present contrasting views of the United States.

This sentence focused on Perez's topic but did not specify what the contrasting views are. Nor did it convey Perez's purpose in writing or her attitude toward her topic. Realizing as much, Perez rewrote the sentence.

> The media image of the United States is unrealistic, and people are depicted as being either in ethnic conflict or blissfully all the same.

This sentence solved the problems with the previous try: Perez clearly wanted to explain a media image that she disputed (she found it *unrealistic*). But Perez now needed to make a unified statement by pulling together the two halves separated by *and*.

> Judging from the unrealistic images projected by the media, the United States is a nation either of constant ethnic conflict or of untroubled homogeneity.

In this sentence Perez succeeded in stating her topic succinctly and specifically, while also conveying her attitude and purpose. (Notice that she substituted the word *homogeneity,* which she learned from her sociology textbook, for the phrase *all the same. Homogeneity* means "similarity in kind.") In specifying the contrasting false images, Perez also forecast the organization of her essay.

When you are writing and revising your thesis sentence, check it against the following questions.

dev

1f

STUDENT MODELS

You may wish to copy effective thesis statements from student papers to use in class discussion or small-group work. The statements will provide positive models and may suggest topics for future essays. You can vary this exercise by copying ineffective statements and discussing how they may be revised. Be sure to keep the discussion of ineffective statements positive in tone, however.

SUPPLYING AN OMITTED THESIS STATEMENT

Ask students to read their papers to the class or to a peer group, deliberately leaving out the thesis statement. Ask the other students to supply a thesis for the essay. If the original thesis and the one supplied by the students match, fine. If not, the thesis a student has chosen may be inappropriate for the paper and the discussion that follows can suggest possible revisions.

ASKING READERS TO AGREE ON THE THESIS

Ask students to read an essay from a collection or a fellow student's paper and then to state its thesis in their own words. If students are working in groups, ask the group members whether they can agree on the thesis. Next have the students try to identify a thesis statement in the essay. If the essay has an explicit thesis statement, ask if they consider it effective or if the thesis statement they produced would be more effective. If the thesis is implicit, ask students whether or not the essay would benefit from an explicit thesis statement.

TRANSPARENCY MASTER
AVAILABLE

COLLABORATIVE LEARNING

ANSWERS: EXERCISE 14

1. The sentence lacks unity because the two halves do not seem to relate to each other. *Possible revision:* We should channel our natural feelings of aggression toward constructive rather than destructive ends.

2. Both halves of the sentence need to be more specific: What kind of gun control? essential for what end?
Possible revision: To curb the rising rate of murder with handguns, restrictions on the sale of handguns should be legislated and strictly enforced.

3. Good thesis sentence: limited, specific, and unified.

4. Both *good manners* and *make our society work* need to be more specific.
Possible revision: Courtesy between people makes human interaction smoother and more efficient.

5. The sentence simply states a fact.
Possible revision: The poem makes motherhood seem a saintly calling.

6. *Different* needs limiting.
Possible revision: City people are different from country people in their attitudes toward strangers, politicians, and money.

7. The sentence lacks unity because the first half is positive but not very specific, while the second half is negative and specific. Making the first half more specific and the second half positive would unify the sentence.
Possible revision: Television is both a useful baby sitter for children, offering them education and entertainment, and a good escape for adults, providing them with relief from their own problems.

8. The sentence is a flat statement of personal preference that provides no preview of reasons for the preference.
Possible revision: Although I liked American history in high school because the teacher focused on social trends and events, I do not like it in college because the teacher focuses on political events and personalities.

9. The sentence lacks unity because the two halves do not clearly relate to each other.

Checklist for revising the thesis sentence

1. Does it make an *assertion* about your topic?
2. Does it convey your *purpose,* your *opinion,* and your *attitude?*
3. Is it *limited* to an assertion of only one idea?
4. Is the assertion *specific?*
5. Is the sentence *unified* in that the parts relate to each other?

Here are other examples of thesis sentences revised to meet these requirements:

Original	Revised
This new product brought in over $300,000 last year. [A statement of fact, not an assertion: what is significant about the product's success?]	This new product succeeded because of its innovative marketing campaign.
People should not go on fad diets. [A vague statement that needs limiting with one or more reasons: what's wrong with fad diets?]	Fad diets can be dangerous when they deprive the body of essential nutrients or rely on excessive quantities of potentially harmful foods.
Televised sports are different from live sports. [A general statement that needs to be made more specific: how are they different, and why is the difference significant?]	Although television cannot transmit all the excitement of being in a crowd during a game, its close-ups and slow-motion replays more than compensate.
Seat belts can save lives, but now car makers are installing air bags. [Not unified: how do the two parts of the sentence relate to each other?]	If drivers more often used lifesaving seat belts, car makers might not need to install air bags.

Exercise 14
Evaluating thesis sentences

Evaluate the following thesis sentences, considering whether each one is sufficiently limited, specific, and unified. Rewrite the sentences as necessary to meet these goals.

1. Aggression usually leads to violence, injury, and even death, and we should use it constructively.
2. Gun control is essential. *what kind   why*
3. One evening of a radio talk show amply illustrates both the appeal of such shows and their silliness.
4. Good manners make our society work.
5. The poem is about motherhood.
6. City people are (different) from country people. *too broad*
7. Television is a useful baby sitter and an escape for people who do not want to think about their own problems.
8. I liked American history in high school, but not in college.
9. We are encouraged to choose a career in college, but people change jobs frequently. *unity*
10. Drunken drivers, whose perception, coordination, and reaction time are impaired, should receive mandatory suspensions of their licenses.

Exercise 15
Drafting thesis sentences

Write limited, specific, and unified thesis sentences for three of the following topics. Each of your sentences should convey the purpose given in parentheses and your own attitude.

1. Why (or why not) major in business (*persuasion*)
2. A frustrating experience (*self-expression*)
3. Why cable television should be free (*persuasion*)
4. How an old house or apartment is better than a new one (or vice versa) (*explanation*)
5. The sounds of the city or country (*self-expression or entertainment*)
6. How to care for a plant (*explanation*)
7. Why students attend college (*explanation*)
8. How a rumor spreads (*explanation*)
9. Why divorce laws should be tougher (or looser) (*persuasion*)
10. A disliked person (*explanation*)

Exercise 16
Drafting and revising your own thesis sentence

Continuing from Exercise 13 (p. 28), write a limited, specific, and unified thesis sentence for your essay-in-progress.

1g Organizing your ideas

An effective essay has a recognizable shape—an arrangement of parts that guides readers, helping them see how ideas and details relate to each other and contribute to the whole. If readers

Possible revision: Because a person should delay a career decision until he or she has worked in several jobs, students should not be encouraged to choose a career while they are in college.

10. The sentence lacks unity because the clause *whose . . . impaired* is not directly related to the opinion being stated.
Possible revision: Drivers who have demonstrated bad judgment and lack of control by operating a car under the influence of alcohol should receive mandatory suspension of their licenses.

COLLABORATIVE LEARNING

ANSWERS: EXERCISE 15
Possible Answers

1. If more students majored in business, U.S. corporations would be run more efficiently.
2. Helping my friend overcome drug dependency taught me how to be patient and consistent in my dealings with others.
3. Cable television provides a worthwhile community service and should, like other community services, be delivered by the government at no charge.
4. Everyone should live for a while in an old building, for old walls and floors provide an essential sense of continuity with the past.
5. The sounds of the city at midnight conjure up a dual image of people having fun and people in trouble.
6. To care for a plant, one must understand and fulfill its special needs for sunlight, water, and nutrition.
7. Most students seem to attend college for one of three reasons: to prepare for a career, to enhance social life, or to delay the decisions of adulthood.
8. Tracing the rumor of Mr. Petrieka's secret sin revealed a laughable series of misunderstood conversations.
9. As long as they do not have children, married people should be able to divorce easily so that they can seek happier, more stable relationships elsewhere.
10. For the two months I stayed with my ex-roommate, his slothfulness, rudeness, and deceit caused me constant pain.

ANSWERS: EXERCISE 16

Individual response.

dev

1g

can't see a clear order in your material or how each new idea or piece of information develops your thesis, they will have difficulty understanding you and they may mistrust what you say.

Writers sometimes let an effective organization emerge over one or more drafts. But many writers find that organizing ideas to some extent before drafting can provide a helpful sense of direction, as a map can help a driver negotiate a half-familiar system of roads. If you feel uncertain about the course your essay should follow or have a complicated topic with many parts, devising a shape for your material can clarify your options.

Before you begin organizing your material, look over all the writing you've done so far—freewriting, notes from reading, lists, whatever. Pull together a master list of all the ideas and details you think you may want to include, leaving blank margins for further notes, connecting arrows, and other additions that will occur to you as you think about shape.

RESOURCES AND IDEAS

Edward Lotto, "Utterance and Text in Freshman English," *College English* 51 (1989): 677–87. Lotto analyzes the differences between spoken and written language as they relate to the difficulties students have in supporting generalizations with concrete examples. He makes suggestions for helping students become aware of text and concrete expression.

Virginia Perdue, "The Politics of Teaching Detail," *Rhetoric Review* 8 (1990): 280–88. Perdue provides methods for using detail to arrive at broader thoughts in the composing process.

 1   Distinguishing the general and the specific

To organize material for an essay, you need to distinguish general and specific ideas and see the relations between ideas. **General** and **specific** refer to the number of instances or objects included in a group signified by a word. *Plant,* for example, is general because it encompasses all kinds of plants; *rose* is specific because it refers to a certain kind of plant. But *general* and *specific* are actually relative terms—that is, something is one or the other only in relation to something else. Thus *plant* is general in relation to *rose,* but it is specific in relation to the broader category of *life form.* Here is a "ladder" that places these three terms in a general-to-specific hierarchy.

Most general
life form
plant
flowering plant
rose
American Beauty rose
Uncle Dan's prize-winning American Beauty rose
Most specific

When you arrange your ideas, pick out the most general ones. (Your thesis sentence may help you identify your most important points.) Underline or circle these ideas, and connect each one by arrows to the specific ideas and details that support it. Or start over with a fresh sheet of paper, write each general idea down with space beneath it, and add specific information in the appropriate spaces.

As you sort ideas, respect their meanings. Otherwise, your hierarchies could become jumbled, with *rose* illogically subordinated to *animal,* or *life form* somehow subordinated to *rose.* See the following section for various tools and guidelines that can help you organize ideas.

 2   Choosing an organizing tool
Outlining

RESOURCES AND IDEAS

Karla F. C. Holloway, "Teaching Composition Through Outlining," *Teaching the Basics— Really!* ed. Ouida Clapp (Urbana: NCTE, 1977) 36–39. Holloway suggests using outlines as a critical tool to teach writing.

Some writers view outlines as chores and straitjackets, but they need not be dull or confining. There are many different kinds of outlines, some more flexible than others. All of them can enlarge and toughen your thinking, showing you patterns of general and specific, suggesting proportions, highlighting gaps or overlaps in coverage.

Many writers use outlines for another purpose as well—to check the underlying structure of a draft when revising it (see p. 51). No matter when it's made, though, an outline can change to reflect changes in your thinking. You should view any outline you make as a tentative sketch, not as a fixed paint-by-numbers diagram.

Using a scratch or informal outline

For many essays, especially those with a fairly straightforward structure, a simple listing of ideas and perhaps their support may provide adequate direction for your writing. A **scratch outline** lists the key points of the paper in the order they will be covered.

Here is Terry Perez's scratch outline for her essay on diversity in the media.

Thesis sentence

Judging from the unrealistic images projected by the media, the United States is a nation either of constant ethnic conflict or of untroubled homogeneity.

Scratch outline

Media images—
    Ethnic conflict
        —news stories—examples
        —the real story—examples
    Sameness—homogeneity
        —TV sitcoms and ads: the happy (white) family
        —the real story—examples

dev

1g

Perez put more into this outline than its simplicity might indicate. She worked out the order in which she would cover the media's contradictory images. And under each type of image she established a pattern of contrasting examples from the media and from real life.

With this much thought, such a scratch outline may be all you need to begin drafting. Sometimes, though, it may prove too skimpy a guide, and you may want to use it as a preliminary to a more detailed outline. Indeed, Terry Perez used her scratch outline as a base for a detailed formal outline that gave her an even more definite sense of direction (see p. 38).

An **informal outline** is usually more detailed than a scratch outline, including key general points and the specific evidence for them. Here is a student's informal outline for a thesis sentence we saw earlier. The writer set up topic headings that would correspond to separate paragraphs of her essay, and she added the examples.

Thesis sentence

The main street of my neighborhood contains enough variety to make almost any city dweller feel at home.

Informal outline

The beginning of the street
    high-rise condominium occupied by well-to-do people
    ground floor of building: an art gallery
    across the street: a delicatessen
    above the delicatessen: a tailor's shop, a camera-repair shop,
        a lawyer's office
The middle of the street
    four-story brick apartment buildings on both sides
    at ground level: an Italian bakery and a Spanish bodega
    people sitting on steps
    children playing
The end of the street
    a halfway house for drug addicts
    a boarding house for retired men
    a discount drugstore
    an expensive department store
    a wine shop
    another high-rise condominium

Using a tree diagram

In a **tree diagram** ideas and details branch out in increasing specificity. Like any outline, the diagram can warn of gaps, overlaps, and digressions. But unlike more linear outlines, it can be supplemented and extended indefinitely, so it is easy to alter for new ideas and arrangements discovered during drafting and revision.

Below is a tree diagram prepared from the earlier list of ideas on a summer job (p. 23). Each main part of the four-part diagram represents a different general idea about the summer-job experience. Notice that the diagram also helped the student to drop irrelevant ideas from her earlier list. In addition, the structure of the diagram showed where she needed more details than she originally had, such as effects of the office pecking order.

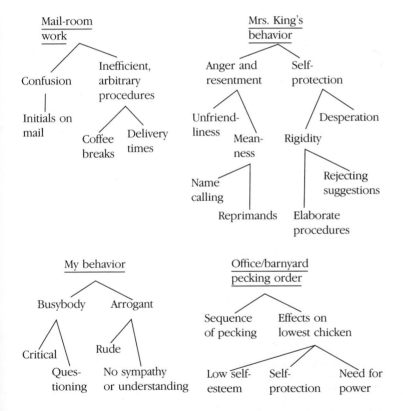

PURPOSE OUTLINES

Some students have trouble maintaining unity of purpose and coherent organization even after they have outlined an essay because the outline describes the content of the essay but does not indicate the function of each part. To help students overcome this problem, ask them to add a statement of purpose to each major section of their outlines and to indicate how the section will carry out the purpose of the paper, as in this example:

In this section I plan to explain how much money industries lose by failing to treat industrial waste to recover precious metals like chromium, gold, silver, and platinum. This will be the second of the three little-known costs of pollution that my thesis statement promises the paper will discuss.

Statements of purpose can alert students to potential problems in the organization or unity of an essay, and they can provide instructors with a quick way to spot the problems. Some instructors even ask students to submit "purpose outlines" in place of formal outlines:

In this section of the paper, I plan to show that there is a real need for this university to provide more funds for the library. To support my point, I plan to explore three serious effects of underfunding—lack of basic reference materials, lack of staff to shelve books properly and check for missing volumes, and poor maintenance of the library building.

Using a formal outline

For complex topics requiring complex arrangements of ideas and support, you may want or be required to construct a **formal outline** either before you began drafting or afterward, as a check on what you have done (see p. 51). More rigidly arranged and more detailed than other outlines, a formal outline not only lays out main ideas and their support but also shows the relative importance of all the essay's elements and how they connect with each other.

On the basis of her scratch outline (p. 35), Terry Perez prepared this formal outline for her essay on cultural diversity in the media.

Thesis sentence

Judging from the unrealistic images projected by the media, the United States is a nation either of constant ethnic conflict or of untroubled homogeneity.

Formal outline

I. Images of ethnic conflict
  A. News stories
    1. Hispanic-black gang wars in L.A.
    2. Defaced synagogues in Chicago
    3. Korean-black disputes in N.Y.
  B. The real story
    1. No war among groups
    2. Groups coexisting
II. Images of untroubled homogeneity
  A. Those pictured in TV shows and ads
    1. White
    2. Middle class
    3. Attractive
  B. Those missing from TV shows and ads
    1. Ethnic
    2. Poor
    3. Handicapped
    4. Other groups

In this outline Perez refined her thinking even further, organizing more tightly and adding examples. Though she knew her outline might change as she drafted and revised her essay, she thought it would set a course for her to follow.

Perez's outline illustrates several principles of outlining that can help ensure completeness, balance, and clear relationships. (These principles largely depend on distinguishing between the general and the specific. See p. 34.)

Principles of the formal outline

1. Labels and indentions indicate order and relative importance.
2. Sections and subsections reflect logical relationships.
3. Topics of equal generality appear in parallel headings.
4. Each subdivision has at least two parts.
5. Headings are expressed in parallel grammatical form.
6. The introduction and conclusion may be omitted (though not, of course, from the essay).

1. So that the outline both clarifies the order of ideas and details and indicates their relative importance, all its parts are systematically indented and numbered or lettered: Roman numerals (I, II) for primary divisions of the essay; indented capital letters (A, B) for secondary divisions; further indented Arabic numerals (1, 2) for principal supporting examples. A level of detail below the Arabic numbers would be indented further still and labeled with small letters (a, b). Each succeeding level contains more specific information than the one before it.
2. The outline divides the material into several groups. An uninterrupted listing of ideas like the one following would indicate a need for tighter, more logical relationships among ideas. (Compare this example with part II of Perez's actual outline.)

> II. Images of untroubled homogeneity
>   A. White people
>   B. Middle-class people
>   C. Attractive people
>   D. No ethnics
>   E. No poor
>   F. No handicapped

3. Within each part of the outline, distinct topics of equal generality appear in parallel headings (with the same indention and numbering or lettering). In the following example points C and D are more specific than point B, not equally general, so they should be subheadings 1 and 2 under it. (See section IB of Perez's outline.)

> B. The real story
> C. No war among groups
> D. Groups coexisting

4. All subdivided headings in the outline break into at least two parts because a topic cannot logically be divided into only one part. The following example violates this principle.

    B. The real story: no war among groups
        1. Groups coexisting

Any single subdivision should be matched with another subdivision (as in part IB of Perez's outline), combined with the heading above it, or rechecked for its relevance to the heading above it.

5. All headings are expressed in parallel grammatical form. Perez's is a topic outline, in which each heading consists of a noun plus modifiers. In a sentence outline all headings are expressed as full sentences (see 36e and pp. 634–35 for discussion and an example). Compare the mixture of forms below with section IB of Perez's actual outline.

    B. The real story
        1. Groups are not at war with each other.
        2. Groups coexisting

6. The outline covers only the body of the essay, omitting the introduction and the conclusion (see below, 1g-3). The beginning and the ending are important in the essay itself, but you need not include them in the outline unless you are required to do so or anticipate special problems with their organization.

3   Choosing a structure

Most essays share a basic shape consisting of an introduction, a body, and a conclusion. The **introduction** draws readers into the world of the essay, stating the topic and often the thesis sentence. It makes a commitment that the rest of the essay delivers on. The **conclusion** generally gives readers something to take away from the essay—a summary of ideas, for instance, or a suggested course of action. (Both introductory and concluding paragraphs are discussed with other special kinds of paragraphs in 3d, pp. 109–13.) The **body** of the essay is its center, the part offering ideas and supporting details, examples, and reasons to develop the thesis and thus fulfill the commitment of the introduction. In an essay of two or three pages, the body may contain three to five substantial paragraphs, each presenting and supporting a part of the thesis.

The organization of the body of your essay will depend on your topic, your purpose, and your sense of what your readers need and expect from you. In almost any writing situation, at least one of the organizing schemes listed below will be appropriate. These schemes are so familiar that readers expect them and look for them. Thus the schemes both help you arrange your material and help readers follow you.

Schemes for organizing ideas in an essay

- Space
- Time
- Emphasis

General to specific   Decreasing familiarity
Specific to general   Increasing complexity
Increasing importance
   (climactic)

Organizing by space or time

Two organizational schemes—spatial and chronological—grow naturally out of the topic. A **spatial organization** is especially appropriate for expository essays that describe a place, an object, or a person. Following the way people normally survey something, you move through space from a chosen starting point to other features of the subject. Describing a friend, for instance, you might begin with his shoes and move upward or begin with his face and move downward. If, instead, you moved from hands to face to shoes to arms, your arrangement might be less effective because your readers would have to work harder to stay with you. The informal outline on page 36 illustrates a spatial organization, moving from one end of the street to the other.

A **chronological organization** reports events as they occurred in time, usually from first to last. This pattern, like spatial organization, corresponds to readers' own experiences and expectations. It suits expository essays in which you recount a historical or more recent sequence of events or explain a process from beginning to end (for instance, how to run a marathon). And it suits the retelling of more personal stories for the purpose of self-expression or entertainment. In an essay developed from the following thesis sentence, the author would probably proceed chronologically through the event, emphasizing the difficulties and the effects they had on his friends.

The surest way to lose good friends is to enlist their help in a move from one fourth-floor walkup to another.

A chronological organization structures the essay on pages 67–68.

Organizing for emphasis

Several other organizational schemes do not so much grow out of the topic as they are imposed on it to aid readers' understanding and achieve a desired emphasis. Two of these depend on the distinction between the general and the specific as discussed on page 34. The **general-to-specific scheme** is common in expository and argumentative essays that start with a general discussion of the main points and then proceed to specific examples, facts, or other evidence. The following thesis sentences forecast expository and argumentative essays with general-to-specific organizations:

> In families consisting of a single parent and a single child, the boundaries between parent and child often disappear, so that the two interact as siblings or as a married couple.

> If it hopes to win the technological race, the United States must make higher education possible for any student who qualifies academically.

Following from the first sentence, the body of the essay might first discuss generally the dynamics of the families in question and then provide specific examples of the two forms of interaction. Following the second sentence, the body of the essay might first elaborate on the basic argument and then provide the supporting data.

In some expository or argumentative essays, a **specific-to-general scheme** can arouse readers' interest in specific examples or other evidence, letting the evidence build to more general ideas. The following thesis sentence could be developed in this way.

> Although most of us are unaware of the public relations campaigns directed at us, they can significantly affect the way we think and live.

The writer might devote most of the essay to a single specific example of a public relations campaign, showing how it influenced people without their knowledge. Then he could explain more generally how the example typifies public relations campaigns.

In a **climactic organization,** ideas unfold in order of increasing drama or importance to a climax. For example, the following thesis sentence lists three effects of strip-mining in order of their increasing severity, and the essay would cover them in the same order.

> Strip-mining should be tightly controlled in this region to reduce its pollution of water resources, its permanent destruction of the land, and its devastating effects on people's lives.

As this example suggests, the climactic organization works well in arguments because it leaves readers with the most important point freshest in their minds. In exposition such an arrangement can create suspense and thus hold readers' attention.

Expository essays can also be arranged in variations of the climactic pattern. An essay on learning to play the guitar might proceed from **most familiar to least familiar,** that is, from simply plucking strings and sliding the hand up and down the instrument's neck, which most people have seen, to the less familiar styles of picking and chording. Similarly, an essay on various computer languages might proceed from **simplest to most complex,** so that the explanation of each language provides a basis for readers to understand the more difficult one following.

 4   Checking for unity and coherence

In conceiving your organization and writing your essay, you should be aware of two qualities of effective writing that relate to organization: unity and coherence. When you perceive that someone's writing "flows well," you are probably appreciating these two qualities. An essay has **unity** if all its parts support the thesis sentence and relate to each other. It has **coherence** if readers can see the relations and move easily from one thought to the next. A unified and coherent outline will not necessarily guide you to a unified and coherent essay. Much depends on how you specify connections in sentences and paragraphs, and the very process of specifying connections may lead you to see different relations and arrangements from those suggested by the outline. Still, checking your outline for unity and coherence will help you spot and solve obvious problems and thus perhaps avoid unnecessary distractions during drafting.

To check your outline for unity, ask these questions:

- Is each main section relevant to the thesis sentence?
- Within main sections of the outline, does each example or detail support the principal idea of that section?

dev

1g

Don't be too hard on your information at this stage: you may find a way to use an apparently wayward idea or example while drafting. But do cut anything that is clearly irrelevant and likely to sidetrack you during drafting.

To check your outline for coherence, ask the following questions about it:

- Does your arrangement suit your purpose?
- Does the arrangement fulfill your readers' needs and expectations?
- Will readers recognize the shape of your material?

The unity and coherence of an essay begin in its paragraphs, so the two are treated in greater detail in Chapter 3 (see 3a and 3b).

COLLABORATIVE LEARNING

ANSWERS: EXERCISE 17
Possible Answers

I. Fans resist [new general idea].
  A. Sports seasons are already too crowded for fans.
    1. Baseball, football, hockey, and basketball seasons already overlap.
    2. Fans have limited time to watch.
    3. Fans have limited money to pay for sports.
  B. Soccer is unfamiliar [new general idea].
    1. A lot of kids play soccer in school, but the game is still "foreign."
    2. Soccer rules are unfamiliar.
II. Backers resist [new general idea].
  A. Sports money goes where the money is.
    1. Soccer fans couldn't fill huge stadiums.
    2. Backers are concerned with TV contracts.
    3. TV contracts almost matter more than live audiences.
    4. American soccer fans are too few for TV interest.
  B. Backers are wary of losing money on new ventures.
    1. Failure of the U.S. Football League was costly.
    2. Previous attempts to start a pro soccer league failed.

Exercise 17
Distinguishing the general and the specific

The following list of ideas was extracted by a student from freewriting he did for a brief paper on soccer in the United States. Using his thesis sentence as a guide, pick out the general ideas and arrange the relevant specific points under them. In some cases you may have to invent general ideas to cover specific points already in the list.

Thesis sentence

Despite the 1994 World Cup competition to be held in the United States, soccer may never be the sport here that it is elsewhere because both the potential fans and the potential backers resist it.

List of ideas

Sports seasons are already too crowded for fans
Soccer rules are confusing to Americans
A lot of kids play soccer in school, but the game is still "foreign"
Sports money goes where the money is
Backers are wary of losing money on new ventures
Fans have limited time to watch
Fans have limited money to pay for sports
Backers are concerned with TV contracts
Previous attempts to start a pro soccer league failed
TV contracts almost matter more than live audiences
Failure of the U.S. Football League was costly
Baseball, football, hockey, and basketball seasons already overlap
Soccer fans couldn't fill huge stadiums
American soccer fans are too few for TV interest

Exercise 18
Revising a formal outline

Revise the following outline so that it adheres to the principles of the formal outline given on pages 39–40. Use the thesis sentence as a guide to appropriate divisions in the outline.

Thesis sentence

Strip-mining should be tightly controlled in this region to reduce its pollution of water resources, its permanent destruction of the land, and its devastating effects on people's lives.

Formal outline

I. Effects of strip-mining in this region
   A. Causes of water pollution
      1. Soil acids are leached by rainwater.
      2. Run-off of acids into streams
   B. Disappearance of fish
   C. Poisoning of water supply
   D. Appearance of hills caused by mining
      1. Scarring
      2. Vegetation is destroyed
   E. Erosion of the land
      1. Topsoil removed
      2. Mud slides are very common.
   F. Elimination of people's forms of recreation
   G. Health problems
      1. Polluted water causes illness.
   H. Destruction of people's farmland and homes
      1. Acid soil
      2. Mud slides
   I. Inadequate compensation for destruction of farmland and homes
II. Possible controls on strip-mining
   A. Regulate mining techniques.
      1. To limit erosion
      2. Limitations on pollution
   B. Mining companies should be required to replace topsoil.
      1. Restore vegetation to prevent erosion
   C. Compensation for destruction of farmland and homes
      1. Cash payments
      2. Rebuilding

Exercise 19
Arranging ideas

Choose three of the following topics and list four to six specific points for each one. Then arrange the ideas in an appropriate and effective order.

ANSWERS: EXERCISE 18
Possible Revision (Changes Underlined):

I. Effects of strip-mining in this region
   A. Pollution of water resources
      1. Causes
         a. Leaching of soil acids by rainwater
         b. Run-off of acids into streams
      2. Results
         a. Disappearance of fish
         b. Poisoning of water supply
   B. Destruction of the land
      1. Appearance of hills
         a. Scarring
         b. Destruction of vegetation
      2. Erosion
         a. Removal of topsoil
         b. Frequent mud slides
      3. Elimination of people's forms of recreation
   C. Devastation of people's lives
      1. Illness from water pollution
      2. Destruction of farmland and homes
         a. Acid soil
         b. Mud slides
         c. Inadequate compensation
II. Possible controls on strip-mining
   A. Regulation of mining techniques
      1. Limitations on erosion
      2. Limitations on pollution
   B. Mandatory replacement of topsoil and restoration of vegetation
   C. Compensation for destruction of farmland and homes
      1. Cash payments
      2. Rebuilding

ANSWERS: EXERCISE 19
Possible Answers

1. A block party, seen from above: the activity and bright colors of the scene as a whole; gatherings of people on the doorsteps lining

the street; children playing games in the street; in the center, people buzzing around the barbecues where food is being prepared.

2. First, an objective view of those left behind; second, a gradual fading of the earthly world; third, an expanding bright light from above; fourth, a brilliant, peaceful, eternal presence.

3. The occasional class missed because of inadequate parking; the frequent need to walk long distances from the remote lots; the common difficulty of wasting time hunting for a parking space; the unfairness to all commuting students in comparison with resident students.

4. Swimming laps, dancing, listening to loud music, attending movies, fighting with your roommate.

5. Failure: a personal, not societal, judgment; an opportunity lost because of inattention, laziness, or confused priorities; a prerequisite to success.

6. Parts of a ten-speed bicycle: frame, handlebars, seat, wheels, brakes, derailleur, gear shift, and cables.

7. Kinds of students: partiers, scholars, leaders, followers, wallflowers.

8. Two newspapers, serious paper versus tabloid: political versus human-interest news; liberal versus conservative bias; sedate versus loud design; no gimmicks versus frequent promotional games.

9. Causes of cheating: pressure from parents, pressure from peers, lack of self-confidence, laziness, immorality.

10. Making a triple play in baseball: the basic play, with players on first and second (second baseman or shortstop catches a line drive, steps to second base, throws to first baseman); other plays.

ANSWERS: EXERCISE 20

Individual response.

1. A festive or depressing place
2. My view of what happens after death
3. Why parking facilities for commuting students should be expanded
4. Ways to release frustration or tension
5. The meaning of success or failure
6. The parts of a religious service, a ten-speed bicycle, a camera, or a baseball
7. Kinds of self-help books, students on campus, joggers, part-time jobs, or teachers
8. The differences or similarities between two television sitcoms, grandparents, newspapers, magazines, or cars
9. The causes or effects of an accident, quitting smoking, playing a sport, or cheating
10. How to make a great dessert, take a photograph, make a triple play in baseball, train a dog, or study for an examination

Exercise 20
Organizing your own essay

Continuing from Exercise 16 (p. 33), choose an appropriate organization for your essay-in-progress. Then, to discover whether and to what extent an outline can help you plan and draft an essay, prepare a tree diagram or a scratch, informal, or formal outline, as specified by your instructor.

Chapter 2

Drafting and Revising the Essay

HIGHLIGHTS

This chapter continues the exploration, begun in Chapter 1, of writing as a flexible process and looks in detail at strategies for drafting, revising, editing, and proofreading. The journey from initial draft to finished essay may involve many decisions and changes of direction for which there are no firm rules. To alert student writers to the options available to them, the chapter provides lists of strategies for drafting an essay and checklists for revising and editing. It also provides concrete advice for the stages of composing that many writers find the most difficult: getting started and completing the initial draft.

Students who view revising as an expendable stage in the writing process may benefit from following, draft by draft, the development of Terry Perez's essay (begun in Chapter 1) on media diversity in the portrayal of ethnic groups. Like most initial efforts, Perez's early draft can benefit from revisions in organization, content, tone, and approach to clarify the essay's purpose and the relationships among its ideas and also to make it easier for readers to share Perez's perspective. The revised draft, in turn, needs editing for clarity, style, and correction of errors in grammar, usage, punctuation, and spelling—changes that appear in the final version of the essay, along with the instructor's corrections and comments.

Teachers who draw on the handbook in correcting and commenting on student papers may wish to direct students' attention to the instructor's corrections on Terry Perez's full essay (pages 61–64); these corrections use a combination of the number-and-letter codes, symbols, and written comments. To familiarize students with use of the handbook, you can assign Exercise 7, which asks them to revise Perez's essay by making use of the instructor's comments. The two additional student papers at the end of the chapter (Exercise 9) are also appropriate for class discussion and criticism. All three papers can provide material for small-group discussion and evaluation, and the section on benefiting from criticism (2e) can help students learn to work effectively in peer critique groups. "Guidelines for Criticizing Others' Work" and "Guidelines for Benefiting from Criticism" on pages 65 and 66 clarify peer review in a helpful list format.

The separation of drafting and revising from the planning activities discussed in Chapter 1 is somewhat artificial because the stages almost always overlap during the writing process. Eventually, though, your primary goal will shift from planning toward forming connected sentences and paragraphs in a draft and then restructuring and rewriting the draft.

2a Writing the first draft

The only "correct" drafting style is the one that works for you, whether that means drafting and revising at the same time, pushing through without rereading at all, or something in between. Just keep in mind that writers do not transcribe fully formed, coherent, polished thoughts into words but strive to find and convey their meaning through the act of writing.

Starting to draft sometimes takes courage, even for seasoned professionals. Students and pros alike find elaborate ways to procrastinate—rearranging shelves, napping, lunching with friends. Such procrastination may actually help you if you let ideas for writing simmer at the same time. At some point, though, enough is enough: the deadline looms; you've got to get started. If the blankness still stares back at you, then try one of the following techniques for unblocking.

rev
2a

OVERCOMING WRITING BLOCKS

Many students have a hard time writing first drafts because they try to get everything right the first time. They end up writing sentences and then crossing out what they have written so often that they have no time left to revise their thoughts in a second draft. Sometimes the pressure of perfection is so great that students become blocked writers, unable to finish even a single draft before the deadline. Here are four ways to help students get started and to help them develop flexibility and self-confidence in their approach to the task:

1. Show them copies of your own first and final drafts to indicate that you were not afraid to make mistakes in the initial draft because you had a chance to correct them in the later versions.

2. Give students a time limit for the first draft, perhaps an hour and a half or two hours, depending on the length of the assignment. Require them to hand in the draft with the final paper so that you can see how they approached the task of writing.

3. Have students start writing in class, where you can encourage them to get ideas down on paper before they try to perfect the wording.

4. Require students to spend some time either jotting down ideas and phrases or freewriting so that they will be loosened up before tackling the initial draft.

RESOURCES AND IDEAS

Mike Rose, *Writer's Block: The Cognitive Dimension* (Carbondale: Southern Illinois UP, 1983). The case studies of student writers that Rose discusses demonstrate that blocked writers often follow rigid, absolute rules about the forms and process of writing, whereas fluent writers use flexible, enabling strategies.

Lynn Z. Bloom, "Research on Writing Blocks, Writing Anxiety, and Writing Apprehension," *Research in Composition and Rhetoric,* ed. Michael G. Moran and Ronald F. Lunsford (Westport: Greenwood, 1984) 71–91. Bloom surveys research on the fears and blocks that many writers encounter and examines strategies, similar to those presented in this chapter, for overcoming the difficulties.

 Ways to start drafting

- Read over what you've already written—notes, outlines, and so on—and immediately start your draft with whatever comes to mind.
- Freewrite (see 1e-3).
- Write scribbles or type nonsense until usable words start coming.
- Pretend you're writing to a friend about your topic.
- Conjure up an image that represents your topic—a physical object, a facial expression, two people arguing over something, a giant machine gouging the earth for a mine, whatever. Describe that image.
- Skip the opening and start in the middle. Or write the conclusion.
- Write a paragraph on what you think your essay will be about when you finish it.
- Using your outline, divide your essay into chunks—say, one for the introduction, another for the first example or reason, and so on. Start writing the chunk that seems most eager to be written, the one you understand best or feel most strongly about.

You should find some momentum once you've started writing. If not, however, or if your energy flags, try one or more of these techniques to keep moving ahead.

 Ways to *keep* drafting

- Set aside enough time for yourself. (For a brief essay, a first draft is likely to take at least an hour or two.)
- Work in a place where you won't be interrupted.
- Make yourself comfortable.
- If you must stop working, jot a note before leaving the draft about what you expect to do next. Then you can pick up where you left off.
- Be as fluid as possible. Spontaneity will allow your attitudes toward your subject to surface naturally in your sentences. It will also make you receptive to ideas and relations you haven't seen before.
- Keep going. Skip over sticky spots; leave a blank if you can't find the right word. If an idea pops out of nowhere but doesn't seem to fit in, quickly jot it down on a separate sheet, or write it into the draft and bracket it for later attention.

- Resist self-criticism. Don't worry about your style, grammar, spelling, and the like. Don't worry what your readers will think. These are very important matters, but save them for revision.
- Use your thesis sentence and outline to remind you of your planned purpose, organization, and content.
- But don't feel constrained by your thesis and outline. If your writing leads you in a more interesting direction, follow.

To accommodate later changes, write or type your first draft only on one side of the paper, leave wide margins, and double- or triple-space all lines. Then you will find it easy to change words or whole sentences and to cut the draft apart and rearrange it without tedious recopying or retyping.

Terry Perez's first draft on diversity in the media appears below. She retyped the completed draft so that her class and she herself would have clean copy to work on.

First draft

Title?

In "America: The Multinational Society," Ishmael Reed

mentions that the communications media sensationalizes the

"conflict between people of different backgrounds." Either

that, or it depicts Americans as homogeneous. Judging

from the unrealistic images projected by television, news-

papers, and magazines, the U.S. is a nation either of con-

stant ethnic conflict or untroubled homogeneity.

It is easy to find examples of the emphasizing of

conflict among ethnic groups. The news is full of stories

of Hispanic gangs fighting black gangs in Los Angeles or

Korean shopkeepers pitted against black and Hispanic

customers in New York City. In fact, New York City, with

the densest and most ethnically diverse population in the

country, regularly supplies stories for other cities' news

media when they run out of local stories of hate and mayhem. My brother who lives in California is always complaining about all the New York stories in the news. What he doesn't realize is that it's not New York's fault, it's the media's for always playing up the bad news. Bad news is what the media specializes in--as everyone is always complaining. When it comes to ethnic relations, this is certainly the case. All sorts of different people mingle together peacefully, but not in the media.

There the only peace belongs to a very narrow band of people. Especially in television fiction and advertising. They have usual characteristics: they are white, married or expecting to be someday, unethnic, white collar, well-to-do, settled, materialistic, good looking, and thin. Many, many groups are excluded from this TV type, such as ethnic groups, poor people, and the handicapped. A certain commercial is typical of TV with the happy prosperous nuclear family enjoying breakfast together.

The problem with this media image, with its extremes of peace and conflict, is that it is untrue. It caters to the ones who feel that the U.S. should be a "monoculture" and would be. If only we could battle down the ones who don't belong or won't. A different picture is possible, but we aren't getting it.

COLLABORATIVE LEARNING

ANSWERS: EXERCISE 1
Possible Answers

Some significant differences between Perez's outline and her first draft:

In paragraph 2 Perez followed a thread about the media and New York City.

In paragraph 3 she expanded the description of the typical media presentation and added an example.

In paragraph 4 she broached the idea of a "different picture" the media could be presenting.

Exercise 1
Analyzing a first draft

Compare Perez's draft with the last step in her planning (her formal outline) on page 38. List the places in the draft where the act of drafting led Perez to rearrange her information, add or delete material, or explore new ideas.

Exercise 2
Drafting your own essay

Prepare a draft of the essay you began in Chapter 1. Use your thesis sentence (Exercise 16, p. 33) and your outline (Exercise 20, p. 46) as guides, but don't be unduly constrained by them. Concentrate on opening up options, not on closing them down.

2b Revising the first draft

Revision literally means "re-seeing"—looking anew at ideas and details, their relationships and arrangement, the degree to which they work or don't work for the thesis. While drafting, you have been focused inwardly, concentrating on pulling your topic out of yourself. In revising, you look out to your readers, trying to anticipate how they will see your work. You examine your draft as a pole-vaulter or dancer would examine a videotape of his or her performance, or as you might examine a photograph of yourself.

Obtaining the needed distance for revision can be difficult, even for experienced writers. Here are some techniques that may help you.

Ways to gain distance from your work

- Take a break after finishing the draft to pursue some other activity. A few hours may be enough; a whole night or day is preferable. The break will clear your mind, relax you, and give you some objectivity.
- Ask someone to read and react to your draft. Many writing instructors ask their students to submit their first drafts so that the instructors and, often, the other members of the class can serve as an actual audience to help guide revision. (See also 2e on receiving and benefiting from criticism.)
- Outline your draft. A formal outline, especially, with its careful structure and many possible levels of detail, can show where organization is illogical or support is skimpy. (See 1g-2 for a discussion of outlining.)
- Listen to your draft: read it out loud, read it into a tape recorder and play the tape, or have someone read the draft to you. Experiencing your words with ears instead of eyes can alter your perceptions.
- Ease the pressure. Don't try to re-see everything in your draft at once. Use a checklist like the one on page 53, making a separate pass through the draft for each numbered item.

RESOURCES AND IDEAS

Linda Flower, "Writer-Based Prose: A Cognitive Basis for Problems in Writing," *College English* 41 (1979): 19–37. Flower argues that writers must learn to transform what they have to say from the form in which they came to understand it (writer-based prose) to the form in which readers can understand it (reader-based prose).

Diane P. Thompson, "Using a Local Area Network to Teach Computer Revision Skills," *Journal of Teaching Writing* 8 (1989): 77–85. Thompson describes how by rewriting stories from different characters' points of view, students were exposed to a number of their own writing problems and discovered revision strategies. This process was facilitated by the networked classroom and video switching equipment.

> TRANSPARENCY MASTER
> AVAILABLE

REVISING ACTIVITIES

Here are a few revising activities for students working on their own or in groups:

Making out an inventory. After students have written an initial draft, ask them to complete a brief version of the audience inventory described in Chapter 1 (page 13). Their completed inventory can help guide the choices they make during revision. Students may wish to share drafts and inventories with other students.

Using dialogue. For narrative writing, ask students to circle every use of "He said that" and "She thought that" or similar phrases in their own or someone else's paper. Then ask them to consider replacing the indirect discourse with dialogue and direct quotations to make the writing more vivid and realistic.

Using the senses. For narrative and descriptive writing, ask students to check how many of the senses they have drawn on; then ask them to consider making use of the other senses.

Adding other arguments. For argumentative essays, have students list all the arguments they

rev
2b

could use but have not yet included in the paper; they may wish to turn to other students for advice about including these arguments.

Soliciting class suggestions. For argumentative essays, ask students to summarize their theses and supporting arguments for their classmates. Then ask the other students to suggest more supporting arguments and opposing arguments the writer might consider during revision.

Answering more questions. For expository essays, ask students to answer these questions for their own or someone else's paper: What five things do you know about this topic that are not included in the draft? Which ones could be put into the essay without harming its unity or coherence? What three things are readers most likely to find interesting, useful, or surprising about this topic? Could these three things be given more emphasis without disrupting the organization or clarity of the essay?

RESOURCES AND IDEAS

Peter Elbow, *Writing with Power: Techniques for Mastering the Writing Process* (New York: Oxford UP, 1981). Elbow's book offers detailed, practical, and often innovative advice on drafting, revising, shaping for an audience, and making use of feedback, including several chapters on revising ("Quick Revising," "Thorough Revising," "Revising with Feedback," and "Cut and Paste Revising and the Collage").

Nancy Sommers, "Revising Strategies of Student Writers and Experienced Adult Writers," *College Composition and Communication* 31 (1980): 378–88. According to Sommers, students see revision as changes in small units—words and sentences. Experienced writers see it as a recursive process directed at larger units of the text and the meaning it conveys.

P. C. Wason, "Specific Thoughts on the Writing Process," *Cognitive Processes in Writing*, ed. Lee W. Gregg and Erwin R. Steinberg (Hillsdale: Erlbaum, 1980) 129–37. Wason argues that multiple drafts are often necessary because writing consists of two processes hard to undertake at the same time: saying (or discovering) something and saying it correctly.

Strictly speaking, revision includes editing—refining the manner of expression to improve clarity or style or to correct errors. In this chapter, though, revision and editing are treated separately to stress their differences: in revision you deal with the underlying meaning and structure of your essay; in editing you deal with its surface. Often it is tempting to skip the fundamental work of revision and move directly to editing the first draft. But the resulting essay, though perhaps superficially correct, may not show you at your best and may be flawed in ways that will negatively affect readers' responses. You can avoid the temptation to substitute editing for revision and prevent them from interfering with each other by making at least two separate drafts beyond the first: a revised one and then an edited one (p. 57).

Set aside at least as much time to revise your essay as you took to draft it. Plan on going through the draft several times to answer the questions in the checklist opposite and to resolve any problems. (If you need additional information on any of the topics in the checklist, refer to the handbook sections given in parentheses.) Note that the checklist can also help you if you have been asked to comment on another writer's draft (see 2e).

A note on titling your essay   *Essays have titles!*

The revision stage is a good time to consider a title because attempting to sum up your essay in a phrase can focus your attention sharply on your topic, purpose, and audience.

Here are some suggestions for titling an essay:

- A **descriptive title** is almost always appropriate and is often expected for academic writing. It announces the topic clearly, accurately, and as briefly as possible. The title Terry Perez finally chose, "America's Media Image," is an example. Other examples: "Images of Lost Identity in *North by Northwest*"; "An Experiment in Small-Group Dynamics"; "Why Lincoln Delayed Emancipating the Slaves."
- A **suggestive title**—the kind often found in popular magazines—may be appropriate for more informal writing. Examples include "Making Peace" (for an essay on the Peace Corps) and "Royal Pain" (for an essay on Prince Charles of England). For a more suggestive title, Perez might have chosen something like "Distorted Pictures." Such titles convey the writers' attitudes and main concerns but not their precise topics, thereby pulling readers into the essays to learn more. A source for such a title may be a familiar phrase, a fresh image, or a significant expression from the essay itself.
- A title tells readers how big the topic is. For Perez's essay, the

Checklist for revision

1. Does the body of the essay carry out the purpose and central idea expressed by the thesis sentence (1f)?

   Is the reason for writing apparent, not only in the thesis sentence but throughout the essay?

   If the body of the essay does not carry out the thesis sentence, is the problem more with the thesis sentence (because it does not reflect a new and better direction in the draft) or with the body (because it wanders)?

2. Are there adequate details, examples, or reasons to support each of the ideas (1d, 1e)?

   Do readers need more information at any point to understand the meaning or appreciate the point of view?

3. Does the tone of the writing convey a clear and appropriate attitude toward the topic and convey the role assumed (1d-3)?

   Is the tone appropriate for the purpose and audience?

   Is it consistent throughout the essay?

4. Is the essay unified (1g-4)?

   Does each paragraph and sentence relate clearly to the thesis sentence?

5. Is the essay coherent (1g-4)? *transitions*

   Are the relationships within and among its parts apparent?

   Can readers see the shape of the essay, its overall organization?

6. Is each paragraph in the body unified (3a), coherent (3b), and well developed (3c)?

7. Does the title state or hint at the essay's scope and approach (see opposite)?

   Does the introduction engage and focus readers' attention (3c-1)?

   Does the conclusion provide a sense of completion (3c-2)?

title "Watching the Media" or "Cultural Diversity" would have been too broad, whereas "The Media and Cultural Conflict" or "Exclusion in the Media" would have been too narrow.

- A title should not restate the assignment or the thesis sentence, as in "What Ishmael Reed Means by Cultural Diversity" or "How I Feel About Cultural Diversity."

For more information on essay titles, see 12c-4 (avoiding reference to the title in the opening of the paper), 26b (capitalizing words in a title), and Appendix A2-d (the format of a title in the final paper).

TRANSPARENCY MASTER
AVAILABLE

rev
2b

RESOURCES AND IDEAS

Mike Rose, "Writing Around Rules," *Patterns in Action,* 2nd ed., ed. Robert A. Schwegler (New York: HarperCollins, 1988) 473–80. As an illustration of the kinds of rules that block writing and the kinds of strategies that enable it, Rose tells of the difficulties he encountered in titling a poem.

RESOURCES AND IDEAS

Peer editing and collaborative learning have become regular features of many composition courses over the past decade, and these approaches are particularly well suited to drafting and revising activities. Section 2e coaches students in giving and receiving criticism. And the essay "Using Collaborative Learning with the Handbook" at the beginning of this annotated edition offers detailed advice about designing collaborative activities and preparing students to work in groups. It also provides sample reader response forms, which you may wish to copy and use in your class.

Much has been written recently about collaborative learning and peer writing groups. Two recent selections, however, offer good starting points for someone interested in examining both the opportunities offered by this approach and the controversies that it has created:

John Trimbur, "Collaborative Learning and Teaching Writing," *Perspectives on Research and Scholarship in Composition,* ed. Ben W. McClelland and Timothy R. Donovan (New York: MLA, 1985) 87–109. Trimbur offers a compact survey of the history and theories behind collaborative learning and raises important questions about the roles of response and evaluation in a student- (rather than teacher-) centered classroom.

Anne Ruggles Gere, *Writing Groups: History, Theory, and Implications* (Carbondale: Southern Illinois UP, 1987). Gere reviews the history, theory, and practice of writing groups and collaborative learning; she also provides a useful annotated bibliography of research and pedagogy.

RESOURCES AND IDEAS

Even though you encourage students to revise and offer them detailed advice about what and when to revise, you may still find that their revisions are limited to superficial changes. Part of the problem may be that students have not yet become good enough readers of their own texts to identify features that might be altered or dropped and to identify places where something might be added. Here are some resources for helping students to become active readers and writers, aware of what they have written and how it might be changed:

James P. Beck, "Asking Students to Annotate Their Own Papers," *College Composition and Communication* 38 (1982): 322–23. Beck asks students to identify specific techniques they have used in their writing (including features of structure, detail, argument, and style) and to evaluate how well they have used those techniques.

Richard M. Coe and Kris D. Gutierrez, "Using Problem-Solving Procedures and Process Analysis to Help Students with Writing Problems," *College Composition and Communication* 32 (1981): 262–71. Coe and Gutierrez offer assignments and activities designed to make students aware of how they go about writing, to help them understand their strengths and weaknesses as writers, and to give them greater control over their composing processes.

Douglas R. Butturff and Nancy I. Sommers, "Placing Revision in a Reinvented Rhetorical Tradition," *Reinventing the Rhetorical Tradition,* ed. Aviva Freedman and Ian Pringle (Conway: L & S Books, 1980) 99–104. The authors argue that the comments instructors make on papers should help students learn writing procedures that will enable them to make effective revisions.

In revising her first draft, Terry Perez had the help of her instructor and several of her classmates, to whom she showed the draft as part of her assignment. (See 2e for more on this kind of collaboration.) Based on the revision checklist, she felt that the purpose and main idea expressed in her thesis sentence had held up well in the draft. But she also knew without being told that her introduction was too hurried and that the body of the essay was thin: she hadn't supplied enough details to support her ideas and convince her readers.

Perez's readers confirmed her self-criticism: some were confused by the introduction; others were unconvinced by her essay; everyone asked for more examples. And among other comments her readers raised additional points that she had not considered. They are reflected in this comment by a classmate:

> I tend to agree with you about the media, but I'd be more willing to go along if you admitted somewhere that ethnic conflict *does* exist (TV and the papers don't just make it up!). Also, what about exceptions to the "TV type"—what about the Cosbys? Finally, I don't see the point you're trying to make about New York, and your brother doesn't seem relevant at all. How does this relate to your thesis?

While revising, Perez made many changes directly on the draft, but she also inserted new passages. Her revision begins on the next page. The principal changes are explained below and keyed to the revision by numbers (some numbers are used more than once).

1. With a fairly descriptive title, Perez intended to give readers a sense of her topic and also remind them that the media create an image for the nation as well as for politicians and movie stars.
2. Perez rewrote and expanded the previous abrupt introduction to give more of a sense of Reed's essay and to make a clearer transition to her additional point about the media (the new sentence beginning *Another false media picture*).
3. Perez's instructor and one of her classmates pointed out that *media* is a plural noun (*medium* is the singular) and thus takes a plural verb. Hence Perez's change to *the communications media sensationalize*.
4. At these points Perez added examples and other details to support her general statements. This and the following category of changes occupied most of Perez's attention during revision.
5. In response to her classmates, Perez added several concessions and exceptions. As soon as she had written these passages, she saw that they strengthened her essay by balancing it.

6. Perez cut a digression that her readers had found distracting and irrelevant.
7. Her conclusion had received few comments in class, but Perez thought that it, too, needed revision. She concentrated on clarifying the opening of the paragraph and adding detail about her own "picture" to the end.

Revised first draft

~~Title?~~ *America's Media Image*   1

Is the United States a "monoculture," a unified   2

homogeneous society? Many Americans would like it to

be or they think that it is now. But the writer Ishmael

Reed says no. His essay is titled "America: The Multinational

Society." In it he speaks out for cultural diversity. He

thinks it makes the nation stronger. In passing he

~~In "America: The Multinational Society," Ishmael Reed~~

mentions that the communications media sensationalize*s* the   3
Another false media picture can be added to Reed's point. The pic-
"conflict between people of different backgrounds." ^ ~~Either~~
ture of Americans as socially, economically, and ethnically similar.
~~that, or it depicts Americans as homogeneous.~~ Judging

from the unrealistic images projected by television, news-

papers, and magazines, the U.S. is a nation either of con-

stant ethnic conflict or untroubled homogeneity.

It is easy to find examples of the emphasizing of

conflict among ethnic groups. The news is full of stories
swastikas are painted on Jewish synagogues in Chicago, Haitians
of Hispanic gangs fighting black gangs in Los Angeles, *or* ^   4
battle Cubans in Miami,
^Korean shopkeepers pitted against black and Hispanic
These are real stories, and all-to-
customers in New York City. ~~In fact, New York City, with~~   5
real ethnic conflict should not be covered up. However, these
~~the densest and most ethnically diverse population in the~~
stories are blown out of proportion.
~~country, regularly supplies stories for other cities' news~~   6

~~media when they run out of local stories of hate and~~

Terry Perez's essay 55–57

Note her extensive revisions.

rev 2b

mayhem. ~~My brother who lives in California is always complaining about all the New York stories in the news. What he doesn't realize is that it's not New York's fault, it's the media's for always playing up the bad news.~~ Bad ~~news is what the media specializes in—as~~ Everyone ~~is~~
that the news media never present enough good news.
always complain~~ing.~~ When it comes to ethnic relations, this is certainly the case. ~~All sorts of different people mingle together peacefully, but not in the media.~~

Pakistanis, Russians, Mexicans, Chinese, Mayflower **4**
descendants, great grandchildren of African slaves. All
these and more mingle on the nation's streets, attend
school together, work together. Integration is very far **5**
from complete, severe inequality persists. Real conflict
exists. But for the most part, cultural groups are not at war.

However, in the media

~~There~~ the only peace belongs to a very narrow band of people. Especially in television fiction and advertising. They have usual characteristics: they are white, married or expecting to be someday, unethnic, white collar, well-to-do, settled, materialistic, good looking, and thin.
These are but a few of the groups excluded from this TV type:
~~Many, many groups are excluded from this TV type, such as~~ **4**
Polish Americans, homeless families, homosexuals, Lebanese
~~ethnic groups, poor people, and the handicapped. A~~
immigrants, unmarried couples (heterosexual and homosexual),
~~certain commercial is typical of TV with the happy~~
stay-at-home fathers, transients, mentally handicapped people,
~~prosperous nuclear family enjoying breakfast together.~~
elderly, homely people, fat people, small people. Exceptions **5**
come and go, such as the working-class and overweight
Roseanne and her husband, the older women in Golden Girls,
and the Cosbys. However, the norm is easy to recognize.

For example, a cereal commercial that features a mother   4
who is over seeing her husband's and children's breakfasts.
The kitchen is full of the latest appliances and decorations.
Everyone is white. Everyone is fit and cute, beautiful, or
handsome. All well dressed and cheerful.

The media's two extremes of peace and conflict   7
create a composite picture of a nation where

~~The problem with this media image, with its extremes~~
~~of peace and conflict, is that it is untrue.~~ ~~It caters to~~
~~the ones who feel that the U.S. should be~~ a "monoculture"
is desirable and all but achieved.
~~and would be.~~ If only we could battle down the ones who
                        Imagine a   though. In
don't belong or won't. ∧A different picture, ~~is possible,~~
this one people coexist, who have diverse backgrounds,
~~but we aren't getting it.~~   4
interests, incomes, living arrangements, and appearances.
Sometimes they stay apart, sometimes they blend. Sometimes
they clash or prey on each other, sometimes they laugh
together. It all happens now and we could be watching.

Exercise 3
Analyzing a revised draft

Compare Perez's revised draft with her first draft on pages 49–50. Based on the discussion of her intentions for revision (pp. 54–55), can you see the reasons for most of her changes? Do you think she identified and solved all the significant problems in her first draft? If not, where would you suggest further revisions, and why?

ANSWERS: EXERCISE 3

Answers will vary.

Exercise 4
Revising your own draft

Revise your own first draft from Exercise 2 (p. 51). Use the checklist for revision on page 53 as a guide. Concentrate on purpose, content, and organization, leaving smaller problems for the next draft.

ANSWERS: EXERCISE 4

Individual response.

rev
2c

last steps

editing and proofreading

2c   Editing the revised draft

Editing for style, sense, and correctness may come second to more fundamental revision, but it is far from unimportant. A carefully developed, interesting essay will still fall flat with readers if you seem oblivious to or careless about awkwardness, repetition, incorrect grammar, misleading punctuation, misused or misspelled words, and similar problems.

When you have revised your first draft, try the following approaches to editing.

Ways to find what needs editing

- Recopy, retype, or print out your revision so that you can read it easily and have plenty of room for changes.
- As you read the new draft, imagine yourself encountering it for the first time, as a reader will.
- Have a friend or relative read your work. Or, if you share your work in class, listen to the responses of your classmates or instructor. (See 2e.)
- As when revising, read the draft aloud, perhaps into a tape recorder, listening for awkward rhythms, repetitive sentence patterns, and missing or clumsy transitions.
- When reading aloud or silently, be careful to read what you actually see *on the page,* not what you may have intended to write but didn't.

In your editing, work for clarity and a smooth movement among sentences as well as for correctness. Use the questions in the checklist opposite to guide your editing. (Chapter numbers in parentheses indicate where you can look in the handbook for more information.) Note that the checklist may also serve as a guide if you are commenting on another writer's paper (see 2e).

In response to these questions and her own sense of clarity and effectiveness, Terry Perez edited the revised draft of her essay.

Edited draft (excerpts)

First paragraph

Is the United States a "monoculture," a unified, homogeneous society? Many Americans ~~would like it to be~~ *think that it is or*

Checklist for editing

1. Are the sentences grammatical?
   Do they avoid errors in case (6), verb form (7), agreement (8), and adjectives and adverbs (9)?
2. Are the sentences clear?
   Do they avoid sentence fragments (10), comma splices and fused sentences (11), errors in pronoun reference (12), shifts (13), misplaced or dangling modifiers (14), and mixed or incomplete constructions (15)?
3. Are the sentences effective?
   Do they use subordination and coordination (16) and parallelism (17) appropriately?
   Are they emphatic (18) and varied (19)?
4. Is the use of commas, semicolons, colons, periods, and other punctuation correct (20–25)?
5. Are the sentences mechanically correct in the use of capitals, italics, abbreviations, numbers, and hyphens (26–30)?
6. Are the words appropriate to the writing situation (31a)?
   Do the words exactly convey meaning and feeling (31b)?
   Is the writing concise (31c)?
7. Are the words spelled correctly (34)?

no slang, "into" cooking, kids / children

---

should be.

~~or they think that it is now.~~ But the writer Ishmael Reed

says no. ~~His essay is titled~~ *In* "America: The Multinational

Society~~,~~*;*" ~~In it he~~ *Reed* speaks out for cultural diversity. He

thinks it makes the nation stronger. In passing he

mentions that the communications media sensationalize the

"conflict between people of different backgrounds."

To Reed's point can be added the media's other false picture
~~Another false media picture of America can be added to~~
of America, ~~Reed's point.~~ *t*The picture of Americans as socially,

economically, and ethnically similar. Judging from the

unrealistic images projected by television, newspapers,

and magazines, the ~~U.S.~~ *United States* is a nation either of constant

ethnic conflict or *of* ∧untroubled homogeneity.

Fourth paragraph

though, especially television fiction and advertising,
~~However,~~ In the media, the only peace belongs to a

very narrow band of people. ~~Especially in television~~
                                            are   *ly*
~~fiction and advertising.~~ They ~~have~~ usual, characteristics:

~~they are~~ white, married or expecting to be someday,

unethnic, white collar, well-to-do, settled, materialis-

tic, good looking, and thin. These are but a few of the
                                          (some overlap)
groups excluded from this TV type: Polish-Americans,

homeless families, homosexuals, factory workers, Lebanese
teenage mothers, amputees, Japanese-Americans,
immigrants, unmarried couples (heterosexual or homo-
              loners,
sexual), stay-at-home fathers, transients, mentally
                        pensioners,
handicapped people, elderly, homely people, fat people,
                              of course,
small people. Exceptions come and go, such as the

working-class and overweight Roseanne and her husband, the

older women in Golden Girls, and the Cosbys. However,
                                        in
the norm is easy to recognize. For example, a cereal
              they
commercial ~~that~~ features a mother who is over seeing her

husband's and children's breakfasts. The kitchen is full

of the latest appliances and decorations. Everyone is

white. Everyone is fit and cute, beautiful, or handsome.
Everyone is
~~All~~ well dressed and cheerful.

ANSWERS: EXERCISE 5

Individual response.

Exercise 5
Editing your own draft
Use the checklist for editing (p. 59) and your own sense of your
essay's needs to edit the revised draft you prepared in Exercise 4
(p. 57).

2d   Proofreading and submitting the final draft

After editing your essay, recopy, retype, or print it once more for submission to your instructor. Follow the guidelines in Appendix A or the wishes of your instructor for an appropriate manuscript form. Be sure to proofread the final essay several times to spot and correct errors. To increase the accuracy of your proofreading, you may need to experiment with ways to keep yourself from relaxing into the rhythm of your prose. Here are a few tricks used by professional proofreaders.

Techniques for proofreading

- Read the paper aloud, very slowly, and distinctly pronounce exactly what you see.
- Place a ruler under each line as you read it.
- Read "against copy," comparing your final draft one sentence at a time against the edited draft you copied it from.
- Read the essay backward, end to beginning, examining each sentence as a separate unit. (This technique will help keep the content of your writing from distracting you.)   — last step

Terry Perez's final essay, along with her instructor's comments, appears below. The instructor pointed out the strengths he saw in the essay as well as the flaws remaining in it. He used a combination of written comments, correction symbols (from inside the back cover of this handbook), and correction codes (from inside the back cover).

Final draft with instructor's comments

                    America's Media Image

        Is the United States a "monoculture," a unified,

    homogeneous society? Many Americans think that it is or

    should be. But the writer Ishmael Reed says no. In

RESOURCES AND IDEAS

Jeanette Harris, "Proofreading: A Reading/Writing Skill," *College Composition and Communication* 38 (December 1987): 464–66. Harris argues that proofreading is a reading skill, a process of looking at each word and punctuation mark rather than of paying attention to the meaning of the text; and she suggests teaching students strategies like those outlined in this chapter—using a pointer (finger, pencil), reading aloud, reading in reverse order, and letting time elapse between writing and proofreading—in order to develop the specialized skill of proofreading.

Jeffrey Sommers, "The Effects of Tape-Recorded Commentary on Student Revision: A Case Study," *Journal of Teaching Writing* 8 (1989): 49–75. Sommers argues that students can misunderstand instructor response to their writing and demonstrates how tape-recorded responses led one student through a series of successive revisions.

rev
2d

CS "America: The Multinational Society," Reed speaks out for
cultural diversity⊙ he thinks it makes the nation
stronger.   In passing he mentions that the communications
media sensationalize the "conflict between people of
different backgrounds."   To Reed's point can be added the *nice*
sentence
media's other false picture of America, the picture of *except for*
repetition
Americans as socially, economically, and ethnically
similar.   Judging from the unrealistic images projected by
television, newspapers, and magazines, the United States
strong,
is a nation either of constant ethnic conflict or of *clear*
thesis
untroubled homogeneity.

   It is easy to find examples of the emphasizing of *awk*
conflict among ethnic groups.   The news is full of stories
of Hispanic gangs fighting black gangs in Los Angeles,
// swastikas are painted on Jewish synagogues in Chicago,
Haitians battle Cubans in Miami, Korean shopkeepers are
pitted against black and Hispanic customers in New York
City.   It's not that these aren't real stories, or that
CS all-too-real ethnic conflict should be covered up⊙ it's
just that these stories are blown out of proportion.

   Everyone complains that the news media never present
enough good news.   When it comes to ethnic relations, this
is certainly the case.   Pakistanis, Russians, Mexicans,
frag
Chinese, Mayflower descendants, great-grandchildren of
African slaves.   All these and more mingle on the nation's
streets, attend school together, work together.   Granted,
CS integration is very far from complete⊙ severe inequality
persists.   Real conflict exists.   But for the most part,
cultural groups are not at war.

rev
2d

In the media, though, especially television fiction
and advertising, the only peace belongs to a very narrow
band of people. They are usually white, married or
expecting to be someday, unethnic, white collar, well-to-
do, settled, materialistic, good looking, and thin. These
are but a few of the groups excluded from this TV type
(some overlap): Polish-Americans, homeless families,
homosexuals, factory workers, Lebanese immigrants, teenage
mothers, amputees, Japanese-Americans, unmarried couples   *this list may be a bit overdone*
(heterosexual or homosexual), loners, stay-at-home
fathers, transients, mentally handicapped people, elderly
pensioners, homely people, fat people, small people.   *Break this very long*

¶ Exceptions come and go, of course, such as the working-   *¶*
class and overweight Roseanne and her husband, the older
women in <u>Golden Girls</u>, and the Cosbys. However, the norm
see 12d ? is easy to recognize. For example, <u>in a cereal commercial
they feature</u> a mother who is overseeing her husband's and
children's breakfasts. The kitchen is full of the latest
appliances and decorations. Everyone is white. Everyone
is fit and cute, beautiful, or handsome. Everyone is well
dressed and cheerful.

The media's two extremes of peace and conflict create
a composite picture of a nation where a "monoculture" is
desirable and all but achieved. <u>If only we could battle   *frag—
attach to pre-vious sentence for clarity*
down the ones who don't belong or won't belong.</u> Imagine a
different picture, though. In this one$_\circ$people coexist$_\circ$ *2lb   2lj-3*
who have diverse backgrounds, interests, incomes, living
CS arrangements, and appearances. Sometimes they stay apart$_\circ$
sometimes they blend. Sometimes they clash or prey on

COLLABORATIVE LEARNING

ANSWERS: EXERCISE 6

An environmental group, National Resources Defense Council, has estimated that 5500 to 6200 children who are <u>in</u> preschool today may contract cancer dur<u>ing</u> their lives be<u>cause</u> of the pesticides they consume in their food. In addition, these children will be at greater risk for kidney damage, problems with immunity, and other serious impairments. The government bases <u>its</u> pesticide-safety standards on adults, but chil<u>dren</u> consume much more <u>of</u> the fruits and fruit products likely to contain pest<u>i</u>cides.

COLLABORATIVE LEARNING

ANSWERS: EXERCISE 7
Possible Revisions

Paragraph 1

Sentence 4: . . . *Reed speaks out for cultural diversity. He thinks it makes the nation stronger.*
Sentence 6: *To Reed's point can be added the media's other <u>false picture of Americans</u> as socially, economically, and ethnically similar.*

Paragraph 2

Sentence 1: *It is easy to find examples <u>of exaggerated conflict</u> among ethnic groups.* Or: *<u>Examples of exaggerated ethnic conflict are easy to find.</u>*
Sentence 2: *The news is full of stories of Hispanic gangs fighting . . . , swastikas <u>painted</u> . . . , Haitians <u>battling</u> . . . , Korean shopkeepers <u>pitted</u>. . . .*
Sentence 3: *It's not that . . . all-too-real ethnic conflict should be covered up. <u>It's</u> just that these stories are blown out of proportion.*

Paragraph 3

Sentences 3–4: *Pakistanis, Russians, . . . slaves—all these and more mingle. . . .*
Sentence 5: *Granted, integration is very far from complete. <u>Severe</u> inequality exists.*

Paragraph 4

Sentence 6: *For example, <u>a cereal commercial features</u> a mother. . . .*

CS   each other_⊙ sometimes they laugh together. It all happens now_⊙ and we could be watching. [annotation: 21a]

> You did a fine job of adding details and acknowledging exceptions and actual problems. Your introduction and conclusion are also much stronger than in your first draft. This is a solid, convincing essay.
>   In future work, pay attention to your use (and misuse) of commas. A number of comma splices and other comma errors mar the clarity and effectiveness of your paper. I suggest you read and do the exercises in Chapters 11 (splices) and 21 (commas).

Exercise 6
Proofreading

Proofread the following passage, using any of the techniques listed on page 61 to bring errors into the foreground. There are ten errors in the passage: missing and misspelled words, typographical errors, and the like. If you are in doubt about any spellings, consult a dictionary.

An envirnmental group, National Resources Defense Council, has estimated that 5500 to 6200 children who are preschool today may contract cancer durng their lives becuase of the pesticides they consume in their food In addition, these children will be at greater risk for kidney damage, problems with immunity, and other serious imparments. The government bases it pesticide-safety standards on adults, but childen consume much more the fruits and fruit products likely to contain pestcides.

Exercise 7
Revising an essay

To become familiar with the symbols and codes of this handbook, revise Perez's essay wherever her instructor has used a symbol or code to mark a problem.

Exercise 8
Preparing your final draft

Prepare the final draft of the essay you have been working on throughout Chapters 1 and 2. Proofread carefully and correct all errors before submitting your essay for review.

2e Receiving and giving criticism

Almost all the writing you do in college will generate responses from an instructor. In writing courses you may submit early drafts as well as your final paper, and your readers may include your classmates as well as your instructor. Indeed, like Terry Perez's, many writing courses feature **collaborative learning,** in which students work together on writing, from completing exercises to commenting on each other's work. Collaboration is common in business, where workers often meet to solve problems and generate ideas. Whether you participate in collaborative learning as a writer or as a writing "coach," you stand to gain experience in reading written work critically and in reaching others through writing.

If you are the reader of someone else's writing, keep the following principles in mind.

Guidelines for criticizing others' work

1. You are an interested, supportive reader, not a judge. Your comments will be most helpful when you:
   a. Question the writer or explain your reactions in a way that emphasizes the effect of the work *on you,* a reader: for instance, "What do you mean by . . . ?" or "I find this paragraph confusing."
   b. Avoid statements that seem to measure the work against a set of external standards: for instance, "This essay is poorly organized" or "Your thesis sentence is inadequate."
2. Unless you have other instructions, address only the most significant problems in the work. If you point out every flaw you detect, the writer may have trouble sorting out the important from the unimportant.
3. Use the revision checklist on page 53 as a guide to what is significant in a piece of writing.
4. Be specific. Explain the *reasons* for your confusion or *why* you disagree with a conclusion.
5. Remember that you are the reader, not the writer. Resist the temptation to edit sentences, add details, or otherwise assume responsibility for the paper.
6. Be positive as well as honest. Instead of saying "This paragraph doesn't interest me," say "You have a really interesting detail here that seems buried in the rest of the paragraph." And tell the writer what you like about the paper.

Paragraph 5

Sentences 1–2: . . . *is desirable and all but achieved, if only we could.* . . .
Sentence 4: *In this one, people coexist who have diverse backgrounds.* . . .
Sentence 5: *Sometimes they stay apart; sometimes they blend.*
Sentence 6: *Sometimes they clash or prey on each other; sometimes they laugh together.*
Sentence 7: *It all happens now, and we could be watching.*

COLLABORATIVE LEARNING

ANSWERS: EXERCISE 8

Individual response.

TRANSPARENCY MASTER
AVAILABLE

RESOURCES AND IDEAS

Nancy Grimm, "Constructing Ideas of the Social Self," *Journal of Teaching Writing* 8 (1989): 11–19. Social pressures, social rules, and social values are at work in the composition classroom and may interfere in collaborative learning, particularly in classes comprised of a culturally diverse student population. The classroom composition must be considered when instructors expect students to think critically and to question dominant cultural values.

Claudia M. Greenwood, " 'It's Scary at First': Reentry Women in College Composition Classes," *Teaching English in the Two-Year College* 17 (1990): 133–42. Greenwood identifies several constant negative internal factors—feelings of guilt, inferiority, doubt, of being out of place—among women reentering higher education, but she finds that the positive internal factors outweigh the negative.

rev
2e

Thomas F. McKendy, "Legitimizing Peer Response: A Recycling Project for Placement Essays," *College Composition and Communication* 41 (1990): 89–91. McKendy found that when students in a remedial writing course holistically scored placement essays, their scoring correlated closely with that of trained readers. This exercise led to the students being more accepting of their placement in the course and more trusting of each others' responses to their writing.

> TRANSPARENCY MASTER
> AVAILABLE

RESOURCES AND IDEAS

Criticism that is given in a helpful and careful manner is perhaps the easiest kind of criticism to benefit from. The chapter "Using Collaborative Learning with the Handbook" at the beginning of this annotated edition contains a detailed section on "Preparing Students to Provide Peer Criticism." You may wish to draw on this discussion as a way of helping your students learn how to benefit from criticism and learn how to offer their classmates advice that can lead to real improvements in expression.

RESOURCES AND IDEAS

Jeffrey Sirc and Tom Reynolds, "The Face of Collaboration in the Networked Writing Classroom," *Computers and Composition* 7 (1990): 53–70. Sirc and Reynolds discuss the use of networked classrooms in peer response to compositions.

When you *receive* the comments of others, whether your classmates or your instructor, you will get more out of the process if you follow these guidelines.

Guidelines for benefiting from criticism

1. Think of your readers as counselors or coaches who will help you see the virtues and flaws in your work and sharpen your awareness of readers' needs.
2. Read or listen to comments closely.
3. Make sure you know what the critic is saying. If you need more information, ask for it, or consult the appropriate section of this handbook. (See "Using This Book," p. xi, for a guide to the handbook.)
4. Don't become defensive. Letting comments offend you will only erect a barrier to improvement in your writing. As one writing teacher advises, "Leave your ego at the door."
5. When comments seem appropriate, revise your work in response to them, whether or not you are required to do so. You will learn more from the act of revision than from just thinking about changes.
6. Keep track of problems that recur in your work so that you can give them special attention in new essays. In this way your learning on one assignment will carry over to the next one.

Writers use varied devices for tracking their particular writing problems. One such aid is a chart like the one below, with a vertical column for each assignment (or draft) and a horizontal row for each weakness that others and you yourself see in your essays. The handbook section is noted for each problem, and check marks indicate how often the problem occurs in each essay.

	Assignment				
Problems	1	2	3	4	
not enough details for readers (1d)	√	√		√	
unity—wanders away from thesis (1f)	√				
parallelism (17)	√√	√	√		
agreement (8a)	√		√	√	
comma splice (11)	√√	√	√		

The chart also provides a convenient place to keep track of words you misspell so that you can master their spellings.

Exercise 9
Analyzing essays

Carefully read the student essays below, and answer the following questions about each one.

1. What is the writer's purpose?
2. Who do you think constitutes the writer's intended audience? What role does the writer seem to be assuming? What does the tone reveal about the writer's attitude toward the topic?
3. How well does the thesis sentence convey the purpose and attitude? What assertion does the thesis sentence make? How specific is the sentence? How well does it preview the writer's ideas and organization?
4. What organization does the writer use? Is it clear throughout the essay?
5. What details, examples, and reasons does the writer use to support his or her ideas? Where is supporting evidence skimpy?
6. How successful is the writer in making you care about the topic and his or her views of it?

Working in the Barnyard

Until two months ago I thought summer jobs occupied time and helped pay the next year's tuition but otherwise provided no useful training. Then I took a temporary job in a large government agency. Two months there taught me a very valuable lesson about how people work together.

Last May I was hired by the personnel department of the agency to fill in for vacationing workers in the mail room. I had seven coworkers and a boss, Mrs. King. Our job was to sort the huge morning and afternoon mail shipments into four hundred slots, one for every employee in the agency. Then we delivered the sorted mail out of grocery carts that we wheeled from office to office along assigned corridors, picking up outgoing mail as we went along. Each mail delivery took an entire half-day to sort and deliver.

My troubles began almost as soon as I arrived. Hundreds of pieces of mail were dumped on a shallow table against a wall of mail slots. I was horrified to see that the slots were labeled not with people's names but with their initials—whereas the incoming letters, of course, contained full names. Without thinking, I asked why this was a good idea, only to receive a sharp glance from Mrs. King. So I repeated the question. This time Mrs. King told me not to question what I didn't understand. It was the first

ANSWERS: EXERCISE 9
Possible Answers

The numbers below match the question numbers in the exercise instruction. (Note that the ways of linking paragraphs in both essays are analyzed in the answer to Chapter 3, Exercise 18.)

"Working in the Barnyard"

1. The writer's purpose is primarily self-expression but also explanation.

2. The writer seems to conceive of her readers as other inexperienced workers like herself. She assumes the role of a confider, sharing a difficult experience. Her tone is straightforward yet strangely subdued when she tells of Mrs. King's tyranny. We sense from the beginning that the writer was humbled by her experience, and the last paragraph is genuinely humble in tone.

3. The thesis sentence (the last sentence of paragraph 1) clearly and specifically states the writer's topic (a work experience) and perspective on that topic (learning something valuable).

4. The essay's organization is clearly chronological. The writer adheres to the organization throughout, providing ample signals to help the reader follow the narrative (e.g., *Last May, then, as soon as I arrived*).

5. This otherwise competent essay is marred by omissions of concrete details and examples that would give the reader a sense of actually sharing the experience instead of rushing through it. Paragraph 2: What did Mrs. King look like? How huge were the mail shipments? Paragraph 3: What were some of the actual words spoken by the writer and Mrs. King? Paragraph 4: What was inefficient about delivery routes and times for coffee breaks? What exactly did Mrs. King do or say in reacting to the writer's questions? Paragraph 5: In what specific ways did the writer pester Mrs. King? How were the efforts fruitless? How counterproductive? What snide names did Mrs. King use? How did she pick on the writer's work? What reprimands did she issue?

6. Answers will vary.

"The Obsolete Hero"

1. The writer's purpose is explanation.

2. The writer's use of *we, our,* and *us* reveals that he believes his readers will share his sense of loss at the demise of the legendary cowboy. Apparently, though, he does not expect readers to be familiar with the causes of the change, for he gives the historical background. His role is part reporter, part disappointed romantic. His tone is animated yet nostalgic, especially in paragraph 3.

3. The thesis sentence (last sentence of paragraph 1) specifies the topic, forecasts the explanatory purpose and comparison-and-contrast organization, and captures the writer's regretful attitude toward the changes he discusses.

4. The writer uses one of the standard comparison-and-contrast organizational schemes, discussing all of one subject (cowboys before the taming of the West) and then all of the other subject (modern cowboys). (As a result, the essay is also chronological.) To link the two parts of the essay and clarify the contrast, the writer covers points of comparison in roughly the same order and, in the second part (paragraph 4), refers frequently to the earlier material (e.g., *instead of trusting to nature; lean less on survival skills*).

5. Unlike "Working in the Barnyard," this essay contains adequate details and examples to help readers share the writer's attitude toward his topic. Particularly effective in sharpening the contrast are the contrasting details in paragraphs 3 and 4 (e.g., *men who had the stamina to ride in the saddle all day for weeks and sleep on the ground at night* versus *He sleeps in a bed at night and rides to the range in a Jeep or pickup truck*).

6. Answers will vary.

of many such exchanges, and I hadn't been on the job a half-hour.

I mastered the initials and the sorting and delivery procedures after about a week. But the longer I worked at the job, the more I saw how inefficient all the procedures were, from delivery routes to times for coffee breaks. When I asked Mrs. King about the procedures, however, she always reacted the same way: it was none of my business.

I pestered Mrs. King more and more over the next seven weeks, but my efforts were fruitless, even counterproductive. Mrs. King began calling me snide names. Then she began picking on my work and singling me out for reprimands, even though I did my best and worked faster than most of the others.

Two months after I had started work, the personnel manager called me in and fired me. I objected, of course, calling up all the deficiencies I had seen in Mrs. King and her systems. The manager interrupted to ask if I had ever heard of the barnyard pecking order: the top chicken pecks on the one below it, the second pecks on the third, and so on all the way down the line to the lowliest chicken, whose life is a constant misery. Mrs. King, the manager said, was that lowliest chicken at the bottom of the pecking order in the agency's management. With little education, she had spent her entire adult life building up her small domain, and she had to protect it from everyone, especially the people who worked for her. The arbitrariness of her systems was an assertion of her power, for no one should doubt for a moment that she ruled her little roost.

I had a month before school began again to think about my adventure. At first it irritated me that I should be humiliated while Mrs. King continued on as before. But eventually I saw how arrogant, and how unsympathetic, my behavior had been. In my next job, I'll learn the pecking order before I become a crusader, *if* I do.

The Obsolete Hero

Most Americans admire the cowboy as a symbol of our nation's pioneering spirit. The cowboy represents the values of a young country expanding its frontiers across the untamed West: rugged courage, physical strength and skill, and stubborn independence. In our century the West has been tamed, however, and the cowboy's role has changed. The hero who used to ride the range is obsolete in an era when cattle are carefully bred, fed, inoculated, and shipped instead of herded to market.

The kind of cowboy we see in television westerns originated with the Spanish conquistadors, who brought horses and cattle to the New World. Let loose to graze, the cattle gradually multiplied into huge herds. When easterners began flooding westward in the mid-1800s, the demand for beef grew, and so did the need for cowboys to track down the cattle and drive them to market.

As the railroads moved westward after the Civil War, it became possible to ship beef not only locally but to the large cities back East. Vast trail drives grew up in which cattle from several ranches at once were herded from Texas northward to railhead cow towns such as Abilene, Wichita, and Dodge City. Supervising these drives were men who had the stamina to ride in the saddle all day for weeks and sleep on the ground at night. Their meals, cooked over an open fire, consisted of whatever could be caught on the way or carried in a chuck wagon without spoiling. The cowboys had to know how to rope a runaway cow, tie a calf's feet for branding, pull a stray out of a bog, shoot a rattlesnake from the back of a galloping horse, find food and water in unfamiliar territory, and break and ride wild mustangs.

As civilization spread across the West, ranchers began fencing in their land and breeding cattle instead of trusting to nature. Trail drives dwindled as the range was divided into private property and the railroads provided closer outlets for beef. As a result of these changes, today's cowboys lean less on survival skills and more on agriculture and veterinary medicine. They learn to build and mend fences and to drill wells and grease windmills, which provide cattle with water and irrigate the land for a dependable feed supply. Though horses remain important, the modern cowboy typically trains his ponies from colthood instead of busting wild broncos. He sleeps in a bed at night and rides to the range in a Jeep or pickup truck. His midday meals are delivered fresh and hot by truck. Even the cattle he tends are trucked between ranges. When the cowboy needs to search the brush for strays, he can do it in a helicopter. Many of the colorful skills that used to be essential, such as riding a bucking horse and twirling a lasso, now show up mainly in rodeos.

Today our national focus has shifted from geographic frontiers to the frontiers of space and high technology. But many of us, in our hearts, still dream of being as hardy, self-sufficient, and free as that obsolete hero of the Wild West, the cowboy.

Many of the choices writers make in composing paragraphs are similar to those they make in composing whole essays, especially in expository and argumentative writing. Studying the basic features of paragraphs—generalizations supported by details, examples, reasons, or other kinds of specific information—and composing paragraphs that employ these features can be a good way for many students to develop their writing skills.

The pattern of the typical paragraph, consisting of a statement of a topic or opinion followed by concrete comment on it, illustrates an essential essay pattern within a length and degree of complexity that students can manage. Moreover, just as the sentences in a paragraph must be related in ways that are immediately clear to a reader, so the paragraphs within an essay must move clearly from one to another. Thus by examining and constructing well-made paragraphs, students can become more confident and accomplished in managing multiparagraph papers. This, at least, is the assumption behind this chapter of the handbook.

Of course, not all paragraphs in professional writing conform in length, structure, or purpose to the models provided in this chapter. Paragraphs in narrative and descriptive writing, dialogue paragraphs, introductory and concluding paragraphs, and paragraphs for emphasis or transition all frequently differ in some way from the standard pattern, differences noted and discussed in this chapter. Nonetheless, helping students master the so-called standard paragraph can be a good way to help them learn better.

RESOURCES AND IDEAS

Paragraphing strategies and the features of paragraphing have been a subject of considerable debate, particularly over the past two decades. According to Michael Moran, scholars have taken two views of paragraphing:

One argues that the paragraph is a unit—either logical, rhetorical, linguistic, psychological, or a combination of them—that possesses an internal structure that can be described using a finite set of rules. The other view argues that the paragraph is a stretch of discourse that owes its existence to the larger requirements of the whole piece of

Chapter 3

Composing Paragraphs

A **paragraph** is a group of related sentences set off by a beginning indention. For the writer, paragraphing provides a way to break down complex ideas into manageable parts, discuss each part separately and completely, relate each part to the central theme or thesis of the essay, and thus achieve a purpose. For readers, paragraphing focuses attention on one idea at a time and provides the mixture of general statements and specific information needed to understand meaning.

The following paragraph provides a fairly simple illustration of how the paragraph aids the writer and the reader.

> Some people really like chili, apparently, but nobody can   1
> agree how the stuff should be made. C. V. Wood, twice win-   2
> ner at Terlingua, uses flank steak, pork chops, chicken, and
> green chilis. My friend Hughes Rudd of CBS News, who im-   3
> ported five hundred pounds of chili powder into Russia as a
> condition of accepting employment as Moscow correspon-
> dent, favors coarse-ground beef. Isadore Bleckman, the cam-   4
> eraman I must live with on the road, insists upon one-inch
> cubes of stew beef and puts garlic in his chili, an Illinois af-
> fection. An Indian of my acquaintance, Mr. Fulton Batisse,   5
> who eats chili for breakfast when he can, uses buffalo meat
> and plays an Indian drum while it's cooking. I ask you.   6
> —CHARLES KURALT, *Dateline America*

The thesis of the essay in which this paragraph appears is that a Texas chili championship gives undue attention to an unpleasant food. Kuralt begins the paragraph with a general statement that relates to his thesis. That statement leads him directly to four examples—four pieces of evidence for his claim that people disagree over how to make chili (sentences 2–5). He keeps himself focused on his general statement by tying each example back to it with the word *chili* and by starting each example sentence with a name or another identification of a chili maker. At the same time he helps us, his readers, by stating what his paragraph will be about and sticking to that idea, by letting us know that sentences 2–5 serve a similar function, and by giving us plenty of specific details in those sentences so that we can appreciate his point of view.

Most paragraphs you write will, like Kuralt's, be **body paragraphs** that develop some aspect of your topic. Effective body paragraphs have three main characteristics.

Qualities of effective paragraphs

- **Unity:** the paragraph adheres to one idea (see 3a).
- **Coherence:** the parts of the paragraph relate clearly to each other (see 3b).
- **Development:** the idea of the paragraph is well supported with specific evidence such as details, facts, examples, and reasons (see 3c).

Introductions, conclusions, and other kinds of paragraphs serve special functions in essays (see 3d). And all an essay's paragraphs work together (3e).

3a   Maintaining paragraph unity

Since readers expect a paragraph to explore one idea, they will be alert for that idea and will patiently follow its development. In other words, they will seek and appreciate paragraph **unity,** clear identification and clear elaboration of one idea and of that idea only. If readers must constantly shift their focus, their confusion or frustration will impede their understanding and acceptance of the writer's meaning.

In an essay the thesis sentence often announces the main idea as a commitment to readers (see 1f). In a paragraph a **topic sen-** *promise*

---

prose. In this view, the paragraph does not exist as a separate entity but as a flexible and convenient method of marking some stage in a larger organic process. ("The English Paragraph," *Research in Rhetoric and Composition: A Bibliographic Sourcebook,* ed. Michael G. Moran and Ronald F. Lunsford [Westport: Greenwood, 1984] 425.)

Though this chapter blends the two points of view, it takes what might be called a fairly traditional approach to paragraphing, at least in light of the research reviewed by Arthur A. Stern, who concludes that the paragraph is not necessarily a logical pattern with a clear topic sentence but is instead a flexible rhetorical structure that can serve a variety of purposes ("When Is a Paragraph?" *College Composition and Communication* 27 [1976]: 253–57).

TRANSPARENCY MASTER
AVAILABLE

But more recent scholarship suggests the importance of topic sentences and patterns of paragraph coherence, at least in academic writing and other forms of expository and argumentative prose. The following articles are worth investigating:

Randall Popken, "A Study of Topic Sentence Use in Academic Writing," *Written Communication* 4 (1987): 209–28.

William J. Vande Koppel, "Something Old, Something New: Functional Sentence Perspective," *Research in the Teaching of English* 17 (1983): 85–99.

Linda K. Shamoon and Robert A. Schwegler, "Sociologists Reading Student Texts: Expectations and Perceptions," *The Writing Instructor* 7 (1988): 71–81.

HIGHLIGHTS

This section of the chapter (3a) addresses the need for a paragraph to focus on a topic and to make the focus clear to the reader through an explicit statement in the form of a topic sentence. It introduces the basic form of the expository paragraph—topic sentence; optional sentence of clarification or limitation; illustrations and details—and indicates how this pattern can be varied to suit a writer's purpose and to fit within the context created by the surrounding paragraphs.

¶ un
3a

The concept of a clearly stated and variously placed topic sentence that controls the shape of a paragraph is an oversimplification. But it appears to help students a great deal to think of the paragraph as a unit dominated and controlled by an expressly stated generalization. Students can see the topic sentence as a commitment they make to the reader, with the rest of the paragraph following through on the commitment. Seeing the obvious parallel between the paragraph's topic sentence and the essay's thesis statement is also helpful to many students. Finally, stating a central point in a single sentence and marshalling support for it enables students to see more clearly what is required for unity.

The exercises for this section ask students to identify the central idea in unified paragraphs, to revise paragraphs, to build a paragraph by combining and revising kernel sentences, and to write their own paragraphs. These exercises can be easily adapted to small-group work; in coming to understand how others view paragraphs, students may more readily understand the influence of paragraph structure and unity on readers.

RESOURCES AND IDEAS

Harvey S. Wiener, "The Single Narrative Paragraph and College Remediation," *College English* 33 (1972): 660–69. Wiener suggests using paragraph-length narrative themes to help students develop both paragraph and essay skills.

tence often alerts readers to the essence of the paragraph by stating the central idea and expressing the writer's attitude toward it. Each body paragraph is likely to treat one part of the essay's thesis sentence; the topic sentences simply elaborate on parts of the thesis. Like the thesis sentence, the topic sentence is a commitment to readers, and the rest of the paragraph delivers on that commitment. In Kuralt's paragraph on chili the topic sentence or commitment is sentence 1: the author states generally that people disagree about how to make chili. The next four sentences fulfill the commitment with specific examples of chili concoctions. The last sentence (*I ask you*) invites us to consider the examples with amusement, as the writer does.

 Focusing on the central idea

Kuralt's paragraph on chili works because it follows through on the topic sentence. But what if he had written it this way instead?

> Some people really like chili, apparently, but nobody can 1
> agree how the stuff should be made. C. V. Woods, twice win- 2
> ner at Terlingua, uses flank steak, pork chops, chicken, and
> green chilis. My friend Hughes Rudd, who imported five 3
> hundred pounds of chili powder into Russia as a condition
> of accepting employment as Moscow correspondent, favors
> coarse-ground beef. He had some trouble finding the beef 4
> in Moscow, though. He sometimes had to scour all the mar- 5
> kets and wait in long lines. For any American used to over- 6
> stocked supermarkets and department stores, the Soviet
> Union can be quite a shock.

In this altered version, the topic of chili preparation is forgotten after sentence 3, as the paragraph wanders off to consumer deprivation in the Soviet Union. The paragraph lacks unity.

Look again at Charles Kuralt's actual paragraph two pages back. Notice how every one of his sentences relates to the central idea of the topic sentence: every one concerns a different way to make chili and even includes the word *chili*. This is a unified paragraph.

You may opt to follow the central idea in the topic sentence with a **clarifying or limiting sentence.** Such a sentence can help you maintain unity by providing a sharper, clearer focus for the paragraph, and it can help the reader by providing a more precise sense of your idea. In the following paragraph, for instance, sentence 2 clarifies and limits what the writer means in her topic sentence (sentence 1) about chronological time being an anachronism (or something out of its proper era).

¶ un
3a

It's hard to think about Saturday night without realizing   1
that chronological time itself is something of an anachronism these days. Schedules are less rigid now than in the   2
past. When I was a kid, grocery stores closed at 6 and were   3
never open on Sundays. I still remember the first time I   4
went to a 24-hour grocery at 4 in the morning, thinking that
something fundamental had changed forever. You used to   5
be out of luck for money on the weekend if you didn't get to
the bank by 3 on Friday. Now most people I know don't   6
even know when banks are open because they use 24-hour
automatic-teller machines. Most stores are now open every   7
day, since blue laws were repealed.
                                —SUSAN ORLEAN, "Saturday Night"

   2   Placing the topic sentence

The topic sentence of a paragraph (along with any limiting or
clarifying sentence) and its supporting details may be arranged
variously depending on how you want to direct readers' attention
and on how complex your central idea is.

Topic sentence at the beginning

In the most familiar arrangement the topic sentence comes
first, then sometimes a clarifying or limiting sentence, then the
supporting information. With this arrangement, the topic sentence
helps you select details in the rest of the paragraph. For readers
the topic-first model establishes an initial context in which all the
following details can be understood. Look again at the paragraph
on page 70 to see how easily we readers relate each detail or example back to the point made in the first sentence.

The topic-first model is common not only in expository paragraphs, such as the ones quoted earlier, but also in argument
paragraphs, such as the one below. Here the author first states a
misconception and then corrects it.

It is a misunderstanding of the American retail store to   1
think we go there necessarily to buy. Some of us shop.   2
There's a difference. Shopping has many purposes, the least   3,4
interesting of which is to acquire new articles. We shop to   5
cheer ourselves up. We shop to practice decision-making.   6
We shop to be useful and productive members of our class   7
and society. We shop to remind ourselves how much is avail-   8
able to us. We shop to remind ourselves how much is to be   9
striven for. We shop to assert our superiority to the material 10
objects that spread themselves before us.
—PHYLLIS ROSE, "Shopping and Other Spiritual Adventures"

RESOURCES AND IDEAS

A. L. Becker, "A Tagmemic Approach to Paragraph Analysis," *College Composition and
Communication* 16 (1965): 237–42. Becker
observes that expository paragraphs generally
follow a variation of one of two patterns:
topic-restriction-illustration (TRI) or problem-solution (PS).

CREATING UNIFIED PARAGRAPHS

Give the class five topic sentences on different
subjects and ask each student to choose one and
write a unified paragraph based on it. Then split
the class into groups and ask students to read
their paragraphs aloud to the groups. Ask the students in each group to discuss the unity of the
paragraphs and to compare the methods of development among the paragraphs.

COLORING PARAGRAPHS

Bring in copies of sample paragraphs and felt-
tipped pens or pencils in three colors. Split the
class into groups and ask each group to underline topic sentences in one color, sentences of
limitation in another, and examples and details
in the third. Students should then be able to discover the arrangement of each paragraph, the
placement of the topic sentence, and the way the
parts fit together to form a unified whole.

¶ un
3a

SEEING PARAGRAPHS

Visually, students may find it easier to understand topic sentence placement and paragraph arrangement by using these diagrams as guides:

Topic sentence at
   the beginning: △

Topic sentence at the
   beginning and in
   the middle: △
                △

Topic sentence at
   the end: ▽

Topic sentence at
   the beginning
   and the end: ◇

in essays

Topic sentence following transitional sentence

In many paragraphs the opening sentence serves as a transition or bridge from the preceding paragraph, simultaneously pointing back to the previous idea and forward to a new one. The topic sentence is then often the second sentence, with the remaining sentences providing the support. In the following paragraph the first, transitional sentence refers to the assertion in the author's preceding paragraph that the lyrics to popular music can "take us by surprise when we find ourselves singing along to words we didn't realize we knew." Sentence 2 is the topic sentence.

> And listening to the lyrics we find some intriguing factors. 1
> In spite of the growth in political music or music where the 2
> lyrics raise social issues, popular music is still absolutely
> dominated by references to sexual attraction, sexual encounter, and the detailing of a love affair. To listen carefully to the 3
> words of a record can be a curious experience; it is like
> eavesdropping on an intimate conversation or argument between lovers, or like getting a crossed line on the telephone
> and listening, embarrassed and fascinated, to personal revelations. The lyrics detail the burning desire which a lover's 4
> kiss can induce, or stormy nights of unbroken sleep. They 5
> describe sweet dreams of a departed lover, sweet dreams instead of hate and anger. Many current songs are like fragments of a narrative, a sudden exposure of a moment in a 6
> relationship. Don't leave me, the lyrics plead, my life will fall 7
> apart, you'll destroy me, break my heart. Or we hear the 8
> other side: it's painful, I know, but I have to go. We've hurt 9
> each other enough, I have to leave.
> —ROSALIND COWARD, "Our Song"

If you are making a significant change in direction, the transition from a preceding paragraph may require more than one sentence or even a separate short paragraph (see 3d-3). Even for very slight changes, however, writers frequently use words or phrases to link paragraphs so that readers see the progression of ideas. Coward's *And* (sentence 1) works like that. Such brief links are discussed in more detail in the next section (see 3b-6, p. 88).

Topic sentence at the end

In some paragraphs the central idea may be stated at the end, after supporting sentences have made a case for the general statement. Since this model leads the reader to a conclusion by presenting all the evidence first, it can prove effective in argument.

And because the point of the paragraph is withheld until the end, this model can be dramatic in exposition as well. For example, all the details in the following paragraph about the comedian Steve Martin lead up to and support the idea stated in sentence 12.

*example
5-day wk.*

> When Martin comes onstage, he may do, say, just what   1
> Red Skelton used to do, but he gets us laughing at the fact
> that we're laughing at such dumb jokes. Martin simulates be-   2
> ing a comedian, and so, in a way, we simulate being the co-
> median's audience. Martin makes old routines work by let-   3
> ting us know that they're old and then doing them immacu-
> lately. For him, comedy is *all* timing. He's almost a   4,5
> comedy robot. Onstage, he puts across the idea that he's go-   6
> ing to do some cornball routine, and then when he does it it
> has quotation marks around it, and that's what makes it hilar-
> ious. He does the routine straight, yet he's totally facetious. 7
> He lets us know that we're seeing silliness in quotes. There   8,9
> he is, spruced up and dapper in a three-piece white suit;
> even his handsomeness is made facetious. Steve Martin is all   10
> persona. That's what's dizzying about him—and a little   11
> ghoulish. He and some of the other comics of his generation   12
> make the *idea* of doing comedy funny.
> —Pauline Kael, "Silliness"

Expressing the central idea at the end of the paragraph does not eliminate the need to unify the paragraph. The idea in the topic sentence must still govern the selection of all the preceding details.

Topic sentence at the beginning and the end

Sometimes the central idea may be stated at the beginning of the paragraph and then restated at the end. Generally, the first sentence provides a context for the supporting information, and the last sentence provides a new twist based on that information. Just before the following example, the author says that the television game show *Wheel of Fortune* provides a "scenario" of sexual equality and material success.

> The terminology of the rules of the game are consistent   1
> with the scenario being played out. A contestant "*earns* the 2
> right to buy a prize" by solving a puzzle and accumulating
> money by spinning The Wheel. If you win the game, you   3
> take the money you have accumulated and then go shop-
> ping, at the "actual retail prices," for the prizes offered until
> you have exhausted your account. You can also elect to bank   4
> your money, hoping that you can solve another puzzle with-
> out hitting "bankrupt," which wipes out all you've earned

¶ un
3a

but not your merchandise, "because once you buy a prize, it's yours to keep." So whether you can spend only $200 for   5
a framed print or $15,000 for a Mustang convertible depends upon a combination of common sense, basic literacy and luck. It is, plain and simple, a microcosm of the mechanisms   6
operating in the American ideology of an open society and the work ethic.

> —GLORIA NAYLOR, "Sexual Equality in a TV Fantasy"

This model, like the previous one, will not work if you try to make the last sentence rescue a disunified paragraph. To be effective, the final statement must reflect some development in the sentences before it.

Central idea not stated

Occasionally, a paragraph's central idea will be stated in the previous paragraph or will be so obvious that it need not be stated at all. The following paragraph, from an essay on the actor Humphrey Bogart, has no explicit topic sentence.

> Usually he wore the trench coat unbuttoned, just tied with   1
> the belt, and a slouch hat, rarely tilted. Sometimes it was a   2
> captain's cap and a yachting jacket. Almost always his trou-   3
> sers were held up by a cowboy belt. You know the kind: one   4
> an Easterner waiting for a plane out of Phoenix buys just as a
> joke and then takes a liking to. Occasionally, he'd hitch up   5
> his slacks with it, and he often jabbed his thumbs behind it,
> his hands ready for a fight or a dame.
>
> —PETER BOGDANOVICH, "Bogie in Excelsis"

The effectiveness of this paragraph rests on the power of details to describe Bogart. Thus a stated central idea—such as "Bogart's character could be seen in the details of his clothing"—not only would weaken the paragraph but would contradict its intention. Nonetheless, the central idea is clearly implied.

Paragraphs in descriptive writing (like the one above) and in narrative writing (relating a sequence of events) often lack stated topic sentences. But a paragraph without a topic sentence still should have a central idea, and its details should develop that idea.

Exercise 1
Finding the central idea

What is the central idea of each paragraph below? In what sentence or sentences is it expressed?

1. To most strangers they [the Los Angeles freeways] sug-   1
gest chaos, or at least purgatory, and there can certainly be

more soothing notices than the one on the Santa Ana Freeway which announces MERGING BUSES AHEAD. There comes a   2
moment, though, when something clicks in one's own mechanism, and suddenly one grasps the rhythm of the freeway
system, masters its tribal or ritual forms, and discovers it to
be not a disruptive element at all, but a kind of computer
key to the use of Los Angeles. One is processed by the free-   3
ways. Elevated as they generally are above the flat and cen-   4
terless expanse of the city, they provide a navigational aid,
into which one locks oneself for guidance. Everything is   5
clearer then. There are the mountains, to the north and east.   6
There is the glimmering ocean. The civic landmarks of L.A.,   7,8
such as they are, display themselves conveniently for you.
The pattern of the place unfolds until, properly briefed by   9
the experience, the time comes for you to unlock from the
system, undo your safety belt, and take the right-hand lane
into the everyday life below.
                              —JAN MORRIS, "The Know-How City"

2. Advocates of the rights of animals have sabotaged re-   1
search laboratories that experiment with animals, physically
prevented seal hunters from killing seals, freed caged animals from commercial fur farms, harassed whaling vessels,
released animals from zoos, and hindered hunters in their
search for prey. In search of public support for their point of   2
view, they have taken advertisements and distributed printed
fliers and vivid photographs that give graphic examples of
how animals are sometimes inhumanely treated. Such acts   3
represent the philosophy of a growing number of people in
this and other countries who believe nonhuman animals are
sentient creatures that can feel pain, are aware of their
plight, and, like humans, have certain rights.
                       —BAYARD WEBSTER, "Should Vivisection Be Abolished?"

3. Though they do not know why the humpback whale   1
sings, scientists do know something about the song itself.
They have measured the length of a whale's song: from a few   2
minutes to over half an hour. They have recorded and stud-   3
ied the variety and complex arrangements of low moans,
high squeaks, and sliding squeals that make up the song.
And they have learned that each whale sings in its own   4
unique pattern.   —A STUDENT

Exercise 2
Revising paragraphs for unity

The following paragraphs contain ideas or details that do not
support their central ideas. Identify the topic sentence in each
paragraph and delete the unrelated material.

ANSWERS: EXERCISE 1

1. The central idea is in sentence 2: the Los Angeles freeway system is "a kind of computer
   key to the use of Los Angeles."
2. The central idea is in sentence 3: antivivisec-
   tionists are defending the rights of animals in
   varied ways.
3. The central idea is in sentence 1: scientists
   know something about the song of the
   humpback whale.

¶ un
3a

ANSWERS: EXERCISE 2

1. The topic sentence is sentence 1. Unrelated are sentences 4 and 7.
2. The topic sentence is sentence 1, clarified in sentence 2. Unrelated are sentences 5, 6, and 7.

ANSWERS: EXERCISE 3

Delete statements not pertaining to Mozart's accomplishments: when he was born, where he lived, when he married, his debts. Possible paragraph:

Mozart's accomplishments in music seem remarkable even today. At the age of six he made his first concert tour of Europe, playing harpsichord, organ, and violin. He had begun composing music at the age of five, and by adolescence he had published numerous musical compositions. When he died at thirty-five, his work included over six hundred compositions, most notably operas, symphonies, quartets, and piano concertos.

1.　In the southern part of the state, some people still live much as they did a century ago. They use coal- or wood-burning stoves for heating and cooking. Their homes do not have electricity or indoor bathrooms or running water. ~~The towns can't afford to put in sewers or power lines, because they don't receive adequate funding from the state and federal governments.~~ Beside most homes there is a garden where fresh vegetables are gathered for canning. Small pastures nearby support livestock, including cattle, pigs, horses, and chickens. ~~Most of the people have cars or trucks, but the vehicles are old and beat-up from traveling on unpaved roads.~~
(lines 1, 2, 3, 4, 5, 6, 7)

2.　Most people don't realize how difficult it is to work and go to school at the same time. If you want to make good grades but need to pay your own way, the burdens are tremendous. I work in an office sixteen hours a week. Each term I have to work out a tight schedule that will let me take the courses I want and still be at work when I'm needed. ~~I like the job. The people there are pleasant, and they are eager to help me learn.~~ In the end my job will be good training ~~for the kind of managerial position I hope to have some day, because I'm gaining useful experience in office procedures and working with people.~~ It's hard for me to have a job and go to school, but when I graduate both will make me more employable.
(lines 1, 2, 3,4, 5, 6, 7, 8)

Exercise 3
Writing a unified paragraph

Develop the following topic sentence into a unified paragraph by using the relevant information in the statements below it. Delete each statement that does not relate directly to the topic, and then rewrite and combine sentences as appropriate.

Topic sentence

Mozart's accomplishments in music seem remarkable even today.

Supporting information

Wolfgang Amadeus Mozart was born in 1756 in Salzburg, Austria.

He began composing music at the age of five.

He lived most of his life in Salzburg and Vienna.

His first concert tour of Europe was at the age of six.

On his first tour he played harpsichord, organ, and violin.

He published numerous compositions before reaching adolescence.

He married in 1782.

Mozart and his wife were both poor managers of money.
They were plagued by debts.
Mozart composed over six hundred musical compositions.
His most notable works are his operas, symphonies, quartets, and
piano concertos.
He died at the age of thirty-five.

Exercise 4
Turning topic sentences into unified paragraphs

Develop three of the following topic sentences into detailed and
unified paragraphs.

1. Fans of country music (or rock music, classical music, jazz)
   come in [number] varieties.
2. My high school was an ugly (or attractive or homely or whatever) building.
3. Words can hurt as much as sticks and stones.
4. Professional sports have (or have not) been helped by extending the regular season with championship play-offs.
5. Working for good grades can interfere with learning.

3b   Achieving paragraph coherence

A paragraph is unified if it holds together—if all its details
and examples support the central idea. A paragraph is **coherent**
if readers can see *how* the paragraph holds together without having to puzzle out the writer's reasons for adding each new sentence. Each time readers must pause and reread to see how sentences relate to each other, they lose both comprehension and
patience.

Coherent paragraphs convey relations in all the ways summarized below.

Ways to achieve paragraph coherence   √

- Organize effectively (3b-1).
- Use parallel structures (3b-2).
- Repeat or restate words and word groups (3b-3).
- Use pronouns (3b-4).
- Be consistent in nouns, pronouns, and verbs (3b-5).
- Use transitional expressions (3b-6).

ANSWERS: EXERCISE 4

Individual response.

HIGHLIGHTS

This section of the chapter (3b) deals with
paragraph coherence, addressing it from the
reader's perspective as well as the writer's. Students are shown how the devices they use to
achieve paragraph coherence help readers to follow the arguments or information being presented.

The discussion emphasizes the need to maintain a clear organizational pattern as one of the
principal ways to ensure coherence, and it presents examples of two basic ways of organizing
paragraphs: organizing by space or time and organizing for emphasis. Students who have difficulty organizing their own writing can usually
see the pattern of organization in a well-made
paragraph.

Following the discussion of patterns, the section takes up and illustrates other methods of
achieving coherence: parallelism; repetition of
words; careful use of pronouns; consistency in
person, tense, and number; and transitional expressions. Analysis of paragraphs can help students understand these explicit and implicit
means by which individual sentences are held together so that the reader follows effortlessly the
flow of ideas and information.

As in the preceding section, the exercises move
from analysis to revision to production and are
useful in small-group activities as well as individual work.

TRANSPARENCY MASTER
AVAILABLE

RESOURCES AND IDEAS

Two new frameworks for describing patterns of coherence and development in paragraphs have recently been proposed. Both draw on current linguistic and rhetorical theory and are somewhat technical, yet they have considerable (if as yet undeveloped) potential for instruction. Both are worth a close look.

Robin Bell Markels, *A New Perspective on Cohesion in Expository Paragraphs* (Carbondale: Southern Illinois UP, 1984).

Richard M. Coe, *Toward a Grammar of Passages* (Carbondale: Southern Illinois UP, 1988).

Incoherence gives readers the feeling of being yanked around, as the following example shows.

> The ancient Egyptians were masters of preserving dead people's bodies by making mummies of them. Mummies several thousand years old have been discovered nearly intact. The skin, hair, teeth, finger- and toenails, and facial features of the mummies were evident. It is possible to diagnose the diseases they suffered in life, such as smallpox, arthritis, and nutritional deficiencies. The process was remarkably effective. Sometimes apparent were the fatal afflictions of the dead people: a middle-aged king died from a blow on the head, and polio killed a child king. Mummification consisted of removing the internal organs, applying natural preservatives inside and out, and then wrapping the body in layers of bandages.

This paragraph seems to be unified: it sticks to the topic of mummification throughout. But the paragraph is hard to read. All the sentences seem disconnected from each other, so that the paragraph lurches instead of gliding from point to point.

The paragraph as it was actually written is much clearer.

> The ancient Egyptians were masters of preserving dead people's bodies by making mummies of them. Basically, mummification consisted of removing the internal organs, applying natural preservatives inside and out, and then wrapping the body in layers of bandages. And the process was remarkably effective. Indeed, mummies several thousand years old have been discovered nearly intact. Their skin, hair, teeth, finger- and toenails, and facial features are still evident. Their diseases in life, such as smallpox, arthritis, and nutritional deficiencies, are still diagnosable. Even their fatal afflictions are still apparent: a middle-aged king died from a blow on the head; a child king died from polio. —A STUDENT

This paragraph contains the same information and the same number of sentences as the previous one, but now we have no difficulty moving from one sentence to the next, seeing the writer's intentions, understanding the writer's meaning. The initial broad assertion (the topic sentence) is the same, but now the writer responds to the expectations it creates with two more specific statements: first (in sentence 2) he defines the process of making mummies; then (in sentence 3) he notes why the Egyptians were masters of the process (because the process was remarkably effective). Sentence 3 automatically leads us to expect an explanation of how the process was effective, and in sentence 4 the writer proceeds to tell us: ancient mummies have been discovered nearly intact. "How intact?" we want to know. And again the writer responds to our expectation: we can make out features (sentence 5), diseases (sentence 6), and even fatal afflictions (sentence 7).

Here is the same paragraph marked up to show the connections made by the writer. Circled and connected words repeat or restate key terms or concepts. Boxed words link sentences and clarify relationships. Underlined and connected phrases are in parallel grammatical form to reflect their parallel content.

Central idea
The ancient Egyptians were masters of preserving dead 1

people's bodies by making mummies of them. Basically, 2

mummification consisted of removing the internal organs, ap-

plying natural preservatives inside and out, and then wrap-

Explanation
ping the body in layers of bandages. And the process was 3

remarkably effective. Indeed, mummies several thousand 4

Specific examples
years old have been discovered nearly intact. Their skin, hair, 5

teeth, finger- and toenails, and facial features are still evident.

Their diseases in life, such as smallpox, arthritis, and nutri- 6

tional deficiencies, are still diagnosable. Even their fatal af- 7

flictions are still apparent: a middle-aged king died from a

blow on the head; a child king died from polio.

Though some of the connections in this paragraph may have been added in revision, the writer probably attended to them while drafting as well. Not only superficial coherence but also an underlying clarity of relationships can be achieved by tying each sentence to the one before—generalizing from it, clarifying it, qualifying it, adding to it, illustrating it. As we saw just above, each sentence in a paragraph creates an expectation of some sort in the mind of the reader, a question such as "How was a mummy made?" or "How intact are the mummies?" or "What's another example?" When you recognize these expectations and try to fulfill them, readers are likely to understand relationships without struggle.

¶ coh
3b

PARAGRAPH PATTERNS I

Give students a topic sentence and a set of assertions, facts, and details in undeveloped form. Tell them to use the material to write a coherent paragraph, following one of the patterns described in the handbook: spatial, chronological, general-to-specific, specific-to-general, climactic, most familiar to least familiar, or simplest to most complex. Students can manipulate the material however they wish to achieve an effect that is appropriate to the pattern. You may also want to ask for several paragraphs, each using the same content but a different pattern.

PARAGRAPH PATTERNS II

As a quiz or an in-class exercise, ask students to write a paragraph following one of the basic organizational schemes discussed in 3b-1. Leave the subject and content of the paragraph up to the individual student. If they wish, students may make up information, as long as they keep it plausible.

 Organizing the paragraph

The paragraphs on mummies illustrate an essential element of coherence: information must be arranged in an order that readers can follow easily and that corresponds to their expectations. The common organizations for paragraphs correspond to those for entire essays (see 1g-3): by space, by time, and for emphasis. (In addition, the patterns of development also suggest certain arrangements. See 3c-2.)

Organizing by space or time

A paragraph organized **spatially** focuses readers' attention on one point and scans a person, object, or scene from that point. The movement may be from top to bottom, from side to side, from a farther point to a closer one, or from a closer point to a farther one. Donald Hall follows the last pattern in the following paragraph.

> Across the yard, between the cow barn and the road, was   1
> a bigger garden which was bright with phlox and zinnias
> and petunias. Beyond was a pasture where the color   2
> changed as the wild flowers moved through the seasons: yellow and orange paint brushes at first, then wild blue lupines
> and white Queen Anne's lace, and finally the goldenrod of
> August. Mount Kearsarge loomed over the pasture in the   3
> blue distance, shaped like a cone with a flattened point on
> top. We sat on the porch and looked at garden, field, and   4
> mountain.   —DONALD HALL, *String Too Short to Be Saved*

Since a spatial organization parallels the way people actually look at a place for the first time, it conforms to readers' expectations. The spatial relationships can be further clarified with explicit signals, such as Hall's *Across* and *between* (sentence 1), *Beyond* (2), and *over* (3). You may place a topic sentence at the beginning of the paragraph, may (like Hall) pull the scene together at the end, or may omit a topic sentence and let the details speak for themselves.

Another familiar way of organizing the elements of a paragraph is **chronologically**—that is, in order of their occurrence in time. In a chronological paragraph, as in experience, the earliest events come first, followed by more recent ones.

> There is no warning at all—only a steady rising intensity   1
> of the sun's light. Within minutes the change is noticeable;   2
> within an hour, the nearer worlds are burning. The star is   3

¶ coh

3b

expanding like a balloon, blasting off shells of gas at a million miles an hour as it blows its outer layers into space.
Within a day, it is shining with such supernal brilliance that it   4
gives off more light than all the other suns in the Universe
combined. If it had planets, they are now no more than   5
flecks of flame in the still-expanding shells of fire. The con-   6
flagration will burn for weeks before the dying star collapses
back into quiescence.

    —ARTHUR C. CLARKE, "The Star of the Magi"

Like spatial paragraphs, chronological paragraphs can be almost
automatically coherent because readers are familiar with progres-
sions of events. You can help readers by signaling the order of
events and the time that separates them, as Clarke does with
the phrases and words *Within minutes* and *within an hour* (sentence 2), *Within a day* (4), *now* and *still* (5), and *before* (6). Like
Clarke's, a chronological paragraph may lack a topic sentence
when the idea governing the sequence is otherwise clear.

Organizing for emphasis

Whereas the spatial or chronological organization is almost
dictated by the content of the paragraph, other organizational
schemes are imposed on paragraphs to achieve a certain emphasis. These imposed organizations are also familiar to readers.

In the **general-to-specific** scheme the topic sentence generally comes first and then the following sentences become increasingly specific. The paragraph on mummies (p. 81) illustrates this
organization: each sentence is either more specific than the one
before it or at the same level of generality. The following paragraph is a more straightforward illustration.

    Perhaps the simplest fact about sleep is that individual   1
needs for it vary widely. Most adults sleep between seven   2
and nine hours, but occasionally people turn up who need
twelve hours or so, while some rare types can get by on
three or four. Rarest of all are those legendary types who re-   3
quire almost no sleep at all; respected researchers have recently studied three such people. One of them—a healthy,   4
happy woman in her seventies—sleeps about an hour every
two or three days. The other two are men in early middle   5
age, who get by on a few minutes a night. One of them com-   6
plains about the daily fifteen minutes or so he's forced to
"waste" in sleeping.

    —LAWRENCE A. MAYER, "The Confounding Enemy of Sleep"

After the general statement of his topic sentence, the author
moves from common and less common sleep patterns (sentence

¶ coh
3b

EXTRA EXAMPLES

The following examples illustrate the specific-to-general pattern in a sentence and may be extended to short sample paragraphs:

(specific)   good study habits
(specific) + consistent effort
(specific) <u>+ curiosity</u>
(general) = good grades

Good study habits, consistent effort, and intellectual curiosity will result in good grades.

(specific)   seeds
(specific) + soil
(specific) + sunlight
(specific) <u>+ water</u>
(general) = good vegetable crop

A combination of fresh seeds, well-balanced soil, and adequate sunlight and water results in a good vegetable crop.

DRAMATIC EXAMPLES

Climactic order is a form of structuring that moves from least to most important. To help explain this strategy you may wish to draw examples from drama, particularly from the structure of tragedy. *Othello* provides an obvious example of structuring that moves from least dramatic/tension-filled to most dramatic/tension-filled.

Least dramatic—Othello marries Desdemona

More dramatic—Othello suspects Desdemona of infidelity

More dramatic—Desdemona defends her chastity and argues for her life

Most dramatic (climax)—Othello kills Desdemona and then realizes that she has been faithful to him

2) to the rarest pattern (sentence 3) and (in the remaining sentences) to particular people.

In the **specific-to-general** organization the elements of the paragraph build to a general conclusion. Such is the pattern of the next paragraph.

> It's disconcerting that so many college women, when asked how their children will be cared for if they themselves work, refer with vague confidence to "the day care center" as though there were some great amorphous kiddie watcher out there that the state provides. But such places, adequately funded, well run, and available to all, are still scarce in this country, particularly for middle-class women. And figures show that when she takes time off for family-connected reasons (births, child care), a woman's chances for career advancement plummet. In a job market that's steadily tightening and getting more competitive, these obstacles bode the kind of danger ahead that can shatter not only professions, but egos. A hard reality is that there's not much more support for our daughters who have family-plus-career goals than there was for us; there's simply a great deal more self- and societal pressure.   —JUDITH WAX, *Starting in the Middle*
> 1 2 3 4 5

The author first states a common belief (sentence 1) and two reasons why it is a misconception (sentences 2 and 3). Then she explains the implications, first specifically (sentence 4) and then generally (sentence 5). The last sentence is the topic sentence of the paragraph.

When the details of a paragraph vary in significance, they can be arranged in a **climactic** order, from least to most important or dramatic. The following paragraph builds to a climax, saving the most dramatic example for last.

> Nature has put many strange tongues into the heads of her creatures. There is the frog's tongue, rooted at the front of the mouth so it can be protruded an extra distance for nabbing prey. There is the gecko lizard's tongue, so long and agile that the lizard uses it to wash its eyes. But the ultimate lingual whopper has been achieved in the anteater. The anteater's head, long as it is, is not long enough to contain the tremendous tongue which licks deep into anthills. Its tongue is not rooted in the mouth or throat: it is fastened to the breastbone.   —ALAN DEVOE, "Nature's Utmost"
> 1 2 3 4 5 6

Similar to the organizations discussed so far are those which arrange details according to readers' likely understanding of them. In discussing the virtues of public television, for instance, you might proceed from **most familiar to least familiar,** from a well-known program your readers have probably seen to less well-known programs they may not have seen. Or in defending the right of government employees to strike, you might arrange your reasons from **simplest to most complex,** from the employees' need to be able to redress grievances to more subtle consequences for employer-employee relations.

2   Using parallel structures

Another way to achieve coherence, although not necessarily in every paragraph, is through **parallelism**—the use of similar grammatical structures for similar elements of meaning within a sentence or among sentences. (See Chapter 17 for a detailed discussion of parallelism.) Parallel structures help tie together the last three sentences in the paragraph on mummies (p. 81). In the following paragraph the parallel structures of *It is the* and *Democracy is the* link all sentences after the first one, and parallelism also appears within many of the sentences (for instance, *hole in the stuffed shirt* and *dent in the high hat* in sentence 4). The author, writing during World War II, was responding to a request from the Writer's War Board for a statement on the meaning of democracy.

> Surely the Board knows what democracy is. It is the line that forms on the right. It is the don't in Don't Shove. It is the hole in the stuffed shirt through which the sawdust slowly trickles; it is the dent in the high hat. Democracy is the recurrent suspicion that more than half of the people are right more than half of the time. It is the feeling of privacy in the voting booths, the feeling of communion in the libraries, the feeling of vitality everywhere. Democracy is the score at the beginning of the ninth. It is an idea which hasn't been disproved yet, a song the words of which have not gone bad. It's the mustard on the hot dog and the cream in the rationed coffee. Democracy is a request from a War Board, in the middle of a morning in the middle of a war, wanting to know what democracy is.   —E. B. WHITE, *The Wild Flag*

(margin line numbers) 1,2 · 3,4 · 5 · 6 · 7 · 8 · 9 · 10

3   Repeating or restating words and word groups

Since every unified paragraph has only one topic, that topic is bound to recur in many of the sentences. In fact, repeating or restating key words or word groups is an important means of achieving paragraph coherence and of reminding your readers what the topic is. In the next example, notice how repetition and

RESOURCES AND IDEAS

Anita Brostoff, "Coherence: 'Next to' Is Not 'Connected to,'" *College Composition and Communication* 32 (1981): 278–94. Brostoff discusses the causes of lack of coherence in writing and describes a program for helping students achieve coherence.

Francis Christensen, "A Generative Rhetoric of the Paragraph," *Notes Toward a New Rhetoric: Nine Essays for Teachers,* 2nd ed., ed. Francis Christensen and Bonniejean Christensen (New York: Harper, 1978) 74–103. Christensen views paragraphs as a series of statements on differing levels of generality, often moving from the more general toward the specific.

W. Ross Winterowd, "The Grammar of Coherence," *College English* 31 (1971): 828–35. This article describes the kinds of relations that link sentence to sentence and paragraph to paragraph.

¶ coh
3b

YEAH—YEAH—YEAH!

To recognize the power of repetition, students need only turn to rock music. Have them begin by listing the titles of popular songs whose lyrics they know by heart. Then ask them to identify words and phrases that they remember best from the songs or that they learned first. Chances are that they will identify the chorus because it is the element of the song most often repeated. You might point out that choruses help unify songs. Students may also note that the considerable amount of repetition in many songs makes them easy to remember and helps create a unified effect. This exercise may also be used to point out the difference between effective use of repetition and overuse.

HE'S ON SECOND

To illustrate the importance of clear pronoun reference in paragraphs, try to locate a recording or transcript of the famous Abbott and Costello skit "Who's on First." While humorous, this skit demonstrates the frustration a reader can feel when encountering a series of pronouns with unclear antecedents.

restatement tie the sentences together and stress the important words of the paragraph.

> The acceptance of paper money is, of course, an act of blind faith. Unlike coins, printed paper has no intrinsic material value (a characteristic that money shares with art). No longer backed by precious metals, the bank note represents nothing more tangible than a minuscule portion of what some economists and bureaucrats estimate to be the probable value of the nation's economy. In other words, it is representative of nothing but the expectation that, owning it, we will be able to get somebody to give us something in return. And, like Tinkerbelle's life, it works because we all believe it will work. As an intrinsically worthless surrogate, upon which all our welfare depends, it is perhaps surprising that the object itself is not more fetishized than it is.
> —SUSAN TALLMAN, "Money"

(sentence numbers 1 through 6 appear in right margin)

Tallman's repetitions and restatements include these:

paper money (sentence 1), *printed paper* and *money* (2), *bank note* (3), *the object* (6)

blind faith (1), *estimate* (3), *expectation* (4), *believe* (5), *fetishized* (6)

no intrinsic material value (2), *nothing more tangible than a minuscule portion* (3), *nothing* (4), *intrinsically worthless* (6)

Caution: Though planned repetition can be effective, careless or excessive repetition weakens prose (see 31c-2).

 4   Using pronouns

The previous examples illustrate yet another device for achieving paragraph coherence, the use of pronouns such as *it, him, his,* and *they*. **Pronouns** refer to and function as nouns (see 5a-2) and thus can help relate sentences to each other. In the following paragraph the pronouns *he, him,* and *his* indicate that the patient is still the subject while enabling the writer to avoid repeating *the patient* or *the patients*.

> The experience is a familiar one to many emergency-room medics. A patient who has been pronounced dead and unexpectedly recovers later describes what happened to him during those moments—sometimes hours—when his body exhibited no signs of life. According to one repeated account, the patient feels himself rushing through a long, dark tunnel while noise rings in his ears. Suddenly, he finds himself outside his own body looking down with curious detachment at a

¶ coh
3b

medical team's efforts to resuscitate him. He hears what is   5
said, notes what is happening but cannot communicate with
anyone. Soon, his attention is drawn to other presences in   6
the room—spirits of dead relatives or friends—who communicate with him nonverbally. Gradually he is drawn to a   7
vague "being of light." This being invites him to evaluate his   8
life and shows him highlights of his past in panoramic vision.
The patient longs to stay with the being of light but is   9
reluctantly drawn back into his physical body and recovers.
—KENNETH L. WOODWARD, "Life After Death?"

The pronouns in this paragraph give it coherence, in part because they refer clearly to a noun. The opposite effect will occur if
the reader cannot tell exactly what noun a pronoun is meant to
refer to (see Chapter 12).

5   Being consistent

Being consistent is the most subtle way to achieve paragraph
coherence because readers are aware of consistency only when it
is absent. Consistency (or the lack of it) occurs primarily in the
person and number of nouns and pronouns and in the tense of
verbs (see Chapter 13). Although some shifts will be necessary because of meaning, inappropriate shifts will interfere with a reader's ability to follow the development of ideas. The writers of the
following paragraphs destroy coherence by shifting person, number, and tense, respectively.

Shifts in person

An enjoyable form of exercise is modern dance. If *one*   1,2
wants to stay in shape, *you* will find that dance tones and
strengthens most muscles. The leaping and stretching *you*   3
do also improves *a person's* balance and poise. And *I* found   4
that *my* posture improved after only a month of dancing.

Shifts in number

Politics is not the activity for everyone. It requires quick-   1,2
ness and patience at the same time. A *politician* must like   3
speaking to large groups of people and fielding questions
without having time to think of the answers. *Politicians* must   4
also be willing to compromise with the people *they* represent. And no matter how good a *politician* is, *they* must give   5
up being popular with all constituents. It isn't possible.   6

Shifts in tense

I *am developing* an interest in filmmaking. I *tried* to take   1,2
courses that relate to camera work or theater, and I *have*

stay in same person tense number

¶ coh
3b

read books about the technical and artistic sides of movies. Though I *would have liked* to get a job on a movie set right away, *I will* probably *continue* my formal education and training in filmmaking after college. There simply *aren't* enough jobs available for all those who *wanted* to be in films but *have* no direct experience.

3
4

READING ALOUD

Often students can spot a lack of transitions in their own writing if they read their papers aloud. If you ask students to read one another's papers aloud, the student writers will often be able to recognize missing or unclear transitions at those points where the readers stumble over a passage or have to stop to puzzle out the meaning.

 Using transitional expressions

In addition to the methods for achieving coherence discussed above, writers also rely on specific words and word groups to connect sentences whose relationships may not be instantly clear to readers. Sometimes the omission of these words or word groups will make an otherwise coherent paragraph choppy and hard to follow, as the next paragraph shows.

> Medical science has succeeded in identifying the hundreds of viruses that can cause the common cold. It has discovered the most effective means of prevention. One person transmits the cold viruses to another most often by hand. An infected person covers his mouth to cough. He picks up the telephone. His daughter picks up the telephone. She rubs her eyes. She has a cold. It spreads. To avoid colds, people should wash their hands often and keep their hands away from their faces.

1
2
3
4
5
6,7
8,9,10

This paragraph is choppy to read, and we can only guess at the precise relationships spelled out by the italicized words below:

> Medical science has *thus* succeeded in identifying the hundreds of viruses that can cause the common cold. It has *also* discovered the most effective means of prevention. One person transmits the cold viruses to another most often by hand. *For instance,* an infected person covers his mouth to cough. *Then* he picks up the telephone. *Half an hour later,* his daughter picks up the *same* telephone. *Immediately afterward,* she rubs her eyes. *Within a few days,* she, *too,* has a cold. *And thus* it spreads. To avoid colds, *therefore,* people should wash their hands often and keep their hands away from their faces.
> —A STUDENT

1
2
3
4
5,6
7
8
9,10

Now the paragraph is smoother and clearer because the writer added connections that tell us precisely what to make of each sentence.

The linking words and word groups are called **transitional expressions.** They state relationships clearly and thus enhance

Transitional expressions

To add or show sequence

again, also, and, and then, besides, equally important, finally, first, further, furthermore, in addition, in the first place, last, moreover, next, second, still, too

To compare

also, in the same way, likewise, similarly

To contrast

although, and yet, but, but at the same time, despite, even so, even though, for all that, however, in contrast, in spite of, nevertheless, notwithstanding, on the contrary, on the other hand, regardless, still, though, yet

To give examples or intensify

after all, an illustration of, even, for example, for instance, indeed, in fact, it is true, of course, specifically, that is, to illustrate, truly

To indicate place

above, adjacent to, below, elsewhere, farther on, here, near, nearby, on the other side, opposite to, there, to the east, to the left

To indicate time

after a while, afterward, as long as, as soon as, at last, at length, at that time, before, earlier, formerly, immediately, in the meantime, in the past, lately, later, meanwhile, now, presently, shortly, simultaneously, since, so far, soon, subsequently, then, thereafter, until, until now, when

To repeat, summarize, or conclude

all in all, altogether, as has been said, in brief, in conclusion, in other words, in particular, in short, in simpler terms, in summary, on the whole, that is, therefore, to put it differently, to summarize

To show cause or effect

accordingly, as a result, because, consequently, for this purpose, hence, otherwise, since, then, therefore, thereupon, thus, to this end, with this object

PARAGRAPH SCRAMBLES

These activities are suitable for students working individually; when assigned for work in small groups, however, the activities are likely to encourage considerable discussion and discovery.

1. Take a good paragraph, by either a student or a professional, and rearrange the sentences. Then ask students to unscramble the sentences and make a clear, coherent paragraph. This exercise will make students aware of the flow of a coherent paragraph and will alert them to the number of examples and details found in a well-developed paragraph.

2. Choose a paragraph that lacks coherence and rearrange the sentences. Tell students to unscramble the sentences to form a coherent paragraph. Indicate that students are free to add any transitions, sentences, illustrations, or details they feel are necessary to make the paragraph both coherent and well developed. Students will quickly spot any coherence problems in the original paragraph, and unless the topic of the paragraph is quite unusual, they will be able to add any necessary content.

¶ coh
3b

¶ coh

3b

paragraph coherence. On the previous page is a partial list of transitional expressions, arranged by the functions they perform.

(For a discussion of transitional sentences and paragraphs, see pp. 74 and 113, respectively.)

 ### 7 Combining devices to achieve coherence

The devices we have examined for achieving coherence rarely appear in isolation in effective paragraphs. As any example in this chapter shows, writers usually combine sensible organization, parallelism, repetition, pronouns, consistency, and transitional expressions to help readers follow the development of ideas. And the devices also figure, naturally, in the whole essay (see 3e).

COLLABORATIVE LEARNING

ANSWERS: EXERCISE 5

1. Chronological.
2. Spatial.
3. Climactic.

Exercise 5
Analyzing paragraph organization

Which of the organizational schemes discussed on pages 82–85 has been used in each of the following paragraphs?

1. On August 18, 1951, the St. Louis Browns baseball team cracked a joke and forever changed the rules of professional baseball. On that day the Browns were playing the Detroit Tigers. In the first inning the St. Louis manager sent to the plate Eddie Gaedel, a man less than four feet tall. Detroit's pitcher at first did not throw to Gaedel, but the small man held his stance, his child's bat cocked. When the pitcher finally let one fly, the ball sailed over Gaedel's head. The pitcher tried again, and again the ball flew over Gaedel's head. The third pitch, too, was high, and so was the fourth. The pitcher simply could not lower his throws to Gaedel's strike zone. Gaedel walked to first base, where he was replaced by a pinch runner who later scored. Within twenty-four hours baseball had a new rule: no midgets would ever again play professional ball.
                                                      —A STUDENT

2. One must descend to the basement and move along a confusing mazelike hall to reach it. Twice the passage seems to lead against a blank wall; then at last one enters the brightly lighted auditorium. And here, finally, are the social workers at the reception desks; and there, waiting upon the benches rowed beneath the pipes carrying warmth and water to the floors above, are the patients. One sees white-jacketed psychiatrists carrying charts appear and vanish behind screens that form the improvised interviewing cubicles. All is an atmosphere of hurried efficiency; and the concerned faces of the patients are brightened by the friendly

smiles and low-pitched voices of the expert workers. One
has entered the Lafargue Psychiatric Clinic.

> —RALPH ELLISON, *Shadow and Act*

6

3. There are three reasons, quite apart from scientific considerations, that mankind needs to travel in space. The first
reason is the need for garbage disposal: we need to transfer
industrial processes into space, so that the earth may remain
a green and pleasant place for our grandchildren to live in.
The second reason is the need to escape material impover-
ishment: the resources of this planet are finite, and we shall
not forego forever the abundant solar energy and minerals
and living space that are spread out all around us. The third
reason is our spiritual need for an open frontier: the ulti-
mate purpose of space travel is to bring to humanity not
only scientific discoveries and an occasional spectacular
show on television but a real expansion of our spirit.

> —FREEMAN DYSON, "Disturbing the Universe"

1
2

3

4

Exercise 6
Analyzing paragraphs for coherence

Study the paragraphs in Exercise 1 (pp. 76–77) for the authors'
use of various devices to achieve paragraph coherence. Look especially for parallel structures and ideas, repetition and restatement, pronouns, and transitional expressions.

Exercise 7
Arranging sentences coherently

After the topic sentence (sentence 1), the sentences in each student paragraph below have been deliberately scrambled to make
the paragraph incoherent. Using the topic sentence and other
clues as guides, rearrange the sentences in each paragraph to
form a well-organized, coherent unit.

1. We hear complaints about the Postal Service all the time,
but we should not forget what it does *right*. The total volume
of mail delivered by the Postal Service each year makes up
more than half the total delivered in all the world. Its 70,000
employees handle 90,000,000,000 pieces of mail each year.
And when was the last time they failed to deliver yours? In
fact, on any given day the Postal Service delivers almost as
much mail as the rest of the world combined. That means
over 1,250,000 pieces per employee and over 400 pieces per
man, woman, and child in the country.

1
2

3

4,5

6

2. A single visit to New York City will tell you why the city
is both loved and hated by so many people. Whether you arrive by car, bus, train, plane, or boat, the skyline will take

1
2

ANSWERS: EXERCISE 6
Possible Answers

1. Parallelism in sentences 2, 6, 7, 8: *something
clicks . . . one grasps . . . masters; There are the
mountains . . . There is the glimmering ocean;
The civic landmarks . . . display themselves . . .
the pattern of the place unfolds; unlock . . .
undo . . . take.* Repetition and restatement: *free-
way(s)* (1, 2, 3); *system* (2, 8); *key, navigational
aid* (2, 4); *locks, unlock* (4, 8). Pronouns: primarily *it* for *system, they* for *freeways.* Transitional expressions: *though, suddenly* (2); *then* (5).
2. Parallelism in all three sentences: *sabotaged
. . . prevented . . . freed . . . harassed . . . released . . . hindered* (1); *taken . . . distributed*
(2); *can feel . . . are aware . . . have* (3). Repetition and restatement: *animals* (throughout); *Advocates of the rights of animals* and *growing
number of people* (1, 3); *rights* (1, 3); *inhumanely treated* and *pain* (2, 3). Pronouns: primarily *they* for *advocates.* Transitional expression: *Such* (1).
3. Parallelism in sentences 2, 3, 4: *They have
measured . . . recorded and studied . . .
learned.* Repetition: *whale, sings, song* throughout. Pronoun: *they* for *scientists* throughout. Transitional expression: *And* (4).

ANSWERS: EXERCISE 7
Possible Answers

1. The coherent order would be 1, 2, 5, 3, 6, 4.
2. The coherent order would be 1, 2, 5, 7, 6, 4,
3, 8.

¶ coh
3b

your breath away. And the streets seem so dirty: cans and 3
bags and newspapers lie in the gutters and on the sidewalks
or sometimes fly across your path. Even the people who do 4
speak English won't smile or say "Excuse me" or give you
good directions. The thrill will only be heightened when 5
you walk down the skyscraper canyons, look in the shop
windows, go to the theater or a museum, stroll in the neighborhoods where no one speaks English. You start to notice 6
the noise of traffic and get annoyed at the crowds. But all is 7
not perfect—far from it. After a few days, when your reac- 8
tions balance out, you have the same love-hate feelings as everyone else.

Exercise 8
Eliminating inconsistencies

The paragraph below is incoherent because of inconsistencies in
person, number, or tense. Identify the inconsistencies and revise
the paragraph to give it coherence.

> I rebel against the idea of males always being the sole 1
> family provider. For me to be happy, I needed to feel useful, 2
> and so I work to support myself and my daughter. I did not 3
> feel that it is wrong for one to be a housewife while a man
> supports your household, but that way is not for me. I enjoy 4
> the business world, and I have been pleased with my job. 5
> Working, I make enough now to support the two of us, and I
> know that when I graduate, I will be able to earn even more.
> I can do very well as my own provider. 6

Exercise 9
Using transitional expressions

Transitional expressions have been removed from the following
paragraph at the numbered blanks. Fill in each blank with an appropriate transitional expression (1) to contrast, (2) to intensify,
and (3) to show effect. Consult the list on page 89 if necessary.

> All over the country people are swimming, jogging, weightlift-
> ing, dancing, walking, playing tennis—doing anything to keep
> fit. __(1)__ this school has consistently refused to construct and
> equip a fitness center. The school has __(2)__ refused to open
> existing athletic facilities to all students, not just those playing or-
> ganized sports. __(3)__ students have no place to exercise ex-
> cept in their rooms and on dangerous public roads.

Exercise 10
Writing a coherent paragraph

Write a coherent paragraph from the following information, combining and rewriting sentences as necessary. First, begin the

---

ANSWERS: EXERCISE 8

Inconsistency in number: <u>males</u> and <u>provider</u>
(sentence 1). Inconsistency in tense: <u>needed</u> and
<u>work</u> (2); <u>did</u> and <u>is</u> (3); <u>enjoy</u> and <u>have been</u> (4).
Inconsistency in person: <u>one</u> and <u>your</u> (3). Possi-
ble revision:

> I rebel against the idea of <u>the male</u> always be-
> ing the sole family provi<u>der</u>. For me to be
> happy, I <u>need</u> to feel useful, and so I work to
> support my<u>self</u> and my daughter. I <u>do</u> not feel
> that it is wrong for one (or <u>a woman</u>) to be a
> housewife while a man supports <u>one</u> (or
> <u>her</u>), but that way is not for me. I en<u>joy</u> the
> <u>business</u> world, and I <u>am</u> pleased with my
> job. Working, I make enough now to support
> the two of us, and I know that when I gradu-
> ate, I will be able to earn even more. I can do
> very well as my own provider.

ANSWERS: EXERCISE 9
Possible Answers

1. *Yet, However, Even so,* or *Nevertheless*
2. *even, also,* or *further*
3. *As a result, Consequently,* or *Therefore*

paragraph with the topic sentence given and arrange the supporting sentences in a climactic order. Then combine and rewrite the supporting sentences, helping the reader see connections by introducing parallelism, repetition and restatement, pronouns, consistency, and transitional expressions.

Topic sentence

Hypnosis is far superior to drugs for relieving tension.

Supporting information

Hypnosis has none of the dangerous side effects of the drugs that relieve tension.
Tension-relieving drugs can cause weight loss or gain, illness, or even death.
Hypnosis is nonaddicting.
Most of the drugs that relieve tension do foster addiction.
Tension-relieving drugs are expensive.
Hypnosis is inexpensive even for people who have not mastered self-hypnosis.

Exercise 11
Turning topic sentences into coherent paragraphs

Develop three of the following topic sentences into coherent paragraphs. Organize your information by space, by time, or for emphasis, as seems most appropriate. Use parallelism, repetition and restatement, pronouns, consistency, and transitional expressions to link sentences.

1. Of all my courses, _____ is the one that I think will serve me best throughout life.
2. The movie (or book) had an exciting plot.
3. Although we Americans face many problems, the one we should concentrate on solving first is _____.
4. The most dramatic building in town is the _____.
5. Children should not have to worry about the future.

¶ dev
3c

3c Developing the paragraph

A paragraph may be both unified and coherent but still be skimpy, unconvincing, or otherwise inadequate. Take the following paragraph.

Despite complaints from viewers, television commercials aren't getting any more realistic. Their makers still present idealized people in unreal situations. And the advertisers also persist in showing a version of male-female relation-

1
2
3

¶ dev

3c

All of us must grapple with the student essay or single paragraph that is largely a succession of generalizations without support or explanation. Part of the solution to such problem paragraphs is to make students aware of readers as a special kind of audience for ideas. Another part is to make them aware of different strategies for developing paragraphs or essays.

The ways to develop ideas are infinite, but this section focuses on a limited number. The initial emphasis falls on the use of details, examples, and reasons, which are essential to any more specific method of development. Then follow the standard methods or patterns of development, each introduced by questions students can ask about an idea, event, or object to uncover concrete information useful for developing a paragraph.

You may wish to ask students to spend time in class or in groups working with sample topics to discover how the methods of development can be used to probe a topic and how the questions reveal different aspects of a topic. This discussion may help students see how the process of development can be an act of discovery. You will probably want to stress, however, that the methods of development covered in the handbook are not the only ones writers can use and that most paragraphs use more than a single method.

The exercises for this section range from analyzing paragraphs to producing them, and whether used in groups or by students working individually, they encourage students to treat the patterns of development as different ways of viewing a topic.

ships that can't exist in more than two households. What do the advertisers know about us, or about how we see ourselves, that makes them continue to plunge millions of dollars into these kinds of commercials?   4

Sentences 2 and 3 create expectations in our minds: we anticipate that the writer will give examples of commercials showing idealized people and unrealistic male-female relationships. But our expectations are disappointed because the paragraph lacks **development,** completeness. It does not provide enough information for us to evaluate the writer's assertion in sentence 1.

A well-developed paragraph always provides the specific information that readers need and expect in order to understand you and to stay interested in what you say. Often you may develop and arrange this information according to a particular pattern.

   Using specific information

If they are sound, the general statements you make in any writing will be based on what you have experienced, observed, read, and thought. Readers will assume as much and will expect you to provide the evidence for your statements. They need details, examples, and reasons—the heart of paragraph development—to understand and appreciate your meaning.

Here is the actual version of the paragraph discussed above. Notice how the added descriptions of commercials (in italics) turn a sketchy paragraph into an interesting and convincing one.

> Despite complaints from viewers, television commercials   1
> aren't getting any more realistic. Their makers still present   2
> idealized people in unreal situations. *Friendly shopkeepers*   3
> *stock only their favorite brand of toothpaste or coffee or*
> *soup. A mother cleans and buffs her kitchen floor to a mir-*   4
> *ror finish so her baby can play on it. A rosy-cheeked preg-*   5
> *nant woman uses two babies, two packaged diapers neatly*
> *dissected, and two ink blotters to demonstrate one diaper's*
> *superior absorbency to her equally rosy-cheeked and preg-*
> *nant friend.* The advertisers also persist in showing a ver-   6
> sion of male-female relationships that can't exist in more
> than two households. *The wife panics because a meddlesome*   7
> *neighbor points out that her husband's shirt is dirty. Or she*   8
> *fears for her marriage because her finicky husband doesn't*
> *like her coffee.* What do the advertisers know about us, or   9
> about how we see ourselves, that makes them continue to
> plunge millions of dollars into these kinds of commercials?
> —A STUDENT

2   Using a pattern of development

RESOURCES AND IDEAS

Carol Cohan, "Writing Effective Paragraphs," *College Composition and Communication* 27 (1976): 363–65. Cohan suggests encouraging paragraph development by treating topic sentences as questions to be answered by the paragraph that follows.

¶ dev
3c

If you have difficulty developing an idea or don't see the most effective way to shape the information you have, then try using one of the patterns of development. (They correspond to the patterns of essay development discussed on pp. 26–27.) Ask yourself a series of questions about an idea.

How did it happen? (Narration)

Narration retells a significant sequence of events, usually in the order of their occurrence (that is, chronologically). The paragraph by Arthur C. Clarke on pages 82–83 narrates the stages of a star's death. Here is another narrative paragraph in which events occupy not weeks but moments. The author's larger concern is contemporary language such as "sharing feelings" that reduces complex human interactions to formulas.

> Years ago, my husband and I rented a summer place in which we found ourselves surrounded by a tightly knit community that seemed to be speaking some common and slightly alien language. One night, at a party, one of these neighbors complained about the Moonie encampment around the corner and my husband—whose unconscious must surely have known what his conscious mind was slower to suspect—said that the Moonies weren't half so bad as . . . and he mentioned an especially strident human-potential group then receiving a good deal of publicity and notoriety. As a hush fell over the room, it dawned on us that the language we'd been puzzling over all summer was the language of that same group. No one breathed until at last our host turned to my husband and said, "Thank you for sharing that with us."   —FRANCINE PROSE, "Therapy Clichés"

1
2
3
4

As this paragraph illustrates, a narrator is concerned not just with the sequence of events but also with their consequence, their importance to the whole. Thus a narrative rarely corresponds to real time but collapses transitional or background events (as in sentence 1) and then expands the events of particular interest (2–4). In addition, writers often rearrange events, as when they simulate the workings of memory by flashing back to an earlier time.

How does it look, sound, feel, smell, taste? (Description)

Description details the sensory qualities of a person, place, thing, or feeling. You use concrete and specific words to evoke in

¶ dev
3c

readers your own experience of the subject. Some description is **subjective:** the writer filters the subject through his or her biases and emotions. In Donald Hall's subjective description on page 82, the *bright* garden and the mountain that *loomed in the blue distance* indicate Hall's feelings about these physical features of his environment. Similarly, in Pauline Kael's description of Steve Martin (p. 75), such words and phrases as *comedy robot, hilarious,* and *spruced up and dapper* convey Kael's interpretation of what she sees and hears.

In contrast to subjective description, journalists and scientists often favor description that is **objective,** conveying the subject without bias or emotion. As the following example from a psychology paper illustrates, the writer of objective description tries to record all relevant sensory data as specifically as possible without interpretation.

> The two toddlers, both boys, sat together for half an hour   1
> in a ten-foot-square room with yellow walls (one with a two-
> way mirror for observation) and a brown carpet. The room   2
> was unfurnished except for two small chairs and about two
> dozen toys. The boys' interaction was generally tense. They   3,4
> often struggled physically and verbally over several toys, es-
> pecially a large red beach ball and a small wooden fire en-
> gine. The larger of the two boys often pushed the smaller   5
> away or pried his hands from the desired object. This larger   6
> boy never spoke, but he did make grunting sounds when he
> was engaging the other. In turn, the smaller boy twice ut-   7
> tered piercing screams of "No!" and once shouted "Stop that!"
> When he was left alone, he hummed and muttered to   8
> himself.   —A STUDENT

What are examples of it or reasons for it? (Illustration or support)

Some ideas can be developed simply by **illustration or support**—supplying detailed examples or reasons. The writer of the paragraph on television commercials (p. 94) developed her idea with several specific examples of each general statement. You can also supply a single extended example, as the author of the following paragraph does to illustrate his assertion (sentence 1) about cultural differences in the ways people communicate.

> One of my earliest discoveries in the field of intercultural   1
> communication was that the position of the bodies of people
> in conversation varies with the culture. Even so, it used to   2
> puzzle me that a special Arab friend seemed unable to walk
> and talk at the same time. After years in the United States, he   3

could not bring himself to stroll along, facing forward while
talking. Our progress would be arrested while he edged   4
ahead, cutting slightly in front of me and turning sideways so
we could see each other. Once in this position, he would   5
stop. His behavior was explained when I learned that for the 6
Arabs to view the other person peripherally is regarded as
impolite, and to sit or stand band-to-back is considered very
rude. You must be involved when interacting with Arabs   7
who are friends.   —EDWARD T. HALL, *The Hidden Dimension*

The details of this example are arranged in a rough chronological
sequence. In a paragraph containing several examples, a climactic
organization is often effective; see the paragraph by Alan Devoe
on page 84 for an example.

Sometimes you can develop a paragraph by providing your
reasons for stating a general idea. For instance:

> It is time to defend the welfare state—taxes, bureaucrats,   1
> rules and regulations—the whole thing. Not only because it   2
> actually helps people who need help and subsidizes and en-
> ables a range of socially valuable activities—it does all that,
> and all that has to be done. There is another, and ultimately   3
> a more important, reason for defending the welfare state. It   4
> expresses a certain civil spirit, a sense of mutuality, a com-
> mitment to justice. Without that sense, no society can survive 5
> for long as a decent place to live—not for the needy, and
> not for anyone else.   —MICHAEL WALZER, "The Community"

Sentences 2, 4, and 5 provide reasons for the general assertion in
sentence 1. As is often the case in such paragraphs, the reasons
are arranged in a climactic order. (For another example, see the
paragraph by Freeman Dyson on p. 91.)

What is it? What does it encompass, and what does it exclude? (Definition)

A **definition** says what something is and is not, specifying the
characteristics that distinguish the subject from the other members of its class. You can easily define concrete, noncontroversial
terms in a single sentence: *A knife is a cutting instrument* (its
class) *with a sharp blade set in a handle* (the characteristics that
set it off from, say, scissors or a razor blade). But defining a complicated, abstract, or controversial topic often requires extended
explanation, and you may need to devote a whole paragraph or
even an essay to it. Such a definition may provide examples to
identify the subject's characteristics. It may also involve other
methods of development discussed below, such as division (sepa-

¶ dev
3c

rating a thing into its parts), classification (combining things into groups), or comparison and contrast.

The following definition comes from an essay asserting that "quality in product and effort has become a vanishing element of current civilization."

[handwritten margin notes: "Keyword-quality", "def 1", "or. 2", "3-7 comp'r cont."]

> In the hope of possibly reducing the hail of censure   1
> which is certain to greet this essay (I am thinking of going to
> Alaska or possibly Patagonia in the week it is published), let
> me say that quality, as I understand it, means investment of
> the best skill and effort possible to produce the finest and
> most admirable result possible. Its presence or absence in   2
> some degree characterizes every man-made object, service,
> skilled or unskilled labor—laying bricks, painting a picture,
> ironing shirts, practicing medicine, shoemaking, scholarship,
> writing a book. You do it well or you do it half-well. Materi-   3,4
> als are sound and durable or they are sleazy; method is
> painstaking or whatever is easiest. Quality is achieving or   5
> reaching for the highest standard as against being satisfied
> with the sloppy or fraudulent. It is honesty of purpose as   6
> against catering to cheap or sensational sentiment. It does   7
> not allow compromise with the second-rate.
> —BARBARA TUCHMAN, "The Decline of Quality"

To explain just what she means by *quality*—the key word of her essay—the author first provides a general definition (sentence 1) and then refines it with examples of the range of activities in which quality may figure (2), followed by a list of the characteristics that distinguish quality from nonquality (3–7). In this paragraph the sentences after the first move roughly from specific to general, but an arrangement by increasing specificity, importance, or complexity often works in definition as well.

What are its parts or characteristics? (Division or analysis)

Division and **analysis** both involve separating something into its elements, the better to understand it. Here is a simple example:

> A typical daily newspaper compresses considerable infor-   1
> mation into the top of the first page, above the headlines.
> The most prominent feature of this space, the newspaper's   2
> name, is called the *logo* or *nameplate*. Under the logo and   3
> set off by rules is a line of small type called the *folio line,*
> which contains the date of the issue, the volume and issue
> numbers, copyright information, and the price. To the right   4
> of the logo is a block of small type called a *weather ear,* a

EXTRA EXAMPLES

Division: Face

Eyes	Nose	Mouth
Pupil	Nostrils	Lips
Iris	Bridge	Tongue
Cornea		Teeth
		Teeth
		Molars
		Incisors
		Bicuspids

summary of the day's forecast. And above the logo is a *sky-*   5
line, a kind of advertisement in which the paper's editors
highlight a special feature of the issue.   —A STUDENT

The elements of the subject can be arranged spatially, as they are
here, or in order of importance or complexity.

Generally, analysis goes beyond simply identifying elements.
It also interprets the meaning and significance of the elements
and relates them to each other and to the whole subject. The following example comes from an essay asserting that soap operas
provide viewers with a sense of community and continuity missing from their own lives.

> The surface realism of the soap opera conjures up an illu-   1
> sion of "liveness." The domestic settings and easygoing   2
> rhythms encourage the viewer to believe that the drama,
> however ridiculous, is simply an extension of daily life. The   3
> conversation is so slow that some have called it "radio with
> pictures." (Advertisers have always assumed that busy house-   4
> wives would listen, rather than watch.) Conversation is ca-   5
> sual and colloquial, as though one were eavesdropping on
> neighbors. There is plenty of time to "read" the character's   6
> face; close-ups establish intimacy. The sets are comfortably   7
> familiar: well-lit interiors of living rooms, restaurants, offices,
> and hospitals. Daytime soaps have little of the glamour of   8
> their prime-time relations. The viewer easily imagines that   9
> the conversation is taking place in real time.
> —RUTH ROSEN, "Search for Yesterday"

analysis of elements: pace sets conversation

In this paragraph, Rosen looks at pace, sets, and other elements of
the soap opera. She shows how each of these elements relates to
the larger impression of a soap opera's "liveness" (sentence 1).

Analysis is a key skill in critical thinking and so receives much
more attention in Chapter 4 (see p. 126).

What groups or categories can it be sorted into?
(Classification)

Classification involves sorting many things into groups
based on their similarities. Using the pattern, we scan a large
group composed of many members that share at least one characteristic—freshman college students, say—and we assign the
members to smaller groups on the basis of some principle—participation in sports, perhaps, or high school grade average. Here is
a paragraph example.

> In my experience, the parents who hire daytime sitters   1
> for their school-age children tend to fall into one of three

EXTRA EXAMPLES

Classification:

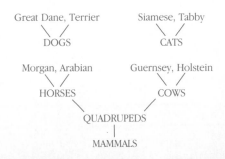

¶ dev
3c

groups. The first group includes parents who work and want someone to be at home when the children return from school. These parents are looking for an extension of themselves, someone who will give the care they would give if they were at home. The second group includes parents who may be home all day themselves but are too disorganized or too frazzled by their children's demands to handle child care alone. They are looking for an organizer and helpmate. The third and final group includes parents who do not want to be bothered by their children, whether they are home all day or not. Unlike the parents in the first two groups, who care for their children whenever and however they can, these parents are looking for a permanent substitute for themselves.   —A Student

The groups in this paragraph are arranged in a climactic order, but complexity or familiarity may also serve to organize a classification.

The preceding paragraph also illustrates two principles of classification. First, the classes or groups are alike in at least one basic way: all hire sitters for their children. And second, the classes do not overlap, as would parents who work and parents who don't because both groups include some uncaring and some caring parents.

How is it like, or different from, other things? (Comparison and contrast)

Asking about similarities and differences leads to **comparison and contrast.** The two may be used separately or together to develop an idea or to relate two or more things. In the following paragraph the author contrasts two kinds of audiences.

Consider the differences also in the behavior of rock and classical music audiences. At a rock concert, the audience members yell, whistle, sing along, and stamp their feet. They may even stand during the entire performance. The better the music, the more active they'll be. At a classical concert, in contrast, the better the performance, the more *still* the audience is. Members of the classical audience are so highly disciplined that they refrain from even clearing their throats or coughing. No matter what effect the powerful music has on their intellects and feelings, they sit on their hands.
—A Student

This paragraph illustrates one of two common ways of organizing a comparison and contrast: **subject-by-subject,** with the two subjects discussed separately, first one and then the other.

The next paragraph illustrates the other common organization: **point-by-point,** with the two subjects discussed side by side and matched feature for feature.

> This emphasis on the unfairness of language to women is misplaced. We should be erasing all bias from language, and that means bias against men as well. If a female pilot should not be stigmatized as an "aviatrix," then a male pilot should not be stigmatized as a "fly-boy." If it is unfair to label disliked women as "witches," then it is equally unfair to label disliked men as "cads." If an unattractive woman should not be called a "dog," then an unattractive man should not be called a "wimp" or a "dweeb." If it demeans the homeless woman to call her "baglady," then it also demeans the homeless man to call him a "bum."   —A STUDENT

IMITATING PARAGRAPHS

Choose a successful paragraph (student or professional) with a clear pattern, and discuss it in class. Then ask students to write paragraphs imitating the pattern but not the content of the model paragraph.

Here are the two organizing schemes in outline form. The one on the left corresponds to the point-by-point paragraph immediately above. The one on the right uses the same information but reorganizes it to cover first one subject, then the other.

Point-by-point

I. Language for pilots
   A. Women: aviatrix
   B. Men: fly-boy
II. Language for disliked people
   A. Women: witch
   B. Men: cad
III. Language for unattractive people
   A. Women: dog
   B. Men: wimp, dweeb
IV. Language for the homeless
   A. Women: baglady
   B. Men: bum

Subject-by-subject

I. Language for women
   A. Pilot: aviatrix
   B. Disliked: witch
   C. Unattractive: dog
   D. Homeless: baglady
II. Language for men
   A. Pilot: Fly-boy
   B. Disliked: cad
   C. Unattractive: wimp, dweeb
   D. Homeless: bum

Is it comparable to something that is in a different class but more familiar to readers? (Analogy)

Whereas we draw comparisons and contrasts between elements in the same general class (audiences, words), we link elements in different classes with a special kind of comparison called **analogy.** Most often in analogy we illuminate or explain an unfamiliar, complex, abstract class of things with a familiar and concrete class of things. In the following paragraph the author devel-

¶ dev
3c

ops an analogy between the Milky Way (abstract) and an atlas (concrete).

> We might eventually obtain some sort of bedrock under-
> standing of cosmic structure, but we will never understand
> the universe in detail; it is just too big and varied for that. If
> we possessed an atlas of our galaxy that devoted but a single
> page to each star system in the Milky Way (so that the sun
> and all its planets are crammed on one page), that atlas
> would run to more than ten million volumes of ten thou-
> sand pages each. It would take a library the size of Harvard's
> to house the atlas, and merely to flip through it, at the rate of
> a page per second, would require over ten thousand years.
> —Timothy Ferris, *Coming of Age in the Milky Way*

1
2
3

COMBINING FOR EMPHASIS

Put together a group of sentences or bits of in-formation about a topic, perhaps drawing the material from an essay in a reader or a magazine article. Ask students, working individually or in groups, to combine the material into a paragraph that has a distinct point of view. You might, for example, provide information about a recent controversial incident and ask for a paragraph emphasizing one perspective toward the incident or one perspective on its causes and effects.

What are its causes or its effects? (Cause-and-effect analysis)

When you use analysis to explain why something happened or what is likely to happen, then you are determining causes and effects. **Cause-and-effect analysis** is especially useful in writing about social, economic, or political events or problems, as the next paragraphs illustrate. In the first, the author looks at the causes of Japanese collectivism, which he elsewhere contrasts with American individualism.

> The *shinkansen* or "bullet train" speeds across the rural
> areas of Japan giving a quick view of cluster after cluster of
> farmhouses surrounded by rice paddies. This particular pat-
> tern did not develop purely by chance, but as a consequence
> of the technology peculiar to the growing of rice, the staple
> of the Japanese diet. The growing of rice requires the con-
> struction and maintenance of an irrigation system, some-
> thing that takes many hands to build. More importantly, the
> planting and the harvesting of rice can only be done effi-
> ciently with the cooperation of twenty or more people. The
> "bottom line" is that a single family working alone cannot
> produce enough rice to survive, but a dozen families work-
> ing together can produce a surplus. Thus the Japanese have
> had to develop the capacity to work together in harmony, no
> matter what the forces of disagreement or social disintegra-
> tion, in order to survive.
> —William Ouchi, *Theory Z: How American Business
> Can Meet the Japanese Challenge*

1
2
3
4
5
6

In sentences 1, 2, and 6 Ouchi specifies an effect: the Japanese live close together and work in harmony. The middle sentences ex-plain the conditions that caused this effect: the Japanese depend heavily on rice, and growing rice demands collective effort.

¶ **dev**
3c

Cause-and-effect paragraphs tend to focus either on causes, as Ouchi's does, or on effects, as the next paragraph does.

> There is something uneasy in the Los Angeles air this af-   1
> ternoon, some unnatural stillness, some tension. What it   2
> means is that tonight a Santa Ana will begin to blow, a hot
> wind from the northeast whining down through the Cajon
> and San Gorgonio Passes, blowing up sandstorms out along
> Route 66, drying the hills and the nerves to the flash point.
> For a few days now we will see smoke back in the canyons,   3
> and hear sirens in the night. I have neither heard nor read   4
> that a Santa Ana is due, but I know it, and almost everyone I
> have seen today knows it too. We know it because we feel it.   5
> The baby frets. The maid sulks. I rekindle a waning argu-   6,7,8
> ment with the telephone company, then cut my losses and
> lie down, given over to whatever it is in the air. To live with   9
> the Santa Ana is to accept, consciously or unconsciously, a
> deeply mechanistic view of human behavior.
> —JOAN DIDION, "Los Angeles Notebook"

Didion's second sentence specifies a cause: the Santa Ana wind. All the sentences in the paragraph describe the effects of the wind.

How does one do it, or how does it work? (Process analysis)

When you analyze how to do something or how something works, you explain the steps in a **process.** Paragraphs developed by process analysis are usually organized chronologically or spatially, as the steps in the process occur. Some process analyses tell the reader how to do a task. For example:

> As a car owner, you waste money when you pay a me-   1
> chanic to change the engine oil. The job is not difficult, even   2
> if you know little about cars. All you need is a wrench   3
> to remove the drain plug, a large, flat pan to collect the
> draining oil, plastic bottles to dispose of the used oil, and
> fresh oil. First, warm up the car's engine so that the oil will   4
> flow more easily. When the engine is warm, shut it off and   5
> remove its oil-filler cap (the owner's manual shows where
> this cap is). Then locate the drain plug under the engine   6
> (again consulting the owner's manual for its location) and
> place the flat pan under the plug. Remove the plug with the   7
> wrench, letting the oil flow into the pan. When the oil stops   8
> flowing, replace the plug and, at the engine's filler hole, add
> the amount and kind of fresh oil specified by the owner's
> manual. Pour the used oil into the plastic bottles and take it   9
> to a waste-oil collector, which any garage mechanic can rec-
> ommend.
> —A STUDENT

Other process analyses explain how a process is done or how it works in nature. The following paragraph, for example, explains how an island of mangrove trees begins "from scratch."

> Nor can a tree live without soil. A hurricane-born man- [1,2]
> grove island may bring its own soil to the sea. But other [3]
> mangrove trees make their own soil—and their own is-
> lands—from scratch. These are the ones which interest me. [4]
> The seeds germinate in the fruit on the tree. The germinated [5,6]
> embryo can drop anywhere—say, onto a dab of floating
> muck. The heavy root end sinks; a leafy plumule unfurls. The [7,8]
> tiny seedling, afloat, is on its way. Soon aerial roots shooting [9]
> out in all directions trap debris. The sapling's networks [10]
> twine, the interstices narrow, and water calms in the lee.
> Bacteria thrive on organic broth; amphipods swarm. These [11,12]
> creatures grow and die at the tree's wet feet. The soil thick- [13]
> ens, accumulating rainwater, leaf rot, seashells, and guano;
> the island spreads.   —ANNIE DILLARD, "Sojourner"

Combining patterns of development

Whatever pattern you choose as the basis for developing a paragraph, other patterns may also prove helpful. We have seen combined patterns often throughout this section: Walzer analyzes effects in providing reasons (p. 97); Tuchman uses contrast to define *quality* (p. 98); Didion uses description to analyze effects (p. 103).

As we will see in 3e, the paragraphs within an essay inevitably will be developed with a variety of patterns, even when one controlling pattern develops and structures the entire essay.

Checking length

The average paragraph contains between 100 and 150 words, or between four and eight sentences. These numbers are averages, of course. The actual length of a paragraph depends on its topic, the role it plays in developing the thesis of the essay, and its position in the essay. Nevertheless, very short paragraphs are often inadequately developed; they may leave readers with a sense of incompleteness. And very long paragraphs often contain irrelevant details or develop two or more topics; readers may have difficulty sorting out or remembering ideas.

When you are revising your essay, reread the paragraphs that seem very long or very short, checking them especially for unity and adequate development. If the paragraph wanders, cut every-

DEVELOPING PARAGRAPHS

Take underdeveloped paragraphs on subjects likely to be familiar to students and ask them to develop the paragraphs fully by drawing on their own knowledge. Student paragraphs often provide good material for this exercise.

thing from it that does not support your main idea (such as sentences that you might begin with *By the way*). If it is underdeveloped, supply the specific details, examples, or reasons needed, or try one of the methods of development we have discussed here.

Exercise 12
Analyzing and revising skimpy paragraphs

The following paragraphs are not well developed. Analyze them, looking especially for general statements that lack support or leave questions in your mind. Then rewrite one into a well-developed paragraph, supplying your own concrete details or examples.

1. One big difference between successful and unsuccessful teachers is the quality of communication. A successful teacher is sensitive to students' needs and excited by the course subject. In contrast, an unsuccessful teacher seems uninterested in students and bored by the subject.

1
2

3

2. Gestures are one of our most important means of communication. We use them instead of speech. We use them to supplement the words we speak. And we use them to communicate some feelings or meanings that words cannot adequately express.

1
2,3
4

3. Children who have been disciplined too much are often easy to spot. Their behavior toward adults may reflect the harsh treatment they have received from adults. And their behavior toward other children may be uncontrolled.

1
2
3

Exercise 13
Analyzing patterns of development

Identify the pattern or patterns of development in each of the following paragraphs. Where does the author supply specific information to achieve development?

1. A century of association has inevitably acculturated both Hispanos and Anglo-Americans to some extent, but there still persist a number of culture traits that neither group has relinquished altogether. Nothing is more disquieting to an Anglo-American who believes that time is money than the time perspective of Hispanos. They usually refer to this attitude as the "*mañana* [tomorrow] psychology." Actually, it is more of a "today psychology," because Hispanos cultivate the present to the exclusion of the future; because the latter has not arrived yet, it is not a reality. They are reluctant to relinquish the present, so they hold onto it until it becomes the

1

2

3
4

5

ANSWERS: EXERCISE 12
Possible Answers

1. Sentence 1 requires some expansion to explain *quality of communication.* Each of the next two sentences needs to be supported with specific examples of the two qualities named.

2. Sentences 2, 3, and 4 should each be followed by at least two specific examples of gestures to make the writer's meaning concrete.

3. Sentences 2 and 3 require specific support, perhaps both citations of studies that have demonstrated the effects mentioned and examples of children's behavior.

ANSWERS: EXERCISE 13

1. The paragraph is developed by comparison and contrast of Hispanos' and Anglo-Americans' attitudes toward time. Specific details appear primarily in sentences 6–10.

2. The paragraph is developed by illustration of the ways in which immigrants are "changing the American landscape." Sentences 2–5 each contain one or two specific examples.

3. The paragraph is developed by a definition of *mooches.* Specific details appear particularly in sentences 3 and 5.

past. To an Hispano, nine is nine until it is ten, so when he 6
arrives at nine-thirty, he jubilantly exclaims: "*¡Justo!*" [right on
time]. This may be why the clock is slowed down to a 7
walk in Spanish while in English it runs. In the United States, 8
our future-oriented civilization plans our lives so far in advance that the present loses its meaning. January magazine 9
issues are out in December; 1973 cars have been out since October; cemetery plots and even funeral arrangements are
bought on the installment plan. To a person engrossed in 10
living today the very idea of planning his funeral sounds like
the tolling of the bells.

—Arthur L. Campa, "Anglo vs. Chicano: Why?"

2.   They [newly arrived ethnic groups] are changing the 1
American landscape, proliferating into unexpected niches,
each following an irresistible ethnic call. Korean greengro- 2
cers have sprouted all over New York City, nestling bins of
knobby and unexplained roots next to red Delicious apples,
while Greeks have all but taken over the coffee shops, con-
quering the quick lunch business under their ubiquitous
symbol: the drink container with a picture of a discus
thrower. In New Orleans, Vietnamese immigrants have con- 3
verted their housing-project lawns into vegetable gardens, ir-
rigating them with the same long-handled canvas buckets
they once dipped into the Mekong. The amplified call of the 4
muezzin echoes through the south end of Dearborn, Michigan, five times a day, calling the faithful to prayer at their
mosque. Just as Americans have finally digested the basics of 5
soccer, cricket has emerged as the avant-garde immigrant
sport, played by exuberant Samoans on the fields of Carson,
California, and earnest Jamaicans and Trinidadians in Brook-
lyn's Prospect Park.   —"The New Immigrants," *Newsweek*

3.   In American society there exist people classified by en- 1
cyclopedia salesmen as "mooches." Mooches can be gener- 2
ally defined as people who like to buy the product; they see
the encyclopedia salesman as the bearer of a rare and desirable gift. Mooches are people whose incomes and occupa- 3
tional levels exceed their educational attainments; persons
whose income is in the middle-middle range but whose education doesn't exceed high school, or may not even attain
that level. Without education, mooches cannot have profes- 4
sional status, although they might make as much money as a
professional; consequently, mooches try to assume profes-
sionalism by accruing what they think are indications of professional status. A conspicuously displayed set of encyclope- 5
dias tells the mooch's friends that he can afford to consume
conspicuously, that he values a highly normative product

¶ dev
3c

over creature comforts, and that he provides for the long-range benefit of his protectorate. The mooch associates all these characteristics with professional persons. For him, then, encyclopedias function as easily interpreted professional-status indicators. —LYNN M. BULLER, "The Encyclopedia Game"

6
7

Exercise 14
Writing a well-developed paragraph

Write a well-developed paragraph on one of the following ideas or an idea of your own. Or take an underdeveloped paragraph from something you have written and revise it. Be sure your paragraph is unified and coherent as well as adequately developed with specific information.

1. How billboards blight (or decorate) the landscape
2. Why you like (or don't like) poetry or song lyrics
3. A place where you feel comfortable (or uncomfortable)
4. An unusual person you know
5. An instance of unusual kindness or cruelty

Exercise 15
Matching topic and development pattern

Identify an appropriate pattern or patterns for developing a paragraph on each of the following topics. (Choose from narration, description, illustration or support, definition, division or analysis, classification, comparison and contrast, analogy, cause-and-effect analysis, and process analysis.) Then write one of the paragraphs.

1. The influences of a person's biorhythms or astrological sign on his or her behavior
2. A typical situation comedy on television
3. Tuning an engine
4. Rock music and country music
5. Why read newspapers
6. What loyalty is
7. The picture of aliens shown by a recent science-fiction movie
8. Dancing as pure motion, like a kite in the wind
9. An especially vivid moment in your life
10. The kinds of fans at a baseball game (or a game in some other sport)

Exercise 16
Writing with the patterns of development

Write ten unified, coherent, and well-developed paragraphs, each one developed with a different pattern. Draw on the topics provided here or in Exercise 15. Or choose your own topics.

ANSWERS: EXERCISE 14

Individual response.

COLLABORATIVE LEARNING

ANSWERS: EXERCISE 15
Possible Answers

1. Cause-and-effect analysis
2. Illustration
3. Process analysis
4. Comparison and contrast
5. Support with reasons
6. Definition
7. Illustration or definition
8. Analogy
9. Narration or description
10. Classification

ANSWERS: EXERCISE 16

Individual response.

¶
3d

1. *Narration*
   An experience of public speaking
   A disappointment
   Leaving home
   Waking up
2. *Description (objective or subjective)*
   Your room
   A crowded or deserted place
   A food
   An intimidating person
3. *Illustration or support*
   Why study
   Having a headache
   The best sports event
   Usefulness (or uselessness) of a self-help book
4. *Definition*
   Humor
   An adult
   Fear
   Authority
5. *Division or analysis*
   A television news show
   A barn
   A movie set
   A piece of music
6. *Classification*
   Factions in a campus controversy
   Styles of playing poker
   Types of street people
   Kinds of teachers

7. *Comparison and contrast*
   Driving a friend's car and driving your own car
   AM and FM radio announcers
   High school and college football
   Movies on TV and in a theater
8. *Analogy*
   Paying taxes and giving blood
   The U.S. Constitution and a building's foundation
   Graduating from high school and being released from prison
9. *Cause-and-effect analysis*
   Connection between tension and anger
   Causes of failing a course
   Connection between credit cards and debt
   Causes of a serious accident
10. *Process analysis*
    Preparing for a job interview
    Making a cabinet
    Protecting your home from burglars
    Making a jump shot

3d   **Writing special kinds of paragraphs**

Several kinds of paragraphs do not always follow the guidelines for unity, coherence, development, and length because they serve special functions. These are the essay introduction, the essay conclusion, the transitional or emphatic paragraph, and the paragraph of spoken dialogue.

1   Opening an essay

read aloud

Most of your essays will open with a paragraph that draws readers from their world into your world. An opening paragraph should focus readers' attention on the topic and arouse their curiosity about what you have to say. It should be concise. It should specify what you will discuss and what your attitude is. It should be sincere. And it should be interesting without misrepresenting the content of the essay that follows. The openers below are illustrated on the next several pages.

Some strategies for opening paragraphs

- State the subject.
- Use a quotation.
- Relate an incident.
- Create an image.
- Ask a question.
- State an opinion.
- Make a historical comparison or contrast.

The most common kind of introduction opens with a statement of the essay's general subject, clarifies or limits the subject in one or more sentences, and then, in the thesis sentence, asserts the point of the essay (see 1f). The following paragraph introduces an essay on the history of American bathing habits.

> We Americans are a clean people. We bathe or shower   1,2
> regularly and spend billions of dollars each year on soaps
> and deodorants to wash away or disguise our dirt and odor.
> Yet cleanliness is a relatively recent habit with us. From the   3,4
> time of the Puritans until the turn of the twentieth century,
> bathing in the United States was rare and sometimes even
> illegal.   —A STUDENT

Sentences 1 and 2 offer the subject and elaborate on it, leading us to focus on something within our experience. Then, by introducing a less familiar but related idea, sentence 3 forms a bridge from common experience to the writer's specific purpose. Sentence 4, the thesis, states that purpose explicitly. Here is another example of this form of introductory paragraph.

> Can your home or office computer make you sterile? Can   1,2
> it strike you blind or dumb? The answer is: probably not.   3
> Nevertheless, reports of side effects relating to computer use   4
> should be examined, especially in the area of birth defects,
> eye complaints, and postural difficulties. Although little con-   5

HIGHLIGHTS

This section addresses introductory and concluding paragraphs, the occasionally useful transitional and short emphatic paragraphs, and the conventions of paragraphing in dialogue. The emphasis you give to introductory and concluding paragraphs may vary with the experience of your students. For some, writing a straightforward introductory paragraph that simply sets the stage for the essay and presents a thesis statement will be an accomplishment. Others will benefit from experimenting with some of the variations illustrated. Most, however, will appreciate the list of "don'ts" for introductory paragraphs.

Because concluding paragraphs often present a special problem, you may wish to highlight the common inept endings that trap students and then suggest satisfactory alternatives.

TRANSPARENCY MASTER
AVAILABLE

¶
3d

MAGAZINE MODELS

Magazines like *Time, Glamour, Outdoor Life,* and *Self* contain a variety of informative articles. The authors of these articles and students writing expository essays face a similar problem—how to get readers interested enough to keep reading. Have students collect effective openings and bring them to class for discussion. Students can also comb editorials and magazine articles for openings of argumentative essays.

clusive evidence exists to establish a causal link between computer use and problems of this sort, the circumstantial evidence can be disturbing.

—THOMAS HARTMANN, "How Dangerous Is Your Computer?"

Several other types of introductions can be equally effective, though they are sometimes harder to invent and control. One kind begins with a quotation that leads into the thesis sentence.

"It is difficult to speak adequately or justly of London," wrote Henry James in 1881. "It is not a pleasant place; it is not agreeable, or cheerful, or easy, or exempt from reproach. It is only magnificent." Were he alive today, James, a connoisseur of cities, might easily say the same thing about New York or Paris or Tokyo, for the great city is one of the paradoxes of history. In countless different ways, it has almost always been an unpleasant, disagreeable, cheerless, uneasy and reproachful place; in the end, it can only be described as magnificent.   —*Time*

Another kind of introduction opens by relating an incident or creating an image that sets the stage for the thesis.

Canada is pink. I knew that from the map I owned when I was six. On it, New York was green and brown, which was true as far as I could see, so there was no reason to distrust the map maker's portrayal of Canada. When my parents took me across the border and we entered the immigration booth, I looked excitedly for the pink earth. Slowly it dawned on me; this foreign, "different" place was not so different. I discovered that the world in my head and the world at my feet were not the same.

—ROBERT ORNSTEIN, *Human Nature*

An introduction may also start with a question, as in the earlier paragraph by Thomas Hartmann, or with an opinion, preferably a startling one that will grab the reader's attention.

Caesar was right. Thin people need watching. I've been watching them for most of my adult life, and I don't like what I see. When these narrow fellows spring at me, I quiver to my toes. Thin people come in all personalities, most of them menacing. You've got your "together" thin person, your mechanical thin person, your condescending thin person, your tsk-tsk thin person. All of them are dangerous.

—SUZANNE BRITT, "That Lean and Hungry Look"

A historical comparison or contrast may make an effective introduction when some background to the essay topic is useful.

¶
3d

Throughout the first half of this century, the American Medical Association, the largest and most powerful medical organization in the world, battled relentlessly to rid the country of quack potions and cure-alls; and it is the AMA that is generally credited with being the single most powerful force behind the enactment of the early pure food and drug laws. Today, however, medicine's guardian seems to have done a complete about-face and become one of the pharmaceutical industry's staunchest allies—often at the public's peril and expense.   —MAC JEFFERY, "Does Rx Spell Rip-off?"   1

2

An effective introductory paragraph need not be long, as the following opener shows.

> I've often wondered what goes into a hot dog. Now I know and I wish I didn't.   1,2
>
> —WILLIAM ZINSSER, *The Lunacy Boom*

When writing and revising an introductory paragraph, avoid the following approaches that are likely to bore readers or make them question your sincerity or control.

LEARNING STRATEGIES

To help students learn effective strategies for writing opening paragraphs, give the class outlines of well-known essays and ask students to construct opening paragraphs based on the information provided. Compare students' opening paragraphs with those of the essays. This exercise will expose students to the numerous possibilities for creating good opening paragraphs and will promote discussion of the relative merits of different techniques for a specific subject, essay, or audience.

Opening paragraphs to avoid

- Don't simply mark time with vague generalities or repetition and then rely entirely on your thesis sentence to get moving. You may have needed a warm-up paragraph to start drafting, but your readers can do without it.
- Don't start with "The purpose of this essay is . . . ," "In this essay I will . . . ," or any similar flat announcement of your intention or topic.
- Don't refer to the title of the essay in the first sentence—for example, "This is my favorite activity" or "This is a big problem."
- Don't start with "According to Webster . . ." or a similar phrase leading to a dictionary definition. A definition can be an effective springboard to an essay, but this kind of lead-in has become dull with overuse.
- Don't apologize for your opinion or for inadequate knowledge with "I'm not sure if I'm right, but I think . . . ," "I don't know much about this, but . . . ," or similar lines.

TRANSPARENCY MASTER
AVAILABLE

 Closing an essay

Most of your essays will end with a closing statement or conclusion, a signal to readers that you have not simply stopped writ-

COMPARING CLOSINGS

Using the same essays gathered for the preceding exercise, ask students to read all but the conclusions. Then have them underline the thesis statement and the main ideas of each paragraph. Finally, have students write their own conclusions. This exercise will help students to recognize the structure, effectiveness, and importance of concluding paragraphs and will provide diverse examples of how key information may be arranged for variety and emphasis.

TRANSPARENCY MASTER
AVAILABLE

IMITATING OPENINGS AND CLOSINGS

When experienced writers have trouble beginning or ending essays, they usually turn to strategies that have been successful on other occasions. To help student writers develop similar resources, distribute opening and closing paragraphs that demonstrate particularly effective strategies and ask students to write their own paragraphs using the same strategies but containing different content.

ing but have actually finished. The conclusion completes the essay, bringing it to a climax while assuring readers that they have understood your intention. Usually set off in its own paragraph, the conclusion may consist of a single sentence or a group of sentences. It may take one or more of the approaches below.

Some strategies for closing paragraphs

- Summarize the paper.
- Echo the introduction.
- Restate the thesis.
- Create an image.
- Strike a note of hope or despair.
- Use a quotation.
- Give a symbolic or powerful fact or other detail.
- Recommend a course of action.

The following paragraph concludes the essay on bathing habits whose introduction we saw on page 109. The writer both summarizes her essay and echoes her introduction by proposing a link between the habits of history and the habits of today.

> Thus changed attitudes and advances in plumbing finally freed us to bathe whenever we want. Perhaps partly to make up for our ancestors' bad habits, we have transformed that freedom into a national obsession. —A STUDENT

Maxine Hong Kingston uses a different technique—a vivid image—to conclude an essay on her aunt, a suicide by drowning.

> My aunt haunts me—her ghost drawn to me because now, after fifty years of neglect, I alone devote pages of paper to her, though not origamied into houses and clothes. I do not think she always means me well. I am telling on her, and she was a spite suicide, drowning herself in the drinking water. The Chinese are always very frightened of the drowned one, whose weeping ghost, wet hair hanging and skin bloated, waits silently by the water to pull down a substitute.
> —MAXINE HONG KINGSTON, "No Name Woman"

In the next paragraph the author concludes an essay on environmental protection with a statement of opinion and, in the last sentence, a call for action.

> Until we get the answers, I think we had better keep on building power plants and growing food with the help of fertilizers and such insect-controlling chemicals as we now have. The risks are well known, thanks to the environmental-

ists. If they had not created a widespread public awareness of   3
the ecological crisis, we wouldn't stand a chance. But such   4
awareness by itself is not enough. Flaming manifestos and   5
prophecies of doom are no longer much help, and a search for
scapegoats can only make matters worse. The time for   6
sensations and manifestos is about over. Now we need rigor-   7
ous analysis, united effort and very hard work.
  —PETER F. DRUCKER,"How Best to Protect the Environment"

These three paragraphs illustrate ways of avoiding several pitfalls of conclusions.

TRANSPARENCY MASTER
AVAILABLE

Closing paragraphs to avoid

- Don't simply restate your introduction—statement of subject, thesis sentence, and all. Presumably the paragraphs in the body of your essay have contributed something to the opening statements, and it's that something you want to capture in your conclusion.
- Don't start off in a new direction, with a subject different from or broader than the one your essay has been about.
- Don't conclude more than you reasonably can from the evidence you have presented. If your essay is about your frustrating experience trying to clear a parking ticket, you cannot reasonably conclude that *all* local police forces are too tied up in red tape to be of service to the people.
- Don't apologize for your essay or otherwise cast doubt on it. Don't say, "Even though I'm no expert," or "This may not be convincing, but I believe it's true," or anything similar. Rather, to win your readers' confidence, display confidence.

Using short transitional or emphatic paragraphs

A short paragraph of a sentence or two may direct readers' attention to a turn in an essay or emphasize an idea that has been or will be developed. A transitional paragraph, because it is longer than a word or phrase and set off by itself, moves a discussion from one point to another more slowly or more completely than does a single transitional expression (3b-6) or even a transitional sentence attached to a paragraph (3a-2).

These, then, are the causes of the current expansion in hospital facilities. But how does this expansion affect the medical costs of the government, private insurers, and individuals?

PAIRS OF IDEAS

Students may hone their skills with transitional paragraphs by being given pairs of seemingly unrelated ideas and being asked to link them. For example, using the topic of capital punishment, have students create a transitional paragraph linking the discussion of legal implications to the discussion of moral implications.

¶

3d

The conclusion would seem to be obvious. To be sure, however, we must look at a few other facts.

So the debates were noisy and emotion-packed. But what did they accomplish? Historians agree on at least three direct results.

Use transitional paragraphs rarely — only to shift readers' attention when your essay makes a significant turn. A paragraph like the one below betrays a writer who is stalling; it does not redirect the flow but stops it altogether.

Now that we have examined these facts, we can look at some others that are equally important to an examination of this issue.

A short, emphatic paragraph gives unusual stress to an important idea, in effect asking the reader to pause and consider before moving on.

In short, all those who might have taken responsibility ducked it, and catastrophe was inevitable.

 4   **Writing dialogue**

When recording a conversation between two or more people, start a new paragraph for each person's speech. The paragraphing establishes for the reader the point at which one speaker stops talking and another begins.

The dark shape was indistinguishable. But once I'd flooded him with light, there he stood, blinking.

"Well," he said eventually, "you're a sight for sore eyes. Should I stand here or are you going to let me in?"

"Come in," I said. And in he came.

—LOUISE ERDRICH, *The Beet Queen*

Though dialogue appears most often in fictional writing (the source of the example above), it may occasionally freshen or enliven narrative or expository essays. (For guidance in using quotation marks and other punctuation in dialogue, see 24c.)

Exercise 17
Analyzing an introduction and conclusion

Analyze the introductory and concluding paragraphs in the first and final drafts of the student essay in Chapter 2, pages 49–50 and 61–64. What is wrong with the first-draft paragraphs? Why are the final-draft paragraphs better? Could they be improved still further?

3e Linking paragraphs in the essay

¶
3e

read *✳*

Paragraphs do not stand alone but contribute to a larger piece of writing. Each unified, coherent, and well-developed paragraph adds something to a unified, coherent, and well-developed essay.

In a two- to four-page essay each paragraph between the introductory and concluding ones will develop and support a part of the essay's central idea, its thesis. The devices for achieving paragraph coherence—organization, transitional expressions, and the like—will also link paragraphs in a coherent whole. And the patterns for developing paragraphs—definition, division, and so on—will work for individual paragraphs in the larger context of the essay. Thus the paragraph patterns may vary and may or may not reflect the overall pattern of the whole essay.

The following essay illustrates the way effective paragraphs can contribute to an effective essay.

1   A hyperactive committee member can contribute to efficiency. A hyperactive salesperson can contribute to profits. But when a child is hyperactive, people—even parents—may wish he had never been born. To understand hyperactivity in children, we can visualize a collage of the thoughts, feelings, and attitudes of those who must cope with the problem: doctors, parents, even the child himself.

— plan of dev.

2   The first part of our collage is the doctors. In their terminology the word *hyperactivity* is short for H-LD, a hyperkinesis–learning disability syndrome. They apply the word to children who are "abnormally or excessively busy." But doctors do not fully understand the problem and thus differ over how to treat it. For example, some recommend a special diet; others, behavior-modifying drugs; and still others, who do not consider hyperactivity to be a medical problem, a psychiatrist for the entire family. The result is a merry-go-round of tests, confusion, and frustration for the parents and the child.

3   As the parent of a hyperactive child, I can say what the word *hyperactivity* means to the parents who form the second part of the collage. It means a worry that is deep and enduring. It means a despair that is a companion on dark and sleepless nights. It means a fear that is heart twisting and constant, for the hyperactive child is most destructive toward himself. It means a mixture of frustration, guilt, and anger. And finally, since there are times when that anger goes out of control and the child is in danger from the parent, it means self-loathing.

‖ ism

4   The weight of hyperactivity, however, rests not on the doctors or the parents but on the child. For him is reserved

¶

3e

the final and darkest part of our collage because he is most affected. From early childhood he is dragged from doctor to doctor, is attached to strange and frightening machines, and is tested or discussed by physicians, parents, neighbors, teachers, peers. His playmates dislike him because of his temper and his unwillingness to follow rules; and even his pets fear and mistrust him, for he treats them erratically, often hurting them without meaning to. As time goes on, he sees his parents more and more often in tears and anger, and he knows that he is the cause. Though he is highly intelligent, he does poorly when he enters school because of his short attention span. He is fond of sports and games but never joins the other children on the playground because he has an uncontrollable temper and poor coordination. By the time he reaches age seven or eight, he is obsessed with one thought: "Mama," my son asks me repeatedly, "why do I have to be hyperactive?"

At last the collage is completed, and it is dark and somber. *Hyperactivity,* as applied to children, is a word with uncertain, unattractive, and bitter associations. But the picture does have a bright spot, for inside every hyperactive child is a loving, trustful, calm person waiting to be recognized.   5

—A STUDENT

The overall pattern of development in this essay is division or analysis: the writer examines the human elements involved in hyperactivity. In addition, the writer creates an analogy, comparing those involved to the pieces in a collage. The essay's basic organization is climactic or general to specific, proceeding from the general notions of the seemingly distant doctors to the more specific and poignant experiences of a single child. Within this general scheme, however, each paragraph follows the course required by its topic and the writer's purpose. For instance, having shown in paragraph 2 that doctors do not agree on what hyperactivity is, the writer develops paragraph 3 by defining the word as she sees it. And she develops paragraph 4 by analyzing the effects of hyperactivity on the one most harmed by it, the child himself. This paragraph also follows a chronological organization in tracing the child's experiences.

Despite the varied organizational schemes and patterns of development in her paragraphs, the writer guides us smoothly and steadily from one paragraph to the next. She recalls the promise of the thesis sentence, a three-part collage, in the topic sentence of every succeeding paragraph. She links paragraphs with transitional words to remind us where we are in the essay: *first* (paragraph 2), *second* (3), *however* and *final* (4), *at last* (5). The entire first sentence of paragraph 4 is a transition from the earlier paragraphs. The writer repeats the key words of the essay, *collage* and *hyperactive* or *hyperactivity,* in the first or second sentence of every paragraph. At the end of paragraph 2, on doctors, she looks ahead to the next two paragraphs, on parents and the child. In the conclusion she echoes the distinction, first made in the introduction, between the useful hyperactivity of adults and the destructive hyperactivity of children. The combination of these techniques produces a tightly woven analysis that readers can easily understand.

Exercise 18
Analyzing paragraphs in essays

Analyze the ways in which paragraphs combine in the three student essays in Chapter 2, pages 61, 67, and 68. With what techniques, if any, does each writer link paragraphs to the thesis sentence and to each other? Where, if at all, does the writer seem to stray from the thesis or fail to show how paragraphs relate to it? How would you revise the essays to solve any problems they exhibit?

Exercise 19
Analyzing unity, coherence, and development

Analyze the following paragraphs for unity, coherence, and development. For each paragraph identify the central idea (even if it is not stated explicitly), the organizational scheme, the devices used to achieve coherence, and the pattern or patterns of development.

1. If it is the very essence of life you seek, visit Japan. The wine is served piping hot in the tiniest thimble bowls, and it is better than gulping beakers of cold sauterne. Some of the finest Japanese sculptures are no larger than a walnut and can be worn as the tassel to one's belt. In the Japanese dance, one tightly controlled gesture stands for an entire routine, and in the theater the merest corner of handkerchief pressed to the eye symbolizes unbearable grief.
— JAMES MICHENER, "Why I Like Japan"

1,2

3

4

2. To feel used is to have a sense of something of ours being taken away. But it is more than that. To feel used is to feel that our services have been separated from ourselves. It is a sense of the violation of our central worth, as though we ourselves are important to the other individual only because we are a vehicle for supplying the stuff that he desires. It may be most graphic and evident when what he desires is a material or physical thing—our money or our possession—but we are equally offended when what is taken or used is our intelligence, our creativity, our companionship, or our love.
— WILLARD GAYLIN, "Feeling Used"

1

2,3

4

5

ANSWERS: EXERCISE 18
Possible Answers

1. Essay on page 61 ("America's Media Image"): Every paragraph after the first is linked to the thesis sentence with the words *conflict, ethnic, media,* or *peace,* so that it is immediately apparent how the paragraph will relate to the thesis. Within paragraphs, too, these key words are repeated and restated so that connections remain clear. In addition, the author uses a transitional expression at the start of paragraph 4 (*though*) to signal a shift. (Further analysis of this essay appears in Chapter 2 of the handbook and in the answer to Exercise 17.)

2. Essay on page 67 ("Working in the Barnyard"): The paragraphs in this narrative essay relate clearly to the thesis and proceed smoothly from one incident to the next. Transitions are provided primarily by time markers such as *Last May* (paragraph 2), *as soon as I arrived* (paragraph 3), *after about a week* (paragraph 4), *over the next seven weeks* (paragraph 5), *Two months after I had started work* (paragraph 6), *a month before school began* (paragraph 7). (Further analysis of this essay appears in the answer to Chapter 2, Exercise 9.)

3. Essay on page 68 ("The Obsolete Hero"): The paragraphs of this essay most obviously are linked by frequent repetition of *cowboy(s)* and by the transitional expressions beginning paragraphs 3–5: *As the railroads moved westward; As civilization spread across the West; Today.* In addition, the main paragraphs (3–4) are linked by a roughly similar arrangement of points of comparison (trail drives, transportation, food, skills) and by frequent echoes of paragraph 3 in paragraph 4 (e.g., *Trail drives dwindled; instead of busting wild broncos; When the cowboy needs to search the bush; skills that used to be essential*). (Further analysis of this essay appears in the answer to Chapter 2, Exercise 9.)

ANSWERS: EXERCISE 19

1. The central idea is in sentence 1. The examples are organized climactically. Coherence is

achieved primarily by repetition and restatement (*Japan, Japanese; tiniest, no larger than a walnut, tightly controlled, merest corner*). The paragraph is developed by illustration.

2. The central idea is in sentence 2. The paragraph is organized from general to specific. Coherence is achieved primarily by repetition and restatement (*To feel used, feel, sense*); by parallelism (*To feel used is to have . . . To feel used is to feel; But it is more . . . It is a sense . . . It may be most graphic*); and by pronouns (*it; ours, ourselves*, etc.; *he*). The paragraph is developed by definition.

3. The central idea is in sentence 2. The organization is chronological. Coherence is achieved by transitional expressions (*First, Second, Finally*); by the pronoun *they*; and by parallelism (*they should shop around . . . they should consult guides . . . they should refuse to accept . . . demand to see . . . decline to sign or accept*). The paragraph is developed by process analysis.

4. The central idea is in sentence 2. The paragraph is organized from general to specific. Coherence is achieved primarily by repetition and restatement (*agriculture's, farm(s); farm boys; technologists, invention, technical, mechanical, invented; Ford, mechanic*); by pronouns (*its; he, his*); and by transitional expressions (*another, Strictly speaking, Years later*). The paragraph is developed by cause-and-effect analysis and illustration.

3.   As more products and services become available to consumers, their quality and effectiveness seem to decline. To avoid unnecessary frustration and expense, consumers should be well informed before buying products and services. First, they should shop around, hunting among dealers for the best quality, price, and service available. Second, they should consult guides, such as *Consumer Reports,* that are published by nonprofit product-testing services. Finally, they should refuse to accept oral promises, demand to see relevant contracts and warranties, and decline to sign or accept any document they do not fully understand.   —A STUDENT

4.   In the nineteenth century one of American agriculture's bumper crops was extraordinary technologists. The revolution that made possible America's great cities was begun on farms. Elias Howe, Eli Whitney, Thomas Alva Edison, Alexander Graham Bell, George Westinghouse, Orville and Wilbur Wright, the American geniuses of invention, manufacturing, transportation, were farm boys all. And not altogether surprisingly. Whatever its limitations as a teacher of culture or sociability, the farm was a superior forcing house of technical ingenuity and mechanical skill. Henry Ford, another American farm boy, born on a farm outside Dearborn, Michigan, in 1863, was the most famous mechanic the world has known. Strictly speaking, Henry Ford invented nothing, but he tinkered with nearly everything. Years later, recalling his early days on his father's farm, Ford said: "My toys were all tools—they still are."   —JOSEPH EPSTEIN, *Ambition*

Chapter 4

Critical Thinking and Argument

This chapter merges two skills that are essential for college, work, and life. One is thinking and reading critically—looking beneath the surface of words and images to gauge their meaning and importance (4a–4d). The second is writing to influence others—composing a sound and convincing argument that will stand up to critical reading (4d–4h).

4a   Thinking and reading critically

Critical thinking and reading are not necessarily *negative* thinking and reading. *Critical* comes from a Greek word meaning "to separate"; someone who thinks or reads critically separates a subject into its parts, sees how the parts work together, and (often) judges the subject's quality and value. Critical thinking is a means of making discoveries and organizing what you find.

You already use critical thinking, perhaps unconsciously, when you probe your relationships ("What did she mean by that?") or when you discuss a movie you just saw ("Don't you think the villain was too obvious?"). Such questioning can help you figure out why things happen to you or what your experiences mean.

The same is true of more deliberate critical thinking. By applying your critical intelligence to all the information and messages you encounter, you assume the independence and power to

HIGHLIGHTS

The special features of this chapter include (1) the treatment of both reading and writing as acts of critical thinking and (2) considerable attention to the construction of arguments as well as to analysis of their logic. In place of an artificial separation of these subjects, as is common among many other texts, *The Little, Brown Handbook* offers a unified view of the various activities involved in critical thinking.

The opening sections of the chapter (4a and 4b) describe detailed and useful procedures for developing a process of critical reading, including keeping a reading journal, previewing, reading, and rereading. Section 4b then moves to a full discussion of summary, analysis, interpretation, synthesis, and evaluation—the full range of the processes involved in critical reading. The aim of these sections is to assist students in coming to an understanding of the main points in a line of reasoning or argument; the habits of critical reading described here can provide a basis for effective reasoning and argumentative writing. Guidelines in list form are given for each aspect that is considered.

Next, this expansive chapter presents a discussion of reading arguments critically: assertions, evidence, and assumptions are presented, followed by techniques for testing assertions; for identifying fact, opinion, belief, and prejudice; and for looking at a writer's definition of terms, use of evidence, and appeals to beliefs or needs (4c). Students are instructed to examine the reliability of evidence as it works to connect assumptions to assertions, to listen for tone, and to question whether a writer is reasonable. Ways for students to recognize logical fallacies—evasions, oversimplifications—comprise the final section on reading critically.

Students are then introduced to conceiving their own written arguments: the topic, thesis, purpose, and audience are considered before the students are introduced to the concepts of arguing inductively and deductively. As they construct their arguments students will consider their own use of evidence, the most effective appeal to their readers, how to deal with opposing views, organizing their argument, and revising their argument. A helpful checklist for revising argument is given on page 166. The chapter concludes with an annotated sample argument.

crit
4b

RESOURCES AND IDEAS

Victoria Aarons, "Ethical Issues: A Rhetorical Methodology," *The Writing Instructor* 4 (1985): 83–88. Aarons suggests that using ethical issues for class discussion and writing engages students' interest and encourages critical thinking.

RESOURCES AND IDEAS

Stephen Hahn, "Counter-Statement: Using Written Dialogue to Develop Critical Thinking and Writing," *College Composition and Communication* 38 (1987): 97–100. Hahn asks students to create short dialogues focusing on an issue, beginning with a counter-statement such as "That's not music—that's junk" and then moving to response and further responses. In so doing, students can come to an understanding of the context of debate surrounding an issue.

Susan H. McLeod, "Cultural Literacy, Curricular Reform, and Freshman Composition," *Rhetoric Review* 8 (1990): 270–78. McLeod argues that students can be successful in going beyond writing about their own experiences in composition courses by reading and then writing in response to works representative of conversations on a specific topic taking place among scholars.

TRANSPARENCY MASTER
AVAILABLE

decide for yourself what's useful and what's not, what's fair and what's not, what's safe and what's not. You channel your curiosity and exercise your skepticism. You may still need to know what the experts say, but thinking critically allows you to evaluate their ideas and resolve conflicting advice.

A relationship, a television commercial, or anything else you think critically about can be considered a "text." Here we concentrate on literal texts—works of writing—because of all the reading you do in college and because the well-established principles of critical reading can be applied to all forms of critical thinking *and* writing.

4b   Developing a process of critical reading

Like all subjects worthy of critical consideration, written texts operate on at least three levels: (1) what the author actually says, (2) what the author does not say but builds into the text (intentionally or not), and (3) what you think. Discovering the text at each level involves a number of techniques.

> ## Techniques of critical reading
>
> 1. **Writing:** annotating; taking notes (4b-1)
> 2. **Previewing:** getting background; skimming (4b-2)
> 3. **Reading:** absorbing and interacting with the text (4b-3)
> 4. **Summarizing:** distilling content (4b-4)
> 5. **Analyzing:** separating into parts (4b-5)
> 6. **Interpreting:** inferring meaning (4b-5)
> 7. **Synthesizing:** reassembling parts; making comparisons (4b5)
> 8. **Evaluating:** judging quality and value (4b-6)

You certainly will not employ all of these techniques for all the reading you do. Which ones you use will depend on the nature of what you are reading and your **purpose**—why you're reading and what use you plan to put your reading to. For instance, if all you want from *People* magazine is some gossip to fill waiting time in the dentist's office, you'll just read quickly, without analyzing, interpreting, or using other critical techniques. But *People* is not only a light, easy read. It is also an immensely successful artifact of our popular culture, reflecting and perhaps even molding contemporary values. If you want to write about this aspect of *People,* then you will have to give the magazine a close, critical look. Course assignments, too, differ in their demands. A book report generally requires the first four techniques—writing, previewing, reading, and summarizing. A critical evaluation of a journal article, in contrast, requires all the techniques.

1 Writing while reading

There are two good reasons to write while you read: to record information and ideas for future use, and to get more out of the text. The first is discussed in detail as part of research writing (see 36b). The second has more to do with critical reading.

Critical reading is *active* reading. You interact with the text, getting involved with it, bringing to it *your* experiences, ideas, and questions. When you use a pen or pencil while reading, you make writing in response to writing. In this way you "translate" the text into your own words and reconstruct it for yourself.

The writing you do while reading may take several forms. *What* you write will depend on your purpose and your findings during the various stages of reading. *Where* you write will depend on whether you own the material and what kind of thinking you do about it. If you do own the text, you may opt to write directly on the pages as you read them (an illustration of this method appears on p. 123). If you don't own the material, make your notes on a separate sheet or, if the material is brief enough, on a photocopy.

Many readers keep a **reading journal,** a notebook in which they regularly work out questions and thoughts about what they read. One technique for keeping such a journal is to divide a blank page in half, on one side dealing with the text itself (notes, questions, doubts) and on the other side recording what the text makes you think (comparisons with other texts, ideas for writing, and so on). See 1e-1 for more on keeping a journal.

2 Previewing the material

Before you begin reading a text word by word, form some expectations about the work and even some preliminary questions. Your reading will be better informed and more fruitful.

One way to preview a text is to **skim** it: go quickly through it looking for clues about its content, its author, and how you will interact with it. Not the same as idly turning pages, skimming is a

RESOURCES AND IDEAS

John A. Walsh, "Circle Diagrams for Narrative Essays," *Journal of Reading* 32 (1989): 366–68. Walsh teaches students to comprehend and analyze narrative events, relationships, and significance by using a graphic technique of concentric circles.

focused, concentrated activity in which you seek information. Use the following questions as a guide. In your journal write down any impressions that you may want to return to later.

Questions for previewing a text

● How long is the material? Can you read it in one sitting, or should you schedule additional time?
● Do you anticipate particular difficulties—for instance, a technical vocabulary that may require a specialized dictionary?
● What can you tell about the material from its title? From any summary or abstract? From headings or illustrations? What questions do these features raise in your mind?
● What do the facts of publication tell you? Does the publisher or publication specialize in particular kinds of material—scholarly articles, say, or popular books? From the date of publication, do you expect the material to be especially recent or out of date?
● What do you know about the author? Look for biographical information at the back of a book, near the start of an article, and in similar places. The author's other publications, interests, and prior work in the field can give you a sense of his or her expertise and biases.

RESOURCES AND IDEAS

Nancy Kline, "Intertextual Trips: Teaching the Essay in the Composition Class," *Journal of Teaching Writing* 8 (1989): 15–37. Kline believes that essay reading requires interaction, that essays are alive with the exploratory rhetorical strategy used by the writer, that they are playful no matter how serious their subject. She uses the writing of Joan Didion, John Berryman, and Martin Luther King as examples.

 Reading

Reading is itself a process involving two steps and maybe more, depending on the complexity of the material. Your primary goal is to understand that first level on which the text operates—what the author actually says.

First reading

The first time through new material, read as steadily and smoothly as possible. Try to get the gist of what the author is saying and a sense of his or her tone. Try to enjoy the work, seeking connections between the text and your own experiences, appreciating forceful writing, humor, good examples.

To keep up a steady reading pace, use your pencil or pen sparingly during this reading. Mark or note major stumbling blocks—such as a paragraph you don't understand—so that you can try to resolve them before rereading. But resist any urge to make frequent or extensive notes until your next pass.

Rereadings

After the first reading, plan on at least one other. This time read *slowly*. Your first priority should be grasping the content and how it is constructed. That means rereading a paragraph if you didn't get the point, or flipping back a few pages to see how ideas are connected, or looking up key words in a dictionary.

Use your pen or pencil freely to annotate the text or make separate notes. If you can write on the material, use any system of annotations that works for you—perhaps "?" in the margin next to passages you don't understand, circles around unfamiliar words, underlining or brackets for main points, "*" for passages you agree with, "!" for those you find startling, "So what?" for those you can't see the point of.

Below is an example of a reader's annotations. The paragraph is from the essay "America: The Multinational Society," by Ishmael Reed. The annotations are those a student, Terry Perez, made in a textbook containing the essay. (Perez's essay in response to Reed's is examined in Chapters 1 and 2.)

> Such blurring of cultural styles occurs in everyday life in the United States to a greater extent than anyone can imagine and is probably more prevalent than the sensational conflict between people of different backgrounds that is played up and often encouraged by the media. The result is what the Yale professor Robert Thompson referred to as a cultural bouillabaisse, yet members of the nation's present educational and cultural Elect still cling to the notion that the United States belongs to some vaguely defined entity they refer to as "Western civilization," by which they mean, presumably, a civilization created by the people of Europe, as if Europe can be viewed in monolithic terms. Is Beethoven's Ninth Symphony, which includes Turkish marches, a part of Western civilization, or the late nineteenth- and twentieth-century French paintings, whose creators were influenced by Japanese art? And what of the Cubists, through whom the influence of African art changed modern painting, or the Surrealists, who were so impressed with the art of the Pacific Northwest Indians that, in their map of North America, Alaska dwarfs the lower forty-eight in size?

*[Margin annotations: * ethnic conflict exaggerated by media; the elite (politics, education, etc.); (mono=one); Who are they?; In other words, Europe itself isn't "pure" Western.]*

Of course, you should try to answer the questions you raise in such annotations, and that may take another reading or some digging in other sources, such as dictionaries and encyclopedias. The effort will resolve any confusion you feel, or it will give you the confidence to say that your confusion is the fault of the author, not the reader.

crit

4b

RESOURCES AND IDEAS

Further advice on writing summaries, along with a number of examples, is available in Leonard J. Rosen and Laurence Behrens, *Writing Papers in College* (Boston: Scott, 1986), ch. 1.

 ### 4   Summarizing

One of the best ways to master the content of written material and see its strengths and weaknesses is to **summarize** it: distill it to its main points, in your own words. Indeed, some assignments call for summary so that you can demonstrate your understanding. Further, summary is an essential tool in writing about other writing, as in research papers (see 36b).

The essence of summary is *conciseness, objectivity,* and *completeness:* you state in as few words as possible the main thrust of a passage. When you need to summarize a few paragraphs or a brief article, your summary should be no longer than one-fifth the length of the original passage. For longer texts, such as chapters of books or whole books, your summary should be quite a bit shorter in proportion to the original.

The following paragraph appears in a book on the architect Frank Lloyd Wright and concerns a project he designed in 1925. As you read the paragraph, think how you would summarize it.

> [Frank Lloyd Wright's] first spiral, the unbuilt Gordon Strong Automobile Objective Project of 1925, is perhaps the first architectural monument, other than a bridge, conceived expressly for the car. As its title suggests, the sole function of this roadway spiraling up a mountainside to a planetarium at the summit was simply to provide an excuse for pleasure driving. Rather than run a highway past a scenic wonder to provide automobile access, Wright's project was designed not to be seen from the car, but to be an extension *of* the car, to express all that Wright felt the car would come to represent in his culture. And the planetarium showed precisely of what cosmic significance Wright knew the car to be: decades before nations had seriously undertaken to explore, much less colonize, outer space, Wright grasped intuitively that the culture of the highway, barely born, would one day come to maturity among the stars.
> —HERBERT MUSCHAMP, *Man About Town*

Capturing the essence of this paragraph in one concise and accurate sentence could easily take a couple of tries. Here's one:

Draft summary

In 1925, according to Muschamp, Wright proposed an unusual architectural structure just for the car, a road that spiraled up a mountain, which he called the Gordon Strong Automobile Objective Project and which demonstrated how important he thought the car was.

Two techniques for writing summaries

Summarizing brief texts (ten pages or fewer)

1. Write a one-sentence summary of every paragraph.
2. Formulate a single sentence that summarizes the whole. (Look at the author's own summary—a thesis or topic sentence—as a guide.)
3. Write a full paragraph (or more, if needed): begin with the overall-summary sentence and follow it with the paragraph-summary sentences.
4. Rewrite and rearrange the paragraph as needed to make it clear and concise, to eliminate repetition and relatively minor points, and to provide transitions (see 3b-6). The final version should be a unified and coherent whole.

Summarizing longer texts (eleven pages or more)

1. Outline the text. Break it down into its component sections— groups of paragraphs focused on a common topic—and list the main supporting points for each section. (A formal outline may help; see 1g-2.)
2. Write a one- or two-sentence summary of each section.
3. Formulate a single sentence to summarize the whole, looking to the author's thesis sentence or topic sentences as a guide.
4. Write a full paragraph (or more, if needed): begin with the overall-summary sentence and follow it with the section-summary sentences.
5. Rewrite and rearrange the paragraph as needed to make it clear and concise, to eliminate repetition and relatively minor points, and to provide transitions (see 3b-6). The final version should be a unified and coherent whole.

This sentence "misreads" the paragraph because it includes some nonessential points, gives undue weight to the name of the project, and omits the information about the planetarium and *why* Wright considered the car important. Revision produces a more concise and accurate summary:

Revised summary

According to Muschamp, Wright's 1925 proposal for a spiral road up a mountain to a planetarium, called the Gordon Strong Automobile Objective Project, symbolized the architect's belief that the car would dominate American culture and his intuition that that culture would take humans into space.

RESOURCES AND IDEAS

Ellen L. Tripp, "Speak, Listen, Analyze, Respond: Problem-Solving Conferences," *Teaching English in the Two-Year College* 17 (1990): 183–86. Tripp argues that teaching critical thinking involves teaching the entire language experience process of talking, listening, writing, and reading. She suggests a collaborative group activity to define, analyze, talk through, and evaluate problems before groups propose solutions. A final group report is suggested.

Caution: When you write a summary, be careful to avoid plagiarism: use your own words and sentence structures (36b), and identify your source both with a text citation (37a) and in your list of works cited (37b).

 Analyzing, interpreting, synthesizing

Once you've got a grip on the content of what you're reading—what the author says—then you can turn to understanding what the author does not say outright but suggests or implies or even lets slip. At this stage you are concerned with the purpose or intention of the author and with how he or she carries it out. Depending on what you are reading, you may examine evidence, organization, attitude, use of language, and other elements of the text. The next section (p. 132) covers the elements to be considered in critically reading an argument, and Chapter 39 discusses critical reading and writing in the academic disciplines. Here we focus on the basic mental operations necessary for critical reading of all texts.

These operations—analyzing, interpreting, and synthesizing—overlap. Indeed, in this handbook and other texts they are often considered under the general label *analysis*. Defined narrowly, though:

- **Analysis** is the separation of something (such as a text) into its parts or elements.
- **Interpretation** is the determination of meaning or significance—in this case, the meaning or significance of the elements and of the whole.
- **Synthesis** is the connection of elements or wholes, as in relating the parts of one text or relating several texts.

When you use these three operations together, you essentially produce a different work from the one you started with. What may seem at first a straightforward article on Native American art turns out to be a subtle condemnation of the way some museums exploit such art. What seems an objective report on a company's new product proves to be a biased promotion of the product.

Analysis

Your purpose for reading will determine a **framework** for your analysis, which in turn will highlight certain features and suggest certain meanings and patterns. Say you have decided to look at *People* magazine seriously and critically as an object of popular culture. More specifically, your purpose in reading *People* is to investigate whether and how its editorial material (mainly articles, and photographs) encourages readers to buy consumer goods. Your framework, then, would restate that purpose: What elements of *People*'s editorial material (if any) encourage readers to buy consumer goods? This framework automatically eliminates many features from consideration—the advertisements, for instance, or uplifting stories about the handicapped. At the same time, the framework concentrates your attention on relevant features, such as items about celebrities' well-appointed homes, photographs of designer clothes, and articles on the authors of best-selling books.

A difference in analytical framework is a key distinction among academic disciplines. A sociologist neatly outlined the frameworks in three disciplines' approaches to poverty:

> Political science does a wonderful job looking at poverty as a policy issue. Economics does an equally wonderful job looking at it from an income-distribution perspective. But sociology asks how people in poverty live and what they aspire to.

Even within disciplines, analytical frameworks may differ. This sociologist may focus on how people in poverty live, but another might be more interested in the effects of poverty on cities or the changes in the poor population over time. (See Chapter 39 for more on the disciplines' analytical frameworks. A sample literary analysis begins on p. 686.)

Interpretation and synthesis

Taking a text apart, distinguishing its elements according to a framework, is of course only part of critical reading. The parts must be interpreted and synthesized into a new whole, again according to the framework. Sometimes the steps will be simultaneous. In critically reading *People,* for instance, you would have to interpret while analyzing, uncovering the commercial messages in certain stories in order to fit them into your framework. Your synthesis—the pattern you find, the way you reassemble the parts—would then be your conclusion about the magazine. You might, for instance, conclude that *People*'s editorial material regularly encourages consumption by glamorizing it and by introducing and displaying consumer goods.

Note that synthesis also comes into play when you draw connections among two or more works—if, say, you were to pull together examples from *People, Us,* and several other publications to make a point about hidden commercialism in magazines.

crit
4b

TRANSPARENCY MASTER
AVAILABLE

Guidelines for analysis, interpretation, and synthesis

- What is the purpose of your reading?
- What is your framework for analysis? Which elements does it highlight for examination? Which elements can be ignored as a result? (See 4c on argument or Chapter 39 on the academic disciplines for specific frameworks.)
- How do you interpret the meaning and significance of the elements, both individually and in relation to the whole text?
- What patterns can you see in (or synthesize from) the elements? How do the elements relate? How does this whole text relate to another text?
- What do you conclude about the text? What does this conclusion add to the text?

A sample literary essay illustrating analysis, interpretation, and synthesis begins on page 686.

6   Evaluating

Many critical reading and writing assignments end at analysis, interpretation, and synthesis: you explain your understanding of what the author says and doesn't say. Only if you are expected to **evaluate** the work will you state and defend the judgments you've made about its quality and its significance. You'll inevitably form such judgments while reading the work: "What a striking series of images," or "That just isn't enough evidence." In evaluating, you collect your judgments, determine that they are generally applicable and are themselves not trivial, and turn them into assertions: "The poet creates fresh, intensely vivid images"; "The author does not summon the evidence to support his case." And you support these statements with citations from the text.

Evaluation takes a certain amount of confidence. You may feel that you lack the expertise to cast judgment on another's writing, especially if the text is difficult or the author well known. True, the more informed you are the better a critical reader you are. But conscientious reading and analysis will give you the internal authority to judge a work *as it stands* and *as it seems to you,* against your own unique bundle of experiences, observations, and attitudes. Following are some questions that may help you evaluate many kinds of texts. (For arguments and in academic disciplines, you'll require additional, more specific criteria. See the next section and Chapter 39.)

Guidelines for evaluation

- What are your reactions to the text? What in the text are you responding to?
- Is the work unified, with all the parts pertaining to a central idea? Is it coherent, with the parts relating clearly to each other?
- Is the work sound in its general idea? In its details and other evidence?
- Has the author achieved his or her purpose? Is the purpose worthwhile?
- Does the author seem authoritative? Trustworthy? Sincere?
- What is the overall quality of the work? What is its value or significance in the larger scheme of things?
- Do you agree or disagree with the work? Can you support, refute, or extend it?

TRANSPARENCY MASTER
AVAILABLE

Exercise 1
Reading

The passage below is by the historian Daniel J. Boorstin. It appeared in his prize-winning book *The Discoverers* (1983), about human exploration of the earth, the universe, and human beings themselves. Read and reread the passage until you understand what the author is saying. Either separately or on these pages, note your questions and reactions. Look up any words you don't know. (Further exercises on this text appear below.)

COLLABORATIVE LEARNING

ANSWERS: EXERCISE 1

Individual response.

1
In Europe the clock very early became a *public* machine. Churches expected communicants to assemble regularly and repeatedly for prayers, and flourishing cities brought people together to share a life of commerce and entertainment. When clocks took their places in church steeples and town belfries, they entered on a public stage. There they proclaimed themselves to rich and poor, awakening the interest even of those who had no personal reason to mark the hours. Machines that began as public instruments gradually became some of the most widely diffused private instruments. But instruments that began their lives in private might never become diffused into the wants and needs of the whole community. The first advertisement for the clock was the clock itself, performing for new publics all over Europe.

2
No self-respecting European town would be without its public clock, which tolled all citizens together to defend, to celebrate, or to mourn. A community that could focus its resources in a dazzling public clock was that much more a

COLLABORATIVE LEARNING

ANSWERS: EXERCISE 2

1. The sentences that do not adequately summarize Boorstin's paragraphs fail for the reasons mentioned.

   Paragraph 1
   The correct answer is a. Sentence b is biased: notice the introduced word *corrupted*; no sense of this word appears in the original.

   Paragraph 2
   The correct answer is b. As a summary, sentence a is incomplete because communal clocks are not mentioned.

   Paragraph 3
   The correct answer is a. Sentence b is incomplete.

   Paragraph 4
   The correct answer is b. Sentence a is incomplete, for it has no mention of the clock evolving from the cloister, through intermediate stages, to the factory.

2. Here is a one-sentence summary, grouped with a slightly edited version of the paragraph summaries:

   The introduction of clocks into Europe altered religious, private, and industrial relations. Found in the churches and town squares of Europe, clocks were at first public machines that announced events of communal interest. European townspeople were proud of these instruments, which summoned individuals to a common cause and reminded them of their interdependence. After a time, the highly valued town clock became an instrument desired by private citizens, whose increasing reliance on "hourly" organization of the day created ever greater demand for timepieces. Uses of the clock grew secular—moving from the church, originally, to the town belfry, to the home, and finally to the factory, when the "machine-made hour" (as opposed to the natural cycles of the sun, moon, and stars) came to organize everyday life.

community. The bell tolled for all and each, as the poet John Donne noted in 1623, and the tolling of the community's bells was a reminder that "I am involved in mankind."

Many communities, even before they had organized sewage disposal or a water supply, offered the town clock as a public service. In due course each citizen wanted a private clock—first for the household, then for his or her person. When more people had their private timepieces, more other people needed timepieces to fulfill their neighbors' expectations at worship, at work, and at play. 3

All the while, the clock was being secularized—another way of saying it was being publicized. The first European clocks, as we have seen, alerted cloistered monks for their regular prayers, but when the clock moved into the church steeple and then into the town belfry, it moved out to a secular world. This larger public soon required the clock for the whole schedule of daily life. In Europe the artificial hour, the machine-made hour, took the calculations of time out of the calendar-universe, out from the penumbra of astrology, into the bright everyday light. When steam power, electric power, and artificial illumination kept factories going around the clock, when night was assimilated into day, the artificial hour, the clock-marked hour became the constant regimen for everyone. The story of the rise of the clock in the West, then, is the story of new modes and widening arenas of publicity. 4

Exercise 2
Summarizing a brief text

Follow the instructions below to compose a summary of the passage on clocks in Exercise 1.

1. From the options below, choose the one sentence for each paragraph that accurately, objectively summarizes the paragraph. Explain why the other sentence is an inappropriate summary.

   Paragraph 1
   a. Found in the churches and town squares of Europe, clocks were at first public machines that announced events of communal interest, but once displayed, they gradually gained value as private machines.
   b. The invention of the clock, once introduced to the public, inevitably corrupted townspeople, who all too easily allowed a machine to dominate their lives.

   Paragraph 2
   a. European townspeople placed great stock in impressing one another and visitors with the grandness of their public clocks.

b. European townspeople were proud of their public clocks, for clocks summoned individuals to a common cause and reminded them that they were interdependent.

Paragraph 3

a. The highly valued town clock after a time became an instrument desired by private citizens, whose increasing reliance on the "hourly" organization of the day created an ever greater demand for timepieces.

b. After a time, townspeople required private clocks.

Paragraph 4

a. The clock, both public and private, was perfectly suited to the advancements of the modern age and soon came to organize everyday life.

b. Uses of the clock grew increasingly secular—moving from the church, originally, to the town belfry, to the home, and finally to the factory, at which point the "machine-made hour" (as opposed to the natural cycles of sun, moon, and stars) came to organize everyday life.

2. Now write your own one-sentence summary of the entire passage on clocks. Following this sentence, place the four sentences you have chosen as appropriate summaries of the separate paragraphs. Rewrite and rearrange the sentences as needed to achieve clarity, to eliminate repetition, and to ensure a smooth final draft.

Exercise 3
Summarizing a long text

Choose a ten- to twelve-page article, essay, or chapter from a book, and write a summary by following the second technique given on page 125. Work on a passage that at least one other student is also summarizing, and compare your results.

Exercise 4
Analyzing, interpreting, synthesizing

In a few paragraphs write a combined analysis, interpretation, and synthesis of the passage on clocks in Exercise 1 (pp. 129–30). For this exercise your purpose is to examine techniques the author uses to lead the reader to accept his final sentence: "The story of the rise of the clock in the West, then, is the story of new modes and widening arenas of publicity." Consider these elements (consulting the sections in parentheses if you need more help):

Organization: arrangement of ideas and evidence (1g)
Evidence: facts and examples (4c-2)
Repetition and restatement of key words and concepts (3b-3)
Connotations of words: their emotional associations (31b-2)

ANSWERS: EXERCISE 3

Individual response.

ANSWERS: EXERCISE 4
Possible Answers

Organization: In a roughly chronological organization, Boorstin pairs increasing use of clocks with increasing publicity. The two developments seem inextricably linked.

Evidence: Boorstin offers varied evidence, from facts and examples to a citation of contemporary poetry (Donne).

Repetition and restatement: Boorstin keeps his twin subjects always before the reader. In paragraph 1, for example, he traces the two threads through every sentence: *clock, clocks, they, machines, instruments, clock*; and *public, assemble, share a life, public, proclaimed, public, whole community, publics*.

Connotations: Boorstin's language conveys a balanced view of the intertwining evolution of clocks and public life. On the one hand, clocks were *dazzling* (paragraph 2) and drew people together, reached everyone, and furthered reason: they *proclaimed themselves to rich and poor* (1), *diffused into the wants and needs of the whole community* (1), and brought time from the *penumbra of astrology* into *bright everyday light* (4). On the other hand, clocks controlled life: they were used to *fulfill . . . neighbors' expectations* (3), they allowed factories to run *around the clock* (4), and they created a *constant regimen for everyone* (4).

COLLABORATIVE LEARNING

ANSWERS: EXERCISE 5

Individual response.

RESOURCES AND IDEAS

Barbara Deane, "Putting the Inferential Process to Work in the Classroom," *College Composition and Communication* 27 (1976): 50–52. Deane describes activities to help students develop their ability to make accurate inferences.

Exercise 5
Evaluating

Write a brief evaluation of the passage on clocks in Exercise 1 (pp. 129–30). Note that the four paragraphs are not an independent essay but a small part of Daniel Boorstin's long book *The Discoverers*. Thus the author's overall thesis and structure have affected the passage in ways not evident to you. Still, the passage is complete enough to judge on its own, using the guidelines on page 129.

4c **Reading arguments critically**

Writing that attempts to change your mind or move you to action is especially worthy of critical reading. Such writing, called **argument,** bombards us through the communications media —in newspaper editorials, magazine articles, televised political speeches, advertising, and many other forms. It also appears regularly in college reading, where, for instance, a psychologist defends a theory or a physicist disputes another's data. Indeed, reading and writing arguments are essential skills for college work. (We'll get to writing arguments in sections 4e–4h.)

Usually in reading arguments you can let the writer's purpose shape yours. If the writer wants to convince you that a tuition increase is justified, then you seek to discover whether you *should* be convinced. If the writer wants to persuade you to vote against a bottle-return referendum, then you seek to discover whether you *should* cast a "no" vote.

In one simple scheme an argument has three parts:

1. **Assertions:** positive statements that require support. In an argument the central assertion is stated outright as the **thesis** (see 1f): it is what the argument is about. For instance:

   The college needs a new chemistry laboratory to replace the existing outdated lab.

   Several minor assertions, such as that the present equipment is inadequate, will contribute to the central assertion.

2. **Evidence:** the facts, examples, expert opinions, and other information that support the assertions. Evidence to support the assertion above might include

   The present lab's age
   An inventory of equipment
   The testimony of chemistry professors

   Like the assertions, the evidence is always stated outright.

3. **Assumptions:** opinions or beliefs held by the writer that tie the evidence to the assertions. For instance, the following assumption might connect the evidence of professors' testimony with the assertion that a new lab is needed:

Chemistry professors are the most capable of evaluating the present lab's quality.

Assumptions are always present in arguments, but they are not always stated outright. Sometimes the writer judges that readers already understand and accept the assumptions (the probable case with the assumption above). Sometimes the writer is not aware of his or her own assumptions. And sometimes the writer deliberately refrains from stating an assumption because it may not appeal to readers. Stated and especially unstated assumptions can strengthen or seriously weaken an argument.

In the following pages, we'll examine each of these components and the ways they are put together.

RESOURCES AND IDEAS

Barbara E. Winder, "The Delineation of Values in Persuasive Writing," *College Composition and Communication* 29 (1978): 55–58. Winder asks writers to spell out both sides of an argument to make them sensitive to their own values and those of their readers.

crit
4c

Questions for critically reading an argument

- What kind of **assertions** does the writer make? (4c-1)
- What kind and quality of **evidence** does the writer use? (4c-2)
- What **assumptions** is the writer making? (4c-3)
- What is the writer's **tone**? How does the writer use **language**? (4c-4)
- Is the writer **reasonable**? (4c-5)
- Is the argument logical? Has the writer committed any **logical fallacies**? (4d)

TRANSPARENCY MASTER
AVAILABLE

 Testing assertions

The assertions in an argument carry specific burdens: they should state arguable opinions, and they should define their terms.

Fact, opinion, belief, and prejudice

Most statements we hear, read, or make in speaking and writing are assertions of fact, opinion, belief, or prejudice. In an argu-

CUT AND PASTE

Ask groups of students to identify an issue, collect newspaper or magazine articles on it, and bring the articles to class (in photocopied form, if possible). Then ask them to identify what the articles say on the different sides of the issue and to cut out the assertions and paste them in columns (or simply write them out) according to the particular perspective on the argument they represent.

ANALYZING ISSUES

Have students, in groups, discuss a campus issue like residential policies, parking arrangements, or library or computer services, trying to
identify the assertions and supporting evidence
on each side of the argument. List the assertions
and evidence on the board so that students can
distinguish fact from opinion and identify terms
that need defining. If students know enough
about issues of public policy (such as gun control, capital punishment, or nuclear disarmament), these topics, too, can be used for discussion.

ment the acceptability of an assertion depends partly on which of
these categories it falls into.

A **fact** is verifiable—that is, one can determine whether it is
true. It may involve numbers or dates: *The football field is 100
yards long. World War II ended in 1945.* Or the numbers may be
implied: *The earth is closer to the sun than Saturn is. The cost of
medical care is rising.* Or the fact may involve no numbers at all:
*The city council adjourned without taking a vote. The President
vetoed the bill.* The truth of the fact is beyond argument if one can
assume that measuring devices or records or memories are correct. Facts provide crucial support for the assertions of an argument. But because they are inarguable, they do not make worthwhile assertions by themselves.

An **opinion** is a judgment *based* on facts, an honest attempt
to draw a reasonable conclusion from evidence. For example, a
writer who knows that millions of people can't afford proper
medical care may form the judgment that the country should institute national health insurance even though it would cost billions
of dollars. This opinion expresses a viewpoint. It is arguable because the same facts might lead another reasonable person to a
different opinion (for instance, that the country simply can't afford
costly national health insurance, even if people must go without
proper medical care). And the opinion is potentially changeable:
with more evidence the writer might conclude that the problem
of inadequate medical care could be solved by other means less
costly than national health insurance.

The main assertion, or thesis, of an argument is always an
opinion. Other, more specific assertions of opinion generally
form the backbone of the argument supporting the thesis. By
themselves, however, opinions do not make arguments. As a critical reader, you must satisfy yourself that the writer has specified
the evidence and that the assumptions linking assertions and evidence are clear and believable.

An opinion is not the same as a **belief,** a conviction based on
cultural or personal faith, morality, or values. Statements such as
Capital punishment is legalized murder and *The primary goal of
government should be to provide equality of opportunity for all*
are often called opinions because they express viewpoints. Unlike
opinions, however, such beliefs are not based on facts and other
evidence. Since they cannot be disproved by facts or even contested on the basis of facts, they are not arguable. Thus they
should not serve as the central assertion of an argument. However, as long as readers share the writer's feelings, statements of
belief can serve an argument as a kind of evidence, and they often
form the assumptions linking assertions and evidence. For instance, a writer might support an argument that the country

should institute national health insurance not only with facts demonstrating the need but also with the assertion that a nation cannot be strong while millions of its citizens suffer needlessly from poor health. If you as reader agree with this assertion, you will probably be more open to other parts of the writer's argument.

One kind of assertion that has no place in argument is **prejudice,** an opinion based on insufficient or unexamined evidence: *Women are bad drivers. Fat people are jolly. Teenagers are irresponsible.* Unlike a belief, a prejudice is testable: it can be contested and disproved on the basis of facts. Very often, however, we form prejudices or accept them from others—parents, friends, the communications media—without questioning their meaning or testing their truth. At best, they are thoughtless oversimplifications: *some* women are bad drivers, but so are *some* men. At worst, assertions of prejudice reflect a narrow-minded view of the world. Writers who display prejudice do not deserve the confidence and agreement of readers. Readers who accept prejudice are not thinking critically.

Defined terms

In any argument, but especially in arguments about abstract ideas, clear and consistent definition of terms is essential. In the following assertion the writer is not clear about what she means by *justice*.

> Over the past few decades justice has deteriorated so badly that it almost does not exist anymore.

We can't tell what the writer is asserting because we don't know what *justice,* the crucial term of the sentence, means to her. The word is **abstract:** it does not refer to anything specific or concrete and in fact has varied meanings. (The seven definitions in *The American Heritage Dictionary* include "the principle of moral rightness" and "the administration and procedure of law.") When the writer specifies her meaning, her assertion is much clearer.

> If by *justice* we mean treating people fairly, punishing those who commit crimes, and protecting the victims of those crimes, then justice has deteriorated badly over the past few decades.

Of course, we need to see how this writer supports her assertion before we can accept it, but at least we now understand her definition of *justice*.

Writers who use highly abstract words such as *justice, equality, success,* and *maturity* have a responsibility to define them. If the word is important to the argument, such a definition may take

crit
4c

an entire paragraph. As a reader you have the obligation to evaluate the writer's definitions before you accept his or her assertions. (See Chapter 3, pp. 97–98, for more on definition and a paragraph defining the abstract word *quality*.)

 Weighing evidence

In argument, evidence demonstrates the validity of the writer's assertions. If the evidence is inadequate or questionable, the assertions are at best doubtful.

Kinds of evidence

Writers draw on several kinds of evidence to support their assertions.

Evidence for argument

- **Facts:** verifiable statements.
- **Statistics:** facts expressed in numbers.
- **Examples:** specific cases.
- **Expert opinions:** the judgments of authorities.
- **Appeals to readers' beliefs or needs.**

Facts are statements whose truth can be verified by observation or research (see p. 134).

> Poland is slightly smaller than New Mexico.
> Insanity is grounds for divorce in a majority of the states.

Facts employing numbers are **statistics.**

> Of those polled, 62 percent stated a preference for a flat tax.
> In 1988 there were 2,138,000 men and women in the U.S. armed forces.
> The average American household consists of 2.64 persons.

Examples are specific instances of the point being made, including historical precedents. The following passage uses a personal narrative as partial support for assertion in the first sentence.

> Besides broadening students' knowledge, required courses can also introduce students to possible careers that they otherwise

---

EVIDENCE IN EDITORIALS

Distribute copies of newspaper editorials, and ask students, in groups, to examine the evidence the editorials contain in order to (1) identify facts, statistics, examples, and expert opinions and (2) evaluate the evidence for accuracy, relevance, representativeness, adequacy, and reliability. Then ask the groups to compare the results of their analysis and evaluation.

TRANSPARENCY MASTER
AVAILABLE

would have known nothing about. Somewhat reluctantly, I en-rolled in a psychology course to satisfy the social science re-quirement. But what I learned in the course about human behav-ior has led me to consider becoming a clinical psychologist instead of an engineer.

Expert opinions are the judgments formed by authorities on the basis of their own examination of the facts. In the following passage the writer cites the opinion of an expert to support the assertion in the first sentence.

> Despite the fact that affirmative action places some individuals at a disadvantage, it remains necessary to right the wrongs inflicted historically on whole groups of people. Howard Glickstein, a past director of the U.S. Commission on Civil Rights, maintains that "it simply is not possible to achieve equality and fairness" unless the previous grounds for discrimination (such as sex, race, and na-tional origin) are now used as the grounds for admission to schools and jobs (26).

As this passage illustrates, a citation of expert opinion should al-ways refer the reader to the source, here indicated by the page number in parentheses, "(26)." Such a citation is also generally ac-companied by a reference to the expert's credentials. See 36g and 37a.

Appeals to beliefs or needs are statements that ask readers to accept an assertion in part because it states something they ac-cept as true without evidence or because it coincides with their needs. Each of the following examples combines such an appeal (second sentence) with a summary of factual evidence (first sen-tence).

> Thus the chemistry laboratory is outdated in its equipment. In addition, its shabby, antiquated appearance shames the school, making it seem a second-rate institution. [Appeals to readers' be-lief that their school is or should be first-rate.]

> That police foot patrollers reduce crime has already been dem-onstrated. Such officers might also restore our sense that our neighborhoods are orderly, stable places. [Appeals to readers' need for order and stability.]

(For more on beliefs, see p. 134. For more on appeals to emotion, see p. 160.)

The reliability of evidence

To support assertions and convince readers, evidence must be reliable. The tests of reliability for appeals to readers' beliefs and needs are specific to the situation: whether they are appropriate for the argument and correctly gauge how readers actually feel (see p. 162). With the other kinds of evidence, the standards are more general, applying to any argument.

Criteria for weighing evidence

- Is it **accurate?**
- Is it **relevant?**
- Is it **representative?**
- Is it **adequate?**

balance of argument

don't take out of context

Accurate evidence is drawn from trustworthy sources, quoted exactly, and presented with the original meaning unchanged. In an essay favoring gun control, for instance, the writer should not rely exclusively on procontrol sources, which are undoubtedly somewhat biased. Instead, the writer should also cite anticontrol sources (representing the opposite bias) and neutral sources (attempting to be unbiased). If the writer quotes an expert, the quotation should present the expert's true meaning, not just a few words that happen to support the writer's argument. (As a reader, you may have difficulty judging the accuracy of quotations if you are not familiar with the expert's opinions.)

Not just opinions but also facts and examples may be misinterpreted or distorted. Suppose you were reading an argument for extending a three-year-old law allowing the police to stop vehicles randomly as a means of apprehending drunk drivers. If the author cited statistics showing that the number of drunk-driving accidents dropped in the first two years of the law, but failed to note that the numbers rose back to the previous level in the third year, then the evidence would be distorted and thus inaccurate. You or any reader would be justified in questioning the entire argument, no matter how accurate the rest seemed.

Relevant evidence comes from sources with authority on a topic and relates directly to the point the writer is making. Unless the writer's uncle is a recognized expert on the disposal of hazardous wastes, or unless the writer establishes the uncle's authority, his opinion that a planned disposal method is safe is not relevant to an argument on the subject. If the writer's aunt is a member of the town council, however, her views may very well be relevant evidence in an argument that a new shopping mall will hurt the town merchants.

Representative evidence reflects the full range of the sample from which it is said to be drawn. For instance, in an essay

RESOURCES AND IDEAS

Kathleen McCormick, "Teaching Critical Thinking and Writing," *The Writing Instructor* 2 (1983): 137–44. McCormick suggests having students develop critical and analytical skills by critiquing flawed essays, and she describes several units in a course employing this strategy.

arguing that dormitories should stay open during school holidays, a writer might say that "the majority of the school's students favor leaving the dormitories open." But that writer would mislead you and other readers if the statement were based only on a poll of her roommates and dormitory neighbors. A few dormitory residents could not be said to represent the entire student body, particularly the nonresident students. To be representative the poll would have to take in many more students in proportions that reflect the numbers of resident and nonresident students on campus.

[**Adequate evidence** is plentiful and specific enough to support a writer's assertions.] A writer arguing against animal abuse cannot hope to win over readers solely with statements such as *Too many animals are deliberately injured or killed by humans every year.* He needs to supply facts instead of the vague *too many.* How many animals are injured? How many die? He needs to specify the conditions under which animals are injured or killed. And he needs to demonstrate that the actions are deliberate, perhaps with examples of animal abuse.

3   Discovering assumptions

[Assumptions connect evidence to assertions: they provide the reason why a particular piece of evidence is relevant to a particular assertion.] In argument the word *assumption* has narrower meanings than in everyday usage, where it may stand for expectation ("I assume you will pay"), speculation ("It was a mere assumption"), or error ("The report was riddled with assumptions"). [Defined more strictly as beliefs or opinions that the writer *supposes* to be true, assumptions are unavoidable in argument, as they are in life. We all adhere to certain values and beliefs; we all form opinions. And we live our lives by such assumptions.]

Their inevitability does not make assumptions neutral, however. For one thing, they can weaken an argument. For instance, a writer may claim that real estate development should be prevented in the town. As evidence for this assertion, the writer offers facts about past developments that have replaced older buildings. But the evidence is relevant to the assertion only if you accept the writer's extreme assumptions that old buildings are always worthy and new development is always bad.

In such a case, the writer's bias may not even be stated. Hence a second problem: in arguments both sound and unsound, assumptions are not always explicit. Here, for example, is a summary of a reasonable argument. What is the unstated assumption?

Assertion

The town should create a plan to manage building preservation and new development.

Evidence

Examples of how such plans work; expert opinions on how and why both preservation and development are needed.

In this instance the assumption is that neither uncontrolled development nor zero development is healthy for the town. If you can accept this assumption, you should be able to accept the writer's claim (though you might still disagree over particulars).

The differences between the two assumptions above can be formulated in a few guidelines.

√ Guidelines for analyzing assumptions

- What are the assumptions underlying the argument? How does the writer connect assertions with evidence?
- Are the assumptions believable? Do they express your values? Do they seem true in your experience?
- Are the assumptions consistent with each other? Is the argument's foundation solid, not slippery?

---

4   Watching language, hearing tone

Tone is the expression of the writer's attitudes toward himself or herself, toward the subject, and toward the reader (see 1d-3, p. 14, for a full discussion). Tone can tell you quite a bit about the writer's intentions, biases, and trustworthiness. For example:

> Some women cite personal growth as a reason for pursuing careers while raising children. Of course, they are equally concerned with the personal growth of the children they relegate to "child-care specialists" while they work.

In the second sentence this writer is being **ironic,** saying one thing while meaning another. The word *relegate* and the quotation marks with *child-care specialists* betray the writer's belief that working mothers may selfishly neglect their children for their own needs. Irony can sometimes be effective in argument, but here it marks the author as insincere in dealing with the complex issues of working parents and child care.

When reading arguments, you should be alert for the author's language. Look for words that **connote,** or suggest, certain attitudes and evoke certain responses in readers. Connotative language is no failure in argument; indeed, the strongest arguments use it skillfully to appeal to readers' hearts as well as their minds (see 4g-1, p. 160). But be suspicious if the language runs counter to the substance of the argument.

Look also for evasive words. **Euphemisms,** such as *peace-keeping force* for a war-making army or *attack of a partly sexual nature* for "rape," are supposedly inoffensive substitutes for words that may frighten or offend readers (see 31a-7). In argument, though, they are sometimes used to hide or twist the truth. An honest, forthright arguer will avoid them.

Finally, watch carefully for sexist, racist, and other biased language that reveals deep ignorance or, worse, entrenched prejudice on the part of the writer. Obvious examples are *broad* for women and *fag* for homosexual. See 31a-8 for more on biased language.

5   Judging reasonableness

The **reasonableness** of an argument is the sense you get as reader that the author is fair and sincere. The reasonable writer does not conceal or distort facts, hide prejudices, mask belief as opinion, manipulate you with language, or resort to any of dozens of devices used unconsciously by those who don't know better and deliberately by those who do.

Reasonableness involves all the elements of argument examined so far: assertions, evidence, assumptions, and language. In addition, the fair, sincere argument always avoids so-called logical fallacies (covered in the next section), and it acknowledges the opposition. Judging whether the opposition is adequately dealt with is a fairly simple matter for the reader of argument. By definition, an arguable issue has more than one side. Even if you have no preconceptions about a subject, you will know that another side exists. If the writer pretends otherwise, or dismisses the opposition too quickly, you are justified in questioning the honesty and fairness of the argument. (For the more complicated business of *writing* an acknowledgment of the opposition, see p. 162.)

Exercise 6
Testing assertions

Identify the assertions of fact, opinion, belief, and prejudice in the following paragraph.

ANSWERS: EXERCISE 6
Possible Answers

The paragraph is reprinted below, with *F* for fact, *O* for opinion, *B* for belief, and *P* for prejudice.

(*F*) Cigarette advertising has already been banned from television and radio, and (*O*) the time has come to ban it from newspapers, magazines, and billboards as well. (*F*) Numerous research studies have linked smoking with disease and death, and (*B*) it is simply wrong to advertise a health- and life-threatening activity. Nonetheless, (*F*) the major tobacco companies continue to spend more than $1.5 billion a year advertising their products. In sharp contrast, (*F*) the federal government and health organizations such as the American Lung Association spend perhaps $20 *million* a year on programs and advertisements designed to educate the public about the dangers of smoking. Clearly, (*O*) these efforts cannot begin to counterbalance the onslaught of the tobacco companies' messages that smoking gives a person romance, beauty, fun, and happiness. And even if there were more balance in what the public is told about smoking, (*P*) people who smoke are so mindless that they would ignore the warnings and heed only the sales pitches.

ANSWERS: EXERCISE 7

Possible Answers

The meaning of *current problems* is vague and shifting. At first, the writer seems to mean the high cost of living caused by scarcities. But in the last sentence a new problem appears: insecurity. *Self-sufficiency* is similarly vague, defined only by the examples of freeing ourselves from grocery and department stores. A possible revision:

The best solution to one current problem— helplessness in the face of rising prices—is one you don't hear very often: self-sufficiency. If we were more self-sufficient, we would not have to rely so much on scarce resources to satisfy basic needs. Instead, we could draw on our innate or easily learned capacities to provide for ourselves. With an inexpensive sewing machine, some fabric, some skill, and time, a person can be at least partly independent of clothing stores. With a good-sized garden, some tools and supplies, and work, a family can grow a year's supply of vegetables and be completely independent of the grocery store's produce section. Any degree of self-sufficiency provides not only the economic reward of avoiding high prices but also the psychological reward of no longer feeling helpless.

ANSWERS: EXERCISE 8

Possible Answers

1. *Facts/statistics:* increase in burglaries and robberies. *Examples:* burglary of parents' house, picking of roommate's pocket, mugging of old man. *Expert opinion:* none. *Appeals:* to readers' disdain for the police and fear of crime.
   Evaluation: The evidence is presumably accurate and seems relevant enough, but it does not support the writer's claim that crime is *rampant*. The examples are unrepresentative and inadequate, and the statistics concern only robberies and burglaries (not crime in general) and do not support the word *rampant.*

2. *Statistics:* 70 billion pieces a year, $200 billion a year return, 4 million tons a year, 45 pounds per adult, half to the dump, 5 percent of available space. *Other facts:* destroys millions of trees, ruins landscape, fouls waterways. *Examples:* none. *Expert opinion:*

Cigarette advertising has already been banned from television and radio, and the time has come to ban it from newspapers, magazines, and billboards as well. Numerous research studies have linked smoking with disease and death, and it is simply wrong to advertise a health- and life-threatening activity. Nonetheless, the major tobacco companies continue to spend more than $1.5 billion a year advertising their products. In sharp contrast, the federal government and health organizations such as the American Lung Association spend perhaps $20 *million* a year on programs and advertisements designed to educate the public about the dangers of smoking. Clearly, these efforts cannot begin to counterbalance the onslaught of the tobacco companies' messages that smoking gives a person romance, beauty, fun, and happiness. And even if there were more balance in what the public is told about smoking, people who smoke are so mindless that they would ignore the warnings and heed only the sales pitches.

Exercise 7
Defining terms

The following paragraph fails to define important words clearly enough for us to pin down the meaning intended. Identify the undefined terms and revise the paragraph as you see fit to eliminate the problems.

The best solution to current problems is one we don't hear of very often: self-sufficiency. If we were more self-sufficient, we would not have to rely so much on scarce resources to satisfy basic needs. Sure, some of us play at gardening, sewing, and other skills, but very few of us try to free ourselves of the grocery store's vegetables or the department store's clothes. If we were more self-sufficient, we would be more secure because independence ultimately creates a bond between individuals.

Exercise 8
Weighing evidence

Locate the statements of evidence in the following passages. Identify each as a fact, statistic, example, expert opinion, or appeal to readers' beliefs or needs. Evaluate the reliability of the evidence: is it accurate, relevant, representative, and adequate to support the writer's assertions?

1. Crime is rampant in this city. Three months ago my parents' house was burglarized. The thieves stole their food processor and their vibrating bed as well as their television and stereo. Then a month ago my roommate had her pocket picked on the bus. And last week I saw a confused old man trying to describe to the police how muggers had stolen his wallet and his groceries as he walked home from the corner market. The police depart-

ment, as usual too ineffectual to do anything about crime, recently announced that since last year burglaries have risen 7 percent and robberies have risen 12 percent. While this may not yet be a tidal wave, at this rate it is inevitable that criminal elements will be running the city before long.

2.   Third-class "junk" mail now circulates at a rate of more than 70 billion pieces a year. According to June B. Hasbah of Market Direct, that number is bound to increase because the direct-mail marketing strategy works for businesses and charities to the tune of $200 billion a year. But all that commerce is working less well for the environment. Producing the paper required destroys millions of trees each year, ruins our beautiful natural landscape, and fouls our waterways. Furthermore, a year's total load of junk mail weighs more than 4 million tons—nearly forty-five pounds per adult American. Half of that goes straight to the dump, where junk mail fills nearly 5 percent of the available space. Junk mail may work for the individual businessperson or fund-raiser, and it may work for the individual consumer, but it does not work for the community.

Exercise 9
Discovering assumptions

Discover and analyze the stated and unstated assumptions in the two passages above (Exercise 8). For each passage, how do the assumptions connect assertions and evidence? Is each assumption believable? Are the assumptions consistent?

Exercise 10
Watching language, hearing tone

Analyze the tone of the two passages in Exercise 8, above. Based on the words in each passage and the way they are used, what do you think is each writer's attitude toward self, subject, and reader? Do you see any instances of evasion or biased language?

4d   Recognizing logical fallacies

This section is positioned between reading and writing arguments because you'll need to know **logical fallacies**—errors in reasoning—as both a reader (to spot them) and a writer (to avoid them). The many common fallacies below fall into two groups. Some evade the issue of the argument. Others treat the argument as if it were much simpler than it is.

*2 groups
1. evasion
2. simplification*

Hasbah. *Appeals*: to readers' concern for the environment and respect for community. *Evaluation*: The writer omits hard statistics on environmental degradation—a serious weakness. Otherwise, the evidence seems accurate, relevant, representative, and adequate to support the claim that junk mail *does not work for the community.*

ANSWERS: EXERCISE 9
Possible Answers

1. Among the assumptions: (1) one's personal connections with crime indicate how much crime there is; (2) crime rises because the police are ineffectual; (3) crime-rate increases of 7 and 12 percent are high; (4) when the crime rate is rising, it will inevitably continue to rise. Although consistent, the assumptions are debatable (1, 3), oversimplified (2), or not believable (4).

2. Among the assumptions: (1) commerce has a price; (2) the environment is worth preserving; (3) the environment is a community concern; (4) the community has needs separate from those of individuals. The assumptions are consistent and would be accepted by many readers.

ANSWERS: EXERCISE 10
Possible Answers

1. The tone is passionate, intemperate: *rampant, too ineffectual to do anything, confused old man, inevitable, running the city.* The writer seems to be caught up in his or her opinions, to be anxious and angry about crime, and to assume that readers already agree and need not be reasoned with.

2. The tone is reasonable but forceful: junk mail *works,* but it also *destroys, ruins,* and *fouls.* The no-nonsense language emphasizes huge quantities: *all that commerce, total load of junk mail.* The writer seems sure of his or her opinion, determined to make a point about junk mail with an abundance of statistics, and yet aware that readers may not necessarily recognize the problem or readily agree.

log
4d

RESOURCES AND IDEAS

Angela A. Rapkin, "The Uses of Logic in the College Freshman English Curriculum," *Activities to Promote Critical Thinking,* ed. Jeff Golub (Urbana: NCTE, 1986) 130–35. Rapkin suggests emphasizing logic in all the papers in a course and describes in detail the use of ads in a final argumentation unit, a strategy that expands awareness of the logical fallacies students have been developing throughout the course.

TRANSPARENCY MASTER
AVAILABLE

Checklist of logical fallacies

Evasions

1. **Begging the question:** treating an opinion that is open to question as if it were already proved or disproved.
2. **Non sequitur** ("it does not follow"): drawing a conclusion from irrelevant evidence.
3. **Inappropriate appeals:**

   Appealing to readers' fear or pity
   Snob appeal: appealing to readers' wish to be like those who are more intelligent, famous, rich, and so on.
   Bandwagon: appealing to readers' wish to be part of the group.
   Flattery: appealing to readers' intelligence, taste, and so on.
   Argument ad populum ("to the people"): appealing to readers' general values such as patriotism or love of family.
   Argument ad hominem ("to the man"): attacking the opponent rather than the opponent's argument.

Oversimplifications

1. **Hasty generalization (jumping to a conclusion):** asserting an opinion based on too little evidence. **Absolute statements** and **stereotypes** are variations.
2. **Reductive fallacy:** generally, oversimplifying causes and effects.
3. **Post hoc fallacy:** assuming that *A* caused *B* because *A* preceded *B*.
4. **Either/or fallacy (false dilemma):** reducing a complicated question to two alternatives.
5. **False analogy:** exaggerating the similarities in an analogy or ignoring key differences.

Recognizing evasions

The central assertion of an argument defines an issue or question: Should real estate development be controlled? Should the country adopt national health insurance? An effective argument faces the central issue squarely with relevant opinions, beliefs, and evidence. An ineffective argument dodges the issue.

Begging the question

A writer **begs the question** by treating an opinion that is open to question as if it were already proved or disproved. (In essence, the writer begs readers to accept his or her ideas from the start.) For example, a writer begs the question when arguing that the expenses of the school library should be reduced by cutting subscriptions to useless periodicals. Without supplying the necessary evidence, the writer asserts that at least some of the library's periodicals are useless and then uses that unproved assertion to support the proposal.

The following sentence begs the question in a slightly different way.

> Teenagers should be prevented from having abortions, for they would not become pregnant in the first place if they weren't allowed to terminate their "mistakes."

The writer assumes—and asks us to agree—that the option of having an abortion leads teenagers to unwanted pregnancies; therefore, removing the option of abortion will remove the problem of pregnancy. But how can we agree when we still have no proof for the fundamental assertion? The writer has merely substituted one debatable assumption for another.

Non sequitur

A **non sequitur** occurs when no logical relation exists between two or more connected ideas. In Latin *non sequitur* means "it does not follow." In the following sentences the second thought does not follow from the first.

> If high school English were easier, fewer students would have trouble with the college English requirement. [Presumably, if high school English were easier, students would have *more* trouble.]

> Kathleen Newsome has my vote for mayor because she has the best-run campaign organization. [Shouldn't one's vote be based on the candidate's qualities, not the campaign organization's?]

Inappropriate appeals

Appeals to readers' emotions are common in effective arguments. But such appeals must be relevant and must supplement rather than substitute for facts, examples, and other evidence.

Writers sometimes ignore the question with **appeals to readers' fear or pity.**

By electing Susan Clark to the city council, you will prevent the city's economic collapse. [Trades on people's fears. Can Clark single-handedly prevent economic collapse?]

She should not have to pay taxes because she is an aged widow with no friends or relatives. [Appeals to people's pity. Should age and loneliness, rather than income, determine a person's tax obligation?]

Sometimes writers ignore the question by appealing to readers' sense of what other people believe or do. One approach is **snob appeal,** inviting readers to accept an assertion in order to be identified with others they admire.

As any literate person knows, James Joyce is the best twentieth-century novelist. [But what qualities of Joyce's writing make him a superior novelist?]

Paul Newman's support for the governor proves that the governor is doing a good job. [What has the governor actually accomplished?]

A similar tactic invites readers to accept an assertion because everybody else does. This is the **bandwagon approach.**

As everyone knows, marijuana use leads to heroin addiction. [What is the evidence?]

No one in this town would consider voting for him. [What is the basis for judging him?]

Yet another diversion involves **flattery** of readers, in a way inviting them to join in a conspiracy.

We all understand campus problems well enough to see the disadvantages of such a backward policy. [What are the disadvantages of the policy?]

The **argument ad populum** ("argument to the people") asks readers to accept a conclusion based on shared values or even prejudices and nothing else.

Any truly patriotic American will support the President's action. [But why is the action worth taking?]

One final and very common kind of inappropriate emotional appeal addresses *not* the pros and cons of the issue itself but the real or imagined negative qualities of the people who hold the opposing view. This kind of argument is called **ad hominem,** Latin for "to the man."

We need not listen to her arguments against national health insurance because she is wealthy enough to afford private insurance. [Her wealth does not necessarily discredit her views on health insurance.]

One of the scientists has been treated for emotional problems, so his pessimism about nuclear war merits no attention. [Do the scientist's previous emotional problems invalidate his current views?]

You'll recognize most of these tricks for evading the issue from advertising and political campaigns. Are your children's teeth cavity-free? Is your kitchen floor as spotless as your neighbor's? Are you the only person who does not eat a certain brand of cereal? Is that candidate as incompetent as his opponent says? Such pitches betray carelessness at best, dishonesty at worst.

 2   **Recognizing oversimplifications**

- To **oversimplify** is to conceal or ignore complexities in a vain attempt to create a neater, more convincing argument than reality allows.

Hasty generalization

A **hasty generalization** is an assertion based on too little evidence or on evidence that is unrepresentative. (This fallacy is also called **jumping to a conclusion.**) For example:

Because it trains one for work, business is the only major worth pursuing. [Other majors train one for work, and other students may have different goals.]

When attendance is down and the team is losing, the basketball coach should be fired. [The sentence does not allow for other influences on the team's performance.]

A variation of the hasty generalization is the **absolute statement** involving words such as *all, always, never,* and *no one* that allow no exceptions. Rarely can evidence support such terms. Moderate words such as *some, sometimes, rarely,* and *few* are more reasonable.

Another common hasty generalization is the **stereotype,** a conventional and oversimplified characterization of a group of people: the British are reserved; the Italians are emotional. Applying such a characterization to an individual Briton or Italian extends a prejudice, an opinion based on insufficient or unexamined evidence (see p. 135). Here are several other stereotypes: *People who live in cities are unfriendly. Californians are fad-crazy. Women are emotional. Men are less expressive than women.* (See also 31a-8 on sexist and other biased language.)

Reductive fallacy

The **reductive fallacy** oversimplifies (or reduces) the relation between causes and their effects. The fallacy (sometimes called **oversimplification**) often involves linking two events as if one caused the other directly, whereas the causes may be more complex or the relation may not exist at all. For example:

> Poverty causes crime. [If so, then why do people who are not poor commit crimes? And why aren't all poor people criminals?]

> The better a school's athletic facilities are, the worse its academic programs are. [The sentence assumes a direct cause-and-effect link between athletics and scholarship.]

Post hoc fallacy

Related to the reductive fallacy is the assumption that because *A* preceded *B,* then *A* must have caused *B.* This fallacy is called in Latin *post hoc, ergo propter hoc,* meaning "after this, therefore because of this," or the **post hoc fallacy** for short.

> In the two months since he took office, Mayor Holcomb has allowed crime in the city to increase 2 percent. [The increase in crime is no doubt attributable to conditions existing before Holcomb took office.]

> The town council erred in permitting the adult bookstore to open, for shortly afterward two women were assaulted. [It cannot be assumed without evidence that the women's assailants visited or were influenced by the bookstore.]

Either/or fallacy

In the **either/or fallacy** (also called **false dilemma**) the writer assumes that a complicated question has only two answers, one good and one bad, both bad, or both good.

> City police officers are either brutal or corrupt. [Most city police officers are neither.]

Either we institute national health insurance or thousands of people will become sick or die. [Allowing people to sicken or die is not necessarily the only alternative to national health insurance.]

False analogy

An **analogy** is a comparison between two essentially unlike things for the purpose of definition or illustration. (See also 3c-2.) In arguing by analogy, a writer draws a likeness between things on the basis of a single shared feature and then extends the likeness to other features. But analogy can only illustrate a point, never prove it: just because things are similar in one respect, they are not *necessarily* alike in other respects. In the fallacy called **false analogy,** the writer makes such an assumption.

The nonhuman primates such as chimpanzees and gorillas care for their young, clean and groom each other, and defend themselves and sometimes the group from attack. Why, then, must the human primates go so much further—Medicare, child care, welfare, Social Security, and so on—to protect the weak? [Taken to its logical extreme, this analogy would lead us to ask why we speak to each other when gorillas do not.]

Exercise 11
Analyzing the questions in assertions

Identify the question implied by each of the following assertions, and evaluate the writer's effectiveness in facing the question.

1. Many woman are bored with their lives because their jobs are tedious.
2. Steven McRae spends too much time making himself look good to be an effective spokesman for the student body.
3. Teenagers are too young to be allowed to use birth control.
4. Giving nuclear capability to emerging nations is dangerous because they will probably use it to wage war.
5. Our souls are immortal because they are not made of matter and thus are indestructible.

Exercise 12
Analyzing advertisements

Leaf through a magazine or watch television for half an hour, looking for advertisements that attempt to sell a product not on the basis of its worth but by snob appeal, flattery, or other inappropriate appeals to emotions. Be prepared to discuss the advertiser's techniques.

ANSWERS: EXERCISE 11
Possible Answers

1. The question is whether many women are bored with their lives. This statement begs the question by assuming the unproved truths that they are bored and that their boredom is caused by tedious jobs.
2. The question is whether Steven McRae is an effective spokesman. The statement ignores the question by presenting an irrelevant observation about his attitude toward himself, an *ad hominem* argument.
3. The question is whether teenagers should be allowed to use birth control. This statement begs the question by asserting that teenagers should not be allowed to use birth control because they are teenagers.
4. The question is what dangers there might be in giving nuclear capability to emerging nations, obviously a complex issue. The statement ignores the complexity of the question by appealing to fear.
5. The question is whether our souls are immortal. The statement begs the question by asserting immortality.

COLLABORATIVE LEARNING

ANSWERS: EXERCISE 12

Individual response.

COLLABORATIVE LEARNING

ANSWERS: EXERCISE 13
Possible Answers

1. Hasty generalization. *No one* is absolute, and *under twenty-five* suggests stereotyping.
   A revision: A successful marriage demands a degree of maturity.
2. Hasty generalization.
   A revision: Students' persistent complaints about the unfairness of the grading system should be investigated.
3. Reductive fallacy.
   A revision: The United States got involved in World War II for many complex reasons. The bombing of Pearl Harbor was a triggering incident.
4. Either/or fallacy.
   A revision: People watch television for many reasons, but some watch because they are too lazy to talk or read or because they want mindless escape from their lives.
5. False analogy
   A revision: Some working people see themselves as slaves to their corporate masters.
6. Hasty generalization.
   A revision: Stories about welfare chiselers show that some people on welfare do shirk and cheat.
7. Post hoc fallacy.
   A revision: We wonder whether my cousin's three recent fainting spells have anything to do with his climbing Pikes Peak.
8. Reductive fallacy.
   A revision: Racial tension may occur when people with different backgrounds live side by side.
9. Either/or fallacy
   A revision: Failing to supply military assistance to our Central and South American allies may endanger those alliances.
10. Non sequitur.
    A revision: She admits to being an atheist, so how can she be a good Sunday school teacher?

Exercise 13
Identifying and revising logical fallacies

The following sentences exemplify some of the fallacies discussed in the text. Determine what is wrong with each sentence, and then revise it to make it more logical.

1. A successful marriage demands a maturity that no one under twenty-five possesses.
2. Students' persistent complaints about the grading system prove that it is unfair.
3. The United States got involved in World War II because the Japanese bombed Pearl Harbor.
4. People watch television because they are too lazy to talk or read or because they want mindless escape from their lives.
5. Working people are slaves to their corporate masters: they have no freedom to do what they want, and they can be traded to other companies.
6. The stories about welfare chiselers show that the welfare system supports only shirkers and cheats.
7. Mountain climbing is more dangerous than people think: my cousin has fainted three times since he climbed Pikes Peak.
8. Racial tension is bound to occur when people with different backgrounds are forced to live side by side.
9. Failing to supply military assistance to our Central and South American allies will destroy those alliances.
10. She admits to being an atheist, so how can she be a good philosophy teacher?

4e   Developing an argument

In composing an argument you put critical thinking to work for your own opinions. You use critical-thinking skills to formulate assertions, find evidence, and analyze readers' beliefs and knowledge. And you use them to evaluate your argument so that it can withstand critical reading by others.

While reading and using sections 4e through 4h, you will fare better if you have read Chapters 1 and 2 on the writing process. References to the earlier material appear throughout the following pages.

1   Finding a topic and conceiving a thesis

An argument topic must be arguable—that is, reasonable people will disagree over it and be able to support their positions with evidence. This sentence implies several *do*'s and *don't*'s.

Tests for an argument topic

A good topic:

- Concerns a matter of opinion—a conclusion drawn from evidence (see 4c-1).
- Can be disputed: others might take a different position.
- *Will* be disputed: it is controversial.
- Is something you care about and know about, or want to research.
- Is narrow enough to argue in the space and time available (see 1b-3).

A bad topic:

- Cannot be disputed because it concerns a fact, such as the distance to Saturn or the functions of the human liver.
- Cannot be disputed because it concerns a personal preference or belief, such as a liking for the color red or a moral commitment to vegetarianism.
- *Will not* be disputed because few if any disagree over it—the virtues of a secure home, for instance.

If you feel uncertain about finding a topic for argument, try some of the techniques listed on page 19 for discovering ideas.

Once you have a topic, you may also have a thesis, or you may need to do some research and writing to find your angle. The **thesis** is the main idea of your paper (see 1f). In an argument the **thesis sentence** states the assertion that you want your readers to accept or act on. Here are two thesis sentences on the same subject.

> The new room fees are unjustified given the condition of the dormitories.

> The administration should postpone the new room fees at least until conditions in the dormitories are improved.

Your thesis sentence must satisfy the same requirements as the topic (see the box above). But it must also specify the grounds of your argument, the general basis for your assertion. In the two thesis sentences above the grounds for protesting the room fees are that the dormitories are in bad condition.

Note that the writer of either of these arguments must clarify the definition of *condition(s)* if the argument is to be clear and reasonable. Always take pains to define abstract and general terms that are central to your argument, preferably in or just after the thesis sentence. (See 4c-1, p. 135.)

RESOURCES AND IDEAS

Charles W. Kneupper, "Teaching Argument: An Introduction to the Toulmin Model," *College Composition and Communication* 29 (1978): 237–41. Kneupper provides a brief review of Stephen Toulmin's simplified, practical logic, a system based primarily on three elements: data, claim, and warrant.

Gerald Levin, "On Freshman Composition and Logical Thinking," *College Composition and Communication* 28 (1977): 359–64. Levin suggests using essays on controversial topics as a basis for class discussion of the features and patterns of argument.

Catherine E. Lamb, "Beyond Argument in Feminist Composition," *College Composition and Communication* 42 (1991): 11–24. Lamb finds that the oral discourse modes of negotiation and mediation can be effectively used in conceiving the purpose and audience of a written argument. She says, "Argument still has a place, although now as a means, not an end. The end—a resolution of conflict that is fair to both sides—is possible even in the one-sidedness of written communication."

Analyzing your purpose and your audience

Your purpose in argument is, broadly, to convince readers to accept your position or to persuade them to act. But arguments have more specific purposes as well. For instance:

To strengthen the commitment of existing supporters
To win new supporters from the undecided
To get the opposition to reconsider
To inspire supporters to act
To deter the undecided from acting

It's no accident that each of these purposes characterizes the audience (*existing supporters, the undecided,* and so on). In argument even more than in other kinds of writing, achieving your purpose depends on the response of your readers, so you need a sense of who they are and where they stand. The "Questions About Audience" on page 13 can help you identify readers' knowledge, beliefs, and other pertinent background. You also need to know their position on your topic—not only whether they agree or disagree generally, but also which specific assertions they will find more or less convincing.

Your purpose can help you fill in this information, for a decision to address supporters or opponents essentially selects readers with certain inclinations and ignores other readers who may tune in. For instance, if you were writing an editorial urging fellow dormitory residents to protest new room fees, you would pitch your arguments to those readers' concerns. If, instead, you wanted to persuade the school administrators who set the fees to postpone them, you'd take a different tack. (For examples of the different approaches a writer might take to two distinct audiences, see p. 14.)

But suppose your purpose is to win new supporters from those who are undecided on your topic. Since it is difficult to guess these readers' special concerns, you'll have to imagine skeptical readers who will be convinced only by an argument that is detailed, logical, and fair. Like you when you read an argument critically, these skeptical readers seek to be reasoned with, not manipulated into a position or hammered over the head.

Exercise 14
Finding a topic; conceiving a thesis sentence

Analyze each topic listed below to determine whether it is appropriate for argument. For each of the topics you deem arguable, draft a thesis sentence that specifies the grounds for an argument. If you prefer, choose five arguable topics of your own and draft a thesis sentence for each one.

1. Granting of athletic scholarships
2. Care of automobile tires
3. History of the town park
4. Housing for the homeless
5. Billboards in urban residential areas or in rural areas
6. Animal testing for cosmetics research
7. Cats versus dogs as pets
8. [Name] for student-government president (or some other elected office)
9. Ten steps in recycling wastepaper
10. Benefits of being a parent

Exercise 15
Analyzing purpose and audience

Specify a purpose and likely audience for an argument on each thesis sentence you drafted in Exercise 14, above. What do purpose and audience suggest about the way each argument should be developed?

4f   Using reason and evidence

1   Reasoning inductively and deductively

The thesis of your argument is a conclusion you reach by reasoning about evidence. Two common processes of reasoning are induction and deduction—methods of thinking that you use all the time even if you don't know their names.

Say, for instance, that you want to buy a reliable used car. In thinking of what kind of car to buy, you follow specific steps of reasoning.

1. You consider your friends' experiences with used cars: one has had to spend a lot of money repairing her Volkswagen, another complains that his Ford handles badly, and three others rave about their Toyotas.
2. You recall an article in *Consumer Reports* rating Toyotas high among used cars.
3. You conclude that Toyota is the most reliable used car.

ANSWERS: EXERCISE 14
Possible Answers

Topics that are not appropriate for argument:

2. A matter of facts, and few people would disagree.
3. A matter of facts, and few people would disagree.
7. A matter of personal preference.
9. A matter of facts.
10. A matter of personal belief.

Possible thesis sentences for appropriate topics:

1. An athletic scholarship should be what the term implies: an award to one who is both a superior athlete and a superior scholar.
4. Until the city can construct private housing for the homeless, it must do more to make public shelters safe and clean.
5. Billboards help to destabilize urban neighborhoods by creating the impression that the neighborhoods are mere roadways.
6. Humane testing methods are adequate, and cosmetics companies do not have to abuse animals in testing.
8. Goldberger has proved successful in representing both resident and commuter students to the administration.

ANSWERS: EXERCISE 15

Individual response.

RESOURCES AND IDEAS

John T. Gage, "Teaching the Enthymeme: Invention and Arrangement," *Rhetoric Review* 2 (1983): 38–50. Gage argues that students can gain awareness and control over the context, logic, and structure of their arguments by stating their reasoning in enthymemic fashion, as a sentence containing an assertion and a because clause.

log
4f

So far your reasoning is **inductive.** You have made a specific observations about the reliability of different ι And from this evidence you have induced, or inferred, a **ization** about Toyotas. In the framework for analyzing arguments discussed earlier (4c), the evidence is connected to the assertion (the generalization) by your assumption that what is true in one set of circumstances (your friends' experiences, *Consumer Reports'* tests) is or will be true in a similar set of circumstances (your own experiences). With induction you create new knowledge out of old.

Having thus reasoned inductively, you then proceed with **deductive** reasoning, from the generalization to specific circumstances.

1. You start with a generalization you believe to be true: Toyota is the most reliable used car.
2. You apply the generalization to new and specific circumstances: you want to buy a reliable used car.
3. You reach a conclusion: buy a used Toyota.

In deduction the assumption is the generalization you believe to be true (number 1 above). It links the evidence (the new information) to the assertion (the conclusion you draw). With deduction you apply old information to new.

As this example demonstrates, we activate induction and deduction effortlessly and habitually in the daily business of living. In argument, though, we have to be more methodical.

Inductive reasoning

Induction is the dominant method of reasoning in two situations: generalizing from observations and attributing a cause to a set of observed circumstances.

We saw an example of generalizing from observations in the identification of a reliable used car. In another case you might observe that few students attend film screenings sponsored by the school, which feature only serious foreign films; that your college friends seem to prefer science-fiction, adventure, and horror movies; and that a magazine article says these three kinds of entertainment films are the most popular with people under twenty-five. From these observations you infer that most college students prefer entertainment movies. The more students you talk to and the more you read about the subject, the more probable it is that your generalization is true. Note, however, that absolute certainty is not possible. At some point you must *assume* that your evidence justifies your assertion, for yourself and for your readers.

Attributing a cause to circumstances is essentially the same process as generalizing from observations. You and your friends, and presumably most students, prefer science-fiction, adventure, and horror movies, which entertain you and offer relief from studying. However, the student who determines the campus film schedule programs only weighty foreign films, and few students attend. From these observations you conclude that this student is unaware of other students' preferences. True, with imagination you could also conclude that she knows students' preferences but is determined to ignore them because she is a snob. You could even conclude that she is ignoring them because she wants to learn foreign languages. But the conclusion you do draw is the most reasonable because it adheres to the available evidence: the student who runs the screenings does not demonstrate awareness of students' preferences. Again, you assume but cannot prove definitively that the evidence justifies the assertion.

Most errors in inductive reasoning involve oversimplifying either the evidence or the assertion. See 4d on logical fallacies.

Deductive reasoning

You reason deductively when you use some assertions to arrive at others. As when you determined that you should buy a used Toyota, in deduction you apply generalizations or conclusions that are accepted as true to slightly different but similar situations or issues. For example, if you know that all male members of your psychology class are on the football squad, and Albert is in the psychology class, then you conclude that Albert must be on the football squad. This group of three statements constitutes a **syllogism,** two premises stating facts or judgments that together lead to a conclusion.

> *Premise:* English papers containing sentence fragments receive
>   poor grades.
> *Premise:* Your English paper contains sentence fragments.
> *Conclusion:* Your English paper will receive a poor grade.

The first premise states a generalization or a belief. The second premise states a specific case of the generalization or belief. As long as the premises are true, the conclusion derives logically and certainly from them.

The force of deductive reasoning depends on the reliability of the premises and the care taken to apply them in drawing conclusions. The reasoning process is **valid** if the premises lead logically to the conclusion. It is **true** if the premises are believable. Sometimes the reasoning is true but *not* valid:

> *Premise:* Student-government presidents must work hard.
> *Premise:* Ti Wong works hard.
> *Conclusion:* Ti Wong is a student-government president.

Both premises are true, but the first does not *necessarily* apply to the second, so the conclusion is invalid.

Sometimes, too, the reasoning is valid but *not* true:

> *Premise:* All bankers are indifferent to poverty.
> *Premise:* DiSantis is a banker.
> *Conclusion:* DiSantis is indifferent to poverty.

This syllogism is valid but useless: because the first premise is an untrue assumption, the entire argument is untrue. Invalid and untrue syllogisms lie behind many of the logical fallacies discussed in 4d.

A particular hazard of deductive reasoning is the **unstated premise:** the basic assumption linking evidence and conclusion is not stated but implied. Here the unstated premise is believable and the argument is reasonable:

> Ms. Stein has worked with drug addicts for fifteen years, so she knows a great deal about their problems. [Unstated premise: Anyone who has worked fifteen years with drug addicts knows about their problems.]

But when the unstated premise is wrong or unfounded, the argument is false. For example:

> Since Jane Lightbow is a senator, she must receive money illegally from lobbyists. [Unstated premise: All senators receive money illegally from lobbyists.]

To avoid such false conclusions, you may be tempted to make your assertions sound more reasonable. But even a reasonable-sounding conclusion must be supportable. For instance, changing *must* to *might* modifies the unstated assumption about Senator Lightbow:

> Since Jane Lightbow is a senator, she might receive money illegally from lobbyists. [Unstated premise: *Some* senators receive money illegally from lobbyists.]

But it does not necessarily follow that Senator Lightbow is one of the "some." The sentence, though logical, is not truly reasonable

---

Tests for inductive and deductive reasoning

Induction

- Have you stated your evidence clearly?
- Is your evidence complete enough and good enough to justify your assertion? What is the assumption that connects evidence and assertion? Is it believable?
- Have you avoided logical fallacies? (See 4d.)

Deduction

- What are the premises leading to your conclusion? Look especially for unstated premises.
- What does the first premise assume? Is the assumption believable?
- Does the first premise necessarily apply to the second premise?
- Is the second premise believable?
- Have you avoided logical fallacies? (See 4d.)

---

unless evidence demonstrates that Senator Lightbow should be linked with illegal activities.

2 Using evidence

Whether your argument is reasonable or not depends heavily on the evidence you marshal to support it. The kinds of evidence and the criteria for evaluating evidence are discussed in detail in 4c-2 (pp. 136–39). How to find evidence is discussed under research writing in 35c.

The kind and quantity of evidence you use should be determined by your purpose, your topic, and the needs of your audience. Some arguments, such as a plea for volunteer help in a soup kitchen, will rely most heavily on appeals to readers' beliefs. Other arguments, such as a proposal for mandatory air bags in cars, will rely much more on statistics and expert opinions. Most arguments, including these, will mingle facts, examples, expert opinions, and appeals to readers' beliefs and needs. (See also p. 160.)

In using evidence for argument, you'll need to be especially wary of certain traps that carelessness or zeal can lure you into. These are listed in the box on the next page.

log
4f

Responsible use of evidence

- **Don't distort.** You mislead readers when you twist evidence to suit your argument—for instance, when you claim that crime in your city occurs five times more often than it did in 1925, without mentioning that the population is also seven times larger.
- **Don't stack the deck.** Ignoring damning evidence is like cheating at cards. You must deal forthrightly with the opposition (see 4g-2).
- **Don't exaggerate.** Watch your language. Don't try to manipulate readers by characterizing your own evidence as *pure* and *rock-solid* and the opposition's as *ridiculous* and *half-baked.* Make the evidence speak for itself.
- **Don't oversimplify.** Avoid forcing the evidence to support more than it can. (See also 4d-2.)
- **Don't misquote.** When you cite experts, quote them accurately and fairly.

Exercise 16
Reasoning inductively

Study the following facts and then evaluate each of the numbered conclusions below them. Which of the generalizations are reasonable given the evidence, and which are not? Why?

Between the 1980 and 1990 national censuses, the population of the United States increased 9.8 percent, to 248,800,000.

The percentage increase from 1960 to 1970 was 13.3 percent; from 1970 to 1980, 11.4 percent.

The population of the South and West regions increased 17.5 percent between 1980 and 1990.

The population of the Northeast and North Central regions increased less than 2 percent between 1980 and 1990.

More than 55 percent of the nation's people now live in the South and the West.

1. During the 1980s the population of the United States continued to grow at the same pace set during the 1960s.
2. During the 1980s increasing numbers of Americans made their homes in the Sun Belt states of the South and West regions rather than in the states of the Northeast and North Central regions.
3. Many Americans prefer the pleasant climate of the South and West regions to the harsh climate of the Northeast and North Central regions.

Exercise 17
Reasoning deductively

Supply the element needed to complete each of the following syllogisms.

1. a. Cigarette smokers risk lung cancer.
   b.
   c. Therefore, cigarette smokers risk death.
2. a. The challenging courses are the good ones.
   b. Biology is a challenging course.
   c.
3. a.
   b. That child receives no individual attention.
   c. Therefore, that child learns slowly.
4. a. Discus throwers develop large pectoral muscles.
   b.
   c. Therefore, Warren has large pectoral muscles.
5. a.
   b. Enrollments will certainly decline.
   c. Therefore, the school will close.

COLLABORATIVE LEARNING

ANSWERS: EXERCISE 17
Possible Answers

1. Lung cancer can cause death.
2. Therefore, biology is a good course.
3. Children who receive no individual attention learn slowly.
4. Warren is a discus thrower.
5. The school will close if enrollments decline.

Exercise 18
Analyzing the reasoning in assertions

At least one of the following assertions is reasonable, but the others either generalize from inadequate evidence or depend on faulty assumptions. Circle the number preceding any sentence that seems reasonable, and explain what is wrong with each of the others.

1. Since capital punishment prevents murder, it should be the mandatory sentence for all murderers.
2. The mayor opposed pollution controls when he was president of a manufacturing company, so he may not support new controls or vigorously enforce existing ones.
3. The only way to be successful in the United States is to make money, because Americans measure success by income.
4. Keeping the library open until midnight has caused the increase in late-night crime on the campus.
5. Government demands so much honesty that we should not leave it to lawyers and professional politicians.

COLLABORATIVE LEARNING

ANSWERS: EXERCISE 18
Possible Answers

1. The assertion depends on the unproved assumption that capital punishment prevents murder.
2. A reasonable assertion.
3. The assertion depends on the overgeneralization that all Americans measure success by income and thus that there is only one way to be successful.
4. The assertion depends on the unproved assumption that the library's late hours have had something to do with the increase in crime.
5. The assertion is based on the faulty assumption that lawyers and politicians are mostly dishonest.

Exercise 19
Supplying evidence

Supply at least two pieces of evidence—examples, facts, expert opinions—to support two of the following assertions. (An exercise on weighing evidence appears on p. 142.)

1. The cost of tuition should be raised before the cost of housing (or vice versa).

COLLABORATIVE LEARNING

ANSWERS: EXERCISE 19

Individual response.

2. _____ is a television program (or book or movie) that should be a model for all entertainment aimed at adolescents (or children or parents).
3. Doctors need (or do not need) more training in counseling patients.
4. Americans must become energy misers instead of energy spendthrifts.
5. Driver education should (or should not) be required of all who receive more than one moving violation.

 4g   Reaching your readers

 Appealing to readers

COLLECTING APPEALS

Ask students to read, on their own, a relatively long and complex argumentative essay from a reader or a magazine of political or social opinion. In class, assign students to groups and ask each group (1) to identify purely logical appeals, purely emotional appeals, and mixed appeals in the essay and (2) to describe, if they can, the effect of each appeal on average readers (like the members of the group).

In forming convictions about arguable issues—capital punishment, gun control, defense spending, the best location for a new town dump—we generally interpret the factual evidence through the filter of our values, beliefs, tastes, desires, and feelings. Mayor Jones may object to placing the new town dump in a particular wooded area because the facts suggest that the site is not large enough and that prevailing winds will blow odors back through the town. But Mayor Jones may also have fond memories of playing in the wooded area as a child, feelings that color her interpretation of the facts and strengthen her conviction that the dump should be placed elsewhere. Her conviction is partly rational, because it is based on evidence, and partly emotional, because it is also based on feelings.

In most arguments you will combine **rational appeals** to readers' capacities for reasoning logically from evidence to a conclusion with **emotional appeals** to readers' beliefs and feelings. The passages below, all expressing the same view on the same subject, illustrate how either a primarily rational or a primarily emotional appeal may be weaker than an approach that uses both.

Rational appeal

In its report the commission expresses too strong a concern for the public image of nuclear power. The commission regards the Howe nuclear plant as now "safe," with the risk of meltdown "an acceptably low 3 in 10,000 per year." Yet it maintains that the general public may not accept the experts' judgments of safety. To "strengthen public faith in nuclear power," the commission calls for additional safety precautions to achieve a "slight" further reduction in risk, to 1 in 10,000. The report does not address the high cost of these additional precautions or how the financially unstable plant is to pay for them.

Emotional appeal

The commission is clearly more intent on improving the public image of nuclear power than on making this much-needed source of energy available for public use. In recommending additional and totally unnecessary safety precautions at the Howe nuclear plant, the commission shows blind unconcern that a minor improvement in public image might be gained at the expense of the plant's being shut down for good.

Rational and emotional appeals

In its report the commission reveals itself to be more intent on improving the public image of nuclear power than on making this much-needed source of energy available for public use. The commission regards the Howe nuclear plant as now "safe," with the risk of meltdown "an acceptably low 3 in 10,000 per year." Yet it worries that the general public may not accept the experts' judgments of safety. To "strengthen public faith in nuclear power," the commission calls for additional safety precautions to achieve a "slight" further reduction in risk, to 1 in 10,000. The report does not acknowledge that these unnecessary precautions would be prohibitively expensive, especially for a plant that is already financially unstable. Apparently the commission is unconcerned that a minor improvement in public image might be gained at the expense of the plant's being shut down for good.

Notice the differences in these three passages. In the first one the writer appeals to readers' reason by making an arguable assertion and then providing the facts to back it up, but he fails to address readers' feelings on the issue. The second passage appeals to readers' emotions—to their desire for more plentiful energy supplies, their receptiveness to nuclear energy, and even their distaste for public relations ploys—but fails to provide supporting evidence. The third passage combines both kinds of appeal. Thus it gives readers both a rational and an emotional basis for accepting the writer's view that the commission is willing to sacrifice nuclear power out of concern for public relations alone, not for actual safety.

As the third passage illustrates, an appeal to emotion is a way to establish common ground between the writer and the reader. For such an appeal to be successful, however, it must be appropriate for the audience and the argument.

- An emotional appeal is *inappropriate for the audience* when it misjudges readers' actual feelings. The writer of the third passage assumed that his readers would want nuclear power to supplement other energy supplies. If, instead, his readers feared nuclear power, finding even a minimal risk too high,

log
4g

then he would fail to convince them that the commission's concerns were misplaced.

- An appeal is *inappropriate for the argument* when it raises emotional issues that are irrelevant to the assertions and the evidence. The writer of the third passage might have tried to bolster his case by stating that one member of the commission was once an executive with the natural-gas company. But the statement would be inappropriate on at least two counts: it would attack a member of the commission rather than the report of the entire commission; and the attack would be based on the unproved assumption that the member's past employment made his current judgment doubtful.

(See 4d-1 for more on inappropriate emotional appeals.)

A third kind of approach to readers, the **ethical appeal,** is the sense you give of being a competent, fair person who is worth heeding. A sound argument backed by ample evidence—a rational appeal—will convince readers of your knowledge and reasonableness. (So will your acknowledging the opposition. See the next section.) Appropriate emotional appeals will demonstrate that you share readers' beliefs and needs. In addition, a sincere and even tone will assure readers that you are a balanced person who wants to reason with them.

A sincere and even tone need not exclude language with emotional appeal—words such as *unnecessary* and *prohibitively* at the end of the third passage above. But avoid certain forms of expression that will mark you as unfair:

- Insulting words such as *idiotic* or *fascist.*
- Biased language such as *fags* or *broads* (see 31a-8).
- Sarcasm—for instance, using the sentence *What a brilliant idea* to indicate contempt for the idea and its originator.
- Exclamation points! They'll make you sound shrill! (See 20f.)

See also 1d-3 on tone.

2   **Answering opposing views**

A good test of your fairness in argument is how you handle possible objections. Assuming your thesis is indeed arguable, then others can marshal their own evidence to support a different view or views. You need to find out what these other views are and what the support is for them. Then, in your argument, you need to take these views on, refute those you can, grant the validity of others, and demonstrate why, despite their validity, the opposing

log
4g

views are less compelling than your own. The student who wrote the following paragraph first stated an opposing view (sentence 1), then conceded its partial validity (sentence 2), and finally demonstrated its irrelevance (sentences 3–5).

> The athletic director argues against reducing university   1
> support for athletic programs on the grounds that they make
> money that goes toward academic programs. It is true that   2
> here at Springfield the surpluses from the football and bas-
> ketball programs have gone into the general university fund,
> and some of that money may have made it into academic de-
> partments (the fund's accounting methods make it impossi-
> ble to say for sure). But the athletic director misses the   3
> point. The problem is not that the athletic programs cost more   4
> than they take in but that they demand too much to begin with.
> For an institution that hopes to become first-rate aca-   5
> demically, too many facilities, too much money, too much en-
> ergy, and too many people are tied up in the effort to produce
> championship sports teams.

Before you draft your essay, list for yourself all the opposing views you can think of. You'll find them in your research, by talking to friends, and by critically thinking about your own ideas. Figure out which opposing views you can refute (do more research if necessary), and prepare to concede those views you can't refute. It's not a mark of weakness or failure to admit that the opposition has a point or two. Indeed, by showing yourself to be honest and fair, you strengthen your ethical appeal and thus your entire argument.

 Organizing your argument

There are organizing schemes for arguments that relate directly to induction and deduction:

- An **inductive organization** moves from specific evidence to a generalization about the evidence.
- A **deductive organization** begins with a commonly held opinion or belief (the first premise of the syllogism), applies it to a new case (the second premise), and draws a conclusion.

In practice, your sense of purpose and audience may dictate that you vary these schemes—for example, stating your generalization (your thesis) first in an inductive argument to secure readers' attention. Further, your arguments may be both inductive and deductive, so that you could not adhere strictly to either scheme.

Because of such variations in subject, purpose, audience, and form of reasoning, arguments can be effectively organized in many different ways. One trusty scheme appears below. Some of the elements can be rearranged.

TRANSPARENCY MASTER
AVAILABLE

Organization of an argument

Introduction

Statement of the significance of the argument; background on the issue; statement of thesis. (See 3d-1 on introductions, 1f and 4e-1 on the thesis sentence.) The introduction may be one or more paragraphs, depending on the complexity of the issue, readers' knowledge of it, and the length of the whole paper.

Body

Assertions relating to the thesis, each perhaps the topic sentence of a paragraph (3a), with the remainder of the paragraph consisting of the evidence for the assertion. This is the meat of the argument and will run as long as needed. Within the body, assertions-with-evidence are usually best arranged in order of increasing importance or persuasiveness.

Answering the opposition

Refutation of opposing views, with evidence; concession to views more valid than your own; demonstration of your argument's greater strength (see 4g-2). This material may come elsewhere in the argument, after the introduction or throughout the body. The choice depends mainly on whether you think readers need the opposition to be dealt with right away or can wait.

Conclusion

Restatement of the thesis; summary of the argument; last appeal to readers. (See 3d-2 on conclusions.) The conclusion may be one or more paragraphs, depending on the complexity and the length of your argument.

Exercise 20
Identifying appeals

Identify each passage below as primarily a rational appeal or primarily an emotional appeal. Which passages make a strong ethical appeal as well?

1. Only complacency, indifference, or selfishness could allow us to ignore these people's hunger. We who have so much cannot in good conscience let others starve.

2. Thus the data collected by these researchers indicate that a mandatory sentence for illegal possession of handguns may lead to reduction in handgun purchases.

3. Most broadcasters worry that further government regulation of television programming could breed censorship—certainly, an undesirable outcome. Yet most broadcasters also accept that children's television is a fair target for regulation.

4. Anyone who cherishes life in all its diversity could not help being appalled by the mistreatment of laboratory animals. The so-called scientists who run the labs are misguided.

5. Many experts in constitutional law have warned that the rule violates the right to free speech. Yet other experts have viewed the rule, however regretfully, as necessary for the good of the community as a whole.

Exercise 21
Imagining opposing views

For one of the arguable topics and thesis sentences you developed in Exercise 14 (p. 152), make a list of possible opposing views. Think freely at first, not stopping to censor views that seem far-fetched or irrational. When your list is complete, decide which views must be taken seriously and why, and develop a response to each one.

4h   Revising your argument

When you revise your argument, do it in at least two stages—revising underlying meaning and structure, and editing more superficial elements. The checklists on pages 53 and 59 can be a guide. Supplement them with the checklist on the next page, which encourages you to think critically about your own argument.

4i   Examining a sample argument

The following student essay illustrates the principles discussed in this section. As you read the essay notice especially the structure, the relation of assertions and supporting evidence, and the kinds of appeals the writer makes.

A Year for America

Among the many problems in the United States today, two are particularly troubling. One is the tendency of people

Introduction: identification of problems

log
4i

Checklist for revising an argument

1. Is your thesis an arguable assertion (4e-1)?
2. Have you considered your readers' needs for information and their probable beliefs and values (4e-2)?
3. Does your thesis derive from induction, deduction, or both (4f-1)? If induction, have you shown how evidence and generalization are related? If deduction, is your syllogism both true and valid?
4. Is your evidence accurate, relevant, representative, and adequate (4c-2)? Is the evidence fairly presented (4f-2)?
5. Have you combined rational, emotional, and ethical appeals appropriately for your subject, your purpose, and your audience (4g-1)?
6. Have you answered the opposition (4g-2)?
7. Have you organized your argument clearly and effectively (4g-3)?
8. Have you avoided logical fallacies (4d)?

to see those with different moral, religious, social, economic, and political views as "the enemy"—absolutely wrong, even somewhat less than human. The other is the tendency to see government not as the resolver of such differences—the place where compromises are hammered out—but as the chief problem itself, either too intrusive or not responsive enough, depending on one's point of view. The loss of respect and sympathy for the "other guy" and the loss of faith in government are depriving us of a sense of community—of belonging to, sharing in, and contributing to our great nation. One step toward restoring this sense of community could be achieved by requiring a year of government service from each citizen.

Thesis: a proposal for a solution

A program of mandatory government service might be set up as follows. On finishing high school or reaching age eighteen, all young adults would be expected to spend one year working for the government (local, state, or federal). The service might be with the military, but it could also be with social-service agencies, hospitals, schools, national parks, data-processing centers, road-maintenance departments, or any other government group. Program participants would be paid the minimum wage and would work full-time throughout the year. There would be no deferments or exemptions from service, except possibly for severe economic hardship or mental or physical disability.

Explanation of the proposal

This program could substantially re-   Support for the produce the present polarization in our soci-   posal: first advantage
ety. In keeping with the United States'
melting-pot heritage, the program would be a great equalizer:
male and female, rich and poor, black and white, urban and rural—all would serve together. Participants would be exposed to
others whose backgrounds, experiences, and values were previously unknown or misunderstood. They would become more
aware and tolerant of diversity, more sympathetic toward "different" people, more respectful of different views.

In addition to learning about each   Support for the pro-
other, the participants would also learn   posal: second advan-
firsthand about their government. They   tage
would see for themselves the huge variety
of services that we as a nation expect our government to deliver,
from keeping roads free of litter to providing health care to the
elderly. In many jobs they would come face to face with the people who benefit from government services—the middle-class
home owner, the school-age child, the disabled veteran, the im-
poverished mother of five. In short, participants would see the
many ways in which their government serves them and others.
And that experience could turn their fear and mistrust of government into healthy appreciation and respect.

The participants would gain personally   Support for the pro-
as well. The year of service would expose   posal: third advan-
them to a broad range of career options,   tage
both in and out of government. They
would gain some of the experience and information necessary to
discover their talents and interests and to make realistic and appropriate decisions about further education and eventual career
paths. They would also acquire marketable skills that would give
them a boost in whatever work they chose. On a less practical
level, participants would begin to see themselves as belonging
and contributing to the larger community of which they were a
part. Such awareness would reduce the sense of isolation and
frustration that often disturbs young adults.

The proposal for a mandatory year of   Responses to proba-
government service is bound to meet at   ble objections
least two objections. First, the young adults
who would be affected might not want to give up a year of their
lives. However, since everyone else in their age group would be
making the same sacrifice, they would not be at any disadvantage.
And with public education, the young adults could be made to
take pride in their sacrifice and service. The second major objection would be cost: with budget deficits already endangering our
economy, how can we possibly afford such a program? Granted,
the program would cost money in its initial stages, as the admin-
istrative machinery was set in motion and the low-level government employees being displaced by participants were retrained

log
4i

for jobs outside government. Eventually, however, the program could save money because the participants, receiving minimum wage, would cost less to do the same work now performed by relatively highly paid government employees. Furthermore, the government labor force would grow temporarily when participants began serving but before existing employees had been retrained and moved out. With a larger labor force, government could do many things it now cannot do because of inadequate labor, such as clean up city streets, give individual attention to disadvantaged children, and help the elderly with daily living. The money would be well spent.

Despite its personal and monetary costs, a program of mandatory government service would be enormously beneficial to the United States. Its citizens, instead of viewing each other as enemies, would learn to work together creatively, despite their differences, to resolve problems. And instead of seeing their government as something *other* than themselves, a faceless giant either too intrusive or too unresponsive to be worth its cost, they would see it as something *of, by,* and *for* themselves and all other Americans.

> Conclusion: summary of how the plan would solve the problems identified in the introduction

ANSWERS: EXERCISE 22
Possible Answers

1. General assertions related to thesis sentence: the first sentence of paragraph 2, the first and last sentences of paragraphs 3 and 4, the last two sentences of paragraph 5, the first sentence of paragraph 6, and the conclusion. Supporting examples and other evidence: paragraph 2, sentences 2–5; paragraph 3, sentences 2–3; paragraph 4, sentences 2–3; paragraph 5, sentences 2–5; paragraph 6, sentences 3–4 and 6–9.

2. Examples of appeals to reason: the explanation of the proposal (paragraph 2); the examples and reasons given as evidence (paragraphs 3–6); the response to probable objections (paragraph 6). Examples of appeals to emotion: *our great nation* (paragraph 1); *melting-pot heritage* (paragraph 3); *sacrifice and service* (paragraph 6); *see [the government] as something of, by, and for themselves and all other Americans* (paragraph 7). Throughout the essay, the writer appeals to readers' feelings of distance from and impatience with government and their wish for community, sense of fairness, pride in their nation, and willingness to make sacrifices for others. In paragraph 5, she appeals specifically to readers' career anxieties.

3. The ethical appeal is that of a patriotic, fair-minded, reasonable citizen willing to make sacrifices.

4. Objections anticipated (paragraph 6): personal sacrifice and monetary cost. However, personal sacrifice would be required of all young adults, not just some, and it could become a source of pride. And cost would be offset by initially improved services and eventual savings.

5. Answers will vary.

6. Individual response.

Exercise 22
Critically reading an argument

Analyze the construction and effectiveness of the preceding essay by answering the following questions.

1. Where does the writer make general assertions related to her thesis sentence, and where does she provide examples or other evidence to support the assertions?

2. Where does the writer appeal primarily to reason, and where does she appeal primarily to emotion? What specific beliefs, values, and desires of readers does the writer appeal to?

3. How would you characterize the writer's ethical appeal?

4. What objections to her plan does the writer anticipate? What reasons does she give for dispensing with them?

5. How effective do you find this argument? To what extent do you agree with the writer about the problems identified in her introduction? To what extent does she convince you that her plan is desirable and workable and would solve those problems? Does she fail to anticipate any major objections to her plan?

6. Write a critical evaluation of "A Year for America." First summarize the writer's views. Then respond to those views by answering the questions posed in item 5 above.

Part II

Grammatical Sentences

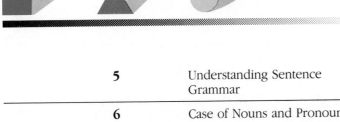

In this chapter, students will encounter a brief descriptive grammar that can serve as a reference for explanations of basic grammatical terms and as a guide to how sentences are constructed and their major elements punctuated. The chapter builds cumulatively from the simplest sentence to increasingly complex expansions rather than compartmentalizing grammar into parts of speech and kinds of phrases, clauses, and sentences. Moreover, it treats punctuation in context, as part of the discussion of word groups and syntactic relationships that may require it.

Because of its whole sentence approach and because of the many sentence-combining and -modeling exercises it contains, this chapter can be useful for a wide range of students. Those whose writing displays fundamental problems with sentences will benefit from its clear treatment of sentence parts and structure and from the exercises that require manipulation of sentence elements. Those who have mastered basic sentence strategies will be able to develop many options for expression through sentence-combining exercises that introduce elements like verbal phrases, absolute phrases, and appositives. And all students will gain a greater understanding of punctuation when they see how it grows out of and communicates a sentence's structure and meaning.

This chapter uses almost entirely traditional terminology because such terminology, despite its weaknesses, is still the most widely used and most likely to be familiar to students and instructors. The overall description largely reflects a structural view of English grammar. It is as simple as possible while still including all the word classes and syntactic structures needed by the student to understand the twenty successive chapters on sentences and punctuation.

You may wish to emphasize or de-emphasize the chapter, depending in part on the preparation of your students and on how much you think an understanding of grammar can contribute to their writing. As may be obvious, this chapter of the handbook was prepared in the belief that a clear understanding of the essential structure of English sentences and of the uses of syntactic groups and compound structures can help many students not only to punctuate correctly but also to gain greater control of subordination and emphasis within their sentences. This process will take place only if students get a chance

Chapter 5

Understanding Sentence Grammar

Grammar describes how language works. Many people who write well would have difficulty explaining in grammatical terms how their sentences work. But when something goes wrong in a sentence, a knowledge of grammar helps in recognizing the problem and provides a language for discussing it.

Grammar can help us understand sentences even if we don't know the meaning of all the words in the sentence.

The rumfrum biggled the pooba.

We don't know what that sentence means. But we can infer that something called a *rumfrum* did something to a *pooba*. He (or she, or it) *biggled* it, whatever that means. We know this because we understand the basic grammar and word order of simple English sentences. We understand that this sentence seems like *The boy kicked the ball* or *The student passed the test*.

In the same way we can understand more complex sentences such as the following:

The stintless rumfrums biggled the jittish poobas who were kerpesting the gloots.

We know that *stintless* and *jittish* describe *rumfrums* and *poobas*, respectively, and that the *poobas were kerpesting* (doing something to) *the gloots*, probably more than one *gloot*. We understand these relations among the words because we recognize structures that recur in everyday talking and writing. Each statement is a **sentence**, the basic unit of writing.

5a Understanding the basic sentence

The basic grammar of sentences consists of the kinds of words that compose them, the functions of those words, the patterns on which sentences are built, and the ways those patterns can be expanded and elaborated. Understanding basic grammar can help you create clear sentences that effectively relate your ideas.

1 Identifying subjects and predicates

Most sentences make statements. First they name something; then they make an assertion about or describe an action involving that something. These two sentence parts are the **subject** and the **predicate.**

Subject	Predicate
Art	can be controversial.
It	has caused disputes in Congress and in artists' studios.
Its meaning and value to society	are often the focus of dispute.

2 Identifying the basic words: nouns and verbs

If we study the following five simple sentences, we find that they consist almost entirely of two quite different kinds of words.

Subject	Predicate
The earth	trembled.
The earthquake	destroyed the city.
The result	was chaos.
The government	sent the city aid.
The citizens	considered the earthquake a disaster.

In these sentences the words in the subject position name things, such as *earth, earthquake,* and *government.* In contrast, the words in the predicate position express actions, such as *trembled, destroyed,* and *sent.* These two groups of words work in different ways. We can have one *citizen* or many *citizens,* but we cannot have one or more *destroyeds.* If we drop the *-ed* from *destroyed,* we change the time of the action. But we cannot add *-ed* to *citizen* and have *citizened.* The word *citizen* just doesn't work that way.

to put knowledge into action through exercises that ask them to manipulate and create sentences. In this regard, the sentence-combining exercises in the chapter can be coordinated with those in other chapters of the text to create a program of sentence combining designed to complement instruction in essay and paragraph writing.

RESOURCES AND IDEAS

Does grammar instruction help? The effectiveness of grammar instruction in improving writing and in helping students achieve correctness in their prose is still a hotly debated issue. Martha Kolln, in "Closing the Books on Alchemy," *College Composition and Communication* 32 (1981): 139–51, defends instruction in formal grammar. The opposite position is articulated by Patrick Hartwell in "Grammar, Grammars, and the Teaching of Grammar," *College English* 47 (February 1985): 105–27 (reprinted in *A Sourcebook for Basic Writing Teachers,* ed. Theresa Enos [New York: Random, 1987] 348–72).

Perhaps the most useful treatment of the issue, however, is Sarah D'Eloia's "The Uses—and Limits—of Grammar," *Journal of Basic Writing* 3 (1977): 1–48 (reprinted in *A Sourcebook for Basic Writing Teachers,* ed. Theresa Enos [New York: Random, 1987] 373–416). D'Eloia argues that grammar instruction can help alert students to errors and suggests ways to integrate instruction in writing and grammar. These methods include dictation, paraphrase and conversion, imitation, follow-ups to writing assignments, and exercises that ask students to "discover" a rule from examples of it in operation. The article also provides a detailed syllabus for teaching the verb phrase.

Grammar reflects these differences by identifying **parts of speech** or **word classes.**

gr
5a

The parts of speech

Nouns name persons, places, things, ideas, or qualities: *Roosevelt, girl, Schuylkill River, coastline, Koran, table, strife, happiness.* (See below.)

Pronouns usually substitute for nouns and function as nouns: *I, you, he, she, it, we, they, myself, this, that, who, which, everyone.* (See p. 174.)

Verbs express actions, occurrences, or states of being: *run, bunt, inflate, become, be.* (See next page.)

Adjectives describe or modify nouns or pronouns: *gentle, small, helpful.* (See p. 180.)

Adverbs describe or modify verbs, adjectives, other adverbs, or whole groups of words: *gently, helpfully, almost, really, someday.* (See p. 180.)

Prepositions relate nouns or pronouns to other words in a sentence: *about, at, down, for, of, with.* (See 5c-1.)

Conjunctions link words, phrases, and clauses. **Coordinating conjunctions** and **correlative conjunctions** link words, phrases, or clauses of equal importance: *and, but, or, nor; both . . . and, not only . . . but also, either . . . or.* (See 5d-1.) **Subordinating conjunctions** introduce subordinate clauses and link them to main clauses: *although, because, if, whenever.* (See 5c-4.)

Interjections express feeling or command attention, either alone or in a sentence: *hey, oh, darn, wow.* (See 20e, 21c-4.)

Except for *the* and *a,* which simply point to and help identify the words after them, the five sentences about the earthquake consist entirely of nouns and verbs. We can identify nouns and verbs both by their meanings and by their forms.

Nouns

Meaning

Nouns name. They may name a person (*Lily Tomlin, Arsenio Hall, astronaut*), a thing (*chair, book, spaceship*), a quality (*pain, mystery, simplicity*), a place (*city, Washington, ocean, Red Sea*), or an idea (*reality, peace, success*). Whatever exists or can be thought to exist has a name. Its name is a noun.

Form

The forms of nouns depend partly on where they fit in certain overlapping groups:

- **Count nouns** name countable things. Most add *-s* or *-es* to distinguish between singular (one) and plural (more than one): *earthquake, earthquakes; city, cities; citizen, citizens.* Some count nouns form irregular plurals: *woman, women; child, children.*
- **Mass nouns** name things that aren't usually countable (*earth, sugar*), or they name qualities (*chaos, fortitude*). Mass nouns do not usually form plurals.
- **Collective nouns** are singular in form but name groups: *army, family, herd.*
- **Common nouns** name general classes of things and do not begin with capital letters. They include all nouns except proper nouns (see below).
- **Proper nouns** name specific people, places, and things and begin with capital letters: *Ann, Cairo, Civil War.*

In addition, most nouns form the **possessive** by adding *-'s* to show ownership (*Nadia's books, citizen's rights*), source (*Auden's poems*), and some other relationships.

Nouns with *the*, *a*, and *an*

Nouns are often preceded by *the* or *a* (*an* before a vowel sound: *an apple*). These words are usually called **articles,** but they may be described as **noun markers** since they always indicate that a noun will soon follow.

Verbs

Meaning

Verbs express an action (*bring, change, grow*), an occurrence (*become, happen*), or a state of being (*be, seem*).

Form

Most verbs can be recognized by two changes in form:

- To indicate a difference between present and past time, most verbs add *-d* or *-ed* to the form listed in the dictionary: *They play today. They played yesterday.* Some verbs indicate past time irregularly: *eat, ate; begin, began* (see 7a).
- When their subjects are singular nouns or some singular pronouns, all present-time verbs except *be* and *have* add *-s* or *-es*

Random, 1987] 348–72), Patrick Hartwell argues that writers struggling to master print literacy display similar patterns of error regardless of dialect.

In contrast, Mary Epes argues that nonstandard dialects have a marked influence on writing and that "direct instruction in the grammar of standard written English is essential for nonstandard dialect speakers" ("Tracing Errors to the Sources: A Study of the Encoding Processes of Adult Basic Writers," *Journal of Basic Writing* 41 [1985]: 4–33).

Though the issue is clearly far from resolved, the perspective offered by Marcia Farr and Harvey Daniels is promising. They look at standard and nonstandard dialects in the context of linguistic research and provide suggestions for shaping writing instruction as a whole (including instruction in formal grammar) in ways that are likely to benefit speakers of nonstandard dialects (*Language Diversity and Writing Instruction* [New York: ERIC Clearinghouse on Urban Education, 1986]).

gr
5a

> TRANSPARENCY MASTER
> AVAILABLE

to the dictionary form: *The bear escapes. It runs. The woman begins. She sings.* The *-s* forms of *be* and *have* are *is* and *has.*

(See Chapter 7, pp. 223–26, for more on verb forms.)

Helping verbs

All verbs can combine with the words *do, does, did, can, could, may, might, will, would, shall, should,* and *must: could run, may escape, must help.* These words are called **helping verbs** or **auxiliary verbs.** They and a few others combine with special forms of verbs to make verb phrases such as *will be running, might have escaped,* and *could have been helped.* (See Chapter 7, pp. 225–26.)

A note on form and function

In different sentences an English word may serve different functions, take correspondingly different forms, and belong to different word classes. For example:

The government sent the city *aid.* [*Aid* functions as a noun.]
Governments *aid* citizens. [*Aid* functions as a verb.]

Because words can function in different ways, we must always determine how a particular word works in a sentence before we can identify what part of speech it is. **The *function* of a word in a sentence always determines its part of speech in that sentence.**

Pronouns

Most **pronouns** substitute for nouns and function in sentences as nouns do. In the sentences below, the pronoun *she* substitutes for *Susanne,* and the pronoun *who* substitutes for *people.*

Susanne enlisted in the Air Force. *She* leaves for her training in two weeks. Susanne is among the people *who* took advanced physics in high school.

Pronouns fall into several subclasses depending on their form or function.

- **Personal pronouns** refer to a specific individual or to individuals: *I, you, he, she, it, we,* and *they.*
- **Indefinite pronouns,** such as *everybody* and *some,* do not substitute for any specific nouns, though they function as nouns (*Everybody speaks*).

- **Demonstrative pronouns,** including *this, that,* and *such,* identify or point to nouns (*This is the problem*).
- **Relative pronouns**—*who, whoever, which, that*—relate groups of words to nouns or other pronouns (*The book that won is a novel*).
- **Intensive pronouns**—a personal pronoun plus *-self* (*himself, myself*)—emphasize a noun or other pronoun (*He asked himself that question*).
- **Reflexive pronouns** have the same form as intensive pronouns but indicate that the sentence subject also receives the action of the verb (*They perjured themselves*).
- **Interrogative pronouns,** such as *who, which,* and *that,* introduce questions (*Who will contribute?*).

The personal pronouns *I, he, she, we,* and *they* and the relative pronoun *who* change form depending on their function in the sentence. (For a discussion of these form changes, see Chapter 6.)

Exercise 1
Identifying subjects and predicates

Identify the subject and the predicate of each sentence below. Then use each sentence as a model to create a sentence of your own.

Example:

An important scientist spoke at commencement.
        SUBJECT   PREDICATE
An important scientist | spoke at commencement.
The hungry family ate at the diner.

1. The leaves fell.
2. October ends soon.
3. The orchard owners made apple cider.
4. They examined each apple carefully before using it.
5. Over a hundred people will buy cider at the roadside stand.

Exercise 2
Identifying nouns, verbs, and pronouns

In the following sentences identify all words functioning as nouns with *N,* all words functioning as verbs with *V,* and all pronouns with *P.*

Example:

We took the tour through the museum.
 P   V   N   N
We took the *tour* through the *museum.*

ANSWERS: EXERCISE 1

            SUBJECT | PREDICATE
1. The leaves|fell.
   Sample imitation: The kite soared.

            SUBJECT | PREDICATE
2. October|ends soon.
   Sample imitation: My class begins soon.

                    SUBJECT | PREDICATE
3. The orchard owners made|apple cider.
   Sample imitation: The couple grew summer squash.

   SUBJECT | PREDICATE
4. They|examined each apple carefully before using it.
   Sample imitation: They dried each glass gingerly after washing it.

                    SUBJECT | PREDICATE
5. Over a hundred people will|buy cider at the roadside stand.
   Sample imitation: Few pool owners will swim at the public beach.

ANSWERS: EXERCISE 2

      N   V
1. The trees died.

   P   V   N
2. They caught a disease.

       N   V   N
3. The disease was a fungus.

   P   V   N   P   V   V
4. It ruined a grove that was treasured.

   P   N   V   N
5. Our great-grandfather planted the grove in

      N
   the last century.

ANSWERS: EXERCISE 3
Possible Answers

1. Noun and verb.
   Blow out the candles and make a <u>wish</u>.
   [Noun.] The child <u>wished</u> for a new bicycle.
   [Verb.]
2. Noun and verb.
   Many people purchase <u>ties</u> as Father's Day
   presents. [Noun.] <u>Tie</u> the rope into a square
   knot. [Verb.]
3. Noun and verb.
   The <u>swing</u> hung from a large oak tree.
   [Noun.] Ted picked up his niece and <u>swung</u>
   her around and around. [Verb.]
4. Noun and verb.
   The <u>mail</u> does not come on national holidays. [Noun.] <u>Mail</u> the package to her home
   address. [Verb.]
5. Verb.
   He <u>spends</u> his free time doing volunteer
   work.
6. Noun and verb.
   The <u>label</u> bore a poison warning. [Noun.]
   The companies must <u>label</u> their products.
   [Verb.]
7. Noun.
   The <u>door</u> flew open by itself.
8. Noun.
   My younger sister was good <u>company</u>.
9. Noun and verb.
   The <u>whistle</u> released us from work. [Noun.]
   We <u>whistle</u> all the way home. [Verb.]
10. Noun and verb.
    The <u>glue</u> stuck to my hands. [Noun.] We <u>glue</u>
    our models together. [Verb.]

1. The trees died.
2. They caught a disease.
3. The disease was a fungus.
4. It ruined a grove that was treasured.
5. Our great-grandfather planted the grove in the last century.

Exercise 3
Using nouns and verbs

Identify each of the following words as a noun, as a verb, or as both. Then create sentences of your own, using each word in each possible function.

Example:
fly
Noun and verb.
The *fly* sat on the meat loaf. [Noun.] The planes *fly* low. [Verb.]

1. wish
2. tie
3. swing
4. mail
5. spend

6. label
7. door
8. company
9. whistle
10. glue

 Forming sentence patterns with nouns and verbs

We build all our sentences, even the most complicated, on five basic patterns. As the following diagrams indicate, the patterns differ in their predicates because the relation between the verb and the remaining words is different.

The Five Basic Sentence Patterns

Predicate

1. Subject → Verb (intransitive)
   The earth   trembled.

2. Subject → Verb (transitive) → Direct object (DO)
   The earthquake   destroyed   the city.

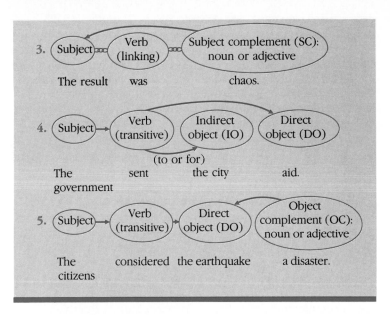

3. Subject — Verb (linking) — Subject complement (SC): noun or adjective

The result   was   chaos.

4. Subject → Verb (transitive) — Indirect object (IO) — Direct object (DO)

(to or for)

The government   sent   the city   aid.

5. Subject → Verb (transitive) — Direct object (DO) — Object complement (OC): noun or adjective

The citizens   considered   the earthquake   a disaster.

RESOURCES AND IDEAS

Andrea Lunsford, "Cognitive Development and the Basic Writer," *College English* 41 (1979): 38–46 (reprinted in *A Sourcebook for Basic Writing Teachers,* ed. Theresa Enos [New York: Random, 1986] 449–59). Lunsford presents exercises and assignments adapted to the cognitive level of basic writers and designed to help students identify sentence parts and functions and to help them write sentences using a number of basic patterns.

Marilyn Sternglass, "Composition Teacher as Reading Teacher," *College Composition and Communication* 27 (1976): 378–82. Sternglass suggests analytical reading as a way to help students understand the varieties of basic sentence structure.

gr
5a

Pattern 1: The earth trembled.

In the simplest pattern the predicate consists only of the verb. Verbs in this pattern do not require following words to complete their meaning and thus are called **intransitive** (from Latin words meaning "not passing over").

Subject	Predicate
	Intransitive verb
The earth	trembled.
Mosquitoes	buzz.
Elections	will have been held.

Pattern 2: The earthquake destroyed the city.

In pattern 2 the predicate consists of a verb followed by a noun that identifies who or what receives the action of the verb. This noun is a **direct object** (DO). Verbs that require direct objects to complete their meaning are called **transitive** ("passing over").

Subject	Predicate	
	Transitive verb	*Direct object*
The earthquake	destroyed	the city.
The people	wanted	peace.
Education	opens	doors.

Pattern 3: The result was chaos.

In pattern 3 the predicate also consists of a verb followed by a single noun. But here the verb *was* serves merely to introduce a word that renames or describes the subject. We could write the sentence *The result = chaos*. The noun following the verb in this kind of sentence is a **subject complement** (SC), or a **predicate noun.** Verbs in this pattern are called **linking verbs** because they link their subjects to the description that follows.

Subject	Predicate	
	Linking verb	*Subject complement*
The result	was	chaos.
The trees	are	elms.
The man	became	an accountant.

Subject complements in this sentence pattern may also be adjectives, words such as *tall* and *hopeful* (see 5b-1). Adjectives serving as complements are often called **predicate adjectives.**

Subject	Predicate	
	Linking verb	*Subject complement*
The result	was	chaotic.
Rents	are	high.
The apartments	seem	expensive.

Pattern 4: The government sent the city aid.

In sentence 4 the predicate consists of a verb followed by two nouns. The second noun is a direct object, identifying what was sent. But the first noun, *city,* is different. This noun is an **indirect object** (IO), identifying to or for whom or what the action of the verb is performed. The direct object and indirect object refer to different things, people, or places.

Subject	Predicate		
	Transitive verb	*Indirect object*	*Direct object*
The government	sent	the city	aid.
Businesses	gave	the museum	money.
One company	offered	its employees	bonuses.

Pattern 5: The citizens considered the earthquake a disaster.

In sentence 5 the predicate again consists of a verb followed by two nouns. But in this pattern the first noun is a direct object and the second noun renames or describes it. Here the second noun is an **object complement** (OC).

Subject	Predicate		
	Transitive verb	*Direct object*	*Object complement*
The citizens	considered	the earthquake	a disaster.
The class	elected	Joan O'Day	president.
Reporters	declared	her	the winner.

Notice that the relation between a direct object and an object complement is the same as that between a subject and a subject complement in pattern 3. Just as the subject complement renames or describes a subject, so an object complement renames or describes a direct object. And just as we can use either nouns or adjectives in pattern 3, so we can use either nouns or adjectives as object complements in this last pattern.

Subject	Predicate		
	Transitive verb	*Direct object*	*Object complement*
The citizens	considered	the earthquake	disastrous.
The results	proved	Sweeney	wrong.
Success	makes	some people	nervous.

However long or complicated a sentence is, one or more of these basic patterns forms its foundation. A question may change the order of the subject and verb (*Is she a doctor?*), a command may omit the subject entirely (*Be quiet!*), and the order of the parts may be different in some statements (see 5e), but the same basic sentence parts will be present or clearly understood.

Exercise 4
Identifying sentence patterns

In the following sentences, identify each verb as intransitive, transitive, or linking. Then identify each direct object (DO), indirect object (IO), subject complement (SC), and object complement (OC).

ANSWERS: EXERCISE 4

1. <u>Find</u> is transitive.

                DO   OC
     Many people find <u>New Orleans</u> <u>exciting</u>.
2. <u>Flock</u> is intransitive.
     No objects or complements.
3. <u>Visit</u> is transitive.

                      DO
     Usually they visit the <u>French Quarter</u> first.
4. <u>Call</u> is transitive.

                        DO
     New Orleans residents also call the <u>Quarter</u>

       OC
     the <u>*Vieux Carré*</u>.
5. <u>Are</u> is linking.

                       SC
     The Quarter's old buildings are <u>magnificent</u>.
6. <u>Is</u> is linking.

                         SC
     The focal point of the Quarter is <u>Jackson</u>
     <u>Square</u>.
7. <u>Sell</u> is transitive.

               IO   DO
     There artists sell <u>tourists</u> their <u>paintings</u>.
8. <u>Buy</u> is transitive.

               IO   DO
     Tourists buy their <u>relatives</u> inexpensive <u>sou-</u>
     <u>venirs</u>.
9. <u>Is</u> is linking.

                       SC
     The large white church is <u>St. Louis Cathedral</u>.
10. <u>Read</u> is transitive.

                   IO
     Parents read their <u>children</u> the church's his-
           DO
     torical <u>marker</u>.

ANSWERS: EXERCISE 5

Possible Answers

1. The audience laughed.
2. The town elected Flynn mayor.
3. Pip stole the pie.
4. Josie caught the ball.
5. My uncle brought me a cake.
6. Marilou seems unhappy.
7. One candidate called the other a crook.
8. We became reckless.
9. We bought ourselves a television set.
10. No one studied.

Example:
Children give their parents both headaches and pleasures.
Give is a transitive verb.

                IO   DO   DO
Children give their *parents* both *headaches* and *pleasures*.

1. Many people find New Orleans exciting.
2. Tourists flock there each year.
3. Usually they visit the French Quarter first.
4. New Orleans residents also call the Quarter the *Vieux Carré*.
5. The Quarter's old buildings are magnificent.
6. The focal point of the Quarter is Jackson Square.
7. There artists sell tourists their paintings.
8. Tourists buy their relatives inexpensive souvenirs.
9. The large white church is St. Louis Cathedral.
10. Parents read their children the church's historical marker.

Exercise 5
Creating sentences

Create sentences by using each of the following verbs in the pattern indicated. You may want to change the form of the verb.

> *Example:*
> give (S–V–IO–DO)
> Sam gave his brother a birthday card.

1. laugh (S–V)
2. elect (S–V–DO–OC)
3. steal (S–V–DO)
4. catch (S–V–DO)
5. bring (S–V–IO–DO)
6. seem (S–V–SC)
7. call (S–V–DO–OC)
8. become (S–V–SC)
9. buy (S–V–IO–DO)
10. study (S–V)

5b   Expanding the basic sentence with single words

Most of the sentences we read, write, or speak are more complex and also more informative and interesting than those examined so far. Most sentences contain one or more of the following: (1) modifying words; (2) word groups, called phrases and clauses; and (3) combinations of two or more words or word groups of the same kind.

1   Using adjectives and adverbs

The simplest expansion of sentences occurs when we add modifying words to describe or limit the nouns and verbs. Modifying words add details.

Recently, the earth trembled.
The earthquake *nearly* destroyed the *old* city.
The *federal* government *soon* sent the city aid.
The grant was a *very generous* one but disappeared *too quickly.*

The italicized words represent two different parts of speech:

- **Adjectives** describe or modify nouns (*old city, federal government*) and pronouns (*generous one*).
- **Adverbs** describe the action of verbs (*nearly destroyed, soon sent*) and also modify adjectives (*very generous*), other adverbs (*too quickly*), and whole groups of words (*Recently, the earth trembled.*).

We cannot always identify adjectives and adverbs by their form. Although an *-ly* ending often signals an adverb, many adverbs—*never* and *always,* for example—have a different form. Moreover, some adjectives end in *-ly: likely candidate* and *lovely breeze.* Therefore, to determine whether a word is an adjective or an adverb, we must identify the word or words it modifies. Adjectives modify only nouns and pronouns; adverbs modify only verbs, adjectives, other adverbs, and word groups.

Adverbs usually indicate where, when, how, or to what extent.

The rocks lie *there.* [*There* = where.]
They cracked *yesterday.* [*Yesterday* = when.]
They cracked *rapidly.* [*Rapidly* = how.]
No one *fully* understands why. [*Fully* = to what extent.]

Adjectives and adverbs appear in three forms:

- The **positive** form is the basic form, the one listed in the dictionary: *good, green, angry; badly, quickly, angrily.*
- The **comparative** form indicates a greater degree of the quality named by the word: *better, greener, angrier; worse, more quickly, more angrily.*
- The **superlative** form indicates the greatest degree of the quality named: *best, greenest, angriest; worst, most quickly, most angrily.*

(For further discussion of these forms, see 9e.)

Exercise 6
Identifying and using adjectives and adverbs

Identify the adjectives and adverbs in the following sentences. Then use each sentence as a model for creating a sentence of your own.

RESOURCES AND IDEAS

Anne J. Herrington, "Grammar Recharted: Sentence Analysis for Writing," *Writing Exercises from "Exercise Exchange,"* vol. 2 (Urbana: NCTE, 1984) 276–87. Herrington suggests using a five-column chart to analyze sentence patterns and help make students aware of syntax. The five columns in the chart—Preceding Subject, Subject, Between Subject and Verb, Verb, and Following Verb—allow the system to account for both relatively simple sentences and those to which considerable information has been added. The columns can be layered as well to account for compound sentences.

gr
5b

ANSWERS: EXERCISE 6

1. The <u>icy</u>^ADJ rain created <u>glassy</u>^ADJ patches on the roads.
   Sample imitation: The blue bird turned graceful circles in the air.

2. <u>Happily</u>,^ADV children played in the <u>slippery</u>^ADJ streets.
   Sample imitation: Quietly, we peeked into the silent cathedral.

3. <u>Fortunately</u>,^ADV <u>no</u>^ADJ cars ventured <u>out</u>.^ADV
   Sample imitation: Impatiently, the old man gazed ahead.

4. <u>Wise</u>^ADJ parents stayed <u>indoors</u>^ADV where they could be <u>warm</u>^ADJ and <u>dry</u>.^ADJ
   Sample imitation: Smart children go outdoors when they feel noisy and rambunctious.

5. The dogs slept <u>soundly</u>^ADV near the <u>warm</u>^ADJ radiators.
   Sample imitation: The babies lay quietly in their small cribs.

ANSWERS: EXERCISE 7

Possible Answers

1. skillfully
   The weaver was <u>skillful</u> at his craft. The waiter <u>skillfully</u> balanced the three trays.
2. wise
   The minister spoke <u>wisely</u> to the congregation. The <u>wise</u> child knows his or her own parent.
3. newly
   The <u>new</u> book smelled of wood. The <u>newly</u> planted petunias wilted in the sun.
4. brightly
   The <u>bright</u> colors were unflattering. The sun glinted <u>brightly</u> off the tin roof.
5. fortunate
   <u>Fortunately</u>, I passed the test. We are <u>fortunate</u> to be living in these times.
6. blunt
   She <u>bluntly</u> stated her opinion. The knife is too <u>blunt</u> to cut the cardboard.
7. happily
   Two <u>happy</u> people left the church. The child skipped <u>happily</u> along the street.
8. painful
   She spoke <u>painfully</u>. It was a <u>painful</u> decision.

Example:

The red barn sat uncomfortably among modern buildings.
The *red*^ADJ barn sat *uncomfortably*^ADV among *modern*^ADJ buildings.
The little girl complained loudly to her busy mother.

1. The icy rain created glassy patches on the roads.
2. Happily, children played in the slippery streets.
3. Fortunately, no cars ventured out.
4. Wise parents stayed indoors where they could be warm and dry.
5. The dogs slept soundly near the warm radiators.

Exercise 7
Using adjectives and adverbs

Change each of the following adjectives into an adverb, and change each adverb into an adjective. Then write one sentence using the adjective and another using the adverb.

Example:

sorrowful: *sorrowfully*

Her expression was *sorrowful.*

David watched *sorrowfully* as the firefighters removed the charred remains of his furniture.

1. skillful　　　5. fortunately　　8. painfully
2. wisely　　　6. bluntly　　　9. stupid
3. new　　　　7. happy　　　10. sturdy
4. bright

2　　**Using other words as modifiers**

We have already observed that a particular word may function sometimes as a noun, sometimes as a verb. Similarly, nouns and special forms of verbs may sometimes serve as modifiers of other nouns. In combinations such as *office buildings, Thanksgiving prayer,* and *shock hazard,* the first noun modifies the second. In combinations such as *singing birds, corrected papers,* and *broken finger,* the first word is a verb form modifying the following noun. (These modifying verb forms are discussed in more detail in 5c-2.) Again, the part of speech to which we assign a word always depends on its function in a sentence.

Exercise 8
Using verb forms as modifiers

Use each of the following verb forms to modify a noun in a sentence of your own.

Example:

smoking
Only a *smoking cigar* remained.

1. scrambled
2. twitching
3. rambling
4. typed
5. painted
6. written
7. charging
8. ripened
9. known
10. driven

Exercise 9
Sentence combining: Single-word modifiers

To practice expanding the basic sentence patterns with single-word modifiers, combine each group of sentences below into one sentence. You will have to delete and rearrange words.

Example:

New Orleans offers tourists food. New Orleans offers food proudly. The food is delicious.

New Orleans *proudly* offers tourists *delicious* food.

1. Tourists visit restaurants. The tourists are hungry. The restaurants are famous.
2. The restaurants fill. The restaurants are expensive. They are French. They fill rapidly.
3. The restaurants' awnings shelter the customers. The awnings are colorful. The customers are waiting.
4. The doors open. The doors are brass. They finally open. They open inward.
5. Waiters seat the customers. The customers are famished. The customers are tired.
6. The dish is salmon. The dish is tastiest. The salmon is poached.
7. Bread creates crumbs. The bread is crusty. The bread is white. The crumbs are many.
8. The desserts are rich. The desserts are chocolate. The desserts are luscious.
9. The patrons sip their coffee. The patrons are satisfied. They sip slowly. The coffee is strong. The coffee is sweet.
10. The customers give the waiters tips. The customers are departing. They give the tips gratefully. The tips are large.

9. stupidly
It was stupid of me to oversleep. He stupidly forgot to make an extra copy.
10. sturdily
The sturdy table was fifty years old. The little boy faced the dog sturdily.

ANSWERS: EXERCISE 8
Possible Answers

1. Jack woke up craving scrambled eggs.
2. The twitching limb relaxed when the sedative took effect.
3. The treasurer's rambling speech covered more topics than I can remember.
4. The typed manuscript contained many errors.
5. Painted birds decorate the window.
6. He wanted to know the origins of the written word.
7. The man escaped the charging animal.
8. We picked the ripened fruit.
9. All the known facts contradict his theory.
10. Driven people may have hypertension.

COLLABORATIVE LEARNING

ANSWERS: EXERCISE 9
Possible Answers

1. Hungry tourists visit famous restaurants.
2. The expensive French restaurants fill rapidly.
3. The restaurants' colorful awnings shelter the waiting customers.
4. The brass doors finally open inward.
5. Waiters seat the famished, tired customers.
6. The tastiest dish is poached salmon.
7. Crusty white bread creates many crumbs.
8. The rich chocolate desserts are luscious.
9. The satisfied patrons slowly sip their strong, sweet coffee.
10. The departing customers gratefully give the waiters large tips.

gr
5c

5c   Expanding the basic sentence with word groups

Most sentences we read or write contain whole word groups that serve as nouns and modifiers. Such word groups enable us to combine several bits of information into one sentence and to make the relations among them clear, as in this sentence:

gr
5c

RESOURCES AND IDEAS
Dealing with Error

David Bartholomae, "The Study of Error," *College Composition and Communication* 31 (1980): 253–69. Bartholomae suggests that asking basic writers to read their papers aloud helps identify sources of error and can contribute to improvement in writing.

Mina P. Shaughnessey, *Errors and Expectations: A Guide for the Teacher of Basic Writing* (New York: Oxford UP, 1977). This valuable book focuses on basic writing but is also an important work for teachers of writing at all levels. It provides a detailed analysis of the causes of student errors as well as useful strategies for dealing with writing problems.

Patricia Laurence, "Error's Endless Train: Why Students Don't Perceive Errors," *Journal of Basic Writing* 1 (1975): 23–42. The author discusses why students do not perceive errors and presents exercises to help make students aware of inflections and easily confused words.

Carroll Viera, "Helping Students to Help Themselves: An Approach to Grammar," *College Composition and Communication* 37 (1986): 94–96. Viera suggests having students analyze their own grammatical problems, do research in their handbooks, and present minilessons in small groups.

When the ice cracked, the skaters, fearing an accident, sought safety at the lake's edge.

The skeleton of this sentence—the basic subject and predicate—is *The skaters sought safety* (subject–verb–direct object). Attached to this skeleton are three other groups of words that add related information: *When the ice cracked, fearing an accident,* and *at the lake's edge.* These constructions are phrases and clauses.

- A **phrase** is a group of related words that lacks either a subject or a predicate or both: *fearing an accident, at the lake's edge.*
- A **clause** contains both a subject and a predicate: *When the ice cracked* and *the skaters sought safety* are both clauses, though only the second can stand alone as a sentence.

1 Using prepositional phrases

Prepositions are connecting words. Unlike nouns, verbs, and modifiers, which may change form according to their meaning and use in a sentence, prepositions never change form. We use many prepositions with great frequency.

Common prepositions

about	beneath	in spite of	round
above	beside	instead of	since
according to	between	into	through
across	beyond	like	throughout
after	by	near	till
against	concerning	next to	to
along	despite	of	toward
along with	down	off	under
among	during	on	underneath
around	except	onto	unlike
as	except for	out	until
aside from	excepting	out of	up
at	for	outside	upon
because of	from	over	with
before	in	past	within
behind	in addition to	regarding	without
below	inside		

A preposition always connects a noun, a pronoun, or a word group functioning as a noun to another word in the sentence: *Robins nest in trees.* The noun, pronoun, or word group so connected (*trees*) is the **object of the preposition.** The preposition plus its object and any modifiers is a **prepositional phrase.**

Preposition	Object
of	spaghetti
on	the surface
with	great satisfaction
upon	entering the room
from	where you are standing

Prepositions normally come before their objects. But in speech and informal writing the preposition sometimes comes after its object.

What do you want to see him *about*?
They know the *town* we are *from*.

Prepositional phrases usually function as adjectives (modifying nouns) or as adverbs (modifying verbs, adjectives, or other adverbs). As modifiers, they add details that make sentences clearer and more interesting for readers.

Prepositional phrases as adjectives

The costs *of the job* rise daily. [Phrase describes *costs*.]

Life *on a raft in the Mississippi* was an opportunity *for adventure*. [*On a raft* describes *life; in the Mississippi* describes *raft;* and *for adventure* describes *opportunity*.]

Prepositional phrases as adverbs

The sun rose *over the dump*. [Phrase describes *rose*.]
After sunset the sky remains light. [Phrase describes *remains*.]

Occasionally, prepositional phrases also function as nouns, though rarely in writing.

Prepositional phrase as noun

Across the river is too far to go for ice cream. [Phrase functions as sentence subject.]

Punctuating prepositional phrases

Since a prepositional phrase lacks a subject and a predicate, it should not be punctuated as a complete sentence. If it is, the result is a **sentence fragment:**

RESOURCES AND IDEAS
Sentence Combining: Background and Suggestions

Much has been written about sentence combining over the past two decades. The twenty-three essays in *Sentence Combining: A Rhetorical Perspective,* ed. Donald A. Daiker, Andrew Kerek, and Max Morenberg (Carbondale: Southern Illinois UP, 1985) provide excellent perspectives on the strengths and weaknesses of sentence combining as a way of improving the quality of writing and of developing an understanding of language and style.

The following articles are also useful resources:

Donald Daiker, Andrew Kerek, and Max Morenberg, "Sentence-Combining and Syntactic Maturity in Freshman English," *College Composition and Communication* 29 (1978): 36–41. The authors discuss the results of an experiment demonstrating the effectiveness of sentence combining over fifteen weeks of intensive instruction.

William Strong, "Sentence Combining: Back to the Basics and Beyond," *English Journal* 65 (1976): 56, 60–64. Strong explains different kinds of exercises and suggests ways to use them in class.

M. Beverly Swan, "Sentence Combining in College Composition: Interim Measures and Patterns," *Research in the Teaching of English* 13 (1979): 217–24. Swan reports that the amount of instruction students receive in sentence combining is less important than the amount of time they are given to absorb the instruction. She suggests that instruction should take place over a relatively long period, perhaps a fifteen-week semester.

RESOURCES AND IDEAS

Many of the exercises in this chapter can be used as the basis for a sequence of sentence-combining activities. The appropriate exercises are 9, 11, 13, 14, 16, 17, 18, 22.

Exercises in other chapters that can be part of a sentence-combining sequence are listed in the discussion "A Sequence for Sentence Combining" in the essay "The Handbook in Composition Courses" at the beginning of this *Annotated Instructor's Edition.*

gr
5c

Fragment   Toward the sun.

The phrase must be attached to another group of words containing both a subject and a predicate:

Revised   The plane turned *toward the sun.*

(See Chapter 10 for a full discussion of how to recognize and revise sentence fragments.)

A prepositional phrase that introduces a sentence is set off with punctuation, usually a comma, unless it is short (see 21b).

> *According to the newspaper and other sources,* the governor has reluctantly decided to veto the bill.
> *In 1865* the Civil War finally ended.

A prepositional phrase that interrupts or concludes a sentence is *not* set off with punctuation when it restricts the meaning of the word or words it modifies (see 21c).

> The announcement *of a tuition increase* surprised no one.
> Students expected new fees *for the coming year.*

When an interrupting or concluding prepositional phrase does *not* restrict meaning, but merely adds information to the sentence, then it *is* set off with punctuation, usually a comma or commas (see 21c).

> The governor, *according to the newspaper and other sources,* has reluctantly decided to veto the bill.
> The governor has reclutantly decided to veto the bill, *according to the newspaper and other sources.*

As all the preceding examples illustrate, a preposition and its object are not separated by a comma (see 21j-1).

ANSWERS: EXERCISE 10

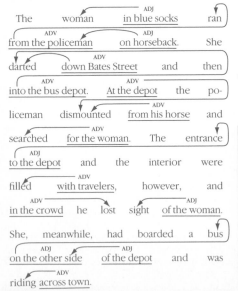

Exercise 10
Identifying prepositional phrases

Identify the prepositional phrases in the following passage. Indicate whether each phrase functions as an adjective or as an adverb, and name the word that the phrase modifies.

Example:
After an hour I finally arrived at the home of my professor.
 ADV PHRASE   ADV PHRASE ADJ PHRASE
After an hour I finally arrived *at the home of my professor.* [*After an hour* and *at the home* modify *arrived*; *of my professor* modifies *home.*]

The woman in blue socks ran from the policeman on horse-back. She darted down Bates Street and then into the bus depot. At the depot the policeman dismounted from his horse and searched for the woman. The entrance to the depot and the interior were filled with travelers, however, and in the crowd he lost sight of the woman. She, meanwhile, had boarded a bus on the other side of the depot and was riding across town.

Exercise 11
Sentence combining: Prepositional phrases

To practice writing sentences with prepositional phrases, combine each group of sentences below into one sentence that includes one or two prepositional phrases. You will have to add, delete, and rearrange words. Some items have more than one possible answer.

> *Example:*
>
> I will start working. The new job will pay the minimum wage.
> I will start working *at a new job for the minimum wage.*

1. Tourists ride the trolley car. The tourists are visiting New Orleans. The Garden District is where the trolley goes.
2. They enter the old cars. They have no hesitation.
3. The trolley tour continues. The tour takes an hour.
4. The passengers travel. They pass Loyola and Tulane universities. They go along Audubon Park's western edge.
5. Audubon Park offers tables. Picnicking families can use the tables.
6. The trolley riders see old homes. The homes have huge yards. Wrought-iron fences surround the yards.
7. Huge oak trees stand. They dot the yards. They also line the trolley rails.
8. The trees bless the homes and the passengers. They provide shade and beauty.
9. Azalea bushes astound the eye. March is when they bloom. They have blazing colors.
10. All the buildings are very old. Only the stores are modern.

ANSWERS: EXERCISE 11
Possible Answers

1. Tourists in New Orleans ride the trolley car to the Garden District.
2. Without hesitation they enter the old cars.
3. The trolley tour continues for an hour.
4. The passengers travel past Loyola and Tulane universities and along Audubon Park's western edge.
5. Audubon Park offers tables for picnicking families.
6. The trolley riders see old homes with huge yards surrounded by wrought-iron fences.
7. Huge oak trees stand in the yards and along the trolley rails.
8. The trees bless the homes and the passengers with shade and beauty.
9. In March azalea bushes astound the eye with their blazing colors.
10. All the buildings except the stores are very old.

2   Using verbals and verbal phrases

Verbals are special verb forms such as *smoking* or *hidden* or *to win* that can function as nouns (*smoking is dangerous*) or as modifiers (*the hidden money, the urge to win*).

Caution: Verbals *cannot* stand alone as the complete verb in the predicate of a sentence. For example, *The man smoking* and *The money hidden* are not sentences but sentence fragments (see

USING READINGS

Students can analyze passages from an essay in a reader (or some other source), looking for verbal phrases, passive sentences, compound and complex sentences, or any other features that you feel contribute to the effect of the essay and should be part of the students' prose style.

REDO THE READINGS

Using the passages from the activity above (or other passages), ask students to transform each occurrence of a structure—verbal phrases or compound sentences, etc.—into alternate structures of their choice without changing the meaning of the passage. Then ask students to comment on how the changes affect the passage, if at all. This activity is particularly well suited for collaborative work.

> TRANSPARENCY MASTER
> AVAILABLE

> TRANSPARENCY MASTER
> AVAILABLE

10a). Any verbal must combine with a helping verb to serve as the predicate of a sentence: *The man was smoking. The money is hidden.*

Because verbals cannot serve alone as sentence predicates, they are sometimes called **nonfinite verbs** (in essence, they are "unfinished"). **Finite verbs,** in contrast, can make an assertion or express a state of being without a helping verb (they are "finished"). Either of two tests can distinguish finite and nonfinite verbs.

Tests for finite and nonfinite verbs (verbals)

Test 1: Does the word require a change in form when a third-person subject changes from singular to plural?

Yes.   Finite verb: *It sings. They sing.*

No.   Nonfinite verb (verbal): *bird singing, birds singing*

Test 2: Does the word require a change in form to show the difference in present, past, and future?

Yes.   Finite verb: *It sings. It sang. It will sing.*

No.   Nonfinite verb (verbal): *The bird singing is/was/will be a robin.*

There are three kinds of verbals: participles, gerunds, and infinitives.

Participles

All verbs have two participle forms, a present and a past. The **present participle** consists of the dictionary form of the verb plus the ending -*ing: beginning, completing, hiding.* The **past participle** of most verbs consists of the dictionary form plus -*d* or -*ed: believed, completed.* Some common verbs have an irregular past participle: *begun, hidden.* (See 7a.)

Both present and past participles function as adjectives to modify nouns and pronouns.

Shopping malls sometimes frustrate shoppers. [Modifies *malls.*]
Shoppers complain of *dizzying* headaches. [Modifies *headaches.*]
Shoppers may feel *trapped.* [Modifies *shoppers.*]
Irritated, they may lash out at companions. [Modifies *they.*]

Gerunds

Gerund is the name given to the *-ing* form of the verb when it serves as a noun.

Strolling through stores can exhaust the hardiest shopper. [Sentence subject.]

Many children learn to hate *shopping.* [Object of *to hate.*]

Present participles and gerunds can be distinguished *only* by their function in a sentence. If the *-ing* form functions as an adjective (*a teaching degree*), it is a present participle. If the *-ing* form functions as a noun (*Teaching is difficult*), it is a gerund.

Infinitives

The **infinitive** is the *to* form of the verb, the dictionary form preceded by the infinitive marker *to: to begin, to hide, to run.* Infinitives may function as nouns, adjectives, or adverbs.

The question *to answer* is why shoppers endure mall fatigue. [The infinitive functions as an adjective, modifying *question.*]

The solution for mall fatigue is *to leave.* [The infinitive functions as a noun, the complement of the subject, *solution.*]

Still, shoppers find it difficult *to quit.* [The infinitive functions as an adverb, modifying *difficult.*]

Verbal phrases

Participles, gerunds, and infinitives—like other forms of verbs—may take subjects, objects, or complements, and they may be modified by adverbs. The verbal and all the words immediately related to it make up a **verbal phrase.** With verbal phrases, we can create concise sentences packed with information.

Like participles, **participial phrases** always serve as adjectives, modifying nouns or pronouns.

Choosing products for purchase, most shoppers feel themselves in control. [Modifies *shoppers.*]

They act on choices *made from personal taste.* [Modifies *choices.*]

Gerund phrases, like gerunds, always serve as nouns.

Shopping for clothing, housewares, and other items also satisfies personal needs. [Sentence subject.]

Malls are good at *creating such needs.* [Object of preposition *at.*]

**gr
5c**

Infinitive phrases may serve as nouns, adverbs, or adjectives.

To design a mall is *to create an artificial environment.* [Both phrases function as nouns, the first as the sentence subject and the second as a subject complement.]

Malls are designed *to make shoppers feel safe.* [Phrase functions as an adverb, modifying *designed.*]

Threats are removed, but so is the option *to act freely.* [Phrase functions as an adjective, modifying *option.*]

Note: When an infinitive or infinitive phrase serves as a noun after verbs such as *hear, let, help, make, see,* and *watch,* the infinitive marker *to* is omitted: *We all heard her (*to*) tell the story.*

Punctuating verbals and verbal phrases

Like prepositional phrases, verbal phrases punctuated as complete sentences are sentence fragments. A complete sentence must contain a subject and a finite verb (p. 188).

Fragment   *Treating* the patients kindly.
Revised   *She treats* the patients kindly.

(See Chapter 10 on sentence fragments.)

A verbal or verbal phrase serving as a modifier is almost always set off with a comma when it introduces a sentence (see 21b).

To pay tuition, some students work at two jobs.
Breathing evenly, the cat lay asleep on the rug.

A modifying verbal or verbal phrase that interrupts or concludes a sentence is *not* set off with punctuation when it restricts the meaning of the word or words it modifies (see 21c).

The boy *selling hot dogs* is my brother.
She worked at two jobs *to pay her tuition.*

When an interrupting or concluding verbal modifier does *not* restrict meaning, but merely adds information to the sentence, it *is* set off with punctuation, usually a comma or commas (see 21c).

The cat, *breathing evenly,* lay asleep on the rug.
The cat lay asleep on the rug, *breathing evenly.*

Exercise 12
Identifying verbals and verbal phrases

The following sentences contain participles, gerunds, and infinitives as well as participial, gerund, and infinitive phrases. First

ANSWERS: EXERCISE 12

1. ^{ADJ}
   <u>Written in 1850 by Nathaniel Hawthorne</u>, *The Scarlet Letter* tells the story of Hester Prynne.
2. ^{ADJ}
   <u>Shunned by the community</u>, Hester endures her loneliness.
3. Hester is humble enough <u>to withstand her Puritan neighbors' cutting remarks</u>.^{ADV}
4. ^N
   <u>Wearing a scarlet *A* on her bosom</u> marks her as a sinner.

identify each verbal or verbal phrase. Then indicate whether it is used as an adjective, an adverb, or a noun.

Example:

Laughing, the talk-show host prodded her guest to talk.
ADJ

Laughing, the talk-show host prodded her guest *to talk*
ADV

1. Written in 1850 by Nathaniel Hawthorne, *The Scarlet Letter* tells the story of Hester Prynne.
2. Shunned by the community, Hester endures her loneliness.
3. Hester is humble enough to withstand her Puritan neighbors' cutting remarks.
4. Wearing a scarlet *A* on her bosom marks her as a sinner.
5. Staring quietly ahead, Hester refuses to name the father of her child.
6. Because the man is a minister, to admit his identity seems impossible.
7. Despite the cruel treatment, the determined young woman refuses to leave her home.
8. Sewing for wealthy townspeople and tending the sick enable Hester to provide a home for her daughter, Pearl.
9. Through the years, Hester resists temptations to remove the glaring *A* from her bosom.
10. By living a life of patience and unselfishness, Hester eventually becomes the community's angel.

Exercise 13
Sentence combining: Verbals and verbal phrases

To practice writing sentences with verbals and verbal phrases, combine each pair of sentences below into one sentence. You will have to add, delete, change, and rearrange words. Each item has more than one possible answer.

Example:

My father took pleasure in mean pranks. For instance, he hid my neighbor's cat.

My father took pleasure in mean pranks such as *hiding the neighbors' cat.*

1. Air pollution is a health problem. It affects millions of Americans.
2. The air has been polluted mainly by industries and automobiles. It contains toxic chemicals.
3. Environmentalists pressure politicians. They think politicians should pass stricter laws.
4. Many politicians waver. They are not necessarily anti-environment.
5. The problems are too complex. They cannot be solved easily.
6. One proposal is that we shut down all industrial polluters. That course could cause economic chaos.

5. Staring quietly ahead, Hester refuses to name
ADJ
the father of her child.
N

6. Because the man is a minister, to admit his
N
identity seems impossible.

7. Despite the cruel treatment, the determined
ADJ
young woman refuses to leave her home.

8. Sewing for wealthy townspeople and tending
N
the sick enable Hester to provide a home for
her daughter, Pearl.

9. Through the years, Hester resists temptations
to remove the glaring *A* from her bo-
ADJ   ADJ
som.

10. By living a life of patience and unselfishness,
N
Hester eventually becomes the community's
angel.

ANSWERS: EXERCISE 13

1. Air pollution is a health problem affecting millions of Americans.
2. Polluted mainly by industries and automobiles, the air contains toxic chemicals.
3. Environmentalists pressure politicians to pass stricter laws.
4. Wavering politicians are not necessarily anti-environment.
5. The problems are too complex to be solved easily.
6. The proposal to shut down all industrial polluters could cause economic chaos.

gr
5c

7. Citizens cherish the convenience of driving their own cars.
8. Yet something must be done to reduce air pollution.
9. Increasing lung illnesses will cost society, too.
10. Found even in rural areas, dangerous air pollutants affect almost everyone.

RESOURCES AND IDEAS

Martha Solomon, "Teaching the Nominative Absolute," *College Composition and Communication* 26 (1975): 356–61. Solomon offers advice on analyzing and teaching the absolute.

7. Citizens cherish the convenience. They drive their own cars.
8. Yet something must be done. Air pollution must be reduced.
9. Lung illnesses will increase. They will cost society, too.
10. Dangerous air pollutants are found even in rural areas. They affect almost everyone.

 Using absolute phrases

Absolute phrases consist of a noun or pronoun and a participle, plus any modifiers.

> Many ethnic groups, *their own place established,* are making way for new arrivals.
>
> *Their native lands left behind, an uncertain future looming ahead,* immigrants face many obstacles.

These phrases are called *absolute* (from a Latin word meaning "free") because they have no specific grammatical connection to any word in the rest of the sentence. Instead, they modify the entire rest of the sentence, adding information or clarifying meaning.

Notice that absolute phrases, unlike participial phrases, always contain a subject. Compare the following.

> For many immigrants *learning English,* the language introduces American culture. [Participial phrase modifying *immigrants.*]
>
> *The immigrants having learned English,* their opportunities widen. [Absolute phrase having its own subject, *immigrants,* and modifying the rest of the sentence.]

We often omit the participle from an absolute phrase when it is some form of *be* such as *being* or *having been.*

> *Two languages* (*being*) *at hand,* bilingual citizens in fact have many cultural and occupational advantages.

Punctuating absolute phrases

Absolute phrases are always set off from the rest of the sentence with punctuation, usually a comma or commas (see 21d).

> *Their future more secure,* these citizens will make room for new arrivals.
>
> These citizens, *their future more secure,* will make room for new arrivals.

Exercise 14
Sentence combining: Absolute phrases

To practice writing sentences with absolute phrases, combine each pair of sentences below into one sentence that contains an absolute phrase. You will have to add, delete, change, and rearrange words.

Example:

The flower's petals wilted. It looked pathetic.
Its petals wilted, the flower looked pathetic.

1. Her husband died in office. Lindy Boggs was elected to his seat as a representative from Louisiana.
2. Representative Barbara Jordan spoke at the national Democratic convention. Her voice thundered through the auditorium.
3. A vacancy had occurred. Sandra Day O'Connor was appointed the first female Supreme Court justice.
4. Geraldine Ferraro enjoyed the crowd's cheers after her nomination for Vice President. Her face beamed joyfully.
5. Pat Schroeder withdrew from the race for President. Her plans had changed.

ANSWERS: EXERCISE 14
Possible Answers

1. Her husband having died in office, Lindy Boggs was elected to his seat as a representative from Louisiana.
2. Representative Barbara Jordan spoke at the national Democratic convention, her voice thundering through the auditorium.
3. A vacancy having occurred, Sandra Day O'Connor was appointed the first female Supreme Court justice.
4. Geraldine Ferraro enjoyed the crowd's cheers after her nomination for Vice President, her face beaming joyfully.
5. Pat Schroeder withdrew from the race for President, her plans having changed.

gr
5c

 4 Using subordinate clauses

As we noted earlier, a **clause** is any group of words that contains both a subject and a predicate. There are two kinds of clauses, and the distinction between them is important.

- A **main** or **independent clause** can stand alone as a sentence: *The sky darkened.*
- A **subordinate** or **dependent clause** is just like a main clause *except* that it begins with a subordinating word: *when the sky darkened.* *When* and other subordinating words such as *because, if, who,* or *that* express particular relationships between the clauses they introduce and the main clauses to which they are attached. Clauses that have been subordinated can *never* stand alone as sentences (see the discussion of punctuation on p. 196).

The following examples show the differences between the two kinds of clauses:

Two main clauses
The school teaches parents. It is unusual.

First clause subordinated
Because the school teaches parents, it is unusual.

Two main clauses

Some parents avoid their children's schools. They are often illiterate.

Second clause subordinated

Parents *who are illiterate* often avoid their children's schools.

We use two kinds of subordinating words to connect subordinate clauses with main clauses. The **subordinating conjunction** or **subordinator** always comes at the beginning of a subordinate clause. Like prepositions, subordinating conjunctions never change form in any way.

Common subordinating conjunctions

after	because	in order that	than	when
although	before	now that	that	whenever
as	even if	once	though	where
as if	even though	rather than	till	whereas
as long as	if	since	unless	wherever
as though	if only	so that	until	while

The **relative pronoun** also introduces a subordinate clause and links it with an independent clause.

Relative pronouns

which	what	who (whose, whom)
that	whatever	whoever (whomever)

Like subordinating conjunctions, relative pronouns link one clause with another. But unlike subordinating conjunctions, relative pronouns also usually act as subjects or objects in their own clauses, and two of them (*who* and *whoever*) change form accordingly (see 6g).

Subordinate clauses function as adjectives, adverbs, and nouns and are described as adjective, adverb, or noun clauses according to their use in a particular sentence. Only by determining its function in a sentence can we identify a particular clause.

Adjective clauses

Adjective clauses modify nouns and pronouns, providing necessary or helpful information about them. They usually begin with the relative pronouns listed above, although a few adjective clauses begin with *when* or *where* (standing for *in which, on which,* or *at which*). The relative pronoun is the subject or object of the clause it begins. The clause ordinarily falls immediately after the noun or pronoun it modifies.

> Parents *who are illiterate* often have bad memories of school. [Modifies *parents.*]
>
> Schools *that involve parents* are more successful with children. [Modifies *Schools.*]
>
> One school, *which is open year-round,* helps parents learn to read. [Modifies *school.*]
>
> The school is in a city *where the illiteracy rate is high.* [Modifies *city.*]

Adverb clauses

Like adverbs, **adverb clauses** modify verbs, adjectives, other adverbs, and whole groups of words. They usually tell how, why, when, where, under what conditions, or with what result. They always begin with subordinating conjunctions.

> The school began teaching parents *when adult illiteracy gained national attention.* [Modifies *began.*]
>
> At first the program was not as successful *as its founders had hoped.* [Modifies *successful.*]
>
> *Because it was directed at people who could not read,* advertising had to be inventive. [Modifies whole clause following.]

An adverb clause can often be moved around in a sentence with no loss of clarity. Compare the example immediately above and this one:

> Advertising had to be inventive *because it was directed at people who could not read.*

Noun clauses

Noun clauses function as subjects, objects, and complements in sentences. They begin either with relative pronouns or with the words *when, where, whether, why,* and *how.* Unlike adjective and adverb clauses, noun clauses *replace* a word (a noun) within a main clause; therefore, they can be difficult to identify.

> *Success* depended on door-to-door advertising. [*Success* is the sentence subject.]
>
> *Whether the program would succeed* depended on door-to-door advertising. [The noun clause replaces *Success* as the sentence subject.]

gr
5c

gr
5c

RESOURCES AND IDEAS

Richard B. Larsen, "Sentence Patterning," *College Composition and Communication* 37 (1986): 103–04. Larsen describes a sequence in which students are introduced to a variety of sentence patterns and then asked to use the patterns in their writing, including paragraph-length compositions.

Here are some typical noun clauses:

> Teachers explained in person *how the program would work.* [Object of *explained.*]
>
> *Whoever seemed slightly interested* was invited to an open meeting. [Sentence subject.]
>
> A few parents were anxious about *what their children would think.* [Object of preposition *about.*]

Elliptical clauses

A subordinate clause that is grammatically incomplete but clear in meaning is an **elliptical clause** (*ellipsis* means "omission"). The meaning of the clause is clear because the missing element can be supplied from the context. Most often the elements omitted are the relative pronouns *that, which,* and *whom* from adjective clauses or the predicate from the second part of a comparison.

> The parents knew their children could read better *than they* (*could read*).
>
> Skepticism and fear were among the feelings (*that*) *the parents voiced.*
>
> *Though* (*they were*) *often reluctant at first,* about a third of the parents attended the meeting.

Punctuating subordinate clauses

Subordinate clauses punctuated as complete sentences are sentence fragments. Though a subordinate clause contains a subject and a predicate and thus resembles a complete sentence, it also contains a subordinating word that makes its meaning dependent on a main clause.

Fragment	Because a door was ajar.
Revised	A door was ajar.
Revised	The secret leaked *because a door was ajar.*

(See Chapter 10 on sentence fragments.)

A subordinate clause serving as an adverb is almost always set off with a comma when it introduces a sentence (see 21b).

> *Although the project was almost completed,* it lost its funding.

A modifying subordinate clause that interrupts or concludes a main clause is *not* set off with punctuation when it restricts the meaning of the word or words it modifies (see 21c).

The woman *who spoke* is a doctor.

The project lost its funding *because it was not completed on time.*

When an interrupting or concluding subordinate clause does *not* restrict meaning, but merely adds information to the sentence, it *is* set off with punctuation, usually a comma or commas (see 21c).

The project lost its funding, *although it was almost completed.*
The woman, *who is a doctor,* cares for her invalid father.

gr
5c

Exercise 15
Identifying subordinate clauses

Identify the subordinate clauses in the following sentences. Then indicate whether each is used as an adjective, an adverb, or a noun. If the clause is a noun, indicate its function in the sentence.

Example:

The article explained how one could build an underground house.

NOUN

The article explained *how one could build an underground house.* [Object of *explained.*]

1. Scientists who want to catch the slightest signals from space use extremely sensitive receivers.
2. That they will hear messages from space is the expectation of many serious scientists.
3. Even though they have had to fight for funding, these scientists have persisted in their research.
4. The research is called SETI, which stands for Search for Extraterrestrial Intelligence.
5. The supposition is that intelligent beings in space are trying to get in touch with us.
6. The challenge is to guess what frequency these beings would use to send signals.
7. The scientists are hopeful because thousands of life-producing planets could exist in the Milky Way.
8. If life could arise on Earth, it could arise elsewhere.
9. The same natural selection that favors complex species here would favor them elsewhere.
10. Although so far no clear messages have been heard, the researchers remain hopeful.

ANSWERS: EXERCISE 15

1. Scientists <u>who want to catch the slightest sig-nals from space</u> use extremely sensitive re-ceivers. [ADJ]
2. <u>That they will hear messages from space</u> is the expectation of many serious scientists. [N (SUBJECT)]
3. <u>Even though they have had to fight for fund-ing</u>, these scientists have persisted in their research. [ADV]
4. The research is called SETI, <u>which stands for Search for Extraterrestrial Intelligence</u>. [ADJ]
5. The supposition is <u>that intelligent beings in space are trying to get in touch with us</u>. [N (SUBJECT COMPLEMENT)]
6. The challenge is to guess <u>what frequency these beings would use to send signals</u>. [N (DIRECT OBJECT)]
7. The scientists are hopeful <u>because thousands of life-producing planets could exist in the Milky Way</u>. [ADV]
8. <u>If life could arise on Earth</u>, it could arise elsewhere. [ADV]
9. The same natural selection <u>that favors com-plex species here</u> would favor them else-where. [ADJ]
10. <u>Although so far no clear messages have been heard</u>, the researchers remain hopeful. [ADV]

Exercise 16
Sentence combining: Subordinate clauses

To practice writing sentences with subordinate clauses, combine each pair of main clauses below into one sentence. Use either

COLLABORATIVE LEARNING

ANSWERS: EXERCISE 16
Possible Answers

1. Moviegoers expect that movie sequels should be as exciting as the original films.
2. Although a few sequels are good films, most are poor imitations of the originals.
3. Whenever a sequel to a blockbuster film arrives in the theater, crowds quickly line up to see it.
4. Viewers pay to see the same villains and heroes whom they remember fondly.
5. Afterward, viewers often grumble about filmmakers who rehash tired plots and characters.
6. The filmmakers seem to be afraid that audiences will not like change.
7. If violence helped the original movie to make money, the director will then put even more in the sequel.
8. The producers depend on the crowds to flock to the theater where they saw the original film.
9. Producers and directors who make trashy sequels may be greedy.
10. When customers demand to see good films, filmmakers will offer something besides cinematic garbage.

CREATE YOUR OWN

Divide the class into groups. Ask each group to create its own set of sentence-combining exercises following the pattern of the exercises in the handbook. Then ask the groups to trade exercises, work on them, and return them to the authors with both positive comments and criticisms.

subordinating conjunctions or relative pronouns as appropriate, referring to the lists on page 194 if necessary. You will have to add, delete, and rearrange words. Each item has more than one possible answer.

> *Example:*
>
> She did not have her tire irons with her. She could not change her bicycle tire.
>
> *Because* she did not have her tire irons with her, she could not change her bicycle tire.

1. Moviegoers expect something. Movie sequels should be as exciting as the original films.
2. A few sequels are good films. Most are poor imitations of the originals.
3. A sequel to a blockbuster film arrives in the theater. Crowds quickly line up to see it.
4. Viewers pay to see the same villains and heroes. They remember these characters fondly.
5. Afterward, viewers often grumble about filmmakers. The filmmakers rehash tired plots and characters.
6. The filmmakers seem to be afraid. Audiences may not like change.
7. Violence may have helped the original movie make money. The director will then put even more in the sequel.
8. The producers depend on the crowds to flock to the theater. The crowds saw the original film there.
9. Producers and directors may be greedy. They make trashy sequels.
10. Customers must demand to see good films. Then filmmakers will offer something besides cinematic garbage.

Using appositives

An **appositive** is a word or word group that renames the word or word group before it. (The word *appositive* derives from a Latin word that means "placed near to" or "applied to.") The most common appositives are nouns that rename other nouns.

> Bizen ware, *a dark stoneware,* has been produced in Japan since the fourteenth century. [Noun phrase as appositive.]
>
> The name *Bizen* comes from the location of the kilns used to fire the pottery. [Proper noun as appositive.]
>
> The process of making Bizen ware, *firing it for many days with no glaze,* produces the dark color. [Gerund phrase as appositive.]

All appositives can replace the words they refer to: *A dark stoneware has been produced in Japan.*

Appositives are often introduced by words and phrases such as *or, that is, such as, for example,* and *in other words.*

> Bizen ware was used in the Japanese tea ceremony, *that is, the Zen Buddhist observance that linked meditation and art.*

Although most appositives are nouns that rename other nouns, they may also be and rename other parts of speech.

> The pottery is thrown, that is, *formed on a potter's wheel.* [The appositive defines the verb *is thrown.*]

Noun appositives can always be stated as clauses with some form of the verb *be.*

> Bizen ware, (*which is*) *a dark stoneware,* has been produced in Japan since the fourteenth century.

Thus appositives are economical alternatives to adjective clauses containing a form of *be.*

gr
5c

Punctuating appositives

Appositives punctuated as complete sentences are sentence fragments (see Chapter 10). Correcting such fragments generally involves connecting the appositive to the main clause containing the word referred to.

Fragment   An exceedingly tall man with narrow shoulders.
Revised   He stood next to a basketball player, *an exceedingly tall man with narrow shoulders.*

An appositive is *not* set off with punctuation when it restricts the meaning of the word it refers to (see 21c).

The verb *howl* comes from the Old English verb *houlen.*

When an appositive does *not* restrict the meaning of the word it refers to, it *is* set off with punctuation, usually a comma or commas (see 21c).

An aged elm, the tree was struck by lightning.
The tree, *an aged elm,* was struck by lightning.
Lightning struck the tree, *an aged elm.*

A nonrestrictive appositive is sometimes set off with a dash or dashes, especially when it contains commas (see 25b-2).

Three people—*Will, Carolyn, and Tom*—object to the new procedure.

A concluding appositive is sometimes set off with a colon (see 25a-1).

Two principles guide the judge's decisions: *justice and mercy.*

gr
5d

COLLABORATIVE LEARNING

ANSWERS: EXERCISE 17
Possible Answers

1. Some people, geniuses from birth, perform amazing feats when they are very young.
2. John Stuart Mill, a British philosopher, had written a history of Rome by age seven.
3. Paul Klee and Gustav Mahler, two great artists, began their work at age four.
4. Mahler, a Bohemian composer of intensely emotional works, was also the child of a brutal father.
5. As a child the Swiss painter Paul Klee was frightened by his own drawings of devils.

Exercise 17
Sentence combining: Appositives

To practice writing sentences with appositives, combine each pair of sentences into one sentence that contains an appositive. You will have to delete and rearrange words. Some items have more than one possible answer.

Example:

The largest land animal is the elephant. The elephant is also one of the most intelligent animals.

The largest land animal, *the elephant,* is also one of the most intelligent animals.

1. Some people perform amazing feats when they are very young. These people are geniuses from birth.
2. John Stuart Mill was a British philosopher. He had written a history of Rome by age seven.
3. Two great artists began their work at age four. They were Paul Klee and Gustav Mahler.
4. Mahler was a Bohemian composer of intensely emotional works. He was also the child of a brutal father.
5. Paul Klee was a Swiss painter. As a child he was frightened by his own drawings of devils.

5d Compounding words, phrases, and clauses

We often combine words and word groups that are closely related and parallel in importance.

Headaches can be controlled by biofeedback. Heart rate can be controlled by biofeedback.

Headaches and heart rate can be controlled by biofeedback. [A **compound subject** with a common predicate.]

People learn to recognize body states. They learn to control their responses.

People learn *to recognize body states and to control their responses.* [A **compound direct object** of the verb *learn.*]

Without medication, biofeedback cures headaches. It steadies heart rate. It lowers blood pressure. It relaxes muscles.

Without medication, biofeedback *cures headaches, steadies heart rate, lowers blood pressure, and relaxes muscles.* [A **compound predicate** with a common subject, *biofeedback.*]

As the examples show, compounding makes writing more economical and clearer because it pulls together linked information. (See also 16a.)

RESOURCES AND IDEAS

Donna Gorrell, "Controlled Composition for Basic Writers," *College Composition and Communication* 32 (1981): 308–16. Gorrell suggests having students manipulate and alter previously written material to develop basic skills.

gr
5d

 1 **Using coordinating conjunctions and correlative conjunctions**

The word *and* is a **coordinating conjunction.** Like prepositions and subordinating conjunctions, coordinating conjunctions are few and do not change form.

> ## Coordinating conjunctions
>
> | and | nor | for | yet |
> |-----|-----|-----|-----|
> | but | or | so | |

The coordinating conjunctions *and, but, nor,* and *or* always connect words or word groups of the same kind—that is, two or more nouns, verbs, adjectives, adverbs, phrases, subordinate clauses, or main clauses.

> Biofeedback *or* simple relaxation can relieve headaches.
> Biofeedback is effective *but* costly.
> Relaxation also works well, *and* it is inexpensive.

The conjunctions *for* and *so* cannot connect words, phrases, or subordinate clauses, but they can connect main clauses. *For* may also function as a preposition (*a present for the girls*). When it functions as a conjunction, it indicates cause. *So* indicates result.

> Biofeedback can be costly, *for* the training involves technical equipment and specialists.
> Relaxation can be difficult to learn alone, *so* some people do seek help.

The word *yet* often functions as an adverb (*She has not left yet*), but it can also function as a coordinating conjunction. Like *but,* it indicates contrast.

Relaxation instruction does cost, *yet* it is usually cheaper than biofeedback training.

Some conjunctions pair up with other words to form **correlative conjunctions.**

Common correlative conjunctions

both . . . and	neither . . . nor
not only . . . but also	whether . . . or
not . . . but	as . . . as
either . . . or	

Both biofeedback *and* relaxation can relieve headaches.

The techniques require *neither* psychotherapy *nor* medication.

The headache sufferer learns *not only* to recognize the causes of headaches *but also* to control those causes.

Punctuating compounded words, phrases, and clauses

Two words, phrases, or subordinate clauses that are connected by a coordinating conjunction are *not* separated by a comma (see 21j-2).

The *boys and girls* segregated themselves.
The cat jumped *off the roof and into the tree.*
The robbery occurred *after I left but before Kim arrived.*

When two *main* clauses are joined into one sentence with a coordinating conjunction, a comma precedes the conjunction (see 21a).

The test is difficult, *but* a good driver will pass.

When two main clauses are joined *without* a coordinating conjunction, they must be separated with a semicolon to avoid the error called a **comma splice** (see 11a).

The joke was not funny; it was insulting.

The semicolon sometimes separates two main clauses joined by a coordinating conjunction when the clauses are long or contain commas (see 22c). The semicolon *always* separates two main clauses related by a conjunctive adverb (see the next section).

In a series of three or more items, commas separate the items, with *and* usually preceding the last item (see 21f-1).

The curtains were mostly white with splotches of pink, yellow, *and* brown.

Semicolons sometimes separate the items in a series if they are long or contain commas (see 22d).

The comma also separates coordinate adjectives (those which modify a noun or pronoun equally) when the adjectives are not joined by a coordinating conjunction (see 21f-2).

Wet, *slick* roads made driving dangerous.

The comma does *not* separate adjectives when the one nearer the noun is more closely related to it in meaning (see 21f-2).

She gave the teacher a *large red* apple.

 2 Using conjunctive adverbs

gr
5d

One other kind of connecting word, called a **conjunctive adverb,** relates only main clauses, not words, phrases, or subordinate clauses.

Common conjunctive adverbs

accordingly	furthermore	moreover	similarly
also	hence	namely	still
anyway	however	nevertheless	then
besides	incidentally	next	thereafter
certainly	indeed	nonetheless	therefore
consequently	instead	now	thus
finally	likewise	otherwise	undoubtedly
further	meanwhile		

Unlike coordinating and subordinating conjunctions, conjunctive adverbs do not bind the two clauses into a grammatical unit. Rather, as adverbs, they describe the relation of the *ideas* in two clauses. Compare the following examples:

Relaxation techniques have improved; *however,* few people know them. [*However* describes how the second main clause relates to the first, but it does not form the two clauses into a grammatical unit.]

Relaxation techniques have improved, *but* few people know them. [The coordinating conjunction *but* joins the two clauses into a unit.]

Although relaxation techniques have improved, few people know them. [The subordinating conjunction *Although* reduces the first clause from an independent clause to an adverb modifier.]

A simple test can distinguish a conjunctive adverb from a coordinating or subordinating conjunction. Remember that a conjunctive adverb is an adverb and does not form clauses into a grammatical unit. As a result, it can be moved around inside a clause.

Relaxation techniques have improved; *however,* few people know them.

Relaxation techniques have improved; few people, *however,* know them.

Relaxation techniques have improved; few people know them, *however.*

In contrast, subordinating and coordinating conjunctions *cannot* be moved. We would not write *Few people although know them* or *Few people know them but.*

These differences among connecting words are important because they determine very different punctuation between clauses. (See the discussion of punctuation below.)

Note: Just as some words may serve as nouns, verbs, or modifiers depending on their function in a sentence (see pp. 174 and 182), so some connecting words may have more than one use. *After, before, until,* and some other words may be either prepositions or subordinating conjunctions. Some prepositions, such as *behind, in,* and *outside,* can serve also as adverbs, as in *He trailed behind.* Most relative pronouns are used also as interrogative pronouns to ask questions: *Who left?* And some conjunctive adverbs, particularly *however,* may also serve simply as adverbs in sentences such as *However much it costs, we must have it.* Again, the part of speech of a word depends on its function in a sentence.

Punctuating sentences containing conjunctive adverbs

Because the two main clauses related by a conjunctive adverb remain independent units, they must be separated by a semicolon (see 22b). If they are separated by a comma, the result is a **comma splice.**

Comma splice	We hoped for sunshine, *instead,* we got rain.
Revised	We hoped for sunshine; *instead,* we got rain.

(See Chapter 11 for a full discussion of comma splices.)

DECODING THE SENTENCE

Divide the class into small groups, and have each group write a set of nonsense sentences that conform to English syntax and punctuation. Students should be sure to include nonsense prepositional phrases, verbals, appositives, absolutes, and subordinate and coordinate structures. Warn students to punctuate the sentences carefully. Students can use the nonsense sentences at the beginning of Chapter 5 as models.

Once the sentences are written, have groups exchange sentences or write them on the board and try to identify the part of speech for each nonsense word. If the creators of the sentences have made any errors in punctuation, the puzzle-solvers should be prepared to correct them. This exercise should help students see how grammar and punctuation work together to define a word's role in a sentence and to create different kinds of sentences.

A conjunctive adverb is almost always set off from its clause with a comma or commas.

No one was injured; *however,* the car was totaled.
No one was injured; the car, *however,* was totaled.
No one was injured; the car was totaled, *however.*

The comma or commas are optional with some one-syllable conjunctive adverbs (especially *hence, now, then,* and *thus*) and are not used with a few others when they appear inside or at the ends of clauses.

Interest rates rose; *thus* real estate prices declined.

All the performances were sold out; the play *therefore* made a profit.

We hoped for sunshine; we got rain *instead.*

Exercise 18
Sentence combining: Compound constructions

To practice compounding words, phrases, and clauses, combine each pair of sentences below into one sentence that is as short as possible without altering meaning. Use an appropriate connecting word of the type specified in parentheses, referring to the lists on pages 201–03 if necessary. You will have to add, delete, and rearrange words, and you may have to change or add punctuation.

Example:

The encyclopedia had some information. It was not detailed enough. (*Conjunctive adverb.*)

The encyclopedia had some information; *however,* it was not detailed enough.

1. All too often people assume that old age is not a productive time. Many people in their nineties have made great achievements. (*Conjunctive adverb.*)
2. Norman Angell was an English political commentator who won a Nobel Peace Prize in 1933. During his last years he lectured on education for the nuclear age. (*Coordinating conjunction.*)
3. In his nineties the philosopher Bertrand Russell spoke vigorously for international peace. He spoke for nuclear disarmament. (*Correlative conjunction.*)
4. George Bernard Shaw changed his vegetarian diet to include meat. He attributed his long life to the change. (*Coordinating conjunction.*)
5. Shaw wrote brilliant plays. They were often controversial. (*Coordinating conjunction.*)

ANSWERS: EXERCISE 18
Possible Answers

1. All too often people assume that old age is not a productive time; <u>however,</u> many people in their nineties have made great achievements.
2. Norman Angell was an English political commentator who won a Nobel Peace Prize in 1933 <u>and</u> during his last years lectured on education for the nuclear age.
3. In his nineties the philosopher Bertrand Russell spoke vigorously for <u>both</u> international peace <u>and</u> nuclear disarmament.
4. George Bernard Shaw changed his vegetarian diet to include meat <u>and</u> attributed his long life to the change.
5. Shaw wrote brilliant <u>but</u> often controversial plays.

gr
5e

6. Shaw could tolerate <u>neither</u> hypocrisy <u>nor</u> stupidity.
7. Grandma Moses did not retire to an easy chair; <u>instead</u>, she began painting at age seventy-six and was still going at one hundred.
8. The British general George Higginson <u>and</u> the British archaeologist Margaret Murray published <u>their</u> memoirs after they were ninety.
9. The architect Frank Lloyd Wright designed his first building at age twenty <u>and</u> his last at age ninety.
10. Wright obscured many facts of his biography; <u>still</u>, the building dates are known from other sources.

6. Shaw could not tolerate hypocrisy. He could not tolerate stupidity. (*Correlative conjunction.*)
7. Grandma Moses did not retire to an easy chair. She began painting at age seventy-six and was still going at one hundred. (*Conjunctive adverb.*)
8. The British general George Higginson published his memoirs after he was ninety. The British archaeologist Margaret Murray published her memoirs after she was ninety. (*Coordinating conjunction.*)
9. The architect Frank Lloyd Wright designed his first building at age twenty. He designed his last building at age ninety. (*Coordinating conjunction.*)
10. Wright obscured many facts of his biography. The building dates are known from other sources. (*Conjunctive adverb.*)

5e Changing the usual order of the sentence

So far, all the examples of basic sentence grammar have been similar: the subject of the sentence comes first, naming the performer of the predicate's action, and the predicate comes second. This arrangement of subject and predicate describes most sentences that occur in writing, but four other kinds of sentences alter the basic pattern.

1 Forming questions

We form questions in one of several ways. We may invert the normal subject-verb arrangement of statements:

The rate is high. Is the rate high?

We may use a question word such as *how, what, who, when, where, which,* or *why:*

What rate is high?

Or we may use some combination of the two methods:

Why is the rate high?

In each case a question mark signals that the sentence is a question.

Forming commands

We construct commands even more simply than we construct questions: we merely delete the subject of the sentence, *you.*

Think of options.   Eat your spinach.
Watch the news.   Leave me alone.

 Writing passive sentences

In any sentence that uses a transitive verb—that is, in any sentence where the verb takes an object—we can move the object to the position of the subject and put the subject in the predicate. The result is a **passive sentence,** using the **passive voice** of the verb rather than the **active voice.**

Kyong *wrote* the paper. [Active voice.]

The paper *was written* by Kyong. [Passive voice.]

A sentence is called passive because its subject does not perform or initiate the action indicated by the verb. Rather, the subject *receives* the action. In passive sentences the verb is always a phrase consisting of some form of the verb *be* and the past participle of the main verb (*paper was written, exams are finished*). The prepositional phrase specifying the subject of the active verb (the actor) may be omitted entirely if the actor is unknown or unimportant: *The house was flooded.*

(For more on the passive voice see Chapter 7, pp. 242–44. Also see 7h and 31c-3 concerning overuse of the passive voice.)

 Writing sentences with postponed subjects

The subject follows the predicate in two sentence patterns that are not questions, commands, or passive sentences. In one pattern the normal word order is reversed for emphasis: *Then came the dawn.* This pattern occurs most often when the normal order is subject–intransitive verb–adverb. Then the adverb moves to the front of the sentence while subject and predicate reverse order.

gr
5e

gr
5e

Henry comes there. [Normal order.]
There comes Henry. [Reversed order.]

A second kind of sentence with a postponed subject begins with either *it* or *there,* as in the following:

$$\overset{\text{V}}{\text{There will}} \text{ be eighteen } \overset{\text{S}}{\text{people}} \text{ attending the meeting.}$$

$$\overset{\text{V}}{\text{It was surprising}} \overset{\text{S}}{\text{that Marinetti was nominated.}}$$

The words *there* and *it* in such sentences are **expletives.** Their only function is to postpone the sentence subject. Expletive sentences are common, but they can be unemphatic because they add words and delay the sentence subject. Usually, the normal subject-predicate order is more effective: *Eighteen people will attend the meeting. Marinetti's nomination was surprising.* (See also 31c-3.)

ANSWERS: EXERCISE 19
Possible Answers

1. Will the water boil?
   Boil the water, please.
2. Did the music stop?
   Stop the music.
3. Have you set the table?
   Set the table.
4. Have you rolled the dice yet?
   Roll the dice.
5. Who can use the telephone?
   Use the telephone.

ANSWERS: EXERCISE 20

1. Ron Kovic cowrote the screenplay for *Born on the Fourth of July.*
2. Oliver Stone directed the film with amazing realism.
3. The Academy of Motion Picture Arts and Sciences nominated Tom Cruise for an Oscar.
4. Whether Tom Cruise will ever have a better role is uncertain.
5. Thousands of people were lined up at theaters on opening day.

Exercise 19
Forming questions and commands

Form a question and a command from the following noun and verb pairs.

Example:
wood, split
Did you *split* all this *wood*?
Split the *wood* for our fire.

1. water, boil   4. dice, roll
2. music, stop   5. telephone, use
3. table, set

Exercise 20
Rewriting passives and expletives

Rewrite each passive sentence below as active, and rewrite each expletive construction to restore normal subject-predicate order. (For additional exercises with the passive voice and with expletives, see pp. 244, 360, and 500.)

1. The screenplay for *Born on the Fourth of July* was cowritten by Ron Kovic.
2. The film was directed with amazing realism by Oliver Stone.
3. Tom Cruise was nominated for an Oscar by the Academy of Motion Picture Arts and Sciences.
4. It is uncertain whether Tom Cruise will ever have a better role.
5. There were thousands of people lined up at theaters on opening day.

5f   Classifying sentences

We describe and classify sentences in two different ways: by function (statement, question, command, exclamation, and so forth) or by structure. Four basic sentence structures are possible: simple, compound, complex, and compound-complex.

1   Writing simple sentences

Simple sentences consist of a single main clause. The clause may contain phrases, and the subject, the verb, and its objects may be compound, but the sentence is simple as long as it contains only one complete main clause and no surbordinate clause.

Last July was unusually hot.

In fact, both July and August were vicious months.

The summer made farmers leave the area for good or reduced them to bare existence. [Two predicates but only one subject.]

2   Writing compound sentences

A **compound sentence** consists of two or more main clauses. The clauses may be joined by a coordinating conjunction and a comma, by a semicolon alone, or by a conjunctive adverb and a semicolon.

Last July was hot, but August was even hotter.

The hot sun scorched the land to powder; the lack of rain made the soil untillable.

The government later provided assistance; consequently, the remaining farmers gradually improved their lot.

3   Writing complex sentences

A sentence is **complex** if it contains one main clause and one or more subordinate clauses.

Rain finally came, although many had left the area by then. [Main clause, then subordinate clause.]

gr
5f

When the rain came, people rejoiced. [Subordinate clause, then main clause.]

Those who remained were able to start anew because the government came to their aid. [Main clause containing subordinate clause, then another subordinate clause.]

Notice that length does not determine whether a sentence is complex or simple; both kinds can be short or long.

 4   Writing compound-complex sentences

A **compound-complex sentence** has the characteristics of both the compound sentence (two or more main clauses) and the complex sentence (at least one subordinate clause).

Even though government aid finally came, many people had already been reduced to poverty, and others had been forced to leave the area. [Subordinate clause, then main clause, then another main clause.]

Some of the farmers who had left the area moved back gradually to their original homes, but several years passed before the land became as fertile as before. [Main clause containing subordinate clause, then another main clause, then another subordinate clause.]

Exercise 21
Identifying sentence structures

Mark the main clauses and subordinate clauses in the following sentences. Identify each sentence as simple, compound, complex, or compound-complex.

Example:

The police began patrolling more often when crime in the neighborhood increased.

Complex: The police began patrolling more often
————————— MAIN —————————

————————— SUBORDINATE —————————
when crime in the neighborhood increased.

1. Joseph Pulitzer endowed the Pulitzer Prizes.
2. Pulitzer, incidentally, was the publisher of the New York newspaper *The World*.
3. Although the first prizes were for journalism and letters only, Pulitzers are now awarded in music and other areas.
4. For example, Berke Breathed won for his *Bloom County* comic strip, and Roger Reynolds won for his musical composition *Whispers Out of Time*.

ANSWERS: EXERCISE 21

————— MAIN —————
1. *Simple:* Joseph Pulitzer endowed the Pulitzer Prizes.

————— MAIN —————
2. *Simple:* Pulitzer, incidentally, was the publisher of the New York newspaper *The World*.

————— SUBORDINATE —————
3. *Complex:* Although the first prizes were for journalism and letters only, Pulitzers are now awarded in music and other areas.
————— MAIN —————

————— MAIN —————
4. *Compound:* For example, Berke Breathed won for his *Bloom County* comic strip, and
————— MAIN —————
Roger Reynolds won for his musical composition *Whispers Out of Time*.

————— SUBORDINATE —————
5. *Compound-complex:* Although only one prize is usually awarded in each category, in
————— MAIN —————
1989 Taylor Branch's *Parting the Waters* won
————— MAIN —————
a history prize, and it shared the honor with James M. McPherson's *Battle Cry of Freedom*.

5. Although only one prize is usually awarded in each category, in 1989 Taylor Branch's *Parting the Waters* won a history prize, and it shared the honor with James M. McPherson's *Battle Cry of Freedom.*

Exercise 22
Sentence combining: Sentence structures

Combine each set of simple sentences below to produce the kind of sentence specified in parentheses. You will have to add, delete, change, and rearrange words.

Example:

The traffic passed the house. It never stopped. (*Complex.*)
The traffic that passed the house never stopped.

1. Recycling takes time. It reduces garbage in landfills. (*Compound.*)
2. People begin to recycle. They generate much less trash. (*Complex.*)
3. White tissues and paper towels biodegrade more easily than dyed ones. People still buy dyed papers. (*Complex.*)
4. The cans are aluminum. They bring recyclers good money. (*Simple.*)
5. Environmentalists have hope. Perhaps more communities will recycle newspaper and glass. Many citizens refuse to participate. (*Compound-complex.*)

gr
5f

ANSWERS: EXERCISE 22
Possible Answers

1. Recycling takes time, but it reduces garbage in landfills.
2. After people begin to recycle, they generate much less trash.
3. Although white tissues and paper towels biodegrade more easily than dyed ones, people still buy dyed papers.
4. Aluminum cans bring recyclers good money.
5. Environmentalists hope that more communities will recycle newspaper and glass, but many citizens refuse to participate.

SUMMARY GUIDES

The guides on the next six pages do not appear in the students' edition. They are included here for use in conferences and labs. Each guide collects all the descriptions and conventions for a different element: nouns, pronouns, verbs and verbals, and modifiers. Thus the guides provide convenient indexes or texts for students having difficulty with, say, identifying and placing modifiers or distinguishing verbs and verbals. The listings under "Conventions" in each guide contain at least one example showing correct or preferred usage. For additional examples or detailed explanations, consult the sections or pages given in parentheses.

gr

Guide to nouns

Summary and index of information in this book (consult sections or pages in parentheses).

Description of nouns

Nouns as sentence subjects (5a-1, 5a-2)

Nouns as direct and indirect objects (5a-3), object complements (5a-3), objects of prepositions (5c-1), appositives (5c-5), modifiers (9g)

Classes of nouns: proper, common, collective, count, mass, concrete, abstract (5a-2)

Forms of nouns: subjective and objective case (p. 213), possessive case (23a), and plural (34b-6)

Other structures serving as nouns: gerunds and gerund phrases (5c-2), infinitives and infinitive phrases (5c-2), subordinate clauses (5c-4)

Conventions regarding nouns

Forms of nouns

Possessive forms: *boy's* vs. *boys'*; *Park's* vs. *Parks's* vs. *Parkses'* (23a)

Possessives before gerunds: *Nguyen's writing is clear.* (6h)

Plurals of nouns and compound nouns: *dish, dishes; child, children; mother-in-law, mothers-in-law* (34b-6)

Nouns and other sentence parts

Agreement of subjects and verbs: *The towel was wet. The towels were wet.* (8a)

Agreement of antecedents and pronouns: *The children surrounded their father.* (8b)

Grammatical fit between subjects and predicates (avoiding mixed grammar): *In the supervision of others is the best preparation for a management career.→The supervision of others is the best preparation for a management career.* (15a)

Fit in meaning of subjects and predicates (avoiding faulty predication): *The use of the airwaves is the ideal medium for campaigning.→The airwaves are the ideal medium for campaigning.* (15b)

Clarity and effectiveness

Nouns as modifiers (avoiding overuse): *adult education grants workshop→workshop on grants for adult education* (9g)

Consistency in subjects and the voice of verbs: *Tony woke suddenly, but his eyes were kept shut.→Tony woke suddenly, but he kept his eyes shut.* (13c)

A

Guide to pronouns

Summary and index of information in this book (consult sections or pages in parentheses).

NOTE

This page does not appear in the students' edition.

Description of pronouns

Pronouns as substitutes for nouns (5a-2, 8b)

Pronouns as subjects, objects, complements, appositives, modifiers (pp. 212–14)

Case forms of pronouns: subjective, objective, possessive (pp. 212–14)

Person, number, and gender of personal pronouns (8b)

Classes of pronouns: personal, relative, interrogative, demonstrative, reflexive, intensive, indefinite (5a-2)

Conventions regarding pronouns

Forms of pronouns

Subjective case for subjects and subject complements: *You and I can talk. It was she.* (6a)

Objective case for objects: *Ken gave me a dog. He gave her to me.* (6b)

We or *us* with nouns: *We drivers like highways. Many of us drivers like highways.* (6c)

Case in appositives: *Two drivers, she and Nell, won the award. The state rewarded two drivers, her and Nell.* (6d)

Case after *than* or *as*: *Nell likes Buddy more than (she likes) him. Nell likes Buddy more than he (likes Buddy).* (6e)

Objective case for subjects and objects of infinitives: *We invited him to meet her.* (6f)

Who vs. *whom*: *Who can predict whom he will ask?* (6g)

Possessives before gerunds: *his working* (6h)

Possessive forms of personal pronouns: *hers* (not *her's*); *theirs* (not *their's*) (23b)

Possessive pronouns vs. contractions: *its* vs. *it's; your* vs. *you're; their* vs. *they're* (23c)

Pronouns and other sentence parts

Agreement of pronoun subjects and verbs: *Neither he nor they are late. Everybody is finished.* (8a)

Agreement of pronouns and antecedents: *Everybody finished his/her/his or her paper. Lisa or Maria left her notebook.* (8b)

Reference of pronouns to antecedents (avoiding unclear or remote reference): *The first act of the play seemed weak, but then it improved.→The first act of the play started weakly but then improved. Or: Though the first act was weak, the play then improved.* (12a–12f)

gr

 Guide to verbs and verbals

Summary and index of information in this book (consult sections or pages in parentheses).

Description of verbs and verbals

Verb as sentence predicate (5a-1, 5a-2, 5a-3)
Transitive, intransitive, and linking verbs (5a-3)
Forms of verbs: infinitive, past tense, past participle, present participle, -s form (pp. 223–25)
Regular vs. irregular verbs (7a)
Finite vs. nonfinite verbs (5c-2)
Helping (auxiliary) verbs (pp. 225–26)
Tense of verbs: present, past, future, etc. (pp. 232–35)
Mood of verbs: indicative, imperative, subjunctive (p. 240)
Voice of verbs: active and passive (pp. 242–44)
Verbals and verbal phrases: participles, gerunds, infinitives (5c-2)

Conventions regarding verbs and verbals

Forms and tenses of verbs

Principal parts of common irregular verbs: e.g., *begin, began, begun; run, ran, run* (7a)
Sit vs. *set* and *lie* vs. *lay* (7b)
Needed -s and -ed endings: *He asks/asked too much.* (7c)
Needed helping verbs: *He is asking too much.* (7d)
Present tense (*runs*) and perfect tenses (*has/had/will have run*) (7e)
Sequence of tenses: e.g., *We would like to have gone* vs. *We would have liked to go.* (7f)
Subjunctive mood: *I wish I were there.* (7g)

Verbs and other sentence parts

Agreement of verbs and subjects: *The guests are here. Nobody is missing.* (8a)
Unseparated verb phrases and infinitives: *They had before long agreed to voluntarily surrender.*→*Before long they had agreed to surrender voluntarily.* (14e)
Grammatical fit between subjects and predicates (avoiding mixed grammar): *By saving is how they could buy a car.*→*By saving, they could buy a car.* (15a)
Fit in meaning of subjects and predicates (avoiding faulty predication): *The reason is because they were frugal.*→*The reason is that they were frugal.* (15b)

C

Problems with verbals

Verbs required in complete sentences (avoiding sentence fragments with verbals): *Rain falling silently.→Rain fell silently.* (10a, 10c)

Clear and logical modifiers (avoiding dangling modifiers): *Flying home, her thoughts remained behind.→As she flew home, her thoughts remained behind.* (14f)

Punctuation with verbals

Commas after introductory verbal modifiers: *Struggling for air, the climbers reached the summit.* (21b)

Commas to set off nonrestrictive verbal modifiers: *The climbers, struggling for air, reached the summit.* (21c)

Clarity and effectiveness

Active rather than passive voice: *Hands were raised by the students.→The students raised their hands.* (7h)

Consistency in voice: *Before you tighten the bolts, the car should be lowered to the ground.→Before you tighten the bolts, you should lower the car to the ground.* (13c)

Consistency in tense: *The hero escapes, but he was captured.→The hero escapes, but he is captured.* (13b)

Consistency in mood: *Unscrew the bolts, and then you remove the wheel.→Unscrew the bolts, and then remove the wheel.* (13b)

Strong rather than weak verbs (avoiding wordiness): *The book is a depiction of family strife.→The book depicts family strife.* (31c-3)

gr

D

gr

Guide to modifiers

Summary and index of information in this book (consult the sections or pages in parentheses).

Description of modifiers

Functions of adjectives: modifying nouns and pronouns (p. 261)

Functions of adverbs: modifying verbs, adjectives, other adverbs, phrases, and clauses (p. 261)

Forms of adjectives and adverbs: positive, comparative, superlative (9e)

Irregular adjectives and adverbs (9e-2)

Classes of adjectives: descriptive, limiting, proper, attributive, predicate (p. 766–67)

Classes of adverbs: modifiers of verbs, adjectives, and other adverbs (p. 261); sentence modifiers (21b); conjunctive adverbs (5d-2)

Other structures serving as modifiers: nouns (9g); prepositional phrases (5c-1); participles and participial phrases (5c-2); infinitives and infinitive phrases (5c-2); subordinate clauses (5c-4)

Conventions regarding modifiers

Distinctions between adjectives and adverbs

Adverbs (not adjectives) to modify verbs, adjectives, adverbs: *Susan writes well* (not *good*). (9a)

Adjectives after linking verbs, adverbs to modify other verbs: *I feel bad. She sings badly.* (9b)

Adjectives to modify objects, adverbs to modify verbs: *We believed him honest. We treated him honestly.* (9c)

Forms of adjectives and adverbs

Short vs. *-ly* forms of adverbs: *slow* vs. *slowly* (9d)

Comparatives and superlatives: *steady, steadier/more steady, steadiest/most steady* (9e-1); *good/well, better, best* (9e-2); *most steadiest→most steady* (9e-3); *the bigger of two* and *the biggest of three* (9e-4); *most unique→unique* (9e-5)

Modifiers and other sentence parts

Clear placement of modifiers: *We waited for the rain to stop in a doorway.→We waited in a doorway for the rain to stop.* (14a–14e)

Clear and logical modifiers (avoiding dangling modifiers): *Watching the rain, our hands and feet froze.→As we watched the rain, our hands and feet froze.* (14f)

E

Punctuation and mechanics with modifiers

Commas after most introductory modifiers: *Happily, we have friends.* (21b)

Commas to set off nonrestrictive modifiers: *Ellen, who is our best friend, checks in every day.* (21c)

Commas to set off absolute phrases: *Her workday finished, she calls us.* (21d)

Commas for coordinate adjectives: *She is a steady, reliable friend.* (21f-2)

Commas with conjunctive adverbs: *Traffic was bad; we left, however, before it could get worse.* (5d-2, 22b)

Semicolons between clauses related by conjunctive adverbs: *We did not leave right away; instead, we waited for Ellen.* (11b, 22b)

Capital letters for proper adjectives: *Indian tea; Buddhist chant* (26d)

Figure vs. words for numbers: *327* vs. *twenty-three* (29a)

Hyphens in compound adjectives and numbers: *well-spoken words* vs. *words well spoken* (34d-1); *thirty-two minutes* (34d-2)

Clarity and effectiveness

Clear negation (avoiding double negatives): *They don't want no interruptions.→They don't want any interruptions.* Or: *They want no interruptions.* (9f)

Nouns as modifiers (avoiding overuse): *business managers spreadsheet analysis seminar→seminar in spreadsheet analysis for business managers* (9g)

Complete and logical comparisons: *The value of friendship is greater than money.→The value of friendship is greater than the value of* (or *that of*) *money.* (15d)

gr

The forms that nouns and pronouns take according to their role in a sentence are relatively few in English when compared with some other languages. Nonetheless, most students are likely to find compound subjects and objects or questions of *who* and *whom* occasionally troublesome. Others may need to review pronoun forms more extensively to gain control over this part of their writing.

This chapter opens with a review of the functions a pronoun can perform, functions that determine the form, or case, of the pronoun. In addition to the familiar list of forms of the personal pronouns, the chapter provides sentences illustrating the wide variety of uses for pronouns. Following this are brief discussions of the proper case for pronouns in contexts that usually cause difficulty for student writers, including compound subjects and objects, appositives, comparisons using *than* or *as*, possessive case with gerunds, and the different uses of *who* and *whom*.

The exercises ask students to select the appropriate forms of pronouns in the troublesome contexts treated in the discussion, to correct any case errors in a paragraph, and to combine sentences so as to use *who* or *whom* in relative clauses.

BACK TO NOUNS

Distribute copies of a paragraph taken from a magazine article, an essay in a reader, or a student paper. Ask students to rewrite it, substituting the appropriate noun for each pronoun. This exercise will help students to understand the role of pronouns and see the relationship between the case of a pronoun and the function of the noun it stands for.

Chapter 6

Case of Nouns and Pronouns

Case is the form of a noun or pronoun that shows the reader how it functions in a sentence—that is, whether it functions as a subject, as an object, or in some other way. As shown in the box on the facing page, only *I, we, he, she, they,* and *who* change form for each case. Thus these pronouns are the focus of this chapter.

The **subjective case** is used when a pronoun is the subject of a sentence, the subject of a clause, the complement of a subject, or an appositive identifying a subject. (See 5a and 5c.)

Subject of sentence

She and *he* discussed the issue.
They had not been convincing.

Subject of subordinate clause

The proposal ignores many *who* deserve help.

Subject of understood verb

The others have more advantages than *they* (have).

Subject complement

The most disgruntled ones were *she* and *he.*
Most assumed it was only *she.*

Appositive identifying subject

Only two members, *she* and *he,* protested.

The **objective case** is used when a pronoun is the direct or indirect object of a verb or verbal, the object of a preposition, the subject of an infinitive, or an appositive identifying an object. (See 5a and 5c.)

Object of verb

The proposal disappointed *her* and *him.*
A man *whom* they respected let *them* down.

Object of preposition

The others did not care *whom* the proposal was for.
Most of *them* were preoccupied.

Object of verbal

The committee avoided hearing *them* out. [Object of gerund.]

Having elected *them,* the members turned to other business. [Object of participle.]

ca

6

Case forms of nouns and pronouns

	Subjective	Possessive	Objective
Nouns	boy	boy's	boy
	Jessie	Jessie's	Jessie
Personal pronouns			
Singular			
1st person	**I**	**my, mine**	**me**
2nd person	you	your, yours	you
3rd person	**he**	**his**	**him**
	she	**her, hers**	**her**
	it	its	it
Plural			
1st person	**we**	**our, ours**	**us**
2nd person	you	your, yours	you
3rd person	**they**	**their, theirs**	**them**
Relative and interrogative pronouns			
	who	**whose**	**whom**
	whoever	—	**whomever**
	which, that, what	—	which, that, what
Indefinite pronouns			
	everybody	everybody's	everybody

TRANSPARENCY MASTER
AVAILABLE

THE CHART

Students may be tempted to skip over this chart of the case forms of nouns and pronouns. Get them to pay attention by asking them to fill out the whole chart in class—without looking at the text. The act of remembering the forms or figuring them out will be more valuable than listening to an explanation. Students who have trouble completing the chart probably need to spend time reviewing the chapter.

Subject of infinitive

The others asked *them* to approve the proposal.

Appositive identifying object

The proposal will not be approved by two members, *her* and *him*.

The **possessive case** of a pronoun is used before nouns and gerunds.

Before a noun

Her counterproposal is in preparation.

Before a gerund

Their standing firm will influence the others.

In addition, the possessive forms *mine, ours, yours, his, hers,* and *theirs* (and only those forms) may be used without a following noun, in the position of a noun.

In noun positions

Theirs is the more defensible position.
The problem is not *his.*

Caution: Do not use an apostrophe to form the possessive of personal pronouns: *yours* (not *your's*); *theirs* (not *their's*). (See 23b. See also 23a for the possessive forms of nouns, which do use apostrophes.)

6a Use the subjective case for all parts of compound subjects and for subject complements.

In compound subjects use the same pronoun form you would use if the pronoun stood alone as a subject.

Subjects

She and *he* will persist.
The others will come around when *she* and *he* get a hearing.

If you are in doubt about the correct form, try the test in the box on the next page.

A pronoun following the forms of the verb *be* (*am, is, are, was, were*) is a subject complement (see 5a-3). Since it renames the subject, the pronoun is in the subjective case.

A test for case forms in compound constructions

1. Identify a compound construction (one connected by *and, but, or, nor*).

   (*He, Him*) and (*I, me*) won the prize.
   The prize went to (*he, him*) and (*I, me*).

2. Write a separate sentence for each part of the compound.

   (*He, Him*) won the prize. (*I, Me*) won the prize.
   The prize went to (*he, him*). The prize went to (*I, me*).

3. Choose the pronouns that sound correct.

   He won the prize. *I* won the prize. [Subjective.]
   The prize went to *him*. The prize went to *me*. [Objective.]

4. Put the separate sentences back together.

   He and *I* won the prize.
   The prize went to *him* and *me*.

Subject complements

The ones who care most are *he* and *she*.
It was *they* whom the mayor appointed.

Sentences like these may sound stilted because expressions such as *It's me* and *It was her* are common in speech. In writing, unless you seek special emphasis, use the more natural order: <u>*He and she*</u> *are the ones who care most. The mayor appointed* <u>*them*</u>.

6b Use the objective case for all parts of compound objects.

In compound objects use the same pronoun form you would use if the pronoun stood alone as an object.

Objects of verbs

The mayor nominated *her* and *him*. [Direct object.]
The mayor gave *her* and *him* awards. [Indirect object.]

Objects of prepositions

The alternative proposal is by *her* and *him*.
Credit goes equally to *them* and *the mayor*.

If you are in doubt about the correct form, try the test in the box above.

ANSWERS: EXERCISE 1

1. I
2. she, I, we
3. her, me
4. she, I, we
5. us, we

6. her, me
7. her, me
8. she, I
9. I, we
10. her, me

Exercise 1
Choosing between subjective and objective pronouns

From the pairs in parentheses, select the appropriate subjective or objective pronoun(s) for each of the following sentences.

Example:

"Between you and (*I, me*), the seller said, "this deal is a steal."
"Between you and *me*," the seller said, "this deal is a steal."

1. Jody and (*I, me*) had been hunting for jobs.
2. The best employees at our old company were (*she, her*) and (*I, me*), so (*we, us*) expected to find jobs quickly.
3. One company did offer jobs to both (*she, her*) and (*I, me*).
4. After (*she, her*) and (*I, me*) had discussed the offers with several people, however, (*we, us*) both decided to decline.
5. The jobs did not seem appropriate for (*we, us*) if (*we, us*) wanted to become management trainees.
6. That left (*she, her*) with only one offer and (*I, me*) with none.
7. Between (*she, her*) and (*I, me*) the job search had lasted two months, and still it had barely begun.
8. Slowly, (*she, her*) and (*I, me*) stopped sharing leads.
9. It was obvious that Jody and (*I, me*) could not be as friendly as (*we, us*) had been.
10. Sadly, money seemed to mean more to (*she, her*) and (*I, me*) than our friendship.

US THE PEOPLE

If students try out pronoun forms in sentences, they can often "hear" the contrast between correct and incorrect forms by relying on their implicit understanding of the language or by using familiar phrases as touchstones:

Us the people.
Us are the world.
Are you going with *we*?
Take *we* to the movies.

This approach will not work with students for whom standard English is a second language or a second dialect.

6c   **Use the appropriate case when the plural pronoun *we* or *us* occurs with a noun.**

The case of the first-person plural pronoun used with a noun depends on the use of the noun.

Freezing weather is welcomed by *us* skaters. [*Skaters* is the object of the preposition *by.*]

We skaters welcome freezing weather. [*Skaters* is the subject of the sentence.]

6d   **In appositives the case of a pronoun depends on the function of the word it describes or identifies.**

The class elected two representatives, Debbie and *me*. [*Representatives* is the object of the verb *elected,* so the words in the appositive, *Debbie and me,* take the objective case.]

Two representatives, Debbie and *I,* were elected. [*Representatives* is the subject of this sentence, so the words in the appositive, *Debbie and I,* take the subjective case.]

If you are in doubt about case in an appositive, try the sentence without the word the appositive identifies: *The class elected Debbie and me; Debbie and I were elected.*

Exercise 2
Choosing between subjective and objective pronouns

From the pairs in parentheses, select the appropriate subjective or objective pronoun for each of the following sentences.

Example:

Convincing (*we, us*) veterans to vote yes on this issue will be difficult.

Convincing *us* veterans to vote yes on this issue will be difficult.

1. Obtaining enough protein is important to (*we, us*) vegetarians.
2. Instead of obtaining protein from meat (*we, us*) vegetarians get our protein from other sources.
3. Jeff claims to know only two vegetarians, Helena and (*he, him*), who avoid all animal products, including milk.
4. Some of (*we, us*) vegetarians eat fish, which is a good source of protein.
5. (*We, Us*) vegetarians in my family, my parents and (*I, me*), drink milk and eat fish.

ANSWERS: EXERCISE 2

1. us
2. we
3. him
4. us
5. we, I

ca

6e

6e The case of a pronoun after *than* or *as* in a comparison depends on the meaning.

When we use *than* and *as* in comparisons, we often do not complete the clauses they introduce: *Joe likes spaghetti more than (he likes) ravioli.* Without the words in parentheses, this sentence is clear because it can have only one sensible meaning. But in *Annie liked Ben more than Joe,* we cannot tell whether *Annie liked Ben more than (she liked) Joe* or *Annie liked Ben more than Joe (liked him).*

When such sentences end with a pronoun, the case of the pronoun indicates what words have been omitted. When the pronoun is subjective, it must serve as the subject of the omitted verb.

Annie liked Ben more than *he* (liked Ben).

When the pronoun is objective, it must serve as the object of the omitted verb.

Annie liked Ben more than (she liked) *him.*

Be careful to choose the pronoun form that fits your meaning.

MAKE UP YOUR OWN TEST

Give students time in class to write out five to ten sentences in quiz form. The easiest way for students to do this is to pattern their questions after the exercises and sample sentences in the handbook:

Most of (we, us) college students realize that finding a good job isn't easy.

There is a five-hundred-dollar reward for (whomever, whoever) finds the missing stock certificates.

Students can use the handbook in preparing the questions, and as long as they know that one of the possible answers they have provided must be right, they need not be sure which one it is.

When the tests are completed, students should exchange them and fill them out. Correcting the tests is best done in small groups so that students can help one another or turn to the instructor for any information necessary to provide answers to the toughest questions.

ca

6g

 6f Use the objective case for pronouns that are subjects or objects of infinitives.

Subject of infinitive

The school asked Carlos and *him* to speak. [*Carlos and him* is the compound subject of *to speak.*]

Object of infinitive

Students chose to invite *them.* [*Them* is the object of *to invite.*]

 6g The form of the pronoun *who* depends on its function in its clause.

 1 At the beginning of questions use *who* for a subject and *whom* for an object.

The form of *who* at the beginning of a question depends on whether it is a subject or an object.

Who wrote the policy? [Subject of *wrote.*]
Whom does it affect? [Object of *affect.*]

To help find the correct case of *who* in a question, try the test in the box below.

Note: In speech the subjective case *who* is commonly used whenever it is the first word of a question, regardless of whether

TRANSPARENCY MASTER
AVAILABLE

A test for *who* versus *whom* in questions

1. Pose the question.

   (*Who, Whom*) makes that decision?
   (*Who, Whom*) does one ask?

2. Answer the question, using a personal pronoun. Choose the pronoun that sounds correct, and note its case.

   (*She, Her*) makes that decision. *She* makes that decision. [Subjective.]

   One asks (*she, her*). One asks *her.* [Objective.]

3. Use the same case (*who* or *whom*) in the question.

   Who makes that decision? [Subjective.]
   Whom does one ask? [Objective.]

it is a subject or an object. But writing requires a distinction between the forms.

Spoken   *Who* should we blame?
Written *Whom* should we blame? [Object of *blame.*]

 In subordinate clauses use *who* and *whoever* for all subjects, *whom* and *whomever* for all objects.

The case of a pronoun in a subordinate clause depends on its function in the clause, regardless of whether the clause itself functions as a subject, an object, or a modifier. (See 5c-4.)

Give clothes to *whoever* needs them. [*Whoever* is the subject of *needs.* The entire clause *whoever needs them* is the object of the preposition *to.*]

I don't know *whom* the mayor appointed. [*Whom* is the object of *appointed: the mayor appointed whom.* The whole clause *whom the mayor appointed* is the object of the verb *know.*]

He is the man *whom* most people prefer. [*Whom* is the object of *prefer: people prefer whom.* The clause *whom most people prefer* modifies the noun *man.*]

If you have trouble determining which form to choose, try the test in the box below.

A test for *who* versus *whom* in subordinate clauses

1. Locate the subordinate clause.

   Few people know (*who, whom*) they should ask.
   They are unsure (*who, whom*) makes the decision.

2. Rewrite the subordinate clause as a separate sentence, substituting a personal pronoun for *who, whom.* Choose the pronoun that sounds correct, and note its case.

   They should ask (*she, her*). They should ask *her.* [Objective.]
   (*She, her*) makes the decision. *She* makes the decision. [Subjective.]

3. Use the same case (*who* or *whom*) in the subordinate clause.

   Few people know *whom* they should ask. [Objective.]
   They are unsure *who* makes the decision. [Subjective]

ca
6g

Note: Don't let expressions such as *I think* and *she says* confuse you when they come between the subject *who* and its verb.

He is the one *who* I think is best qualified. [*Who* is the subject of *is,* not the object of *think.*]

He is also the one who the mayor says should win. [*Who* is the subject of *should win,* not the object of *says.*]

To choose between *who* and *whom* in such constructions, delete the interrupting phrase: *He is the one who should win.*

COLLABORATIVE LEARNING

ANSWERS: EXERCISE 3

1. whom	6. whom
2. who	7. who
3. whoever	8. whomever
4. Who	9. who
5. Whom	10. whom

Exercise 3
Choosing between *who* and *whom*

From the pairs in parentheses, select the appropriate form of the pronoun in each of the following sentences.

Example:

My mother asked me (*who, whom*) I was going out with.
My mother asked me *whom* I was going out with.

1. The school administrators suspended Jurgen, (*who, whom*) they suspected of setting the fire.
2. Jurgen had been complaining to other custodians, (*who, whom*) reported him.
3. He constantly complained of unfair treatment from (*whoever, whomever*) happened to be passing in the halls, including pupils.
4. "(*Who, Whom*) here has heard Mr. Jurgen's complaints?" the police asked.
5. "(*Who, Whom*) did he complain most about?"
6. His coworkers agreed that Jurgen seemed less upset with the staff or students, most of (*who, whom*) he did not even know, than with the building itself.
7. "He took out his aggressions on the building," claimed one coworker (*who, whom*) often witnessed Jurgen's behavior.
8. "He cursed and kicked the walls and (*whoever, whomever*) he saw nearby."
9. The coworker thought that Jurgen might have imagined people (*who, whom*) instructed him to behave the way he did.
10. "He's someone (*who, whom*) other people can't get next to," said the coworker.

Exercise 4
Sentence combining: *Who* versus *whom*

Combine each pair of sentences below into one sentence that contains a clause beginning with *who* or *whom.* Be sure to use the appropriate case form. You will have to add, delete, and rearrange words. Each item may have more than one possible answer.

Example:

David is the candidate. We think David deserves to win.
David is the candidate *who* we think deserves to win.

1. Some children have undetected hearing problems. These children may do poorly in school.
2. They may not hear important instructions and information from teachers. Teachers may speak softly.
3. Classmates may not be audible. The teacher calls on those classmates.
4. Some hearing-impaired children may work harder to overcome their handicap. These children get a lot of encouragement at home.
5. Some hearing-impaired children may take refuge in fantasy friends. They can rely on these friends not to criticize or laugh.

ANSWERS: EXERCISE 4

Possible Answers

1. Some children who have undetected hearing problems may do poorly in school.
2. They may not hear important instructions and information from teachers who speak softly.
3. Classmates whom the teacher calls on may not be audible.
4. Some hearing-impaired children who get a lot of encouragement at home may work harder to overcome their handicap.
5. Some hearing-impaired children may take refuge in fantasy friends whom they can rely on not to criticize or laugh.

6h **Ordinarily, use the possessive form of a pronoun or noun immediately before a gerund.**

A **gerund** is the *-ing* form of the verb (*running, sleeping*) used as a noun (see 5c-2). Like nouns, gerunds are commonly preceded by possessive nouns and pronouns: *our vote* (noun), *our voting* (gerund).

The coach disapproved of *their* lifting weights.
The *coach's* disapproving was a surprise.

Notice the difference between the gerund and the present participle. Both have the same *-ing* form. But whereas the gerund serves as a subject or object, the participle serves as an adjective.

Team members had often seen *the coach* lifting weights. [*Lifting* is a participle modifying *coach*.]
The *coach's* weightlifting seemed somewhat obsessive. [*Weightlifting* is a gerund, the subject of the sentence.]

The case of a noun or pronoun before the *-ing* form of a verb can subtly influence the meaning of a sentence.

Everyone had noticed the *coach* weightlifting. [The emphasis is on the coach, who happened to be weightlifting. *Weightlifting* is a participle.]
Everyone had noticed the *coach's* weightlifting. [The emphasis is on the coach's activity. *Weightlifting* is a gerund.]

Note that a gerund usually is not preceded by the possessive when the possessive would create an awkward construction.

CREATE A STORY

On the board, write a sentence or two that introduces as many people's names as possible. For example, you might write,

Bob went to a party last night, and there he saw his first-grade teacher, Mrs. West; his neighbor George; his old girlfriend Sarah; and her children Susan and Jason. In the middle of the party, Bob's dog Bowser came racing into the living room.

Divide the class into small groups and ask each group to write a one-paragraph story that grows out of the sentences on the board. (In the example above, students would probably describe what happened after the dog's entrance.) In writing their story, students should try to use as many pronouns as possible without introducing any ambiguity into the tale.

Groups should then read their stories aloud or write them on the board so that other students can try to understand the stories and verify that all the pronoun cases are accurate.

Awkward	A rumor spread about everybody's on the team wanting to quit.
Less awkward	A rumor spread about everybody on the team wanting to quit.
Better	A rumor spread that everybody on the team wanted to quit.

COLLABORATIVE LEARNING

ANSWERS: EXERCISE 5

Written four thousand years ago, *The Epic of Gilgamesh* tells of the friendship of Gilgamesh and Enkidu. Gilgamesh was a bored king who his people thought was too harsh. But he soon found a source of entertainment when he met Enkidu, a wild man <u>who</u> had lived with the animals in the mountains. Immediately, <u>he</u> and Gilgamesh wrestled to see <u>who</u> was more powerful. After hours of struggle, Enkidu admitted that Gilgamesh was stronger than <u>he</u>. Now the friends needed adventures worthy of the two strongest men on earth. Gilgamesh said, "Between you and <u>me</u>, mighty deeds will be accomplished, and our fame will be everlasting." Among their glorious acts, Enkidu and <u>he</u> defeated the giant bull, Humbaba, and cut down the bull's cedar forests. <u>Their</u> bringing back cedar logs to the treeless plains of Gilgamesh's land won great praise from the people. When Enkidu died, Gilgamesh mourned his death, realizing that no one had been a better friend than <u>he</u>. When Gilgamesh himself died many years later, his people raised a monument praising Enkidu and <u>him</u> for their friendship and their mighty deeds of courage.

Exercise 5
Revising: Case

Revise all inappropriate case forms in the following paragraph, and explain the function of each case form.

Written four thousand years ago, *The Epic of Gilgamesh* tells of the friendship of Gilgamesh and Enkidu. Gilgamesh was a bored king who his people thought was too harsh. But he soon found a source of entertainment when he met Enkidu, a wild man whom had lived with the animals in the mountains. Immediately, him and Gilgamesh wrestled to see whom was more powerful. After hours of struggle, Enkidu admitted that Gilgamesh was stronger than him. Now the friends needed adventures worthy of the two strongest men on earth. Gilgamesh said, "Between you and I, mighty deeds will be accomplished, and our fame will be everlasting." Among their glorious acts, Enkidu and him defeated the giant bull, Humbaba, and cut down the bull's cedar forests. Them bringing back cedar logs to the treeless plains of Gilgamesh's land won great praise from the people. When Enkidu died, Gilgamesh mourned his death, realizing that no one had been a better friend than him. When Gilgamesh himself died many years later, his people raised a monument praising Enkidu and he for their friendship and their mighty deeds of courage.

Note: See page 270 for an exercise involving case along with other aspects of grammar.

Chapter 7

Verb Forms, Tense, Mood, and Voice

HIGHLIGHTS

Verbs can cause trouble for writers regardless of their level of skill. For some inexperienced writers, choosing the correct tense or form of a verb is a challenge. Verb endings and the forms of irregular verbs (inflections) can be quite confusing, especially if the writer's spoken dialect employs differing forms of a verb. Even experienced writers may occasionally stumble over the forms of *lie* and *lay* or worry about maintaining a correct sequence of tenses in a complicated writing task, such as a summary of a secondary source in a research paper.

For all these needs (and many others as well) this chapter can be useful, though it cannot provide the kind of sustained support and practice some students may require. (Students who need additional work may benefit from tutoring in a writing center or from the supplemental exercises available in *The Little, Brown Workbook* or *The Little, Brown ESL Workbook.*)

Students looking for help with verb *forms* will benefit from the chapter's thorough explanations, list of the principal parts of frequently used irregular verbs, discussion of the troublesome pairs *sit/set* and *lie/lay,* and treatment of two problems often associated with dialect interference: omitted *-s* and *-ed* endings and omitted helping verbs.

Students looking for help with verb *tense* can make use of the chapter's discussion of the major tenses and of appropriate sequences of tenses. Tense sequence becomes increasingly important as students begin to write ambitious narratives and expository or argumentative essays.

The closing sections of the chapter deal with mood and voice, reviewing uses of the subjunctive and placing special emphasis on appropriate and inappropriate uses of the passive voice.

If you can speak English, you already know a great deal about verbs. Still, even experienced writers occasionally stumble over this most complicated part of speech, which changes form to express a wide range of information.

VERB FORMS

All verbs except *be* have five basic forms. The first three are the verb's **principal parts.**

- The **plain form** is the dictionary form of the verb. It indicates action in the present when the subject is a plural noun or the pronoun *I, we, you,* or *they.*

  We *live* in the city.
  Examinations *frighten* me.
  They *go* downtown.

- The **past-tense form** indicates that the action of the verb occurred in the past. It usually adds *-d* or *-ed* to the plain form, although for some irregular verbs it forms in other ways (see 7a).

  We *lived* in the city.
  Examinations *frightened* me.
  They *went* downtown. [Irregular verb.]

223

vb

7

 Terms used to describe verbs

Form

The spelling of the verb that conveys time, mood, and other information. *Kick, kicked, kicking,* and *kicks* are forms of *kick.* (See p. 223.)

Tense

The time of the verb's action—for instance, present (*kick*), past (*kicked*), future (*will kick*). (See p. 232.)

Mood

The attitude of the verb's speaker or writer—the difference, for example, in *I kick the ball, Kick the ball,* and *I suggest that you kick the ball.* (See p. 240.)

Voice

The distinction between the **active,** in which the subject performs the verb's action (*I kick the ball*), and the **passive,** in which the subject is acted upon (*The ball is kicked by me*). (See p. 242.)

Person

The verb form that reflects whether the subject is speaking (*I/we kick the ball*), spoken to (*You kick the ball*), or spoken about (*She kicks the ball*). (See 7c, 8a.)

Number

The verb form that reflects whether the subject is singular (*The girl kicks the ball*) or plural (*Girls kick the ball*). (See 7c, 8a.)

- The **past participle** uses *have, has,* or *had* (*have climbed*); uses a form of *be* in the passive voice (*was created*); or appears by itself to modify nouns and pronouns (*sliced bread*). Except for some irregular verbs, the past participle is the same as the past-tense form.

  We have *lived* in the city.
  Examinations have *frightened* me.
  They had *gone* downtown. [Irregular verb.]

- The **present participle** adds *-ing* to the verb's plain form (*acting, studying*). The present participle can modify nouns and pronouns (*boiling water*); and, as a gerund, the same form functions as a noun (*Running exhausts me*). Note, how-

Verb forms

Plain form: close, run
Past tense: closed, ran
Past participle: closed, run
Present participle: closing, running
-*s* form: closes, runs

vb
7

ever, that the present participle *cannot* serve as a sentence predicate unless it combines with a form of the verb *be* (*am, is, are, was, were*) to indicate continuing action (*is buying, was finishing*). (See 10a.)

- The **-*s* form** ends in *-s* or *-es* (*begs, lives, has*). It indicates action in the present when the subject is third-person singular.

The dog *begs*.   Everybody *likes* popcorn.
Harry *lives* in town.   She *has* a car.

The verb *be* has eight forms rather than the five forms of most other verbs.

Plain form	be		
Present participle	being		
Past participle	been		
	I	*he, she, it*	*we, you, they*
Present tense	am	is	are
Past tense	was	was	were

Helping verbs

Helping verbs, also called **auxiliary verbs,** combine with a verb's plain form, present participle, or past participle to indicate time and other kinds of meaning, as in *can run, was sleeping, had been eaten*. These combinations are **verb phrases** (see also 7d). Since the plain form, present participle, or past participle in any verb phrase always carries the principal meaning, it is sometimes called the **main verb.**

Verb phrase

Helping	*Main*
The music *is*	*playing.*
The sounds *can be*	*heard.*
The doors *should be*	*closed.*

Shall, will, and forms of *have, do,* and *be* combine with main verbs to indicate time and voice (see pp. 232 and 242).

I *will go.*	The doors *were opened.*
She *had run.*	The child *was awakened.*
Sylvia *did* not *want* grapes.	They *have been seen.*

Be changes form as a helping verb to indicate changes in subject and time, as shown in the chart on the previous page. *Have* and *do* also change form as helping verbs:

	I	he, she, it	we, you, they
Present tense	have/do	has/does	have/do
Past tense	had/did	had/did	had/did

Helping verbs such as *can, could, may, might, must, ought, shall, should, will,* and *would* combine with main verbs to indicate necessity, obligation, permission, possibility, and other conditions. The helping verbs do not change form for different subjects.

I/She *can* write.	He/You *must* go.
They/I *should* study.	It/They *might* come.

 7a Use the correct form of regular and irregular verbs.

Most verbs are **regular;** that is, they form their past tense and past participle by adding *-d* or *-ed* to the plain form.

Plain form	Past tense	Past participle
live	lived	lived
act	acted	acted

Since the past tense and past participle are created simply by adding to the plain form and since the two are identical, the forms of regular verbs do not often cause problems in speech and writing (but see 7c).

About two hundred English verbs are **irregular;** that is, they form their past tense and past participle in some irregular way. We have to learn the parts of the verbs by memorizing them, just as we learn new words.

Most irregular verbs form the past tense and the past participle by changing an internal vowel.

Plain form	Past tense	Past participle
begin	began	begun
come	came	come

Some irregular verbs change an internal vowel and add an *-n* in the past participle.

Plain form	Past tense	Past participle
break	broke	broken
draw	drew	drawn

Some irregular verbs have the same form in both the past tense and the past participle or in all three forms.

Plain form	Past tense	Past participle
sleep	slept	slept
let	let	let

vb
7a

Check a dictionary if you have any doubt about a verb's principal parts. The form listed there is the plain form. If no other forms are listed, the verb is regular; that is, both the past tense and the past participle add *-d* or *-ed* to the plain form. If the verb is irregular, the dictionary will list the plain form, the past tense, and the past participle in that order (*go, went, gone*). If the dictionary gives only two forms (as in *think, thought*), then the past tense and the past participle are the same.

The following list includes the most common irregular verbs. (When two forms are possible, as in *dove* and *dived,* both are included.) Look over this list to find verbs whose parts you are unsure of. Then spend some time memorizing the parts and trying them in sentences.

Principal parts of common irregular verbs

Plain form	Past tense	Past participle
arise	arose	arisen
become	became	become
begin	began	begun
bid	bid	bid
bite	bit	bitten, bit
blow	blew	blown
break	broke	broken
bring	brought	brought
burst	burst	burst
buy	bought	bought
catch	caught	caught
choose	chose	chosen
come	came	come
cut	cut	cut

(continued)

vb
7a

ONE-FORM PARAGRAPHS

Choose groups of three to five verbs, and have students create paragraphs using only one form of the verbs. Then have students rewrite the paragraphs using a different verb form. This exercise will reinforce consistent use of form and may make students more aware of the element of time in verb usage. Following are student-written examples that use the past-participle form of the verbs *break, bring, burst, buy,* and *catch.*

Because his bubble had burst and she had broken his heart, he had caught the next train home and had brought his mother some flowers.   —Jennifer Haas

We had brought the dishes out to the table to set it. When we looked we realized that we had broken some of them. We had burst out laughing, but it wasn't too funny when we realized that my mother had caught us.— Nicole Hanna

He had broken the vase that she had brought. She had burst into tears. If only he had caught it.   —Jim Rosen

Principal parts of common irregular verbs
(continued)

Plain form	Past tense	Past participle
dive	dived, dove	dived
do	did	done
draw	drew	drawn
dream	dreamed, dreamt	dreamed, dreamt
drink	drank	drunk
drive	drove	driven
eat	ate	eaten
fall	fell	fallen
find	found	found
flee	fled	fled
fly	flew	flown
forget	forgot	forgotten, forgot
freeze	froze	frozen
get	got	got, gotten
give	gave	given
go	went	gone
grow	grew	grown
hang (suspend)	hung	hung
hang (execute)	hanged	hanged
hear	heard	heard
hide	hid	hidden
hold	held	held
keep	kept	kept
know	knew	known
lay	laid	laid
lead	led	led
leave	left	left
let	let	let
lie	lay	lain
lose	lost	lost
pay	paid	paid
prove	proved	proved, proven
ride	rode	ridden
ring	rang	rung
rise	rose	risen
run	ran	run
say	said	said
see	saw	seen
set	set	set
shake	shook	shaken
sing	sang, sung	sung

Plain form	Past tense	Past participle
sink	sank, sunk	sunk
sit	sat	sat
slide	slid	slid
speak	spoke	spoken
spring	sprang, sprung	sprung
stand	stood	stood
steal	stole	stolen
swim	swam	swum
take	took	taken
tear	tore	torn
throw	threw	thrown
wear	wore	worn
write	wrote	written

vb

7a

Exercise 1
Using irregular verbs

For each irregular verb in parentheses, supply either the past tense or past participle, as appropriate, and identify the form you used.

> *Example:*
>
> Though we had (*hide*) the cash box, it was (*steal*).
>
> Though we had *hidden* the cash box, it was *stolen*. [Two past participles.]

1. The world population has (*grow*) by two-thirds of a billion people in less than a decade.
2. Recently it (*break*) the 5 billion mark.
3. Experts have (*draw*) pictures of a crowded future.
4. They predict that the world population may have (*slide*) up to as much as 16 billion by the year 2100.
5. Though the food supply (*rise*) in the last decade, the share to each person (*fall*).
6. At the same time the water supply, which had actually (*become*) healthier over the previous century, (*sink*) in size and quality.
7. The number of animal species on earth (*shrink*) by 20 percent.
8. Changes in land use (*run*) nomads and subsistence farmers off the land.
9. Yet all has not been (*lose*).
10. Recently human beings have (*begin*) to heed these and other problems and to explore how technology can be (*drive*) to help the earth and all its populations.

ANSWERS: EXERCISE 1

1. The world population has grown by two-thirds of a billion people in less than a decade. (Past participle.)
2. Recently it broke the 5 billion mark. (Past tense.)
3. Experts have drawn pictures of a crowded future. (Past participle.)
4. They predict that the world population may have slid up to as much as 16 billion by 2100. (Past participle.)
5. Though the food supply rose in the last decade, the share to each person fell. (Both past tense.)
6. At the same time the water supply, which had actually become healthier over the previous century, sank in size and quality. (Past participle and past tense.)
7. The number of animal species on earth shrank by 20 percent. (Past tense.)
8. Changes in land use ran nomads and subsistence farmers off the land. (Past tense.)
9. Yet all has not been lost. (Past participle.)
10. Recently human beings have begun to heed these and other problems and to explore how technology can be driven to help the earth and all its populations. (Both past participles.)

vb
7c

7b Distinguish between *sit* and *set* and between *lie* and *lay*.

The principal parts of *sit* and *set* and of *lie* and *lay* are easy to confuse. Here are the forms of the four verbs.

Plain form	Past tense	Past participle
sit	sat	sat
set	set	set
lie	lay	lain
lay	laid	laid

Sit and *lie,* as in *Sit down* and *Lie down,* mean "be seated" and "recline," respectively. They are both **intransitive verbs:** they cannot take objects. *Set* and *lay,* as in *Set the eggs down carefully* and *Lay the floor boards there,* mean "put" or "place." They are **transitive verbs** and usually take objects. (See 5a-3.)

Angela *lies* down every afternoon. [No object.]
Jose *lays* the plans on the table. [*Plans* is the object of *lays.*]
The dog *sits* by the back door. [No object.]
Mr. Flood *sets* the jug down roughly. [*Jug* is the object of *sets.*]

ANSWERS: EXERCISE 2

1. Last Christmas, Jay lay in bed all day with a fever.
2. When he awoke, Millard sat up in his chair, picked up the fallen book, and set it on the table.
3. The spider sat in its web and lay in wait for its prey.
4. After she had set the table, she laid a cloth over it.
5. Joan's wallet had lain in the street for two days.

Exercise 2
Distinguishing *sit/set, lie/lay*

Choose the correct verb from the pair given in parentheses and then supply the past tense or past participle, as appropriate.

Example:

After I washed all the windows, I (*lie, lay*) down the squeegee and then I myself (*lie, lay*) down for a nap.

After I washed all the windows, I *laid* down the squeegee and then I myself *lay* down for a nap.

1. Last Christmas, Jay (*lie, lay*) in bed all day with a fever.
2. When he awoke, Millard (*sit, set*) up in his chair, picked up the fallen book, and (*sit, set*) it on the table.
3. The spider (*sit, set*) in its web and (*lie, lay*) in wait for its prey.
4. After she had (*sit, set*) the table, she (*lie, lay*) a cloth over it.
5. Joan's wallet had (*lie, lay*) in the street for two days.

7c Use the *-s* and *-ed* forms of the verb when they are required.

Some English dialects use the plain form of the verb instead of the *-s* form that is required by standard English whenever the subject is third-person singular and the verb's action occurs in the present.

The roof *leak* (*leaks*).   Nobody *have* (*has*) a car.
Harry *live* (*lives*) in town.   She *be* (*is*) happy.
He *don't* (*doesn't*) care.

In sentences like these, standard English requires the forms in parentheses.

Some dialects also omit the *-ed* or *-d* ending from the past tense or past participle of regular verbs when the ending is not clearly pronounced.

We *bag* (*bagged*) groceries.   I bought a *use* (*used*) book.
He was *suppose* (*supposed*) to   Sue has *ask* (*asked*) for help.
call.

In standard English, however, the *-ed* or *-d* ending is required for regular verbs whenever (1) the verb's action occurred in the past (*we bagged*), (2) the past participle functions as a modifier (*used book*), or (3) the past participle combines with a form of *be* or *have* (*was supposed, has asked*).

Exercise 3
Using *-s* and *-ed* verb endings

Supply the correct form of each verb in parentheses. Be careful to include *-s* and *-ed* (or *-d*) endings where they are needed for standard English.

A teacher sometimes (*ask*) too much of a student. In high school I was once (*punish*) for being sick. I had (*miss*) some school, and I (*realize*) that I would fail a test unless I had a chance to make up the class work. I (*discuss*) the problem with the teacher, but he said I was (*suppose*) to make up the work while I was sick. At that I (*walk*) out of the class. I (*receive*) a failing grade then, but it did not change my attitude. Today I still balk when a teacher (*make*) unreasonable demands or (*expect*) miracles.

7d   Use helping verbs when they are required.

Helping verbs combine with the plain forms, present participles, and past participles of verbs to indicate time and other kinds of meaning (see p. 225). In some English dialects the helping verb is omitted:

The owl (*is*) *hooting*.   Sara (*has*) *been* at home.
I (*have*) *taken* French.   That (*would*) *be* awful.

RESOURCES AND IDEAS

Speakers of black English vernacular may tend to use the verb forms of this dialect in their writing rather than those of standard written English, particularly by dropping *-s* and *-ed* endings. Becoming aware of the verb system of standard written English and the differences between it and the verb system of black English vernacular is an important step for students seeking control over their writing. But as Marcia Farr and Harvey Daniels point out in *Language Diversity and Writing Instruction* (New York: ERIC Clearing House on Urban Education and Urbana: NCTE, 1986), awareness of and practice in identifying and using the verb forms are useful only if they take place in a context that includes a wide range of reading and writing experiences; substantial practice in writing; collaborative activities; sentence combining or similar activities; and flexible, sensitive feedback from the instructor. Farr and Daniels also offer a detailed discussion of dialects and language variations, along with concrete suggestions for teaching.

ANSWERS: EXERCISE 3

A teacher sometimes <u>asks</u> too much of a student. In high school I <u>was</u> once <u>punished</u> for being sick. I had <u>missed</u> some school, and I <u>realized</u> that I would fail a test unless I had a chance to make up the class work. I <u>discussed</u> the problem with the teacher, but he said I was <u>supposed</u> to make up the work while I was sick. At that I <u>walked</u> out of the class. I <u>received</u> a failing grade then, but it did not change my attitudes. Today I still balk when a teacher <u>makes</u> unreasonable demands or <u>expects</u> too much.

t
7e

However, standard English requires the helping verbs in these sentences and in others like them.

Often, the omission of a helping verb creates an incomplete sentence, or **sentence fragment,** because a present participle (*hooting*) or an irregular past participle (*taken, been*) cannot stand alone as the only verb in a sentence (see Chapter 10).

Fragments	Few people *smoking.* The toy *broken.*
Revised	Few people *were smoking.* The toy *was broken.*

Smoking and *broken* are **nonfinite,** or "unfinished," verbs: they can modify other words, but they cannot serve as sentence predicates. Only a **finite,** or "finished," verb can serve as a sentence predicate. To be made finite, a nonfinite verb must be combined with a helping verb. (See p. 188.)

ANSWERS: EXERCISE 4

1. Each year thousands of new readers <u>have</u> been discovering Agatha Christie's mysteries.
2. The books <u>were</u> written by a prim woman who had worked as a nurse during World War I.
3. Christie never expected that her play *The Mousetrap* <u>would</u> be performed for decades.
4. During her life Christie <u>was</u> always complaining about movie versions of her stories.
5. Readers of her stories <u>have</u> been delighted to be baffled by her.

Exercise 4
Using helping verbs

Add helping verbs in the following sentences where they are needed for standard English.

1. Each year thousands of new readers been discovering Agatha Christie's mysteries.
2. The books written by a prim woman who had worked as a nurse during World War I.
3. Christie never expected that her play *The Mousetrap* be performed for decades.
4. During her life Christie always complaining about movie versions of her stories.
5. Readers of her stories been delighted to be baffled by her.

TENSE

Tense shows the time of a verb's action. The table on the next two pages shows all the tense forms for a regular and an irregular verb in the active voice. (See pp. 242–44 on voice.)

The **simple tenses** indicate that an action is present, past, or future relative to the speaker or writer. The present tense uses the verb's plain form (*work, write*), or, for third-person singular subjects, its *-s* form (*he works, she writes*). The past tense uses the verb's past-tense form (*worked, wrote*). The future tense uses the helping verb *will* or *shall* and the verb's plain form.

The **perfect tenses** indicate that an action was or will be completed before another time or action. (The term *perfect* derives from the Latin *perfectus,* meaning "completed.") The perfect tenses consist of the verb's past participle (*worked, written*) preceded by a form of the helping verb *have.*

Tenses of a regular and an irregular verb (active voice)

	Singular	Plural

Simple tenses

Present

1st person	I work/write	we work/write
2nd person	you work/write	you work/write
3rd person	he/she/it works/writes	they work/write

Past

1st person	I worked/wrote	we worked/wrote
2nd person	you worked/wrote	you worked/wrote
3rd person	he/she/it worked/wrote	they worked/wrote

Future

1st person	I will work/write	we will work/write
2nd person	you will work/write	you will work/write
3rd person	he/she/it will work/write	they will work/write

Perfect tenses

Present perfect

1st person	I have worked/written	we have worked/written
2nd person	you have worked/written	you have worked/written
3rd person	he/she/it has worked/written	they have worked/written

Past perfect

1st person	I had worked/written	we had worked/written
2nd person	you had worked/written	you had worked/written
3rd person	he/she/it had worked/written	they had worked/written

Future perfect

1st person	I will have worked/written	we will have worked/written
2nd person	you will have worked/written	you will have worked/written
3rd person	he/she/it will have worked/written	they will have worked/written

(continued)

t
7e

t
7e

Tenses of a regular and an irregular verb (active voice)

(continued)

	Singular	**Plural**
Progressive tenses		
Present progressive		
1st person	I am working/writing	we are working/writing
2nd person	you are working/writing	you are working/writing
3rd person	he/she/it is working/writing	they are working/writing
Past progressive		
1st person	I was working/writing	we were working/writing
2nd person	you were working/writing	you were working/writing
3rd person	he/she/it was working/writing	they were working/writing
Future progressive		
1st person	I will be working/writing	we will be working/writing
2nd person	you will be working/writing	you will be working/writing
3rd person	he/she/it will be working/writing	they will be working/writing
Present perfect progressive		
1st person	I have been working/writing	we have been working/writing
2nd person	you have been working/writing	you have been working/writing
3rd person	he/she/it has been working/writing	they have been working/writing
Past perfect progressive		
1st person	I had been working/writing	we had been working/writing
2nd person	you had been working/writing	you had been working/writing
3rd person	he/she/it had been working/writing	they had been working/writing
Future perfect progressive		
1st person	I will have been working/writing	we will have been working/writing
2nd person	you will have been working/writing	you will have been working/writing
3rd person	he/she/it will have been working/writing	they will have been working/writing

The **progressive forms,** sometimes called the **progressive tenses,** indicate continuing (therefore progressive) action. The progressive uses the *-ing* form of the verb plus a form of *be (is working, were writing).* Regular and irregular verbs do not differ.

We use the helping verb *do (does)* or its past tense *did,* together with the plain form of the verb, in asking questions, making negative statements, and showing emphasis.

Does he *write* every day? [Question.]
He *did* not *write* every day. [Negation.]
He *does write* every day. [Emphasis.]

7e Use the appropriate tense to express your meaning.

For native speakers of English, most errors in tense are actually errors in verb form like those discussed earlier. Still, errors in tense do sometimes occur, so edit your work to ensure that the tenses of verbs accurately express your meaning.

Any problems in verb tense are most likely to occur with some special uses of the present tense and with the perfect tenses.

 Observe the special uses of the present tense.

The present tense generally indicates action occurring at the time of speaking, as in *She <u>understands</u> what you mean.* It is also used in several special situations.

To indicate habitual or recurring action

Abby *goes* to New York every Friday.
The store *opens* at ten o'clock.

To state a general truth

The mills of the gods *grind* slowly.
The earth *is* round.

To discuss the content of literature, film, and so on
(see also p. 682)

Huckleberry Finn *has* adventures we all envy.
In that article the author *examines* several causes of crime.

To indicate future time

Our friends *arrive* tomorrow.
Ted *leaves* in an hour.

(Time is really indicated here by *tomorrow* and *in an hour.*)

MEMORY AID

To help students remember special uses of the present tense, you might suggest that they use the acronym *FACT* as a memory aid:

*F*uture time
*A*ction recurring
*C*ontent of literature
*T*ruth, general

t
7e

Observe the uses of the perfect tenses.

The perfect tenses generally indicate an action completed before another specific time or action. The present perfect tense also indicates action begun in the past and continued into the present.

Present perfect

The dancer *has performed* here only once. [The action is completed at the time of the statement.]

Critics *have written* about the performance ever since. [The action began in the past and continues now.]

Past perfect

The dancer *had trained* in Asia before his performance. [The action was completed before another past action.]

Future perfect

He *will have performed* here again by next month. [The action begins now or in the future and will be completed by a specified time in the future.]

Then he *will have performed* here twice in his life. [The action began in the past and will be completed by a specified time in the future.]

PICTURES AND EVENTS—VERB TENSE AND SEQUENCE

Show students a picture containing a scene that suggests some preceding events as well as some that might follow. Ask students to write a brief narrative describing the sequence of events and making use of proper verb forms and the correct sequence of tenses.

 7f Use the appropriate sequence of verb tenses.

The term **sequence of tenses** refers to the relation between the verb in a main clause and the verbs or verbals in subordinate clauses or verbal phrases (see 5c). The tenses need not be identical as long as they reflect changes in actual or relative time: in *He had left before I arrived,* the verbs are in clear sequence. The principal conventions governing tense sequence are discussed below. (For a discussion of tense shifts—changes *not* required by meaning—see 13b.)

 Generally, the verb in a subordinate clause may be in any tense required by meaning.

As long as the tense of the verb in the main clause is neither past nor past perfect (see 7f-2 below), the tense in the subordinate clause need only reflect your meaning. In the following sentences all the verb forms follow a clear and natural sequence, though the tenses in main and subordinate clauses are different.

> Most people *do know* that Lincoln *was* President during the Civil War.
>
> That fact *will be recorded* when the study *is* complete.

Note: Any change of tense between a main and a subordinate clause must be logical. The sentence *My family always keeps pets because we liked them* does not seem logical because *liked* indicates that the liking is past and thus is not a reason to keep pets in the present.

 The verb in a subordinate clause must be past or past perfect if the verb in the main clause is past or past perfect.

The past or past perfect tense in a main clause refers to an action already completed (*smiled, had smiled*). Since the meaning of a subordinate clause depends on that of the main clause, the verb in the subordinate clause must also be completed and thus past or past perfect.

> People *differed* widely in what they *knew* about public events. [Since people differed in the past, their knowing must also have occurred in the past.]
>
> Only a few *knew* when Harding *had been* President. [The past perfect *had been* indicates that Harding's Presidency occurred before people knew of it.]
>
> None of them *had been born* when Harding *was* President. [The past perfect *had been born* indicates an occurrence before Harding's Presidency.]

Exception: When a subordinate clause expresses a general truth such as *The earth is round,* use the present tense even though the verb of the main clause is in the past or past perfect tense.

> Few *understood* that popular Presidents *are* not necessarily good Presidents.

 Observe the appropriate tense sequence with infinitives.

The tense of an infinitive is determined by the tense of the verb in the predicate. The **present infinitive** is the verb's plain

CREATING A STORY

Write on the board a sentence containing one or more characters and an action. Here are some examples:

> As he rounded the corner, John heard a loud noise, somewhere between a crash and a bang.
>
> As he came into the classroom, Jim noticed that Carolyn was already there reviewing her notes.

Ask students to form groups, and then require the groups to write paragraph-length (seven to eight sentences) stories. The stories should begin with the sentence you have provided, and individual members of the group should add sentences to the narrative one by one until it is complete. The final story should maintain a correct sequence of tenses, contain proper verb forms, and use a variety of action verbs.

DISCUSSION STORY

Put a lead sentence (as in *Creating a Story*—above) on the board, and ask the class as a whole to decide on the events that follow it. Summarize the events briefly; then ask groups of students to write out the story as in the preceding activity, making it as vivid as they can. This entire exercise will provide both oral and written practice with verb tense and sequence.

form preceded by *to* (see 5c-2). It indicates action *at the same time* as or *later* than that of the verb.

> The researcher *expects to see* change. [The expectation is in the present; the seeing is still to come.]

> She *would have liked to see* (not *to have seen*) more change before. [The present infinitive indicates the same past time as *would have liked*.]

The verb's **perfect infinitive** consists of *to have* followed by the past participle, as in *to have talked, to have won.* It indicates action *earlier* than that of the verb.

> Other researchers *would like* (not *would have liked*) *to have seen* change as well. [The liking occurs in the present; the seeing would have occurred in the past.]

> They *judge* the data *to have been interpreted* correctly. [The interpretation occurred before the judgment about it.]

 Observe the appropriate tense sequence with participles.

The tense of a participle is determined by the tense of the verb in the predicate. The present participle shows action occurring *at the same time* as that of the verb.

> *Testing* a large group, the researcher *had posed* multiple-choice questions. [Testing and posing occurred at the same time.]

The past participle and the present perfect participle show action occurring *earlier* than that of the verb.

> *Prepared* by earlier failures, she *knew* not to ask open questions. [Preparing occurred before knowing.]

> *Having tested* many people, she *understood* the process. [Testing preceded understanding.]

Exercise 5
Adjusting tense sequence

The tenses in each sentence below are in correct sequence. Change the tense of one verb as instructed. Then change the tense of infinitives, participles, and other verbs to restore correct sequence. Some items have more than one possible answer.

Example:

He will call when he reaches his destination. (*Change will call to called.*)

He called when he *reached* (or *had reached*) his destination.

1. Diaries that Adolf Hitler is supposed to have written have surfaced in Germany. (*Change have surfaced to had surfaced.*)
2. Many people believe that the diaries are authentic because a well-known historian has declared them so. (*Change believe to believed.*)
3. However, the historian's evaluation has been questioned by other authorities, who call the diaries forgeries. (*Change has been questioned to was questioned.*)
4. They claim, among other things, that the paper is not old enough to have been used by Hitler. (*Change claim to claimed.*)
5. Eventually, the doubters will win the debate because they have the best evidence. (*Change will win to won.*)

Exercise 6
Revising: Tense sequence

Revise the following sentences so that the sequence of verb tenses is appropriate. If a sentence is already correct as given, circle its number. Some items have more than one possible answer.

Example:

Hedy had hoped to have been elected.
Hedy had hoped *to be elected.*

1. In a history of hospitals in the United States, Charles E. Rosenberg describes how changes in medicine and in American society have fostered increasing dependence on hospitals.
2. Until well into the nineteenth century, hospitals were mainly places to house the desperately sick who have been poor and alone.
3. The sick in hospitals usually received little professional care and usually improved, if at all, simply because time has elapsed.
4. As doctors learned more about infectious disease, they also decided that the hospital was the best place to have trained young doctors and to have conducted medical research.
5. Tending the wounded in the Crimean War, the British nurse Florence Nightingale then campaigned for hospital improvements and training of nurses.
6. Surgeons increasingly believed that to have performed their work properly required a hospital setting.
7. In addition, doctors of all kinds saw hospitals as places to improve their knowledge and to gain new patients.
8. Before World War I had begun, the number of hospitals in the U.S. reaches more than 4400.
9. Having learned to depend heavily on hospitals, Americans soon found that the services were very expensive.
10. Now many Americans would have liked to have reconsidered whether it is healthy to rely so heavily on hospitals.

ANSWERS: EXERCISE 5

1. Diaries that Adolf Hitler was supposed to have written had surfaced in Germany.
2. Many people believed that the diaries were authentic because a well-known historian had declared them so.
3. The historian's evaluation was questioned, however, by other authorities who called the diaries forgeries.
4. They claimed, among other things, that the paper was not old enough to have been used by Hitler.
5. Eventually, the doubters won the debate because they had the best evidence.

t seq

7f

ANSWERS: EXERCISE 6

1. Sentence correct.
2. Until well into the nineteenth century, hospitals were mainly places to house the desperately sick who were poor and alone.
3. The sick in hospitals usually received little professional care and usually improved, if at all, simply because time elapsed.
4. As doctors learned more about infectious disease, they also decided that the hospital was the best place to train young doctors and to conduct medical research.
5. Having tended the wounded in the Crimean War, the British nurse Florence Nightingale then campaigned for hospital improvements and training of nurses.
6. Surgeons increasingly believed that to perform their work properly required a hospital setting.
7. Sentence correct.
8. Before World War I had begun, the number of hospitals in the U.S. had reached more than 4400.
9. Sentence correct.
10. Now many Americans would like to reconsider whether it is healthy to rely so heavily on hospitals.

vb

7g

MOOD

Mood in grammar is a verb form that indicates the writer's or speaker's attitude toward what he or she is saying. The **indicative mood** states a fact or opinion or asks a question.

The theater *needs* help. [Opinion.]
The ceiling *is falling* in. [Fact.]
Will you *contribute* to the theater? [Question.]

The **imperative mood** expresses a command or gives a direction. It omits the subject of the sentence, *you.*

Donate money or time. [Command.]
Send contributions to the theater. [Direction.]

The **subjunctive mood** expresses a suggestion, a requirement, or a desire, or it states a condition that is contrary to fact (that is, imaginary or hypothetical). The subjunctive mood uses distinctive verb forms.

● *Suggestion or requirement:* plain form with all subjects.

The manager asked that he *donate* money [Suggestion.]
Rules require that donations *be* mailed. [Requirement.]

● *Desire or present condition contrary to fact:* past tense; for *be,* the past tense *were.*

We wish that the theater *had* more money. [Desire.]
It would be in better shape if it *were* better funded. [Present condition contrary to fact.]

● *Past condition contrary to fact:* past perfect.

The theater could have been better funded if it *had been* better managed.

With conditions contrary to fact, the verb in the main clause also expresses the imaginary or hypothetical with the helping verb *could* or *would,* as in the last two sample sentences above.

(For a discussion of keeping mood consistent within and among sentences, see 13b.)

7g   Use the subjunctive verb forms appropriately.

Contemporary English uses distinctive subjunctive verb forms only in two kinds of constructions and in a few idiomatic expressions.

Use the subjunctive in contrary-to-fact clauses beginning with *if* or expressing desire.

If the theater *were* saved, the town would benefit.
We all wish the theater *were* not so decrepit.

Note: The indicative form *was* (*We all wish the theater was not so decrepit*) is common in speech and in some informal writing, but the subjunctive *were* is usual in formal English.

Not all clauses beginning *if* express conditions contrary to fact. In the sentence *If Joe is out of town, he hasn't heard the news,* the verb *is* is correct because the clause refers to a condition presumed to exist.

vb

7g

 Use *would* or *could* only in the main clause of a conditional statement.

The helping verb *would* or *could* appears in the main clause of a sentence expressing a condition contrary to fact. The helping verb does *not* appear in the subordinate clause beginning with *if.*

Not   Many people would have helped if they *would have* known.

But   Many people would have helped if they *had* known.

Use the subjunctive in *that* clauses following verbs that demand, request, or recommend.

Verbs such as *ask, insist, urge, require, recommend,* and *suggest* often precede subordinate clauses beginning with *that* and containing the substance of the request or suggestion. The verb in such *that* clauses should be in the subjunctive mood.

The board urged that everyone *contribute.*
The members insisted that they themselves *contribute.*
They suggested that each *donate* both time and money.

Note: These constructions have widely used alternative forms that do not require the subjunctive, such as *The board urged everyone to contribute* or *The members insisted on donating.*

 Use the subjunctive in some set phrases and idioms.

Several English expressions commonly use the subjunctive. For example:

Come rain or *come* shine.
Be that as it may.
The people *be* damned.

ANSWERS: EXERCISE 7

1. If she <u>were</u> still alive, Agatha Christie would probably be pleased by David Suchet's performance as her detective Hercule Poirot.
2. Suchet is determined that his performance <u>be</u> accurate.
3. Christie would have been gratified if she <u>had</u> known about Suchet's attention to Poirot's appearance and behavior.
4. The role requires that Suchet <u>speak</u> with a Belgian accent and <u>wear</u> an elaborate waxed mustache.
5. Christie's fans can only wish that Suchet <u>play</u> Poirot more often.

Exercise 7
Revising: Subjunctive mood

Revise the following sentences with appropriate subjunctive verb forms.

Example:

I would help the old man if there was a way I could reach him.

I would help the old man if there *were* a way I could reach him.

1. If she was still alive, Agatha Christie would probably be pleased by David Suchet's performance as her detective Hercule Poirot.
2. Suchet is determined that his performance is accurate.
3. Christie would have been gratified if she would have known about Suchet's attention to Poirot's appearance and behavior.
4. The role requires that Suchet speaks with a Belgian accent and wears an elaborate waxed mustache.
5. Christie's fans can only wish that Suchet plays Poirot often.

PASSIVE SENTENCES—COUNT THE WORDS

Write on the board a number of sentences in the active voice, the sentences ranging from simple to relatively complex. Ask students to change the sentences into the passive voice and then to count the number of words in each version. Finally, ask students to read some of the passive sentences aloud and comment on their effectiveness. This exercise will allow you to check students' understanding of the passive voice and at the same time demonstrate its wordiness.

VOICE

The **voice** of a verb tells whether the subject of the sentence performs the action or is acted upon.

Bookies coordinate illegal bets. [The subject acts.]

Illegal *bets are coordinated* by bookies. [The subject is acted upon: it is the object of the action *coordinate*.]

Verbs whose subjects perform the action are in the **active voice.** Verbs whose subjects are acted upon are in the **passive voice.** The actor in a passive sentence may be named in a prepositional phrase (as in the second example above), or the actor may be omitted:

Illegal *bets are coordinated*.

A passive verb always consists of a form of *be* plus the past participle of the main verb: *bets <u>are coordinated</u>, people <u>were inspired</u>*. Other helping verbs may also be present: *bets <u>have been coordinated</u>, people <u>would have been inspired</u>*.

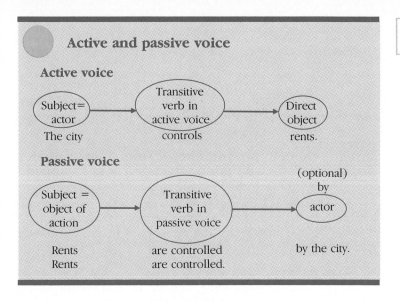

Active and passive voice

Active voice

Subject= actor → Transitive verb in active voice controls → Direct object rents.

The city   controls   rents.

Passive voice

Subject = object of action → Transitive verb in passive voice → (optional) by actor

Rents   are controlled   by the city.
Rents   are controlled.

pass
7h

Converting active to passive

A sentence can be changed from active to passive voice only if the verb is **transitive**—that is, it can take an object (see p. 177). For example:

	Subject	Transitive verb	Indirect object	Direct object
Active	Bookies	give	debtors	no freedom.

To make the verb passive, convert either of the objects into the subject of the sentence, and use the appropriate verb form.

	New subject	Passive verb		Old subject
Passive	Debtors	are given	no freedom	by bookies.
Passive	No freedom	is given	debtors	by bookies.

Converting passive to active

Changing a sentence from passive to active voice requires naming the verb's actor as subject, converting the verb to active voice, and making the old subject into a direct or indirect object (or omitting it).

		Passive verb	
	Subject		
Passive	Gamblers	are hounded	by bookies.

	New subject	*Active verb*	*Old subject*
Active	Bookies	hound	gamblers.

 7h **Generally, prefer the active voice. Use the passive voice when the actor is unknown or unimportant.**

Because the passive omits or de-emphasizes the actor (the performer of the verb's action), it can deprive writing of vigor and is often vague or confusing. The active voice is usually stronger, clearer, and more forthright.

Weak passive The exam was thought by us to be unfair because we were tested on material that was not covered in the course.

Strong active We thought the exam unfair because it tested us on material the course did not cover.

The passive voice is useful in two situations: when the actor is unknown and when the actor is unimportant or less important than the object of the action.

Ray Appleton *was murdered* after he returned home. [The murderer is presumably unknown, and in any event Ray Appleton's death is the point of the sentence.]

In the first experiment acid *was added* to the solution. [The person who added the acid, perhaps the writer, is less important than the fact that acid was added. Passive sentences are common in scientific writing.]

Except in such situations, however, you should prefer the active voice in your writing. (See 31c-3 for additional cautions against the passive voice.)

Exercise 8
Converting between active and passive voices

To practice using the two voices of the verb, convert the following sentences from active to passive or from passive to active. (In converting from passive to active, you may have to add a subject for the new sentence.) Which version of each sentence seems more effective, and why? (For additional exercises with the passive voice, see pp. 208, 360, and 500.)

Example:

The aspiring actor was discovered in a nightclub.
A *talent scout discovered* the aspiring actor in a nightclub.

1. When the Eiffel Tower was built in 1889, it was thought by the French to be ugly.
2. At that time many people still resisted industrial technology.
3. The tower's naked steel construction epitomized this technology.
4. Beautiful ornament was expected to grace fine buildings.
5. Further, the tower could not even be called a building because it had no solid walls.

Exercise 9
Revising: Verb forms, tense, mood

Circle all the verbs and verbals in the following paragraph and correct their form, tense, or mood if necessary.

For centuries the natives of Melanesia, a group of islands laying northeast of Australia, have practice an unusual religion. It began in the eighteenth century when European explorers first have visited the islands. The natives were fascinated by the rich goods or "cargo" possessed by the explorers. They saw the wealth as treasures of the gods, and cargo cults eventually had arisen among them. Over the centuries some Melanesians turned to Christianity in the belief that the white man's religion will bring them the white man's treasures. During World War II, American soldiers, having arrived by boat and airplane to have occupied some of the islands, introduced new and even more wonderful cargo. Even today some leaders of the cargo cults insist that the airplane is worship as a vehicle of the Melanesians' future salvation.

Note: See page 270 for an exercise involving verbs along with other aspects of grammar.

ANSWERS: EXERCISE 8
Possible Answers

1. When engineers built the Eiffel Tower in 1889, the French thought it was ugly.
2. At that time industrial technology was still resisted by many people.
3. The technology was epitomized by the tower's naked steel construction.
4. People expected beautiful ornament to grace fine buildings.
5. Further, people could not even call the tower a building because it had no solid walls.

ANSWERS: EXERCISE 9

For centuries the natives of Melanesia, a group of islands (lying) northeast of Australia, (have practiced) an unusual religion. It (began) in the eighteenth century when European explorers first (visited) the islands. The natives (were fascinated) by the rich goods or "cargo" (possessed) by the explorers. They (saw) the wealth as treasures of the gods, and cargo cults eventually (arose) among them. Over the centuries some Melanesians (turned) to Christianity in the belief that the white man's religion (would bring) them the white man's treasures. During World War II, American soldiers (having arrived) by boat and airplane (to occupy) some of the islands, (introduced) new and even more wonderful cargo. Even today some leaders of the cargo cults (insist) that the airplane (be worshipped) as a vehicle of the Melanesians' future salvation.

pass

7h

Some students may have difficulty with basic subject-verb agreement, particularly with the -s or -es endings that mark plural nouns and singular verbs in English. Almost all students encounter problems with subject-verb and pronoun-antecedent agreement when they begin writing complicated, information-filled sentences. This chapter addresses the needs of both groups of writers, paying special attention to sentence structures that make it difficult for student writers to determine the correct relationship in number between subjects and verbs or pronouns and antecedents.

Rather than treating agreement problems as errors resulting from ignorance, the chapter treats such problems as areas requiring special attention, even by experienced writers. Among the troublesome structures covered are compound subjects, collective nouns, relative and indefinite pronouns, phrases like "one of the," and widely separated subjects and verbs.

Recent changes in the language have given rise to some confusion over pronoun-antecedent agreement with indefinite pronouns. Moreover, in English, subjects that are singular in form, like *audience* or *the faculty,* may be plural in meaning. In speech, even educated speakers sometimes treat indefinite pronouns like *anybody* and *everybody* as plural: "Everybody ought to pay attention to their own business." This change in part reflects a desire to avoid the generic *he,* a form of usage many people regard as sexist. The discussions present alternatives designed to avoid sexist language, while at the same time making clear the need to treat *everybody, someone,* and the like as singular, at least in the more conservative written medium.

TRANSPARENCY MASTER
AVAILABLE

Chapter 8   *Agreement*

Agreement helps readers understand the relations between elements in a sentence. Subjects and verbs agree in number and person:

More *Japanese-Americans live* in Hawaii and California than elsewhere. [Both subject and verb are third-person plural.]

Daniel Inouye was the first Japanese-American in Congress. [Both subject and verb are third-person singular.]

Pronouns and their **antecedents**—the words they refer to—agree in person, number, and gender.

Inouye makes *his* home in Hawaii. [Both pronoun and antecedent are masculine and third-person singular.]

Hawaiians value his work for *them.* [Both pronoun and antecedent are third-person plural.]

8a   **Make subjects and verbs agree in number.**

Most subject-verb agreement problems arise when endings are omitted from subjects or verbs or when the relation between sentence parts is uncertain.

Use the verb ending *-s* or *-es* with all third-person singular subjects. Use the noun ending *-s* or *-es* to make most nouns plural.

An *-s* or *-es* ending does opposite things to nouns and verbs: it usually makes a noun *plural,* but it always makes a present-tense verb *singular.* Thus if the subject noun is plural, it will end in *-s* or *-es* and the verb will not. If the subject is singular, it will not end in *-s* and the verb will.

agr
8a

Singular	Plural
The boy eats.	The boys eat.
The bird soars.	The birds soar.

The only exceptions to these rules involve the nouns that form irregular plurals, such as *child/children, woman/women.* The irregular plural still requires a plural verb: *The children play.*

Writers often omit *-s* and *-es* endings from nouns or verbs because they are not pronounced clearly in speech (as in *asks* and *lists*) or because they are not used regularly in some English dialects. However, the endings are required in standard English.

Aspects of agreement

Person

1st person, the speaker(s): *I, we*
2nd person, the person(s) spoken to: *you*
3rd person, the person(s) or thing(s) spoken about: *he, she, it, they;* nouns; indefinite and relative pronouns

Number

Singular, one: *I, you, he, she, it;* nouns naming one; indefinite and relative pronouns referring to singular nouns and pronouns
Plural, more than one: *we, you, they;* nouns naming more than one; indefinite and relative pronouns referring to plural nouns and pronouns

Gender

Masculine: *he;* nouns naming males; indefinite and relative pronouns referring to males
Feminine: *she;* nouns naming females; indefinite and relative pronouns referring to females
Neuter: *it;* nouns naming places, things, qualities, and ideas; indefinite and relative pronouns referring to same

agr
8a

Summary of subject-verb agreement

- Basic subject-verb agreement (8a-1):

Singular	Plural
The kite flies.	The kites fly.

- Words between subject and verb (8a-2):

The kite with two tails *flies* badly. The tails of the kite *compete*.

- Subjects joined by *and* (8a-3):

The kite and the bird *are* almost indistinguishable.

- Subjects joined by *or* or *nor* (8a-4):

The kite or the bird *dives*. Kites or birds *fill* the sky.

- Indefinite pronouns as subjects (8a-5):

No one *knows*. All the spectators *wonder*.

- Collective nouns as subjects (8a-6):

A flock *appears*. The flock *disperse*.

- Inverted word order (8a-7):

Is the kite or the bird blue? *Are* the kite and the bird both blue?

- Linking verbs (8a-8):

The kite *is* a flier and a dipper.

- *Who, which, that* as subjects (8a-9):

The kite that *flies* longest wins. Kites that *fall* lose.

- Subjects with plural form and singular meaning (8a-10):

Aeronautics *plays* a role in kite flying.

- Titles and words named as words (8a-11):

Kite Dynamics *is* one title. Vectors *is* a key word.

Nonstandard	The voter *resist* change.
Standard	The voter *resists* change.

Nonstandard	Such *action* demand a response.
Standard	Such *actions* demand a response.

Remember that the verb *be* is irregular.

Present tense

he, she, it, } *is*   all plurals } *are*
singular nouns }

Past tense

he, she, it, } *was*   all plurals } *were*
singular nouns }

Note: In a verb phrase (verb plus helping verb), the helping verb sometimes reflects the number of the subject and sometimes does not: *The car does run; The cars do run; the car/cars will run.* The verb itself (*run*) does not change in any way. (See p. 225.)

agr
8a

 Subject and verb should agree even when other words come between them.

When the subject and verb are interrupted by other words, particularly nouns, then agreement errors may result from connecting the verb to the nearest noun instead of the actual subject.

A catalog of courses and requirements often *baffles* (not *baffle*) students. [The verb must agree with the subject, *catalog,* not the nearer noun, *requirements.*]

The requirements stated in the catalog *are* (not *is*) unclear. [The subject is *requirements,* not *catalog.*]

Note: Phrases beginning with *as well as, together with, along with, in addition to,* and similar expressions do not change the number of the subject.

The president, as well as the deans, *has* (not *have*) agreed to revise the catalog.

If you really mean *and* in such a sentence, you can avoid awkwardness by using it. Then the subject is compound, and the verb should be plural: *The president and the deans have agreed to revise the catalog.*

3 **Subjects joined by *and* usually take plural verbs.**

Two or more subjects joined by *and* usually take a plural verb, whether one or all of the subjects are singular.

Frost and Roethke *were* contemporaries.

Frost, Roethke, Stevens, and Pound *are* among the great American poets.

TRUE COMPLEXITY

Sometimes the sample sentences we offer to students by way of illustrating a point of grammar or style seem a bit artificial or a bit too simple. Writers such as Charles Dickens and Henry James offer sentences with considerable variety and flair in structure that can be used either as models themselves or as patterns for sentences with a more contemporary content and cast. The following sentence, from James's preface to *The Princess Casamassima*, illustrates tight control of subject-verb and pronoun-antecedent agreement:

> The troubled life mostly at the center of our subject—whatever our subject, for the artistic hour, happens to be—embraces them [fools] and deals with them for its amusement and its anguish: they are apt largely indeed, on a near view, to be all the cause of its trouble.

Exceptions: When the parts of the subject form a single idea or refer to a single person or thing, they take a singular verb.

Avocado and bean sprouts *is* a California sandwich.
The winner and new champion *remains* unconscious.

When a compound subject is preceded by the adjective *each* or *every,* the verb is usually singular.

At customs every box, bag, and parcel *is* inspected.
Each man, woman, and child *has* a right to be heard.

But a compound subject *followed* by *each* takes a plural verb.

The man and the woman each *have* different problems.

 When parts of a subject are joined by *or* or *nor*, the verb agrees with the nearer part.

When all parts of a subject joined by *or* or *nor* are singular, the verb is singular; when all parts are plural, the verb is plural.

Either the painter or the carpenter *knows* the cost.
The cabinets or the bookcases *are* too costly.

Problems with subjects joined by *or* or *nor* occur most often when one part of the subject is singular and the other plural. In that case the verb should agree with the subject part closer to it. To avoid awkwardness, place the plural part closer to the verb.

Awkward   Neither the owners nor the contractor *agrees*.
Improved   Neither the contractor nor the owners *agree*.

When the subject consists of nouns and pronouns of different person requiring different verb forms, the verb agrees with the part of the subject nearer to it.

Either Juarez or I *am* responsible.

Since observing this convention often results in awkwardness, avoid the problem altogether by rewording the sentence.

Improved   Either Juarez *is* responsible, or I *am*.

 Generally, use singular verbs with indefinite pronouns.

An **indefinite pronoun** is one that does not refer to a specific person or thing.

Common indefinite pronouns

all	each	neither	one
any	either	nobody	some
anybody	everybody	none	somebody
anyone	everyone	no one	someone
anything	everything	nothing	something

ARE EVERYONE READY?

Though many students will not, at first, hear anything wrong with sentences like "Everyone ought to pay attention to their own business" (a pattern that has wide acceptance in speech), almost all will find sentences like these unacceptable: "Are everyone ready for lunch?" "Do everybody have enough money to buy tickets for the rides?" Anyone who finds the latter sentences acceptable is probably having trouble recognizing the singular and plural forms of verbs. Sample sentences can, therefore, help you identify the real source of a student's problems with agreement.

Most indefinite pronouns are singular in meaning (they refer to a single unspecified person or thing), and they take singular verbs.

Something *smells.*   Neither *is* right.

A few indefinite pronouns such as *all, any, none,* and *some* may be either singular or plural in meaning. The verbs you use with these pronouns depend on the meaning of the nouns or pronouns they refer to.

All of the money *is* reserved for emergencies. [*All* refers to the singular noun *money,* so the verb is singular.]

All of the funds *are* reserved for emergencies. [*All* refers to the plural noun *funds,* so the verb is plural.]

 6 **Collective nouns take singular or plural verbs depending on meaning.**

A **collective noun** has singular form but names a group of individuals or things—for example, *army, audience, committee, crowd, family, group, team.* As a subject, a collective noun may take a singular or plural verb, depending on the context. When considering the group as one unit, use a singular verb.

The group *agrees* that action is necessary.
Any band *sounds* good in that concert hall.

But when considering the group's members as individuals who act separately, use the plural form of the verb.

The old group *have* gone their separate ways.
The band *do* not agree on where to play.

Note: Even when the plural verb form is properly used, as in these examples, it often sounds awkward. For this reason you may prefer to rephrase such sentences with plural subjects, as in *The members of the old group have gone their separate ways.*

The collective noun *number* may be singular or plural. Preceded by *a,* it is plural; preceded by *the,* it is singular.

A number of people *are* in debt.
The number of people in debt *is* very large.

 7 **The verb agrees with the subject even when the normal word order is inverted.**

Inverted subject-verb order occurs in questions.

Is voting a right or a privilege? [*Voting* is the subject; *is* is the verb. Compare *Voting is a right or a privilege.*]

Are a right and a privilege the same thing? [*A right and a privilege* is the compound subject; *are* is the verb. Compare *A right and a privilege are the same thing.*]

Inverted subject-verb order also occurs in expletive constructions beginning with *there* or *it* and a form of *be* (see 5e-4).

There *are* differences between them. [*Differences* is the subject; *are* is the verb. Compare *Differences are between them.*]

There *is* the key difference of whether the power is earned. [*Difference* is the subject; *is* is the verb. Compare *The key difference is whether the power is earned.*]

In expletive constructions *there is* may be used before a compound subject when the first element in the subject is singular.

There *is* much work to do and little time to do it.

Word order may sometimes be inverted for emphasis. The verb still agrees with its subject.

From the mountains *comes* an eerie, shimmering light.

 8 **A linking verb agrees with its subject, not the subject complement.**

When a linking verb is followed by a subject complement, make the verb agree with its subject, the first element, not with the noun or pronoun serving as a subject complement (see 5a-3).

Henry's sole support *is* his mother and father. [The subject is *support.*]

Henry's mother and father *are* his sole support. [The subject is *mother and father.*]

9 **When used as subjects, *who, which,* and *that* take verbs that agree with their antecedents.**

The relative pronouns *who, which,* and *that* do not have different singular and plural forms. When one of these pronouns serves as a subject, its verb should agree with the noun or other pronoun that the relative pronoun refers to (its antecedent).

Mayor Garber ought to listen to the people who *work* for her. [*Who* refers to the plural *people,* so the verb is plural.]
Bardini is the only aide who *has* her ear. [*Who* refers to the singular *aide,* so the verb is singular.]

Agreement problems often occur with relative pronouns when the sentence includes *one of the* or *the only one of the* before the pronoun.

Bardini is one of the aides who *work* unpaid. [*Who* refers to the plural *aides,* so the verb is plural. Of the aides who work unpaid, Bardini is one.]
Bardini is the only one of the aides who *knows* the community. [*Who* refers to *one*. Of the aides, only one, Bardini, knows the community.]

 10 **Nouns with plural form but singular meaning take singular verbs.**

Some nouns with plural form (that is, ending in *-s*) are usually regarded as singular in meaning. They include *athletics, economics, mathematics, measles, news, physics, politics,* and *statistics.*

After so long a wait, the news *has* to be good.
Statistics *is* required of psychology majors.

Measurements and figures ending in *-s* may also be singular when the quantity they refer to is a unit.

Three years *is* a long time to wait.
Three-fourths of the library *consists* of reference books.

These words and amounts are plural in meaning when they describe individual items rather than whole groups or whole bodies of activity or knowledge.

The statistics *prove* him wrong. [*Statistics* refers to facts, individual items.]
Two-fifths of the cars on the road *are* unsafe. [The cars are unsafe separately.]

agr
8a

11 Titles and words named as words take singular verbs.

When your sentence subject is the title of a corporation or a work (such as a book or a movie) or a word you are defining or describing, the verb should be singular even if the title or the word is plural.

Hakada Associates *is* a new firm.
Dream Days *remains* a favorite book.
Folks *is* a down-home word for people.

Exercise 1
Revising: Subject-verb agreement

Revise the verbs in the following sentences as needed to make subjects and verbs agree in number. If the sentence is already correct as given, circle the number preceding it.

Example:

Each of the job applicants type sixty words per minute.
Each of the job applicants *types* sixty words per minute.

1. Weinstein & Associates are a consulting firm that try to make businesspeople laugh.
2. Statistics from recent research suggests that humor relieves stress.
3. Reduced stress in businesses in turn reduce illness and absenteeism.
4. Reduced stress can also reduce friction within an employee group, which then work together more productively.
5. In special conferences held by one consultant, each of the participants practice making the others laugh.
6. "Isn't there enough laughs within you to spread the wealth?" the consultant asks his students.
7. The consultant quotes Casey Stengel's rule that the best way to keep your management job is to separate the underlings who hate you from the ones who have not decided how they feel.
8. Such self-deprecating comments in public is uncommon among business managers, the consultant says.
9. Each of the managers in a typical firm take the work much too seriously.
10. The humorous boss often feels like the only one of the managers who have other things in mind besides profits.
11. One consultant to many companies suggest cultivating office humor with practical jokes such as a rubber fish in the water cooler.
12. When employees or their manager regularly post cartoons on the bulletin board, office spirit usually picks up.

13. When someone who has seemed too easily distracted is entrusted with updating the cartoons, his or her concentration often improves.
14. In the face of levity, the former sourpuss becomes one of those who hides bad temper.
15. Every one of the consultants caution, however, that humor has no place in life-affecting corporate situations such as employee layoffs.

8b **Make pronouns and their antecedents agree in person and number.**

The **antecedent** of a pronoun is the noun or other pronoun it refers to.

Home owners fret over *their* tax bills. [*Home owners* is the antecedent of *their*.]

Its constant increases make the *tax bill* a dreaded document. [*Tax bill* is the antecedent of *its*.]

As these examples show, a pronoun agrees with its antecedent in gender (masculine, feminine, neuter), person (first, second, third), and number (singular, plural). (See p. 247 for an explanation of these terms.) Since pronouns derive their meaning

---

Summary of pronoun-antecedent agreement

- Basic pronoun-antecedent agreement:
  Old Faithful spews *its* columns of water, each of *them* over 115 feet high.
- Antecedents joined by *and* (8b-1):
  Old Faithful and Giant are geysers known for *their* height.
- Antecedents joined by *or* or *nor* (8b-2):
  Either Giant or Giantess ejects *its* column the highest.
- Indefinite pronouns as antecedents (8b-3):
  Each of the geysers has *its* own personality. Anyone who visits has *his or her* memories.
- Collective nouns as antecedents (8b-4):
  A crowd amuses *itself* watching Old Faithful. The crowd go *their* separate ways.

USING MAGAZINES OR A READER

Using essays from a reader or magazine articles, have students work in groups to find sentence structures often associated with agreement problems. Ask the groups to decide how important these structures are for expository prose and to write out what they consider to be the rules governing agreement within these structures.

from their antecedents, pronoun-antecedent agreement is essential for the reader to understand what you are saying.

 Antecedents joined by *and* usually take plural pronouns.

Two or more antecedents joined by *and* usually take a plural pronoun, whether one or all of the antecedents are singular.

Mr. Bartos and I cannot settle *our* dispute.
The dean and my adviser have offered *their* help.

Exceptions: When the compound antecedent refers to a single idea, person, or thing, then the pronoun is singular.

My friend and adviser offered *her* help.

When the compound antecedent follows *each* or *every,* the pronoun is singular.

Every girl and woman took *her* seat.

 When parts of an antecedent are joined by *or* or *nor,* the pronoun agrees with the nearer part.

When the parts of an antecedent are connected by *or* or *nor,* the pronoun should agree with the part closer to it.

Tenants or owners must present *their* grievances.
Either the tenant or the owner will have *her* way.

When one subject is plural and the other singular, the sentence will be awkward unless you put the plural subject second.

Awkward   Neither the tenants nor the owner has yet made *her* case.

Revised   Neither the owner nor the tenants have yet made *their* case.

 Generally, use a singular pronoun when the antecedent is an indefinite pronoun.

Indefinite pronouns such as *anybody* and *something* refer to persons or things in general rather than to a specific person or thing. (See p. 251 for a list.) Most indefinite pronouns are singular in meaning. When these indefinite pronouns serve as antecedents to other pronouns, the other pronouns are singular.

Everyone on the team had *her* own locker.
Each of the boys likes *his* teacher.

Using a singular pronoun to refer to an indefinite pronoun may result in an awkward sentence when the indefinite pronoun clearly means "many" or "all."

Awkward   Everyone on board feared for *his* life.

In speech we commonly avoid such awkwardness with a plural pronoun: *Everyone feared for their lives.* In writing, however, you should rewrite the sentence to avoid the ungrammatical *Everyone . . . their*.

Rewritten   *All the riders* feared for *their* lives.

The generic *he*

The meaning of an indefinite pronoun often includes both masculine and feminine genders, not one or the other. The same is true of other indefinite words such as *child, adult, individual,* and *person.* In such cases tradition has called for *he* (*him, his*) to refer to the antecedent. But this so-called **generic *he*** (or generalized *he*) appears to exclude females. In speech we often get around this problem by combining a plural pronoun with an indefinite pronoun, as in *None of the students had the credits they needed.* But many readers view this construction as incorrect, so it should be avoided in writing. Instead, follow the practice of many writers by creating grammatical sentences without the generic *he,* as shown in the box below.

For more on avoiding bias in writing, see 31a-8.

RESOURCES AND IDEAS

Martha Kolln, "Everyone's Right to Their Own Language," *College Composition and Communication* 37 (February 1986): 100–02. The frequency with which students treat indefinite pronouns as plural suggests that the widely accepted rules of usage discussed in this section may in some ways conflict with practice. Kolln takes a radical stance, arguing that "dicta that designate all indefinite pronouns as singular have no basis either in actual usage or in the rules of logic" (102).

agr
8b

Ways to avoid the generic *he*

Generic *he*   Nobody in the class had the credits *he* needed.

● Substitute *he or she.*

Revised   Nobody in the class had the credits *he or she* needed.

To avoid awkwardness, don't use *he or she* more than once in several sentences.

● Recast the sentence using a plural antecedent and pronoun.

Revised   *All the students* in the class lacked the credits *they* needed.

● Rewrite the sentence to avoid the pronoun.

Revised   Nobody in the class had the *needed credits.*

TRANSPARENCY MASTER
AVAILABLE

Collective noun antecedents take singular or plural pronouns depending on meaning.

Collective nouns such as *army, committee, family, group,* and *team* have singular form but may be referred to by singular or plural pronouns, depending on the meaning intended. When you are referring to the group as a unit—all its members acting together—then the pronoun is singular.

> The committee voted to disband *itself.*
> The team attended a banquet in *its* honor.

When you are referring to the individual members of the group, the pronoun is plural.

> The audience arose quietly from *their* seats.
> The old group have gone *their* separate ways.

In the last example, note that the verb and pronoun are consistent in number (see also 8a-6).

Inconsistent	The old group *has* gone *their* separate ways.
Consistent	The old group *have* gone *their* separate ways.

ANSWERS: EXERCISE 2

1. Almost any child will quickly astound observers with <u>his or her</u> capabilities. *Or:* <u>Most children</u> will quickly astound observers with their capabilities.
2. Sentence correct.
3. Of course, the family has a tremendous influence on the development of a child in <u>its</u> midst.
4. Each of the members of the immediate family exerts <u>his or her</u> own unique pull on the child.
5. Other relatives, teachers, and friends can also affect <u>children's</u> view of the world and themselves. (Avoiding the generic <u>he</u>, the only alternative to a plural antecedent is the awkward <u>the world and himself or herself</u>.)
6. Genetics and physiology also strongly influence child development, but <u>they</u> may never be fully understood.
7. The psychology community often cannot agree in <u>their</u> views of whether nurture or nature is more important in a child's development.

Exercise 2
Revising: Pronoun-antecedent agreement

Revise the following sentences so that pronouns and their antecedents agree in person and number. Some items have more than one possible answer. Try to avoid the generic *he* (see p. 257). If you change the subject of a sentence, be sure to change verbs as necessary for agreement. If the sentence is already correct as given, circle the number preceding it.

Example:

Each of the Boudreaus' children brought their laundry home at Thanksgiving.

Each of the Boudreaus' children brought *his or her* laundry home at Thanksgiving. *Or: All* of the Boudreaus' children brought *their* laundry home at Thanksgiving.

1. Almost any child will quickly astound observers with their capabilities.
2. Despite their extensive research and experience, neither child psychologists nor parents have yet figured out how children work.
3. Of course, the family has a tremendous influence on the development of a child in their midst.
4. Each of the members of the immediate family exerts their own unique pull on the child.

5. Other relatives, teachers, and friends can also affect the child's view of the world and themselves.
6. Genetics and physiology also strongly influence child development, but it may never be fully understood.
7. The psychology community often cannot agree in its views of whether nurture or nature is more important in a child's development.
8. Another debated issue is whether the child's emotional development or their intellectual development is more central.
9. Just about everyone has their strong opinion on these issues, often backed up by evidence.
10. Neither the popular press nor scholarly journals devote much of their space to the wholeness of the child.

Exercise 3
Adjusting for agreement

In the following sentences subjects agree with verbs, and pronouns agree with antecedents. Make the change specified in parentheses after each sentence, and then revise the sentence as necessary to maintain agreement. Try to avoid the generic *he* (see p. 257). Some items have more than one possible answer.

> *Example:*
>
> The student attends weekly conferences with her teacher. (*Change* The student *to* Students.)
>
> Students *attend* weekly conferences with *their* teacher.

1. Recently, one psychologist has published his ideas about the entire process of child development. (*Change* one psychologist *to* some psychologists.)
2. This theory meshes social and intellectual development and illuminates the connection between them. (*Change* This theory *to* These theories.)
3. Stanley Greenspan, a child psychiatrist, proposes that children proceed through stages in their first ten years. (*Change* children *to* the child.)
4. Each stage integrates emotions and cognition, and it prepares the way for following stages. (*Change* Each stage *to* The stages.)
5. In the first stage, for example, the child learns some self-regulation as a means of protecting himself from overstimulation. (*Change* the child *to* children.)
6. But self-regulation also helps the child organize his immediate experience, so it serves a cognitive purpose for him as well. (*Change* the child *to* children.)
7. At a much later stage, around age nine, children identify strongly with adults of the same sex and imitate their roles and behaviors. (*Change* children *to* the child.)
8. Children also become preoccupied with their peers at this

8. Another debated issue is whether <u>children's</u> emotional development or their intellectual development is more central. *Or:* . . . whether the child's <u>emotional or intellectual development</u> is more central. *Or:* . . . whether the child's emotional development or <u>his or her</u> intellectual development is more central.
9. Just about everyone has <u>his or her</u> strong opinion on these issues, often backed up by evidence.
10. Sentence correct.

ANSWERS: EXERCISE 3

1. Recently, <u>some psychologists have</u> published <u>their</u> ideas about the entire process of child development.
2. <u>These theories mesh</u> social and intellectual development and illuminate the connection between them.
3. Stanley Greenspan, a child psychiatrist, proposes that <u>the child proceeds</u> through stages in <u>his or her</u> first ten years. (<u>His</u> would also be correct, but some would consider it sexist.)
4. <u>The stages integrate</u> emotions and cognition, and <u>they prepare</u> the way for following stages.
5. In the first stage, for example, <u>children learn</u> some self-regulation as a means of protecting <u>themselves</u> from overstimulation.
6. But self-regulation also helps children organize <u>their</u> immediate experience, so it serves a cognitive purpose for <u>them</u> as well.
7. At a much later stage, around age nine, <u>the child identifies</u> strongly with adults of the same sex and <u>imitates</u> their roles and behaviors.
8. <u>The child</u> also <u>becomes</u> preoccupied with <u>his or her</u> peers at this stage and <u>begins</u> to seek stable relationships.

agr
8b

9. Yet the child's <u>interactions</u> with peers <u>are</u> often guided by strict rules, indicating that <u>they have</u> a cognitive function.
10. The child is organizing <u>experiences</u> that <u>are</u> abstract and complex, not just immediate and concrete as in infancy.

COLLABORATIVE LEARNING

ANSWERS: EXERCISE 4

Everyone has *his* (or *his or her*) favorite view of professional athletes. A common view is that the athletes are like well-paid children who have no real work to do, have no responsibilities, and simply enjoy the game and the good money. But this view of professional athletes *fails* to consider the grueling training the athletes have to go through to become professionals. Either training or competing *leads* each athlete to take risks that can result in *his* (or *his or her*) serious injury. The athletes have tremendous responsibility to the team they play on, which *needs* to function as a unit at all times to win *its* games. Most athletes are finished as active team players by the age of forty, when *they are* too stiff and banged-up to go on. Rather than just listening to any of the people who *criticize* professional athletes, everyone interested in sports *needs* to defend the athletes. They take stiff physical punishment so neither the sports fanatic nor the casual observer *is* deprived of *his* (or *his or her*) pleasure.

stage and begin to seek stable relationships. (*Change Children to The child.*)
9. Yet the <u>child</u>'s interaction with peers is often guided by strict rules, indicating that it has a cognitive function. (*Change interaction to interactions.*)
10. The <u>child</u> is <u>organizing</u> experience that is abstract and complex, not just immediate and concrete as in infancy. (*Change experience to experiences.*)

Exercise 4
Revising: Agreement

Revise the sentences in the following paragraph to correct errors in agreement between subjects and verbs or between pronouns and their antecedents.

Everyone has their favorite view of professional athletes. A common view is that the athletes are like well-paid children who have no real work to do, have no responsibilities, and simply enjoy the game and the good money. But this view of professional athletes fail to consider the grueling training the athletes have to go through to become professionals. Either training or competing lead each athlete to take risks that can result in their serious injury. The athletes have tremendous responsibility to the team they play on, which need to function as a unit at all times to win their games. Most athletes are finished as active team players by the age of forty, when he is too stiff and banged-up to go on. Rather than just listening to any of the people who criticizes professional athletes, everyone interested in sports need to defend the athletes. They take stiff physical punishment so neither the sports fanatic nor the casual observer are deprived of their pleasure.

Note: See page 270 for an exercise involving agreement along with other aspects of grammar.

Chapter 9

Adjectives and Adverbs

HIGHLIGHTS

Many readers view misuse of adjectives and adverbs as a sign of ignorance or carelessness. You should alert students to the potential effect of errors, of course, and remind them that this text offers helpful advice.

Yet fear of failure can disrupt the writing process and cause students to drop effective phrases and sentences from an essay because they are uncertain about the correct form of a word. This chapter therefore takes a positive approach, showing students the correct way to use adjectives and adverbs rather than emphasizing the "don'ts." It also offers easily remembered advice to guide writers over trouble spots. The exercises in the chapter ask students not only to recognize errors but also to revise sentences to make sure adjectives and adverbs are used appropriately.

Adjectives and adverbs are modifiers that describe, restrict, or otherwise qualify the words to which they relate.

Functions of adjectives and adverbs

Adjectives modify nouns: *serious* student
pronouns: *ordinary* one
Adverbs modify verbs: *warmly* greet
adjectives: *only* three people
adverbs: *quite* seriously
phrases: *nearly* to the edge of the cliff
clauses: *just* when we arrived
sentences: *Fortunately*, she is employed.

TRANSPARENCY MASTER
AVAILABLE

Many of the most common adjectives are familiar one-syllable words such as *bad, strange, large,* and *wrong.* Many others are formed by adding endings such as *-al, -able, -ful, -less, -ish, -ive,* and *-y* to nouns or verbs: *optional, fashionable, beautiful, fruitless, selfish, expressive, dreamy.*

Most adverbs are formed by adding *-ly* to adjectives: *badly, strangely, largely, beautifully.* But note that we cannot depend on *-ly* to identify adverbs, since some adjectives also end in *-ly (fatherly, lonely)* and since some common adverbs do not end in *-ly (always, here, not, now, often, there).* Thus the only sure way to

ad
9b

distinguish between adjectives and adverbs is to determine how an individual word functions in its sentence. If a word modifies a noun or pronoun, it is an adjective; if it modifies a verb, an adjective, another adverb, or an entire word group, it is an adverb.

9a Use adjectives only to modify nouns and pronouns.

Adjectives modify only nouns and pronouns. Using adjectives instead of adverbs to modify verbs, adverbs, or other adjectives is nonstandard.

Nonstandard	They took each other *serious.*
Standard	They took each other *seriously.*

The adjectives *good* and *bad* often appear where standard English requires the adverbs *well* and *badly.*

Nonstandard	Playing *good* is the goal of practicing baseball.
Standard	Playing *well* is the goal of practicing baseball.

Nonstandard	The band played *bad.*
Standard	The band played *badly.*

Although in informal speech the adjective forms *real* and *sure* are often used in place of the adverb forms *really* and *surely,* formal speech and writing require the *-ly* adverb form.

Informal	After a few lessons Dan drove *real* well.
Formal	After a few lessons Dan drove *really* well.

Informal	The officer *sure* was amazed.
Formal	The officer *surely* was amazed.

9b Use an adjective after a linking verb to modify the subject. Use an adverb to modify a verb.

A **linking verb** is one that links, or connects, a subject and its complement: *They are golfers* (noun complement); *He is lucky* (adjective complement). (See also 5a-3.) Linking verbs are forms of *be,* the verbs associated with our five senses (*look, sound, smell, feel, taste*), and a few others (*appear, seem, become, grow, turn, prove, remain*).

Some of these verbs may or may not be linking, depending on their meaning in the sentence. When the word after the verb modifies the subject, the verb is linking and the word should be an adjective. When the word modifies the verb, however, it should be an adverb.

> The evidence proved *conclusive*. [Adjective *conclusive* modifies *evidence*.]
>
> The evidence proved *conclusively* that the defendant was guilty. [Adverb *conclusively* modifies *proved*.]

Two word pairs are especially troublesome in this context, *bad/badly* and *good/well*.

> Decker felt *bad* after she lost the race. [Adjective *bad,* meaning "unhappy" or "ill," modifies *Decker*.]
>
> She lost the race *badly*. [Adverb *badly* modifies *lost*.]

Well may serve as an adverb with a host of meanings or as an adjective meaning only "fit" or "healthy." *Good* serves only as an adjective.

> Decker had trained *well*. [*Well* is an adverb modifying *trained*.]
>
> She had felt *well*. [*Well* is an adjective modifying *She*.]
>
> Her prospects had been *good*. [*Good* is an adjective modifying *prospects*.]

HOMEMADE QUIZZES

Ask students to follow the pattern of the sample sentences and exercises in the chapter and make up sentences containing common errors in the use of adjectives and adverbs. The uses of *well* and *good, bad* and *badly* are good starters. Collect the papers and distribute them as quizzes during the next class. Correct them in small groups.

ad
9c

9c   **After a direct object, use an adjective to modify the object and an adverb to modify the verb.**

If the direct object of a verb is followed by a word that modifies the verb, that word must be an adverb: *Mungo repeated the words angrily*. If, in contrast, the direct object is followed by a word that modifies the object itself (an object complement), that word must be an adjective: *Campus politics made Mungo angry*. (See also 5a-3.)

You can test whether a modifier should be an adjective or an adverb by trying to separate it from the direct object. If you can separate it, it should be an adverb: *Mungo angrily repeated the words*. If you cannot separate it, it is probably an adjective.

> The instructor considered the student's work *thorough*. [The adjective can be moved in front of *work* (*student's thorough work*), but it cannot be separated from *work*.]
>
> The instructor considered the student's work *thoroughly*. [The adverb can be separated from *work*. Compare *The instructor thoroughly considered the student's work*.]

ad
9d

ANSWERS: EXERCISE 1

1. The <u>reverent</u> tourists <u>slowly</u> file past the
   <u>long</u> <u>black</u> monument.
   Sample imitation: The happy children
   quickly skip into the big circular tent.

2. Down the <u>gentle</u> slope of the <u>narrow</u> walkway, visitors whisper <u>quietly</u> among themselves.
   Sample imitation: In the dark hallways of the
   ancient palace, tourists peer excitedly at the
   armor.

3. As they read the <u>many</u> names on the panels
   that rise <u>high</u> above them, the tourists become <u>increasingly</u> sober.
   Sample imitation: As the children read the
   exciting stories about the superhero who
   fights bravely against crime, they become
   very engrossed.

4. Leaving the <u>shiny</u> <u>black</u> wall, <u>most</u> visitors
   feel <u>sad</u>.
   Sample imitation: Taking a difficult mathematics exam, many students are anxious.

5. Seeing the <u>somber</u> memorial and thinking
   of the Americans honored <u>there</u> can be an
   <u>overwhelming</u> experience.
   Sample imitation: Visiting the huge building
   and feeling its spaciousness can be a thrilling
   experience.

9d **When an adverb has a short form and an *-ly* form, distinguish carefully between the forms.**

Some adverbs have two forms, one with an *-ly* ending and one without. These include the following:

cheap, cheaply	loud, loudly	sharp, sharply
high, highly	near, nearly	slow, slowly
late, lately	quick, quickly	wrong, wrongly

With some of these pairs the choice of form is a matter of idiom, for the two forms have developed entirely separate meanings.

He went *late*.   Winter is drawing *near*.
Lately he has been eating more.   Winter is *nearly* here.

In other pairs the long and short forms have the same meaning. However, the short forms generally occur in informal speech and writing. The *-ly* forms are preferable in formal writing.

Informal   Drive *slow*.
Formal   The funeral procession moved *slowly* through town.

Informal   Jones wants to get rich *quick*.
Formal   Harrison became rich *quickly*.

Exercise 1
Identifying adjectives and adverbs

Identify the adjectives and adverbs in the following sentences, and determine what part of speech each one modifies. Then compose a sentence of your own that parallels each sentence.

Example:

The *angry* man shouted *loudly* and moved *inside*.
The *angry* man shouted *loudly* and moved *inside*.
The *hungry* child cried *plaintively* and fussed *loudly*.

1. The reverent tourists slowly file past the long black monument.
2. Down the gentle slope of the narrow walkway, visitors whisper quietly among themselves.
3. As they read the many names on the panels that rise high
   above them, the tourists become increasingly sober.
4. Leaving the shiny black wall, most visitors feel sad.
5. Seeing the somber memorial and thinking of the Americans
   honored there can be an overwhelming experience.

Exercise 2
Revising: Adjectives and adverbs

Revise the following sentences so that adjectives and adverbs are used appropriately. If any sentence is already correct as given, circle the number preceding it.

Example:

The announcer warned that traffic was moving very slow.
The announcer warned that traffic was moving very *slowly.*

1. The eighteenth-century essayist Samuel Johnson was real surprised when he received a pension from King George III.
2. Thinking about his meeting with the king, Johnson felt proudly.
3. Johnson was relieved that he had not behaved badly in the king's presence.
4. If he had worked more diligent, Johnson might have made money faster.
5. After living cheap for over twenty years, Johnson finally had enough money from the pension to eat and dress good.

ANSWERS: EXERCISE 2

1. The eighteenth-century essayist Samuel Johnson was <u>really</u> surprised when he received a pension from King George III.
2. Thinking about his meeting with the king, Johnson felt <u>proud</u>.
3. Sentence correct.
4. If he had worked more <u>diligently</u>, Johnson might have made money faster.
5. After living <u>cheaply</u> for over twenty years, Johnson finally had enough money from the pension to eat and dress <u>well</u>.

ad

9e

9e Use the comparative and superlative forms of adjectives and adverbs appropriately.

Adjectives and adverbs can show degrees of quality or amount with the endings *-er* and *-est* or with the words *more* and *most* or *less* and *least*. Most modifiers have three forms. The **positive form** is the dictionary form. It describes without comparing.

a *big* book   spoke *forcefully*

The **comparative form** compares the thing modified with one other thing.

a *bigger* book   spoke *more* (or *less*) *forcefully*

The **superlative form** compares the thing modified with two or more other things.

the *biggest* book   spoke *most* (or *least*) *forcefully*

 When word length or sound requires, use *more* and *most* instead of the endings *-er* and *-est*.

Most one-syllable adjectives and adverbs and many two-syllable adjectives take the endings *-er* and *-est*: *red, redder, reddest; lucky, luckier, luckiest; fast, faster, fastest*.

ad
9e

CORRECTING ERRORS

Take an acceptable passage from a student pa-per, an essay in a reader, or a magazine article and rewrite it to introduce errors in the use of adjectives and adverbs. Distribute the passage to students and ask them to correct it. Then distrib-ute the original version and ask students to com-ment on any differences between their correc-tions and the original version.

Many two-syllable adjectives can either add *-er* and *-est* or use the words *more* and *most: steady, steadier* or *more steady, steadi-est* or *most steady.* The use of *more* or *most* tends to draw the comparison out and so places more emphasis on it.

Using *more* and *most* is the only way to form the comparative and superlative for adjectives of three or more syllables and for most adverbs of two or more syllables (including nearly all end-ing in *-ly*): *beautiful, more beautiful, most beautiful; often, more often, most often; sadly, more sadly, most sadly.* For negative com-parisons, all adjectives and adverbs use *less* for the comparative (*less open*) and *least* for the superlative (*least open*).

If you are in doubt about how to form a comparative or su-perlative, consult a dictionary. It will supply *-er* and *-est* forms if they can be used. Otherwise, use *more* and *most.*

Use the correct forms of irregular adjectives and adverbs.

The irregular modifiers change the spelling of their positive form to show comparative and superlative degrees.

Degrees of irregular adjectives and adverbs

Positive	Comparative	Superlative
Adjectives		
good	better	best
bad	worse	worst
little	littler, less	littlest, least
many ⎫		
some ⎬	more	most
much ⎭		
Adverbs		
well	better	best
badly	worse	worst

Use either *-er/-est* or *more/most,* not both.

A double comparative or double superlative combines the *-er* or *-est* ending with the word *more* or *most.* It is redundant.

Chang was the *wisest* (not *most wisest*) person in town.
He was *smarter* (not *more smarter*) than anyone else.

4 **In general, use the comparative form for comparing two things and the superlative form for comparing three or more things.**

She was the *taller* of the two girls. [Comparative.]
Of all those books, *The Yearling* is the *best*. [Superlative.]

In conversation the superlative form is often used even though only two things are being compared: *When two people argue, the angriest one is usually wrong.* But the distinction between the forms should be observed in writing.

5 **Use comparative or superlative forms only for modifiers that can logically be compared.**

Some adjectives and adverbs cannot logically be compared— for instance, *perfect, unique, dead, impossible, infinite.* These words are absolute; that is, they are not capable of greater or lesser degrees because their positive form describes their only state. Although they can be preceded by adverbs like *nearly* or *almost* that mean "approaching," they cannot logically be modified by *more* or *most* (as in *most perfect*). This distinction is sometimes ignored in speech, but it should always be made in writing.

Not He was the *most unique* teacher we had.
But He was a *unique* teacher.

Exercise 3
Using comparatives and superlatives

Write the comparative and superlative forms of each adjective or adverb below. Then use all three forms in your own sentences.

Example:

heavy: heavier (comparative), heaviest (superlative)

The barbells were too *heavy* for me. The magician's trunk was *heavier* than I expected. Joe Clark was the *heaviest* person on the team.

1. badly   5. some   8. well
2. great   6. often   9. elegant
3. lively   7. good   10. understanding
4. steady

Exercise 4
Revising: Comparatives and superlatives

Revise the following sentences so that the comparative and superlative forms of adjectives and adverbs are appropriate for formal usage.

---

ad
9e

ANSWERS: EXERCISE 3
Possible Answers

1. badly, worse, worst
   The favored horse performed <u>badly</u> in the race. He performed <u>worse</u> than all but one other horse. The horse that performed <u>worst</u> broke stride and left the race.
2. great, greater, greatest
   A <u>great</u> tremor shook the earth. The tremor was <u>greater</u> than the earlier one. The <u>greatest</u> tremor was still to come.
3. lively, livelier, liveliest
   The children were <u>lively</u> yesterday. They are <u>livelier</u> today. The <u>liveliest</u> child sets the pattern for the others.
4. steady, steadier, steadiest
   The stool was not <u>steady</u>. It's <u>steadier</u> now that I've planed one leg. But it's still not the <u>steadiest</u> stool in the house.
5. some, more, most
   <u>Some</u> apples are in the basket. <u>More</u> apples are in the cooler. <u>Most</u> apples are red or green.
6. often, more often, most often
   We do not see our grandparents <u>often</u>. We would like to see them <u>more often</u>. <u>Most often</u>, we see our cousins.
7. good, better, best
   The fruit tasted <u>good</u>. The cheese tasted <u>better</u>. The chocolate pie tasted <u>best</u>.
8. well, better, best
   Julie did <u>well</u> on the test. Jack did <u>better</u> than Julie. Ellen did <u>best</u> of all.
9. elegant, more elegant, most elegant
   The Princess of Wales is an <u>elegant</u> woman. She is <u>more elegant</u> than the Queen. Of all the members of the Royal Family, she is the <u>most elegant</u>.
10. understanding, more understanding, most understanding
    Professor Najarian was <u>understanding</u> about my late paper. She was <u>more understanding</u> than I had expected. She must be the <u>most understanding</u> professor in the department.

ad
9g

ANSWERS: EXERCISE 4

1. Charlotte was the <u>oldest</u> of the three Brontë sisters, all of whom were novelists.
2. Some readers think Emily Brontë's *Wuthering Heights* is the <u>saddest</u> novel they have ever read.
3. Of the other two sisters, Charlotte and Anne, Charlotte was probably the <u>more</u> talented.
4. Critics still argue about whether Charlotte or Emily wrote <u>better</u>.
5. Certainly, this family of woman novelists was <u>unique</u>.

Example:

Attending classes full-time and working at two jobs was the most impossible thing I ever did.

Attending classes full-time and working at two jobs was *impossible* (or *the hardest thing I ever did*).

1. Charlotte was the older of the three Brontë sisters, all of whom were novelists.
2. Some readers think Emily Brontë's *Wuthering Heights* is the most saddest novel they have ever read.
3. Of the other two sisters, Charlotte and Anne, Charlotte was probably the most talented.
4. Critics still argue about whether Charlotte or Emily wrote more better.
5. Certainly this family of women novelists was the most unique.

9f Avoid double negatives.

A **double negative** is a nonstandard construction in which two negative words such as *no, none, neither, barely, hardly,* or *scarcely* cancel each other out. For instance, in *Jenny did not feel nothing,* the negatives *not* and *nothing* in essence produce a positive: the sentence asserts that Jenny felt other than nothing, or something. For the opposite meaning, one of the negatives must be eliminated or changed to a positive: *She felt <u>nothing</u>* or *She did <u>not</u> feel anything.*

Faulty	We could *not hardly* hear the speaker. *None* of her ideas *never* made it to the back of the room.
Revised	We could *hardly* hear the speaker. *None* of her ideas made it to the back of the room.
Revised	We could *not* hear the speaker. Her ideas *never* made it to the back of the room.

9g Use nouns sparingly as modifiers.

We often use one noun to modify another. For example:

father figure	slave trade	child care
flood control	truth serum	security guard

Carefully conceived, such phrases can be both clear and concise: *security guard* seems preferable to *guard responsible for security*. But overuse of noun modifiers can lead to flat, even senseless, writing. To avoid awkwardness or confusion, observe two principles. First, prefer possessives or adjectives as modifiers.

Not	A student takes the state medical *board* exams to become a *dentist* technician.
But	A student takes the state medical *board's* exams to become a *dental* technician.

Second, use only short nouns as modifiers and use them only in two- or three-word sequences.

Confusing	Minimex maintains a *plant employee relations improvement* program.
Revised	Minimex maintains a program *for improving* relations *among plant employees*.

Exercise 5
Revising: Adjectives and adverbs

Revise the following paragraph so that it conforms to formal usage of adjectives and adverbs.

Americans often argue about which professional sport is better: basketball, football, or baseball. Basketball fans contend that their sport offers more action because the players are constant running and shooting. Because it is played indoors in relative small arenas, basketball allows fans to be more closer to the action than the other sports do. Fans point to how graceful the players fly through the air to the hoop. Football fanatics say they don't hardly stop yelling once the game begins. They cheer when their team executes a real complicated play good. They roar more louder when the defense stops the opponents in a goal-line stand. They yell loudest when a fullback crashes in for a score. In contrast, the supporters of baseball believe that it might be the most perfect sport played. It combines the one-on-one duel of pitcher and batter struggling valiant with the tight teamwork of double and triple plays. Because the game is played slow and careful, fans can analyze and discuss the manager's strategy. Besides, they don't never know when they might catch a foul ball as a souvenir. However, no matter what the sport, all fans feel happily only when their team wins!

Note: See the next page for an exercise involving adjectives and adverbs along with other aspects of grammar.

ANSWERS: EXERCISE 5

Americans often argue about which professional sport is <u>best</u>: basketball, football, or baseball. Basketball fans contend that their sport offers more action because the players are <u>constantly</u> running and shooting. Because it is played indoors in <u>relatively</u> small arenas, basketball allows fans to be <u>closer</u> to the action than the other sports do. Fans point to how <u>gracefully</u> the players fly through the air to the hoop. Football fanatics say they <u>hardly</u> stop yelling once the game begins. They cheer when their team executes a <u>really</u> complicated play <u>well</u>. They roar more <u>loudly</u> when the defense stops the opponents in a goal-line stand. They yell <u>most loudly</u> when a fullback crashes in for a score. In contrast, the supporters of baseball believe that it might be the most <u>nearly</u> perfect sport played. It combines the one-on-one duel of pitcher and batter struggling <u>valiantly</u> with the tight teamwork of double and triple plays. Because the game is played <u>slowly</u> and <u>carefully</u>, fans can analyze and discuss the manager's strategy. Besides, they <u>never</u> know when they might catch a foul ball as a souvenir. However, no matter what the sport, all fans feel <u>happy</u> only when their team wins!

ANSWERS: EXERCISE ON CHAPTERS 6–9

Occasionally, musicians become "crossover artists" who can perform well in more than one field of music. For example, Wynton and Branford Marsalis were trained in jazz by their father, the great pianist Ellis Marsalis. Both of the sons have recently become successful classical artists. Branford's saxophone captures the richness of pieces by Ravel and Stravinsky. Wynton's albums of classical trumpet music from the Baroque period have brought him many awards. Still, if he were to choose which kind of music he likes better, Wynton would probably choose jazz. In contrast to the Marsalises, Yo-Yo Ma and Jean Pierre Rampal grew up studying classical music. Then in the 1980s they were invited by Claude Bolling, a French pianist, to record Bolling's jazz compositions. In fact, Rampal's flute blended with Bolling's music so well that the two men have done three albums.

Such crossovers are often harder for vocalists. Each type of music has its own style and feel that are hard to learn. For example, Luciano Pavarotti and Placido Domingo, two great opera tenors, have sung popular music and folk songs in concerts and on albums. On each occasion, their technique was nearly perfect, yet each sounded as if he were simply trying to sing properly. It is even more difficult for pop or country vocalists to sing opera, as Linda Ronstadt and Gary Morris found when they appeared in *La Bohème*. Each of them has a clear, pure voice, but a few critics said that he and she lacked the vocal power necessary for opera. However, Bobby McFerrin has been successful singing both pop and classical pieces. He won a Grammy award for his song "Don't Worry, Be Happy." But he is equally able to sing classical pieces *a cappella* (without musical accompaniment). His voice's remarkable range and clarity allow him to imitate many musical instruments.

No matter how successful, all of these musicians have shown great courage by performing in a new field. They are willing to test and stretch their talents, and we music fans benefit.

Exercise on Chapters 6–9
Revising: Grammatical sentences

The paragraphs below contain errors in pronoun case, verb forms, subject-verb agreement, pronoun-antecedent agreement, and the forms of adjectives and adverbs. Revise the paragraphs to correct the errors.

Occasionally, musicians become "crossover artists" whom can perform good in more than one field of music. For example, Wynton and Branford Marsalis was train in jazz by their father, the great pianist Ellis Marsalis. Both of the sons has recent became successful classical artists. Branford's saxophone captures the richness of pieces by Ravel and Stravinsky. Wynton's albums of classical trumpet music from the Baroque period has brung him many awards. Still, if he was to choose which kind of music he likes best, Wynton would probable choose jazz. In contrast to the Marsalises, Yo-Yo Ma and Jean Pierre Rampal growed up studying classical music. Then in the 1980s they was invited by Claude Bolling, a French pianist, to record Bolling's jazz compositions. In fact, Rampal's flute blended with Bolling's music so good that the two men have did three albums.

Such crossovers are often more harder for vocalists. Each type of music has their own style and feel that is hard to learn. For example, Luciano Pavarotti and Placido Domingo, two great opera tenors, have sang popular music and folk songs in concerts and on albums. On each occasion, their technique was the most perfect, yet each sounded as if he was simply trying to sing proper. It is even more difficulter for pop or country vocalists to sing opera, as Linda Ronstadt and Gary Morris founded when they appear in *La Bohème*. Each of them have a clear, pure voice, but a few critics said that him and her lacked the vocal power necessary for opera. However, Bobby McFerrin been successful singing both pop and classical pieces. He won a Grammy award for his song "Don't Worry, Be Happy." But he is equal able to sing classical pieces *a cappella* (without musical accompaniment). His voice's remarkable range and clarity allows him to imitate many musical instruments.

No matter how successful, all of these musicians has shown great courage by performing in a new field. They are willing to test and stretch their talents, and us music fans benefits.

Part III

Clear Sentences

This chapter opens with a positive approach, showing students how to test sentences for completeness, revise any fragments, and punctuate revised fragments. Following the opening section are discussions of particular structures that are often mispunctuated as complete sentences: subordinate clauses; verbal and prepositional phrases; and other word groups such as appositives, parts of compound predicates, and nouns plus modifiers. The chapter concludes with a discussion of the acceptable uses of incomplete sentences.

Chapter 10 — *Sentence Fragments*

A **sentence fragment** is part of a sentence that is set off as if it were a whole sentence by an initial capital letter and a final period or other end punctuation. Unlike a complete sentence, a sentence fragment lacks a subject or a verb or both, or it is a subordinate clause not attached to a complete sentence.

Fragment	The baboon in the cage. [The word group lacks a verb.]
Fragment	Leaning over. [The word group lacks both a subject and a verb.]
Fragment	When he eats. [The word group is a subordinate clause.]

TRANSPARENCY MASTER
AVAILABLE

Complete sentences versus sentence fragments

A **complete sentence**

1. contains a subject and a verb (*Candy is sweet*);
2. *and* is not a subordinate clause (beginning with a subordinating conjunction such as *because* and *whereas* or a relative pronoun such as *who* and *that*).   *p. 194*

A **sentence fragment**

1. lacks a verb (*The horse running away*);
2. *or* lacks a subject (*And ran away*);
3. *or* is a subordinate clause not attached to a complete sentence (*Because it was confused*).

make a note

Although writers occasionally use fragments deliberately and effectively (see 10e), readers perceive most fragments as serious errors because they are distracting or confusing. (Before reading further, you may find it helpful to review 5a and 5c on sentences and clauses.)

 10a **Test your sentences for completeness, and revise any fragments.**

The following three tests will help you determine whether a word group punctuated as a sentence is actually a complete sentence. If the word group does not pass *all three* tests, it is a fragment and needs to be revised.

> ## Tests for sentence fragments
>
> A sentence is complete only when it passes *all three* tests.
> 1. Find the verb.
> 2. Find the subject.
> 3. Make sure the clause is not subordinate.

Test 1: Find the verb.

Look for a verb in the group of words. If you do not have one, the word group is a fragment.

Fragment	The baboon with a stick in his mouth. [The word group contains no verb. Compare a complete sentence: *The baboon held a stick in his mouth.*]

To function as the verb in a complete sentence, any verb form you find must be a **finite verb,** one that is capable of making an assertion without the aid of a helping verb. (See also 5c-2). A finite verb changes form at least once to show the difference in present, past, and future time. Verbals such as *looking* and *to look* do not change and thus are not finite verbs.

	Finite verbs	**Verbals in fragments**
Present	The baboon *looks.*	The baboon *looking.*
Past	The baboon *looked.*	The baboon *looking.*
Future	The baboon *will look.*	The baboon *looking.*

A finite verb in the present tense also changes form when the subject changes from singular to plural. A verbal does not.

RESOURCES AND IDEAS

Ann Schlumberger and Diane Clymer, "Tailoring Composition Classes to ESL Students' Needs," *Teaching English in the Two-Year College* 16 (1989): 121–28. Schlumberger and Clymer provide suggestions for instructors who have no training in teaching English as a second language but have students in their composition classes whose first language is not English. They also provide a bibliography for curriculum design, cultural aspects of writing, and reading.

frag 10a

> TRANSPARENCY MASTER
> AVAILABLE

RESOURCES AND IDEAS

Muriel Harris, "Mending the Fragmented Free Modifier," *College Composition and Communication* 32 (1981): 175–82. Harris presents strategies for identifying kinds of fragments and correcting them.

	Finite verbs	**Verbals in fragments**
Singular	The baboon *looks.*	The baboon *looking.*
Plural	The baboons *look.*	The baboons *looking.*

Fragments like those above require a change in the verbal or the addition of a helping verb to become complete sentences.

Fragment   The animal crouching by the door. [Compare a complete sentence: *The animal is (was, will be) crouching by the door.*]

Test 2: Find the subject.

If you find a finite verb, look for its subject by asking who or what performs the action or makes the assertion of the verb. The subject will usually come before the verb. If there is no subject, the word group is a fragment unless it is a command.

Fragment   Eyed the guard nervously. [The word group lacks a subject. Compare a complete sentence: *The ba-boon eyed the guard nervously.*]

In one kind of complete sentence, a command, the subject *you* is understood.

(You) Move away from the cage.

NEWSCASTERS

The breathless style of radio and television newscasters often includes fragments. Ask students to write down examples from the evening news. Newspapers, especially tabloids, can be a good source, too.

Test 3: Make sure the clause is not subordinate.

If you find a finite verb and its subject, look for a subordinating conjunction or a relative pronoun, such as those below:

Subordinating conjunctions			**Relative pronouns**	
after	once	until	that	who
although	since	when	which	whoever
as	than	where		
because	that	whereas		
if	unless	while		

p. 194 more complete list.

These words almost always signal **subordinate clauses,** which do not express complete, independent thoughts and must be attached to main clauses. (See p. 194 for a longer list of subordinating conjunctions.)

Fragment   When the next cage rattled. [The word group has a subject and a verb, *cage rattled,* but begins with a subordinating conjunction, *When.* Compare a complete sentence: *The next cage rattled.*]

Fragment   The rival that the baboon hated. [The verb, *hated,* is in a subordinate clause beginning *that,* so the thought about the rival is incomplete. Compare a complete sentence: *The rival that the baboon hated <u>rattled the cage</u>.*]

Some words may introduce either subordinate clauses or complete questions:

how	where	whom
what	which	whose
when	who	why

A word group beginning with one of these words is a fragment *unless* (1) it is attached to a complete main clause or (2) it asks a question.

Fragment   When their rivalry began. [The word group is not attached to a main clause, nor is it a question, so it is a fragment. Compare a complete sentence: *<u>No one knows</u> when their rivalry began.*]

Question   When *did* their rivalry *begin*?

Revising sentence fragments

Almost all sentence fragments can be corrected in one of two ways, the choice depending on the importance of the information in the fragment.

Revision of sentence fragments

- Rewrite the fragment as a complete sentence.
- Combine the fragment with the appropriate main clause.

Rewriting the fragment as a complete sentence gives the information in the fragment the same importance as that in other complete sentences.

Fragment   The baboon stared at his challenger. *Poised for combat.*

Revised   The baboon stared at his challenger. *He was* poised for combat.

Fragment   The animals acted out a rivalry. *Which mystified their keepers.*

Revised   The animals acted out a rivalry. *It* mystified their keepers.

frag

10a

Two main clauses may be separated by a semicolon instead of a period (see 22a).

The second method of correcting a fragment, combining it with a main clause, subordinates the information in the fragment to the information in the main clause.

| **Fragment** | The baboon stared at his challenger. *Poised for combat.* |
| **Revised** | The baboon, poised for combat, stared at his challenger. |

In this example, commas separate the inserted phrase from the rest of the sentence because the phrase does not restrict the meaning of any word in the main clause but simply adds information (see 21c). When a phrase or subordinate clause *does* restrict the meaning of a word in the main clause, a comma or commas do not separate the two elements.

| **Fragment** | The challenger was a newcomer. *Who was unusually fierce.* |
| **Revised** | The challenger was a newcomer who was unusually fierce. |

Sometimes a fragment may be combined with the main clause using a colon or a dash (see 25a and 25b, respectively).

Fragment	The rivalry may have begun with a specific cause. *Territory, dominance, or a female baboon.*
Revised	The rivalry may have begun with a specific cause: territory, dominance, or a female baboon.
Fragment	Now the rivalry was constant and vicious. *A threat to both animals.*
Revised	Now the rivalry was constant and vicious—a threat to both animals.

ANSWERS: EXERCISE 1

Possible Answers

1. Lacks a subject and a verb.
   Complete: An <u>article</u> about vandalism against works of art <u>was</u> interesting.
   Combined: In an interesting article about vandalism against works of art, <u>the author says the vandals' motives vary widely</u>.
2. Lacks a verb.
   Complete: The motives of the vandals <u>vary</u> widely.
   Combined: The motives of the vandals varying widely, researchers can make few generalizations.

Exercise 1
Identifying and revising sentence fragments

Apply the tests for completeness to each of the following word groups. If a word group is a complete sentence, circle the number preceding it. If it is a sentence fragment, revise it in two ways: by making it a complete sentence, and by combining it with a main clause written from the information given in other items.

Example:

And could not find his money.

The word group has a verb (*could . . . find*) but no subject.

Revised into a complete sentence: And *he* could not find his money.

Combined with a new main clause: *He was lost* and could not find his money.

1. In an interesting article about vandalism against works of art.
2. The motives of the vandals varying widely.
3. Those who harm artwork are usually angry.
4. But not necessarily at the artist or the owner.
5. For instance, a man who hammered at Michelangelo's *Pietà*.
6. And knocked off the Virgin Mary's nose.
7. Because he was angry at the Roman Catholic Church.
8. Which knew nothing of his grievance.
9. Although many damaged works can be repaired.
10. Usually even the most skillful repairs are forever visible.

10b   A subordinate clause is not a complete sentence.

Subordinate clauses contain both subjects and verbs, but they always begin with a subordinating conjunction (*although, if,* and so on) or a relative pronoun (*who, which, that*). (See p. 193.) Subordinate clauses cannot stand alone as complete sentences.

To correct a subordinate clause set off as a sentence, combine it with the main clause or remove or change the subordinating word to create a main clause.

Fragment   Many pine trees bear large cones. *Which appear in August.* [The fragment is a subordinate clause modifying *cones.*]

Revised   Many pine trees bear large cones, which appear in August. [The subordinate clause is combined with the main clause.]

Revised   Many pine trees bear large cones. *They* appear in August. [Substituting *They* for *Which* makes the fragment into a complete sentence.]

3. Complete sentence.
4. Lacks a subject and a verb.
    Complete: But the vandal is not necessarily angry at the artist or the owner.
    Combined: Whoever harms artwork is usually angry, but not necessarily at the artist or the owner.
5. Lacks a verb for the subject man.
    Complete: For instance, a man hammered at Michelangelo's *Pietà.*
    Combined: For instance, a man who hammered at Michelangelo's *Pietà* was angry at the Roman Catholic Church.
6. Lacks a subject.
    Complete: He knocked off the Virgin Mary's nose.
    Combined: A man hammered at Michelangelo's *Pietà* and knocked off the Virgin Mary's nose.
7. Begins with subordinating conjunction.
    Complete: He was angry at the Roman Catholic Church.
    Combined: A man hammered at Michelangelo's *Pietà* because he was angry at the Roman Catholic Church.
8. Begins with *which* but is not a question.
    Complete: The Church knew nothing of his grievance.
    Combined: He was angry at the Roman Catholic Church, which knew nothing of his grievance.
9. Begins with subordinating conjunction.
    Complete: Many damaged works can be repaired.
    Combined: Although many damaged works can be repaired, even the most skillful repairs are forever visible.
10. Complete sentence.

frag
10b

Correct any sentence fragment below either by combining it with a main clause or by making it a main clause. If an item contains no sentence fragment, circle the number preceding it.

Example:

Jujitsu can be an excellent form of self-protection. Because it enables one to overcome an opponent without the use of weapons.

Jujitsu can be an excellent form of self-protection because it enables one to overcome an opponent without the use of weapons.

COLLABORATIVE LEARNING

ANSWERS: EXERCISE 2
Possible Answers

1. In the nineteenth century chemists began synthesizing perfume oils, which previously could be made only from natural sources.
2. After medieval crusaders returned from the East, European perfumers began using animal oils as well as plant oils in their mixtures.
3. The most popular animal oil for perfume today is musk, although some people dislike its heavy, sweet odor.
4. No sentence fragment.
5. Synthetic musk oil would preserve a certain species of deer whose gland is the source of musk.

CREATING PROBLEMS

If students have been assigned Chapter 11, "Comma Splices and Fused Sentences," along with this chapter, ask them to write sample sentences containing fused sentences, comma splices, and fragments. Then have them exchange papers and check to see if the errors have been executed properly. This exercise will help students recognize fused sentences, comma splices, and fragments. (It's much harder to create intentional errors, particularly sentence fragments, than most students will think.)

1. In the nineteenth century chemists began synthesizing perfume oils. Which previously could be made only from natural sources.
2. After medieval crusaders returned from the East. European perfumers began using animal oils as well as plant oils in their mixtures.
3. The most popular animal oil for perfume today is musk. Although some people dislike its heavy, sweet odor.
4. Musk oil goes a long way. Because of its pungency very little is needed to make a strong perfume.
5. Synthetic musk oil would help conserve a certain species of deer. Whose gland is the source of musk.

 10c **A verbal phrase or a prepositional phrase is not a complete sentence.**

A **verbal phrase** consists of an infinitive (*to choose*), a past participle (*chosen*), or a present participle or gerund (*choosing*) together with any objects and modifiers it may have (see 5c-2). Verbal phrases cannot serve as the verbs in complete sentences. Fragments consisting of verbal phrases are most easily corrected by combining them with the main clauses they are related to. Verbal phrases can be converted into main clauses only by rewriting.

Fragment	She backed closer and closer to the end of the diving board. *At last falling into the water.*
Revised	She backed closer and closer to the end of the diving board**,** at last falling into the water. [The phrase is combined with the main clause.]
Revised	She backed closer and closer to the end of the diving board**.** At last *she fell* into the water. [The phrase is made into a complete sentence by changing *falling* to the verb *fell* and by adding the subject *she.*]

A **prepositional phrase** consists of a preposition (such as *in, on, to,* and *with*) together with its object and any modifier (see 5c-1). A prepositional phrase cannot stand alone as a complete sentence. It may be combined with a main clause or rewritten as a main clause.

Fragment	Falling gave her confidence. *In her strength.*
Revised	Falling gave her confidence in her strength.
Revised	Falling gave her confidence. *She learned to trust her strength.*

Exercise 3
Identifying and revising phrase fragments

Correct any sentence fragment below either by combining it with a main clause or by rewriting it as a main clause. If an item contains no sentence fragment, circle the number preceding it.

Example:

A hobby can contribute to a fulfilling life. Engaging one in activities outside work.

A hobby can contribute to a fulfilling life, engaging one in activities outside work.

1. Deliberately scenting the air. It is a behavior that originated in prehistory.
2. Some sources say that the custom arose as an attempt to cover up the smell of burning flesh. During sacrifices to the gods.
3. The sacred use of perfume survives. In the incense burned during religious services.
4. Perfumes became religious offerings in their own right. Being expensive to make, they were highly prized.
5. The earliest historical documents from the Middle East record the use of fragrances. Not only in religious ceremonies but on the body.

10d   **Any word group lacking a subject or a verb or both is not a complete sentence.**

We often follow a noun with a phrase or subordinate clause that modifies the noun. No matter how long the noun and its modifier are, they cannot stand alone as a sentence.

Fragments	*People waving flags and cheering. Lined the streets for the parade.*
Revised	People waving flags and cheering lined the streets for the parade. [The two fragments are combined into one sentence.]
Fragment	*Veterans who fought in Vietnam.* They are finally being honored.
Revised	Veterans who fought in Vietnam are finally being honored. [The fragment replaces *They* as the modified subject of the main clause.]

Appositives are nouns, or nouns and their modifiers, that rename or describe other nouns (see 5c-5). They cannot stand alone as sentences.

ANSWERS: EXERCISE 3
Possible Answers

1. Deliberately scenting the <u>air is</u> a behavior that originated in prehistory.
2. Some sources say that the custom arose as an attempt to cover up the smell of burning <u>flesh</u> during sacrifices to the gods.
3. The sacred use of perfume <u>survives</u> in the incense burned during religious services.
4. No sentence fragment.
5. The earliest historical documents from the Middle East record the use of <u>fragrances,</u> not only in religious ceremonies but on the body.

ADVERTISING

Advertisements and public announcements frequently contain fragments, fused sentences, and comma splices. In fact, some people speculate that this incidence may be one source of problems in student writing. Ask students to read Chapters 10 and 11 carefully. Then collect examples from magazine ads, junk mail, signs, and similar sources, and ask students to spot and correct the errors. Here are two examples, the first from an advertisement, the second from a hotel restaurant's menu.

Introducing the Satellite
News Channel.
The first all-live, all-news TV channel. News with no fillers. No reruns. No nonsense. No fat.
SNC is live-action news, delivered fresh every 18 minutes. Powered by the worldwide resources of ABC Television and Group W. Broadcasting. With the depth of 24 award-winning regional news teams.
Available 24-hours a day. Seven days a week.

Picnic Lunch Available
Please give your order 1 hour in advance. Before 10:00 A.M. Good Morning we hope you will have a pleasant day.

This activity is particularly effective in groups because some students may wish to argue that

frag
10d

the fragments they find are used appropriately, while others will insist on a strict interpretation of the rules they find in the handbook. The ensuing discussion is likely to be worthwhile, particularly if it touches on the importance of rhetorical context and convention in determining punctuation rules.

frag
10d

Fragment	When I was a child, my favorite adult was an old uncle. *A retired sea captain who always told me long stories of wild adventures in faraway places.*
Revised	When I was a child, my favorite adult was an old uncle, a retired sea captain who always told me long stories of wild adventures in faraway places. [The appositive is combined with the main clause.]

Compound predicates are predicates made up of two or more verbs and their objects, if any. A verb or its object cannot stand alone as a sentence.

Fragment	Uncle Marlon drew out his tales. *And embellished them.* [The fragment is part of a compound predicate.]
Revised	Uncle Marlon drew out his tales and embellished them.
Fragment	He described characters he had met. *And storms at sea.* [The fragment is part of a compound object.]
Revised	He described characters he had met and storms at sea.

Note: Beginning a sentence with a coordinating conjunction such as *and* and *but* can lead to a sentence fragment. Check every sentence you begin with a coordinating conjunction to be sure it is complete.

ANSWERS: EXERCISE 4
Possible Answers

1. Human beings who perfume themselves are not much different from other animals.
2. Animals as varied as insects and dogs release pheromones, chemicals that signal other animals.
3. No sentence fragment.
4. Human beings have a diminished sense of smell and do not consciously detect most of their own species' pheromones.
5. The human substitute for pheromones may be perfumes, especially musk and other fragrances derived from animal oils.

Exercise 4 ✓
Identifying and revising other fragments

Correct any sentence fragment below either by combining it with a main clause or by rewriting it as a main clause. If an item contains no sentence fragment, circle the number preceding it.

Example:

Lynn graduated from college in 1989. But did not begin working until 1991.

Lynn graduated from college in 1989 but did not begin working until 1991.

Lynn graduated from college in 1989. But *she* did not begin working until 1991.

1. Human beings who perfume themselves. They are not much different from other animals.
2. Animals as varied as insects and dogs release *pheromones.* Chemicals that signal other animals.
3. The chemicals sometimes repel other animals. But more often they perform a sexual function by attracting a member of the opposite sex.

4. Human beings have a diminished sense of smell. And do not consciously detect most of their own species' pheromones.
5. The human substitute for pheromones may be perfumes. Especially musk and other fragrances derived from animal oils.

 10e   **Be aware of the acceptable uses of incomplete sentences.**

A few word groups lacking the usual subject-predicate combination are incomplete sentences, but they are not fragments because they conform to the expectations of most readers. They include exclamations (*Oh no!*); questions and answers (*Where next? To Kansas.*); and commands (*Move along. Shut the window.*). Exclamations and questions and answers occur most often in speech or in writing that records speech; commands occur in speech and in written directions. Another kind of incomplete sentence, which occurs in special situations, is the transitional phrase (*So much for the causes, now for the results. One final point.*).

Experienced writers sometimes use incomplete sentences that *are* sentence fragments when they want to achieve a special effect. Such fragments appear more in informal than in formal writing. Unless you are experienced and thoroughly secure in your own writing, you should avoid all fragments and concentrate on writing clear, well-formed sentences.

Exercise 5
Revising: Sentence fragments

Revise the following paragraph to eliminate sentence fragments by combining them with main clauses or rewriting them as main clauses.

   Hiring Steele as the manager of the baseball team was a stupid move. Or a very clever maneuver. Depending on whether one is thinking like a fan or like the team's owner. Fans claim it was stupid. Because Steele is hard to get along with and unfair. They say he is also a poor manager. Failing to make the best use of the team's talents. And creating friction among the players. But the team's owner may have had a good reason for hiring such a manager. Some people think the owner hired Steele only temporarily. In order to make the team less attractive to unfriendly buyers. Who have been threatening a hostile takeover of the team. Hiring Steele could have been intended to prevent the takeover. And in the long run save the team. Not ruin it.

Note: See page 326 for an exercise involving sentence fragments along with comma splices, fused sentences, and other sentence errors.

RESOURCES AND IDEAS

Charles R. Kline, Jr., and W. Dean Memering, "Formal Fragments: The English Minor Sentence," *Research in the Teaching of English* 11 (1977): 97–110. The authors identify the kinds of fragments (minor sentences) often used and considered acceptable in formal writing.

frag
10e

COLLABORATIVE LEARNING

ANSWERS: EXERCISE 5
Possible Revision

   Hiring Steele as manager of the baseball team was a stupid move or a very clever maneuver, depending on whether one is thinking like a fan or like the team's owner. Fans claim it was stupid because Steele is hard to get along with and unfair. They say he is also a poor manager, failing to make the best use of the team's talents and creating friction among the players. But the team's owner may have had a good reason for hiring such a manager. Some people think the owner hired Steele only temporarily in order to make the team less attractive to unfriendly buyers who have been threatening a hostile takeover of the team. Hiring Steele could have been intended to prevent the takeover and in the long run save the team, not ruin it.

This chapter begins with a summary of the accepted methods for punctuating consecutive main clauses and follows with advice for recognizing and correcting comma splices and fused sentences. Correction of comma splices and fused sentences may involve strategies that students should employ more frequently in their sentences, particularly subordination and use of the semicolon. To encourage variety in sentence structure along with the avoidance of error, exercises for the chapter ask students to combine sentences following different strategies as well as to recognize and revise comma splices and fused sentences.

Comma Splices and Fused Sentences

Chapter 11

> TRANSPARENCY MASTER
> AVAILABLE

Two or more consecutive main clauses may be separated from each other in one of four ways:

- With a period:

  The ship was huge. Its mast stood thirty feet high.

- With a semicolon:

  The ship was huge; its mast stood thirty feet high.

- With a comma preceding a coordinating conjunction that joins the clauses and specifies the relation between them:

  The ship was huge, *and* its mast stood thirty feet high.

- Occasionally with a colon when the second clause explains the first (see 25a):

  The ship was huge: its mast stood thirty feet high.

Two problems commonly occur in punctuating consecutive main clauses. One is the **comma splice,** in which the clauses are joined (or spliced) *only* with a comma.

Comma splice

The ship was huge, its mast stood thirty feet high.

The other problem is the **fused sentence,** in which no punctuation or coordinating conjunction appears between the clauses.

Fused sentence

The ship was huge its mast stood thirty feet high.

Comma splices and fused sentences are serious errors because they generally force the reader to reread for sense.

COMMA SPLICES

11a   **Separate two main clauses with a comma *only* when they are joined by a coordinating conjunction.**

A comma cannot separate main clauses unless they are linked by a coordinating conjunction (*and, but, or, nor, for, so, yet*). Readers expect the same sentence to continue after a comma. When they find themselves reading a second sentence before they

RESOURCES AND IDEAS

Teachers and tutors who have little trouble punctuating sentences themselves may find it difficult to understand why some students have such difficulty with punctuation. In *The Practical Tutor* (New York: Oxford UP, 1987, 177–201), Emily Meyer and Louise Z. Smith offer detailed explanations of the causes of error and advice for diagnosing the roots of a student's punctuation difficulties. The teaching strategies they suggest include reading aloud, reading unpunctuated passages, asking probing questions (examples provided), and using simple diagrams.

Situations that may produce comma splices and fused sentences

- The first clause is negative; the second, positive.

  Splice   Petric is not a nurse, she is a doctor.
  Revised   Petric is not a nurse; she is a doctor.

- The second clause amplifies or illustrates the first.

  Fused   She did well in college her average was 3.9.
  Revised   She did well in college: her average was 3.9.

- The second clause contains a conjunctive adverb such as *however, therefore,* or *instead* (see 11b).

  Splice   She had intended to become a biologist, *however,* medicine seemed more exciting.

  Revised   She had intended to become a biologist; *however,* medicine seemed more exciting.

- Both clauses have the same subject.

  Fused   Petric is an internist *she* practices in Topeka.
  Revised   Petric is an internist. *She* practices in Topeka.

- Splicing or fusing is an attempt to link related ideas or to smooth choppy sentences.

  Splice   She is very committed to her work, she devotes almost all her time to patient care.

  Revised   *Because* she is very committed to her work, she devotes almost all her time to patient care.

cs
11a

realize they have finished the first, they may have to reread to understand the writer's meaning.

> **Comma splice**   Rain had fallen steadily for sixteen hours,
> many basements were flooded.

Exception: Experienced writers sometimes use commas between very brief main clauses that are grammatically parallel.

> He's not a person, he's a monster.

However, many readers view such punctuation as incorrect. Unless you are certain that your readers will not object to the comma
in a sentence like this one, separate the clauses with periods or
semicolons, as described below.

You have four main options for correcting a comma splice.
The option you choose depends on the relation you want to establish between the clauses.

cs
11a

Revision of comma splices

- Make the clauses into separate sentences.
- Insert an appropriate coordinating conjunction after the comma between clauses.
- Insert a semicolon between clauses.
- Subordinate one clause to the other.

RESOURCES AND IDEAS

Betty Bamberg, "Periods Are Basic: A Strategy
for Eliminating Comma Faults and Run-On
Sentences," *Teaching the Basics—Really!* ed.
Ouida Clapp (Urbana: NCTE, 1977) 97–99.
Bamberg suggests using oral reading to iden-
tify and correct problems.

Making separate sentences

Revising a comma splice by making separate sentences from
the main clauses will always be correct.

> Rain had fallen steadily for sixteen hours. Many basements were
> flooded.

The period is not only correct but preferable when the ideas expressed in the two main clauses are only loosely related.

> **Comma splice**   Chemistry has contributed much to our un-
> derstanding of foods, many foods such as
> wheat and beans can be produced in the lab-
> oratory.
>
> **Revised**   Chemistry has contributed much to our un-
> derstanding of foods. Many foods such as
> wheat and beans can be produced in the lab-
> oratory.

Inserting a coordinating conjunction

When the ideas in the main clauses are closely related and equally important, you may choose to correct a comma splice by inserting the appropriate coordinating conjunction immediately after the comma to join the clauses.

Rain had fallen steadily for sixteen hours, and many basements were flooded.

Comma splice   Some laboratory-grown foods taste good, they are nutritious.

Revised   Some laboratory-grown foods taste good, *and* they are nutritious.

Notice that the relation indicated by a coordinating conjunction can be complementary (*and*), contradictory (*but, yet*), causal (*for, so*), or alternate (*or, nor*).

Many people were late to work, *for* cars would not start.

People were late to work, *or* they stayed home to pump out flooded basements.

Using a semicolon

If the relation between the ideas expressed in the main clauses is very close and obvious without a conjunction, you can separate the clauses with a semicolon. (See also 11b.)

Rain had fallen steadily for sixteen hours; many basements were flooded.

Comma splice   Good taste is rare in laboratory-grown vegetables, they are usually bland.

Revised   Good taste is rare in laboratory-grown vegetables; they are usually bland.

Subordinating one clause

When the idea in one clause is more important than that in the other, you can express the less important idea in a phrase or a subordinate clause. (See p. 194 for a list of subordinating conjunctions.)

After rain had fallen steadily for sixteen hours, many basements were flooded. [The addition of the subordinating conjunction *After* reduces the first sentence to a subordinate clause indicating time.]

cs

11a

After sixteen hours of steady rain, many basements were flooded. [The clause is reduced to a prepositional phrase.]

Subordination is often more effective than forming separate sentences because it defines the relation between ideas more precisely.

Comma splice	The vitamins are adequate, the flavor is deficient.
Revised	The vitamins are adequate. The flavor is deficient. [Both ideas receive equal weight.]
Improved	*Even though* the vitamins are adequate, the flavor is deficient. [Emphasis on the second idea.]

 11b Use a period or semicolon to separate main clauses related by conjunctive adverbs.

Conjunctive adverbs are modifiers that describe a relation between two clauses:

anyway	hence	meanwhile	still
consequently	however	moreover	then
finally	indeed	nonetheless	therefore
furthermore	instead	otherwise	thus

(See p. 203 for a longer list.)

When two clauses are related by a conjunctive adverb, they must be separated by a period (forming two separate sentences) or by a semicolon (see 22b). The adverb is also generally set off by a comma or commas.

Comma splice	Most Americans refuse to give up unhealthful habits, consequently our medical costs are higher than those of many other countries.
Revised	Most Americans refuse to give up unhealthful habits. Consequently, our medical costs are higher than those of many other countries.
Revised	Most Americans refuse to give up unhealthful habits; consequently, our medical costs are higher than those of many other countries.

Unlike coordinating and subordinating conjunctions, conjunctive adverbs do not join two clauses into a grammatical unit but merely describe the way the clauses relate in meaning. Also unlike conjunctions, which must be placed between the word groups they join (coordinating) or at the beginning of the word group they introduce (subordinating), conjunctive adverbs may usually

cs
11b

CREATING PROBLEMS

If students have been assigned Chapter 10, "Sentence Fragments," along with this chapter, ask them to write sample sentences containing comma splices, fused sentences, and fragments. Then have them exchange papers and check to see if the errors have been executed properly. This exercise will help students recognize comma splices, fused sentences, and fragments. (It's much harder to create intentional errors, particularly fused sentences and sentence fragments, than most students will think.)

be moved from one place to another in the clause (see 5d-2). No matter where in the clause a conjunctive adverb appears, however, the clause must be separated from another main clause by a period or a semicolon.

Comma splice

The increased time devoted to watching television is not the only cause of the decline in reading ability, however, it is one of the important causes.

Period and conjunctive adverb

The increased time devoted to watching television is not the only cause of the decline in reading ability. *However*, it is one of the important causes.

Semicolon and conjunctive adverb

The increased time devoted to watching television is not the only cause of the decline in reading ability; *however*, it is one of the important causes.

The increased time devoted to watching television is not the only cause of the decline in reading ability; it is, *however*, one of the important causes.

The increased time devoted to watching television is not the only cause of the decline in reading ability; it is one of the important causes, *however*.

Exercise 1
Identifying and revising comma splices

Correct each comma splice below in *two* of the following ways: (1) make separate sentences of the main clauses; (2) insert an appropriate coordinating conjunction after the comma; (3) substitute a semicolon for the incorrect comma; or (4) subordinate one clause to another. If an item contains no comma splice, circle the number preceding it.

Example:

Carolyn still had a headache, she could not get the child-proof cap off the aspirin bottle.

Carolyn still had a headache *because* she could not get the child-proof cap off the aspirin bottle. [Subordination.]

Carolyn still had a headache, *for* she could not get the child-proof cap off the aspirin bottle. [Coordinating conjunction.]

1. Money has a long history, it goes back at least as far as the earliest records.
2. Many of the earliest records concern financial transactions, indeed, early history must often be inferred from commercial activity.

cs
11b

IN CONTEXT

Identifying sentence problems in the context of an essay can be more challenging and rewarding than working with single-sentence examples. The content and flow of an essay can draw attention away from punctuation and sentence structure, making it hard to identify errors but also providing an experience similar to that of proofreading. To supplement the paragraph exercise at the end of this chapter (or at the end of Chapter 10), revise part of a professional essay to introduce errors (or find an error-filled student essay), and then distribute the essay to the class, asking students to locate and revise the errors.

COLLABORATIVE LEARNING

ANSWERS: EXERCISE 1
Possible Answers

1. Money has a long history. It goes back at least as far as the earliest records.
   Money has a long history that goes back at least as far as the earliest records.
2. Many of the earliest records concern financial transactions; indeed, early history must often be inferred from commercial activity.
   Many of the earliest records concern financial transactions. Indeed, early history must often be inferred from commercial activity.

3. No comma splice.
4. Sometimes the objects have had real value. In modern times, however, their value has been more abstract.

   Sometimes the objects have had real value; in modern times, however, their value has been more abstract.
5. Cattle, fermented beverages, and rare shells have served as money, and each one had actual value for the society.

   Cattle, fermented beverages, and rare shells have served as money. Each one had actual value for the society.
6. No comma splice.
7. Today money may be made of worthless paper; it may even consist of a bit of data in a computer's memory.

   Today money may be made of worthless paper. It may even consist of a bit of data in a computer's memory.
8. Although we think of money as valuable, only our common faith in it makes it valuable.

   We think of money as valuable, but only our common faith in it makes it valuable.
9. That faith is sometimes fragile; consequently, currencies themselves are valuable.

   That faith is sometimes fragile. Consequently, currencies themselves are valuable.
10. Economic crises often shake the belief in money. Such weakened faith helped cause the Great Depression of the 1930s.

    Economic crises often shake the belief in money; such weakened faith helped cause the Great Depression of the 1930s.

3. Every known society has had a system of money, though the objects serving as money have varied widely.
4. Sometimes the objects have had real value, in modern times, however, their value has been more abstract.
5. Cattle, fermented beverages, and rare shells have served as money, each one had actual value for the society.
6. As money, however, these objects acquired additional value because they represented other goods.
7. Today money may be made of worthless paper, it may even consist of a bit of data in a computer's memory.
8. We think of money as valuable, only our common faith in it makes it valuable.
9. That faith is sometimes fragile, consequently, currencies themselves are fragile.
10. Economic crises often shake the belief in money, such weakened faith helped cause the Great Depression of the 1930s.

FUSED SENTENCES

11c **Combine two main clauses only with an appropriate conjunction or punctuation mark between them.**

When two main clauses are joined without a word to connect them or a punctuation mark to separate them, the result is a **fused sentence.** Fused sentences can rarely be understood on first reading, and they are never acceptable in standard written English.

Fused   Our foreign policy is not well defined it confuses many countries.

Fused sentences may be corrected in the same ways as comma splices.

> ### Revision of fused sentences
>
> - Make the clauses into separate sentences.
> - Insert a comma and an appropriate coordinating conjunction between clauses.
> - Insert a semicolon between clauses.
> - Subordinate one clause to the other.

Separate sentences

Our foreign policy is not well defined. It confuses many countries. [The two main clauses are made into separate sentences.]

Comma and coordinating conjunction

Our foreign policy is not well defined, *and* it confuses many countries. [The two main clauses are separated by a comma and a coordinating conjunction.]

Semicolon

Our foreign policy is not well defined; it confuses many countries. [The two main clauses are separated by a semicolon.]

Subordinating conjunction

Because our foreign policy is not well defined, it confuses many countries. [*Because* subordinates the first clause to the second.]

Exercise 2
Identifying and revising fused sentences ✓

Revise each of the fused sentences below in *two* of the four ways shown above.

> *Example:*
> Tim was shy he usually refused invitations.
> Tim was shy, *so* he usually refused invitations.
> Tim was shy; he usually refused invitations.

1. Throughout history money and religion were closely linked there was little distinction between government and religion.
2. The head of state and the religious leader were often the same person all power rested in one ruler.
3. These powerful leaders decided what objects would serve as money their backing encouraged public faith in the money.
4. Coins were minted of precious metals the religious overtones of money were then strengthened.
5. People already believed the precious metals to be divine their use in money intensified its allure.

Exercise 3
Sentence combining: Comma splices and fused sentences

Combine each pair of sentences below into one sentence without creating a comma splice or fused sentence. Combine sentences by (1) supplying a comma and coordinating conjunction, (2) supplying a semicolon, or (3) subordinating one clause to the other. You will have to add, delete, or change words as well as punctuation.

> *Example:*
> The sun sank lower in the sky. The colors gradually faded.
> As the sun sank lower in the sky, the colors gradually faded.
> [The first clause is subordinated to the second.]

cs/fs
11

ANSWERS: EXERCISE 2
Possible Answers

1. Throughout history money and religion were closely linked <u>because</u> there was little distinction between government and religion.
   Throughout history money and religion were closely linked<u>; for</u> there was little distinction between government and religion.
2. The head of state and the religious leader were often the same person.<u> All</u> power rested in one ruler.
   The head of state and the religious leader were often the same person<u>;</u> all power rested in one ruler.
3. These powerful leaders decided what objects would serve as money,<u> and</u> their backing encouraged public faith in the money.
   These powerful leaders decided what objects would serve as money.<u> Their</u> backing encouraged public faith in the money.
4. <u>When</u> coins were minted of precious metals, the religious overtones of money were then strengthened.
   Coins were minted of precious metals.<u> The</u> religious overtones of money were then strengthened.
5. People already believed the precious metals to be divine,<u> so</u> their use in money intensified its allure.
   People already believed the precious metals to be divine<u>;</u> their use in money intensified its allure.

ANSWERS: EXERCISE 3
Possible Answers

1. The exact origin of paper money is unknown <u>because</u> it has not survived as coins, shells, and other durable objects have.
2. Scholars disagree over where paper money originated<u>;</u> many scholars believe it was first used in Europe, however.
3. Perhaps goldsmiths were also bankers<u>;</u> thus they held the gold of their wealthy customers.

4. The goldsmiths probably gave customers receipts for their gold; and these receipts were then used in trade.
5. The goldsmiths were something like modern-day bankers; their receipts were something like modern-day money.
6. The goldsmiths became even more like modern-day bankers when they began issuing receipts for more gold than they actually held in their vaults.
7. Today's bankers owe more to their customers than they actually have in reserve, but they keep enough assets on hand to meet reasonable withdrawals.
8. In economic crises bank customers sometimes fear the loss of their money; consequently, they demand their deposits.
9. If depositors' demands exceed a bank's reserves, the bank may collapse.
10. The government now regulates banks to protect depositors, so bank failures are less frequent than they once were.

COLLABORATIVE LEARNING

ANSWERS: EXERCISE 4
Possible Revision

A good way to learn new subjects and to meet new people is to take evening courses. Many colleges, high schools, and adult-education centers offer them. Such courses attract different kinds of people who share common interests. For example, students, secretaries, teachers, and businesspeople can enroll in word-processing courses, for they all need to use computers to improve their work. Courses in photography bring together people interested in taking vivid, striking pictures. The students sometimes go out in pairs or groups to shoot the same site; then they all enjoy passing around and discussing their photographs. By studying subjects ranging from cooking and wine tasting to enhancing reading and study skills, students can improve themselves and meet new friends. These classes clearly enrich the students' lives.

1. The exact origin of paper money is unknown. It has not survived as coins, shells, and other durable objects have.
2. Scholars disagree over where paper money originated. Many scholars believe it was first used in Europe, however.
3. Perhaps goldsmiths were also bankers. Thus they held the gold of their wealthy customers.
4. The goldsmiths probably gave customers receipts for their gold. These receipts were then used in trade.
5. The goldsmiths were something like modern-day bankers. Their receipts were something like modern-day money.
6. The goldsmiths became even more like modern-day bankers. They began issuing receipts for more gold than they actually held in their vaults.
7. Today's bankers owe more to their customers than they actually have in reserve. They keep enough assets on hand to meet reasonable withdrawals.
8. In economic crises bank customers sometimes fear the loss of their money. Consequently, they demand their deposits.
9. Depositors' demands may exceed a bank's reserves. The bank may collapse.
10. The government now regulates banks to protect depositors. Bank failures are less frequent than they once were.

Exercise 4
Revising: Comma splices and fused sentences

Identify and revise the comma splices and fused sentences in the following paragraph.

A good way to learn new subjects and to meet new people is to take evening courses, many colleges, high schools, and adult-education centers offer them. Such courses attract different kinds of people who share common interests, for example, students, secretaries, teachers, and businesspeople can enroll in word-processing courses they all need to use computers to improve their work. Courses in photography bring together people interested in taking vivid, striking pictures, the students sometimes go out in pairs or groups to shoot the same site, then they all enjoy passing around and discussing their photographs. By studying subjects ranging from cooking and wine tasting to enhancing reading and study skills, students can improve themselves and meet new friends, these classes clearly enrich the students' lives.

Note: See page 326 for an exercise involving comma splices and fused sentences along with other sentence errors.

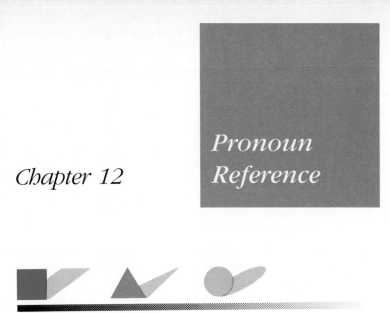

Chapter 12

Pronoun Reference

HIGHLIGHTS

Writers at all levels—advanced or struggling—will be likely to consult this chapter often, for problems with pronoun reference can arise in short, uncomplicated sentences as well as in papers that are ambitious in style and content. The discussion covers a number of particularly troublesome problems: unclear or ambiguous antecedents; broad reference with *this, that, which,* and *it;* indefinite use of *it* and *they;* and inappropriate use of *who, which,* and *that.* In each case, the discussion stresses the need for precision in reference as a way of ensuring that readers can follow the meaning of a passage. The examples and exercises mostly show reference problems within sentences as a way of keeping the discussion as simple and accessible as possible; however, the text points out that reference problems are just as likely to occur between sentences, and the paragraph exercise at the end of the chapter stresses this fact. Because strings of pronouns are an important device for creating coherence over long stretches of discourse, reference problems between or among sentences can cause considerable misunderstanding.

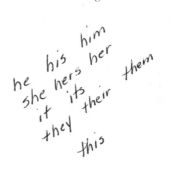

A **pronoun** such as *it* or *they* derives its meaning from its **antecedent,** the noun it substitutes for. Therefore, a pronoun must refer clearly and unmistakably to its antecedent in order for the meaning to be clear. A sentence such as *Jim told Mark he was not invited* is not clear because the reader does not know whether *he* refers to Jim or to Mark.

One way to make pronoun reference clear is to ensure that the pronoun and antecedent agree in person and number (see 8b). The other way is to ensure that the pronoun refers unambiguously to a single, close, specific antecedent.

12a Make a pronoun refer clearly to one antecedent.

A pronoun may, of course, refer to two or more nouns in a compound antecedent, as in *Jenkins and Wilson pooled their resources and became partners.* But when either of two nouns can be a pronoun's antecedent, the reference will not be clear.

Confusing	The workers removed all the furniture from the room and cleaned *it.* [Does *it* refer to the room or to the furniture?]
Clear	The workers removed all the furniture from the room and cleaned *the room* (or *the furniture*).

291

ref
12a

Principal causes of unclear pronoun reference

● More than one possible antecedent (12a):

> **Confusing** To keep birds from eating seeds, soak *them* in blue food coloring.
>
> **Clear** To keep birds from eating seeds, soak *the seeds* in blue food coloring.

● Antecedent too far away (12b):

> **Confusing** Employees should consult with their supervisor *who* require personal time.
>
> **Clear** Employees *who* require personal time should consult with their supervisor.

● Antecedent only implied (12c):

> **Confusing** Many children begin reading on their own by watching television, but *this* should be discounted in government policy.
>
> **Clear** Many children begin reading on their own by watching television, but *such self-instruction* should be discounted in government policy.

See also 12d, 12e, and 12f.

> **Clear** After removing all the furniture from it, the workers cleaned the room.
>
> **Clear** The workers cleaned all the furniture after removing it from the room.

You can revise sentences with unclear pronoun reference in two ways:

● Replace the pronoun with the appropriate noun (as in the revision on the previous page).
● To avoid repetition of the appropriate noun, rewrite the sentence with the pronoun but with only one possible antecedent (as in the revisions above).

Sentences that report what someone said, using verbs such as *said* or *told,* often require direct rather than indirect quotation.

> **Confusing** Juliet Noble told Susan Torre that she was mistaken.
>
> **Clear** Juliet Noble told Susan Torre, "I am mistaken."
>
> **Clear** Juliet Noble told Susan Torre, "You are mistaken."

Note: Avoid the awkward device of using a pronoun followed by the appropriate noun in parentheses.

Weak	Noble should apologize to Torre, and *she (Noble)* should notify the press.
Improved	Noble should apologize to Torre and notify the press.

12b Place a pronoun close enough to its antecedent to ensure clarity.

When the relative pronoun *who, which,* or *that* introduces a clause, the pronoun generally should fall immediately after its antecedent to prevent confusion. (See also 14b.)

Confusing	Jody found a dress in the attic *that* her aunt had worn. [Her aunt had worn the attic?]
Clear	In the attic Jody found a *dress that* her aunt had worn.

Even when only one word could possibly serve as the antecedent of a pronoun, the relationship between the two may still be unclear if they are widely separated.

Confusing	Denver, where my grandmother grew up, was once the scene of a mad gold rush with fortune seekers, plush opera houses, makeshift hotels, noisy saloons, and dirt streets. When I was a child, *she* often retold the stories she had heard.
Clear	Denver, where my grandmother grew up, was once the scene of a mad gold rush with fortune seekers, plush opera houses, makeshift hotels, noisy saloons, and dirt streets. When I was a child, *my grandmother* often retold the stories she had heard. [The noun is repeated for clarity.]

The confusing separation of pronoun and antecedent is most likely to occur in long sentences and, as illustrated by the preceding example, in adjacent sentences within a paragraph.

Exercise 1
Revising: Ambiguous and remote pronoun reference

Rewrite the following sentences to eliminate unclear pronoun reference. If you use a pronoun in your revision, be sure that it refers to only one antecedent and that it falls close enough to its antecedent to ensure clarity.

RETRIEVING SENTENCES

Reverse the process of sentence combining by asking students to reconstruct (or retrieve) the shorter (kernel) sentences that lie behind a long sentence containing a reference error. You may wish to use sentences from the text as a basis for the exercise. This activity will help students spot ambiguity or vague reference in the long sentence. After they have found the shorter sentences, ask students to recombine, this time avoiding the reference problem.

Original sentence: After the van hit John's car, its engine stopped running and its radiator started leaking.
Kernels: The van hit John's car. The van's engine stopped running. The van's radiator started leaking.
Recombined sentence: After the van hit John's car, the van's engine stopped running and its radiator started leaking.

ref
12b

ANSWERS: EXERCISE 1
Possible Answers

1. There is a difference between the heroes of the twentieth century and the heroes of earlier times: twentieth-century heroes have flaws in their characters.
2. Sports fans still admire Pete Rose, Babe Ruth, and Joe Namath even though none of these heroes could be perfect.
3. Fans liked Rose for having his young son serve as bat boy when Rose was in Cincinnati.
4. Rose's reputation as a gambler and tax evader may overshadow his reputation as a ball player, but the latter will survive.
5. Rose amassed an unequaled record as a hitter, using his bat to do things no one else has ever done. The record stands even though Rose has been banned from baseball.
6. Babe Ruth's drinking and carousing did not stop fans from cheering him.
7. Fans were happy if Ruth hit home runs and won games, and the Yankee owners wanted to fill the stadium. "The Bambino" seldom failed to satisfy the fans (or the owners or both the fans and the owners).
8. With his bat Ruth achieved the record for most home runs in a career. Nearly half a century passed before Henry Aaron broke the record.
9. When he was quarterback of the New York Jets, Joe Namath told a reporter, "I will have to quit because I am part-owner of a restaurant that mobsters supposedly also own."
10. Choosing between restaurant and career, Namath sold the restaurant.

Example:

Saul found an old gun in the rotting shed that was just as his grandfather had left it.

In the rotting shed Saul found an old gun that was just as his grandfather had left it.

1. There is a difference between the heroes of the twentieth century and the heroes of earlier times: they have flaws in their characters.
2. Sports fans still admire Pete Rose, Babe Ruth, and Joe Namath even though they could not be perfect.
3. Fans liked Rose for having his young son serve as bat boy when he was in Cincinnati.
4. Rose's reputation as a gambler and tax evader may overshadow his reputation as a ball player, but it will survive.
5. Rose amassed an unequaled record as a hitter, using his bat to do things no one else has ever done. It stands even though Rose has been banned from baseball.
6. Fans knew about Babe Ruth's drinking and carousing, but it did not stop them from cheering him.
7. Fans were happy if Ruth hit home runs and won games, and the Yankee owners wanted to fill the stadium. "The Bambino" seldom failed to satisfy them.
8. With his bat Ruth achieved the record for most home runs in a career. Nearly half a century passed before Henry Aaron broke it.
9. When he was quarterback of the New York Jets, a reporter was told by Joe Namath that he would have to quit football because he was part-owner of a restaurant that mobsters supposedly also owned.
10. Choosing between restaurant and career, Namath sold it.

 12c **Make a pronoun refer to a specific antecedent rather than to an implied one.**

A pronoun should refer to a specific noun or other pronoun. When the antecedent is not specifically stated but is implied by the context, the reference can only be inferred by the reader.

 1 Use *this, that, which,* and *it* cautiously in referring to whole statements.

The most common kind of implied reference occurs when the pronoun *this, that, which,* or *it* refers to a whole idea or situation described in the preceding clause, sentence, or even paragraph. Such reference, often called **broad reference,** is acceptable only when the pronoun refers clearly to the entire preceding clause. In the following sentence, *which* could not possibly refer to anything but the whole preceding clause.

> I can be kind and civil to people, *which* is more than you can.
> —GEORGE BERNARD SHAW

But if a pronoun might confuse a reader, you should avoid using it or provide an appropriate noun.

Confusing	I knew nothing about economics, *which* my instructor had not learned. [*Which* could refer to *economics* or to the whole preceding clause.]
Clear	I knew nothing about economics, *a fact* my instructor had not learned.
Clear	I knew nothing about economics *because* my instructor knew nothing about it.
Confusing	The faculty agreed on a change in the requirements, but *it* took time. [Does *it* refer to the faculty, to reaching agreement, or to the change?]
Clear	The faculty agreed on a change in the requirements, but *arriving at agreement* took time.
Clear	The faculty agreed on a change in the requirements, but *the change* took time to implement.
Confusing	The British knew little of the American countryside and had no experience with the colonists' guerrilla tactics. *This* gave the colonists an advantage. [Does *This* refer to the whole preceding sentence, to the ignorance alone, or to the inexperience alone?]
Clear	The British knew little of the American countryside and had no experience with the colonists' guerrilla tactics. *Their ignorance and inexperience* gave the colonists an advantage.

2   Implied nouns are not clear antecedents.

A noun may be implied in a modifier, a possessive, another noun, or some other word or phrase: *happiness* is implied in *happy, girl* in *girl's, news* in *newspaper, bite* in *bitten.* But a pronoun cannot refer clearly to such an implied noun; it must refer to a specific, stated antecedent.

Confusing	The speaker discussed ways to tap creative powers, but she did not define *it*. [*It* refers to *creativity,* the noun implied by the modifier *creative.*]

RESOURCES AND IDEAS

Leonard Moskovit, "When Is Broad Reference Clear?" *College Composition and Communication* 34 (1983): 454–469. The question of the acceptability of broad reference is a complicated one, as Moskovit points out, and anyone interested in looking at how broad reference operates in sophisticated prose will enjoy his essay.

ref
12c

ref
12d

Clear	The speaker discussed ways to tap creative powers, but she did not define *creativity*.
Confusing	In the speaker's advice *she* was not concrete enough. [*She* refers to *speaker,* implied by the possessive *speaker's.*]
Clear	In *her* advice *the speaker* was not concrete enough.
Better	The *speaker's advice* was not concrete enough.
Confusing	She spoke once before, but *it* was sparsely attended. [*It* refers to *speech,* implied by the verb *spoke.*]
Clear	She spoke once before, but *the speech* was sparsely attended.

3   Titles of papers are not clear antecedents.

The title of a paper is entirely separate from the paper itself, so a pronoun should not be used in the opening sentence of a paper to refer to the title. If you must refer to the title, repeat whatever part of the title is necessary for clarity.

Title	How to Row a Boat
Not	*This* is not as easy as it looks.
But	*Rowing a boat* is not as easy as it looks.

12d   Use *it* and *they* to refer to definite antecedents. Use *you* only to mean "you, the reader."

In conversation we commonly use expressions such as *It says in the paper* or *In Texas they say*. But such indefinite use of *it* and *they* is inappropriate in writing. The constructions are not only unclear but wordy.

Don't use you.

Confusing	In Chapter 4 of this book *it* describes the early flights of the Wright brothers.
Clear	*Chapter 4* of this book describes the early flights of the Wright brothers.
Confusing	In the average television drama *they* present a false picture of life.
Clear	The average television *drama* presents a false picture of life.

Using *you* with indefinite reference to people in general is also well established in conversation: *You can tell that my father was a military man.* The indefinite *you* frequently occurs in informal writing, too. And in all but very formal writing, *you* is acceptable when the meaning is clearly "you, the reader," as in *You can learn the standard uses of pronouns.* But the context must be appropriate for such a meaning. Consider this example:

Inappropriate	In the fourteenth century *you* had to struggle simply to survive. [Clearly, the meaning cannot be "you, the reader."]
Revised	In the fourteenth century *one* (or *a person* or *people*) had to struggle simply to survive.

12e   Use the pronoun *it* only one way in a sentence.

We use *it* idiomatically in expressions such as *It is raining.* We use *it* to postpone the subject in sentences such as *It is true that more jobs are available to women today.* And, of course, we use *it* as a personal pronoun in sentences such as *Joan wanted the book, but she couldn't find it.* All these uses are standard, but two of them in the same sentence can confuse the reader.

Confusing	When *it* is rainy, shelter your bicycle and wipe *it* often. [The first *it* is idiomatic; the second refers to *bicycle*.]
Revised	*In rainy weather,* shelter your bicycle and wipe *it* often.

12f   Use *who, which,* and *that* for appropriate antecedents.

The relative pronouns *who, which,* and *that* commonly refer to persons, animals, or things. *Who* refers most often to persons but may also refer to animals that have names.

Dorothy is the girl *who* visits Oz.
Her dog, Toto, *who* accompanies her, gives her courage.

Which refers to animals and things.

The Orinoco River, *which* is 1600 miles long, flows through Venezuela into the Atlantic Ocean.

IT, WHICH, AND THEY

Distribute copies of a student paper that uses *it, which, they,* and other pronouns in sentences without supplying clear antecedents in preceding sentences. Ask students to work in groups to correct the reference problems. Ask them also to construct an explanation of how a string of pronouns can be used properly to bring coherence to writing.

CORRECTING A NARRATIVE

Find or write a brief narrative containing several events and more than one character. Introduce enough reference problems so that readers have difficulty unraveling the events. If you wish, include dialogue in the narrative in such a way that the reference problems make it hard to identify the speakers. (Using "He said" as a tag when there are two men in the narrative is one possibility.) Ask students to work in groups to untangle the problems in the narrative and to rewrite it, removing vague and ambiguous references.

**ref
12f**

That refers to animals and things and occasionally to persons when they are collective or anonymous.

The rocket *that* failed cost millions.
Infants *that* walk need constant tending.

(See also 21c-1 for the use of *which* and *that* in nonrestrictive and restrictive clauses.)

The possessive *whose* generally refers to people but may refer to animals and things to avoid awkward and wordy *of which* constructions.

The book *whose* binding broke was rare. [Compare *The book of which the binding broke was rare.*]

ref
12f

ANSWERS: EXERCISE 2
Possible Answers

1. "Life begins at forty" is a cliché many people live by, and this <u>saying</u> may or may not be true.
2. <u>Its validity</u> depends on how one lives.
3. When <u>Pearl Buck</u> was forty, <u>her</u> novel *The Good Earth* won the Pulitzer Prize.
4. Buck was a novelist <u>who</u> wrote primarily about China.
5. In *The Good Earth* <u>the characters</u> have to struggle, but fortitude is rewarded.
6. Buck received much critical praise and earned over $7 million, but she was very modest about <u>her success</u> (or <u>the praise</u> or <u>the money</u>).
7. Pearl Buck donated most of her earnings to a foundation for Asian-American children, <u>thus proving</u> her generosity.
8. Kenneth Kaunda was elected to <u>the Presidency of Zambia</u> in 1964, at age forty.
9. When Catherine I became Empress of Russia at age forty, <u>the Russians</u> feared more than loved her.
10. At forty, Paul Revere made his famous ride to warn American revolutionary leaders that the British were going to arrest them. <u>His warning</u> gave the colonists time to prepare for battle.
11. <u>The members of the British House of Commons</u> did not welcome forty-year-old Nancy Astor as the first female member when she entered in 1919.

Exercise 2
Revising: Indefinite and inappropriate pronoun reference

Many of the pronouns in the following sentences do not refer to specific, appropriate antecedents. Revise the sentences as necessary to make them clear.

Example:

In Grand Teton National Park they have moose, elk, and trumpeter swans.

Moose, elk, and trumpeter swans live in Grand Teton National Park.

1. "Life begins at forty" is a cliché many people live by, and this may or may not be true.
2. It all depends on how one lives it.
3. When she was forty, Pearl Buck's novel *The Good Earth* won the Pulitzer Prize.
4. Buck was a novelist which wrote primarily about China.
5. In *The Good Earth* you have to struggle, but fortitude is rewarded.
6. Buck received much critical praise and earned over $7 million, but she was very modest about it.
7. Pearl Buck donated most of her earnings to a foundation for Asian-American children that proves her generosity.
8. Kenneth Kaunda, President of Zambia, was elected to it in 1964, at age forty.
9. When Catherine I became Empress of Russia at age forty, they feared more than loved her.
10. At forty, Paul Revere made his famous ride to warn American revolutionary leaders that the British were going to arrest them. This gave the colonists time to prepare for battle.
11. In the British House of Commons they did not welcome

forty-year-old Nancy Astor as the first female member when she entered in 1919.

12. In A.D. 610 Muhammad, age forty, began to have a series of visions that became the foundation of the Muslim faith. Since then, millions of people have become one.

13. In the *Book of Romance* it reserves a chapter for the story of forty-year-old Elizabeth Barrett, who married Robert Browning against her father's wishes.

14. In the 1840s they did not normally defy their fathers, but Elizabeth was too much in love to obey.

15. She left a poetic record of her love for Robert, and readers still enjoy reading them.

Exercise 3
Revising: Pronoun reference

Revise the following paragraph so that each pronoun refers clearly to a single specific and appropriate antecedent.

In Charlotte Brontë's *Jane Eyre* she is a shy young woman that takes a job as governess. Her employer is a rude, brooding man named Rochester. He lives in a mysterious mansion on the English moors, which contributes an eerie quality to Jane's experience. Eerier still are the fires, strange noises, and other unexplained happenings in the house; but Rochester refuses to discuss this. Eventually, they fall in love. On the day they are to be married, however, she learns that he has a wife hidden in the house. She is hopelessly insane and violent and must be guarded at all times, which explains his strange behavior. Heartbroken, Jane leaves the moors, and many years pass before they are reunited.

Note: See page 326 for an exercise involving unclear pronoun reference along with sentence fragments, comma splices, and other sentence errors.

12. In A.D. 610 Muhammad, age forty, began to have a series of visions that became the foundation of the Muslim faith. Since then, millions of people have become <u>Muslims</u>.

13. The <u>*Book of Romance* reserves</u> a chapter for the story of forty-year-old Elizabeth Barrett, who married Robert Browning against her father's wishes.

14. In the 1840s <u>children</u> did not normally defy their fathers, but Elizabeth was too much in love to obey.

15. She left a poetic record of her love for Robert, and readers still enjoy reading <u>the poems</u>.

ref
12f

ANSWERS: EXERCISE 3
Possible Revision

In Charlotte Brontë's *Jane Eyre,* Jane is a shy young woman <u>who</u> takes a job as governess. Her employer is a rude, brooding man named Rochester. He lives in a mysterious mansion on the English moors, <u>and both the mansion and the moors</u> contribute an eerie quality to Jane's experience. Eerier still are the fires, strange noises, and other unexplained happenings in the house; but Rochester refuses to discuss <u>them</u>. Eventually, <u>Jane and Rochester</u> fall in love. On the day they are to be married, however, Jane learns that <u>Rochester</u> has a wife hidden in the house. <u>The wife</u> is hopelessly insane and violent and must be guarded at all times, <u>circumstances that explain</u> Rochester's strange behavior. Heartbroken, Jane leaves the moors, and many years pass before <u>she and Rochester</u> are reunited.

Shifts in person and number, in tense and mood, in subject and voice, or between direct and indirect quotation can be irritating to readers and occasionally make it hard to follow the meaning of a passage. Often, however, students are not fully aware of the shifts or their effect on a reader. This chapter describes in detail and illustrates the various shifts so that students can learn to identify the problems in their own writing. The exercises ask students to revise sentences and a longer passage, much as they will need to in revising their own work.

Chapter 13   **Shifts**

A sentence or a group of related sentences should be consistent: grammatical elements such as tense, mood, voice, person, and number should remain the same unless grammar or meaning requires a shift. Unnecessary shifts in these elements confuse readers and distort meaning.

13a Keep a sentence or related sentences consistent in person and number.

Person in grammar refers to the distinction among the person talking (first person), the person spoken to (second person), and the person, object, or concept being talked about (third person). **Number** refers to the distinction between one (singular) and more than one (plural). Both nouns and personal pronouns change form to show differences in number, but only personal pronouns have distinctive forms for the three persons.

Shifts in person

The most common faulty shifts in person are from second to third and from third to second person. They occur because we can refer to people in general, including our readers, either in the third person (*a person, one; people, they*) or in the second person (*you*).

People should not drive when *they* have been drinking.
One should not drive when *he or she* has been drinking.
You should not drive when *you* have been drinking.

Although any one of these possibilities is acceptable in an appropriate context, a mixture of them is inconsistent.

Inconsistent	If a *person* works hard, *you* can accomplish a great deal.
Revised	If *you* work hard, *you* can accomplish a great deal.
Revised	If a *person* works hard, *he or she* can accomplish a great deal.
Better	If *people* work hard, *they* can accomplish a great deal.

Shifts in number

Inconsistency in number occurs most often between a pronoun and its antecedent (see 8b).

Inconsistent	If a *student* does not understand a problem, *they* should consult the instructor.
Revised	If a *student* does not understand a problem, *he or she* should consult the instructor.
Better	If *students* do not understand a problem, *they* should consult the instructor.

Inconsistency in number can also occur between other words (usually nouns) that relate to each other in meaning.

Inconsistent	All the *boys* have a good *reputation.*
Revised	All the *boys* have good *reputations.*

The consistency in the revised sentence is called **logical agreement** because the number of the nouns is logically consistent.

Exercise 1
Revising: Shifts in person and number

Revise the following sentences to make them consistent in person and number.

Example:
A plumber will fix burst pipes, but they won't repair waterlogged appliances.

Plumbers will fix burst pipes, but they won't repair waterlogged appliances.

CHECK YOUR OWN

If shifts are a problem in the essays your class submits, go over the chapter in detail in class, and then ask students to go through their papers and circle each shift they find. This activity can be done on the day papers are to be handed in or with a set of graded papers on which you have not marked the shifts. The activity is also a good small-group exercise; students are often good at spotting shifts in someone else's writing.

shift
13a

shift
13b

ANSWERS: EXERCISE 1

1. When a taxpayer is waiting to receive a tax refund from the Internal Revenue Service, <u>he or she begins</u> to notice what time the mail carrier arrives. *Or:* When <u>taxpayers are</u> waiting to receive <u>tax refunds, they</u> begin to notice what time the mail carrier arrives.

2. If the taxpayer does not receive a refund check within six weeks of filing a return, <u>he or she</u> may not have followed the rules of the IRS. *Or:* If <u>taxpayers do</u> not receive <u>refund checks</u> within six weeks of filing a return, they may not have followed the rules of the IRS.

3. If <u>taxpayers do</u> not include <u>their</u> Social Security <u>numbers</u> on <u>returns, they</u> will have to wait for <u>refunds</u>. *Or:* If a taxpayer does not include <u>his or her</u> Social Security number on a return, <u>he or she</u> will have to wait for a refund.

4. When taxpayers do not file their <u>returns</u> early, they will not get <u>refunds</u> quickly.

5. If one has made errors on the tax form, <u>one</u> might even be audited, thereby delaying a refund even longer. *Or:* If one has made errors on the tax form, <u>he or she</u> might even be audited, thereby delaying a refund even longer.

1. When a taxpayer is waiting to receive a tax refund from the Internal Revenue Service, you begin to notice what time the mail carrier arrives.

2. If the taxpayer does not receive a refund check within six weeks of filing a return, they may not have followed the rules of the IRS.

3. If a taxpayer does not include the Social Security number on a return, you will have to wait for a refund.

4. When taxpayers do not file their return early, they will not get a refund quickly.

5. If one has made errors on the tax form, they might even be audited, thereby delaying a refund even longer.

13b **Keep a sentence or related sentences consistent in tense and mood.**

Shifts in tense

Certain changes in tense within a sentence or from one sentence to another may be required to indicate changes in actual or relative time (see 7f). For example:

Ramon *will graduate* from college twenty-three years after his father *arrived* in the United States. [Ramon's graduation is still in the future, but his father arrived in the past.]

But changes that are not required by meaning distract readers. Unnecessary shifts from past to present or from present to past in passages narrating a series of events are particularly confusing.

Inconsistent	Immediately after Booth *shot* Lincoln, Major Rathbone *threw* himself upon the assassin. But Booth *pulls* a knife and *plunges* it into the major's arm. [Tense shifts from past to present.]
Revised	Immediately after Booth *shot* Lincoln, Major Rathbone *threw* himself upon the assassin. But Booth *pulled* a knife and *plunged* it into the major's arm.

The present tense is used to describe what an author has written, including the action in literature or a film (see also 39b-3).

Inconsistent	The main character in the novel *suffers* psychologically because he *has* a clubfoot, but he eventually *triumphed* over his handicap.
Revised	The main character in the novel *suffers* psychologically because he *has* a clubfoot, but he eventually *triumphs* over his handicap.

Shifts in mood

Shifts in the mood of verbs occur most frequently in directions when the writer moves between the imperative mood (*Unplug the appliance*) and the indicative mood (*You should unplug the appliance*). (See 7g.) Directions are usually clearer and more concise in the imperative, as long as its use is consistent.

Inconsistent   *Cook* the mixture slowly, and *you should stir* it until the sugar is dissolved. [Mood shifts from imperative to indicative.]

Revised   *Cook* the mixture slowly, and *stir* it until the sugar is dissolved. [Consistently imperative.]

shift
13c

Exercise 2
Revising: Shifts in tense and mood

Revise the following sentences to make them consistent in tense and mood.

Example:

Lynn ran to first, rounded the base, and keeps running until she slides into second.

Lynn ran to first, rounded the base, and *kept* running until she *slid* into second.

1. When your cholesterol count is too high, adjusting your diet and exercise level reduced it.
2. After you lowered your cholesterol rate, you decrease the chances of heart attack and stroke.
3. First eliminate saturated fats from your diet; then you should consume more whole grains and raw vegetables.
4. To avoid saturated fats, substitute turkey and chicken for beef, and you should use cholesterol-free margarine, salad dressing, and cooking oil.
5. A regular program of aerobic exercise, such as walking or swimming, improves your cholesterol rate and made you feel much healthier.

ANSWERS: EXERCISE 2

1. When your cholesterol count is too high, adjusting your diet and exercise level <u>reduces</u> it.
2. After you <u>lower</u> your cholesterol rate, you decrease the chances of heart attack and stroke.
3. First eliminate saturated fats from your diet; then <u>consume</u> more whole grains and raw vegetables.
4. To avoid saturated fats, substitute turkey and chicken for beef, and <u>use</u> cholesterol-free margarine, salad dressing, and cooking oil.
5. A regular program of aerobic exercise, such as walking or swimming, improves your cholesterol rate and <u>makes</u> you feel much healthier.

13c   **Keep a sentence or related sentences consistent in subject and voice.**

When a verb is in the **active voice,** the subject names the actor: *Linda passed the peas.* When a verb is in the **passive voice,** the subject names the receiver of the action: *The peas were passed (by Linda).* The actor may not be mentioned or may be mentioned in a prepositional phrase. (See pp. 242–44.)

CLASS READING

Use the passage below, or find or write another that contains several kinds of shifts. Distribute copies to the class and read through the passage with students, asking them to identify the problems. This exercise will help make students aware of the different kinds of shifts as they appear in the context of an essay.

As soon as the avalanche was over, Jim pulls himself out of the snowbank and yells, "Where's everybody?" and were we still alive. As each of us in turn started digging out, you could see the damage the huge wall of snow had caused. The snow had destroyed the lodge and cars were swept away.

Compare to parallelism

COLLABORATIVE LEARNING

ANSWERS: EXERCISE 3

1. If students learn how to study efficiently, they will make much better grades on tests.
2. Conscientious students begin to prepare for tests immediately after they attend the first class.
3. Before each class the students complete all reading assignments and outline the material and answer any study questions.
4. In class they listen carefully and take good notes.
5. The students ask questions when they do not understand the professor.

A shift in voice may sometimes help focus the reader's attention on a single subject, as in *The candidate campaigned vigorously and was nominated on the first ballot*. However, most shifts in voice also involve shifts in subject. They are unnecessary and confusing.

Inconsistent	In the morning the *children rode* their bicycles; in the afternoon *their skateboards were given* a good workout. [The shift in subject from *children* to *skateboards* is confusing. Without a named actor the second clause implies that people other than the children used the skateboards.]
Revised	In the morning the *children rode* their bicycles; in the afternoon *they gave* their skateboards a good workout.
Inconsistent	As *we looked* out over the ocean, *ships could be seen* in the distance. [Since the main clause does not name an actor, the reader cannot be sure who is looking.]
Revised	As *we looked* out over the ocean, *we could see* ships in the distance.

Exercise 3
Revising: Shifts in subject and voice

Make the following sentences consistent in subject and voice.

Example:

At the reunion they ate hot dogs and volleyball was played.
At the reunion they ate hot dogs and *played volleyball.*

1. If students learn how to study efficiently, much better grades will be made on tests.
2. Conscientious students begin to prepare for tests immediately after the first class is attended.
3. Before each class all reading assignments are completed, and the students outline the material and answer any study questions.
4. In class they listen carefully and good notes are taken.
5. Questions are asked by the students when they do not understand the professor.

13d **Keep a quotation consistently indirect or direct.**

Direct quotation reports, in quotation marks, the exact words of a speaker: *He said, "I am going."* **Indirect quotation** reports what was said but not necessarily in the speaker's exact words: *He said that he was going*.

Inconsistent	Kapek reported that the rats avoided the maze and "None of them responds to conditioning."
Revised	Kapek reported that the rats avoided the maze and thus did not respond to conditioning.
Revised	Kapek reported, "The rats do not go near the maze. . . . None of them responds to conditioning."

For information on integrating quotations into your writing, see 21h and 36g.

Exercise 4
Using direct and indirect quotation

Each passage below comes from the British essayist Charles Lamb (1775–1834). Quote each passage in two sentences of your own, once using direct quotation consistently and once using indirect quotation consistently.

Example:

"The greatest pleasure I know is to do a good action by stealth and to have it found out by accident."

Direct: "The greatest pleasure I know," said Charles Lamb, "is to do a good action by stealth and to have it found out by accident."

Indirect: Charles Lamb said that the greatest pleasure he knew was to do a good action by stealth and to have it found out by accident.

1. "Coleridge holds that a man cannot have a pure mind who refuses apple-dumplings. I am not certain but that he was right."
2. "The human species, according to the best theory I can form of it, is composed of two distinct races, the men who borrow, and the men who lend."
3. "Nothing puzzles me more than time and space; and yet nothing troubles me less, as I never think about them."
4. "When I am not walking, I am reading; I cannot sit and think."
5. "Sentimentally I am disposed to harmony. But organically I am incapable of a tune."

Exercise 5
Revising: Shifts

Revise the following paragraph to eliminate unnecessary shifts in person, number, tense, mood, and voice.

shift

13d

ANSWERS: EXERCISE 4
Possible Answers

1. *Direct:* Charles Lamb once said, "Coleridge holds that a man cannot have a pure mind who refuses apple-dumplings. I am not certain but he was right."
   Indirect: Charles Lamb once quoted Coleridge as saying that a man cannot have a pure mind who refuses apple-dumplings, and Lamb said he was not certain but that Coleridge was right.
2. *Direct:* Lamb wrote, "The human species, according to the best theory I can form of it, is composed of two distinct races, the men who borrow, and the men who lend."
   Indirect: Lamb wrote that the human species, according to the best theory he could form of it, was composed of two distinct races, those who borrow, and those who lend.
3. *Direct:* Lamb said, "Nothing puzzles me more than time and space; and yet nothing troubles me less, as I never think about them."
   Indirect: Lamb said that nothing puzzled him more than time and space, and yet that nothing troubled him less, as he never thought about them.
4. *Direct:* According to Lamb, "When I am not walking, I am reading; I cannot sit and think."
   Indirect: According to Lamb, when he was not walking, he was reading; he could not sit and think.
5. *Direct:* "Sentimentally I am disposed to harmony," said Lamb. "But organically I am incapable of a tune."
   Indirect: Lamb said that he was sentimentally disposed to harmony but organically incapable of a tune.

shift
13d

COLLABORATIVE LEARNING

ANSWERS: EXERCISE 5
Possible Revision

Driving in snow need not be dangerous if you practice a few simple rules. First, <u>avoid</u> fast starts, which prevent the wheels from gaining traction and may result in the car's getting stuck. Second, drive more slowly than usual, and <u>pay</u> attention to the feel of the car: if the steering <u>seems</u> unusually loose or the wheels <u>do</u> not seem to be grabbing the road, slow down. Third, avoid fast stops, which lead to skids. <u>Be alert</u> for other cars and intersections that may necessitate <u>applying the brakes</u> suddenly. If you need to slow down, <u>reduce the car's momentum</u> by downshifting as well as by applying the brakes. When braking, don't press the pedal to the floor but <u>pump it</u> in short bursts. If you feel the car skidding, <u>release the brakes</u> and <u>turn the wheel</u> into the direction of the skid, and then <u>pump the brakes</u> again. <u>Repeating</u> these motions <u>will stop the skid</u> and <u>reduce the speed</u> of the car.

Driving in snow need not be dangerous if you practice a few rules. First, one should avoid fast starts, which prevent the wheels from gaining traction and may result in the car's getting stuck. Second, drive more slowly than usual, and you should pay attention to the feel of the car: if the steering seemed unusually loose or the wheels did not seem to be grabbing the road, slow down. Third, avoid fast stops, which lead to skids. One should be alert for other cars and intersections that may necessitate that the brakes be applied suddenly. If you need to slow down, the car's momentum can be reduced by downshifting as well as by applying the brakes. When braking, don't press the pedal to the floor, but it should be pumped in short bursts. If you feel the car skidding, the brakes should be released and the wheel should be turned into the direction of the skid, and then the brakes should be pumped again. If one repeated these motions, the skid would be stopped and the speed of the car would be reduced.

Note: See page 326 for an exercise involving shifts along with sentence fragments, comma splices, and other sentence errors.

Chapter 14

Misplaced and Dangling Modifiers

HIGHLIGHTS

Misplaced and dangling modifiers often interest students because the faulty constructions can be amusing. To tie together all the different problems discussed in the chapter, however, you may want to point out that they all illustrate the importance of position and arrangement in sentences. Split constructions (14d and 14e) conveniently emphasize the need to keep the parts of related syntactic groups clearly unified. Yet both standard speech and formal writing provide frequent examples of freely placed limiting modifiers and of split infinitives. Part of our difficulty in teaching composition is in giving students effective advice about when freedom is constructive and when it is confusing. As in all such matters, the advice of the handbook is largely conservative; you may therefore want to modify it somewhat.

In reading a sentence in English, we depend principally on the arrangement of the words to tell us how they are related. In writing, we may create confusion if we fail to connect modifiers to the words they modify.

MISPLACED MODIFIERS

We say that a modifier is **misplaced** if it appears to modify the wrong part of the sentence or if we cannot be certain what part of the sentence the writer intended it to modify. Misplaced modifiers may be awkward, unintentionally amusing, or genuinely confusing.

14a   **Place modifiers where they will clearly modify the words intended.**

Readers tend to link a modifying word, phrase, or clause to the nearest word it could modify: *I saw a man in a green hat.* Thus the writer must place the phrase so that it clearly modifies the intended word and not some other.

> **Confusing**   She served hamburgers to the men *on paper plates.* [Surely the hamburgers, not the men, were on paper plates.]

307

Clear	She served the men hamburgers *on paper plates.*
Confusing	He was unhappy that he failed to break the record *by a narrow margin.* [The sentence implies that he wanted to break the record only by a narrow margin.]
Clear	He was unhappy that he failed *by a narrow margin* to break the record.
Confusing	According to police records, many dogs are killed by automobiles and trucks *roaming unleashed.* [The phrase appears to modify *automobiles and trucks.*]
Clear	According to police records, many dogs *roaming unleashed* are killed by automobiles and trucks.
Confusing	The mayor was able to cut the ribbon and then the band played *when someone found scissors.* [The clause appears to modify *the band played.*]
Clear	*When someone found scissors,* the mayor was able to cut the ribbon and then the band played.

Exercise 1
Revising: Misplaced clauses and phrases

Revise the following sentences so that prepositional phrases and subordinate clauses clearly modify the words they are intended to modify.

    Example:

I came to enjoy flying over time.
Over time I came to enjoy flying.

1. Women have contributed much to American culture of great value.
2. For example, Elizabeth Pinckney introduced indigo, the source in the colonies of a valuable blue dye.
3. Emma Willard founded the Troy Female Seminary, the first institution to provide a college-level education for women in 1821.
4. Sixteen years later Mary Lyon founded Mount Holyoke Female Seminary, the first true women's college with directors and a campus who would sustain the college even after Lyon's death.
5. *Una* was the first American newspaper, which was founded by Pauline Wright Davis in 1853, that was dedicated to gaining women's rights.
6. Mitchell's Comet was discovered in 1847, which was named for Maria Mitchell.
7. Mitchell was the first American female astronomer who lived from 1818 to 1889.

ANSWERS: EXERCISE 1

1. Women have contributed much <u>of great value</u> to American culture.
2. For example, Elizabeth Pinckney introduced indigo, the source <u>of a valuable blue dye</u> in the colonies.
3. <u>In 1821</u> Emma Willard founded the Troy Female Seminary, the first institution to provide a college-level education for women.
4. Sixteen years later Mary Lyon founded Mount Holyoke Female Seminary, the first true women's college with <u>a campus and directors</u> who would sustain the college even after Lyon's death.
5. *Una,* <u>which was founded by Pauline Wright Davis in 1853,</u> was the first American newspaper that was dedicated to gaining women's rights.
6. Mitchell's Comet, <u>which was named for Maria Mitchell,</u> was discovered in 1847.
7. Mitchell, <u>who lived from 1818 to 1889,</u> was the first American female astronomer.

8. She was a member at Vassar College of the first faculty.
9. She was also the first woman elected in 1848 to the American Academy of Arts and Sciences.
10. Mitchell said, "I was born of only ordinary capacity, but of extraordinary persistency" when asked about her many accomplishments.

8. She was a member <u>of the first faculty</u> at Vassar College.
9. <u>In 1848</u> she was also the first woman elected to the American Academy of Arts and Sciences.
10. <u>When asked about her many accomplishments,</u> Mitchell said, "I was born of only ordinary capacity, but of extraordinary persistency."

14b Place limiting modifiers carefully.

Limiting modifiers include *almost, even, exactly, hardly, just, merely, nearly, only, scarcely,* and *simply.* They modify the expressions that immediately follow them. Compare the uses of *just* in the following sentences:

The instructor *just nodded* to me as he came in.
The instructor nodded *just to me* as he came in.
The instructor nodded to me *just as he came in.*

In speech several of these modifiers frequently occur before the verb, regardless of the words they are intended to modify. In writing, however, these modifiers should fall immediately before the word or word group they modify to avoid any ambiguity.

Unclear   They *only* saw each other during meals. [They had eyes only for each other, or they met only during meals?]

Clear   They saw *only* each other during meals.

Clear   They saw each other *only* during meals.

Note: *Only* is acceptable immediately before the verb when it modifies a whole statement.

He *only* wanted his guest to have fun.

Exercise 2
Using limiting modifiers

Use each of the following limiting modifiers in two versions of the same sentence.

Example:

only
He is the *only* one I like.
He is the one *only* I like.

1. almost
2. even
3. hardly
4. simply
5. nearly

MOVING *ONLY*

Ask students to create sentences whose meaning changes as a modifier like *only* moves from place to place:

Only students were asked to bring gym shorts and running shoes.

Students were *only* asked to bring gym shorts and running shoes.

Students were asked *only* to bring gym shorts and running shoes.

Students were asked to bring *only* gym shorts and running shoes.

[handwritten: Only I ate the cake. I only ate the cake. I ate only the cake. I ate the only cake. stop here]

ANSWERS: EXERCISE 2
Possible Answers

1. <u>Almost</u> everybody hates him.
   Everybody <u>almost</u> hates him.
2. <u>Even</u> now I remember the details of the event.
   Now I remember <u>even</u> the details of the event.
3. We <u>hardly</u> heard him call our names.
   We heard him <u>hardly</u> call our names.
4. Write <u>simply</u>.
   <u>Simply</u> write.
5. I <u>nearly</u> missed the performance that was booed off the stage.
   I missed the performance that was <u>nearly</u> booed off the stage.

mm
14d

 14c **Make each modifier refer to only one grammatical element.**

A modifier can modify only *one* element in a sentence—the subject, the verb, or some other element. A **squinting modifier** seems confusingly to refer to either of two words.

Squinting	Snipers who fired on the soldiers *often* escaped capture. [Does *often* modify *fired* or *escaped?*]
Clear	Snipers who *often* fired on the soldiers escaped capture.
Clear	Snipers who fired on the soldiers escaped capture *often*.

When an adverb modifies an entire main clause, as in the last example, it can usually be moved to the beginning of the sentence: *Often, snipers who fired on the soldiers escaped capture.*

ANSWERS: EXERCISE 3

1. People who <u>often</u> sunbathe can damage their skin. *Or:* People who sunbathe can <u>often</u> damage their skin.
2. Sunbathers who <u>frequently</u> apply a sun screen avoid some of the sun's harmful rays. *Or:* <u>Frequently</u>, sunbathers who apply a sun screen avoid some of the sun's harmful rays.
3. Men and women who <u>much of the time</u> lie out in the sun have leathery, dry skin. *Or:* <u>Much of the time</u> men and women who lie out in the sun have leathery, dry skin.
4. Doctors tell sunbathers they risk skin cancer <u>when they are older</u>. *Or:* Doctors tell <u>older</u> sunbathers they risk skin cancer.
5. People who <u>usually</u> stay out of the sun will have better skin and fewer chances of skin cancer. *Or:* People who stay out of the sun will <u>usually</u> have better skin and fewer chances of skin cancer.

Exercise 3
Revising: Squinting modifiers

Revise each sentence twice so that the squinting modifier applies clearly first to one element and then to the other.

Example:

The work that he hoped would satisfy him completely frustrated him.

The work that he hoped would *completely* satisfy him frustrated him.

The work that he hoped would satisfy him frustrated him *completely*.

1. People who sunbathe often can damage their skin.
2. Sunbathers who apply a sunscreen frequently block some of the sun's harmful ultraviolet rays.
3. Men and women who lie out in the sun much of the time have leathery, dry skin.
4. Doctors tell sunbathers when they are older they risk skin cancer.
5. People who stay out of the sun usually will have better skin and fewer chances of skin cancer.

14d **Keep subjects and verbs, verbs and objects, and verbs and complements together.**

When we read a sentence, we expect the subject, verb, and object or complement to be close to each other. If adjective phrases or clauses separate these parts, the meaning is usually clear to us.

> The wreckers who were demolishing the old house discovered a large box of coins. [The subject, *wreckers,* and the verb, *discovered,* are separated by the adjective clause beginning *who.*]

However, if an adverb phrase or clause interrupts the movement from subject to verb to object or complement, the resulting sentence is likely to be awkward and confusing.

Awkward	The *wreckers,* soon after they began demolishing the old house, *discovered* a large box of coins. [The clause beginning *soon after* interrupts the movement from subject to verb.]
Revised	Soon after they began demolishing the old house, the *wreckers discovered* a large box of coins.
Awkward	Three of the wreckers *lifted,* with great effort, *the heavy box.* [The phrase beginning *with* interrupts the movement from verb to object.]
Revised	Three of the wreckers *lifted the heavy box* with great effort.

14e Keep parts of verb phrases and infinitives together.

A **verb phrase** consists of a helping verb plus a main verb, as in *will call, was going, had been writing.* Such phrases constitute close grammatical units. We regularly insert single-word adverbs in them without causing awkwardness: *Joshua had almost completed his assignment.* But when longer word groups interrupt verb phrases, the result is almost always awkward.

Awkward	Many students *had,* by spending most of their time on the assignment, *completed* it.
Revised	By spending most of their time on the assignment, many students *had completed* it.
Revised	Many students *had completed* the assignment by spending most of their time on it.

An **infinitive** consists of the marker *to* plus the plain form of a verb: *to produce, to enjoy.* The two parts of the infinitive are widely regarded as a grammatical unit that should not be split.

Awkward	The weather service expected temperatures *to not rise.*
Revised	The weather service expected temperatures not *to rise.*

THE MEDIA

Radio and television newscasts are rich sources of dangling and misplaced modifiers, perhaps because reporters have little time to pay attention to the structure of their sentences. Have students listen to newscasts and record errors; doing so will help them to understand the perspective of a reader who comes across similar errors in an essay. Newspaper headlines and public announcements are also rich sources; from time to time, magazine articles and paperback books appear with collections of particularly humorous errors. But students will be able to find many on their own by looking at the newspaper for headlines like "Young Man, 17, Slain by Road."

HOME-GROWN STAR REPORTERS

Ask students to form groups in order to write their own newscasts filled with the kinds of errors they might spot through the activity above. The newscasts (and the errors) should be plausible in style and content, though the content will probably have to be the product of students' imaginations. Having heard many newscasts, however, students will probably have little trouble parodying them in form and matter.

Note, however, that a split infinitive may sometimes be natural and preferable, though it may still bother some readers.

Several U.S. industries expect *to* more than *triple* their use of robots within the next decade.

We could recast the sentence entirely: *Several U.S. industries expect to increase their use of robots by more than three times within the next decade.* But the split construction is more economical.

COLLABORATIVE LEARNING

ANSWERS: EXERCISE 4

1. <u>In 1868</u> Myra Bradwell founded the *Chicago Legal News.*
2. <u>Although she had qualified,</u> Bradwell was later denied admission to the Illinois Bar Association.
3. In an attempt <u>finally</u> to gain admission to the bar, she carried the case to the Supreme Court, but the Justices decided against her.
4. Bradwell was determined that no other woman would be denied entrance to a profession <u>if she were qualified.</u>
5. <u>In response to Bradwell's persuasion,</u> the Illinois legislature finally passed a bill ensuring that no one would be restricted from a profession <u>on the basis of gender.</u>

RESOURCES AND IDEAS

Elaine Chaika, "Grammars and Teaching," *College English* 39 (1978): 770–83. Chaika offers fresh explanations from a linguistic perspective for a number of standard errors, including dangling modifiers.

William H. Pixton, "The Dangling Gerund: A Working Definition," *College Composition and Communication* 24 (1973): 193–99. Pixton reviews discussions of dangling modifiers and, using a variety of sample sentences, formulates a definition of the dangling gerund.

Exercise 4
Revising: Separated sentence parts

Revise the following sentences to connect separated parts (subject-predicate, verb-object-complement, verb phrase, infinitive).

> *Example:*
> Most children have by the time they are seven lost a tooth.
> *By the time they are seven,* most children have lost a tooth.

1. Myra Bradwell founded in 1868 the *Chicago Legal News.*
2. Bradwell was later denied, although she had qualified, admission to the Illinois Bar Association.
3. In an attempt to finally gain admission to the bar, she carried the case to the Supreme Court, but the justices decided against her.
4. Bradwell was determined that no other woman would, if she were qualified, be denied entrance to a profession.
5. The Illinois legislature finally passed, in response to Bradwell's persuasion, a bill ensuring that no one on the basis of gender would be restricted from a profession.

DANGLING MODIFIERS

14f   **Relate dangling modifiers to their sentences.**

A **dangling modifier** does not sensibly modify anything in its sentence.

Dangling   *Passing the building,* the vandalism was clearly visible. [The modifying phrase seems to describe *vandalism,* but vandalism does not pass buildings. Who was passing the building? Who saw the vandalism?]

Dangling   *To understand the causes,* vandalism has been extensively investigated. [The modifying phrase again seems to describe *vandalism,* but vandalism does not understand causes. Who wants to understand?]

Dangling modifiers occur most often when certain kinds of modifiers precede the main clause of the sentence. As in the examples above, each of these modifiers has an implied, or unnamed, subject that readers assume to be the same as the subject of the following main clause. When the two subjects are not the same, the modifier "dangles" unconnected to the rest of the sentence, and the sentence is illogical. The modifiers most likely to dangle are listed and illustrated below.

dm
14f

- Participial phrases:

  Dangling   *Passing the building,* the vandalism was clearly visible. [Implied subject of modifier: the people passing.]

  Revised   *As we passed* the building, the vandalism was clearly visible.

- Infinitive phrases:

  Dangling   *To understand the causes,* vandalism has been extensively investigated. [Implied subject of modifier: the people seeking to understand.]

  Revised   To understand the causes, *researchers have* extensively *investigated* vandalism.

- Prepositional phrases in which the object of the preposition is a gerund:

  Dangling   *After studying the problem,* vandals are now thought to share certain characteristics. [Implied subject of modifier: the people studying.]

  Revised   After studying the problem, *researchers think* that vandals share certain characteristics.

- Elliptical clauses in which the subject and perhaps the verb are omitted:

  Dangling   *When destructive,* researchers have learned that vandals are more likely to be in groups. [Implied subject and verb in modifier: *vandals are.*]

  Revised   When *vandals are* destructive, researchers have learned that *they* are more likely to be in groups.

Dangling modifiers are especially likely when the verb in the main clause is in the **passive voice** instead of the **active voice**—that is, when the verb expresses what is *done to* the subject instead of what the subject *does* (see p. 242). The passive voice appears in the second and third examples above: *vandalism has been investigated; vandals are thought.* The revisions recast the verbs and subjects as active: *researchers have investigated; researchers think.*

---

dm
14f

 Identifying and revising dangling modifiers

1. If the modifier lacks a subject of its own (e.g., *when in diapers*), identify what it describes.
2. Verify that what the modifier describes is in fact the subject of the main clause. If it is not, the modifier is probably dangling.
3. Revise a dangling modifier (*a*) by recasting it with a subject of its own or (*b*) by changing the subject of the main clause.

	Modifier	**Subject**
Dangling	*When in diapers,* my mother remarried.	
Revision A	When *I was* in diapers, my mother remarried.	
Revision B	When in diapers, *I attended my mother's second wedding.*	

Note that a modifier may be dangling even when the sentence elsewhere contains a word the modifier might seem to describe, such as *vandals* below:

Dangling   *When destructive,* researchers have learned that vandals are more likely to be in groups.

In addition, a dangling modifier may fall at the end of a sentence:

Dangling   The vandalism was visible *passing the building.*

Revising dangling modifiers

Revise dangling modifiers by recasting the sentences in which they appear.

- Change the subject of the main clause to a word the modifier properly describes.
- Rewrite the dangling modifier as a complete clause with its own stated subject and verb.

The choice of method depends on what you want to emphasize in the sentence.

Dangling   *To express themselves,* graffiti decorate walls.

Revised   To express themselves, *some youths decorate* walls with graffiti. [New subject, stresses *some youths.*]

Revised   *Because some youths need to express themselves,* graffiti decorate walls. [Rewritten modifier, stresses *graffiti.*]

Exercise 5
Revising: Dangling modifiers

Revise the following sentences to eliminate any dangling modifiers. Each item has more than one possible answer.

Example:

Driving north, the vegetation became increasingly sparse.

Driving north, *we noticed* that the vegetation became increasingly sparse.

As we drove north, the vegetation became increasingly sparse.

1. After accomplishing many deeds of valor, Andrew Jackson's fame led to his election to the Presidency in 1828 and 1832.
2. While still very young, both of Jackson's parents had died.
3. To aid the American Revolution, service as a mounted courier was chosen by Jackson.
4. A scar marred Jackson's craggy face after being struck with a saber by a British officer.
5. Though not well educated, a successful career as a lawyer and judge proved Jackson's ability.
6. Winning many military battles, the American public believed in Jackson's leadership.
7. Earning the nicknames "Old Hickory" and "Sharp Knife," the War of 1812 established Jackson's military prowess.
8. On January 8, 1815, the Battle of New Orleans was won without losing more than six American dead and ten wounded.
9. After putting down raiding parties from Florida, Jackson's victories helped pressure Spain to cede that territory.
10. The U.S. Presidency became Jackson's goal while briefly governor of Florida.

Exercise 6
Sentence combining: Placing modifiers

Combine each pair of sentences below into a single sentence by rewriting one as a modifier. Make sure the modifier applies clearly to the appropriate word. You will have to add, delete, and rearrange words, and you may find that more than one answer is possible in each case.

ANSWERS: EXERCISE 5

Possible Answers

1. After he had accomplished many deeds of valor, Andrew Jackson's fame led to his election to the Presidency in 1828 and 1832.
2. While Jackson was still very young, both of his parents had died.
3. To aid the American Revolution, Jackson chose service as a mounted courier.
4. A scar marred Jackson's craggy face after he was struck with a saber by a British officer.
5. Though not well educated, Jackson proved his ability in a successful career as a lawyer and judge.
6. Because Jackson had won many military battles, the American public believed in his leadership.
7. Earning the nicknames "Old Hickory" and "Sharp Knife," Jackson established his military prowess during the War of 1812.
8. On January 8, 1815, Jackson won the Battle of New Orleans without losing more than six American dead and ten wounded.
9. After Jackson had put down raiding parties from Florida, his victories helped pressure Spain to cede that territory.
10. The U.S. Presidency became his goal while Jackson was briefly governor of Florida.

SENTENCE COMBINING

Exercise 6 requires students to combine pairs of sentences whose content and structure make them likely causes of misplaced or dangling modifiers. Extend this activity by having students create their own sentences that would be easy to miscombine. Choose the best pairs, copy them, and have the class do them for an exercise. This activity leads to considerable discussion and some imaginative and amusing results when the students work in groups.

dm

14f

mm/dm
14f

ANSWERS: EXERCISE 6
Possible Answers

1. As evening falls in the Central American rain forests, the tungara frogs begin their croaking chorus.
2. Croaking loudly at night, male tungara frogs sing "songs" designed to attract female frogs.
3. But predators, also hearing the croaking, gather to feast on the frogs.
4. Lured by their croaking dinners, the predators include bullfrogs, snakes, bats, and opossums.
5. Although the frogs hope to mate, their nightly chorus can result in death instead.
6. Several nights a week the frogs rest their voices, reducing their chances of being eaten and of mating.
7. Protected by rain and clouds, all the frogs join in the singing.
8. Relatively safe on moonless nights, the frogs croak loudly and lustily.
9. Tungara frogs, seeming to believe in "safety in numbers," are more likely to croak along with a large group than to sing by themselves.
10. These frogs apparently know that they must forgo croaking on some evenings to prevent their species from "croaking."

ANSWERS: EXERCISE 7
Possible Revision

When she was only twenty-eight, Elizabeth Blackwell (1821–1910) became the first woman to earn a medical degree from a medical school in the United States. In 1857 Blackwell founded the New York Infirmary for Women and Children, [which was] staffed entirely by women. To prepare women in medicine fully, Blackwell included at the hospital a complete course in medical training, which became the Women's Medical College in 1868. Blackwell's full-time work as a physician, lecturer, and author was stopped when she reached age eighty-six only by a serious accident.

Example:

Bob demanded a hearing from the faculty. Bob wanted to appeal the decision.

Wanting to appeal the decision, Bob demanded a hearing from the faculty.

1. Evening falls in the Central American rain forests. The tungara frogs begin their croaking chorus.
2. Male tungara frogs croak loudly at night. The "songs" they sing are designed to attract female frogs.
3. But predators also hear the croaking. They gather to feast on the frogs.
4. The predators are lured by their croaking dinners. The frogs are prey to bullfrogs, snakes, bats, and opossums.
5. The frogs hope to mate. Their nightly chorus can result in death instead.
6. Several nights a week the frogs rest their voices. They reduce their chances of being eaten and of mating.
7. The frogs are protected by rain and clouds. The singing is then joined in by all the frogs.
8. The frogs are relatively safe on moonless nights. Their croaks are loud and lusty.
9. Tungara frogs seem to believe in "safety in numbers." They are more likely to croak along with a large group than to sing by themselves.
10. These frogs apparently know that they must forgo croaking on some evenings. The behavior is necessary to prevent their species from "croaking."

Exercise 7
Revising: Misplaced and dangling modifiers

Revise the following paragraph to eliminate any misplaced or dangling modifiers.

Elizabeth Blackwell (1821–1910) became the first woman to earn a medical degree when she only was twenty-eight from a medical school in the United States. Staffed entirely by women, Blackwell founded the New York Infirmary for Women and Children in 1857. To fully prepare women in medicine, Blackwell included a complete course in medical training at the hospital, which became the Women's Medical College in 1868. Blackwell's full-time work as a physician, lecturer, and author was only stopped at age eighty-six by a serious accident.

Note: See page 326 for an exercise involving misplaced and dangling modifiers along with other sentence errors.

Chapter 15

Mixed and Incomplete Sentences

HIGHLIGHTS

The first two sections of Chapter 15 treat sentences whose subjects and predicates are incompatible. The tangled sentences in some student writing have more complex causes than this brief discussion of mixed sentences can address. But the two most common problems do seem to be subjects and predicates that are incompatible in grammar and in meaning.

The third section deals with compound constructions that are grammatically or idiomatically incomplete. Ill-prepared students seem to encounter this problem less often than better-prepared students do, perhaps because only the latter use such constructions. On the other hand, incomplete comparisons (15d) are common, and you may wish to call particular attention to them.

The final section, covering omission of needed words, is designed primarily as an aid to grading papers. Instructors who notice words missing in a student essay can call attention to the problem by using the number-and-letter code to refer students to this section.

MIXED SENTENCES

A **mixed sentence** contains two or more parts that are incompatible—that is, the parts do not fit together. The misfit may be in grammar or in meaning.

Mixed grammar

After watching television for twelve hours was the reason the children fought.

Mixed meaning

The work involved in directing the use of resources is the definition of management.

15a   **Be sure that the parts of your sentences, particularly subjects and predicates, fit together grammatically.**

Many mixed sentences occur when we start a sentence with one grammatical plan or construction in mind but end it with a different one. Such sentences often result from a confusion between two ways of making a statement.

    Mixed   In all her efforts to please others got her into trouble.

In this mixed sentence the writer starts with a modifying prepositional phrase and then tries to make that phrase

ACTIVITIES AND ASSIGNMENTS

Because the mixed and incomplete sentences in student writing have complicated causes and because the problems in one student's essay are likely to differ widely from those in another student's paper, most instructors choose simply to discuss the chapter and use some of the exercises rather than elaborate with classroom activities and assignments. In working with individual students, however, most instructors are able to devise activities that suit individual needs. Instructors who wish to alert students to the problem of incomplete compound constructions, incomplete comparisons, and omission of needed words can draw from a student paper or write a passage containing these problems and then ask students to work with the passage, perhaps in small groups, proofreading it and correcting the errors.

ject of the verb *got*. But prepositional phrases can very seldom function as sentence subjects. The sentence needs a new subject for *got*.

Revised   In all her efforts to please others, *she* got into trouble. [The necessary subject *she* is added to the main clause.]

Revised   *All her efforts* to please others got her into trouble. [The preposition *In* is dropped, leaving the subject *All her efforts.*]

Each group of sentences below illustrates a similar confusion between two sentence plans and gives ideas for revising the subject and sometimes the predicate so that they fit grammatically.

Mixed   Although he was seen with a convicted thief does not make him a thief. [The writer has used an adverb clause, beginning *Although,* as the subject of *does.* An adverb clause cannot serve as a subject.]

Revised   *That* he was seen with a convicted thief does not make him a thief. [*That* changes the clause into a noun clause, a grammatical subject.]

Revised   Although he was seen with a convicted thief, *he is* not necessarily a thief. [A new subject and verb are supplied for the main clause.]

Mixed   Among those who pass the entrance examinations, they do not all get admitted to the program. [The modifying phrase beginning *Among* demands a subject that gives an amount, such as *all* or *many,* not the general *they.*]

Revised   Among those who pass the entrance examinations, *not all* get admitted to the program.

Revised   Among those who pass the entrance examinations, *many* do not get admitted to the program.

Revised   *Not all those* who pass the entrance examinations get admitted to the program.

15b **Be sure that the subjects and predicates of your sentences fit together in meaning.**

In a sentence with mixed meaning, the subject is said to be or do something it cannot logically be or do. Such a mixture is sometimes called **faulty predication** because the predicate conflicts with the subject.

Illogical equation with *be*

The most common form of faulty predication occurs when the linking verb *be* connects a subject and its complement. Since such a sentence forms a kind of equation, the subject and complement must be items that can be sensibly equated. If they are not, the sentence goes awry.

Faulty	A *compromise* between the city and the town would be the ideal *place* to live.

This sentence says that *a compromise is a place,* clearly not a sensible statement. The writer tried to compress too many ideas into a single word. Here is the sentence revised to state the writer's meaning more exactly.

Revised	A *community* that offered the best qualities of both city and town would be the ideal *place* to live.

Is when, is where

A special kind of faulty predication occurs when a clause beginning *when* or *where* follows a form of *be* in a definition, as in *Suffrage is where you have the right to vote.* Though the construction is common in speech, written definitions require nouns or noun clauses on both sides of *be: Suffrage is the right to vote.*

Faulty	*An examination* is *when you are tested* on what you know.
Revised	*An examination* is *a test* of what you know.
Revised	*In an examination you are tested* on what you know.

Reason is because

A similar kind of faulty predication occurs when a *because* clause follows the subject-verb pattern *The reason is,* as in *The reason is because I don't want to.* This construction is common in speech, but it is redundant since *because* means "for the reason that." The construction should not appear in writing.

Faulty	The *reason* the temple requests donations *is because* the school needs expanding.
Revised	The reason the temple requests donations is *that* the school needs expanding.
Revised	The temple requests donations *because* the school needs expanding.

RESOURCES AND IDEAS

Valerie Krishna, "The Syntax of Error," *Journal of Basic Writing* 1 (1975): 43–49. The author views problems like mixed constructions and shifts as the result of a weak sentence core, and she encourages teachers to pay attention to this underlying problem in helping students avoid such errors.

mixed
15b

Other mixed meanings

Faulty predications are not confined to sentences with *be*.

Faulty	The *use* of emission controls *was created* to reduce air pollution. [The controls, not their use, were created.]
Revised	Emission *controls were created* to reduce air pollution.
Faulty	The *area* of financial mismanagement *poses* a threat to small businesses. [Mismanagement, not the area, poses the threat.]
Revised	Financial *mismanagement poses* a threat to small businesses.

In some mixed sentences the combination of faults is so confusing that the writer has little choice but to start over.

Mixed	My long-range goal is through law school and government work I hope to deal with those problems I deal with more effectively.
Possible revision	My long-range goal is to go to law school and then work in government so that I can deal more effectively with problems I face.

Exercise 1
Revising: Mixed sentences

Revise the following sentences so that their parts fit together both in grammar and in meaning. Each item has more than one possible answer.

Example:

When they found out how expensive pianos are is why they were discouraged.

They were discouraged *because* they found out how expensive pianos are.

When they found out how expensive pianos are, *they* were discouraged.

1. A hurricane is when the winds in a tropical depression rotate counterclockwise at more than seventy-four miles per hour.
2. Because hurricanes can destroy so many lives and so much property is why people fear them.
3. Through high winds, storm surge, floods, and tornadoes is how a hurricane can kill thousands of people.
4. Among the hurricanes in history, they have become less deadly since 1950.

5. The reason for the lower death rates is because improved communication systems and weather satellites warn people early enough to escape the hurricane.
6. Storm surge is where the hurricane's winds whip up a tide that spills over sea walls and deluges coastal islands.
7. By simply boarding up a house's windows will not protect a family from a major hurricane.
8. The immediate strength and danger of a hurricane is in how strong its winds are.
9. A hurricane that packs winds of 150 to 200 miles per hour, it can inflict terrible damage even on inland towns.
10. However, the worst damage to inland areas is when tornadoes and floods strike.

5. The death rates are lower because improved communication systems and weather satellites warn people early enough to escape the hurricane.
6. Storm surge occurs when the hurricane's winds whip up a tide that spills over sea walls and deluges coastal islands.
7. Simply boarding up a house's windows will not protect a family from a major hurricane.
8. The immediate danger of a hurricane comes from the strength of its winds.
9. A hurricane that packs winds of 150 to 200 miles per hour can inflict terrible damage even on inland towns.
10. However, the worst damage to inland areas occurs when tornadoes and floods strike.

inc
15c

INCOMPLETE SENTENCES

The most serious kind of incomplete sentence is the fragment (see Chapter 10). But sentences are also incomplete when the writer omits one or more words needed to make a phrase or clause clear or accurate.

15c   **Omissions from compound constructions should be consistent with grammar or idiom.**

In both speech and writing we commonly use **elliptical constructions,** which omit words not necessary for meaning (see 5c-4). In the following sentences the words in parentheses can be omitted without confusing or distracting the reader. Notice that they all involve compound constructions.

By 1993 automobile-emission standards will be tougher, and by 1996 (automobile-emission standards will be) tougher still.

Some cars will run on electricity; some (will run) on methane.

Environmentalists have hopes for alternative fuels and (for) public transportation.

Such omissions are possible only when the words omitted are common to all the parts of a compound construction. When the parts differ in grammar or idiom, all words must be included in all parts.

One new car *gets* eighty miles per gallon; some old cars *get* as little as five miles per gallon. [One verb is singular, the other plural.]

Environmentalists *were* invited to submit proposals and *were* ea-

inc
15d

ger to do so. [Each *were* has a different grammatical function: the first is a helping verb; the second is a linking verb.]

They believe *in* and work *for* fuel conservation. [Idiom requires different prepositions with *believe* and *work*.]

Notice that in the sentence *My brother and friend moved to Dallas,* the omission of *my* before *friend* indicates that *brother* and *friend* are the same person. If two different persons are meant, the modifier or article must be repeated: *My brother and my friend moved to Dallas.*

(See 31b-3 for a list of English idioms and 17a for a discussion of grammatical parallelism.)

 15d **All comparisons should be complete and logical.**

Comparisons make statements about the relation between two or more things, as in *Dogs are more intelligent than cats* or *Bones was the most intelligent dog we ever had.* To be complete and logical, a comparison must (1) state the relation fully enough to ensure clarity, (2) compare only items that can sensibly be compared, and (3) include all and only the items being compared.

 State a comparison fully enough to ensure clarity.

In a comparison such as *John likes bowling better than (he likes) tennis,* we can omit *he likes* because only one meaning is possible. But sentences such as *John likes bowling better than Jane* may mean either "better than he likes Jane" or "better than Jane likes bowling." Therefore, we must be careful to state such sentences fully enough to prevent any misreading.

> **Unclear**　　Car makers worry about their industry more than environmentalists.
>
> **Clear**　　Car makers worry about their industry more than environmentalists *do.*
>
> **Clear**　　Car makers worry about their industry more than *they worry about* environmentalists.

 The items being compared should in fact be comparable.

A comparison is logical only if it compares items that can sensibly be compared.

Illogical   The cost of an electric car is greater than a gasoline-powered car. [Illogically compares a cost and a car.]

Revised   The cost of an electric car is greater than *the cost of* (or *that of*) a gasoline-powered car.

 In comparing items in the same class, use *other* or *any other*. In comparing items in different classes, use *any*.

When we compare a person or thing with all others in the same group, we form two units: (1) the individual person or thing and (2) all *other* persons or things in the group: *Joshua* (the individual) *was more stubborn than any other child in the family* (all the others in the group). The two units need to be distinguished.

Illogical   Los Angeles is larger than *any* city in California. [Since Los Angeles is itself a city in California, the sentence seems to say that Los Angeles is larger than itself.]

Logical   Los Angeles is larger than *any other* city in California. [Adding *other* excludes Los Angeles from the group of the state's other cities.]

When a person or thing is compared with the members of a *different* group, the two units are logically separate: *Some American cars* (one group) *are cheaper than any foreign car* (a different group).

Illogical   Los Angeles is larger than *any other* city in Canada. [The cities in Canada constitute a group to which Los Angeles does not belong.]

Logical   Los Angeles is larger than *any* city in Canada. [Omitting the word *other* makes a separate group of the Canadian cities.]

 Comparisons should state what is being compared.

Brand X gets clothes *whiter*. [Whiter than what?]
Brand Y is so much *better*. [Better than what?]

 15e   Include all needed articles, prepositions, and other words.

In haste or carelessness writers sometimes omit small words such as articles and prepositions that are needed for clarity.

inc
15e

Incomplete   Regular payroll deductions are a type painless savings. You hardly notice missing amounts, and after period of years the contributions can add a large total.

Revised   Regular payroll deductions are a type *of* painless savings. You hardly notice *the* missing amounts, and after *a* period of years the contributions can add *up to* a large total.

Writers whose first language is not English often omit the articles *a, an,* and *the* because their native language uses such words differently or not at all. For guidelines on when to use articles, see the Glossary of Terms, page 768.

In both speech and writing we often omit *that* when it introduces a noun clause following a verb: *We knew (that) he was coming.* But such an omission can sometimes be confusing.

Incomplete   The personnel director expects many employees will benefit from the plan. [*Many employees* seems to be the object of *expects,* not the subject of the subordinate clause.]

Revised   The personnel director expects *that* many employees will benefit from the plan.

Attentive proofreading is the only insurance against the kind of omissions described in this section. (See 2d.) *Proofread all your papers carefully.* See page 61 for tips.

Exercise 2
Revising: Incomplete sentences

Revise the following sentences so that they are complete, logical, and clear. Some items have more than one possible answer.

Example:

Our house is closer to the courthouse than the subway stop.

Our house is closer to the courthouse than *it is* to the subway stop.

Our house is closer to the courthouse than the subway stop *is.*

1. The first ice cream, eaten in China in about 2000 B.C., was more lumpy than the modern era.
2. The Chinese made their ice cream of milk, spices, and overcooked rice and packed in snow to solidify.
3. The Chinese believed anyone who ate this dessert at their tables would be impressed by their wealth.
4. In about A.D. 1000 the Chinese developed better ways transporting and preserving snow from the mountains.
5. Then they made fruit ices by combining fruit juice, including the pulp, with snow or adding to ice milk.

---

inc
15e

COLLABORATIVE LEARNING

ANSWERS: EXERCISE 2
Possible Answers

1. The first ice cream, eaten in China in about 2000 B.C., was more lumpy than <u>ice cream in</u> (or <u>that in</u>) the modern era.
2. The Chinese made their ice cream of milk, spices, and overcooked rice and packed <u>it</u> in snow to solidify.
3. The Chinese believed <u>that</u> anyone who ate this dessert at their tables would be impressed by their wealth.
4. In about A.D. 1000 the Chinese developed better ways <u>of</u> transporting and preserving snow from the mountains.
5. Then they made fruit ices by combining fruit juice, including the pulp, with snow or adding <u>it</u> to ice milk.

6. In the fourteenth century ice milk and fruit ices appeared in Italy and the tables of the wealthy.
7. At her wedding in 1533 to the king of France, Catherine de Médicis offered more flavors of fruit ices than any hostess offered.
8. Modern sherbets resemble her ices; modern ice cream her soft dessert of thick, sweetened cream.
9. Americans consume more ice cream than any dessert.
10. Most Americans would probably believe that their ice cream tastes better.

Exercise 3
Revising: Mixed and incomplete sentences

Revise the following paragraph to eliminate mixed or incomplete constructions.

The Hancock Tower in Boston is thin mirror-glass slab that rises almost eight hundred feet. When it was being constructed in the early 1970s was when its windows began cracking, and some fell crashing to the ground. In order to minimize risks is why the architects and owners replaced over a third the huge windows with plywood until the problem could be found and solved. With its plywood sheath, the building was homelier than any skyscraper, the butt of many jokes. Eventually, however, it was discovered that the reason the windows cracked was because joint between the double panes of glass was too rigid. The solution of thicker single-pane windows was installed, and the silly plywood building crystallized into a reflective jewel.

Note: See the next page for an exercise involving mixed and incomplete sentences along with sentence fragments, comma splices, and other sentence errors.

6. In the fourteenth century ice milk and fruit ices appeared in Italy and <u>on</u> the tables of the wealthy.
7. At her wedding in 1533 to the King of France, Catherine de Médicis offered more flavors of fruit ices than any <u>other</u> hostess offered.
8. Modern sherbets resemble her ices; modern ice cream <u>resembles</u> her soft dessert of thick, sweetened cream.
9. Americans consume more ice cream than any <u>other</u> dessert.
10. Most Americans would probably believe that their ice cream tastes better <u>than Chinese ice cream</u> (or <u>Catherine de Médicis's</u>).

ANSWERS: EXERCISE 3
Possible Revision

The Hancock Tower in Boston is <u>a</u> thin mirror-glass slab that rises almost eight hundred feet. When it was being constructed in the early 1970s<u>,</u> <u>its</u> windows began cracking, and some fell crashing to the ground. In order to minimize risks<u>, the</u> architects and owners replaced over a third <u>of</u> the huge windows with plywood until the problem could be found and solved. With its plywood sheath, the building was homelier than any <u>other</u> skyscraper, the butt of many jokes. Eventually, however, it was discovered <u>that the</u> windows <u>cracked because the</u> joint between the double panes of glass was too <u>rigid.</u> <u>Thicker</u> single-pane windows <u>were</u> installed, and the silly plywood building crystallized into <u>a</u> reflective jewel.

ANSWERS: EXERCISE ON CHAPTERS 10–15
Possible Answers

Many people who are physically challenged have accomplished much, which proves that they are not "handicapped." Confined to wheelchairs, Bob Sampson and Stephen Hawking have forged successful careers. Despite his muscular dystrophy, Sampson has earned a law degree; he has also worked for United Airlines for more than thirty years. Stephen Hawking is most famous for his book *A Brief History of Time*. Hawking is unable to speak, but his voice synthesizer allows him to dictate his books, conduct public lectures, and teach mathematics classes at Cambridge University.

Franklin D. Roosevelt, Ann Adams, and Itzhak Perlman all refused to let polio destroy their lives. Indeed, as President, Roosevelt led the United States during two of the worst periods of its history: the Great Depression and World War II. Roosevelt inspired hope and determination in the American public, who were reassured by his strong, firm voice. Ann Adams, who was talented in art before polio paralyzed her, knew she had to continue to be an artist. Having retrained herself to draw with a pencil grasped in her teeth, she produced sketches of children and pets. These drawings were turned into greeting cards whose profits sustained her. Roosevelt and Adams were stricken with polio when they were adults; Itzhak Perlman was stricken when he was a child. He was unable to play sports; instead, he studied the violin. Now many think he is greater than any other violinist in the world.

Like Perlman, many physically challenged individuals turn to the arts. Perhaps they do so because the joy of artistic achievement compensates for other pleasures they cannot experience. Ray Charles, Stevie Wonder, José Feliciano, and Ronnie Milsap all express their souls through their music. Although they are physically blind, their music reveals how well they truly see. Deafness struck Ludwig van Beethoven and Marlee Matlin, but it did not stop them from developing their talents. Already a successful composer, Beethoven wrote many of his best, most powerful pieces after he became deaf. Similarly, Matlin has had excellent acting roles in movies, plays, and television programs; indeed, she won an Oscar for *Children of a Lesser God*. She encourages other deaf actors to develop their abilities, and she has inspired many deaf actors.

mng

Exercise on Chapters 10–15
Revising: Clear sentences

Clarify meaning in the following paragraphs by revising sentence fragments, comma splices, fused sentences, problems with pronoun reference, awkward shifts, misplaced and dangling modifiers, and mixed and incomplete sentences. Most errors can be corrected in more than one way.

Many people who are physically challenged. They have accomplished much. Which proves that they are not "handicapped." Confined to wheelchairs, successful careers have been forged by Bob Sampson and Stephen Hawking. Despite his muscular dystrophy, he has earned a law degree he has also worked for United Airlines for more than thirty years. Stephen Hawking most famous for his book *A Brief History of Time*. Unable to speak, Hawking's voice synthesizer allows him to dictate his books and conduct public lectures. And teach mathematics classes at Cambridge University.

Franklin D. Roosevelt, Ann Adams, and Itzhak Perlman all refused let polio destroy their lives. Indeed, Roosevelt led the United States during two of the worst periods of its history as President. The Great Depression and World War II. Reassured by his strong, firm voice, Roosevelt inspired hope and determination in the American public. Ann Adams, who was talented in art before polio paralyzed her, knew she had to continue to be one. Having retrained herself to draw with a pencil grasped in her teeth. She produces sketches of children and pets. That were turned into greeting cards. The profits from the cards sustained her. Roosevelt and Adams were stricken with polio when they were adults; Itzhak Perlman when a child. He was unable to play sports, instead he studied the violin, now many think he is greater than any violinist in the world.

Like Perlman, many physically challenged individuals turn to the arts. Perhaps the reason is because the joy of artistic achievement compensates for other pleasures they cannot experience. Ray Charles, Stevie Wonder, José Feliciano, and Ronnie Milsap all express, through their music, their souls. Although physically blind, their music reveals truly how well they see. Deafness struck Ludwig van Beethoven and Marlee Matlin it did not stop them from developing their talents. Already a successful composer, many of Beethoven's best, most powerful pieces were written after he became deaf. Similarly, Matlin has had excellent acting roles in movies, plays, and television programs, indeed she won an Oscar for *Children of a Lesser God*. She encourages others to develop their ability, and many deaf actors have been inspired by her.

Part IV

Effective Sentences

The discussion in this chapter emphasizes how writers can use coordination and subordination to relate ideas and distinguish central ideas from less important material. The opening section illustrates how coordination relates facts and ideas and then goes on to address the problems of excessive and faulty coordination. The second section follows a parallel pattern in discussing subordination, focusing on subordinate clauses. But since effective writing depends on a writer's ability to work with the whole range of subordinate structures, the uses of single words; appositives; and prepositional, verbal, and absolute phrases are also illustrated. The final section cautions briefly against the often unclear and misused connectors *like, while,* and *as.*

Included in this chapter are subsections on punctuating coordinated elements (16a), designed to help students not only punctuate correctly but also see punctuation as an instrument and extension of effective sentence structure. The exercises in this chapter ask students to revise sentences and longer passages and to combine sentences in ways that implement the sentence strategies introduced in the chapter.

RESOURCES AND IDEAS

Evelyn B. Melamed and Harvey Minkoff, "Transitions: A Key to Mature Reading and Writing," *Teaching the Basics—Really!* ed. Ouida Clapp (Urbana: NCTE, 1977) 17–21. The authors describe exercises to help students make logical links between sentences and parts of sentences with transitions.

Chapter 16

Using Coordination and Subordination

To help readers see the relative importance of ideas, you coordinate or subordinate information in sentences.

- **Coordination** gives ideas equal stress (see 5d).

  Car and *medical* insurance are modern necessities.

  Car insurance is costly, but *medical insurance is almost a luxury.*

- **Subordination** de-emphasizes less important ideas so that the more important ones stand out (see 5c).

  Many people *applying for insurance* are jolted by the cost.

  Because accidents and thefts are frequent, car insurance is expensive.

16a Coordinating to relate equal ideas

Two or more simple sentences in a row will seem roughly equal in importance but distinct, even if they are related in content. By linking equally important information with coordinating conjunctions or conjunctive adverbs, you can emphasize the relations for readers. Compare the following passages.

String of simple sentences

We should not rely so heavily on oil. Coal and uranium are also overused. We have a substantial energy resource in the moving waters of our rivers. Smaller streams add to the total volume of

Principal ways to coordinate and subordinate information in sentences

Use **coordination** to relate ideas of equal importance (16a).

- Link main clauses with a comma and a coordinating conjunction: *and, but, or, nor, for, so, yet* (5d-1).

  Independence Hall in Philadelphia is now restored, but *fifty years ago it was in bad shape.*

- Relate main clauses with a semicolon alone or a semicolon and a conjunctive adverb: *however, indeed, thus,* etc. (5d-2).

  The building was standing; however, *it suffered from decay and vandalism.*

- Within clauses, link words and phrases with a coordinating conjunction: *and, but, or, nor* (5d-1).

  The *people* and *officials* of Philadelphia *were indifferent to Independence Hall* or *took it for granted.*

Use **subordination** to de-emphasize ideas (16b).

- Use a subordinate clause beginning with a subordinating conjunction: *although, because, if, whereas,* etc. (5c-4).

  Although some citizens had tried to rescue the building, they had not gained substantial public support.

- Use a subordinate clause beginning with a relative pronoun: *who, whoever, which, that* (5c-4).

  The first strong step was taken by the federal government, *which made the building a national monument.*

- Use a prepositional, verbal, or absolute phrase (5c-1 to 5c-3).

  Like most national monuments, Independence Hall is protected by the National Park Service. [Prepositional phrase.]

  Protecting many popular tourist sites, the service is a highly visible government agency. [Verbal phrase.]

  Visitors can always learn something at national parks, *the rangers being helpful and informative.* [Absolute phrase.]

- Use an appositive (5c-5).

  The National Park Service, *a branch of the Department of Interior,* also runs Yosemite and other wilderness parks.

- Use a modifying word.

  At the *red brick* Independence Hall, park rangers give *guided* tours and protect the *irreplaceable* building from vandalism.

TRANSPARENCY MASTER
AVAILABLE

TRANSPARENCY MASTER
AVAILABLE

coord
16a

RESOURCES AND IDEAS

You may wish to remind students that section 5d of the handbook contains a detailed discussion of coordinating conjunctions. If students make a simple list of the conjunctions, they may find themselves becoming more aware of the words and their functions as they read and write:

and	or
but	for
nor	so
yet	

coord
16a

water. The resource renews itself. Coal and oil are irreplaceable. Uranium is also irreplaceable. The cost of water does not increase much over time. The costs of coal, oil, and uranium rise dramatically.

Ideas coordinated

We should not rely so heavily on coal, oil, and uranium, for we have a substantial energy resource in the moving waters of our rivers and streams. Coal, oil, and uranium are irreplaceable and thus subject to dramatic cost increases; water, however, is self-renewing and more stable in cost.

The information in both passages is essentially the same, but the second is shorter and considerably easier to read and understand. The difference is that the second passage builds connections among coordinate ideas: the overuse of some resources and the availability of water in rivers and streams (first sentence); the relation between renewal and cost (second sentence); and the contrast between water and the other resources (both sentences).

Punctuating coordinated words, phrases, and clauses

Most coordinated words, phrases, and subordinate clauses are not punctuated with commas (see 21j-2). The exceptions are items in a series and coordinate adjectives.

> We rely heavily on *coal, oil, and uranium.* [A series; see 21f-1.]
> *Dirty, unhealthy* air is one result. [Coordinate adjectives; see 21f-2.]

In a sentence consisting of two main clauses, punctuation depends on whether a coordinating conjunction, a conjunctive adverb, or no connecting word links the clauses.

> Oil is irreplaceable, *but* water is self-renewing. [See 21a.]
> Oil is irreplaceable; *however,* water is self-renewing. [See 22b.]
> Oil is irreplaceable; water is self-renewing. [See 22a.]

 Using coordination effectively

Coordination can appropriately stress the equality of ideas. But a string of coordinated elements—especially main clauses—creates the same effect as a string of simple sentences: it obscures the relative importance of ideas and details.

Excessive coordination We were near the end of the trip, and the storm kept getting worse, and the snow and ice covered the windshield, and I could hardly see the road ahead, and I knew I should stop, but I kept on driving, and once I barely missed a truck.

This sentence contains two main assertions: *the storm kept getting worse* and *I kept on driving*. All the rest is detail elaborating on these simple statements. When the information in the sentence is recombined using subordination, main assertions and supporting details become distinct.

Revised As we neared the end of the trip, *the storm kept getting worse,* covering the windshield with snow and ice until I could barely see the road ahead. Even though I knew I should stop, *I kept on driving,* once barely missing a truck.

So is often overused as a connector.

Excessive coordination The experience was a frightening one, so I am afraid to drive in bad weather, so I had to leave my job, so now I work closer to home.

As before, revision separates the most important information from the supporting details.

Revised The experience was so frightening that I am afraid to drive in bad weather and had to leave my job for one closer to home.

RESOURCES AND IDEAS

You may wish to remind students that section 5d of the handbook contains a detailed discussion of conjunctive adverbs. You can help create awareness of conjunctive adverbs by asking students to make a list of the words. As they read and write later, students may pay greater attention to the conjunctive adverbs and their functions:

also	further
next	then
certainly	likewise
similarly	undoubtedly
however	anyway
therefore	now
meanwhile	finally
namely	still
besides	indeed
otherwise	thus

coord
16a

2 Coordinating logically

Coordinated sentence elements should be logically equal and related, and the relation between them should be the one expressed by the connecting word. If either principle is violated, the result is **faulty coordination.**

Faulty John Stuart Mill was a nineteenth-century utilitarian, and he believed that actions should be judged by their usefulness or by the happiness they cause. [Mill's utilitarianism is not separate from and equal to his belief; rather, it *labels* his belief.]

Revised John Stuart Mill, *a nineteenth-century utilitarian,* believed that actions should be judged by their usefulness or by the happiness they cause.

Faulty   Mill is recognized as a utilitarian, and he did not found the utilitarian school of philosophy. [The two clauses seem to contrast, requiring *but* or *yet* between them.]

Revised   Mill is recognized as a utilitarian, *but* he did not found the utilitarian school of philosophy.

Sometimes faulty coordination occurs because the writer omits necessary information.

Faulty   Jeremy Bentham founded the utilitarian school, and Mill was precocious. [The two clauses seem unrelated.]

Revised   Jeremy Bentham founded the utilitarian school *before Mill was born,* and Mill *joined at the precocious age of twenty.*

COLLABORATIVE LEARNING

ANSWERS: EXERCISE 1

Possible Revisions

1. Many chronic misspellers do not have the time or motivation to master spelling rules. They rely on dictionaries to catch misspellings, but most dictionaries list words under their correct spellings. One kind of dictionary is designed for chronic misspellers. It lists each word under its common *mis*spellings and then provides the correct spelling and definition.

2. Henry Hudson was an English explorer, but he captained ships for the Dutch East India Company. On a voyage in 1610 he passed Greenland and sailed into a great bay in today's northern Canada. He thought he and his sailors could winter there, but the cold was terrible and food ran out. The sailors mutinied and cast Hudson and eight others adrift in a small boat. Hudson and his companions perished.

Exercise 1
Sentence combining: Coordination

Combine sentences in the following passages to coordinate related ideas in the way that seems most effective to you. You will have to apply coordinating conjunctions or conjunctive adverbs and the appropriate punctuation.

1. Many chronic misspellers do not have the time to master spelling rules. They may not have the motivation. They rely on dictionaries to catch misspellings. Most dictionaries list words under their correct spellings. One kind of dictionary is designed for chronic misspellers. It lists each word under its common *mis*spellings. It then provides the correct spelling. It also provides the definition.

2. Henry Hudson was an English explorer. He captained ships for the Dutch East India Company. On a voyage in 1610 he passed by Greenland. He sailed into a great bay in today's northern Canada. He thought he and his sailors could winter there. The cold was terrible. Food ran out. The sailors mutinied. The sailors cast Hudson adrift in a small boat. Eight others were also in the boat. Hudson and his companions perished.

Exercise 2
Revising: Excessive or faulty coordination

Revise the following sentences to eliminate excessive or faulty coordination. Relate ideas effectively by adding or subordinating information or by forming more than one sentence. Each item has more than one possible answer.

Example:

My dog barks, and I have to move out of my apartment.

Because my dog's barking *disturbs my neighbors,* I have to move out of my apartment.

1. Often soldiers admired their commanding officers, and they gave them nicknames, and these names frequently contained the word "old," but not all of the commanders were old.
2. General Thomas "Stonewall" Jackson was also called "Old Jack," and he was not yet forty years old.
3. Another Southern general in the Civil War was called "Old Pete," and his full name was James Longstreet.
4. The Union general Henry W. Halleck had a reputation as a good military strategist, and he was an expert on the work of a French military authority, Henri Jomini, and Halleck was called "Old Brains."
5. Andrew Jackson was physically tough, and he was determined to defeat the enemy, and he was called "Old Hickory," and his character was just as firm as that wood.
6. Jackson fought Native Americans in the War of 1812, and he earned the nickname then, but it stuck with him in later years, and even as President he was called "Old Hickory."
7. General Zachary Taylor's soldiers called him "Old Rough and Ready," and he was rough in appearance, and his informality with the soldiers caused them to respect him.
8. General Winfield Scott was a contemporary of "Old Rough and Ready," and he was less respected than Taylor.
9. Scott was a good organizer and strategist, but he was a stern disciplinarian, and he was vain and formal, and the soldiers called him "Old Fuss and Feathers."
10. General William Henry Harrison won the Battle of Tippecanoe, and he received the nickname "Old Tippecanoe," and he used the name in his Presidential campaign slogan "Tippecanoe and Tyler, Too," and he won the election in 1840, but he died of pneumonia a month after taking office.

16b   Subordinating to distinguish main ideas

Many sentences consist of a main idea amplified and supported by details. Usually, the main idea appears in the main clause, and the details appear in subordinate structures such as phrases or subordinate clauses. This arrangement helps readers distinguish principal ideas from supporting information. In the following sentence the writer does not provide such assistance.

ANSWERS: EXERCISE 2
Possible Answers

1. Because soldiers admired their commanding officers, they often gave them nicknames containing the word "old," even though not all of the commanders were old.
2. General Thomas "Stonewall" Jackson was also called "Old Jack," although he was not yet forty years old.
3. Another Southern general, whose full name was James Longstreet, was called "Old Pete."
4. The Union General Henry W. Halleck had a reputation as a good military strategist, and he was an expert on the work of a French military authority, Henri Jomini. Therefore, Halleck was called "Old Brains."
5. Since Andrew Jackson was physically tough and determined to defeat the enemy, he was called "Old Hickory." His character was just as firm as that wood.
6. Jackson earned his nickname fighting Native Americans in the War of 1812, but it stuck with him in later years. Even as President he was called "Old Hickory."
7. General Zachary Taylor's soldiers called him "Old Rough and Ready" because he was rough in appearance. His informality with the soldiers caused them to respect him.
8. Although General Winfield Scott was a contemporary of "Old Rough and Ready," he was less respected than Taylor.
9. Scott was a good organizer and strategist. But because he was a stern disciplinarian and vain and formal, the soldiers called him "Old Fuss and Feathers."
10. After General William Henry Harrison won a victory at the Battle of Tippecanoe, he received the nickname "Old Tippecanoe." He used the name in his Presidential campaign slogan "Tippecanoe and Tyler, Too." Although he won the election in 1840, he died of pneumonia a month after taking office.

sub
16b

IDENTIFYING

Have students, working in groups, identify the connectors (subordinating and coordinating conjunctions) in several essays: an essay from a reader, a news item in a newspaper, or a student essay. If the uses of subordination and coordination and the kinds of connectors differ in each kind of essay, ask students to try to account for the differences.

sub
16b

Excessive coordination

In recent years computer prices have dropped, and production costs have dropped more slowly, and computer manufacturers have had to contend with shrinking profits.

By loosely coordinating the three facts in the three main clauses, the writer suggests some relation among them. But we do not know which fact the writer considers most important or how the others qualify or support it. Look at the improvement in these revisions.

Revised

Because production costs have dropped more slowly than computer prices in recent years, computer manufacturers have had to contend with shrinking profits.

In recent years computer manufacturers have had to contend with shrinking profits *on account of* a slower drop in production costs than in computer prices.

Faced with a slower drop in production costs than in computer prices, computer manufacturers have had to contend with shrinking profits in recent years.

Each revision indicates a specific cause-and-effect relation among the three facts, but the emphasis varies from one version to another.

No rules can specify what information in a sentence you should make primary and what you should subordinate; the decision will depend on your meaning. But, in general, you should consider using subordinate structures for details of time, cause, condition, concession, purpose, and identification (size, location, and the like). Consider the use of subordinate clauses in the following pairs of examples. (Some appropriate subordinating conjunctions and relative pronouns are listed in parentheses.)

Time (*after, before, since, until, when, while*)

The mine explosion killed six workers. The owners adopted safety measures.

After the mine explosion killed six workers, the owners adopted safety measures.

Cause (*because, since*)

Jones had been without work for six months. He was having trouble paying his bills.

Because Jones had been without work for six months, he was having trouble paying his bills.

Condition (*if, provided, since, unless*)

Forecasters predicted a mild winter. Farmers hoped for an early spring.

Since forecasters predicted a mild winter, farmers hoped for an early spring.

Concession (*although, as if, even though, though*)

The horse looked gentle. It proved high-spirited and hard to manage.

Although the horse looked gentle, it proved high-spirited and hard to manage.

Purpose (*in order that, so that, that*)

Congress passed new immigration laws. Many Vietnamese refugees could enter the United States.

Congress passed new immigration laws *so that* many Vietnamese refugees could enter the United States.

Identification (*that, when, where, which, who*)

The old factory now manufactures automobile transmissions. It stands on the south side of town and covers three acres.

The old factory, *which* stands on the south side of town and covers three acres, now manufactures automobile transmissions.

Phrases and single words can also indicate the subordinate role of information. Subordinate clauses generally place the greatest emphasis on such information because they are longer and grammatically more like main clauses. Verbal phrases, appositives, and absolute phrases give less weight; prepositional phrases still less; and single words the least.

Old barns are common in New England. They are often painted red. [Separate sentences.]

Old barns, *which are often painted red,* are common in New England. [Subordinate clause.]

Old barns, *often painted red,* are common in New England. [Verbal phrase.]

Old *red* barns are common in New England. [Single word.]

The horse looked gentle. It proved high-spirited and hard to manage. [Separate sentences.]

Although the horse looked gentle, it proved high-spirited and hard to manage. [Subordinate clause.]

Despite its gentle appearance, the horse proved high-spirited and hard to manage. [Prepositional phrase.]

sub
16b

GETTING A NEW LOOK AT YOUR WRITING

Give students a fresh look at their own writing by asking them to revise a portion of a graded essay following specific directions, such as "Add subordination" or "Use more imaginative subordinating words."

REDUCING

To help students practice subordination, create several groups, and give each group a different passage. Ask the groups to first reduce sentences to clauses and then, if possible, to phrases and words. After they have reduced the modifiers in these stages, ask the students in each group to reach consensus on the version they find most effective. At the end of the activity, the groups can explain to the rest of the class the changes they made. Or the groups can exchange passages and repeat the process, comparing their work at the end with the work of the prior group.

The horse, *a gentle-looking animal,* proved high-spirited and hard to manage. [Appositive.]

The *gentle-looking* horse proved high-spirited and hard to manage. [Single word.]

sub
16b

Punctuating subordinate constructions

A modifying word, phrase, or clause that introduces a sentence is usually set off from the rest of the sentence with a comma (see 21b).

Unfortunately, the bank failed.
In a little over six months, the bank became insolvent.
When the bank failed, many reporters investigated.

A modifier that interrupts or concludes a main clause is *not* set off with punctuation when it restricts the meaning of a word or words in the clause (see 21c).

One article *about the bank failure* won a prize.

The article *that won the prize* appeared in the local newspaper.

The reporter wrote the article *because the bank failure affected many residents of the town.*

When an interrupting or concluding modifier does *not* restrict meaning, but simply adds information to the sentence, it *is* set off with punctuation, usually a comma or commas (see 21c).

The bank, *over forty years old,* never reopened.

The bank managers, *who were cleared of any wrongdoing,* all found new jobs.

The customers of the bank never recovered all their money, *though most of them tried to do so.*

Like a modifier, an appositive is set off with punctuation (usually a comma or commas) only when it does *not* restrict the meaning of the word it refers to (see 21c-2).

The bank, *First City,* was the oldest in town.

The newspaper *the Chronicle* was one of the several reporting the story.

A dash or dashes may also be used to set off a nonrestrictive appositive, particularly when it contains commas (see 25b-2). A concluding appositive is sometimes set off with a colon (see 25a-1).

Subordinating logically

Subordination works only when used for the less important information in a sentence. **Faulty subordination** reverses the dependent relation the reader expects.

Faulty	Ms. Angelo was in her first year of teaching, although she was a better instructor than others with many years of experience. [The sentence suggests that Angelo's inexperience is the main idea, whereas the writer almost certainly intended to stress her skill *despite* her inexperience.]
Revised	Although Ms. Angelo was in her first year of teaching, *she was a better instructor than others with many years of experience.*
Faulty	Her class, which won a national achievement award, had twenty students. [Common sense says the important fact is the award.]
Revised	Her class of twenty students *won a national achievement award.*

sub
16b

 Using subordination effectively

Subordination can do much to organize and emphasize information. But it loses that power when a writer tries to cram too much loosely related detail into one long sentence.

Overloaded	The boats that were moored at the dock when the hurricane, which was one of the worst in three decades, struck were ripped from their moorings, because the owners had not been adequately prepared, since the weather service had predicted the storm would blow out to sea, which they do at this time of year.

Since such sentences usually have more than one idea that deserves a main clause, they are best revised by sorting their details into more than one sentence.

Revised	Struck by one of the worst hurricanes in three decades, *the boats at the dock were ripped from their moorings. The owners were unprepared* because the weather service had said that hurricanes at this time of year blow out to sea.

AVOIDING EXCESSIVE SUBORDINATION

Choose paragraphs from student essays that demonstrate overuse or faulty use of subordination, and distribute them to the class. Have students rewrite the paragraphs and then compare their versions to determine which are the most clear and effective revisions. This exercise may be used for small-group or individual work.

A common form of excessive subordination occurs with a string of adjective clauses beginning *which, who,* or *that,* as in the following:

Stringy   Every Christmas we all try to go to my grandfather's house, which is near Louisville, which is an attractive city where my parents now live.

To revise such sentences, recast some of the subordinate clauses as other kinds of modifying structures.

Revised   Every Christmas we all try to go to my grandfather's house *near Louisville, an attractive city* where my parents now live.

Exercise 3
Sentence combining: Subordination

Combine each of the following pairs of sentences twice, each time using one of the subordinate structures in parentheses to make a single sentence. You will have to add, delete, change, and rearrange words.

   Example:

   During the late eighteenth century, workers carried beverages in brightly colored bottles. The bottles had cork stoppers. (*Clause beginning that. Phrase beginning with.*)

   During the late eighteenth century, workers carried beverages in brightly colored bottles *that had cork stoppers.*

   During the late eighteenth century, workers carried beverages in brightly colored bottles *with cork stoppers.*

1. The bombardier beetle sees an enemy. It shoots out a jet of chemicals to protect itself. (Clause beginning *when.* Phrase beginning *seeing.*)
2. The beetle's spray is very potent. It consists of hot and irritating chemicals. (Phrase beginning *consisting.* Phrase beginning *of.*)
3. The spray is a most dangerous weapon against enemies. It is harmless to the beetle. (Clause beginning *although.* Appositive beginning *a most.*)
4. The beetle's spray is a series of tiny chemical explosions. The spray is discharged as a pulsed jet. (Phrase beginning *discharged.* Appositive beginning *a series.*)
5. Scientists filmed the beetle. They discovered that this jet pulses five hundred times each second. (Clause beginning *who.* Phrase beginning *filming.*)
6. The jet's two chemicals are stored separately in the beetle's body and mixed in the spraying gland. The chemicals resem-

COLLABORATIVE LEARNING

ANSWERS: EXERCISE 3
Possible Answers

1. When the bombardier beetle sees an enemy, it shoots out a jet of chemicals to protect itself.
   Seeing an enemy, the bombardier beetle shoots out a jet of chemicals to protect itself.
2. Consisting of hot and irritating chemicals, the beetle's spray is very potent.
   The beetle's spray of hot and irritating chemicals is very potent.
3. Although it is harmless to the beetle, the spray is a most dangerous weapon against enemies.
   A most dangerous weapon against enemies, the spray is harmless to the beetle.
4. The beetle's spray is a series of tiny chemical explosions discharged as a pulsed jet.
   A series of tiny chemical explosions, the beetle's spray is discharged as a pulsed jet.
5. Scientists who filmed the beetle discovered that this jet pulses five hundred times each second.
   Filming the beetle, scientists discovered that this jet pulses some five hundred times each second.
6. Stored separately in the beetle's body and mixed in the spraying gland, the jet's two chemicals resemble a nerve-gas weapon.
   The jet's two chemicals, which are stored separately in the beetle's body and mixed in the spraying gland, resemble a nerve-gas weapon.
7. Revolving like a turret on a World War II bomber, the tip of the beetle's abdomen sprays the chemicals.
   Spraying the chemicals, the tip of the beetle's abdomen revolves like a turret on a World War II bomber.

ble a nerve-gas weapon. (Phrase beginning *stored*. Clause beginning *which*.)
7. The tip of the beetle's abdomen sprays the chemicals. The tip revolves like a turret on a World War II bomber. (Phrase beginning *revolving*. Phrase beginning *spraying*.)
8. The spray is accompanied by a popping sound. It travels twenty-six miles per hour. (Phrase beginning *accompanied*. Clause beginning *which*.)
9. The beetle is less than an inch long. It has many enemies. (Clause beginning *because*. Phrase beginning *less*.)
10. The beetle defeats most of its enemies. It is still eaten by spiders and birds. (Clause beginning *although*. Phrase beginning *except*.)

Exercise 4
Revising: Subordination

Rewrite the following paragraph in the way you think most effective to subordinate the less important ideas to the more important ones. Use subordinate clauses and other subordinate constructions as appropriate.

Many students today are no longer majoring in the liberal arts. I mean by "liberal arts" such subjects as history, English, and the social sciences. Students think a liberal arts degree will not help them get jobs. They are wrong. They may not get practical, job-related experience from the liberal arts, but they will get a broad education, and it will never again be available to them. Many employers look for more than a technical, professional education. They think such an education can make an employee's views too narrow. The employers want open-minded employees. They want employees to think about problems from many angles. The liberal arts curriculum instills such flexibility. The flexibility is vital to the health of our society.

Exercise 5
Revising: Faulty or excessive subordination

Revise the following sentences to eliminate faulty or excessive subordination by reversing main and subordinate ideas, by coordinating ideas, or by making separate sentences. Some items have more than one possible answer.

Example:
Terrified to return home, he had driven his mother's car into a corn field.
Having driven his mother's car into a corn field, he was terrified to return home.

1. Genaro González is blessed with great writing talent, which

8. Accompanied by a popping sound, the spray travels twenty-six miles per hour.
The spray, which is accompanied by a popping sound, travels twenty-six miles per hour.
9. Because the beetle is less than an inch long, it has many enemies.
Less than an inch long, the beetle has many enemies.
10. Although the beetle defeats most of its enemies, it is still eaten by spiders and birds.
The beetle defeats most of its enemies except spiders and birds.

ANSWERS: EXERCISE 4
Possible Revision

Many students today are no longer majoring in the liberal arts—that is, in such subjects as history, English, and the social sciences. Although students think a liberal arts degree will not help them get jobs, they are wrong. They may not get practical, job-related experience from the liberal arts, but they will get a broad education that will never again be available to them. Many employers look for more than a technical, professional education because they think such an education can make an employee's views too narrow. Instead, they want open-minded employees who can think about problems from many angles. This sort of flexibility—vital to the health of our society—is just what the liberal arts curriculum instills.

sub
16b

ANSWERS: EXERCISE 5
Possible Answers

1. Because Genaro González is blessed with great writing talent, several of his stories and his novel *Rainbow's End* have been published.
2. Although he loves to write, he has also earned a doctorate in psychology.
3. His first story, which is entitled "Un Hijo del Sol," reflects his growing consciousness of his Aztec heritage and place in the world.
4. González writes equally well in English and Spanish. In 1990 he received a large fellowship enabling him to take a leave of absence from Pan American University, where he teaches psychology. During that year he could write without worrying about an income.
5. González wrote the first version of "Un Hijo del Sol" while he was a sophomore at Pan American. The university is in the Rio Grande valley of southern Texas, which González calls "el Valle" in the story.

sub
16c

means that several of his stories and his novel *Rainbow's End* have been published.
2. He loves to write, although he has also earned a doctorate in psychology.
3. His first story, which reflects his growing consciousness of his Aztec heritage and place in the world, is entitled "Un Hijo del Sol."
4. In 1990 González, who writes equally well in English and Spanish, received a large fellowship that enabled him to take a leave of absence from the Pan American University, where he teaches psychology, so that he could write without worrying about an income.
5. González wrote the first version of "Un Hijo del Sol" while he was a sophomore at Pan American, which is in the Rio Grande valley of southern Texas, which González calls "el Valle" in the story.

16c Choosing clear connectors

Most connecting words signal specific and unambiguous relations; for instance, the coordinating conjunction *but* clearly indicates contrast, and the subordinating conjunction *because* clearly indicates cause. A few connectors, however, require careful use, either because they are ambiguous in many contexts or because they are often misused.

 Using unambiguous connectors: *as* and *while*

The subordinating conjunction *as* can indicate several kinds of adverbial relations, including comparison and time.

Comparison	He was working *as* rapidly as he could.
Time	The instructor finally arrived *as* the class was leaving.

As is sometimes used to indicate cause, but in that sense it is often ambiguous and should be avoided.

Ambiguous	*As* I was in town, I visited some old friends. [Time or cause intended?]
Clear	*When* I was in town, I visited some old friends. [Time.]
Clear	*Because* I was in town, I visited some old friends. [Cause.]

The subordinating conjunction *while* can indicate either time or concession. Unless the context makes the meaning of *while* unmistakably clear, choose a more exact connector.

Ambiguous   *While* we were working nearby, we did not hear the burglars enter. [Time or concession?]

Clear   *When* we were working nearby, we did not hear the burglars enter. [Time.]

Clear   *Although* we were working nearby, we did not hear the burglars enter. [Concession.]

 2   Using correct connectors: *as, like,* and *while*

The use of *as* as a substitute for *whether* or *that* is nonstandard—that is, it violates the conventions of spoken and written standard English.

Nonstandard   He was not sure *as* he could come.

Revised   He was not sure *whether* (or *that*) he could come.

Although the preposition *like* is often used as a conjunction in informal speech and in advertising (*Dirt-Away works like a soap should*), writing generally requires the conjunction *as, as if, as though,* or *that.*

Speech   It seemed *like* the examination would never end.

Writing   It seemed *as if* (*as though*) the examination would never end.

The subordinating conjunction *while* is sometimes carelessly used in the sense of *and* or *but,* creating false subordination.

Faulty   My sister wants to study medicine *while* I want to study law.

Revised   My sister wants to study medicine, *and* I want to study law.

Exercise 6
Revising: Clear connectors

Substitute a clear or correct connector in the following sentences where *as, while,* and *like* are ambiguous or misused.

Example:

He looked to me like he had slept in his clothes.
He looked to me *as if* he had slept in his clothes.

REWRITING

Give students a passage from a student or professional essay, and ask them to rewrite it following a specified strategy: adding subordination, using different subordinators, or adding coordination. This exercise can be extended by having students rewrite the passage to change its emphasis.

sub
16c

ANSWERS: EXERCISE 6

1. Many writers use *he* to denote both males and females, <u>but</u> others avoid the usage.
2. Some writers feel <u>that</u> substituting *he* for *a doctor* or *the engineer* insults female members of those professions.
3. <u>Because</u> women more frequently enter such fields now, writers can no longer safely use *he* to refer to a white-collar professional.
4. Nor can writers automatically use *she* to refer to a nurse or secretary, <u>as if</u> a man would not enter such a career.
5. <u>Since</u> they desire to be fair to both genders, many writers prefer plural nouns (for example, *doctors*) and *they*.

ANSWERS: EXERCISE 7
Possible Revision

Sir Walter Raleigh personified the Elizabethan Age, <u>the</u> period during which Elizabeth I ruled England, <u>in</u> the last half of the sixteenth century. Raleigh was a <u>courtier, a poet, an explorer, and an entrepreneur.</u> Supposedly, he gained Queen Elizabeth's favor by throwing his cloak beneath her feet at the right moment, <u>just as she was</u> about to step over a puddle. <u>Although</u> there is no evidence for this <u>story, it</u> illustrates Raleigh's dramatic and dynamic personality. His energy drew others to <u>him, and</u> he was one of Elizabeth's favorites. She supported <u>him and</u> dispensed favors to him. However, he lost his queen's good <u>will when without</u> her permission he <u>seduced and eventually married</u> one of her maids of honor. <u>After Elizabeth died,</u> her successor, <u>James I,</u> imprisoned Raleigh in the Tower of London <u>on false charges of treason.</u> Raleigh was released after thirteen <u>years but</u> arrested again two years later on the old treason charges. At the age of sixty-six he was beheaded.

1. Many writers use *he* to denote both males and females, while others avoid the usage.
2. Some writers feel like substituting *he* for *a doctor* or *the engineer* insults female members of those professions.
3. As women more frequently enter such fields now, writers can no longer safely use *he* to refer to a white-collar professional.
4. Nor can writers automatically use *she* to refer to a nurse or secretary, like a man would not enter such a career.
5. As they desire to be fair to both genders, many writers prefer plural nouns (for example, *doctors*) and *they*.

Exercise 7
Revising: Coordination and subordination

The following paragraph consists entirely of simple sentences. Use coordination and subordination to combine sentences in the way you think most effective to emphasize main ideas.

Sir Walter Raleigh personified the Elizabethan Age. That was the period of Elizabeth I's rule of England. The period occurred in the last half of the sixteenth century. Raleigh was a courtier and poet. He was also an explorer and entrepreneur. Supposedly, he gained Queen Elizabeth's favor. He did this by throwing his cloak beneath her feet at the right moment. She was just about to step over a puddle. There is no evidence for this story. It does illustrate Raleigh's dramatic and dynamic personality. His energy drew others to him. He was one of Elizabeth's favorites. She supported him. She also dispensed favors to him. However, he lost his queen's good will. Without her permission he seduced one of her maids of honor. He eventually married the maid of honor. Elizabeth died. Then her successor imprisoned Raleigh in the Tower of London. Her successor was James I. Raleigh was charged falsely with treason. He was released after thirteen years. He was arrested again two years later on the old treason charges. At the age of sixty-six he was beheaded.

Note: See page 372 for an exercise involving coordination and subordination along with parallelism and other techniques for effective sentences.

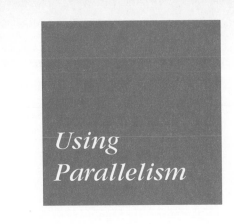

Chapter 17

Using Parallelism

HIGHLIGHTS

This discussion of parallelism is divided into two sections, and it moves from correctness to effective style. The opening section addresses the obligatory use of parallelism in coordinate constructions—those linked by coordinating conjunctions and correlative conjunctions; those in comparisons and contrasts; and those in lists, outlines, and the like. The second section examines how parallelism can be used within and among sentences to increase coherence, emphasize meaning, and heighten the effect. For some students you may wish to emphasize the items in the opening section. But students who have no trouble maintaining obligatory parallelism can often profit by working more creatively with parallelism to tighten and clarify their writing. Exercise 3, a sentence-combining exercise, is designed to give students a chance to explore the options for expression that parallelism provides. The exercise is likely to be most effective when students are given a chance to (1) discuss with one another the impact of various combinations or (2) work collaboratively in exploring various sentence-combining options.

Parallelism is a similarity of grammatical form between two or more coordinated elements.

The air is dirtied by ‖ factories ‖ belching ‖ smoke
and ‖ cars ‖ spewing ‖ exhaust.

Parallel structure reinforces and highlights a close relation or a contrast between compound sentence elements, whether words, phrases, or entire clauses.

The principle underlying parallelism is that form should reflect meaning: since the parts of compound constructions have the same function and importance, they should have the same grammatical form.

17a Using parallelism for coordinate elements

Parallel structure is necessary wherever coordination exists:

- Wherever elements are connected by coordinating or correlative conjunctions.
- Wherever elements are compared or contrasted.
- Wherever items are arranged in a list or outline.

(See the box on the next page.)

<table>
<tr><td>TRANSPARENCY MASTER
AVAILABLE</td></tr>
</table>

 Patterns of parallelism

Use parallel structures for all coordinated elements.

● For elements connected by coordinating or correlative conjunctions (17a-1, 17a-2):

In 1988 a Greek cyclist, backed up by ‖ *engineers,*
‖ *physiologists,*
and ‖ *athletes,*
broke the world's record for human flight
with <u>neither</u> ‖ *a boost*
<u>nor</u> ‖ *a motor.*

● For elements being compared or contrasted (17a-3):

‖ *Pedal power*
<u>rather than</u> ‖ *horse power*
propelled the plane.

● For items arranged in a series or outline (17a-4):

The four-hour flight was successful because
‖ (1) *the cyclist was very fit,*
‖ (2) *he flew a straight course over water,*
and ‖ (3) *he kept the aircraft near the water's surface.*

Parallel elements match each other in structure, though they do not always match word for word.

We passed *through the town* <u>and</u> *into the vast, unpopulated desert.*

 Using parallelism for elements linked by coordinating conjunctions

The coordinating conjunctions *and, but, or, nor,* and *yet* always signal a need for parallelism.

The industrial base is *shifting* <u>and</u> *shrinking.* [Parallel words.]
Politicians rarely *acknowledge the problem* <u>or</u> *propose alternatives.* [Parallel phrases.]
Industrial workers are understandably disturbed *that they are losing their jobs* <u>and</u> *that no one seems to care.* [Parallel clauses.]

Sentence elements that are linked by coordinating conjunctions should be parallel in structure; otherwise, their coordination will be weakened and the reader distracted.

// 17a

RESOURCES AND IDEAS

Phyllis Brooks, "Mimesis: Grammar and the Echoing Voice," *College English* 35 (1973): 161–68. Brooks suggests the writing of paragraphs that imitate the style of a writer but use different content. She indicates that the practice helps students learn to use a variety of structures, including parenthetical expressions, appositives and modifiers, and parallelism plus reference.

Robert L. Walker, "The Common Writer: A Case for Parallel Structure," *College Composition and Communication* 21 (1970): 373–79. Walker believes that students should be encouraged to use a variety of sentence structures and parallelism, which he considers important features of mature sentences.

PATTERNS FOR PARALLELISM

Working on their own, students might find it difficult to write many sentences containing correlative conjunctions, lists, and coordinate structures that require parallelism, but if you ask them to do this in groups, they can probably generate quite a few. As part of the assignment, ask students to vary the sentences as much as they can in content and in use of parallelism. Then ask the groups to judge each other's work for originality, clarity, and effectiveness.

Faulty Three reasons why steel companies keep losing money are that their plants are inefficient, high labor costs, <u>and</u> foreign competition is increasing.

Revised Three reasons why steel companies keep losing money are *inefficient plants, high labor costs,* and *increasing foreign competition.*

All the words required by idiom or grammar must be stated in compound constructions (see also 15c).

Faulty Given training, workers can acquire the skills <u>and</u> interest in other jobs. [Idiom dictates different prepositions with *skills* and *interest.*]

Revised Given training, workers can acquire the skills *for* and interest in other jobs.

Often, the same word must be repeated to avoid confusion.

Confusing Thoreau stood up for his principles by not paying his taxes <u>and</u> spending a night in jail. [Did he spend a night in jail or not?]

Revised Thoreau stood up for his principles by not paying his taxes and *by* spending a night in jail.

Be sure that clauses beginning *and who* or *and which* are coordinated only with preceding *who* and *which* clauses.

Faulty Thoreau was the nineteenth-century writer <u>and</u> who retired to the woods.

Revised Thoreau was the nineteenth-century writer *who* retired to the woods.

SAMPLE ESSAYS

Ask students to look for parallelism in essays from a reader or a similar source. If the students are working in groups, ask them not only to reach consensus on which elements are parallel but also to decide what functions the parallelism performs.

//
17a

▲
2 **Using parallelism for elements linked by correlative conjunctions**

Correlative conjunctions are pairs of connectors. For example:

both . . . and	neither . . . nor	not only . . . but also
either . . . or	not . . . but	whether . . . or

They stress equality and balance and thus emphasize the relation between elements, even long phrases and clauses. The elements should be parallel to confirm their relation.

It is <u>not</u> *a tax bill* <u>but</u> *a tax relief bill,* providing relief <u>not</u> *for the needy* <u>but</u> *for the greedy.*   —FRANKLIN DELANO ROOSEVELT

// 17a

ADDING PARALLELISM

Take a loose-jointed student essay or a professional essay and distribute it to students (working individually or in groups), asking them to make the sentences denser by adding parallelism wherever possible. Ask them also to decide when the parallelism adds to the essay and when it detracts.

At the end of the novel, Huck Finn <u>both</u> *rejects society's values by turning down money and a home* <u>and</u> *affirms his own values by setting out for "the territory."*

Most errors in parallelism with correlative conjunctions occur when the element after the second connector does not match the element after the first connector.

Nonparallel Mark Twain refused <u>either</u> to ignore the moral blindness of his soci<u>ety</u> <u>or</u> spare the reader's sensibilities. [Since *to* follows *either,* it must also follow *or.*]

Revised Mark Twain refused either to ignore the moral blindness of his society or *to* spare the reader's sensibilities.

Nonparallel Huck Finn learns <u>not only</u> that human beings have an enormous capacity for folly <u>but also</u> enormous dignity. [A clause follows *not only,* whereas only a phrase follows *but also.*]

Revised Huck Finn learns *that human beings have not only* an enormous capacity for folly but also enormous dignity. [Repositioning *not only* makes the two elements parallel.]

 Using parallelism for elements being compared or contrasted

Elements being compared or contrasted should ordinarily be cast in the same grammatical form.

It is better *to live rich* than *to die rich.*   —SAMUEL JOHNSON

Weak The study found that most welfare recipients wanted to work <u>rather than</u> handouts.

Revised The study found that most welfare recipients wanted *work* rather than handouts.

Revised The study found that most welfare recipients wanted to work rather than *to accept handouts.*

 Using parallelism for items in lists or outlines

The elements of a list or outline that divides a larger subject are coordinate and should be parallel in structure. Parallelism is essential in a formal topic outline (see 1g-2):

Faulty

Changes in Renaissance England

1. An extension of trade routes
2. Merchant class became more powerful
3. The death of feudalism
4. Upsurging of the arts
5. The sciences were encouraged
6. Religious quarrels began

Improved

Changes in Renaissance England

1. The extension of trade routes
2. The increasing power of the merchant class
3. The death of feudalism
4. The upsurge of the arts
5. The encouragement of the sciences
6. The rise of religious quarrels

Exercise 1
Identifying parallel elements

Identify the parallel elements in the following sentences. How does parallelism contribute to the effectiveness of each sentence?

1. While not as pointless as *The Three Musketeers* or as lengthy as *Harrigan 'n' Hart* or as becalmed as *Quilters,* this show does lead the pack in such key areas as incoherence (total), vulgarity (boundless), and decibel level (stratospheric, with piercing electronic feedback).   —FRANK RICH
2. This apparent amnesia, which Freud labelled infantile or childhood amnesia, applies only to our memories about the self, not to our memory for words learned or objects and people recognized.   —PATRICK HUYGHE
3. They [pioneer women] rolled out dough on the wagon seats, cooked with fires made out of buffalo chips, tended the sick, and marked the graves of their children, husbands and each other.   —ELLEN GOODMAN
4. The mornings are the pleasantest times in the apartment, exhaustion having set in, the sated mosquitoes at rest on ceiling and walls, sleeping it off, the room a swirl of tortured bedclothes and abandoned garments, the vines in their full leafiness filtering the hard light of day, the air conditioner silent at last, like the mosquitoes.   —E. B. WHITE
5. Aging paints every action gray, lies heavy on every movement, imprisons every thought.   —SHARON CURTIN

Exercise 2
Revising: Parallelism

Revise the following sentences to make coordinate, compared, or listed elements parallel in structure. Add or delete words or rephrase as necessary.

COLLABORATIVE LEARNING

ANSWERS: EXERCISE 1

1. The two sets of parallel constructions (*pointless . . . lengthy . . . becalmed* and *incoherence . . . , vulgarity . . . , decibel level*) condemn the reviewed show by repeated association with other inept shows and then separate it into its own realm of ineptness. After such a tight sentence structure, the final break in parallelism (*stratospheric, with piercing electronic feedback*) gives a sense of the writer's exasperation and pain.
2. The parallel phrases (*applies only to our memories about . . . not to our memory for*) clarify what the definition includes and excludes.
3. The parallel verbs (*rolled out . . . cooked . . . tended . . . marked*) stress the number and variety of the women's responsibilities.
4. Supporting *pleasantest* is a wealth of detail expressed in five parallel absolute phrases: *exhaustion . . . in; the sated mosquitoes . . . off; the room . . . garments; the vines . . . day;* and *the air conditioner . . . mosquitoes.* The phrases convey no action, emphasizing the stillness of the scene.
5. The limiting effects of aging are emphasized by the increasingly narrow parallel verbs—*pants, lies, imprisons*—and the parallel objects—*every action, every movement,* and *every thought.*

//
17a

ANSWERS: EXERCISE 2
Possible Answers

1. The ancient Greeks celebrated four athletic contests: the Olympic Games at Olympia, the Isthmian <u>Games near</u> Corinth, <u>the Pythian Games at Delphi</u>, and the Nemean <u>Games at</u> Cleonae.
2. Each day of the games consisted of either athletic events or <u>ceremonies</u> and sacrifices to the gods.
3. In the years between the games, competitors were taught <u>boxing</u>, wrestling, and javelin throwing.
4. <u>Competitors ran</u> sprints, <u>participated in</u> spectacular chariot and horse races, and <u>ran</u> long distances while wearing full armor.
5. The purpose of such events was developing physical strength, demonstrating skill and endurance, and <u>sharpening</u> the skills needed for war.
6. Events were held <u>both for</u> men and for boys.
7. At the Olympic Games the spectators cheered their favorites to victory, attended sacrifices to the gods, and <u>feasted</u> on the meat not burned in offerings.
8. The athletes competed less to achieve great wealth than <u>to gain</u> honor <u>for both</u> themselves and their cities.
9. Of course, exceptional athletes received financial support from patrons, poems and statues by admiring artists, and <u>even lavish</u> living quarters from their sponsoring cities.
10. With the medal counts and flag ceremonies, today's Olympians often seem not so much to be demonstrating individual talent as <u>to be proving</u> their countries' superiority.

Example:

After emptying her bag, searching the apartment, and having called the library, Jennifer realized she had lost the book.

After emptying her bag, searching the apartment, and *calling* the library, Jennifer realized she had lost the book.

1. The ancient Greeks celebrated four athletic contests: the Olympic Games at Olympia, the Isthmian Games were held near Corinth, at Delphi the Pythian Games, and the Nemean Games were sponsored by the people of Cleonae.
2. Each day of the games consisted of either athletic events or holding ceremonies and sacrifices to the gods.
3. In the years between the games, competitors were taught how to box and wrestling and javelin throwing.
4. Competitors participated in running sprints, spectacular chariot and horse races, and running long distances while wearing full armor.
5. The purpose of such events was developing physical strength, demonstrating skill and endurance, and to sharpen the skills needed for war.
6. Events were held for both men and for boys.
7. At the Olympic Games the spectators cheered their favorites to victory, attended sacrifices to the gods, and they feasted on the meat not burned in offerings.
8. The athletes competed less to achieve great wealth than for gaining honor both for themselves and their cities.
9. Of course, exceptional athletes received financial support from patrons, poems and statues by admiring artists, and they even got lavish living quarters from their sponsoring cities.
10. With the medal counts and flag ceremonies, today's Olympians often seem not so much to be demonstrating individual talent as to prove their countries' superiority.

17b Using parallelism to increase coherence

Parallelism not only ensures similarity of form for coordinated structures but also enhances coherence by clearly relating paired or opposed units. Consider this sentence:

Nonparallel   During the early weeks of the semester, the course reviews fundamentals, <u>but</u> little emphasis is placed on new material.

Here "the course" is doing two things—or doing one thing and not doing the other—and these are opposites. But the nonparallel construction of the sentence (*the course reviews . . . little emphasis is placed*) does not make the connection clear.

| **Revised** | During the early weeks of the semester, the course reviews fundamentals but *places little emphasis* on new material. |

Effective parallelism will enable you to combine in a single, well-ordered sentence related ideas that you might have expressed in separate sentences. Compare the following three sentences with the original single sentence written by H. L. Mencken.

Slang originates in the effort of ingenious individuals to make language more pungent and picturesque. They increase the store of terse and striking words or widen the boundaries of metaphor. Thus a vocabulary for new shades and differences in meaning is provided by slang.

Slang originates in the effort of ingenious individuals to make the language more pungent and picturesque—to increase the store of terse and striking words, to widen the boundaries of metaphor, and to provide a vocabulary for new shades and differences in meaning.   —H. L. MENCKEN

Parallel structure works as well to emphasize the connections among related sentences in a paragraph (see 3b-2).

Style is an extraordinary thing. It is one of the subtlest secrets of all art. . . . *In painting, it is* composition, colour-sense, and brushwork. *In sculpture, it is* the treatment of depths and surfaces and the choice of stones and metals. *In music, it is* surely the melodic line, the tone-colour, and the shape of the phrase. . . . *In prose and poetry, it is* the choice of words, their placing, and the rhythms and melodies of sentence and paragraph.   — GILBERT HIGHET

Here, Highet clarifies and emphasizes his assertion that style is common to all forms of art by casting four successive sentences in the same structure (*In . . . , it is . . .*).

//
17b

Exercise 3
Sentence combining: Parallelism

Combine each group of sentences below into one concise sentence in which parallel elements appear in parallel structures. You will have to add, delete, change, and rearrange words. Each item has more than one possible answer.

Example:

Christin sorted the books neatly. She was efficient, too.
Christin sorted the books neatly *and efficiently.*

1. People can develop Post-Traumatic Stress Disorder (PTSD). They develop it after experiencing a dangerous situation. They will also have felt fear for their survival.

ANSWERS: EXERCISE 3
Possible Answers

1. People can develop Post-Traumatic Stress Disorder (PTSD) after experiencing a dangerous situation and fearing for their survival.
2. The disorder can be triggered by a wide variety of events, such as combat, natural disasters, or a hostage situation.

3. PTSD can occur immediately after the stressful incident or sometimes not until many years later.
4. Sometimes people with PTSD will act irrationally and angrily.
5. Other symptoms include dreaming that one is reliving the experience, hallucinating that one is back in the terrifying place, and imagining that strangers are actually one's former torturers.
6. Victims of the disorder might isolate themselves from family and friends, stop going to work, commit criminal acts, or do violence to themselves or others.
7. Victims might need private counseling or hospitalization.
8. The healing process is terrifying when the patients begin but becomes exciting when they improve.
9. After treatment many patients overcome their fears and seldom experience any recurrence of the symptoms.
10. When victims learn the roots of their fears, they are relieved of their pain, restored to their families, and returned to a productive place in society.

ANSWERS: EXERCISE 4

Possible Revision

The great white shark has an undeserved bad reputation. Many people consider the great white not only swift and powerful <u>but also a</u> cunning and cruel predator on humans. However, scientists claim that the great white attacks humans not by choice <u>but by</u> chance. To a shark, our behavior in the water is similar to that of porpoises, seals, and sea lions—the shark's favorite foods. These sea mammals are both agile enough <u>and fast</u> enough to evade the shark. Thus the shark must attack <u>swiftly</u> and noiselessly to surprise the prey and <u>give</u> it little chance to escape. Humans become the shark's victims not because the shark has any preference <u>for</u> or hatred of humans but because humans can neither outswim <u>nor outmaneuver</u> the shark. If the fish were truly a cruel human-eater, it would prolong the terror of its attacks, perhaps by circling or bumping into its intended victims before <u>attacking them</u>.

2. The disorder can be triggered by a wide variety of events. Combat is a typical cause. Similarly, natural disasters can result in PTSD. Some people experience PTSD after a hostage situation.
3. PTSD can occur immediately after the stressful incident. Sometimes it will not appear until many years later.
4. Sometimes people with PTSD will act irrationally. Moreover, they often become angry.
5. Other symptoms include dreaming that one is reliving the experience. They include hallucinating that one is back in the terrifying place. In another symptom one imagines that strangers are actually one's former torturers.
6. Victims of the disorder might isolate themselves from family and friends. They can stop going to work. Criminal acts might be committed. Or doing violence to themselves or others is a possibility.
7. Victims might need private counseling. Some might need to be hospitalized.
8. The healing process is terrifying when the patients begin. But it becomes exciting when they improve.
9. After treatment many patients overcome their fears. And they seldom experience any recurrence of the symptoms.
10. Victims learn the roots of their fears. Then they are relieved of their pain. Usually they are restored to their families. And they return to a productive place in society.

Exercise 4

Revising: Parallelism

Revise the following paragraph to create parallelism wherever it is required for grammar or for coherence.

The great white shark has an undeserved bad reputation. Many people consider the great white not only swift and powerful but also to be a cunning and cruel predator on humans. However, scientists claim that the great white attacks humans not by choice but as a result of chance. To a shark, our behavior in the water is similar to that of porpoises, seals, and sea lions—the shark's favorite foods. These sea mammals are both agile enough and can move fast enough to evade the shark. Thus the shark must attack with swiftness and noiselessly to surprise the prey and giving it little chance to escape. Humans become the shark's victims not because the shark has any preference or hatred of humans but because humans can neither outswim nor can they outmaneuver the shark. If the fish were truly a cruel human-eater, it would prolong the terror of its attacks, perhaps by circling or bumping into its intended victims before they were attacked.

Note: See page 372 for an exercise involving parallelism along with other techniques for effective sentences.

Chapter 18

Emphasizing Main Ideas

HIGHLIGHTS

This chapter looks at two ways to achieve emphasis within sentences: by the distribution of information and by the choice of strategies to create a specific effect. Special features of the chapter are its treatment of cumulative and periodic sentences and discussion that stresses the rhetorical effect of each sentence pattern. The sentence-combining exercises that accompany the discussion are designed to help students feel comfortable using these patterns in their writing. The opening discussion also looks at the importance of sentence beginnings and endings and at the effective arrangement of items in a series. Most students benefit from some work with these basic ways of controlling emphasis as well as from discussion of using the active voice (18d) and of being concise (18e). Students who have problems with sentence structure, however, may have more difficulty with the effective uses of repetition (18b) and separation (18c) for emphasis.

Effective writing emphasizes the important information in sentences by making it readily apparent to readers.

Ways to emphasize ideas

- Put important ideas in the beginnings or endings of sentences (18a-1).
- Arrange series items in order of increasing importance (18a-2).
- Use an occasional balanced sentence (18a-2).
- Carefully repeat key words and phrases (18b).
- Set off important ideas with punctuation (18c).
- Use the active voice (18d).
- Write concisely (18e).

18a Arranging ideas effectively

In arranging ideas within sentences for emphasis, you should keep two principles in mind.

- The beginnings and endings of sentences are the most emphatic positions, and endings are generally more emphatic than beginnings.

351

- A parallel series of words, phrases, or clauses will be emphatic if the elements appear in order of increasing importance.

emph
18a

 Using sentence beginnings and endings

Readers automatically seek a writer's principal meaning in the basic sentence—that is, in the subject that names a topic and the predicate that comments on the topic (see 5a). Thus you can help ensure that readers understand your intended meaning by controlling the relation of the basic sentence to any other words, phrases, or clauses that modify all or parts of it.

The most effective way to call attention to information is to place it first or last in the sentence, reserving the middle for incidentals.

Unemphatic	Education remains the most important single means of economic advancement, in spite of its shortcomings.
Revised	In spite of its shortcomings, education remains the most important single means of economic advancement.
Revised	Education remains, in spite of its shortcomings, the most important single means of economic advancement.

The first sentence focuses our attention on education's shortcomings, even though the writer clearly wished to emphasize its importance. The first revision stresses the shortcomings a bit by placing them at the beginning but emphasizes education's importance by reserving it for the end. The second revision de-emphasizes the shortcomings by placing them in the middle.

Many sentences begin with the subject and predicate plus their modifiers and then add more modifiers. Such sentences are called **cumulative** (because they accumulate information as they proceed) or **loose** (because they are not tightly structured).

Cumulative	Education has no equal in opening minds, instilling values, and creating opportunities.
Cumulative	Most of the Great American Desert is made up of bare rock, rugged cliffs, mesas, canyons, mountains, separated from one another by broad flat basins covered with sun-baked mud and alkali, supporting a sparse and measured growth of sagebrush or creosote or saltbush, depending on location and elevation. —EDWARD ABBEY

A cumulative sentence completes its main statement (topic and comment) and then explains, amplifies, or illustrates it. By thus accumulating information, the sentence parallels the way we naturally think.

The opposite kind of sentence, called **periodic,** saves the main clause until just before the end (the period) of the sentence. Everything before the main clause points toward it.

Periodic	In opening minds, instilling values, and creating opportunities, education has no equal.
Periodic	In the Mason jars stacked up dusty and fly-specked on the side shelves, in the broken-webbed snowshoes hung there, the heap of rusty hinged traps waiting this long to be oiled and set to catch something in the night, was the visible imprint of the past we were rooted in.

—JOAN CHASE

A variation of the periodic sentence names the subject at the beginning, follows it with a modifier, and then finishes with the predicate.

Thirty-eight-year-old Dick Hayne, who works in jeans and loafers and likes to let a question cure in the air for a while before answering it, bears all the markings of what his generation used to call a laid-back kind of guy. — GEORGE RUSH

The periodic sentence creates suspense for the reader by reserving important information for the end. But it requires careful planning so that the reader can remember all the information leading up to the main clause. Most writers save periodic sentences for when their purpose demands climactic emphasis.

2 **Arranging parallel elements effectively**

Series

Parallelism requires that you express coordinate ideas in similar grammatical structures (see Chapter 17). In addition, you should arrange the coordinate ideas in order of importance.

Unemphatic	The storm ripped the roofs off several buildings, killed ten people, and knocked down many trees in town.

In this sentence the most serious damage (*killed ten people*) is

---

MEMORY AID

Thinking About Cumulative and Periodic Sentences

The following examples may help students remember how to formulate and how to distinguish between cumulative and periodic sentences:

1. *Cumulative sentences*

A cumulative sentence is created much like a portrait, detail by detail. The diver (for example) paused at the end of the board, gazing down at the smooth, greenish-blue water meters below, his arms stretched out in front, his legs trembling slightly with anticipation and tension, drops of water falling from his fingertips into the swirling wind filled with murmurs from the crowd below and behind his solitary figure.

2. *Periodic sentences*

In a form that parallels the dramatic movement of a tragedy, the meaning of a periodic sentence is built from words and phrases preceding the main clause. In Shakespeare's play *Othello,* step by step, with slowly gathering force and filled with increasing tension and foreboding, the opening scenes create a situation that makes the tragic events inevitable.

emph
18a

MORE COMBINING

Give students a list of information about a topic, and ask them to combine the information to emphasize certain features or to achieve a particular rhetorical purpose. They can do the combining in groups or meet together to discuss the results.

buried in the middle. The revised sentence below presents the items in order of increasing importance.

Emphatic   The storm knocked down many trees in town, ripped the roofs off several buildings, and killed ten people.

You may want to use an unexpected item at the end of a series for humor or for another special effect.

Early to bed and early to rise makes a man healthy, wealthy, and dead.   —JAMES THURBER

But be careful not to use such a series unintentionally. The following series seems thoughtlessly random rather than intentionally humorous.

Unemphatic   The painting has subdued tone, great feeling, and a length of about three feet.

Emphatic   The painting, about three feet long, has subdued tone and great feeling.

Balanced sentences

When the clauses of a compound or complex sentence are parallel, the sentence is **balanced.**

The fickleness of the women I love is equalled only by the infernal constancy of the women who love me.
                                              —GEORGE BERNARD SHAW

In a pure balanced sentence two main clauses are exactly parallel: they match item for item.

The love of liberty is the love of others; the love of power is the love of ourselves.   —WILLIAM HAZLITT

But the term is commonly applied to sentences that are only approximately parallel or that have only some parallel parts.

If thought corrupts language, language can also corrupt thought.
                                              —GEORGE ORWELL

The secret of learning to act lies not in the study of methods but in the close observation of those who have already learned.

Balanced sentences are heavily emphatic but require thoughtful planning. When used carefully, they can be an especially effective way to alert readers to a strong contrast between two ideas.

Exercise 1
Writing cumulative and periodic sentences

Underline the main clause in each sentence below, and identify the sentence as cumulative or periodic. Then rewrite each cumulative sentence as a periodic one and each periodic sentence as a cumulative one.

1. One of the most disastrous cultural influences ever to hit America was Walt Disney's Mickey Mouse, that idiot optimist who each week marched forth in Technicolor against a battalion of cats, invariably humiliating them with one clever trick after another. —JAMES A. MICHENER
2. At length, in the beginning of May, with the help of some of my acquaintances, rather to improve so good an occasion for neighborliness than from any necessity, I set up the frame of my house. —HENRY DAVID THOREAU
3. Thirty years later, when the country was aroused by a rash of political assassinations—the Kennedys, King, Malcolm X—Congress passed the Gun Control Act of 1968. —JERVIS ANDERSON
4. Matthew's children worked two years to get him out of jail—writing letters, seeing lawyers, attending meetings—because they knew him to be honest and believed him to be innocent.
5. Aspiring writers can learn much from waiting on tables, eavesdropping on conversations to sharpen their ear for dialogue and to pick up promising story material.

Exercise 2
Sentence combining: Cumulative and periodic sentences

Combine each group of sentences below into a single cumulative sentence and then into a single periodic sentence. You will have to add, delete, change, and rearrange words. Each item has more than two possible answers. Does the cumulative or the periodic sentence seem more effective to you?

Example:

The woman refused any treatment. She felt that her life was completed. She wished to die.

Cumulative: The woman refused any treatment, feeling that her life was completed and wishing to die.

Periodic: Feeling that her life was completed and wishing to die, the woman refused any treatment.

1. Pat Taylor strode into the packed room. He was greeting "Taylor's Kids." He was nodding to their parents and teachers.
2. This wealthy Louisiana oilman had promised his "Kids" free

ANSWERS: EXERCISE 1

1. The main clause is *One . . . Mouse*. The sentence is cumulative. Rewritten as a periodic sentence:
   An idiot optimist, each week marching forth in Technicolor against a battalion of cats, invariably humiliating them with one clever trick after another, Walt Disney's Mickey Mouse was one of the most disastrous influences ever to hit America.
2. The main clause is *I . . . house*. The sentence is periodic. Rewritten as a cumulative sentence:
   I set up the frame of my house at length, in the beginning of May, with the help of some of my acquaintances, rather to improve so good an occasion for neighborliness than from any necessity.
3. The main clause is *Congress . . . 1968*. The sentence is periodic. Rewritten as a cumulative sentence:
   Congress passed the Gun Control Act of 1968 thirty years later, when the country was aroused by a rash of political assassinations—the Kennedys, King, Malcolm X.
4. The main clause is *Matthew's . . . jail*. The sentence is cumulative. Rewritten as a periodic sentence:
   Writing letters, seeing lawyers, and attending meetings—because they knew their father to be honest and believed him to be innocent—Matthew's children worked two years to get him out of jail.
5. The main clause is *Aspiring . . . tables*. The sentence is cumulative. Rewritten as a periodic sentence:
   Eavesdropping on conversations to sharpen their ear for dialogue and to pick up promising story materials, aspiring writers can learn much from waiting on tables.

emph
18a

COLLABORATIVE LEARNING

ANSWERS: EXERCISE 2
Possible Answers

1. *Cumulative:* Pat Taylor strode into the packed room, greeting "Taylor's Kids" and nodding to their parents and teachers.
   Periodic: Greeting "Taylor's Kids" and nodding to their parents and teachers, Pat Taylor strode into the packed room.

2. *Cumulative:* This wealthy Louisiana oilman had promised his "kids" free college educations because he was determined to make higher education available to all qualified but disadvantaged students.
   Periodic: Because he was determined to make higher education available to all qualified but disadvantaged students, this wealthy Louisiana oilman had promised his "kids" free college educations.

3. *Cumulative:* The students sang "You Are the Wind Beneath My Wings," their faces beaming with hope, their eyes flashing with self-confidence.
   Periodic: Their faces beaming with hope, their eyes flashing with self-confidence, the students sang "You Are the Wind Beneath My Wings."

4. *Cumulative:* A college education had been beyond their dreams, seeming too costly and too demanding.
   Periodic: Seeming too costly and too demanding, a college education had been beyond their dreams.

5. *Cumulative:* Taylor created a bold plan for free college educations, rewarding good students, encouraging greater involvement of parents, and inspiring teachers to work more imaginatively.
   Periodic: Rewarding good students, encouraging greater involvement of parents, and inspiring teachers to work more imaginatively, Taylor created a bold plan for free college educations.

COLLABORATIVE LEARNING

ANSWERS: EXERCISE 3
Possible Answers

1. Remembering her days as a "conductor" on the Underground Railroad made Harriet Tubman proud, but <u>remembering</u> her years as a slave made her angry.
2. Harriet wanted freedom regardless of personal danger, whereas her husband, John, <u>wanted</u> personal safety regardless of freedom.
3. Harriet proved her fearlessness in many ways: she disobeyed John's order not to run away, she led hundreds of other slaves to freedom, and she was a spy for the North during the Civil War.

college educations. He was determined to make higher education available to all qualified but disadvantaged students.

3. The students sang "You Are the Wind Beneath My Wings." Their faces beamed with hope. Their eyes flashed with self-confidence.
4. A college education had been beyond their dreams. It had seemed too costly. It had seemed too demanding.
5. Taylor created a bold plan for free college educations. He rewarded good students. He encouraged greater involvement of parents. He inspired teachers to work more imaginatively.

Exercise 3
Revising: Series and balanced elements

Revise the following sentences so that elements in a series or balanced elements are arranged to give maximum emphasis to main ideas.

Example:

The campers were stranded without matches, without food or water, and without a tent.

The campers were stranded without matches, without a tent, and without food or water.

1. Remembering her days as a "conductor" on the Underground Railroad made Harriet Tubman proud, but she got angry when she remembered her years as a slave.
2. Harriet wanted freedom regardless of personal danger, whereas for her husband, John, personal safety was more important than freedom.
3. Harriet proved her fearlessness in many ways: she led hundreds of other slaves to freedom, she was a spy for the North during the Civil War, and she disobeyed John's order not to run away.
4. To conduct slaves north to freedom, Harriet risked being returned to slavery, being hanged for a huge reward, and being caught by Southern patrollers.
5. After the war Harriet worked tirelessly for civil rights and women's suffrage; raising money for homes for needy former slaves was something else she did.

18b **Repeating ideas**

Although repetition often clutters and weakens sentences, careful repetition of key words and phrases can be an effective means of emphasis. Such repetition often combines with parallelism. It may occur in a series of sentences within a paragraph (see

3b-3). Or it may occur in a series of words, phrases, or clauses within a sentence, as in the following examples.

> We have the tools, all the tools—we are suffocating in tools—but we cannot find the actual wood to work or even the actual hand to work it. —ARCHIBALD MACLEISH

> Government comes from below, not above; government comes from men, not from kings or lords or military masters; government looks to the source of all power in the consent of men. —HENRY STEELE COMMAGER

18c Separating ideas

When you save important information for the end of a sentence, you can emphasize it even more by setting it off from the rest of the sentence. The second example below illustrates how putting an important idea in a separate sentence can highlight it.

> Boys are wild animals, rich in the treasures of sense, but the New England boy had a wider range of emotions than boys of more equable climates, for he felt his nature crudely, as it was meant.

> Boys are wild animals, rich in the treasures of sense, but the New England boy had a wider range of emotions than boys of more equable climates. He felt his nature crudely, as it was meant. —HENRY ADAMS

You can vary the degree of emphasis by varying the extent to which you separate one idea from the others. A semicolon provides more separation than a comma, and a period provides still more separation. Compare the following sentences.

> Most of the reading which is praised for itself is neither literary nor intellectual, but narcotic.

> Most of the reading which is praised for itself is neither literary nor intellectual; it is narcotic.

> Most of the reading which is praised for itself is neither literary nor intellectual. It is narcotic. —DONALD HALL

Sometimes a dash or a pair of dashes will isolate and thus emphasize a part of a statement (see also 25b).

> His schemes were always elaborate, ingenious, and exciting—and wholly impractical.

> Athletics—that is, winning athletics—have become a profitable university operation.

4. To conduct slaves north to freedom, Harriet risked being caught by Southern patrollers, being returned to slavery, and being hanged for a huge reward.
5. After the war, Harriet worked tirelessly for civil rights and women's suffrage; she also raised money for homes for needy former slaves.

REWRITE

Take a passage from a student essay or a professional essay and ask students to rewrite it, using different sentence patterns that give different emphasis to the content of the sentences. Split the class into groups and have them compare their versions with the original, trying to identify a new version that is in some ways clearer than the original and that contains more appropriate emphasis on the main ideas. Since students may well have decided to emphasize different ideas from those emphasized by the original writer, their analysis of the versions may involve matters of content as well as style.

emph
18c

emph
18d

ANSWERS: EXERCISE 4
Possible Answers

1. One of the few worthwhile habits is daily reading: <u>reading for</u> information, <u>reading for</u> entertainment, <u>reading for</u> a broader view of the world.
2. Reading introduces new words and introduces <u>varied styles of expression</u>.
3. Students who read a great deal will write essays that are vivid, well structured, and grammatically correct. <u>These students will have absorbed the style and sentence structures of other authors.</u>
4. Reading gives <u>knowledge about</u> other cultures, <u>knowledge about</u> history and current events, and <u>knowledge about</u> human nature.
5. As a result of reading, writers have more resources and more flexibility. <u>Thus, reading creates better writers.</u>

Exercise 4
Emphasizing with repetition or separation

Emphasize the main idea in each sentence or group of sentences below by following the instructions in parentheses: either combine sentences so that parallelism and repetition stress the main idea, or place the main idea in a separate sentence. Each item has more than one possible answer.

Example:

I try to listen to other people's opinions. When my mind is closed, I find that other opinions open it. And they can change my mind when it is wrong. (*Parallelism and repetition.*)

I try to listen to other people's opinions, for they can open my mind when it is closed and they can change my mind when it is wrong.

1. One of the few worthwhile habits is daily reading. One can read for information. One can read for entertainment. Reading can give one a broader view of the world. (*Parallelism and repetition.*)
2. Reading introduces new words. One encounters varied styles of expression through reading. (*Parallelism and repetition.*)
3. Students who read a great deal will write essays that are vivid, well structured, and grammatically correct, for these students will have absorbed the style and sentence structures of other authors. (*Separation.*)
4. Reading gives knowledge. One gets knowledge about other cultures. One will know about history and current events. One gains knowledge about human nature. (*Parallelism and repetition.*)
5. As a result of reading, writers have more resources and more flexibility, and thus reading creates better writers. (*Separation.*)

18d **Preferring the active voice**

In the **active voice** of the verb, the subject acts: *I peeled the onions.* In the **passive voice** the subject is acted upon: *The onions were peeled by me.* In the passive voice the actor is either relegated to a phrase (*by me*) or omitted entirely: *The onions were peeled.* (See pp. 242–44 for a more detailed explanation of voice.)

<u>The passive voice is indirect</u> because it obscures or removes the actor. The active voice is more direct, vigorous, and emphatic. Further, all sentences turn on their verbs, which give sentences

their motion, pushing them along. And active verbs push harder than passive ones.

Passive	For energy conservation it is urged that all lights be turned off when not being used. [Who is urging? Who is to turn the lights off?]
Active	To save energy, *students should turn off* all lights they are not using.
Passive	The new outpatient clinic was opened by the hospital administration so that the costs of nonemergency medical care would be reduced.
Active	The hospital *administration opened* the new outpatient clinic to reduce the costs of nonemergency medical care.

Sometimes the actor is unknown or unimportant, and many technical writers deliberately omit the actor in order to give impersonal emphasis to what is being acted upon. In these cases the passive voice can be useful.

Wellington was called the "Iron Duke."
Thousands of people are killed annually in highway accidents.
The mixture was then stirred.

Except in these situations, however, rely on the active voice. It is economical and creates movement. (See also 31c-3.)

emph
18e

18e   Being concise

Conciseness—brevity of expression—aids emphasis no matter what the sentence structure. Unnecessary words detract from necessary words. They clutter sentences and obscure ideas.

Weak	In my opinion the competition in the area of grades is distracting. It distracts many students from their goal, which is to obtain an education that is good. There seems to be a belief among a few students that grades are more important than what is measured by them.
Emphatic	The competition for grades distracts many students from their goal of obtaining a good education. A few students seem to believe that grades are more important than what they measure.

Because conciseness comes mainly from deleting unneeded words, it receives detailed coverage in Chapter 31, on choosing and using words (see 31c). The box below summarizes that discussion.

Ways to achieve conciseness

- Cut or shorten empty words or phrases (31c-1).
  Shorten filler phrases, such as *by virtue of the fact that.*
  Cut all-purpose words, such as *area, factor.*
  Cut unneeded qualifiers, such as *in my opinion, for the most part.*
- Cut unnecessary repetition (31c-2).
- Simplify word groups and sentences (31c-3).
  Combine sentences.
  Replace clauses with phrases and phrases with single words.
  Use strong verbs.
  Rewrite passive sentences as active.
  Avoid expletive constructions beginning *there is* or *it is.*
- Cut or rewrite jargon (31c-4).

ANSWERS: EXERCISE 5
Possible Answers

1. <u>Customers in restaurants</u> must be wary of suggestive selling.
2. In suggestive selling, <u>the waiter asks diners</u> to buy additional menu selections <u>besides</u> what <u>they ordered.</u>
3. For each item on the menu, <u>another food will</u> naturally complement it.
4. For example, <u>the waiter will ask</u> customers if they want French fries with a sandwich or salad with a steak dinner.
5. <u>Customers who</u> give in to suggestive <u>selling often</u> find that their restaurant meals <u>cost more</u> than they had intended to pay.

Exercise 5
Revising: Active voice; conciseness

Revise the following sentences to make them more emphatic by converting passive to active voice and by eliminating wordiness. (For additional exercises with the passive voice, see pp. 208, 244, and 500.)

Example:

The problem in this particular situation is that we owe more money than we can afford under present circumstances.

The *problem is* that we owe more money than we can afford.

1. As far as I am concerned, customers who are dining out in restaurants in our country must be wary of suggestive selling, so to speak.
2. In suggestive selling, diners are asked by the waiter to buy additional menu selections in addition to what was ordered by them.
3. For each item on the menu, there is another food that will naturally complement it.
4. For example, customers will be asked if they want French fries with a sandwich or salad with a steak dinner.

5. Due to the fact that customers often give in to suggestive sell-ing, they often find that their restaurant meals are more costly than they had intended to pay.

Exercise 6
Revising: Emphasizing main ideas

Drawing on the advice in this chapter, rewrite the following para-graph to emphasize main ideas and to de-emphasize less impor-tant information.

In preparing pasta, there is a requirement for common sense and imagination rather than for complicated recipes. The key to success in this area is fresh ingredients for the sauce and per-fectly cooked pasta. The sauce may be made with just about any fresh fish, meat, cheese, herb, or vegetable. As for the pasta itself, it may be dried or fresh, although fresh pasta is usually more del-icate and flavorful, as many experienced cooks have found. Dried pasta is fine with zesty sauces; with light oil and cream sauces fresh pasta is best used. There is a difference in the cooking time for dried and fresh pasta, with dried pasta taking longer. It is im-portant that the package directions be followed by the cook and that the pasta be tested before the cooking time is up. The pasta is done when the texture is neither tough nor mushy but *al dente,* or "firm to the bite," according to the Italians, who ought to know.

Note: See page 372 for an exercise involving emphasis along with parallelism and other techniques for effective sentences.

See page 372 for an exercise involving emphasis

COLLABORATIVE LEARNING

ANSWERS: EXERCISE 6
Possible Revision

Preparing pasta requires common sense and imagination rather than complicated recipes. The key to success is fresh ingredients for the sauce and perfectly cooked pasta. The sauce may con-tain just about any fresh fish, meat, cheese, herb, or vegetable. The pasta itself may be dried or fresh, although many experienced cooks find fresh pasta more delicate and flavorful. Dried pasta is fine with zesty sauces; fresh pasta is best with light oil and cream sauces. Dried pasta takes longer to cook than fresh pasta does. The cook should follow the package directions and should test the pasta before the cooking time is up. Ac-cording to the Italians, who ought to know, the pasta is done when the texture is neither tough nor mushy but al dente, or "firm to the bite."

emph
18e

This chapter asks students to think of sentences not as single units but as a sequence of ideas working together. Coordination, subordination, parallelism, and emphasis—topics covered in the preceding chapters—all come into play in the examples in this chapter. You will probably want to direct attention to the introduction to this chapter and to the first two sections, covering strategies for varying the length and structure of sentences and for varying sentence beginnings. You may have to decide, though, how much time to devote to the last two sections, which cover the occasional uses of inverted sentence order and of minor sentence types such as questions and commands.

Chapter 19

Achieving Variety

In a paragraph or an essay, sentences do not stand one by one. Rather, each stands in relation to those before and after it. To make sentences work together effectively, the writer must vary their length, structure, and word order to reflect the importance and complexity of ideas. Although experienced writers generally find that variety takes care of itself as they commit ideas to paper, inexperienced writers often have difficulty achieving variety without guidance and practice.

Ways to achieve variety among sentences

- Vary the length and structure of sentences so that important ideas stand out (19a).
- Vary the beginnings of sentences with modifiers, transitional words and expressions, and occasional expletive constructions (19b).
- Occasionally, invert the normal order of subject, predicate, and object or complement (19c).
- Use an occasional command, question, or exclamation (19d).

A series of similar sentences will prove monotonous and ineffective, as this passage illustrates:

Ulysses S. Grant and Robert E. Lee met on April 9, 1865. Their meeting place was the parlor of a modest house at Appomattox Court House, Virginia. They met to work out the terms for the surrender of Lee's Army of Northern Virginia. One great chapter of American life ended with their meeting, and another began. Grant and Lee were bringing the Civil War to its virtual finish. Other armies still had to surrender, and the fugitive Confederate government would struggle desperately and vainly. It would try to find some way to go on living with its chief support gone. Grant and Lee had signed the papers, however, and it was all over in effect.

These eight sentences are all between twelve and sixteen words long (counting initials and dates), they are about equally detailed, and they all consist of one or two main clauses beginning with the subject. At the end of the passage we have a sense of names, dates, and events but no sure sense of how they relate.

Now compare the preceding passage with the actual passage written by Bruce Catton. Here the few sentences range from eleven to fifty-five words, and only one of the sentences begins with its subject.

When Ulysses S. Grant and Robert E. Lee met in the parlor of a modest house at Appomattox Court House, Virginia, on April 9, 1865, to work out the terms for the surrender of Lee's Army of Northern Virginia, a great chapter in American life came to a close, and a great new chapter began.

> Suspenseful periodic sentence (18a-1) focuses attention on meeting. Details of place, time, and cause are in opening subordinate clause.

These men were bringing the Civil War to its virtual finish. To be sure, other armies had yet to surrender, and for a few days the fugitive Confederate government would struggle desperately and vainly, trying to find some way to go on living now that its chief support was gone. But in effect it was all over when Grant and Lee signed the papers.

> Short sentence sums up.
>
> Cumulative sentence (18a-1) reflects lingering obstacles to peace.
>
> Short final sentence indicates futility of further struggle.

——Bruce Catton, "Grant and Lee"

In these paragraphs the sentence variety underscores, even dramatizes, the fact that the meeting ended the war and marked a turning point in American history.

The rest of this chapter suggests how you can vary your sentences for the kind of interest and clarity achieved by Catton.

RESOURCES AND IDEAS

Jane R. Walpole, "The Vigorous Pursuit of Grace and Style," *The Writing Instructor* 1 (1982): 163–69. Walpole describes six ways students can manipulate a good but not great passage (improving their own prose in the process), along with an example to show how the procedure works.

var
19

var
19a

19a   Varying sentence length and structure

The sentences of a stylistically effective essay will differ most obviously in their length. Further, some sentences will consist only of one main clause with modifiers, others of two main clauses; some will be cumulative, and a few perhaps will be periodic. (See 18a-1.) This variation in length and structure marks mature writing, making it both readable and clear.

1   Varying length

In most contemporary writing, sentences tend to vary from about ten words on the short side to about forty words on the long. The average is between fifteen and twenty-five words, depending on the writer's purpose and style.

Your sentences should not be all at one extreme or the other; if they are, your readers may have difficulty focusing on main ideas and seeing the relations among them. If most of your sentences contain thirty-five words or more, you probably need to break some up into shorter, simpler sentences. If most of your sentences contain fewer than ten or fifteen words, you probably need to add details to them or combine them through coordination and subordination. Examine your writing particularly for a common problem: strings of main clauses, subjects first, in either simple or compound sentences.

2   Rewriting strings of brief and simple sentences

A series of brief and simple sentences is both monotonous and hard to understand because it forces the reader to sort out relations among ideas. If you find that you depend on brief, simple sentences, work to increase variety by combining some of them into longer units that emphasize and link new and important ideas while de-emphasizing old or incidental information. (See 16a, 16b, and 18a.)

The following example shows how a string of simple sentences can be revised into an effective piece of writing.

Weak

The moon is now drifting away from the earth. It moves away at the rate of about one inch a year. Our days on earth are getting longer. They grow a thousandth of a second longer every cen-

tury. A month might become forty-seven of our present days
long. We might eventually lose the moon altogether. Such great
planetary movement rightly concerns astronomers. It need not
worry us. The movement will take 50 million years.

Revised

The moon is now drifting away from the earth, moving at the rate
of about one inch a year. And at the rate of a thousandth of a second or so every century, our days on earth are getting longer.
Someday, a month will be forty-seven of our present days long, if
we don't eventually lose the moon altogether. Such great planetary movement rightly concerns astronomers, but it need not
concern us. It will take 50 million years.

In the first passage the choppy movement of the nine successive
simple sentences leaves the reader with nine independent facts
and a lame conclusion. The revision retains all the facts of the
original but compresses them into five sentences that are structured to emphasize and show relations among main ideas: the
moon's movement (sentence 1), our lengthening days (2), and the
enormous span of time involved (5).

var

19a

 3   **Rewriting strings of compound sentences**

Because compound sentences are usually just simple sentences linked with conjunctions, a series of them will be as weak
as a series of brief simple sentences, especially if the clauses of
the compound sentences are all about the same length.

Weak

The hotel beach faces the south, and the main street runs along
the north side of the hotel. The main street is heavily traveled
and often noisy, but the beach is always quiet and sunny. It was a
Sunday afternoon, and we were on the hotel beach. We lay
stretched out on the sand, and the sun poured down on us.

Revised

The main street, heavily traveled and often noisy, runs along the
north side of the hotel. But on the south side the hotel beach is
always quiet and sunny. On a Sunday afternoon we lay there
stretched out on the sand, letting the sun pour down on us.

The first passage creates a seesaw effect. The revision, with some
main clauses changed into modifiers and repositioned, is both
clearer and more emphatic. (See 16a-2 for additional discussion of
how to avoid excessive coordination within sentences.)

ANSWERS: EXERCISE 1
Possible Revisions

1. Charlotte Perkins Gilman was a leading intellectual in the women's movement during the first decades of this century. Her book *Women and Economics* challenged Victorian assumptions about the differences between the sexes and explored the economic root of women's oppression. Gilman wrote little about gaining the vote for women, the issue that then preoccupied feminists and that historians have since focused their analyses on. As a result, Gilman's contribution to today's women's movement has often been overlooked.

2. Nathaniel Hawthorne was one of America's first great writers. He was descended from a judge who had presided at some of the Salem witch trials and had condemned some men and women to death. Hawthorne could never forget about this piece of family history, and he always felt guilty about it. Though he never wrote about his ancestor directly, he did write about the darkness of the human heart. In *The Scarlet Letter* and *The House of the Seven Gables,* he demonstrated his favorite theme: a secret sin.

RESOURCES AND IDEAS

William J. Vande Kopple, *Clear and Coherent Prose: A Functional Approach* (New York: HarperCollins, 1989). Vande Kopple offers detailed advice about creating clear and emphatic sentences, including helpful suggestions for sentence beginnings.

var
19b

Exercise 1
Revising: Varied sentence structures

Rewrite the following paragraphs to increase variety so that important ideas receive greater emphasis than supporting information does. You will have to change some main clauses into modifiers and then combine and reposition the modifiers and the remaining main clauses.

1. Charlotte Perkins Gilman was a leading intellectual in the women's movement during the first decades of this century. She wrote *Women and Economics*. This book challenged Victorian assumptions about differences between the sexes. It explored the economic roots of women's oppression. Gilman wrote little about gaining the vote for women. Many feminists were then preoccupied with this issue. Historians have since focused their analyses on this issue. As a result, Gilman's contribution to today's women's movement has often been overlooked.

2. Nathaniel Hawthorne was one of America's first great writers, and he was descended from a judge. The judge had presided at some of the Salem witch trials, and he had condemned some men and women to death. Hawthorne could never forget this piece of family history, and he always felt guilty about it. He never wrote about his ancestor directly, but he did write about the darkness of the human heart. He wrote *The Scarlet Letter* and *The House of the Seven Gables,* and in those books he demonstrated his favorite theme of a secret sin.

19b Varying sentence beginnings

Most English sentences begin with their subjects.

The defendant's lawyer relentlessly cross-examined the stubborn witness for two successive days.

However, an unbroken sequence of sentences beginning with the subject quickly becomes monotonous, as shown by the passage on Grant and Lee that opened this chapter (p. 363). Your final arrangement of sentence elements should always depend on two concerns: the relation of a sentence to those preceding and following it and the emphasis required by your meaning. When you do choose to vary the subject-first pattern, you have several options.

Adverb modifiers

Adverb modifiers can often be placed at a variety of spots in a sentence. Consider these different emphases:

For two successive days, the defendant's lawyer *relentlessly* cross-examined the stubborn witness.

Relentlessly, the defendant's lawyer cross-examined the stubborn witness *for two successive days.*

Relentlessly, for two successive days, the defendant's lawyer cross-examined the stubborn witness.

Notice that the last sentence, with both modifiers at the beginning, is periodic and thus highly emphatic (see 18a-1).

Participial phrases

Beginning a sentence with a participial phrase also postpones the subject and sometimes creates a periodic sentence.

The lawyer thoroughly cross-examined the witness and then called the defendant herself to testify.

Having thoroughly cross-examined the witness, the lawyer called the defendant herself to testify.

Coordinating conjunctions and transitional expressions

When the relation between two successive sentences demands, you may begin the second with a coordinating conjunction or with a transitional expression such as *first, for instance, however, in addition, moreover,* or *therefore.* (See 3b-6 for a list of transitional expressions.)

The witness expected to be dismissed after his first long day of cross-examination. He was not; the defendant's lawyer called him again the second day.

The witness expected to be dismissed after his first long day of cross-examination. *But* he was not; the defendant's lawyer called him again the second day.

The price of clothes has risen astronomically in recent years. The cheap cotton shirt that once cost $6.00 and now costs $25.00 is an example.

The price of clothes has risen astronomically in recent years. *For example,* a cheap cotton shirt that once cost $6.00 now costs $25.00.

Occasional expletive constructions

An expletive construction—*it* or *there* plus a form of *be*—may occasionally be useful to delay and thus emphasize the subject of the sentence.

His judgment seems questionable, not his desire.
It is his judgment that seems questionable, not his desire.

However, expletive constructions are more likely to flatten writing by adding extra words. You should use them rarely, only when you can justify doing so. (See also 31c-3.)

ANSWERS: EXERCISE 2

1. Some people are champion procrastinators. Consequently, they seldom complete their work on time.
2. If procrastinators fear criticism, they will delay completing an assignment.
3. Procrastinators often desire to please a boss or a teacher. Yet they fear failure so much that they cannot do the work.
4. Although procrastination seems a hopeless habit, it is conquerable.
5. Helpfully encouraging procrastinators, teachers or employers can give them the confidence to do good work on time.

COLLABORATIVE LEARNING

ANSWERS: EXERCISE 3
Possible Revision

When scientists in Egypt dug up 40-million-year-old fossil bones, they had evidence of primitive whales. Called mesonychids, the whale ancestors were small, furry land animals with four legs. These limbs were complete with kneecaps, ankles, and little toes. In contrast, gigantic modern whales have tiny hind legs inside their bodies and flippers instead of front legs. But scientists are certain that these two very different creatures share the same family tree.

Exercise 2
Revising: Varied sentence beginnings

Revise each pair of sentences below, following the instructions in parentheses to make a single sentence that begins with an adverb modifier or a participial phrase, or to make one of the two sentences begin with an appropriate coordinating conjunction or transitional expression.

> *Example:*
> The *Seabird* took first place. It moved quickly in the wind. (*One sentence with participial phrase beginning moving.*)
> *Moving quickly in the wind,* the *Seabird* took first place.

1. Some people are champion procrastinators. They seldom complete their work on time. (*Two sentences with transitional expression.*)
2. Procrastinators may fear criticism. They will delay completing an assignment. (*One sentence with adverb modifier beginning if.*)
3. Procrastinators often desire to please a boss or a teacher. They fear failure so much that they cannot do the work. (*Two sentences with coordinating conjunction.*)
4. Procrastination seems a hopeless habit. It is conquerable. (*One sentence with adverb modifier beginning although.*)
5. Teachers or employers can be helpful as they encourage procrastinators. The teachers or employers can give them the confidence to do good work on time. (*One sentence with participial phrase beginning helpfully.*)

Exercise 3
Revising: Varied sentence beginnings

Revise the following paragraph to vary sentence beginning by using each of the following at least once: an adverb modifier, a participial phrase, a coordinating conjunction, and a transitional expression.

Scientists in Egypt dug up 40-million-year-old fossil bones. They had evidence of primitive whales. The whale ancestors are called mesonychids. They were small, furry land mammals with four legs. These limbs were complete with kneecaps, ankles, and little toes. Gigantic modern whales have tiny hind legs inside their bodies and flippers instead of front legs. Scientists are certain that these two very different creatures share the same family tree.

19c   Inverting the normal word order

Inverted sentences such as *Up came the dawn* and *Mutton he didn't like* are infrequent in modern prose. Because the word order of subject, verb, and object or complement is so strongly fixed in English, an inverted sentence can be emphatic.

Harry had once been a dog lover. Then his neighbor's barking dogs twice raced through his garden. Now *all dogs,* especially barking dogs, *Harry detests.*

Inverting the normal order of subject, verb, and complement can be useful in two successive sentences when the second expands on the first.

Critics have not been kind to Presidents who have tried to apply the ways of private business to public affairs. Particularly *explicit was the curt verdict* of one critic of President Hoover: Mr. Hoover was never President of the United States; he was four years chairman of the board.   —Adapted from EMMET JOHN HUGHES, "The Presidency vs. Jimmy Carter"

Inverted sentences used without need are artificial. Avoid descriptive sentences such as *Up came Larry and down went Cindy's spirits.*

19d   Mixing types of sentences

var
19d

Most written sentences make statements. Occasionally, however, questions, commands, or, more rarely, exclamations may enhance variety.

Questions may set the direction of a paragraph, as in *What does a detective do?* or *How is the percentage of unemployed workers calculated?* More often, though, the questions used in exposition or argument do not require answers but simply emphasize ideas that readers can be expected to agree with. Such **rhetorical questions** are illustrated in the following passage.

Another word that has ceased to have meaning due to overuse is *attractive. Attractive* has become verbal chaff. Who, by some

USING FORMS

Tell students to write a paragraph making use of the strategies suggested in this chapter. Leave the content of the paragraph up to them; they will discover how form can help suggest content.

stretch of language and imagination, cannot be described as attractive? And just what is it that attractive individuals are attracting?
—DIANE WHITE

Commands occur frequently in an explanation of a process, particularly in directions, as this passage on freewriting illustrates.

The idea is simply to write for ten minutes (later on, perhaps fifteen or twenty). Don't stop for anything. Go quickly, without rushing. Never stop to look back, to cross something out, to wonder how to spell something, to wonder what word or thought to use, or to think about what you are doing.   —PETER ELBOW

Notice that the authors of these examples use questions and commands not merely to vary their sentences but to achieve some special purpose. Variety occurs because a particular sentence type is effective for the context, not because the writer set out to achieve variety for its own sake.

var
19d

Exercise 4
Writing varied sentences

Imagine that you are writing an essay either on the parking problem at your school or on the problems of living in a dormitory. Practice varying sentences by composing a sentence or passage to serve each purpose listed below.

1. Write a question that could open the essay.
2. Write a command that could open the essay.
3. Write an exclamation that could open the essay.
4. For the body of the essay, write an appropriately varied paragraph of at least five sentences, including at least one short and one long sentence beginning with the subject; at least one sentence beginning with an adverb modifier; at least one sentence beginning with a coordinating conjunction or transitional expression; and one rhetorical question or command.

Exercise 5
Analyzing variety

Examine the following paragraph for sentence variety. By analyzing your own response to each sentence, try to explain why the author wrote each short or long sentence, each cumulative or periodic sentence, each sentence beginning with its subject or beginning some other way, and each question.

That night in my rented room, while letting the hot water run over my can of pork and beans in the sink, I opened [H. L. Mencken's] *A Book of Prefaces* and began to read. I was jarred and shocked by the style, the clear, clean, sweeping sentences. Why did he write like that? And how did one write like that? I pictured the man as a raging demon, slashing with his pen, consumed with hate, denouncing everything American, extolling everything European or German, laughing at the weaknesses of people, mocking God, authority. What was this? I stood up, trying to realize what reality lay behind the meaning of the words. Yes, this man was fighting, fighting with words. He was using words as a weapon, using them as one would use a club. Could words be weapons? Well, yes, for here they were. Then, maybe, perhaps, I could use them as a weapon? No. It frightened me. I read on and what amazed me was not what he said, but how on earth anybody had the courage to say it.   —RICHARD WRIGHT, *Black Boy*

Exercise 6
Revising: Variety

The following paragraph consists entirely of simple sentences that begin with their subjects. As appropriate, use the techniques discussed in this chapter to vary sentences so that the paragraph is more readable and its important ideas stand out clearly. You will have to delete, add, change, and rearrange words.

The Italian volcano Vesuvius had been dormant for many years. It then exploded on August 24 in the year A.D. 79. The ash, pumice, and mud from the volcano buried two busy towns. Herculaneum is one. The more famous is Pompeii. The ruins of both towns lay undiscovered for many centuries. Herculaneum and Pompeii were discovered in 1709 and 1748, respectively. The excavation of Pompeii was the more systematic. It was the occasion for initiating modern methods of conservation and restoration. The methods replaced earlier practices. Herculaneum was simply looted of its most valuable finds. It was then left to disintegrate. Pompeii appears much as it did before the eruption. A luxurious house opens onto a lush central garden. An election poster decorates a wall. A dining table is set for breakfast.

Note: See the next page for an exercise involving variety along with parallelism and other techniques for effective sentences.

ANSWERS: EXERCISE 5
Possible Answers

The shortest sentence is one word: *No.* The longest is sentence 5, *I pictured the man as . . . .* The opening periodic sentence sets the scene before coming to the point. The longest sentence gains its length and power from the six modifying verbal phrases that convey Wright's first impression of Mencken. Wright relies on questions interspersed with tentative answers to show his own incremental awakening on discovering Mencken. Repetition—*fighting, fighting; using . . . using; maybe, perhaps*—also shows Wright wrestling with what he has found. The last question leads to the conclusion of the final three sentences, which gradually increase in length and complexity.

ANSWERS: EXERCISE 6
Possible Revision

After being dormant for many years, the Italian volcano Vesuvius exploded on August 24 in the year A.D. 79. The ash, pumice, and mud from the volcano buried two towns—Herculaneum and the more famous Pompeii—which lay undiscovered until 1709 and 1748, respectively. The excavation of Pompeii was the more systematic, the occasion for initiating modern methods of conservation and restoration. Whereas Herculaneum was simply looted of its most valuable finds and then left to disintegrate, Pompeii appears much as it did during the eruption. A luxurious house opens onto a lush central garden. An election poster decorates a wall. And a dining table is set for breakfast.

var
19d

ANSWERS: EXERCISE ON CHAPTERS
16–19

Possible Revision

Modern Americans owe many debts to Native Americans, including several pleasures. Native Americans originated two fine junk foods: popcorn and potato chips.

Native Americans introduced popcorn to the European settlers, Massasoit providing popcorn at the first Thanksgiving feast and the Aztecs offering popcorn to the Spanish explorer Hernando Cortés. The Aztecs and natives of the West Indies wore popcorn necklaces. Native Americans popped the corn in three ways. First, they roasted an ear skewered on a stick over the fire and ate the corn that fell outside the flames. Second, they scraped the corn off the cob, threw the kernels into a low fire, and ate the popped kernels that did not fall into the fire. Third and most sophisticated, they heated a shallow pottery vessel containing sand, stirred corn kernels into the hot sand, and ate what popped up to the surface.

A Native American chef named George Crum devised the crunchy potato chip. In 1853 Crum was cooking at Moon Lake Lodge in Saratoga Springs, New York. A customer complained that Crum's French-fried potatoes were too thick. Crum tried a thinner batch, but these were also unsuitable. Frustrated, Crum deliberately made the potatoes so thin and crisp that they could not be cut with a knife and fork. Crum's joke backfired, for the customer raved about the potato chips. Soon these Saratoga Chips appeared on the lodge's menu and throughout New England. Crum later opened his own restaurant, of course offering potato chips.

Now all Americans munch popcorn in movies, crunch potato chips at parties, and gorge on both when alone and bored. They can be grateful to Native Americans for these guilty pleasures.

eff

Exercise on Chapters 16–19
Revising: Effective sentences

Revise the paragraphs below to emphasize main ideas, de-emphasize supporting information, and achieve a pleasing, clear variety in sentences. As appropriate, use subordination, coordination, parallelism, and cumulative, periodic, and balanced sentences. Cut wordiness. Use the active voice. Edit the finished product for punctuation.

Modern Americans owe many debts to Native Americans. Several pleasures are among the debts. Native Americans originated two fine junk foods. They discovered popcorn. Potato chips were also one of their contributions.

Native Americans introduced popcorn to the European settlers. Massasoit provided popcorn at the first Thanksgiving feast. The Aztecs offered popcorn to the Spanish explorer Hernando Cortés. The Aztecs wore popcorn necklaces. So did the natives of the West Indies. There were three ways that the Native Americans popped the corn. First, they roasted an ear over the fire. The ear was skewered on a stick. They ate only some of the popcorn. They ate the corn that fell outside the flames. Second, they scraped the corn off the cob. The kernels would be thrown into the fire. Of course, the fire had to be low. Then the popped kernels that did not fall into the fire were eaten. The third method was the most sophisticated. It involved a shallow pottery vessel. It contained sand. The vessel was heated. The sand soon got hot enough. Corn kernels were stirred in. They popped to the surface of the sand and were eaten.

A Native American chef devised the crunchy potato chip. His name was George Crum. In 1853 Crum was cooking at Moon Lake Lodge. The lodge was in Saratoga Springs, New York. Complaints were sent in by a customer. The man thought Crum's French-fried potatoes were too thick. Crum tried a thinner batch. These were also unsuitable. Crum became frustrated. He deliberately made the potatoes thin and crisp. They could not be cut with a knife and fork. Crum's joke backfired. The customer raved about the potato chips. The chips were named Saratoga Chips. Soon they appeared on the lodge's menu. They also appeared throughout New England. Crum later opened his own restaurant. Of course, he offered potato chips.

Now all Americans munch popcorn in movies. They crunch potato chips at parties. They gorge on both when alone and bored. They can be grateful to Native Americans for these guilty pleasures.

Part V

Punctuation

HIGHLIGHTS

This chart provides sentence examples covering the main features of sentence punctuation, including the comma, the semicolon, the colon, dashes, and parentheses. It also provides a quick reference for such troublesome features as restrictive and nonrestrictive modifiers and items in a series. Students can locate on the chart a sentence like one they have just written to determine how to punctuate it, or they can look at the chart for a particular feature of punctuation whose name they have forgotten and therefore cannot locate in the handbook's index or table of contents.

Because the various punctuation strategies appear together in a short space in this list, students will be able to see the options available to them as they write. In addition, the cross-references give students a chance to explore these options in depth. Instructors, too, should be able to find many uses for the chart, both in class and in working with individual students.

USING THE PUNCTUATION CHAPTERS

The use you make of the chapters in this unit of the text is likely to depend partly on your students and partly on whether you choose to use the chapters solely to teach punctuation or as part of a sentence-combining program. Many college students should need no formal instruction in punctuation, although they, like all of us, will need to check on particular conventions as they write. Other students may

Major internal sentence punctuation
Commas, semicolons, colons, dashes, parentheses
(For explanations, consult the sections in parentheses.)

Sentences with two main clauses

The bus stopped, *but* no one got off. (21a)
The bus stopped; no one got off. (22a)
The bus stopped; *however,* no one got off. (22b)
The mechanic replaced the battery, the distributor cap, and the starter; *but* still the car would not start. (22c)
His duty was clear: he had to report the theft. (25a-1)

Introductory elements

Modifiers (21b)
After the argument was over, we laughed at ourselves.
Racing over the plain, the gazelle escaped the lion.
To dance in the contest, he had to tape his knee.
Suddenly, the door flew open.
With 125 passengers aboard, the plane was half full.
In 1983 he won the Nobel Prize.

Absolute phrases (21d)
Its wing broken, the bird hopped around on the ground.

Interrupting and concluding elements

Nonrestrictive modifiers (21c-1)
Jim's car, *which barely runs,* has been impounded.
We consulted the dean, *who had promised to help us.*
The boy, *like his sister,* wants to be a pilot.
They moved across the desert, *shielding their eyes from the sun.*
The men do not speak to each other, *although they share a car.*

Nonrestrictive appositives
Bergen's daughter, *Candice,* became an actress. (21c-2)
The residents of three counties—*Suffolk, Springfield, and Morrison*—were urged to evacuate. (25b-2)
Father demanded one promise: *that we not lie to him.* (25a-1)

Restrictive modifiers (21j-3)
The car *that hit mine* was uninsured.
We consulted a teacher *who had promised to help us.*
The boy *in the black hat* is my cousin.
They were surprised to find the desert *teeming with life.*
The men do not speak to each other *because they are feuding.*

Restrictive appositives (21j-3)

Shaw's play *Saint Joan* was performed last year.

Their sons *Tony, William, and Steve* all chose military careers, leaving only Joe to run the family business.

Parenthetical expressions

We suspect, *however,* that he will not come. (21c-3)

Jan is respected by many people—*including me.* (25b-2)

George Balanchine (*1904–1983*) was a brilliant choreographer. (25c-1)

Absolute phrases (21d)

The bird, *its wing broken,* hopped about on the ground.

The bird hopped about on the ground, *its wing broken.*

Phrases expressing contrast (21e)

The humidity, *not just the heat,* gives me headaches.

My headaches are caused by the humidity, *not just the heat.*

Concluding summaries and explanations

The movie opened to bad notices: *the characters were judged shallow and unrealistic.* (25a-1)

We dined on gumbo and jambalaya—*a Cajun feast.* (25b-3)

Items in a series

Three or more items

Chimpanzees, gorillas, orangutans, and gibbons are all apes. (21f-1)

The cities singled out for praise were *Birmingham, Alabama; Lincoln, Nebraska; Austin, Texas; and Troy, New York.* (22d)

Two or more adjectives before a noun (21f-2)

Dingy, smelly clothes decorated their room.

The luncheon consisted of *one tiny watercress* sandwich.

Introductory series (25b-3)

Appropriateness, accuracy, and necessity—these criteria should govern your selection of words.

Concluding series

Every word should be *appropriate, accurate, and necessary.* (25a-3)

Every word should meet three criteria: *appropriateness, accuracy, and necessity.* (25a-1)

Pay attention to your words—*to their appropriateness, their accuracy, and their necessity.* (25b-3)

require specific work with the principal uses of the comma, the semicolon, and the apostrophe, and some students may profit from a review of end punctuation.

Almost all students, however, find punctuation of restrictive and nonrestrictive elements a problem, and the extensive discussion in Chapter 21 should prove helpful. Two special features of this discussion are the practical tests for determining whether an element is restrictive or nonrestrictive and the discussion of how the context of a sentence helps determine the role an element plays.

The sentence-combining exercises in Chapters 21 and 22 give students a chance to practice using the comma and the semicolon. These exercises also ask students to create sentences with the structures those marks of punctuation make possible, such as independent clauses joined with a semicolon, nonrestrictive clauses and phrases, and compound sentences. By asking students to complete these exercises, you can encourage variety in sentence structure and style.

If time allows, you might wish to point out to your class how punctuation marks often substitute for other grammatical and semantic signals used in speech.

p

This chapter discusses the three marks of end punctuation: the period, the question mark, and the exclamation point. Although many college students will need no formal instruction in punctuation, some students will benefit from a review of end punctuation. Such a review might emphasize the important role punctuation plays in conveying meaning and in creating subtle shades of meaning—a role students often overlook.

Chapter 20

End Punctuation

THE PERIOD

20a Use a period to end a statement, mild command, or indirect question.

Statements

These are exciting and trying times.
The airline went bankrupt.
The violins played quietly in the background.

Mild commands

Please do not smoke.
Think of the possibilities.
Turn to page 146.

If you are unsure whether to use an exclamation point or a period after a command, use a period. The exclamation point should be used only rarely (see 20f).

An **indirect question** reports what someone has asked but not in the original speaker's own words.

Indirect questions

The judge asked why I had been driving with my lights off in the middle of the night.

Students sometimes wonder whether their teachers read the papers they write.

Abused children eventually stop asking why they are being punished.

20b Use periods with most abbreviations.

Ordinarily, use periods with abbreviations.

p.	B.C.	B.A.	Mr.
D.C.	A.D.	Ph.D.	Mrs.
M.D.	A.M., a.m.	e.g.	Ms.
Dr.	P.M., p.m.		

When an abbreviation falls at the end of a sentence, use only one period: *Government is the business of Washington, D.C.*

Periods are usually dropped from abbreviations for organizations, corporations, and government agencies when more than two words are abbreviated. For example:

IBM	USMC	NFL	AFL-CIO

Check a dictionary for the preferred form of such abbreviations, and see Chapter 28 on abbreviations.

Note that **acronyms**—pronounceable words, such as UNESCO, NATO, VISTA, and WHO, formed from the initial letters of the words in a name—never require periods (see 28b).

Exercise 1
Revising: Periods

Revise the following sentences so that periods are used correctly.

Example:

Several times I wrote to ask when my subscription ended?
Several times I wrote to ask when my subscription ended.

1. The instructor asked when Plato wrote *The Republic?*
2. Give the date within one century
3. The exact date is not known, but it is thought to be around 370 BC..
4. Dr Arn will lecture on Plato at 7:30 PM.
5. The area of the lecture hall is only 1600 sq ft

THE QUESTION MARK

20c Use a question mark after a direct question.

Direct questions

Who will follow her?
What is the difference between these two people?
Will economists ever really understand the economy?

After indirect questions, use a period: *My mother asked why I came in so late.* (See 20a.)

Questions in a series are each followed by a question mark.

The officer asked how many times the suspect had been arrested. Three times? Four times? More than that?

The use of capital letters for questions in a series is optional (see 26a).

Caution: Question marks are never combined with other question marks, exclamation points, periods, or commas.

Faulty	I finally asked myself, "Why are you working at a job you hate?."
Revised	I finally asked myself, "Why are you working at a job you hate?"

 20d Use a question mark within parentheses to indicate doubt about the correctness of a number or date.

The Greek philosopher Socrates was born in 470 (?) B.C. and died in 399 B.C. from drinking poison after having been condemned to death.

Note: Don't use a question mark within parentheses to express sarcasm or irony. Express these attitudes through sentence structure and diction. (See Chapters 18 and 31.)

Faulty	Her friendly (?) criticism did not escape notice.
Revised	Her criticism, *too rough to be genuinely friendly,* did not escape notice.

ANSWERS: EXERCISE 2

1. In Homer's *Odyssey,* Ulysses took seven years to travel from Troy to Ithaca. Or was it eight years? Or more?
2. Ulysses must have wondered whether he would ever make it home.
3. "What man are you and whence?" asks Ulysses's wife, Penelope.
4. Why does Penelope ask, "Where is your city? Your parents?"
5. Penelope does not recognize Ulysses and asks who this stranger is.

Exercise 2
Revising: Question marks

Revise the following sentences so that question marks (along with other punctuation marks) are used correctly.

Example:
"When will it end?," cried the man dressed in rags.
"When will it end?" cried the man dressed in rags.

1. In Homer's *Odyssey,* Ulysses took seven years to travel from Troy to Ithaca. Or was it eight years. Or more?
2. Ulysses must have wondered whether he would ever make it home?
3. "What man are you and whence?," asks Ulysses's wife, Penelope.

4. Why does Penelope ask, "Where is your city? Your parents?"?
5. Penelope does not recognize Ulysses and asks who this stranger is?

EXTRA HELP

The *Little, Brown Workbook* provides additional exercises for students who need more practice with the end marks of punctuation.

THE EXCLAMATION POINT

20e Use an exclamation point after an emphatic statement, interjection, or command.

No! We must not lose this election!
When she saw her rain-soaked term paper, she gasped, "Oh, no!"
Come here immediately!
"Stop!" he yelled.

Follow mild interjections and commands with commas or periods, as appropriate.

No, the response was not terrific.
To prolong your car's life, change its oil regularly.

Caution: Exclamation points are never combined with other exclamation points, question marks, periods, or commas.

Faulty   My father was most emphatic. "I will not give you any more money!," he roared.

Revised   My father was most emphatic. "I will not give you any more money!" he roared.

20f Use exclamation points sparingly.

Don't express sarcasm, irony, or amazement with the exclamation point. Rely on sentence structure and diction to express these attitudes. (See Chapters 18 and 31.)

Faulty   After traveling 4.4 billion miles through space, *Voyager 2* was off-target by 21 miles (!).

Revised   After traveling 4.4 billion miles through space, *Voyager 2* was off target by *a mere* 21 miles.

Relying on the exclamation point for emphasis is like crying wolf: the mark loses its power to impress the reader. Frequent exclamation points can also make writing sound overemotional. In the following passage, the writer could have conveyed ideas more effectively by punctuating sentences with periods.

!
20f

Our city government is a mess! After just six months in office, the mayor has had to fire four city officials! In the same period the city councilors have done nothing but argue! And city services decline with each passing day!

ANSWERS: EXERCISE 3

1. As the firefighters moved their equipment into place, the police shouted, "Move back!"
2. A child's cries could be heard from above: "Help me! Help!"
3. When the child was rescued, the crowd called, "Hooray!"
4. The rescue was the most exciting event of the day.
5. Correct.

Exercise 3
Revising: Exclamation points

Revise the following sentences so that exclamation points (along with other punctuation marks) are used correctly. If a sentence is punctuated correctly as given, circle the number preceding it.

> *Example:*
>
> "Well, now!," he said loudly.
> "Well, now!" he said loudly.

1. As the firefighters moved their equipment into place, the police shouted, "Move back!."
2. A child's cries could be heard from above: "Help me. Help."
3. When the child was rescued, the crowd called "Hooray."
4. The rescue was the most exciting event of the day!
5. Let me tell you about it.

Exercise 4
Revising: End punctuation

Insert appropriate punctuation (periods, question marks, or exclamation points) where needed in the following paragraph.

! 20f

ANSWERS: EXERCISE 4

When visitors first arrive in Hawaii, they often encounter an unexpected language barrier. Standard English is the language of business and government, but many of the people speak Pidgin English. Instead of an excited "Aloha!" the visitors may be greeted with an excited Pidgin "Howzit!" or asked if they know "how fo' find one good hotel." Many Hawaiians question whether Pidgin will hold children back because it prevents communication with the *baoles,* or Caucasians, who run businesses. Yet many others feel that Pidgin is a last defense of ethnic diversity on the islands. To those who want to make Standard English the official language of the state, these Hawaiians may respond, "Just 'cause I speak Pidgin no mean I dumb." They may ask, "Why you no listen?" or, in Standard English, "Why don't you listen?"

COLLABORATIVE LEARNING

When visitors first arrive in Hawaii, they often encounter an unexpected language barrier Standard English is the language of business and government, but many of the people speak Pidgin English Instead of an excited "Aloha" the visitors may be greeted with an excited Pidgin "Howzit" or asked if they know "how fo' find one good hotel" Many Hawaiians question whether Pidgin will hold children back because it prevents communication with the *baoles,* or Caucasians, who run businesses Yet many others feel that Pidgin is a last defense of ethnic diversity on the islands To those who want to make standard English the official language of the state, these Hawaiians may respond, "Just 'cause I speak Pidgin no mean I dumb" They may ask, "Why you no listen" or, in standard English, "Why don't you listen"

Note: See page 450 for a punctuation exercise combining periods with other marks of punctuation.

Chapter 21

The Comma

HIGHLIGHTS

This chapter deals with one of the most frequently misused marks of punctuation—the comma. Although some of the trouble that students have with comma usage may stem from speech patterns (ill-timed pauses, for example) and may be corrected through attention to speech patterns and sentence rhythm, the remainder of the problems generally arise from unfamiliarity with the rules of punctuation. One way to overcome this trouble is to memorize the rules. The chapter, therefore, provides both the rules and examples of the rules in use in a format designed for easy notation and memorization.

The comma is the most frequently used—and misused—mark of internal punctuation. In general, commas function within sentences to separate elements (see the box on the next page). Omitting needed commas or inserting needless ones can confuse the reader, as the following sentences show.

Comma needed	Though very tall Abraham Lincoln was not an overbearing man.
Revised	Though very tall, Abraham Lincoln was not an overbearing man.
Unneeded commas	The hectic pace of Beirut, broke suddenly into frightening chaos when the city became, the focus of civil war.
Revised	The hectic pace of Beirut broke suddenly into frightening chaos when the city became the focus of civil war.

 21a **Use a comma before a coordinating conjunction linking main clauses.**

The coordinating conjunctions are

for	and	or
so	but	nor
yet		

21a

Principal uses of the comma

● To separate main clauses linked by a coordinating conjunction (21a).

The steering was stiff, *but* the car rode smoothly.

● To set off most introductory elements (21b).

Fortunately, the ride would be comfortable.

● To set off nonrestrictive elements (21c).

We dreaded the trip, *which would take sixteen hours.*

Our destination, *Oklahoma City,* was unfamiliar to us.

● To separate items in a series (21f-1).

We would need *a new home, new schools, and new friends.*

● To separate coordinate adjectives (21f-2).

A *bumpy, cramped* ride would have been unbearable.

Other uses of the comma:
   To set off absolute phrases (21d).
   To set off phrases expressing contrast (21e).
   To separate parts of dates, addresses, long numbers (21g).
   To separate quotations and explanatory words (21h).
   To prevent misreading (21i).

See also 21j for when *not* to use the comma.

Words or phrases joined by a coordinating conjunction are *not* separated by a comma: *Bill plays and sings Irish and English folk songs* (see 21j-2). However, main clauses joined by a coordinating conjunction *are* separated by a comma. **Main clauses** are those which have a subject and a predicate (but no subordinating word at the beginning) and make complete statements (see 5c).

> She was perfectly at home in what she knew, *and* what she knew has remained what all of us want to know.
> —EUDORA WELTY on Jane Austen

> He would have turned around again without a word, *but* I seized him.
> —FYODOR DOSTOYEVSKY

> Seventeen years ago this month I quit work, *or,* if you prefer, I retired from business.
> —F. SCOTT FITZGERALD

> They made their decision with some uneasiness, *for* they knew that in such places any failure to conform could cause trouble.
> —RICHARD HARRIS

> In putting on trousers a man always inserts the same old leg first. . . . All men do it, *yet* no man thought it out and adopted it of set purpose.
> —MARK TWAIN

> Near evening I was too jittery to attend to chores, *so* Bailey volunteered to do all before his bath.
> —MAYA ANGELOU

Exceptions: Some writers prefer to use a semicolon before *so* and *yet.*

> Many people say that the institution of marriage is in decline; *yet* recent evidence suggests that the institution is at least holding steady.

When the main clauses in a sentence are very long or grammatically complicated, or when they contain internal punctuation, a semicolon before the coordinating conjunction will clarify the division between clauses (see 22c).

> Life would be dull without its seamier side, its violence, filth, and hatred; *for* otherwise how could we appreciate the joys?
> —ELLEN STEPIK

When main clauses are very short and closely related in meaning, you may omit the comma between them as long as the resulting sentence is clear.

> She opened her mouth *but* no sound came out of it.
> —FLANNERY O'CONNOR

> My heart raced *and* I felt ill.

If you are in doubt about whether to use a comma in such sentences, use it. It will always be correct.

RESOURCES AND IDEAS

Though writing instructors often treat commas and other marks of punctuation as if they were primarily cues to grammatical structures, these marks also function legitimately as stylistic cues, as indicators of the writer's voice—or so argues Wallace Chafe in "What Good Is Punctuation?" (*The Quarterly of the National Writing Project and the Center for the Study of Writing* 10 [1988]: 8–11). Chafe supports his argument with examples from the work of Herman Melville and James Agee and concludes with some useful advice for teaching:

Students, in addition to being sensitized to their inner voices, will benefit from knowing the range of punctuating options that are available, and from being shown, through examples, what is most appropriate to one style and another. They can learn from practice in writing advertising copy as well as the more academic kinds of exposition, and from experimenting with fiction that mimics the very different punctuation styles of, say, Melville and Agee. At the same time, developing writers need to know that there are certain specific rules for punctuating that violate the prosody of their inner voices and that simply have to be learned. These arbitrary rules are few in number and well defined, and to learn them need be no burden. . . . The bottom line is that punctuation contributes substantially to the effectiveness of a piece of writing, and that its successful use calls for an awareness of something that is, for this and other reasons, essential to good writing: a sensitivity to the sound of written language. (11)

RESOURCES AND IDEAS

Emily Meyer and Louise Z. Smith, "Punctuation," *The Practical Tutor* (New York: Oxford, 1987). The authors offer detailed advice for the often frustrating task of helping students develop effective punctuation skills.

$\hat{,}$

21a

ANSWERS: EXERCISE 1

1. Parents once automatically gave their children the father's surname, but some no longer do.
2. Instead, they bestow the mother's name, for they believe that the mother's importance should be recognized.
3. The child's surname may be just the mother's, or it may link the mother's and the father's with a hyphen.
4. Sometimes the first and third children will have the mother's surname, and the second child will have the father's.
5. Occasionally the mother and father combine parts of their names, and a new hybrid surname is born.

⌃
,
21a

ANSWERS: EXERCISE 2
Possible Answers

1. Parents were once legally required to bestow the father's surname on their children, but these laws have been contested in court and found invalid.
2. Parents may now give their children any surname they choose, and the arguments for bestowing the mother's surname are often strong and convincing.
3. Critics sometimes question the effects of unusual surnames on children, or they wonder how confusing or fleeting the new surnames will be.
4. Children with surnames different from their parents' may suffer embarrassment or identity problems, for giving children their father's surname is still very much the norm.
5. Hyphenated names are awkward and difficult to pass on, so some observers think they will die out in the next generation or before.

Exercise 1
Punctuating linked main clauses

Insert a comma before each coordinating conjunction that links main clauses in the following sentences.

Example:

I would have attended the concert and the reception but I had to baby-sit for my niece.

I would have attended the concert and the reception, but I had to baby-sit for my niece.

1. Parents once automatically gave their children the father's surname but some no longer do.
2. Instead, they bestow the mother's name for they believe that the mother's importance should be recognized.
3. The child's surname may be just the mother's or it may link the mother's and the father's with a hyphen.
4. Sometimes the first and third children will have the mother's surname and the second child will have the father's.
5. Occasionally the mother and father combine parts of their names and a new hybrid surname is born.

Exercise 2
Sentence combining: Linked main clauses

Combine each group of sentences below into one sentence that contains only two main clauses connected by the coordinating conjunction in parentheses. Separate the main clauses with a comma. You will have to add, delete, and rearrange words.

Example:

The circus had come to town. The children wanted to see it. Their parents wanted to see it. (*and*)

The circus had come to town, *and* the children and their parents wanted to see it.

1. Parents were once legally required to bestow the father's surname on their children. These laws have been contested in court. They have been found invalid. (*but*)
2. Parents may now give their children any surname they choose. The arguments for bestowing the mother's surname are often strong. They are often convincing. (*and*)
3. Critics sometimes question the effects of unusual surnames on children. They wonder how confusing the new surnames will be. They wonder how fleeting the surnames will be. (*or*)
4. Children with surnames different from their parents' may suffer embarrassment. They may suffer identity problems. Giving children their father's surname is still very much the norm. (*for*)

5. Hyphenated names are awkward. They are also difficult to pass on. Some observers think they will die out in the next generation. Or they may die out before. (*so*)

21b Use a comma to set off most introductory elements.

RESOURCES AND IDEAS

Joseph Collignon, "Why Leroy Can't Write," *College English* 39 (1978): 852–59. Collignon suggests using oral reading to help students punctuate correctly and to provide them with models for writing.

An introductory element modifies a word or words in the main clause that follows. These elements are usually set off from the rest of the sentence with a comma.

Subordinate clauses serving as adverbs (5c-4, 16b)

If Ernest Hemingway had written comic books, they would have been just as good as his novels.   —STAN LEE

After the rains came, the country turned green.

Verbals and verbal phrases (5c-2)

Exhausted, the runner collapsed at the finish line. [Participle.]

To win the most important race of her career, she had nearly killed herself. [Infinitive phrase.]

Prepositional phrases (5c-1)

From Columbus and Sir Walter Raleigh onward, America has been traveling the road west.   —PETER DAVISON

With the end of the century in sight, futurists are multiplying.

Sentence modifiers

Unfortunately, the diamond was fake.

Of course, everyone should have known.

The comma may be omitted after short introductory elements if its omission does not create confusion. (If you are in doubt, however, the comma is always correct.)

Clear	*By the year 2000* the world population will be more than 6 billion.
Clear	*When snow falls* the city collapses.
Confusing	At eighteen people are considered young adults.
Revised	At eighteen, people are considered young adults.

Caution: Take care to distinguish verbals used as modifiers from verbals used as subjects. The former almost always take a comma; the latter never do.

$\overset{\wedge}{,}$
21b

Jogging through the park, I was unexpectedly caught in a downpour. [Participial phrase used as modifier.]

Jogging through the park has become a popular form of recreation for city dwellers. [Gerund phrase used as subject.]

To dance professionally, he trained for years. [Infinitive phrase used as modifier.]

To dance professionally is his one desire. [Infinitive phrase used as subject.]

In addition, do not use a comma to separate a verbal from the noun or pronoun it modifies when the verbal restricts the meaning of the noun or pronoun (see also 21c).

Shuttered houses lined the street. [*Shuttered* restricts *houses.*]

Shuttered, the houses were protected from the elements. [*Shuttered* does not restrict *houses.*]

ANSWERS: EXERCISE 3

1. Veering sharply to the right, a large flock of birds neatly avoids a high wall.
2. Correct.
3. With the help of complex computer simulations, zoologists are learning more about this movement.
4. Because it is sudden and apparently well coordinated, the movement of flocks and schools has seemed to be directed by a leader.
5. Almost incredibly, the group could behave with more intelligence than any individual seemed to possess.
6. However, new studies have discovered that flocks and schools are leaderless.
7. Correct.
8. When each bird or fish senses a predator, it follows individual rules for fleeing.
9. To keep from colliding with its neighbors, each bird or fish uses other rules for dodging.
10. Multiplied over hundreds of individuals, these responses look as if they have been choreographed.

Exercise 3
Punctuating introductory elements

Insert commas where needed after introductory elements in the following sentences. If a sentence is punctuated correctly as given, circle the number preceding it.

Example:

After the new library opened the old one became a student union.

After the new library opened, the old one became a student union.

1. Veering sharply to the right a large flock of birds neatly avoids a high wall.
2. Moving in a fluid mass is typical of flocks of birds and schools of fish.
3. With the help of complex computer simulations zoologists are learning more about this movement.
4. Because it is sudden and apparently well coordinated the movement of flocks and schools has seemed to be directed by a leader.
5. Almost incredibly the group could behave with more intelligence than any individual seemed to possess.
6. However new studies have discovered that flocks and schools are leaderless.
7. Evading danger turns out to be an individual response.
8. When each bird or fish senses a predator it follows individual rules for fleeing.
9. To keep from colliding with its neighbors each bird or fish uses other rules for dodging.

10. Multiplied over hundreds of individuals these responses look as if they have been choreographed.

Exercise 4
Sentence combining: Introductory elements

Combine each pair of sentences below into one sentence that begins with an introductory phrase or clause as specified in parentheses. Follow the introductory element with a comma. You will have to add, delete, change, and rearrange words.

Example:

The girl was humming to herself. She walked upstairs. (*Phrase beginning Humming.*)

Humming to herself, the girl walked upstairs.

1. Scientists have made an effort to explain the mysteries of flocks and schools. They have proposed bizarre magnetic fields and telepathy. (*Phrase beginning In.*)
2. Scientists developed computer models. They have abandoned earlier explanations. (*Clause beginning Since.*)
3. The movement of a flock or school starts with each individual. It is rapidly and perhaps automatically coordinated among individuals. (*Phrase beginning Starting.*)
4. One zoologist observes that human beings seek coherent patterns. He suggests that investigators saw purpose in the movement of flocks and schools where none existed. (*Phrase beginning Observing.*)
5. One may want to study the movement of flocks or schools. Then one must abandon a search for purpose or design. (*Phrase beginning To.*)

ANSWERS: EXERCISE 4
Possible Answers

1. In an effort to explain the mysteries of flocks and schools, scientists have proposed bizarre magnetic fields and telepathy.
2. Since scientists developed computer models, they have abandoned earlier explanations.
3. Starting with each individual, the movement of a flock or school is rapidly and perhaps automatically coordinated among individuals.
4. Observing that human beings seek coherent patterns, one zoologist suggests that investigators saw purpose in the movement of flocks and schools where none existed.
5. To study the movement of flocks or schools, one must abandon a search for purpose or design.

21c Use a comma or commas to set off nonrestrictive elements.

Restrictive and nonrestrictive sentence elements contribute differently to meaning and require different punctuation. A **restrictive element** limits, or restricts, the meaning of the word or words it applies to. Thus it is essential to the meaning of the sentence and cannot be omitted without significantly changing that meaning. Restrictive elements are never set off with punctuation.

Restrictive element

Employees *who work hard* will receive raises. [Not all employees will receive raises. *Who work hard* specifies which ones will.]

A **nonrestrictive element** gives added information about the word or words it applies to, but it does not limit the word or

RESTRICTIVE AND NONRESTRICTIVE PAIRS

Give students a sentence containing a modifying element and ask them to write two brief groups of sentences, one providing a context that requires that the element in the original sentence be restrictive, another requiring a nonrestrictive element.

,
21c

TRANSPARENCY MASTER
AVAILABLE

 A test for restrictive and nonrestrictive elements

1. Identify the element.

   Hai Nguyen *who emigrated from Vietnam* lives in Denver.
   Those *who emigrated with him* live elsewhere.

2. Remove the element. Does the fundamental meaning of the sentence change?

   Hai Nguyen lives in Denver. **No.**
   Those live elsewhere. **Yes.** [Who are *Those?*]

3. If **no,** the element is *nonrestrictive* and *should* be set off with punctuation.

   Hai Nguyen, who emigrated from Vietnam, lives in Denver.

   If **yes,** the element is *restrictive* and should *not* be set off with punctuation.

   Those who emigrated with him live elsewhere.

̂
;
21c

words. It can be omitted from the sentence without changing the essential meaning. Nonrestrictive elements are always set off with punctuation.

Nonrestrictive element

Molly Berman, *who works hard,* got a raise. [The information that Molly Berman works hard is not essential to identify who she is. Without that information, the essential meaning of the sentence does not change: *Molly Berman got a raise.*]

The relation of restriction and punctuation is an inverse one: when the element is *not* essential, the punctuation *is;* and when the element *is* essential, the punctuation is *not.*

Note: Commas are most commonly used to set off nonrestrictive elements, although dashes or parentheses are sometimes used to emphasize or de-emphasize them (see 25b-2 and 25c-1, respectively, especially the box on p. 442). Whatever punctuation mark you select, be sure to use a pair if the nonrestrictive element falls in the middle of a sentence—one *before* and another *after* the element.

Meaning and context

The same element in the same sentence may be restrictive or nonrestrictive depending on your intended meaning and the context in which the sentence appears. For example, look at the second sentence in each passage below.

Restrictive

Not all the bands were equally well received, however. The band *playing old music* held the audience's attention. The other groups created much less excitement. [The absence of punctuation restricts the subject to a particular band, the one playing old music. As the context indicates, other groups played other kinds of music.]

Nonrestrictive

A new band called Fats made its debut on Saturday night. The band, *playing old music*, held the audience's attention. If this performance is typical, the group has a bright future. [The punctuation indicates that only one band performed and that, incidentally, it played old music.]

1   **Use a comma or commas to set off nonrestrictive clauses and phrases.**

Clauses and phrases serving as adjectives and adverbs may be either nonrestrictive or restrictive. Only nonrestrictive clauses and phrases are set off with punctuation, as the following examples illustrate.

Nonrestrictive clauses

The American farming system, *which is the envy of the world,* is the despair of the American farmer. [Compare *The American farming system is the despair of the American farmer*. The meaning of the subject is unchanged.]   —CHARLES KURALT

Puerto Rico was a Spanish colony until 1898, *when it was ceded to the United States*. [Compare *Puerto Rico was a Spanish colony until 1898*. The meaning of the main clause remains the same without the deleted clause.]

Note: Most subordinate clauses serving as adverbs are restrictive because they describe conditions necessary to the main clause. They are set off by a comma only when they introduce sentences (see 21b) and when they are truly nonrestrictive, adding incidental information (as in the second example above) or expressing a contrast beginning *although, even though, though, whereas,* and the like.

Nonrestrictive phrases

The Capitol, *at one end of Independence Mall,* is an imposing sight. [Compare *The Capitol is an imposing sight*. The building's

RESOURCES AND IDEAS

Francis Christensen, "Restrictive and Nonrestrictive Modifiers Again," *Notes Toward a New Rhetoric: Nine Essays for Teachers,* ed. Francis Christensen and Bonniejean Christensen, 2nd ed. (New York: Harper, 1978) 117–32. Christensen discusses and illustrates uses of the comma with a variety of modifying elements.

$\hat{,}$
21c

WORD PUZZLES

Divide the class into small groups, and give them word puzzles like the following. Each of these puzzles can be solved only if the reader knows how restrictive and nonrestrictive phrases are punctuated.

1. You are a CIA agent whose job is to keep track of all the Russian spies in Melopolia. One day you receive this telegram from Washington: "All the Russian spies, formerly residing in the Russian embassy, have been sent home."
Is there anyone left for you to watch?

2. After a long and successful season the university basketball team played its cross-state rival for the conference championship. Pandemonium broke out when a long shot dropped in at the buzzer to give the university the victory. Parties were held all over campus.
When Professor Kean arrived at class the next morning, the students, who had celebrated long into the night, were fast asleep at their desks.
Can you tell what portion of the class was asleep?

3. A severe electrical storm swept through town just after noon. Lightning struck several buildings, including the computer center. Technicians repairing damage there found that the microcomputers which were not equipped with electrical surge protectors needed to have their circuit boards replaced.
Are any of the microcomputers still usable?

name identifies it; its location does not supply further restriction.]

He beat the other runners**,** *reaching the finish line in record time.* [Compare *He beat the other runners.* The meaning of the main clause remains the same.]

Note: When a participial phrase is separated from the noun or pronoun it modifies, as in the second example above, a comma is essential to clarify that the phrase does not modify the word closest to it. Without the comma, the reader automatically connects the phrase to *runners: He beat the other runners reaching the finish line in record time.*

Restrictive clauses

Every question *that has a reasonable answer* is justifiable. [Compare *Every question is justifiable,* which clearly alters the writer's meaning.]   —KONRAD LORENZ

Books fall apart *when they are not well bound.* [Compare *Books fall apart,* which omits the limiting circumstances and thus implies that all books always fall apart. See the note on the preceding page about adverb clauses.]

Restrictive phrases

A student *seeking an easy course* should not enroll *in History 101.* [Compare *A student should not enroll,* which fails to limit the kind of student who should not enroll and does not specify the course to be avoided.]

The ongoing taboo *against women dating men shorter than themselves* is among the strictest of this society. [Compare *The ongoing taboo is among the strictest of this society,* which no longer specifies what taboo.]   —RALPH KEYES

Note: Whereas both nonrestrictive and restrictive clauses may begin with *which,* only restrictive clauses begin with *that.* Some writers prefer *that* exclusively for restrictive clauses and *which* exclusively for nonrestrictive clauses. See the Glossary of Usage, page 763, for advice on the use of *that* and *which.*

 Use a comma or commas to set off nonrestrictive appositives.

An **appositive** is a noun or noun substitute that renames and could substitute for another noun immediately preceding it. (See 5c-5.) Many appositives are nonrestrictive; thus they are set off, usually with commas. Take care *not* to set off restrictive appositives; like restrictive phrases and clauses, they limit or define the noun or nouns they refer to.

Nonrestrictive appositives

The Chapman lighthouse, *a three-legged thing erect on a mud-flat,* shone strongly. [Compare *The Chapman lighthouse shone strongly.*]   —JOSEPH CONRAD

John Kennedy Toole's only novel, *A Confederacy of Dunces,* won the Pulitzer Prize. [Compare *John Kennedy Toole's only novel won the Pulitzer Prize.*]

Restrictive appositives

The philosopher *Alfred North Whitehead* once wrote that the history of philosophy was a series of footnotes to Plato. [Compare *The philosopher once wrote that the history of philosophy was a series of footnotes to Plato.*]

Our language has adopted the words *garage, panache, and fanfare* from French. [Compare *Our language has adopted the words from French.*]

3   **Use a comma or commas to set off parenthetical expressions.**

Parenthetical expressions are explanatory, supplementary, or transitional words or phrases. (Transitional expressions include *however, indeed, consequently, as a result, of course, for example,* and *in fact;* see 3b-6 for a longer list.) Parenthetical expressions are usually set off by a comma or commas.

> The Cubist painters, *for example,* were obviously inspired by the families of crystals.   —JACOB BRONOWSKI
>
> The only option, *besides locking him up,* was to release him to his parents' custody.
>
> Any writer, *I suppose,* feels that the world into which he was born is nothing less than a conspiracy against the cultivation of his talent.   —JAMES BALDWIN

(Dashes and parentheses may also set off parenthetical elements. See 25b-2 and 25c-1, respectively, and see especially the box on p. 442.)

4   **Use a comma or commas to set off *yes* and *no,* tag questions, words of direct address, and mild interjections.**

Yes and no

Yes, the editorial did have a point.
No, that can never be.

,
21c

21c

Tag questions

Jones should be allowed to vote, *should he not?*
They don't stop to consider others, *do they?*

Direct address

Cody, please bring me the newspaper.
With all due respect, *sir,* I will not do that.

Mild interjections

Well, you will never know who did it.
Oh, they forgot all about the baby.

(You may want to use an exclamation point to set off a forceful interjection. See 20e.)

ANSWERS: EXERCISE 5

1. Italians insist that Marco Polo, the thirteenth-century explorer, did not import pasta from China.
2. Pasta, which consists of flour and water and often egg, existed in Italy long before Marco Polo left for his travels.
3. Correct.
4. Most Italians dispute this account, although their evidence is shaky.
5. Wherever it originated, the Italians are now the undisputed masters in making and cooking pasta.
6. Correct.
7. Most cooks must buy dried pasta, lacking the time to make their own.
8. Correct.
9. Pasta manufacturers choose hard durum wheat because it makes firmer cooked pasta than common wheat does.
10. Pasta made from common wheat tends to get soggy in boiling water.

Exercise 5
Punctuating restrictive and nonrestrictive elements

Insert commas in the following sentences to set off nonrestrictive elements, and delete any commas that incorrectly set off restrictive elements. If a sentence is correct as given, circle the number preceding it.

Example:

Elizabeth Blackwell who attended medical school in the 1840s was the first American woman to earn a medical degree.

Elizabeth Blackwell, who attended medical school in the 1840s, was the first American woman to earn a medical degree.

1. Italians insist that Marco Polo the thirteenth-century explorer did not import pasta from China.
2. Pasta which consists of flour and water and often egg existed in Italy long before Marco Polo left for his travels.
3. A historian who studied pasta places its origin in the Middle East in the fifth century.
4. Most Italians dispute this account although their evidence is shaky.
5. Wherever it originated, the Italians are now the undisputed masters, in making and cooking pasta.
6. Marcella Hazan, who has written several books on Italian cooking, insists that homemade and hand-rolled pasta is the best.
7. Most cooks must buy dried pasta lacking the time to make their own.
8. The finest pasta is made from semolina, a flour from hard durum wheat.
9. Pasta manufacturers choose hard durum wheat, because it makes firmer cooked pasta than common wheat does.
10. Pasta, made from common wheat, tends to get soggy in boiling water.

Exercise 6
Sentence combining: Restrictive and nonrestrictive elements

Combine each pair of sentences below into one sentence that uses the element described in parentheses. Insert commas as appropriate. You will have to add, delete, change, and rearrange words. Some items have more than one possible answer.

Example:

Mr. Ward's oldest sister helped keep him alive. She was a nurse in the hospital. (*Nonrestrictive clause beginning who.*)

Mr. Ward's oldest sister, *who was a nurse in the hospital,* helped keep him alive.

1. Most sources say it was the Italians. The Italians introduced pasta as a main dish. (*Restrictive clause beginning who.*)
2. The Italians use the word to mean only tubular pasta. The word is *maccheroni.* (*Restrictive appositive.*)
3. American manufacturers use *macaroni* to mean all flour-and-water pasta. These manufacturers are unlike the Italians. (*Nonrestrictive phrase beginning unlike.*)
4. Americans also use *spaghetti* for all flour-and-water pasta. The meaning is "little strings" in Italian. (*Nonrestrictive phrase beginning meaning.*)
5. American colonists first imported pasta from the English. The English had discovered it as tourists in Italy. (*Nonrestrictive clause beginning who.*)
6. The English returned from their grand tours of Italy. They were called *macaronis* because of their fancy airs. (*Restrictive phrase beginning returning.*)
7. A hair style was also called *macaroni.* It had elaborate curls. (*Restrictive phrase beginning with.*)
8. The song "Yankee Doodle" refers to this hairdo. It reports that Yankee Doodle "stuck a feather in his cap and called it macaroni." (*Restrictive clause beginning when.*)
9. The song was actually intended to poke fun at unrefined American colonists. It was a creation of the English. (*Nonrestrictive appositive.*)
10. The colonists adopted the jolly tune. They turned it to their advantage. (*Nonrestrictive phrase beginning turning.*)

ANSWERS: EXERCISE 6
Possible Answers

1. Most sources say it was the Italians who introduced pasta as a main dish.
2. The Italians use the word *maccheroni* to mean only tubular pasta.
3. American manufacturers, unlike the Italians, use *macaroni* to mean all flour-and-water pasta.
4. Americans also use *spaghetti,* meaning "little strings" in Italian, for all flour-and-water pasta.
5. American colonists first imported pasta from the English, who discovered it as tourists in Italy.
6. The English returning from their grand tours of Italy were called *macaronis* because of their fancy airs.
7. A hair style with elaborate curls was also called *macaroni.*
8. The song "Yankee Doodle" refers to this hairdo when it reports that Yankee Doodle "stuck a feather in his cap and called it macaroni."
9. The song, a creation of the English, was actually intended to poke fun at unrefined American colonists.
10. The colonists adopted the jolly tune, turning it to their advantage.

˄
,
21d

21d Use a comma or commas to set off absolute phrases.

An **absolute phrase** modifies a whole main clause rather than any word or word group in the clause; it is not connected to the rest of the sentence by a conjunction, preposition, or relative pronoun. (See 5c-3.) Absolute phrases usually consist of at least a participle and its subject (a noun or pronoun), as in the following:

Their work finished, the men quit for the day.

Absolute constructions can occur at almost any point in the sentence. Whatever their position, they are always set off by a comma or commas.

Their homework done, the children may watch whatever they want on television.

After reaching Eagle Rock, we pointed our canoes toward shore, *the rapids ahead being rough.*

His clothes, *the fabric tattered and the seams ripped open,* looked like Salvation Army rejects.

ANSWERS: EXERCISE 7

1. Prices having risen rapidly, the government debated a price freeze.
2. Businesses, their profits otherwise made vulnerable, would demand a wage freeze as well.
3. The President would have to persuade businesses to accept a price freeze, his methods depending on their recalcitrance.
4. No doubt the President, his advisers having urged it, would first try a patriotic appeal.
5. Arm-twisting having worked for previous Presidents, this one might resort to it.

Exercise 7
Punctuating absolute phrases

Insert commas in the following sentences to set off absolute phrases.

Example:

The recording contract was canceled the band having broken up.

The recording contract was canceled, the band having broken up.

1. Prices having risen rapidly the government debated a price freeze.
2. Businesses their profits otherwise made vulnerable would demand a wage freeze as well.
3. The President would have to persuade businesses to accept a price freeze his methods depending on their recalcitrance.
4. No doubt the President his advisers having urged it would first try a patriotic appeal.
5. Arm-twisting having worked for previous Presidents this one might resort to it.

21e **Use a comma or commas to set off phrases expressing contrast.**

The essay needs less wit, *more pith.*

His generosity, *not his good looks,* won him friends.

Style is the manner of a sentence, *not its matter.* —DONALD HALL

It is not light that is needed, *but fire;* it is not the gentle shower, *but thunder.*

—FREDERICK DOUGLASS

Note: Writers often omit commas around contrasting phrases beginning *but.*

His life was long *but sadly empty.*   —HERMAN CRATSLEY

Exercise 8
Punctuating phrases expressing contrast

Insert commas in the following sentences to set off phrases that express contrast.

Example:

Susan not her sister was the one who attended college in Michigan.

Susan, not her sister, was the one who attended college in Michigan.

1. The expense of heating homes not just the cold makes the winter months difficult in northern states.
2. Many people must forgo necessities not just luxuries to pay their heating bills.
3. People use their gas ovens more for heat less for cooking.
4. Using a gas oven for heat is extremely dangerous not safe as many people believe.
5. The gas fumes not the flames are the source of danger.

ANSWERS: EXERCISE 8

1. The expense of heating homes, not just the cold, makes the winter months difficult in northern states.
2. Many people must forego necessities, not just luxuries, to pay their heating bills.
3. People use their gas ovens more for heat, less for cooking.
4. Using a gas oven for heat is extremely dangerous, not safe as many people believe.
5. The gas fumes, not the flames, are the source of danger.

21f Use commas between items in a series and between coordinate adjectives.

 1 Use commas between words, phrases, or clauses forming a series.

Place commas between all elements of a **series**—that is, three or more items of equal importance.

The names *Belial, Beelzebub, and Lucifer* sound ominous.

He felt cut off from them *by age, by understanding, by sensibility, by technology, and by his need to measure himself against the mirror of other men's appreciation.*   —RALPH ELLISON

The ox *was solid black, stood five feet high at the shoulder, had a five-foot span of horns, and must have weighed 1,200 pounds on the hoof.*   —RICHARD B. LEE

Though some writers omit the comma before the coordinating conjunction in a series (*Breakfast consisted of coffee, eggs and kippers*), the final comma is never wrong and it always helps the

SAMPLE PAPERS

Take one of the sample papers from the chapter on "Evaluating and Responding to Student Writing" at the beginning of this annotated edition and revise it to introduce punctuation errors of the kind you have been emphasizing in class. Distribute copies of the altered paper, and ask students to correct it. You may also wish to use a student paper from one of your own classes.

21f

reader see the last two items as separate. Use it consistently and your writing will be clearer, as the following example shows.

| **Confusing** | The job involves typing, answering the phone, filing and reading manuscripts. |
| **Clear** | The job involves typing, answering the phone, filing, and reading manuscripts. |

Exception: When items in a series are long and grammatically complicated, they may be separated by semicolons. When the items contain commas, they must be separated by semicolons. (See 22d.)

 Use commas between coordinate adjectives not linked by conjunctions.

Coordinate adjectives are two or more adjectives that modify equally the same noun or pronoun. The individual adjectives are separated either by coordinating conjunctions or by commas.

The *sleek* and *shiny* car was a credit to the neighborhood.
The *dirty, rusty, dented* car was an eyesore.
Nothing is more essential to *intelligent, profitable* reading than sensitivity to connotation. —RICHARD ALTICK

 Tests for coordinate adjectives

1. Identify the adjectives.
   She was a *faithful sincere* friend.
   They are *dedicated medical* students.
2. Can the adjectives be reversed without changing meaning?
   She was a *sincere faithful* friend. **Yes.**
   They are *medical dedicated* students. **No.**
3. Can the word *and* be inserted between the adjectives without changing meaning?
   She was a *faithful and sincere* friend. **Yes.**
   They are *dedicated and medical* students. **No.**
4. If **yes** to *both* questions, the adjectives *are* coordinate and *should* be separated by a comma.
   She was a *faithful, sincere* friend.

   If **no** to both questions, the adjectives are *not* coordinate and should *not* be separated by a comma.
   They are *dedicated medical* students.

Adjectives are not coordinate—and should *not* be separated by commas—when the one nearer the noun is more closely related to the noun in meaning.

> The house overflowed with *ornate electric* fixtures. [*Ornate* modifies *electric fixtures.*]
>
> The museum's most valuable object is a *sparkling diamond* necklace. [*Sparkling* modifies *diamond necklace.*]

Caution: Numbers are not coordinate with other adjectives.

Faulty	Among the junk in the attic was *one, lovely* vase.
Revised	Among the junk in the attic was *one lovely* vase.

Do not use a comma between the final coordinate adjective and the noun.

Faulty	Spring evenings in the South are *warm, sensuous,* experiences.
Revised	Spring evenings in the South are *warm, sensuous* experiences.

Exercise 9
Punctuating series and coordinate adjectives

Insert commas in the following sentences to separate coordinate adjectives or elements in series. Circle the number preceding each sentence whose punctuation is already corrrect.

Example:

Although quiet by day, the club became a noisy smoky dive at night.

Although quiet by day, the club became a noisy, smoky dive at night.

1. Shoes with high heels originated to protect feet from the mud garbage and animal waste in the streets.
2. The first known high heels worn strictly for fashion appeared in the sixteenth century.
3. The heels were worn by men and made of colorful silk brocades soft suedes or smooth leathers.
4. High-heeled shoes received a boost when the short powerful King Louis XIV of France began wearing them.
5. Louis's influence was so strong that men and women of the court priests and cardinals and even household servants donned high heels.
6. Eventually only wealthy fashionable French women wore high heels.
7. In the seventeenth and eighteenth centuries, French culture represented the one true standard of elegance and refinement.

⌃
,
21f

ANSWERS: EXERCISE 9

1. Shoes with high heels originated to protect feet from the mud, garbage, and animal waste in the streets.
2. Correct.
3. The heels were worn by men and made of colorful silk brocades, soft suedes, or smooth leathers.
4. High-heeled shoes received a boost when the short, powerful King Louis XIV of France began wearing them.
5. Louis's influence was so strong that men and women of the court, priests and cardinals, and even household servants donned high heels.
6. Eventually only wealthy, fashionable French women wore high heels.
7. Correct.

8. High-heeled shoes for women spread to other courts‸ most European and North American countries‸ and almost all social classes.
9. Now high heels are commonplace, though their heights and shapes undergo wide‸ often baffling swings.
10. Correct.

8. High-heeled shoes for women spread to other courts most European and North American countries and almost all social classes.
9. Now high heels are commonplace, though their heights and shapes undergo wide often baffling swings.
10. A Paris store recently showed a pair of purple satin pumps with tiny jeweled bows and four-inch stiletto heels.

21g Use commas according to convention in dates, addresses, place names, and long numbers.

The items in a date, address, or place name are conventionally separated with commas, as illustrated below. When they appear within sentences, dates, addresses, and place names punctuated with commas are also ended with commas.

Dates

July 4, 1776, was the day the Declaration of Independence was signed.

The bombing of Pearl Harbor on Sunday, December 7, 1941, prompted American entry into World War II.

Commas are not used between the parts of a date in inverted order: *Their anniversary on 15 December 1991 was their fiftieth.* Commas need not be used in dates consisting of a month or season and a year: *For the United States the war began in December 1941 and ended in August 1945.*

Addresses and place names

Use the address 5262 Laurie Lane, Memphis, Tennessee, for all correspondence.

Send inquiries to Box 3862, Pasadena, California.

Columbus, Ohio, is the location of Ohio State University.

The population of Garden City, Long Island, New York, is 30,000.

Commas are not used between state names and zip codes in addresses: *Berkeley, California 94720, is the place of my birth.*

Long numbers

Use the comma to separate the figures in long numbers into groups of three, counting from the right. The comma with numbers of four digits is optional.

A kilometer is 3,281 feet (*or* 3281 feet).

Russia's 8,649,490 square miles make it the largest country in the world.

‸
,
21g

Exercise 10
Punctuating dates, addresses, place names, numbers

Insert commas as needed in the following sentences.

Example:

The house cost $27000 fifteen years ago.
The house cost $27,000 fifteen years ago.

1. The festival will hold a benefit dinner and performance on March 10 1992 in Asheville.
2. The organizers hope to raise more than $100000 from donations and ticket sales.
3. Performers are expected from as far away as Milan Italy and Kyoto Japan.
4. All inquiries sent to Mozart Festival P.O. Box 725 Asheville North Carolina 28803 will receive a quick response.
5. The deadline for ordering tickets by mail is Monday February 10 1992.

ANSWERS: EXERCISE 10

1. The festival will hold a benefit dinner and performance on March 10, 1992, in Asheville.
2. The organizers hope to raise more than $100,000 from donations and ticket sales.
3. Performers are expected from as far away as Milan, Italy, and Kyoto, Japan.
4. All inquiries sent to Mozart Festival, P.O. Box 725, Asheville, North Carolina 28803, will receive a quick response.
5. The deadline for ordering tickets by mail is Monday, February 10, 1992.

21h   Use commas with quotations according to standard practice.

The words used to explain a quotation (*he said, she replied,* and so on) may come before, after, or in the middle of the quotation. They must always be separated from the quotation by punctuation, usually a comma or commas. (See pp. 428–29 for a summary of conventions regarding quotations.)

1   Ordinarily, use a comma to separate introductory and concluding explanatory words from quotations.

General Sherman summed up the attitude of all thoughtful soldiers when he said, "War is hell."

"Knowledge is power," wrote Francis Bacon.

Exceptions: Do not use a comma when explanatory words follow a quotation ending in an exclamation point or a question mark (see 20c and 20e).

"Claude!" Mrs. Harrison called.
"Why must I come home?" he asked.

Do not use commas with a quotation introduced by *that* or with a short quotation that is merely one element in a longer sentence.

The warning that "cigarette smoking is dangerous to your health" has fallen on many deaf ears.

People should always say "Excuse me" when they bump into fellow pedestrians.

Use a colon instead of a comma to separate explanatory words from a quotation when there is an emphatic break between them in meaning or in grammar or when the quotation is very formal or longer than a sentence. (See also 25a.)

The Bill of Rights is unambiguous: "Congress shall make no law respecting an establishment of religion, or prohibiting the free exercise thereof."

RESOURCES AND IDEAS

Kenneth S. Benson, "Profitable Proofreading," *Teaching the Basics—Really!* ed. Ouida Clapp (Urbana: NCTE, 1977) 80–81. Benson describes exercises in proofreading and in getting students to pay attention to correction symbols.

2 Use a comma after the first part of a quotation interrupted by explanatory words. Follow the explanatory words with the punctuation required by the quotation.

Quotation

"When you got nothin', you got nothin' to lose."

Explanatory words

"When you got nothin'," Kris Kristofferson sings, "you got nothin' to lose." [The explanatory words interrupt the quotation at a comma and thus end with a comma.]

Quotation

"That part of my life was over; his words had sealed it shut."

Explanatory words

"That part of my life was over," she wrote; "his words had sealed it shut." [The explanatory words interrupt the quotation at a semicolon and thus end with a semicolon.]

Quotation

"This is the faith with which I return to the South. With this new faith we will be able to hew out of the mountain of despair a stone of hope."

Explanatory words

"This is the faith with which I return to the South," Martin Luther King, Jr., proclaimed. "With this new faith we will be able to hew out of the mountain of despair a stone of hope." [The explanatory words interrupt the quotation at the end of a sentence and thus end with a period.]

Caution: Using a comma instead of a semicolon or a period in the last two examples would result in the error called a comma splice: two main clauses separated only by a comma, without a linking coordinating conjunction. (See 11a.)

 3   **Place commas that follow quotations within quotation marks.**

"That's my seat," she said coldly.
"You gave it up," I replied evenly, "so you have no right to it."

Exercise 11
Punctuating quotations

Insert commas or semicolons in the following sentences to correct punctuation with quotations. Circle the number preceding any sentence whose punctuation is already correct.

> *Example:*
> The shoplifter declared "I didn't steal anything."
> The shoplifter declared, "I didn't steal anything."

1. The writer and writing teacher Peter Elbow suggests that an "open-ended writing process . . . can change you, not just your words."
2. "I think of the open-ended writing process as a voyage in two stages" Elbow says.
3. "The sea voyage is a process of divergence, branching, proliferation, and confusion" Elbow continues "the coming to land is a process of convergence, pruning, centralizing, and clarifying."
4. "Keep up one session of writing long enough to get loosened up and tired" advises Elbow "long enough in fact to make a bit of a voyage."
5. "In coming to new land" Elbow says "you develop a new conception of what you are writing about."

ANSWERS: EXERCISE 11

1. Correct.
2. "I think of the open-ended writing process as a voyage in two stages," Elbow says.
3. "The sea voyage is a process of divergence, branching, proliferation, and confusion," Elbow continues; "the coming to land is a process of convergence, pruning, centralizing, and clarifying."
4. "Keep up one session of writing long enough to get loosened up and tired," advises Elbow, "long enough in fact to make a bit of a voyage."
5. "In coming to new land," Elbow says, "you develop a new conception of what you are writing about."

,
21i

21i   Use commas to prevent misreading.

The comma tells the reader to pause slightly before moving on. In some sentences words may run together in unintended and confusing ways unless a comma separates them. Use a comma in such sentences even though no rule requires one.

Confusing   Soon after she left town for good. [A short introductory phrase does not require a comma, but clarity requires it in this sentence.]

Revised   Soon after, she left town for good.

Confusing	The students who can usually give some money to the United Fund. [Without a comma the sentence seems incomplete.]
Revised	The students who can**,** usually give some money to the United Fund.

Exercise 12
Punctuating to prevent misreading

Insert commas in the following sentences to prevent misreading.

Example:

To Laura Ann symbolized decadence.
To Laura**,** Ann symbolized decadence.

1. Though happy people still have moments of self-doubt.
2. In research subjects have reported themselves to be generally happy people.
3. Yet those who have described sufferings as well as joys.
4. Of fifty eight subjects reported bouts of serious depression.
5. For half the preceding year had included at least one personal crisis.

21j Use commas only where required.

Commas can make sentences choppy and even confusing if they are used more often than needed or in violation of rules 21a through 21h. Examine every sentence you write to be sure you have used commas appropriately.

 Delete any comma that separates subject and verb, verb and object, or preposition and object unless the words between them require punctuation.

Faulty	The returning *soldiers, received* a warmer welcome than they expected. [Separation of subject and verb.]
Revised	The returning *soldiers received* a warmer welcome than they expected.
Faulty	They had *chosen, to fight* for their country *despite, the risks and low pay.* [Separation of verb *chosen* and its object, of preposition *despite* and its object.]
Revised	They had chosen to fight for their country despite the risks and low pay.

In the following sentence, commas are needed to set off the nonrestrictive clause that interrupts subject and verb (see 21c).

Principal misuses of the comma

● To separate subject-verb, verb-object, or preposition-object (21j-1).

Faulty   *Anyone* with breathing problems, *should not exercise* during smog alerts.

Revised   Anyone with breathing problems should not exercise during smog alerts.

● To separate pairs of words, phrases, or subordinate clauses joined by coordinating conjunctions (21j-2).

Faulty   Asthmatics are affected by *ozone, and sulfur oxides.*

Revised   Asthmatics are affected by ozone and sulfur oxides.

● To set off restrictive elements (21j-3).

Faulty   Even people, *who are healthy,* should be careful.

Revised   Even people who are healthy should be careful.

● Before or after a series (21j-4).

Faulty   *Cars, factories, and even bakeries,* contribute to smog.

Revised   Cars, factories, and even bakeries contribute to smog.

● To set off an indirect quotation or a single word that isn't a non-restrictive appositive (21j-5).

Faulty   Experts *say, that* the pollutant, *ozone,* is especially damaging.

Revised   Experts say that the pollutant ozone is especially damaging.

no ˆ
21j

Americans, who are preoccupied with other sports, have not developed a strong interest in professional soccer.

 2   **Delete any comma that separates words, phrases, or subordinate clauses joined by coordinating conjunctions.**

Faulty   Banks *could, and should* help older people manage their money. [Compound helping verb.]

Revised   Banks could and should help older people manage their money.

CREATING SENTENCES

Choose a mark of punctuation you wish to emphasize in class—the comma, for this chapter—and ask students to write sentences using the punctuation strategy correctly. You may wish to use this activity as a quiz.

no ^,
21j

Faulty   Older people need special assistance *because they live* on fixed incomes, *and because they are not familiar* with new *accounts, and rates.* [Compound subordinate clauses *because . . . because* and compound object of preposition *with.*]

Revised   Older people need special assistance because they live on fixed incomes and because they are not familiar with new accounts and rates.

Faulty   *Banks, and community groups* can eliminate the *confusion, or distress* many of the elderly feel about their money. [Compound subject and compound objects of verb *eliminate.*]

Revised   Banks and community groups can eliminate the confusion or distress many of the elderly feel about their money.

Faulty   One bank *established* special accounts for older depositors, *and counseled* them on investments. [Compound predicate.]

Revised   One bank established special accounts for older depositors and counseled them on investments.

(See 21a and 21f-1, respectively, for the appropriate use of commas with coordinating conjunctions when they link main clauses or elements in a series.)

 3   **Delete any commas that set off restrictive elements.**

Faulty   Hawthorne's work, *The Scarlet Letter,* was the first major American novel. [The title of the novel is essential to distinguish the novel from the rest of Hawthorne's work.]

Revised   Hawthorne's work *The Scarlet Letter* was the first major American novel.

Faulty   The theme, *of secret sin,* figures in much of Hawthorne's work. [The phrase specifies the theme.]

Revised   The theme of secret sin figures in much of Hawthorne's work.

Faulty   The symbols, *that Hawthorne used,* influenced other novelists. [The clause identifies which symbols were influential.]

Revised   The symbols that Hawthorne used influenced other novelists.

(See 21c for further discussion of identifying and punctuating nonrestrictive and restrictive elements in sentences.)

4   **Delete any comma before or after a series unless a rule requires it.**

Faulty   *Agriculture, herding, and hunting,* sustained the Native Americans. [The comma after *hunting* separates subject and verb.]

Revised   Agriculture, herding, and hunting sustained the Native Americans.

Faulty   Among other things, the Europeans brought to the New World, *horses, advanced technology, and new diseases.* [The comma after *World* separates verb and object.]

Revised   Among other things, the Europeans brought to the New World horses, advanced technology, and new diseases.

In the following sentence the commas before and after the series are appropriate because the series is a nonrestrictive appositive (see 21c-2).

The three major television networks, *ABC, CBS, and NBC,* face fierce competition from the cable networks.

However, many writers prefer to use dashes rather than commas to set off series functioning as appositives (see 25b-2).
(See 21f-1 for further discussion of punctuating series.)

5   **Delete any comma setting off an indirect quotation or a single word that isn't a nonrestrictive appositive.**

Indirect quotation

Faulty   The report *concluded, that* dieting could be more dangerous than overeating.

Revised   The report concluded that dieting could be more dangerous than overeating.

Faulty   The students asked, why they had to take a test the day before vacation.

Revised   The students asked why they had to take a test the day before vacation.

no ⌃
21j

Quoted or italicized word

Faulty   James Joyce's story, "Araby," was assigned last year. [The story title is a restrictive appositive. The commas imply wrongly that Joyce wrote only one story.]

Revised   James Joyce's story "Araby" was assigned last year.

Faulty   The word, *open,* can be both a verb and an adjective. [*Open* is a restrictive appositive.]

Revised   The word *open* can be both a verb and an adjective.

The following sentence requires commas because the quoted title is a nonrestrictive appositive.

Her only poem about death, "Mourning," was printed in *The New Yorker*.

(See 21c-2 for more on punctuating appositives.)

Exercise 13
Revising: Needless or misused commas

Revise the following sentences to eliminate needless or misused commas. Circle the number preceding each sentence that is already punctuated correctly.

Example:

The portrait of the founder, that hung in the dining hall, was stolen by pranksters.

The portrait of the founder that hung in the dining hall was stolen by pranksters.

1. In Greek mythology Theseus is protected by the god, Poseidon.
2. Theseus is an adventurer, and a hero of the Athenians.
3. In one of his adventures Theseus sails, to Crete, to kill the Minotaur, which has been devouring young Athenians.
4. The Minotaur, half bull and half human, is kept by the king of Crete, Minos, in his mazelike palace.
5. Each year Minos captures fourteen young Athenians, and throws them to the Minotaur in revenge for the death of his son in Athens.
6. When Theseus arrives in Crete, Minos challenges him by, throwing a gold ring into the sea and ordering him to retrieve it.
7. Under the water Theseus meets a woman, who is Poseidon's wife and who hands him the ring to return to Minos.
8. Theseus later meets Minos's only daughter, Ariadne, and she gives him a ball of string so that he can find his way out of the maze.
9. She warns, that the Minotaur's victims have been too exhausted from being lost in the maze to fight for their lives.

ANSWERS: EXERCISE 13

1. In Greek mythology Theseus is protected by the god Poseidon.
2. Theseus is an adventurer and a hero of the Athenians.
3. In one of his adventures Theseus sails to Crete to kill the Minotaur, which has been devouring young Athenians.
4. Correct.
5. Each year Minos captures fourteen young Athenians and throws them to the Minotaur in revenge for the death of his son in Athens.
6. When Theseus arrives in Crete, Minos challenges him by throwing a gold ring into the sea and ordering him to retrieve it.
7. Under the water Theseus meets a woman who is Poseidon's wife and who hands him the ring to return to Minos.
8. Correct.
9. She warns that the Minotaur's victims have been too exhausted from being lost in the maze to fight for their lives.
10. With a ball of string Theseus can leave a trail behind him and find his way through and out of the maze.
11. Theseus does as Ariadne urges and conserves the energy needed to kill the Minotaur.

10. With a ball of string Theseus can leave a trail behind him, and find his way through, and out of the maze.

11. Theseus does, as Ariadne urges, and conserves the energy, needed to kill the Minotaur.

12. He also rescues some youths, whom the Minotaur has not yet killed.

13. Theseus, the youths, and Ariadne, all flee from Crete in Theseus's ship.

14. They travel to the island, of Naxos, where Theseus deserts Ariadne.

15. One version of the myth explains, that another god, Dionysus, orders Theseus away so that he can have Ariadne for himself.

Exercise 14
Revising: Commas

Insert commas in the following paragraphs wherever they are needed, and eliminate any misused or needless commas.

Ellis Island New York has reopened for business but now the customers are tourists not immigrants. This spot which lies in New York Harbor was the first American soil seen, or touched by many of the nation's immigrants. Though other places also served as ports of entry for foreigners none has the symbolic power of, Ellis Island. Between its opening in 1892 and its closing in 1954, over 20 million people about two-thirds of all immigrants were detained there before taking up their new lives in the United States. Ellis Island processed over 2000 newcomers a day when immigration was at its peak between 1900 and 1920.

As the end of a long voyage and the introduction to the New World Ellis Island must have left something to be desired. The "huddled masses" as the Statue of Liberty calls them indeed were huddled. New arrivals were herded about kept standing in lines for hours or days yelled at and abused. Assigned numbers they submitted their bodies to the pokings and proddings of the silent nurses and doctors, who were charged with ferreting out the slightest sign of sickness, disability or insanity. That test having been passed the immigrants faced interrogation by an official through an interpreter. Those, with names deemed inconveniently long or difficult to pronounce, often found themselves permanently labeled with abbreviations, of their names, or with the names, of their hometowns. But of course millions survived the examination humiliation and confusion, to take the last short boat ride to New York City. For many of them and especially for their descendants Ellis Island eventually became not a nightmare but the place where life began.

Note: See page 450 for a punctuation exercise combining commas with other marks of punctuation.

---

12. He also rescues some youths whom the Minotaur has not yet killed.

13. Theseus, the youths, and Ariadne all flee from Crete in Theseus's ship.

14. They travel to the island of Naxos, where Theseus deserts Ariadne.

15. One version of the myth explains that another god, Dionysus, orders Theseus away so that he can have Ariadne for himself.

ANSWERS: EXERCISE 14

Ellis Island, New York, has reopened for business, but now the customers are tourists, not immigrants. This spot, which lies in New York Harbor, was the first American soil seen or touched by many of the nation's immigrants. Though other places also served as ports of entry for foreigners, none has the symbolic power of Ellis Island. Between its opening in 1892 and its closing in 1954, over 20 million people about two-thirds of all immigrants, were detained there before taking up their new lives in the United States. Ellis Island processed over 2000 [or 2,000] newcomers a day when immigration was at its peak between 1900 and 1920.

As the end of a long voyage and the introduction to the New World, Ellis Island must have left something to be desired. The "huddled masses," as the Statue of Liberty calls them, indeed were huddled. New arrivals were herded about, kept standing in lines for hours or days, yelled at, and abused. Assigned numbers, they submitted their bodies to the pokings and proddings of the silent nurses and doctors who were charged with ferreting out the slightest sign of sickness, disability, or insanity. That test having been passed, the immigrants faced interrogation by an official through an interpreter. Those with names deemed inconveniently long or difficult to pronounce often found themselves permanently labeled with abbreviations of their names or with the names of their hometowns. But, of course, millions survived the examination, humiliation, and confusion to take the last short boat ride to New York City. For many of them, and especially for their descendants, Ellis Island eventually became not a nightmare, but the place where life began.

no ⌃
21j

The semicolon is frequently ignored or misused in student writing, as is the comma. This chapter is divided into four sections that explain appropriate uses of the semicolon: to separate main clauses not joined by a coordinating conjunction; to separate main clauses joined by a conjunctive adverb; to separate main clauses if they are very long and complex or if they contain commas, even when they are joined by a coordinating conjunction; and to separate items in a series if they are long or contain commas. The final section explains the most frequent misuses of the semicolon.

Chapter 22

The Semicolon

| **22a** | **Use a semicolon to separate main clauses not joined by a coordinating conjunction.** |

Main clauses contain a subject and a predicate and do not begin with a subordinating word (see 5c). They may be linked by a coordinating conjunction such as *and* or *but* and then separated by a comma (see 21a). But when no coordinating conjunction is present, the clauses should be separated by a semicolon.

I was not led to the university by conventional middle-class ambitions; my grip on the middle class was more tenuous than that on the school system.
—ROBIN FOX

The box opposite distinguishes among the principal uses of three often-confused marks: semicolon, comma, and colon. In choosing among these or the period to separate main clauses, you need to decide how much separation you want and what your meaning is. Generally, the semicolon is most appropriate when the first clause creates some suspense—some expectation in the reader that an equally important and complementary statement is coming. The semicolon then provides a pause before the second clause fulfills the expectation.

Directing movies was only one of his ambitions; he also wanted to direct theatrical productions of Shakespeare's plays.

Caution: If you do not link main clauses with a coordinating conjunction and you separate them only with a comma or with no punctuation at all, you will produce a comma splice or a fused sentence. See Chapter 11.

Exception: Writers sometimes use a comma instead of a semicolon between very short and closely parallel main clauses.

The poor live, the rich just exist.

But a semicolon is safer, and it is always correct.

Distinguishing the comma, the semicolon, and the colon

The **comma** chiefly separates both equal and unequal sentence elements.

- It separates main clauses when they are linked by a coordinating conjunction (21a).

  An airline once tried to boost sales by advertising the tense alertness of its crews, *but* nervous fliers did not want to hear about pilots' sweaty palms.

- It separates subordinate information that is part of or attached to a main clause, such as a nonrestrictive modifier or an introductory element (21b–21h).

  Although the airline campaign failed, many advertising agencies, including some clever ones, copied its underlying message.

The **semicolon** chiefly separates equal and balanced sentence elements.

- It separates complementary main clauses that are *not* linked by a coordinating conjunction (22a).

  The airline campaign had highlighted only half the story; the other half was buried in the copy.

- It separates complementary main clauses that are related by a conjunctive adverb (22b).

  The campaign should not have stressed the pilots' insecurity; *instead,* the campaign should have stressed the improved performance resulting from that insecurity.

The **colon** chiefly separates unequal sentence elements.

- It separates a main clause from a following explanation or summary, which may or may not be a main clause (25a).

  Many successful advertising campaigns have used this message: the anxious seller is harder working and smarter than the competitor.

;
22a

ANSWERS: EXERCISE 1

1. More and more musicians are playing computerized instruments; more and more listeners are worrying about the future of acoustic instruments.
2. The computer is not the first new technology in music; the pipe organ and saxophone were also technological breakthroughs in their day.
3. Musicians have always experimented with new technology; audiences have always resisted the experiments.
4. Most computer musicians are not merely following the latest fad; they are discovering new sounds and new ways to manipulate sound.
5. Few musicians have abandoned acoustic instruments; most value acoustic sounds as much as electronic sounds.

;
22a

COLLABORATIVE LEARNING

ANSWERS: EXERCISE 2
Possible Answers

1. Electronic instruments are prevalent in jazz and rock music; they are less common in classical music.
2. Jazz and rock change rapidly; they nourish experimentation and improvisation.
3. Traditional classical music does not change; its notes and instrumentation were established by a composer writing decades or centuries ago.
4. Contemporary classical music not only can draw on tradition; it also can respond to innovations such as jazz rhythms and electronic sounds.
5. Much contemporary electronic music is more than just jazz, rock, or classical; it is a fusion of all three.

Exercise 1
Punctuating between main clauses

Insert semicolons to separate main clauses in the following sentences.

Example:

One man at the auction bid prudently another did not.
One man at the auction bid prudently; another did not.

1. More and more musicians are playing computerized instruments more and more listeners are worrying about the future of acoustic instruments.
2. The computer is not the first new technology in music the pipe organ and saxophone were also technological breakthroughs in their day.
3. Musicians have always experimented with new technology audiences have always resisted the experiments.
4. Most computer musicians are not merely following the latest fad they are discovering new sounds and new ways to manipulate sound.
5. Few musicians have abandoned acoustic instruments most value acoustic sounds as much as electronic sounds.

Exercise 2
Sentence combining: Related main clauses

Combine each set of three sentences below into one sentence containing only two main clauses, and insert a semicolon between the clauses. You will have to add, delete, change, and rearrange words. Most items have more than one possible answer.

Example:

The painter Andrew Wyeth is widely admired. He is not universally admired. Some critics view his work as sentimental.

The painter Andrew Wyeth is widely but not universally admired; some critics view his work as sentimental.

1. Electronic instruments are prevalent in jazz. They are also prevalent in rock music. They are less common in classical music.
2. Jazz and rock change rapidly. They nourish experimentation. They nourish improvisation.
3. Traditional classical music does not change. Its notes and instrumentation were established by a composer. The composer was writing decades or centuries ago.
4. Contemporary classical music not only can draw on tradition. It also can respond to innovations. These are innovations such as jazz rhythms and electronic sounds.
5. Much contemporary electronic music is more than just one type of music. It is more than just jazz, rock, or classical. It is a fusion of all three.

22b Use a semicolon to separate main clauses related by a conjunctive adverb.

Conjunctive adverbs include *consequently, hence, however, indeed, instead, nonetheless, otherwise, still, then, therefore,* and *thus.* (See p. 203 for more explanation and a fuller list.) When a conjunctive adverb relates two main clauses, the clauses should be separated by a semicolon.

> The Labor Department lawyers will be here in a month; *therefore,* the grievance committee should meet as soon as possible.

> For the first time in twenty years, the accident rate in St. Louis did not rise; *indeed,* it actually declined.

The position of the semicolon between main clauses never changes, but the conjunctive adverb may move around within a clause. The adverb is usually set off with a comma or commas.

> Blue jeans have become fashionable all over the world; *however,* the American originators still wear more jeans than anyone else.

> Blue jeans have become fashionable all over the world; the American originators, *however,* still wear more jeans than anyone else.

> Blue jeans have become fashionable all over the world; the American originators still wear more jeans than anyone else, *however.*

Commas are optional with *thus, then,* and some other one-syllable conjunctive adverbs; and commas are usually omitted when *therefore, instead,* and a few other adverbs fall inside or at the ends of clauses.

> She skipped first grade; *thus* she is younger than her classmates.

> She skipped first grade; she is *therefore* younger than her classmates.

> I did not buy the book; I borrowed it *instead.*

Caution: If you use a comma or no punctuation at all between main clauses connected by a conjunctive adverb, you will produce a comma splice or a fused sentence. See Chapter 11.

Exercise 3
Punctuating main clauses related by conjunctive adverbs

Insert a semicolon in each sentence below to separate main clauses related by a conjunctive adverb, and insert a comma or commas where needed to set off the adverb.

ADDITIONAL PRACTICE

The Little, Brown Workbook offers additional practice in using the semicolon.

;
22b

ANSWERS: EXERCISE 3

1. Music is a form of communication like language; the basic elements, however, are not letters but notes.
2. Computers can process any information that can be represented numerically; consequently, they can process musical information.
3. A computer's ability to process music depends on what software it can run; furthermore, it must be connected to a system that converts electrical vibration into sound.
4. Computers and their sound systems can produce many different sounds; indeed, the number of possible sounds is infinite.
5. The powerful music computers are very expensive; they are therefore used only by professional musicians. *Or:* . . . they are, therefore, used by professional musicians.

COLLABORATIVE LEARNING

ANSWERS: EXERCISE 4
Possible Answers

1. Most music computers are too expensive for the average consumer; however, digital keyboard instruments can be inexpensive and are widely available.
2. Inside the keyboard is a small computer that controls a sound synthesizer; consequently, the instrument can both process and produce music.
3. The person playing the keyboard presses keys or other controls; then the computer and synthesizer convert these signals into vibrations and sounds.
4. The inexpensive keyboards can perform only a few functions; still, to the novice computer musician the range of drum rhythms and simulated instruments is exciting.
5. Would-be musicians can orchestrate whole songs from just the melody lines; thus they need never again play "Chopsticks."

;
22b

Example:

He knew that tickets for the concert would be scarce therefore he arrived at the box office hours before it opened.

He knew that tickets for the concert would be scarce; therefore, he arrived at the box office hours before it opened.

1. Music is a form of communication like language the basic elements however are not letters but notes.
2. Computers can process any information that can be represented numerically consequently they can process musical information.
3. A computer's ability to process music depends on what software it can run furthermore it must be connected to a system that converts electrical vibration into sound.
4. Computers and their sound systems can produce many different sounds indeed the number of possible sounds is infinite.
5. The powerful music computers are very expensive they are therefore used only by professional musicians.

Exercise 4
Sentence combining: Main clauses related by conjunctive adverbs

Combine each set of three sentences below into one sentence containing only two main clauses. Connect the clauses with the conjunctive adverb in parentheses, and separate them with a semicolon. (Be sure conjunctive adverbs are punctuated appropriately.) You will have to add, delete, change, and rearrange words. Each item has more than one possible answer.

Example:

The Albanians censored their news. We got little news from them. And what we got was unreliable. (*therefore*)

The Albanians censored their news; *therefore*, the little news we got from them was unreliable.

1. Most music computers are too expensive for the average consumer. Digital keyboard instruments can be inexpensive. They are widely available. (*however*)
2. Inside the keyboard is a small computer. The computer controls a sound synthesizer. The instrument can both process and produce music. (*consequently*)
3. The person playing the keyboard presses keys or manipulates other controls such as switches. The computer and synthesizer convert these signals. The signals are converted into vibrations and sounds. (*then*)
4. The inexpensive keyboards can perform only a few functions. To the novice computer musician, the range is exciting. The

range includes drum rhythms and simulated instruments. (*still*)

5. Would-be musicians can orchestrate whole songs. They start from just the melody lines. They need never again play "Chopsticks." (*thus*)

 22c **Use a semicolon to separate main clauses if they are long and complex or if they contain commas, even when a coordinating conjunction joins them.**

You would normally use a comma with the coordinating conjunctions *and, but, or, nor,* and *for* between main clauses. But placing semicolons between clauses punctuated with commas or between long and grammatically complicated clauses makes a sentence easier to read.

> Lewis and Clark led the men of their party with consummate skill, inspiring and encouraging them, doctoring and caring for them; *and* they kept voluminous notes and journals.
> —PAGE SMITH

> By a conscious effort of the mind, we can stand aloof from actions and their consequences; *and* all things, good and bad, go by us like a torrent.   —HENRY DAVID THOREAU

Many writers prefer to use a semicolon instead of a comma between main clauses joined by the coordinating conjunctions *so* and *yet,* even when the clauses are not complicated or internally punctuated.

> The day was rainy and blustery; *so* the food vendors kept their fruits and vegetables indoors.

> It seemed an unlikely day for shopping; *yet* buyers flocked to the market for fresh, inexpensive produce.

Exercise 5
Punctuating between long main clauses

Substitute semicolons for commas in the following sentences to separate main clauses that are long or grammatically complicated or that are internally punctuated.

Example:

> She enjoyed dancing to rock music, often joined a group for square dancing, and even danced the fox trot with her father and brothers, but she preferred ballet.

> She enjoyed dancing to rock music, often joined a group for square dancing, and even danced the fox trot with her father and brothers; but she preferred ballet.

(handwritten margin note) I used to live at 4408 Morgal Street, Rockville, Maryland, but now I live at 110 Wye Road, Queenstown, Maryland.

;
22c

; 22d

ANSWERS: EXERCISE 5

1. Legends of the towns of the Old West create a lively picture of constant saloon brawls, bank robberies, and gunfights; but the picture is distorted.
2. Many of the towns lacked saloons or banks, not to mention gun-toting strangers; and they were sparsely populated.
3. For towns such as Last Chance, with a population of sixty, the arrival of a stagecoach bearing supplies and mail was the only excitement; and that event occurred only once a month.
4. In between stagecoach visits, the townspeople worked hard at their business, whether ranching, homemaking, shopkeeping, or preaching; but they rarely caroused.
5. Gambling, dancing, drinking, fighting, and other forms of fast living were not the style of the citizens of Last Chance and similar Old West towns; for eking out a living took most of their energy.

1. Legends of the towns of the Old West create a lively picture of constant saloon brawls, bank robberies, and gunfights, but the picture is distorted.
2. Many of the towns lacked saloons or banks, not to mention gun-toting strangers, and they were sparsely populated.
3. For towns such as Last Chance, with a population of sixty, the arrival of a stagecoach bearing supplies and mail was the only excitement, and that event occurred only once a month.
4. In between stagecoach visits, the townspeople worked hard at their business, whether ranching, homemaking, shopkeeping, or preaching, but they rarely caroused.
5. Gambling, dancing, drinking, fighting, and other forms of fast living were not the style of the citizens of Last Chance and similar Old West towns, for eking out a living took most of their energy.

 22d   Use semicolons to separate items in a series if they are long or contain commas.

You normally use commas to separate items in a series (see 21f-1). But use semicolons instead when the items are long or internally punctuated. The semicolons help the reader identify the items.

> The custody case involved Amy Dalton, the child; Ellen and Mark Dalton, the parents; and Ruth and Hal Blum, the grandparents.

> One may even reasonably advance the claim that the sort of communication that really counts, and is therefore embodied into permanent records, is primarily written; that "words fly away, but written messages endure," as the Latin saying put it two thousand years ago; and that there is no basic significance to at least fifty per cent of the oral interchange that goes on among all sorts of persons, high and low.
> —MARIO PEI

Exercise 6
Punctuating long items in series

Substitute semicolons for commas in the following sentences to separate long or internally punctuated items in a series.

Example:

After graduation he debated whether to settle in San Francisco, which was temperate but far from his parents, New York City, which was exciting but expensive, or Atlanta, which was close to home but already familiar.

After graduation he debated whether to settle in San Francisco, which was temperate but far from his parents; New

York City, which was exciting but expensive; or Atlanta, which was close to home but already familiar.

1. The Indian subcontinent is separated from the rest of the world by clear barriers: the Bay of Bengal and the Arabian Sea to the east and west, respectively, the Indian Ocean to the south, and 1600 miles of mountain ranges to the north.

2. For thousands of years the subcontinent attracted immigrants, who fled poverty or oppression in their own lands, invaders, who aimed to conquer and rule the vast territory, and colonizers, who sought to enrich their own countries with India's labor and resources.

3. As a result, India is a nation of ethnic and linguistic diversity, with numerous religions, including Hinduism, Islam, and Christianity, with distinct castes as well as Aryan, Dravidian, and Mongoloid ethnic groups, and with sixteen languages, including the official Hindi and the "associate official" English.

4. Between the seventeenth and nineteenth centuries the British colonized most of India, taking control of government and the bureaucracy, running all significant mining, farming, industry, and trade, and assuming a social position above all Indians.

5. During British rule the Indians' own unresolved differences and their frustrations with the British erupted in violent incidents such as the Sepoy Mutiny that began on February 26, 1857, and lasted two years, the Amritsar Massacre on April 13, 1919, and violence between Hindus and Moslems during World War II that resulted in the division of India into India and Pakistan.

Exercise 7
Sentence combining: Long main clauses; items in series

Combine each set of sentences below into a single sentence with the structure indicated in parentheses, and punctuate with semicolons as appropriate. For items in series, rewrite into parallel constructions (see 17a). You will have to add, delete, change, and rearrange words. Each item has more than one possible answer.

Example:

He lived in a dream world. It was populated by chauffeurs who drove him about in expensive, fast cars. Servants fulfilled his every wish. Politicians sought his advice and money. (*Series punctuated with semicolons.*)

He lived in a dream world populated by chauffeurs who drove him about in expensive, fast cars; servants who fulfilled his every wish; and politicians who sought his advice and money.

1. India's geography is varied. It includes the world's highest mountains, the Himalayas, in the north. Some of the world's most fertile farmland is farther south. And still farther south

ANSWERS: EXERCISE 6

1. The Indian subcontinent is separated from the rest of the world by clear barriers: the Bay of Bengal and the Arabian Sea to the east and west, respectively; the Indian Ocean to the south; and 1600 miles of mountain ranges to the north.

2. For thousands of years the subcontinent attracted immigrants, who fled poverty or oppression in their own lands; invaders, who aimed to conquer and rule the vast territory; and colonizers, who sought to enrich their own countries with India's labor and resources.

3. As a result, India is a nation of ethnic and linguistic diversity, with numerous religions, including Hinduism, Islam, and Christianity; with distinct castes as well as Aryan, Dravidian, and Mongoloid ethnic groups; and with sixteen languages, including the official Hindi and the "associate official" English.

4. Between the seventeenth and nineteenth centuries the British colonized most of India, taking control of government and the bureaucracy; running all significant mining, farming, industry, and trade; and assuming a social position above all Indians.

5. During British rule the Indians' own unresolved differences and their frustrations with the British erupted in violent incidents such as the Sepoy Mutiny that began on February 26, 1857, and lasted two years; the Amritsar Massacre on April 13, 1919; and violence between Hindus and Moslems during World War II that resulted in the division of India into India and Pakistan.

;
22d

COLLABORATIVE LEARNING

ANSWERS: EXERCISE 7
Possible Answers

1. India's geography is varied, including the world's highest mountains, the Himalayas, in the north; some of the world's most fertile farmland farther south; still farther south, unpopulated deserts and tropical rain forests.
2. In the village of Cherrapunji the annual rainfall is 451 inches, one of the highest on earth; and raindrops are sometimes as big as marbles.
3. Monsoon winds drive India's climate, bringing the hot, dry season between October and May; the cool, rainy season between June and September; and the short spells of moderate rain and temperature as the seasons change.
4. The monsoon is a central fact of life in much of India, determining feast or famine; yet it cannot be predicted.
5. In ancient Indian religions the moods of the monsoon were attributed to the moods of the gods: their pleasure with human beings brought the good monsoon of moderate rains; their anger at human trangressions brought scorching drought; their grief over still other transgressions brought crop-killing rains.

MEMORY AID

Students may benefit from this brief list of ways *not* to use the semicolon:

Do not use a semicolon to separate a subordinate clause from a main clause.
Do not use a semicolon to introduce a series.
Do not overuse a semicolon.

are unpopulated deserts and tropical rain forests. (*Series punctuated with semicolons.*)
2. In the village of Cherrapunji the annual rainfall is 451 inches. It is one of the highest rainfalls on earth. Raindrops are sometimes as big as marbles. (*Main clauses linked by <u>and</u> and a semicolon.*)
3. Monsoon winds drive India's climate. The winds bring the hot, dry season between October and May. They bring the cool, rainy season between June and September. And they bring the short spells of moderate rain and temperature as the seasons change. (*Series punctuated with semicolons.*)
4. The monsoon is a central fact of life in much of India. It determines feast or famine. It cannot be predicted. (*Main clauses linked by <u>yet</u> and a semicolon.*)
5. In ancient Indian religions the moods of the monsoon were attributed to the moods of the gods. One mood was their pleasure with human beings. It brought the good monsoon of moderate rains. Another mood was their anger at human transgressions. It brought scorching drought. And another mood was their grief over still other transgressions. It brought crop-killing rains. (*Series punctuated with semicolons.*)

22e Use the semicolon only where required.

1 Delete any semicolon that separates a subordinate clause or a phrase from a main clause.

The semicolon separates only equal sentence parts: main clauses and sometimes items in series. It does not separate unequal parts: subordinate clauses and main clauses, or phrases and main clauses.

Faulty	According to African authorities; only about 35,000 Pygmies exist today.
Revised	According to African authorities, only about 35,000 Pygmies exist today.
Faulty	The world would be less interesting; if clothes were standardized.
Revised	The world would be less interesting if clothes were standardized.

Caution: Many readers regard a phrase or subordinate clause set off with a semicolon as a sentence fragment. See Chapter 10.

2 **Delete any semicolon that introduces a series or explanation.**

Colons and dashes, not semicolons, introduce series, explanations, and so forth. (See 25a and 25b.)

Faulty   Teachers have heard all sorts of reasons why students do poorly; psychological problems, family illness, too much work, too little time.

Revised   Teachers have heard all sorts of reasons why students do poorly: psychological problems, family illness, too much work, too little time.

Revised   Teachers have heard all sorts of reasons why students do poorly—psychological problems, family illness, too much work, too little time.

3 **Use the semicolon sparingly.**

Use the semicolon only occasionally. Too many semicolons, even when they are required by rule, often indicate repetitive sentence structure. Compare two versions of the same information.

Semicolon overused

The Make-a-Wish Foundation helps sick children; it grants the wishes of children who are terminally ill. The foundation learns of a child's wish; the information usually comes from parents, friends, or hospital staff; the wish may be for a special toy, perhaps, or a visit to Disneyland. The foundation grants some wishes with its own funds; for other wishes it appeals to those who have what the child desires.

Revised

The Make-a-Wish Foundation grants the wishes of children who are terminally ill. From parents, friends, or hospital staff, the foundation learns of a child's wish for a special toy, perhaps, or a visit to Disneyland. It grants some wishes with its own funds; for other wishes it appeals to those who have what the child desires.

;
22e

Exercise 8
Revising: Misused or overused semicolons

Revise the following sentences or groups of sentences to eliminate misused or overused semicolons, substituting other punctuation as appropriate.

COLLABORATIVE LEARNING

ANSWERS: EXERCISE 8

1. The main religion in India is Hinduism, a way of life as well as a theology and philosophy.
2. Unlike Christianity and Judaism, Hinduism is a polytheistic religion, with deities numbering in the hundreds.
3. Unlike many other religions, Hinduism allows its creeds and practices to vary widely from place to place and person to person. Whereas other religions have churches and principal prophets and holy books, Hinduism does not. And whereas other religions are centered on specially trained priests or other leaders, in Hinduism the individual is his or her own priest.
4. In Hindu belief there are four types of people: reflective, emotional, active, and experimental.
5. Each type of person has a different technique for realizing the true, immortal self, which has infinite existence, infinite knowledge, and infinite joy.

COLLABORATIVE LEARNING

ANSWERS: EXERCISE 9

The set, sounds, and actors in the movie captured the essence of horror films. The set was ideal: dark, deserted streets; trees dipping their branches over the sidewalks; mist hugging the ground and creeping up to meet the trees; looming shadows of unlighted, turreted houses. The sounds, too, were appropriate; especially terrifying was the hard, hollow sound of footsteps echoing throughout the film. But the best feature of the movie was its actors, all of them tall, pale, and thin to the point of emaciation. With one exception, they were dressed uniformly in gray and had gray hair. The exception was an actress who dressed only in black, as if to set off her pale yellow, nearly white long hair, the only color in the film. The glinting black eyes of another actor stole almost every scene; indeed, they were the source of all the film's mischief.

Example:

The doctor gave all his patients the same advice; cut back on salt and fats, don't smoke, and exercise regularly.

The doctor gave all his patients the same advice: cut back on salt and fats, don't smoke, and exercise regularly.

1. The main religion in India is Hinduism; a way of life as well as a theology and philosophy.
2. Unlike Christianity and Judaism; Hinduism is a polytheistic religion; with deities numbering in the hundreds.
3. Hinduism is unlike many other religions; it allows its creeds and practices to vary widely from place to place and person to person. Other religions have churches; Hinduism does not. Other religions have principal prophets and holy books; Hinduism does not. Other religions are centered on specially trained priests or other leaders; in Hinduism the individual is his or her own priest.
4. In Hindu belief there are four types of people; reflective, emotional, active, and experimental.
5. Each type of person has a different technique for realizing the true, immortal self; which has infinite existence, infinite knowledge, and infinite joy.

Exercise 9
Revising: Semicolons

Insert semicolons in the following paragraph wherever they are needed. Eliminate any misused or needless semicolons, substituting other punctuation as appropriate.

The set, sounds, and actors in the movie captured the essence of horror films. The set was ideal; dark, deserted streets, trees dipping their branches over the sidewalks, mist hugging the ground and creeping up to meet the trees, looming shadows of unlighted, turreted houses. The sounds, too, were appropriate, especially terrifying was the hard, hollow sound of footsteps echoing throughout the film. But the best feature of the movie was its actors; all of them tall, pale, and thin to the point of emaciation. With one exception, they were dressed uniformly in gray and had gray hair. The exception was an actress who dressed only in black; as if to set off her pale yellow, nearly white, long hair; the only color in the film. The glinting black eyes of another actor stole almost every scene, indeed, they were the source of all the film's mischief.

Note: See page 450 for a punctuation exercise combining semicolons with other marks of punctuation.

Chapter 23

The Apostrophe

HIGHLIGHTS

This chapter deals with the uses of the apostrophe. The format of the chapter presents these uses in a manner suitable for easy memorization. In addition, the chapter points out trouble spots writers often encounter: the distinction between *it's* and *its,* for example.

Unlike other punctuation marks, which separate words, the apostrophe (') appears as *part* of a word to indicate possession, the omission of one or more letters, or (in a few cases) plural number.

23a   **Use the apostrophe to indicate the possessive case for nouns and indefinite pronouns.**

The **possessive case** shows ownership or possession of one person or thing by another. Possession may be shown with an *of* phrase (*the hair of the dog*); or it may be shown with the addition of an apostrophe and, usually, an *-s* (*the dog's hair*). The possessive form functions as an adjective does to limit a noun.

Caution: The apostrophe or apostrophe plus *-s* is an *addition:* everything before this addition should spell the name of the owner or owners without dropped or added letters.

RESOURCES AND IDEAS

Harvey S. Wiener, *The Writing Room: A Resource Book for Teachers of English* (New York: Oxford UP, 1981) 175–80. Wiener offers advice on explaining possession to students and describes several exercises designed to help them master the possessive forms of words.

 1   **Add -'s to form the possessive case of singular or plural nouns or indefinite pronouns that do *not* end in -s.**

Bill *Boughton's* skillful card tricks amaze children.
Children's eyes widen. *Anyone's* eyes would widen.
Most tricks will pique an *adult's* curiosity, too.

TRANSPARENCY MASTER
AVAILABLE

23a

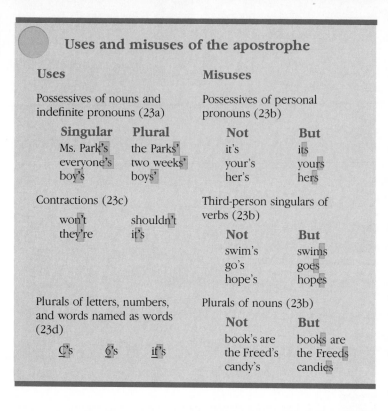

Uses and misuses of the apostrophe

Uses	Misuses
Possessives of nouns and indefinite pronouns (23a)	Possessives of personal pronouns (23b)

Singular	Plural		Not	But
Ms. Park's	the Parks'		it's	its
everyone's	two weeks'		your's	yours
boy's	boys'		her's	hers

Contractions (23c)		Third-person singulars of verbs (23b)

won't	shouldn't
they're	it's

	Not	But
	swim's	swims
	go's	goes
	hope's	hopes

Plurals of letters, numbers, and words named as words (23d)	Plurals of nouns (23b)

	Not	But
C's	6's	if's	book's are	books are

	the Freed's	the Freeds
	candy's	candies

2 **Add -'s to form the possessive case of singular words ending in -s.**

Henry *James's* novels reward the patient reader.
Jane *Gross's* promotion was expected.
Doris's book sells well.
Los *Angeles's* weather is mostly warm.
The *business's* customers filed suit.

Exception: We typically do not pronounce the possessive *-s* of a few singular nouns ending in an *s* or *z* sound, especially names with more than one *s* sound (*Moses*), names that sound like plurals (*Rivers, Bridges*), and other nouns when they are followed by a word beginning in *s*. In these cases, many writers add only the apostrophe to indicate possession.

Moses' mother concealed him in the bulrushes.
Joan *Rivers'* jokes offend many people.
For *conscience'* sake she confessed her lie.

However, usage varies widely, and the final -*s* is not wrong with words like these (*Moses's, Rivers's, conscience's*).

 Add only an apostrophe to form the possessive case of plural words ending in -'s.

Workers' incomes have risen over the past decade, but not fast enough.
Many students actually benefit from several *years'* work after high school.
The *Jameses'* talents are extraordinary.

Note the difference in the possessives of singular and plural words ending in -*s*. The singular form usually takes -'*s: James's* (see 23a-2). The plural takes only the apostrophe: *Jameses'*.

 Add -'s only to the last word to form the possessive case of compound words or word groups.

The *council president's* address was a bore.
The *brother-in-law's* business failed.
Taxes are always *somebody else's* fault.

 When two or more words show individual possession, add -'s to them all. If they show joint possession, add -'s only to the last word.

Individual possession

Youngman's and Mason's comedy techniques are similar. [Each comedian has his own technique.]

Joint possession

The child recovered despite her *mother and father's* neglect. [The mother and father were jointly neglectful.]

Exercise 1
Forming possessives

Form the possessive case of each word or word group in parentheses.

23a

ANSWERS: EXERCISE 1

1. In the myths of the ancient Greeks, the god-desses' roles vary widely.
2. Demeter's responsibility is the fruitfulness of the earth.
3. Athena's role is to guard the city of Athens.
4. Artemis's function is to care for wild animals and small children.
5. Athena and Artemis's father, Zeus, is the king of the gods.
6. Even a single goddess's responsibilities are often varied.
7. Over several centuries' time, Athena changes from a mariner's goddess to the patron of crafts.
8. Athena is also concerned with fertility and with children's well-being, since Athens's strength depended on a large and healthy population.
9. Athena often changes into birds' forms.
10. In Homer's *Odyssey* she assumes a sea eagle's form.
11. In ancient Athens the myths of Athena were part of everyone's knowledge and life.
12. A cherished myth tells how Athena fights to retain possession of her people's land when the god Poseidon wants it.
13. Athena's and Poseidon's skills are different, and each promises a special gift to the Athenians.
14. At the contest's conclusion, Poseidon has given water and Athena has given an olive tree, for sustenance.
15. The other gods decide that the Athenians' lives depend more on Athena than on Poseidon.

Example:

The (*men*) blood pressures were higher than the (*women*). The *men's* blood pressures were higher than the *women's*.

1. In the myths of the ancient Greeks, the (*goddesses*) roles vary widely.
2. (*Demeter*) responsibility is the fruitfulness of the earth.
3. (*Athena*) role is to guard the city of Athens.
4. (*Artemis*) function is to care for wild animals and small children.
5. (*Athena and Artemis*) father, Zeus, is the king of the gods.
6. Even a single (*goddess*) responsibilities are often varied.
7. Over several (*centuries*) time, Athena changes from a (*mariner*) goddess to the patron of crafts.
8. Athena is also concerned with fertility and with (*children*) well-being, since (*Athens*) strength depended on a large and healthy population.
9. Athena often changes into (*birds*) forms.
10. In (*Homer*) *Odyssey* she assumes a (*sea eagle*) form.
11. In ancient Athens the myths of Athena were part of (*everyone*) knowledge and life.
12. A cherished myth tells how Athena fights to retain possession of her (*people*) land when the god Poseidon wants it.
13. (*Athena and Poseidon*) skills are different, and each promises a special gift to the Athenians.
14. At the (*contest*) conclusion, Poseidon has given water and Athena has given an olive tree, for sustenance.
15. The other gods decide that the (*Athenians*) lives depend more on Athena than on Poseidon.

23b **Delete any apostrophe from a plural noun, a singular verb, or a possessive personal pronoun.**

Not all words ending in *-s* take an apostrophe. Three kinds of words are especially likely to attract unneeded apostrophes.

Plural nouns

The plurals of nouns are generally formed by adding *-s* or *-es* (*boys, Smiths, families, Joneses*). Don't mistakenly add an apostrophe to form the plural.

Faulty	The unleashed *dog's* began traveling in a pack.
Revised	The unleashed *dogs* began traveling in a pack.

Faulty   The *Jones'* and *Bass'* were feuding.
Revised   The *Joneses* and *Basses* were feuding.

Singular verbs

Present-tense verbs used with *he, she, it,* and other third-person singular subjects always end in *-s* and *never* take an apostrophe.

Faulty   The subway *break's* down less often now.
Revised   The subway *breaks* down less often now.

Possessives of personal pronouns

His, hers, its, ours, yours, theirs, and *whose* are possessive forms of the personal pronouns. They do not need apostrophes.

Faulty   The credit is *her's,* not *their's.*
Revised   The credit is *hers,* not *theirs.*

The personal pronouns are often confused with contractions. See 23c below.

Exercise 2
Distinguishing between plurals and possessives

Supply the appropriate form—possessive or plural—of each word given in parentheses. Some answers require apostrophes, and some do not.

    Example:

    A dozen Hawaiian (*shirt*), each with (*it*) own loud design, hung in the window.

    A dozen Hawaiian *shirts,* each with *its* own loud design, hung in the window.

1. Demeter may be the oldest of the Greek (*god*), older than Zeus.
2. Many prehistoric (*culture*) had earth (*goddess*) like Demeter.
3. In myth she is the earth mother, which means that the responsibility for the fertility of both (*animal*) and (*plant*) is (*she*).
4. The (*goddess*) power is so great that the world becomes desolate when she neglects (*it*) care.
5. Her (*trouble*) begin with the kidnapping of her daughter, Kore, by the god Hades.

ANSWERS: EXERCISE 2

1. Demeter may be the oldest of the Greek gods, older than Zeus.
2. Many prehistoric cultures had earth goddesses like Demeter.
3. In myth she is the earth mother, which means that the responsibility for the fertility of both animals and plants is hers.
4. The goddess's power is so great that the world becomes desolate when she neglects its care.
5. Her troubles begin with the kidnapping of her daughter, Kore, by the god Hades.

23b

6. Hades's domain is the underworld.
7. Both Demeter and Hades insist that Kore is rightfully theirs.
8. Eventually, like divorced parents, Demeter and Hades agree to share Kore.
9. Demeter restores the earth's fruitfulness.
10. The world owes a debt to Zeus, whose mediation encourages Demeter and Hades to compromise.

6. (*Hades*) domain is the underworld.
7. Both Demeter and Hades insist that Kore is rightfully (*they*).
8. Eventually, like divorced (*parent*), Demeter and Hades agree to share Kore.
9. Demeter restores the (*earth*) fruitfulness.
10. The world owes a debt to Zeus, (*who*) mediation encourages Demeter and Hades to compromise.

23c Use an apostrophe to indicate the omission of one or more letters, numbers, or words in a standard contraction.

it is	it's	does not	doesn't
they are	they're	were not	weren't
you are	you're	class of 1987	class of '87
who is	who's	of the clock	o'clock
cannot	can't	madam	ma'am

Contractions of verb phrases (*don't, weren't, isn't*) and of pronoun-verb pairs (*I'll, we're, she's*) are common in speech and in informal writing. They may also be used to relax style in more formal kinds of writing, as they are in this handbook. But be aware that many people disapprove of contractions in any kind of formal writing.

Caution: Don't confuse the personal pronouns *its, their, your,* and *whose* with the contractions *it's, they're, you're,* and *who's.*

Faulty *It's* messiness is not *you're* problem or *they're* problem. But *whose* going to clean up?

Revised *Its* messiness is not *your* problem or *their* problem. But *who's* going to clean up?

Exercise 3
Forming contractions

Form contractions from each set of words below. Use each contraction in a complete sentence.

Example:
we are: *we're*
We're open to ideas.

1. she would
2. could not
3. they are
4. he is
5. do not
6. she will
7. hurricane of 1962
8. is not
9. we would
10. will not

ANSWERS: EXERCISE 3
Possible Answers

1. she'd
   She'd rather be dancing.
2. couldn't
   He couldn't see her in the crowd.
3. they're
   They're at the front door now.
4. he's
   He's my brother.
5. don't
   We don't like the beach.
6. she'll
   She'll speak her mind.
7. hurricane of '62
   The recent storm was nearly as bad as the hurricane of '62.
8. isn't
   Isn't that your cousin?
9. we'd
   We'd prefer you did not ask.
10. won't
    The door won't budge.

Exercise 4
Revising: Contractions and personal pronouns

Revise the following sentences to correct mistakes in the use of contractions and personal pronouns. Circle the number preceding any sentence that is already correct.

Example:

The company gives it's employees their birthdays off.
The company gives *its* employees their birthdays off.

1. In Greek myth the goddess Demeter has a special fondness for Eleusis, near Athens, and it's people.
2. She finds rest among the people and is touched by their kindness.
3. Arriving in the disguise of an old woman, Demeter cares for a baby who's father is the king.
4. She tries to make the child immortal by laying it in fire to burn away its mortality.
5. Stopped by the baby's mother, the goddess announces, "You're eyes gaze on Demeter."
6. Demeter rewards the Eleusians with the secret for making they're land fruitful.
7. Demeter also presents the Eleusians with corn, and it's they who introduce the new food to the rest of the world.
8. The Eleusians begin a cult in honor of Demeter, whose worshiped in secret ceremonies.
9. At this point the ceremonies leave myth and enter history, for written texts record they're actual occurrence.
10. Yet its unknown what happened in the ceremonies, for no participant ever revealed their rituals.

23d Use an apostrophe plus *-s* to form the plurals of letters, numbers, and words named as words.

That sentence has too many <u>but</u>'s.

Remember to dot your <u>i</u>'s and cross your <u>t</u>'s, or your readers may not be able to distinguish them from <u>e</u>'s and <u>l</u>'s.

At the end of each chapter the author had mysteriously written two <u>3</u>'s and two <u>&</u>'s.

Notice that the letters, numbers, and words are underlined (*italicized*) but the apostrophe and added *-s* are not. (See 27d on this use of underlining or italics.)

Exception: References to the years in a decade are not underlined and often omit the apostrophe. Thus either 1960's or 1960s is acceptable as long as usage is consistent.

ANSWERS: EXERCISE 5

Possible Answers

1. 7's
   She drew 7's four times in a row.
2. q's
   She writes her q's with flourishes.
3. if's
   That's too many if's.
4. and's
   It's easy to use too many and's in writing.
5. stop's
   His job was to paint all the stop's in the parking lot.

COLLABORATIVE LEARNING

ANSWERS: EXERCISE 6

Landlocked Chad is among the world's most troubled countries. The peoples of Chad are poor: their average per capita income equals $73 a year. No more than 15 percent of Chad's population is literate, and every thousand people must share only two teachers. The natural resources of the nation have never been plentiful, and now, as it's [correct] slowly being absorbed into the growing Sahara Desert, even water is scarce. Chad's political conflicts go back beyond the turn of the century, when the French colonized the land by brutally subduing its people. The rule of the French—whose inept government of the colony did nothing to ease tensions among racial, tribal, and religious groups—ended with independence in 1960. But since then the Chadians' experience has been one of civil war and oppression, and now they're threatened with invasions from their neighbors.

23d

Exercise 5
Forming plurals of letters, numbers, words

Form the plural of each letter, number, or word by using an apostrophe and -*s* and by underlining (italicizing) appropriately. Use the new plural in a complete sentence.

Example: x
Erase or white out typing mistakes. Do not use x's.

1. 7   4. and
2. q   5. stop
3. if

Exercise 6
Revising: Apostrophes

Correct any mistakes in the use of the apostrophe or any confusion between personal pronouns and contractions in the following paragraph.

Landlocked Chad is among the worlds most troubled countries. The people's of Chad are poor; they're average per capita income equals $73 a year. No more than 15 percent of Chads population is literate, and every thousand people must share only two teacher's. The natural resources of the nation have never been plentiful, and now, as it's slowly being absorbed into the growing Sahara Desert, even water is scarce. Chads political conflicts go back beyond the turn of the century, when the French colonized the land by brutally subduing it's people. The rule of the French—who's inept government of the colony did nothing to ease tensions among racial, tribal, and religious group's—ended with independence in 1960. But since then the Chadians experience has been one of civil war and oppression, and now their threatened with invasions from they're neighbors.

Note: See page 450 for a punctuation exercise involving apostrophes along with other marks of punctuation.

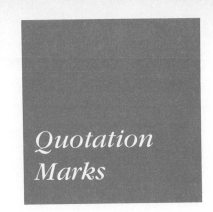

Chapter 24

Quotation Marks

HIGHLIGHTS

The uses of quotation marks are the subject of this chapter. While many students are familiar with the basic rules of punctuation, review of the conventions governing quotation marks will be helpful, especially when the students are preparing papers that require the use of cited material.

Quotation marks—either double (" ") or single (' ')—mainly enclose direct quotations from speech and from writing. The chart on the next two pages summarizes this and other uses.

Caution: Always use quotation marks in pairs, one at the beginning of a quotation and one at the end.

24a Use double quotation marks to enclose direct quotations.

Direct quotations report what someone has said or written in the exact words of the original. Always enclose direct quotations in quotation marks.

> "If a sentence does not illuminate your subject in some new and useful way," says Kurt Vonnegut, "scratch it out."

Indirect quotations report what has been said or written, but not in the exact words of the person being quoted. Indirect quotations are *not* enclosed in quotation marks.

> Kurt Vonnegut advises writers to cross out any sentence that does not say something new and useful about their subject.

(Text continues p. 430)

TRANSPARENCY MASTER
AVAILABLE

" "

24

Handling quotations from speech or writing
(For explanations, consult the sections in parentheses.)

Direct and indirect quotation

Direct quotation (24a)

According to Lewis Thomas, "We are, perhaps uniquely among the earth's creatures, the worrying animal. We worry away our lives."

Quotation within quotation (24b)

Quoting a phrase by Lewis Thomas, the author adds, "We are 'the worrying animal.' "

Indirect quotation (24a)

Lewis Thomas says that human beings are unique among animals in their worrying.

Quotation marks with other punctuation marks

Commas and periods (24g-1)

Human beings are the "worrying animal," says Thomas.
Thomas calls human beings "the worrying animal."

Semicolons and colons (24g-2)

Machiavelli said that "the majority of men live content"; in contrast, Thomas calls us "the worrying animal."

Thomas believes that we are "the worrying animal": we spend our lives afraid and restless.

Question marks, exclamation points, dashes (24g-3)

When part of your own sentence

Who said that human beings are "the worrying animal"?
Imagine saying that we human beings "worry away our lives"!
Thomas's phrase—"the worrying animal"—seems too narrow.

When part of the original quotation

"Will you discuss this with me?" she asked.
"I demand that you discuss this with me!" she yelled.
"Please, won't you—" She paused.

Altering quotations

Brackets for additions (25d)

"We [human beings] worry away our lives," says Thomas.

Brackets for altered capitalization (26a)

"[T]he worrying animal" is what Thomas calls us. He says that "[w]e worry away our lives."

Ellipsis marks for omissions (25e)

"We are . . . the worrying animal," says Thomas.

Our worrying places us "uniquely among the earth's creatures. . . . We worry away our lives."

Punctuating explanatory words

Introductory explanatory words (21h-1)

He says, "We worry away our lives."

An answer is in these words by Lewis Thomas: "We are, perhaps uniquely among the earth's creatures, the worrying animal."

Thomas says that "the worrying animal" is afraid and restless.

Concluding explanatory words (21h-1)

We are "the worrying animal," says Thomas.
"Who says?" she demanded.
"I do!" he shouted.

Interrupting explanatory words (21h-2)

"We are," says Thomas, "perhaps uniquely among the earth's creatures, the worrying animal."

I do not like the idea," she said; "however, I agree with it."

We are "the worrying animal," says Thomas. "We worry away our lives."

See also:

Special kinds of quoted material

Using quotations in your own text

" "
24

24b Use single quotation marks to enclose a quotation within a quotation.

When you quote a writer or speaker, use double quotation marks (see 24a). When the material you quote contains yet another quotation, distinguish the two by enclosing the second quotation in single quotation marks.

> "In formulating any philosophy," Woody Allen writes, "the first consideration must always be: What can we know? . . . Descartes hinted at the problem when he wrote, 'My mind can never know my body, although it has become quite friendly with my leg.' "

Notice that two different quotation marks appear at the end of the sentence—one single (to finish the interior quotation) and one double (to finish the main quotation).

Exercise 1
Using double and single quotation marks

Insert single and double quotation marks as needed in the following sentences. Circle the number preceding any sentence that is already correct.

Example:

The purpose of this book, explains the preface, is to examine the meaning of the phrase Dance is poetry.

"The purpose of this book," explains the preface, "is to examine the meaning of the phrase 'Dance is poetry.' "

1. Why, the lecturer asked, do we say Bless you! or something else when people sneeze but not acknowledge coughs, hiccups, and other eruptions?
2. She said that sneezes have always been regarded differently.
3. Sneezes feel more uncontrollable than some other eruptions, she said.
4. Unlike coughs and hiccups, she explained, sneezes feel as if they come from inside the head.
5. She concluded, People thus wish to recognize a sneeze, if only with a Gosh.

24c Set off quotations of dialogue, poetry, and long prose passages according to standard practice.

Dialogue

When quoting conversations, begin a new paragraph for each speaker.

"What shall I call you? Your name?" Andrews whispered rapidly, as with a high squeak the latch of the door rose.

"Elizabeth," she said. "Elizabeth."

—GRAHAM GREENE, *The Man Within*

Note: When you quote a single speaker for more than one paragraph, put quotation marks at the beginning of each paragraph but at the end of only the last paragraph. The absence of quotation marks at the end of each paragraph but the last tells readers that the speech is continuing.

Poetry

When you quote a single line from a poem, song, or verse play, run the line into your text and enclose it in quotation marks.

Dylan Thomas remembered childhood as an idyllic time: "About the lilting house and happy as the grass was green."

Poetry quotations of two or three lines may be placed in the text or displayed separately. If you place such a quotation in the text, enclose it in quotation marks and separate the lines with a slash surrounded by space (see 25f).

An example of Robert Frost's incisiveness is in two lines from "Death of the Hired Man": "Home is the place where, when you have to go there, / They have to take you in."

Quotations of more than three lines of poetry should always be separated from the text with space and an indention. *Do not add quotation marks.*

Emily Dickinson rarely needed more than a few lines to express her complex thoughts:

> To wait an Hour–is long–
> If Love be just beyond–
> To wait Eternity–is short–
> If Love reward the end–

The *MLA Handbook for Writers of Research Papers,* the standard guide to manuscript format in English and some other disciplines, recommends these spacings for displayed quotations:

- Double-space above and below the quotation.
- Indent the quotation ten spaces from the left margin.
- Double-space the quoted lines.

Unless your instructor specifies otherwise, follow these guidelines for your typewritten or handwritten papers. (See Chapter 38, p. 636, for an example of a displayed quotation in a typed paper.)

NOTE

If you are using this chapter as part of a review of citation, it may be helpful to mention the ellipsis mark (25e) at this point as a means of omitting unnecessary material within a quotation.

" "
24c

Caution: Be careful when quoting poetry to reproduce faithfully all line indentions, space between lines, spelling, capitalization, and punctuation, such as the capitals and dashes in the Dickinson poem above.

Long prose passages

Separate a prose quotation of more than four typed or handwritten lines from the body of your paper. Follow the guidelines of the *MLA Handbook* in the list above. *Do not add quotation marks.*

In his 1967 study of the lives of unemployed black men, Eliot Lebow observes that "unskilled" construction work requires more experience and skill than generally assumed.

> A healthy, sturdy, active man of good intelligence requires from two to four weeks to break in on a construction job. . . . It frequently happens that his foreman or the craftsman he services is not willing to wait that long for him to get into condition or to learn at a glance the difference in size between a rough 2 × 8 and a finished 2 × 10.

Do not use a paragraph indention when quoting a single complete paragraph or a part of a paragraph. Use paragraph indentions only when quoting two or more complete paragraphs.

Exercise 2
Quoting dialogue, poetry, and long prose passages

Practice using quotation marks in quoted dialogue, poetry, and long prose passages by completing each of the exercises below.

1. Write a short sketch of dialogue between two people.
2. Write a sentence that quotes a single line of poetry.
3. Write two sentences, each quoting the same two lines of poetry. In one, place the poetry lines in the text. In the other, separate the two lines from the text.
4. Write a sentence introducing a prose passage of more than four lines, and then set up the quotation appropriately.

24d Put quotation marks around the titles of works that are parts of other works.

Use quotation marks to enclose the titles of short poems, articles in periodicals, short stories, essays, episodes of television and radio programs, the subdivisions of books, and other works that

ANSWERS: EXERCISE 2
Possible Answers

1. "Do you have the tickets?" she asked, as they parked the car and started up the steps through the crowd.
  "Of course," he said. "What do you think I am?" He stopped despite the crowd, patting his pockets. "Oh, no! My wallet!"
2. Do you know a poem that begins, "What is so rare as a day in June"?
3. The sonnet begins: "The world is too much with us; late and soon, / Getting and spending, we lay waste our powers."

The sonnet begins:

> The world is too much with us; late
> [and soon,
> Getting and spending, we lay waste
> [our powers.

4. Everyone should know by heart the first article of the Bill of Rights:

> Congress shall make no law respecting an establishment of religion, or prohibiting the free exercise thereof; or abridging the freedom of speech, or of the press; or the right of the people peaceably to assemble, and to petition the government for a redress of grievances.

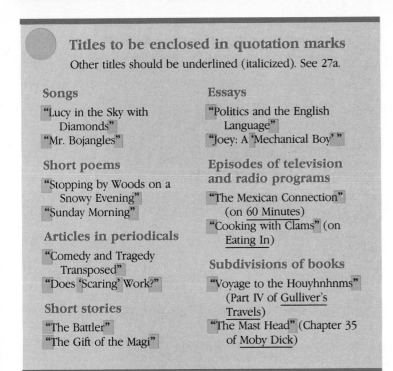

Titles to be enclosed in quotation marks

Other titles should be underlined (italicized). See 27a.

Songs

"Lucy in the Sky with
  Diamonds"
"Mr. Bojangles"

Short poems

"Stopping by Woods on a
  Snowy Evening"
"Sunday Morning"

Articles in periodicals

"Comedy and Tragedy
  Transposed"
"Does 'Scaring' Work?"

Short stories

"The Battler"
"The Gift of the Magi"

Essays

"Politics and the English
  Language"
"Joey: A 'Mechanical Boy'"

**Episodes of television
and radio programs**

"The Mexican Connection"
  (on 60 Minutes)
"Cooking with Clams" (on
  Eating In)

Subdivisions of books

"Voyage to the Houyhnhnms"
  (Part IV of Gulliver's
  Travels)
"The Mast Head" (Chapter 35
  of Moby Dick)

are published or released within larger works. Use quotation
marks for song titles as well. Use underlining (italics) for all other
titles, such as books, plays, periodicals, movies, television programs, and works of art. (See 27a.)

Note: Use single quotation marks for a quotation within a
quoted title, as in the second article and second essay in the box
above.

See 26b for guidelines on the use of capital letters in titles.

24e   Quotation marks may be used to enclose words
being defined or used in a special sense.

By "charity," I mean the love of one's neighbor as oneself.
On movie sets movable "wild walls" make a one-walled room
seem four-walled on film.

Note: In definitions, underlining (italics) is more common
than quotation marks (see 27d).

By charity, I mean the love of one's neighbor as oneself.

ANSWERS: EXERCISE 3

1. In Chapter 8, titled "How to Be Interesting," the author explains the art of conversation.
2. The Beatles' "Let It Be" reminds him of his uncle.
3. "Doom" [or Doom] means simply judgment as well as unhappy destiny.
4. The article that appeared in Mental Health [correct] was titled "Children of Divorce Ask, 'Why?'"
5. In my encyclopedia the discussion under "Modern Art" fills less than a column.

Exercise 3
Quoting titles and words

Insert quotation marks as needed for titles and words in the following sentences. If quotation marks should be used instead of underlining, insert them.

Example:

The students call her professor despite her youth.
The students call her "professor" despite her youth.

1. In Chapter 8, titled How to Be Interesting, the author explains the art of conversation.
2. The Beatles' Let It Be reminds him of his uncle.
3. Doom means simply judgment as well as unhappy destiny.
4. The article that appeared in Mental Health was titled Children of Divorce Ask, "Why?"
5. In the encyclopedia the discussion under Modern Art fills less than a column.

" "
24f

24f **Use quotation marks only where they are required.**

Don't use quotation marks in the titles of your papers unless they contain or are themselves direct quotations.

Not   "The Death Wish in One Poem by Robert Frost"

But   The Death Wish in One Poem by Robert Frost

Or   The Death Wish in "Stopping by Woods on a Snowy Evening"

Don't use quotation marks to enclose common nicknames or technical terms that are not being defined.

Not   Even as President, "Jimmy" Carter preferred to use his nickname.

But   Even as President, Jimmy Carter preferred to use his nickname.

Not   "Mitosis" in a cell is fascinating to watch.

But   Mitosis in a cell is fascinating to watch.

Don't use quotation marks in an attempt to justify or apologize for slang and trite expressions that are inappropriate to your writing. If slang is appropriate, use it without quotation marks.

Not   We should support the President in his "hour of need" rather than "wimp out" on him.

But   We should give the President the support he needs rather than turn away like cowards.

(See 31a-1 and 31b-5 for more on slang and trite expressions.)

 24g **Place other marks of punctuation inside or outside quotation marks according to standard practice.**

NOTE

Students should note that this rule applies even when closing quotation marks are both single and double. Example: "The author of the article pointed out that the rock group The Police coined the word 'synchronicity.'"

 1 **Place commas and periods inside quotation marks.**

Swift uses irony in his essay "A Modest Proposal."

When he says he hopes his proposal "will not be liable to the least objection," he is being ironic.

Many first-time readers are shocked to see infants described as "delicious."

"'A Modest Proposal,'" wrote one critic, is "so outrageous that it cannot be believed."

Notice that periods or commas fall inside closing quotation marks even when only a single word is quoted (third example) or when single and double quotation marks are combined (last example).

(See 21h for the use of commas to separate quotations from words used to introduce or explain them.)

 2 **Place colons and semicolons outside quotation marks.**

A few years ago the slogan in elementary education was "learning by playing"; now educators are concerned with teaching basic skills.

We all know what is meant by "inflation": more money buys less.

3 **Place dashes, question marks, and exclamation points inside quotation marks only if they belong to the quotation.**

When a dash, question mark, or exclamation point is part of the quotation, put it *inside* quotation marks. Don't use any other punctuation such as a period or comma.

" "

24g

"But must you—" Marcia hesitated, afraid of the answer.
Did you say, "Who is she?"
"Go away!" I yelled.

When a dash, question mark, or exclamation point applies only to the larger sentence, not to the quotation, place it *outside* quotation marks—again, with no other punctuation.

One of the most evocative lines in English poetry—"After many a summer dies the swan"—was written by Alfred, Lord Tennyson.
Who said, "Now cracks a noble heart"?
The woman called me "stupid"!

ANSWERS: EXERCISE 4

1. The course reading included Virginia Woolf's essay "The Anatomy of Fiction."
2. "No smoking on this bus!" the driver shouted.
3. The commercial says, "Lite Beer is a third less filling than your regular beer"; but how do they measure that?
4. Wearing calico and lace, she looked like a down-home girl.
5. How can we answer children who ask, "Will there be a nuclear war?"
6. In America the signs say, "Keep off the grass"; in England they say, "Please refrain from stepping on the lawn."
7. In King Richard II [correct] Shakespeare calls England "This precious stone set in the silver sea."
8. The doctors gave my father an electrocardiogram but found nothing wrong.
9. Correct.
10. Must we regard the future with what Kierkegaard called "fear and trembling"?

Exercise 4
Revising: Quotation marks

Revise the following sentences for the proper use of quotation marks. Insert quotation marks where they are needed, remove them where they are not needed, and be sure that other marks of punctuation are correctly placed inside or outside the quotation marks. Circle the number preceding any sentence that is already punctuated correctly.

Example:

The award-winning story was titled How to Say I'm Sorry to a Child.

The award-winning story was titled "How to Say 'I'm Sorry' to a Child."

1. The course reading included Virginia Woolf's essay The Anatomy of Fiction.
2. No smoking on this bus! the driver shouted.
3. The commercial says, Lite Beer is a third less filling than your regular beer; but how do they measure that?
4. Wearing calico and lace, she looked like a "down-home girl."
5. How can we answer children who ask, Will there be a nuclear war?
6. In America the signs say, Keep off the grass; in England they say, Please refrain from stepping on the lawn.
7. In King Richard II Shakespeare calls England This precious stone set in the silver sea.
8. The doctors gave my father an "electrocardiogram" but found nothing wrong.
9. Our forests—in Longfellow's words, "The murmuring pines and the hemlocks"—are slowly succumbing to land development.
10. Must we regard the future with what Kierkegaard called fear and trembling?

" "

24g

Exercise 5
Revising: Quotation marks

Insert quotation marks as needed in the following paragraph.

In one class we talked about a passage from I Have a Dream, the speech delivered by Martin Luther King, Jr., on the steps of the Lincoln Memorial on August 28, 1963:

> When the architects of our republic wrote the magnificent words of the Constitution and the Declaration of Independence, they were signing a promissory note to which every American was to fall heir. This note was a promise that all men would be guaranteed the unalienable rights of life, liberty, and the pursuit of happiness.

What did Dr. King mean by this statement? the teacher asked. Perhaps we should define promissory note first. Then she explained that a person who signs such a note agrees to pay a specific sum of money on a particular date or on demand by the holder of the note. One student suggested, Perhaps Dr. King meant that those who wrote and signed the Constitution and Declaration had stated the country's promise that all people in America should have equal political rights and equal opportunity for the pursuit of happiness. He and over 200,000 people had gathered in Washington, D.C., added another student. Maybe their purpose was to demand payment, to demand those rights for African-Americans. The whole discussion was an eye opener for those of us (including me) who had never considered that those documents make promises that we should expect our country to fulfill.

Note: See page 450 for a punctuation exercise involving quotation marks along with other marks of punctuation.

ANSWERS: EXERCISE 5

In one class we talked about a passage from "I Have a Dream," the speech delivered by Martin Luther King, Jr., on the steps of the Lincoln Memorial on August 28, 1963:

> When the architects of our republic wrote the magnificent words of the Constitution and the Declaration of Independence, they were signing a promissory note to which every American was to fall heir. This note was a promise that all men would be guaranteed the unalienable rights of life, liberty, and the pursuit of happiness.

"What did Dr. King mean by this statement?" the teacher asked. "Perhaps we should define 'promissory note' first." Then she explained that a person who signs such a note agrees to pay a specific sum of money on a particular date or on demand by the holder of the note. One student suggested, "Perhaps Dr. King meant that those who wrote and signed the Constitution and Declaration had stated the country's promise that all people in America should have equal political rights and equal opportunity for the pursuit of happiness." "He and over 200,000 people had gathered in Washington, D.C.," added another student. "Maybe their purpose was to demand payment, to demand those rights for African-Americans." The whole discussion was an eye opener for those of us (including me) who had never considered that those documents make promises that we should expect our country to fulfill.

" "

24g

HIGHLIGHTS

Chapter 25 covers the marks of punctuation not treated in the preceding chapters (20–24): the colon, the dash, parentheses, brackets, the ellipsis mark, and the slash. In addition to exercises for these marks of punctuation, the chapter provides at the end an exercise that asks students to practice using all the punctuation marks covered in Chapters 20–25.

SUMMARY

25a Use the colon to introduce summaries, explanations, series, appositives ending sentences, long or formal quotations, and statements introduced by *the following* or *as follows.*

25b Use a dash or dashes to indicate sudden changes in tone or thought and to set off some sentence elements.

25c Use parentheses to enclose nonessential elements within sentences.

25d Use brackets only within quotations to separate your own comments from the words of the writer you quote.

25e Use the ellipsis mark to indicate omissions within quotations.

25f Use the slash between options and to separate lines of poetry that are run in to the text.

Chapter 25

Other Punctuation Marks

THE COLON

 25a   **Use the colon to introduce and to separate.**

The colon is mainly a mark of introduction: it tells the reader that the preceding statement is about to be explained, amplified, or summarized; or it signals that a list or quotation follows. Occasionally, colons also separate figures and other elements.

In its main use as an introducer, a colon is always preceded by a complete **main clause**—one containing a subject and a predicate and not starting with a subordinating word (see 5c-4). A colon may or may not be followed by a main clause. This is one way the colon differs from the semicolon (see the box on the next page). The colon is often interchangeable with the dash, though the dash is more informal and more abrupt (see 25b).

    Use a colon to introduce a concluding explanation, series, appositive, or long or formal quotation.

Explanation

Soul food has a deceptively simple definition: the ethnic cooking of African-Americans.

Sometimes a concluding explanation is preceded by *the following* or *as follows* and a colon.

A more precise definition might be *the following:* ingredients, cooking methods, and dishes originating in Africa, brought to the New World by black slaves, and modified or supplemented in the Caribbean and the American South.

Series

At least three soul food dishes are familiar to most Americans: fried chicken, barbecued spareribs, and sweet potatoes.

Appositive

Soul food has one disadvantage: fat.

Namely, that is, and other expressions that introduce appositives *follow* the colon: *Soul food has one disadvantage: namely, fat.*

Long or formal quotation

One soul food chef has a solution: "Soul food doesn't have to be greasy to taste good. . . . Instead of using ham hocks to flavor beans, I use smoked turkey wings. The soulful, smoky taste remains, but without all the fat of pork."

  2 **Use a colon to separate two main clauses when the second explains or amplifies the first.**

Explanation

Soul food is a varied cuisine: it includes spicy gumbos, black-eyed peas, collard greens, and sweet potato pie.

:
25a

Distinguishing the colon and the semicolon

- The **colon** separates elements of *unequal* importance, such as statements and explanations or introductions and quotations. The first element must be a complete main clause; the second element need not be. (See 25a.)

  The business school caters to working students: it offers special evening courses in business writing, finance, and management.

  The school has one goal: to train students to be responsible, competent businesspeople.

- The **semicolon** separates elements of *equal* importance, almost always complete main clauses. (See 22a.)

  Few enrolling students know exactly what they want from the school; most hope generally for a managerial career.

Amplification

Soul food recipes, rarely written down, are passed orally from one generation to another: they form part of African-Americans' oral tradition.

Note: Depending on your preference, the complete sentence *after* the colon may begin with a capital letter or a small letter (as in the examples above). Just be consistent throughout an essay.

Use a colon to separate titles and subtitles, the subdivisions of time, and the parts of biblical citations.

Titles and subtitles

Charles Dickens: An Introduction to His Novels
Eros and Civilization: A Philosopical Inquiry into Freud

Time	Biblical citations
1:30	Isaiah 28:1–6
12:26	1 Corinthians 3:6–7

Use the colon only where required.

Use the colon only at the end of a main clause. Avoid using it between a verb and complement, verb and object, or preposition and object.

Not Two entertaining movies directed by Steven Spielberg are: *E.T.* and *Raiders of the Lost Ark.*

But Two entertaining movies directed by Steven Spielberg are *E.T.* and *Raiders of the Lost Ark.*

Not Shakespeare possessed the qualities of a Renaissance thinker, such as: humanism and a deep interest in classical Greek and Roman literature.

But Shakespeare possessed the qualities of a Renaissance thinker, such as humanism and a deep interest in classical Greek and Roman literature.

Exercise 1
Revising: Colons

Insert colons as needed in the following sentences, or delete colons that are misused.

Example:

Mix the ingredients as follows sift the flour and salt together, add the milk, and slowly beat in the egg yolk.

Mix the ingredients as follows: sift the flour and salt together, add the milk, and slowly beat in the egg yolk.

1. In the remote parts of many Third World countries, simple signs mark human habitation a dirt path, a few huts, smoke from a campfire.
2. In the built-up sections of industrialized countries, nature is all but obliterated by signs of human life, such as: houses, factories, skyscrapers, and highways.
3. The spectacle makes many question the words of Ecclesiastes 1:4 "One generation passeth away, and another cometh; but the earth abideth forever."
4. Yet many scientists see the future differently they hold that human beings have all the technology necessary to clean up the earth and restore the cycles of nature.
5. All that is needed is: a change in the attitudes of those who use technology.

ANSWERS: EXERCISE 1

1. In the remote parts of many Third World countries, simple signs mark human habitation: a dirt path, a few huts, smoke from a campfire.
2. In the built-up sections of industrialized countries, nature is all but obliterated by signs of human life, such as houses, factories, skyscrapers, and highways.
3. The spectacle makes many question the words of Ecclesiastes 1:4: "One generation passeth away, and another generation cometh; but the earth abideth forever."
4. Yet many scientists see the future differently: they hold that human beings have all the technology necessary to clean up the earth and restore the cycles of nature.
5. All that is needed is a change in the attitudes of those who use technology.

THE DASH

Use a dash or dashes to indicate sudden changes in tone or thought and to set off some sentence elements.

Dashes are mainly marks of interruption: they signal an insertion or break.

Note: In handwritten and typewritten papers, form a dash with two hyphens (--). Do not add extra space before, after, or between the hyphens.

Use a dash or dashes to indicate sudden shifts in tone, new or unfinished thoughts, and hesitation in dialogue.

Shift in tone

He tells us—does he really mean it?—that he will speak the truth from now on.

Unfinished thought

If she found out—he did not want to think what she would do.

Hesitation in dialogue

"I was worried you might think I had stayed away because I was influenced by—" He stopped and lowered his eyes.

Astonished, Howe said, "Influenced by what?"

"Well, by—" Blackburn hesitated and for answer pointed to the table.
—LIONEL TRILLING

 2 Use a dash or dashes to emphasize nonrestrictive elements.

Dashes may be used in place of commas or parentheses to set off and emphasize nonrestrictive elements such as modifiers, appositives, and parenthetical expressions. (See the box below.) Dashes are especially useful when these elements are internally punctuated. Be sure to use a pair of dashes when the element interrupts a main clause.

Appositive

The qualities Monet painted—sunlight, rich shadows, deep colors—abounded near the rivers and gardens he used as subjects.

Modifier

Though they are close together—separated by only a few blocks —the two neighborhoods could be in different countries.

TRANSPARENCY MASTER
AVAILABLE

Distinguishing dashes, commas, and parentheses

Dashes, commas, and parentheses may all set off nonessential information such as nonrestrictive modifiers and parenthetical expressions.

- **Dashes** give the information the greatest emphasis (25b-2):

  Many students—including some employed by the college—disapprove of the new work rules.

- **Commas** are less emphatic (21c):

  Many students, including some employed by the college, disapprove of the new work rules.

- **Parentheses,** the least emphatic, signal that the information is just worth a mention (25c-1):

  Many students (including some employed by the college) disapprove of the new work rules.

Parenthetical expression

At any given time there exists an inventory of undiscovered embezzlement in—or more precisely not in—the country's businesses and banks. —JOHN KENNETH GALBRAITH

3   Use a dash to set off introductory series and concluding series and explanations.

Introductory series

Shortness of breath, skin discoloration or the sudden appearance of moles, persistent indigestion, the presence of small lumps—all these may signify cancer.

A dash sets off concluding series and explanations more informally and more abruptly than a colon does (see 25a-1).

Concluding series

The patient undergoes a battery of tests—CAT scan, bronchoscopy, perhaps even biopsy.

Concluding explanation

Many patients are disturbed by the CAT scan—by the need to keep still for long periods in an exceedingly small space.

4   Use the dash only where needed.

Don't use the dash when commas, semicolons, and periods are more appropriate. And don't use too many dashes. They can create a jumpy or breathy quality in writing.

Not   In all his life—eighty-seven years—my great-grandfather never allowed his picture to be taken—not even once. He claimed the "black box"—the camera—would steal his soul.

But   In all his eighty-seven years my great-grandfather did not allow his picture to be taken even once. He claimed the "black box"—the camera—would steal his soul.

Exercise 2
Revising: Dashes

Insert dashes as needed in the following sentences.

Example:

What would we do if someone like Adolf Hitler that monster appeared among us?

ANSWERS: EXERCISE 2

1. The movie-theater business is undergoing dramatic changes—changes that may affect what movies are made and shown.
2. The closing of independent theaters, the control of theaters by fewer and fewer owners, and the increasing ownership of theaters by movie studios and distributors—these changes may reduce the availability of non-commercial films.
3. Yet at the same time the number of movie screens is increasing—primarily in multi-screen complexes—so that smaller films may find more outlets.
4. The number of active movie screens—that is, screens showing films or booked to do so—is higher now than at any time since World War II.
5. The biggest theater complexes seem to be something else as well—art galleries, amusement arcades, restaurants, spectacles.

What would we do if someone like Adolf Hitler—that monster—appeared among us?

1. The movie-theater business is undergoing dramatic changes changes that may affect what movies are made and shown.
2. The closing of independent theaters, the control of theaters by fewer and fewer owners, and the increasing ownership of theaters by movie studios and distributors these changes may reduce the availability of noncommercial films.
3. Yet at the same time the number of movie screens is increasing primarily in multiscreen complexes so that smaller films may find more outlets.
4. The number of active movie screens that is, screens showing films or booked to do so is higher now than at any time since World War II.
5. The biggest theater complexes seem to be something else as well art galleries, amusement arcades, restaurants, spectacles.

PARENTHESES

25c Use parentheses to enclose nonessential elements within sentences.

1 Use parentheses to enclose parenthetical expressions.

Parenthetical expressions include explanations, facts, digressions, and examples that may be helpful or interesting but are not essential to meaning. They are emphasized least when set off with a pair of parentheses instead of commas or dashes. (See the box on p. 442.)

The population of Philadelphia (now about 1.6 million) has declined since 1950.

Unlike the creatures (some insects, for instance) that have been unchanged for five, ten, even fifty million years, man has changed over this time-scale out of all recognition.   —JACOB BRONOWSKI

Caution: Don't put a comma before a parenthetical expression enclosed in parentheses.

Not   The dungeon, (really the basement) haunted us.
But   The dungeon (really the basement) haunted us.

A comma or period falling after a parenthetical expression should be placed outside the closing parenthesis.

We received numerous complaints (125 to be exact), but most harped on the same old theme (namely, high prices).

When it falls between other complete sentences, a complete sentence enclosed in parentheses has a capital letter and end punctuation.

In general, coaches will tell you that scouts are just guys who can't coach. (But then, so are brain surgeons.) —ROY BLOUNT, JR.

 2 Use parentheses to enclose letters and figures labeling items in lists within sentences.

My father could not, for his own special reasons, even *like* me. He spent the first twenty-five years of my life acting out that painful fact. Then he arrived at two points in his own life: (1) his last years, and (2) the realization that he had made a tragic mistake.   —RAY WEATHERLY

When lists are set off from the text, the numbers or letters labeling them are usually not enclosed in parentheses.

Exercise 3
Revising: Parentheses

Insert parentheses as needed in the following sentences.

Example:

Students can find good-quality, inexpensive furniture for example, desks, tables, chairs, sofas, even beds in junk stores.

Students can find good-quality, inexpensive furniture (for example, desks, tables, chairs, sofas, even beds) in junk stores.

1. Many of those involved in the movie business agree that multiscreen complexes are good for two reasons: 1 they cut the costs of exhibitors, and 2 they offer more choices to audiences.
2. Those who produce and distribute films and not just the big studios argue that the multiscreen theaters give exhibitors too much power.
3. The major studios are buying movie theaters to gain control over important parts of the distribution process what gets shown and for how much money.
4. For twelve years 1938–50 the federal government forced the studios to sell all their movie theaters.
5. But because they now have more competition television and videocassette recorders, the studios are permitted to own theaters.

ALTERNATE EXAMPLE

When you are enclosing a complete sentence within another complete sentence, you need not start the sentence in parentheses with a capital letter nor end it with a punctuation mark. For example:

I spent the weekend buried in books (this is my usual practice) and emerged on Monday in time to go to the library.

ANSWERS: EXERCISE 3

1. Many of those involved in the movie business agree that multiscreen complexes are good for two reasons: (1) they cut the costs of exhibitors; and (2) they offer more choices to audiences.
2. Those who produce and distribute films (and not just the big studios) argue that the multiscreen theaters give exhibitors too much power.
3. The major studios are buying movie theaters to gain control over important parts of the distribution process (what gets shown and for how much money).
4. For twelve years (1938–50) the federal government forced the studios to sell all their movie theaters.
5. But because they now have more competition (television and videocassette recorders), the studios are permitted to own theaters.

( )
25c

BRACKETS

25d   **Use brackets only within quotations to indicate your own comments or changes.**

If you need to explain, clarify, or correct the words of the writer you quote, place your additions in a pair of brackets.

"That Texaco station [just outside Chicago] is one of the busiest in the nation," said a company spokesperson.

Also use brackets if you need to alter the capitalization of a quotation so that it will fit into your sentence. (See also 26a.)

"[O]ne of the busiest in the nation" is how a company spokesperson described the station.

You may also use a bracketed word or words to substitute for parts of the original quotation that would otherwise be unclear. In the sentence below, the bracketed word substitutes for *they* in the original.

"Despite considerable achievements in other areas, [humans] still cannot control the weather and probably will never be able to do so."

The word *sic* (Latin for "in this manner") in brackets indicates that an error in the quotation appeared in the original and was not made by you.

According to the newspaper report, "The car slammed thru [*sic*] the railing and into oncoming traffic."

But don't use *sic* to make fun of a writer or to note errors in a passage that is clearly nonstandard or illiterate.

ADDITIONAL POINT

Brackets may also be used to supply missing letters to complete names that are given partly in initials in a quotation.

THE ELLIPSIS MARK

25e   **Use the ellipsis mark to indicate omissions within quotations.**

The **ellipsis mark** consists of three spaced periods (. . .). It is used most often to indicate an omission from a quotation, as illustrated in the following excerpts from this quotation about the Philippines:

Original quotation

"It was the Cuba of the future. It was going the way of Iran. It was another Nicaragua, another Cambodia, another Vietnam. But all these places, awesome in their histories, are so different from each other that one couldn't help thinking: this kind of talk was a shorthand for a confusion. All that was being said was that something was happening in the Philippines. Or more plausibly, a lot of different things were happening in the Philippines. And a lot of people were feeling obliged to speak out about it."

—JAMES FENTON, "The Philippine Election"

Omission of the middle of a sentence

"But all these places . . . are so different from each other that one couldn't help thinking: this kind of talk was a shorthand for a confusion."

Omission of the end of a sentence

"It was another Nicaragua. . . ."

Omission of parts of two sentences

"All that was being said was that . . . a lot of different things are happening in the Philippines."

Omission of one or more sentences

"It was the Cuba of the future. It was going the way of Iran. It was another Nicaragua, another Cambodia, another Vietnam. . . . All that was being said was that something was happening in the Philippines."

. . .
25e

Notice that when the ellipsis mark follows a grammatically complete sentence, as in the second and last examples, four equally spaced periods result: the sentence period (closed up to the last word of the sentence) and the three periods of the ellipsis mark. In the last example, notice also that the ellipsis mark is followed by space and that no ellipsis mark ends the quotation even though Fenton's essay goes on. Use a trailing ellipsis mark only when you omit the end of a sentence (second example).

If you omit one or more lines of poetry or paragraphs of prose from a quotation, use a separate line of ellipsis marks across the full width of the quotation to show the omission.

Note: Pauses and unfinished statements in quoted speech may be indicated with an ellipsis mark instead of a dash (25b-1).

"I wish . . ." His voice trailed off.

ANSWERS: EXERCISE 4

1. "The most common trait of all primitive peoples is a reverence for the life-giving earth, and the native American shared this elemental ethic: the land was alive to his loving touch, and he. . . brother to all creatures."

2. "The most common trait of all primitive peoples is a reverence for the life-giving earth, and the native American shared this elemental ethic: the land was alive to his loving touch, and he, its son, was brother to all creatures. . . . During the long Indian tenure the land remained undefiled save for scars no deeper than the scratches of cornfield clearings or the farming canals of the Hohokams on the Arizona desert."

Exercise 4
Using ellipsis marks

To practice using ellipsis marks to show omissions from quotations, follow each instruction below, using the following paragraph by Stewart Udall.

The most common trait of all primitive peoples is a reverence for the life-giving earth, and the native American shared this elemental ethic: the land was alive to his loving touch, and he, its son, was brother to all creatures. His feelings were made visible in medicine bundles and dance rhythms for rain, and all of his religious rites and land attitudes savored the inseparable world of nature and God, the master of life. During the long Indian tenure the land remained undefiled save for scars no deeper than the scratches of cornfield clearings or the farming canals of the Hohokams on the Arizona desert.

—Stewart Udall

1. Quote the first sentence from the paragraph, but omit the words *its son* (and punctuation as necessary). Show the omission with an ellipsis mark.
2. Quote the paragraph, but omit the second sentence. Show the omission with an ellipsis mark.

/
25f

THE SLASH

25f Use the slash between options and to separate lines of poetry that are run in to the text.

Option

I don't know why some teachers oppose pass/fail courses.

When used between options, the slash is not surrounded by extra space.

Note: The options *and/or* and *he/she* should be avoided. (See the Glossary of Usage, pp. 750 and 756.)

Poetry

Many readers have sensed a reluctant turn away from death in Frost's lines "The woods are lovely, dark and deep, But I have promises to keep."

When used to separate lines of poetry, the slash is surrounded by space. (See 24c for more on quoting poetry.)

Exercise 5
Revising: Colons, dashes, parentheses, brackets, ellipsis marks, slashes

Insert colons, dashes, parentheses, brackets, ellipsis marks, or slashes as needed in the following paragraph. When different marks would be appropriate in the same place, be able to defend the choice you make.

"Let all the learned say what they can, 'Tis ready money makes the man." These two lines of poetry by the Englishman William Somerville 1645–1742 may apply to a current American economic problem. Non-American investors with plenty of "ready money" are pouring some of it as much as $1.3 trillion in recent years into the United States. The investments of foreigners are varied stocks and bonds, savings deposits, service companies, factories, art works, even the campaigns of political candidates. Proponents of foreign investment argue that it revives industry, strengthens the economy, creates jobs more than 3 million, they say, and encourages free trade among nations. Opponents discuss the risks of heavy foreign investment it makes the American economy vulnerable to outsiders, sucks profits from the country, and gives foreigners an influence in governmental decision making. Proponents cite the jobs 3500 to be created by a new Japanese automobile factory in Kentucky. Opponents cite an attempt by the Russians the Russians! to buy California banks in order to spy on computer companies. On both sides, it seems, "the learned say 'Tis ready money makes the man or country." The question is, whose money?

Note: See the next page for a punctuation exercise combining colons, dashes, and parentheses with other marks of punctuation, such as commas and semicolons.

ANSWERS: EXERCISE 5

"Let all the learned say what they can,_/_ 'Tis ready money makes the man." These two lines of poetry by the Englishman William Somerville (1645–1742) may apply to a current American economic problem. Non-American investors with plenty of "ready money" are pouring some of it—as much as $1.3 trillion in recent years—into the United States. The investments of foreigners are varied: stocks and bonds, savings deposits, service companies, factories, art works, even the campaigns of political candidates. Proponents of foreign investment argue that it revives industry, strengthens the economy, creates jobs (more than 3 million, they say), and encourages free trade among nations. Opponents discuss the risks of heavy foreign investment: it makes the American economy vulnerable to outsiders, sucks profits from the country, and gives foreigners an influence in governmental decision making. Proponents cite the jobs (3500) to be created by a new Japanese automobile factory in Kentucky. Opponents cite an attempt by the Russians [the Russians!] to buy California banks in order to spy on computer companies. On both sides, it seems "the learned say . . . / 'Tis ready money makes the man [or country]." The question is, whose money?

/
25f

COLLABORATIVE LEARNING

ANSWERS: EXERCISE ON CHAPTERS 20–25

Brewed coffee is the most widely consumed beverage in the world. The trade in coffee beans alone amounts to well over $6,000,000,000 a year, and the total volume of beans traded exceeds 4,250,000 tons a year. It's believed that the beverage was introduced into Arabia in the fifteenth century A.D., probably by Ethiopians. By the middle or late sixteenth century, the Arabs had introduced the beverage to the Europeans, who at first resisted it because of its strong flavor and effect as a mild stimulant. The French, Italians, and other Europeans incorporated coffee into their diets by the seventeenth century; the English, however, preferred tea, which they were then importing from India. Since America was colonized primarily by the English, Americans also preferred tea. Only after the Boston Tea Party (1773) did Americans begin drinking coffee in large quantities. Now, though, the U.S. is one of the top coffee-consuming countries, consumption having been spurred on by familiar advertising claims: "Good till the last drop," "Rich, hearty aroma," "Always rich, never bitter."

Produced from the fruit of an evergreen tree, coffee is grown primarily in Latin America, southern Asia, and Africa. Coffee trees require a hot climate, high humidity, rich soil with good drainage, and partial shade; consequently, they thrive on the east or west slopes of tropical volcanic mountains, where the soil is laced with potash and drains easily. The coffee beans—actually seeds—grow inside bright red berries. The berries are picked by hand, and the beans are extracted by machine, leaving a pulpy fruit residue that can be used for fertilizer. The beans are usually roasted in ovens, a chemical process that releases the beans' essential oil (caffeol), which gives coffee its distinctive aroma. Over a hundred different varieties of beans are produced in the world, each with a different flavor attributable to three factors: the species of plant (*Coffea arabica* and *Coffea robusta* are the most common) and the soil and climate where the variety was grown.

Exercise on Chapters 20–25
Revising: Punctuation

The following paragraphs are unpunctuated except for end-of-sentence periods. Insert periods, commas, semicolons, apostrophes, quotation marks, colons, dashes, or parentheses where they are required. When different marks would be appropriate in the same place, be able to defend the choice you make.

Brewed coffee is the most widely consumed beverage in the world. The trade in coffee beans alone amounts to well over $6000000000 a year and the total volume of beans traded exceeds 4250000 tons a year. Its believed that the beverage was introduced into Arabia in the fifteenth century AD probably by Ethiopians. By the middle or late sixteenth century the Arabs had introduced the beverage to the Europeans who at first resisted it because of its strong flavor and effect as a mild stimulant. The French Italians and other Europeans incorporated coffee into their diets by the seventeenth century the English however preferred tea which they were then importing from India. Since America was colonized primarily by the English Americans also preferred tea. Only after the Boston Tea Party 1773 did Americans begin drinking coffee in large quantities. Now though the US is one of the top coffee-consuming countries consumption having been spurred on by familiar advertising claims Good till the last drop Rich hearty aroma Always rich never bitter.

Produced from the fruit of an evergreen tree coffee is grown primarily in Latin America southern Asia and Africa. Coffee trees require a hot climate high humidity rich soil with good drainage and partial shade consequently they thrive on the east or west slopes of tropical volcanic mountains where the soil is laced with potash and drains easily. The coffee beans actually seeds grow inside bright red berries. The berries are picked by hand and the beans are extracted by machine leaving a pulpy fruit residue that can be used for fertilizer. The beans are usually roasted in ovens a chemical process that releases the beans essential oil caffeol which gives coffee its distinctive aroma. Over a hundred different varieties of beans are produced in the world each with a different flavor attributable to three factors the species of plant *Coffea arabia* and *Coffea robusta* are the most common and the soil and climate where the variety was grown.

Part VI Mechanics

HIGHLIGHTS

Relatively few students will need to study or practice extensively the rules of capitalization covered in this chapter. A brief review, however, will be helpful for most students to clarify the rules for capitalization of titles, historical periods, specific places or institutions, people's titles, and similar matters.

Chapter 26 — *Capitals*

Experienced writers generally agree on when to use capitals, but the conventions are constantly changing. Consult a recent dictionary if you have any doubt about whether a particular word should be capitalized.

RESOURCES AND IDEAS

Relatively little has been written about the teaching of capitalization, and most teachers probably assume that rules and drills are the only available instructional strategies. In *The Writing Room: A Resource Book for Teachers of English* (New York: Oxford UP, 1981, [172–74]), however, Harvey S. Wiener looks at the sources of capitalization problems for many basic writers—particularly problems of misunderstanding the rules governing sentence boundaries, of confusion over the capitalization of *I* and other personal pronouns, and of difficulty with the sometimes inexact categories of words that are to be treated as proper nouns. Wiener suggests looking for patterns of error in a student's writing, creating groups of words illustrating a particular rule, and asking a student to prepare sentences that demonstrate his or her grasp of a particular convention. These strategies can be used for more skilled writers as well.

26a   **Capitalize the first word of every sentence.**

Every writer should own a good dictionary.
Will inflation be curbed?
Watch out!

When quoting other writers, you must reproduce the capital letters beginning their sentences or indicate that you have altered the source. Whenever possible, integrate the quotation into your own sentence so that its capitalization coincides with yours.

"Psychotherapists often overlook the benefits of self-deception," the author argues.

The author argues that "the benefits of self-deception" are not always recognized by psychotherapists.

If you need to alter the capitalization in the source, indicate the change with brackets (see 25d).

"[T]he benefits of self-deception" are not always recognized by psychotherapists, the author argues.

The author argues that "[p]sychotherapists often overlook the benefits of self-deception."

Note: Capitalization of questions in a series is optional. Both of the following examples are correct.

Is the population a hundred? Two hundred? More?
Is the population a hundred? two hundred? more?

Also optional is capitalization of the first word in a complete sentence after a colon (see 25a-2).

 26b **Capitalize most words in titles and subtitles of works.**

In all titles and subtitles of works, capitalize the first and last words and all other words *except* articles (*a, an, the*), *to* in infinitives, and connecting words (prepositions and coordinating and subordinating conjunctions) of fewer than five letters. Capitalize even these short words when they are the first or last word in a title or when they fall after a colon or semicolon.

The Sound and the Fury   *Management: A New Theory*
"Courtship Through the Ages"   "Once More to the Lake"
A Diamond Is Forever   *An End to Live For*
"Knowing Whom to Ask"   *File Under Architecture*
Learning from Las Vegas   *Only when I Laugh*

Note: Always capitalize the prefix or first word in a hyphenated word within a title. Capitalize the second word only if it is a noun or an adjective or is as important as the first word.

"Applying Stage Make-up"   *Through the Looking-Glass*
The Pre-Raphaelites

 26c **Always capitalize the pronoun *I* and the interjection *O*. Capitalize *oh* only when it begins a sentence.**

I love to stay up at night, but, oh, I hate to get up in the morning.
He who thinks himself wise, O heavens, is a great fool.
—Voltaire

cap
26d

 26d Capitalize proper nouns, proper adjectives, and words used as essential parts of proper nouns.

 1 Capitalize proper nouns and proper adjectives.

Proper nouns name specific persons, places, and things: *Shakespeare, California, World War I.* **Proper adjectives** are formed from some proper nouns: *Shakespearean, Californian.* Capitalize all proper nouns and proper adjectives but not the articles (*a, an, the*) that precede them.

Proper nouns and adjectives to be capitalized

Specific persons and things

Stephen King   the Leaning Tower of Pisa
Napoleon Bonaparte   Boulder Dam
Doris Lessing   the Empire State Building

Specific places and geographical regions

New York City   the Mediterranean Sea
China   Lake Victoria
Europe   the Northeast, the South
North America   the Rocky Mountains
But: northeast of the city, going south

Days of the week, months, holidays

Monday   Yom Kippur
May   Christmas
Thanksgiving   Columbus Day

Historical events, documents, periods, movements

World War II   the Middle Ages
the Vietnam War   the Age of Reason
the Boston Tea Party   the Renaissance
the Treaty of Ghent   the Great Depression
the Constitution   the Romantic Movement

Government offices or departments and institutions

House of Representatives   Polk Municipal Court
Department of Defense   Warren County Hospital
Appropriations Committee   Northeast High School
Postal Service   York Board of Education

Political, social, athletic, and other organizations and associations and their members

Democratic Party, Democrats	Rotary Club, Rotarians
Communist Party, Communist	Eastern Star
Sierra Club	League of Women Voters
Girl Scouts of America, Scout	Boston Celtics
B'nai B'rith	Chicago Symphony Orchestra

Races, nationalities, and their languages

Native American	Germans
African-American, Negro	Swahili
Caucasian	Italian
But: blacks, whites	

Religions and their followers

Christianity, Christians	Judaism, Orthodox Jew
Protestantism, Protestants	Hinduism, Hindu
Catholicism, Catholics	Islam, Moslems *or* Muslims

Religious terms for sacred persons and things

God	Buddha
Allah	the Bible (*but* biblical)
Christ	the Koran

Note: Capitalization of pronouns referring to God is optional in most contexts, but it is often used in religious texts and should be used where necessary to avoid confusion.

Ambiguous	Our minister spoke of God as though *he* loved every member of our congregation. [Does *he* refer to the minister or to God?]
Revised	Our minister spoke of God as though *He* loved every member of our congregation.

cap
26d

 2 Capitalize common nouns used as essential parts of proper nouns.

Common nouns name general classes of persons, places, or things, and they generally are not capitalized. However, capitalize the common nouns *street, avenue, park, river, ocean, lake, company, college, county,* and *memorial* when they are part of proper nouns naming specific places or institutions.

Main Street	Lake Superior
Central Park	Ford Motor Company

NOTE

You may wish to point out that when a generic term occurs with a proper name, the generic term is capitalized (the Congo *River*), but when the generic term occurs with two or more proper names, it is usually capitalized when it precedes the proper names but lowercased when it succeeds them (*Lakes* Superior and Ontario; the Congo and Amazon *rivers*).

Mississippi River   Madison College
Pacific Ocean   George Washington Memorial Park

 Capitalize trade names.

Trade names identify individual brands of certain products. When a trade name loses its association with a brand and comes to refer to a product in general, it is not capitalized. Refer to a dictionary for current usage when you are in doubt about a name.

Scotch tape   Xerox
Chevrolet   Bunsen burner
But: nylon, thermos

 26e **Capitalize titles when they precede proper names but generally not when they follow proper names or appear alone.**

Professor Otto Osborne   Otto Osborne, a professor of English
Doctor Jane Covington   Jane Covington, a medical doctor
Senator Robert Dole   Robert Dole, senator from Kansas
the Reverend Ann Cole   Ann Cole, the minister

Exception: Many writers capitalize a title denoting very high rank even when it follows a proper name or is used alone.

Lyndon Johnson, past President of the United States
the Chief Justice of the United States

 26f **Capitalize only when required.**

In general, modern writers capitalize fewer words than earlier writers did. Capitalize only when a rule says you must.

1 **Use small letters for common nouns replacing proper nouns.**

Unnecessary   I am determined to take an Economics course
                   before I graduate from College.

Revised   I am determined to take an economics course
                   before I graduate from college.

Revised   I am determined to take Economics 101 before
                   I graduate from Madison College.

cap
26f

Capitalize compass directions only when they refer to specific geographical areas.

The storm blew in from the northeast and then veered south along the coast. [Here *northeast* and *south* refer to general directions.]

Students from the South have trouble adjusting to the Northeast's bitter winters. [Here *South* and *Northeast* refer to specific regions.]

 Use small letters for the names of seasons or the names of academic years or terms.

spring	autumn	freshman year
fall	winter quarter	summer term

 Capitalize the names of relationships only when they form part of or substitute for proper names.

my mother   the father of my friend
John's brother

But

I remember how Father scolded us.

Aunt Annie, Uncle Jake, and Uncle Irvin died within two months of each other.

Exercise
Revising: Capitals

Capitalize words as necessary in the following sentences, or substitute small letters for unnecessary capitals. Consult a dictionary if you are in doubt. If the capitalization in a sentence is already correct, circle the number preceding the sentence.

Example:

The first book on the reading list is mark twain's *a connecticut yankee in king arthur's court.*

The first book on the reading list is Mark Twain's *A Connecticut Yankee in King Arthur's Court.*

1. Under Henry Cisneros, former mayor, San Antonio, texas, became a thriving city in the southwest.
2. The city has always offered much to tourists interested in the roots of spanish settlement of the new world.
3. The alamo is one of five Catholic Missions built by Priests to

cap
26f

ANSWERS: EXERCISE

1. Under Henry Cisneros, former mayor, San Antonio, <u>T</u>exas, became a thriving city in the <u>S</u>outhwest.
2. The city has always offered much to tourists interested in the roots of <u>S</u>panish settlement of the <u>N</u>ew <u>W</u>orld.

3. The Alamo is one of five Catholic missions built by priests to convert the Native Americans and to maintain Spain's claims in the area.
4. But the Alamo is more famous for being the site of an 1836 battle that helped to create the Republic of Texas.
5. Many of the nearby streets, such as Crockett Street, are named for men who gave their lives in that battle.
6. The Hemisfair Plaza and the San Antonio River link new tourist and convention facilities developed during Mayor Cisneros's terms.
7. Restaurants, hotels, and shops line the river. The haunting melodies of "Una Paloma Blanca" and "Malagueña" lure passing tourists into Casa Rio and other excellent Mexican restaurants.
8. The University of Texas at San Antonio has expanded, and a medical center has been developed in the northwest part of the city.
9. Correct.
10. The city has attracted high-tech industry, creating a corridor of economic growth between San Antonio and Austin and contributing to the Texas economy.

convert native americans and to maintain spain's claims in the area.
4. But the alamo is more famous for being the site of an 1836 battle that helped to create the republic of Texas.
5. Many of the nearby Streets, such as Crockett street, are named for men who gave their lives in that Battle.
6. The Hemisfair plaza and the San Antonio river link new tourist and convention facilities developed during mayor Cisneros's terms.
7. Restaurants, Hotels, and shops line the River. the haunting melodies of "Una paloma blanca" and "malagueña" lure passing tourists into Casa rio and other excellent mexican restaurants.
8. The university of Texas at San Antonio has expanded and a Medical Center has been developed in the Northwest part of the city.
9. Sea World, on the west side of San Antonio, entertains grandparents, fathers and mothers, and children with the antics of dolphins and seals.
10. The City has attracted high-tech industry, creating a corridor of economic growth between san antonio and austin and contributing to the texas economy.

Note: See page 474 for an exercise involving capitals along with underlining (italics) and other mechanics.

Chapter 27

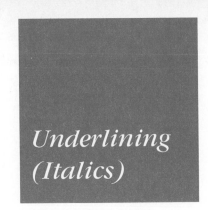

Underlining (Italics)

HIGHLIGHTS

Of all the chapters on mechanics, this chapter, on the uses of italics, most frequently needs to be reviewed, particularly by students writing essays or research papers that require incorporating material from outside the classroom. The chapter includes the rules for underlining titles; the names of various craft; foreign words and phrases that have not yet become part of the English language; and words, letters, numbers, and phrases named as words. It also gives the rules for underlining for emphasis.

Underlining and *italic type* indicate the same thing: the word or words are being distinguished or emphasized. In your papers use a ruler or the underscore on the keyboard to underline. If your typewriter or word processor can produce italic type, consult your instructor about whether to use it. Many instructors prefer underlining. (See also Appendix A, p. 735.)

27a Underline the titles of works that appear independently.

Many works are published, released, or produced separately from other works: books, some long poems, plays, periodicals, pamphlets, published speeches, long musical works, movies, television and radio programs, and works of visual art. Underline the titles of these works. (See the box on the next page.) Use quotation marks for all other titles, such as songs, short poems, short stories, articles in periodicals, essays, and episodes of television and radio programs. (See 24d.)

Note: Be careful to underline marks of punctuation only if they are part of the title: *Did you read Catch-22?* (not *Catch-22?*). In titles of newspapers underline the name of the city only when it is part of the title.

NOTE

When an apostrophe or an apostrophe plus an *s* is added to a title, the addition is not underlined.

> Manchester Guardian
> New York Times

When giving the title of a periodical in your text, you need not capitalize or underline the article *the*, even if it is part of the title.

Titles to be underlined (italicized)

Other titles should be placed in quotation marks. See 24d.

Books

Catch-22
War and Peace
The Promise
The Bonfire of the Vanities

Plays

Equus
Hamlet
Summer and Smoke
The Phantom of the Opera

Pamphlets

The Truth About Alcoholism
On the Vindication of the
 Rights of Women

Long musical works

Tchaikovsky's Swan Lake
Bach's St. Matthew Passion
The Beatles' Revolver
But: Symphony in C

Television and radio programs

60 Minutes
The Shadow
L.A. Law

Long poems

Beowulf
The Song of Roland
Paradise Lost
Song of Myself

Periodicals

Time
Philadelphia Inquirer
Yale Law Review
Mechanical Engineering

Published speeches

Lincoln's Gettysburg Address
Pericles's Funeral Oration

Movies

Gone with the Wind
Star Wars
Invasion of the Body
 Snatchers

Works of visual art

Michelangelo's David
the Mona Lisa
Duchamp's Standard
 Stoppages

und
27a

She has the New York Times delivered to her in Alaska.

Omit the article entirely in source citations (see 37b, p. 613).

 Exceptions: Legal documents, the Bible, and their parts are generally not underlined.

Not They registered their deed.
But They registered their deed.

Not We studied the Book of Revelation in the Bible.
But We studied the Book of Revelation in the Bible.

27b Underline the names of ships, aircraft, spacecraft, and trains.

Queen Elizabeth II   Challenger   Orient Express
Spirit of St. Louis   Apollo XI   Montrealer

27c Underline foreign words and phrases that are not part of the English language.

English has absorbed many foreign words and phrases—such as the French expression "bon voyage"—and these need not be underlined. A foreign phrase should be underlined when it has not been absorbed into our language. A dictionary will say whether a phrase is still considered foreign to English.

The scientific name for the brown trout is Salmo trutta. [The Latin scientific names for plants and animals are always underlined.]

What a life he led! He was a true bon vivant.

The Latin De gustibus non est disputandum translates roughly as "There's no accounting for taste."

27d Underline words, letters, numbers, and phrases named as words.

Some people pronounce th, as in thought, with a faint s or f sound.

Carved into the middle of the column, twenty feet up, was a mysterious 7.

Try pronouncing unique New York ten times fast.

Underlining may also be used instead of quotation marks in definitions (see 24e).

The word syzygy refers to a straight line formed by three celestial bodies, as in the alignment of the earth, sun, and moon.

27e Occasionally, underlining may be used for emphasis.

Underlining can stress an important word or phrase, especially in reporting how someone said something.

"Why on earth would you do that?" she cried.

NOTE

You may wish to remind students that when sounds (e.g., *kerplunk, oof*) are represented in writing, they are usually underlined.

**und
27e**

ADD THE MECHANICS

If you have assigned one or more of Chapters 26–30, this activity may be useful and interesting. Take an essay, either student or professional; remove capitals, italics, and the like; and ask students to work in groups reaching consensus on how to correct the mechanics in the "new" essay. Tell them not to look at the handbook but to decide on their own the best way to serve the readers' needs through mechanics. When the students have finished, they can compare their work with the original and, using the handbook as a reference, decide which choices in mechanics they think best serve the needs of the essay and the readers. If they decide to disagree with the advice given in the handbook, ask them to write out their own rules.

Such emphasis should be used sparingly, though. Excessive underlining will make your writing sound immature or hysterical.

The hunters had <u>no</u> food and <u>no</u> firewood. But they were <u>too</u> tired to do anything more than crawl into their sopping sleeping bags. Had it been ten degrees colder, they might have frozen to death.

If you find that you rely on underlining to achieve emphasis, consult Chapter 18 for other techniques to help you accent your writing.

ANSWERS: EXERCISE

1. Of the many Vietnam veterans who are writers, Oliver Stone is perhaps the most famous for writing and directing the films <u>Platoon</u> and <u>Born on the Fourth of July</u>.
2. Tim O'Brien has written short stories for <u>Esquire</u>, <u>GQ</u>, and <u>Massachusetts Review</u>.
3. <u>Going After Cacciato</u> is O'Brien's dreamlike novel about the horrors of combat.
4. The word <u>Vietnam</u> is technically two words (<u>Viet</u> and <u>Nam</u>), but most American writers spell it as (one) word. [<u>Viet</u> and <u>Nam</u> were correctly underlined.]
5. American writers use words or phrases borrowed from the Vietnamese language, such as <u>di di mau</u> ("go quickly") or <u>dinky dau</u> ("crazy").
6. Philip Caputo's (gripping) account of his service in Vietnam appears in the book <u>A Rumor of War</u>.
7. Sentence correct.
8. David Rabe's plays—including <u>The Basic Training of Pavlo Hummel</u>, <u>Streamers</u>, and <u>Sticks and Bones</u>—depict the effects of the war (not only) on the soldiers (but) on their families.
9. Called ("the poet laureate of the Vietnam war,") Steve Mason has published two collections of poems: <u>Johnny's Song</u> and <u>Warrior for Peace</u>.
10. The <u>Washington Post</u> has published rave reviews of <u>Veteran's Day</u>, an autobiography by Rod Kane.

Exercise
Revising: Underlining (italics)

Underline (italicize) words and phrases as needed in the following sentences, or circle any words or phrases that are underlined unnecessarily. Note that some underlining is correct as given.

Example:

Of Hitchcock's movies, Psycho is the scariest.
Of Hitchcock's movies, <u>Psycho</u> is the scariest.

1. Of the many Vietnam veterans who are writers, Oliver Stone is perhaps the most famous for writing and directing the films Platoon and Born on the Fourth of July.
2. Tim O'Brien has written short stories for Esquire, GQ, and Massachusetts Review.
3. Going After Cacciato is O'Brien's dreamlike novel about the horrors of combat.
4. The word Vietnam is technically two words (<u>Viet</u> and <u>Nam</u>), but most American writers spell it as <u>one</u> word.
5. American writers use words or phrases borrowed from the Vietnamese language, such as di di mau ("go quickly") or dinky dau ("crazy").
6. Philip Caputo's <u>gripping</u> account of his service in Vietnam appears in the book A Rumor of War.
7. Caputo's book was made into a television movie, also titled <u>A Rumor of War</u>.
8. <u>David Rabe's</u> plays—including The Basic Training of Pavlo Hummel, Streamers, and Sticks and Bones—depict the effects of the war <u>not only</u> on the soldiers <u>but</u> on their families.
9. Called <u>poet laureate of the Vietnam war</u>, Steve Mason has published two collections of poems: Johnny's Song and Warrior for Peace.
10. The Washington Post has published rave reviews of Veteran's Day, an autobiography by Rod Kane.

Note: See page 474 for an exercise involving underlining (italics) along with capitals and other mechanics.

Chapter 28

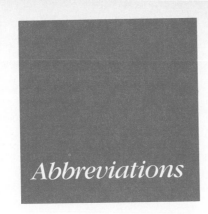

Abbreviations

HIGHLIGHTS

The discussion in this chapter covers the rules for using abbreviations in general writing. The first four sections cover the use of standard abbreviations for titles; the appropriate use of familiar abbreviations and acronyms; the abbreviations that accompany dates and numbers to show time and amount; and the use of common Latin abbreviations. The last two sections deal with the misuse of abbreviations.

The guidelines on abbreviations in this chapter pertain to nontechnical academic writing and most writing for a general audience. Technical writing, such as in the sciences and engineering, generally uses a great many more abbreviations (see 28f). And abbreviations are common in source citations in all disciplines (see 37d, pp. 629–30, for a list).

28a Use standard abbreviations for titles immediately before and after proper names.

Before the name	After the name
Dr. James Hsu	James Hsu, M.D.
Mr., Mrs., Ms., Hon.,	D.D.S., D.V.M., Ph.D.,
St., Rev., Msgr., Gen.	Ed.D., O.S.B., S.J., Sr., Jr.

(Note that the title *Ms.* is followed by a period, even though it is not actually an abbreviation: *Ms. Judith Boyer.*)

Use abbreviations such as *Rev., Hon., Prof., Rep., Sen., Dr.,* and *St.* (for *Saint*) only if they appear with a proper name. Spell them out in the absence of a proper name.

Faulty   We learned to trust the *Dr.*
Revised   We learned to trust the *doctor.*
Revised   We learned to trust *Dr. Kaplan.*

The abbreviations for academic degrees—*Ph.D., M.A., B.A.,* and the like—may be used without a proper name.

ADDITIONAL RULES

Civil and military titles are abbreviated only when used before a full name, not before the last name only.

Scholarly degrees are abbreviated when the degree follows a name. When a name is followed by an abbreviated title, no other title goes before the name.

SCHOLARLY ABBREVIATIONS

anon.	anonymous
b.	born
c	copyright
c. *or* ca.	about (with dates)
cf.	compare
col., cols.	column, columns
d.	died
ed.; eds.	editor, edited by; editors
e.g.	for example
esp.	especially
et al.	and others
i.e.	that is
ms., mss.	manuscript, manuscripts
N.B.	note carefully
n.d.	no date (of publication)
n.p.	no place (of publication), no publisher
p., pp.	page, pages
pref.	preface
rept.	report, reported by
sec., sect.; secs.	section; sections
v. *or* vs.	versus (legal)
vol., vols.	volume, volumes

POSTAL ABBREVIATIONS (U.S. AND CANADA)

AB	Alberta
AL	Alabama
AK	Alaska
AR	Arkansas
AZ	Arizona
BC	British Columbia
CA	California
CO	Colorado
CT	Connecticut
DC	District of Columbia
DE	Delaware
FL	Florida
GA	Georgia
HI	Hawaii
IA	Iowa
ID	Idaho
IL	Illinois
IN	Indiana
KS	Kansas
KY	Kentucky
LA	Louisiana
LB	Labrador
MA	Massachusetts
MB	Manitoba
MD	Maryland
ME	Maine
MI	Michigan
MN	Minnesota
MO	Missouri
MS	Mississippi
NB	New Brunswick
NC	North Carolina
ND	North Dakota
NE	Nebraska
NF	Newfoundland
NH	New Hampshire
NJ	New Jersey
NM	New Mexico
NS	Nova Scotia
NT	Northwest Territories
NV	Nevada
NY	New York
OH	Ohio
OK	Oklahoma
ON	Ontario
OR	Oregon
PA	Pennsylvania
PE	Prince Edward Island
PQ	Quebec, Province du Québec
PR	Puerto Rico
RI	Rhode Island

ab
28c

Abbreviations for nontechnical writing

- Titles before or after proper names: *Dr. Jorge Rodriguez; Jorge Rodriguez, Ph.D.* (28a).
- Familiar abbreviations and acronyms: *U.S.A., U.S.S.R., AIDS* (28b).
- *B.C., A.D., A.M., P.M., no.,* and *$* with specific dates and numbers (28c).
- *I.e., e.g.,* and other Latin abbreviations within parentheses and in source citations (28d).
- *Inc., Bros., Co.,* and *&* with names of business firms (28e).

My brother took seven years to get his *Ph.D.* It will probably take me just as long to earn my *B.A.*

28b Familiar abbreviations and acronyms are acceptable in most writing.

An **acronym** is an abbreviation that spells a pronounceable word, such as WHO, NATO, and AIDS. These abbreviations, written without periods, are acceptable in most writing as long as they are familiar. So are several familiar abbreviations of the names of organizations, corporations, people, and countries. When these abbreviate three or more words, they are usually written without periods.

Organizations	CIA, FBI, YMCA, AFL-CIO
Corporations	IBM, CBS, ITT
People	JFK, LBJ, FDR
Countries	U.S.A. (or USA), U.S.S.R. (or USSR)

(See 20b for more on when to use periods in abbreviations.)

Note: If a name or term (such as *operating room*) appears often in a piece of writing, then its abbreviation (*O.R.*) can cut down on extra words. Spell out the full term at its first appearance, indicate its abbreviation in parentheses, and use the abbreviation from then on.

28c Use *B.C., A.D., A.M., P.M., no.,* and *$* only with specific dates and numbers.

The abbreviation B.C. ("before Christ") always follows a date, whereas A.D. (*anno Domini,* Latin for "year of the Lord") precedes a date.

44 B.C.	8:05 P.M. (*or* p.m.)	no. 36 (*or* No. 36)	SC	South Carolina
A.D. 1492	11:26 A.M. (*or* a.m.)	$7.41	SD	South Dakota
			˙SK	Saskatchewan
			TN	Tennessee
			TX	Texas
			UT	Utah
			VA	Virginia
			VT	Vermont
			WA	Washington
			WI	Wisconsin
			WV	West Virginia
			WY	Wyoming
			YT	Yukon Territory

Faulty   Hospital routine is easier to follow in the A.M. than in the P.M.

Revised   Hospital routine is easier to follow in the *morning* than in the *afternoon or evening.*

Note: The capitalized abbreviations above are often set in small capital letters in publications: B.C., A.D., A.M., P.M. In your papers use B.C. and A.D. and either A.M./P.M. or a.m./p.m. The abbreviation for *number* may either be capitalized or not (No., no.).

28d   **Generally, reserve common Latin abbreviations such as *i.e., e.g.,* and *etc.* for use in source citations and comments in parentheses.**

i.e.	*id est:* that is
cf.	*confer:* compare
e.g.	*exempli gratia:* for example
et al.	*et alii:* and others
etc.	*et cetera:* and so forth
N.B.	*nota bene:* note well

He said he would be gone a fortnight (i.e., two weeks).
Bloom et al., editors, *Anthology of Light Verse*
Trees, too, are susceptible to disease (e.g., Dutch elm disease).

(Note that these abbreviations are generally not italicized or underlined.)

Some writers avoid these abbreviations in formal writing, even within parentheses.

Informal   The cabs of some modern farm machines (e.g., combines) look like airplane cockpits.

Formal   The cabs of some modern farm machines (for example, combines) look like airplane cockpits.

28e   **Reserve *Inc., Bros., Co.,* or *&* (for *and*) for official names of business firms.**

Faulty   *The Santini bros.* operate a large moving firm in New York City.

Revised   *The Santini brothers* operate a large moving firm in New York City.

Revised   *Santini Bros.* is a large moving firm in New York City.

ab
28e

Faulty	We read about the Hardy Boys & Nancy Drew.
Revised	We read about the Hardy Boys *and* Nancy Drew.

 28f **Spell out units of measurement; names of places, calendar designations, people, and courses; and divisions of written works.**

Units of measurement, geographical names, specialized terms, and other words are often abbreviated in technical writing. In other academic writing and general writing, however, such words should be spelled out.

Units of measurement

The dog is thirty *inches* (not *in.*) high.
The building is 150 *feet* (not *ft.*) tall.

Exceptions: Long phrases such as *miles per hour* (m.p.h.) or *cycles per second* (c.p.s.) are usually abbreviated, with or without periods: *The speed limit on that road was once 75 m.p.h.* (or *mph*).

Geographical names

The publisher is in *Massachusetts* (not *Mass.* or *MA*).
He came from Aukland, *New Zealand* (not *N.Z.*).
She lived on Morrissey *Boulevard* (not *Blvd.*).

Exceptions: The United States is often referred to as the U.S.A. (USA) or the U.S., and the Soviet Union as the U.S.S.R. (USSR). In writing of the U.S. capital, we use the abbreviation D.C. for District of Columbia when it follows the city's name: *Washington, D.C.*

Names of days, months, and holidays

The truce was signed on *Tuesday* (not *Tues.*), *April* (not *Apr.*) 16.
The *Christmas* (not *Xmas*) holidays are uneventful.

Names of people

James (not *Jas.*) Bennett ran for that seat.
Robert (not *Robt.*) Frost writes accessible poems.

Courses of instruction

I'm majoring in *political science* (not *poli. sci.*).
Economics (not *Econ.*) is a difficult course.

Divisions of written works

The story begins on *page* (not *p.*) 15 in *volume* (not *vol.*) 2.
Read *Chapter* (not *Ch.*) 6.

Exercise 1
Revising: Abbreviations

Revise the following sentences as needed to correct inappropriate use of abbreviations for nontechnical writing. Circle the number preceding any sentences in which the abbreviations are already appropriate as written.

Example:

One prof. lectured for five hrs.
One *professor* lectured for five *hours*.

1. On Fri., Oct. 26, 1990, astronomers announced the discovery of the largest galaxy in the universe.
2. Measuring 6 million light-yrs. across, the galaxy is sixty times the size of the Milky Way.
3. A light-yr.—i.e., the distance that light can travel in one year in a vacuum—is 5.89 trillion mi.
4. Jeffrey R. Kuhn, Juan M. Uson, & Stephen P. Boughn studied the galaxy at the Kitt Peak Natl. Observatory in AZ.
5. The work of Drs. Kuhn, Uson, and Boughn has brought distinction to astronomers of the U.S.A.

Exercise 2
Revising: Abbreviations

Spell out all inappropriate abbreviations in the following paragraph. If an abbreviation is appropriate in its context, leave it as is.

The advantages of a grad. degree are not lost on me. With a Ph.D. I might become a college prof., a job that would allow me to work only in the P.M., so I wouldn't have to get up before 11:00 A.M., and only on Tues., Wed., and Thurs., my favorite days. Or I could get an M.D. and become a dr. Though I might have to work long hrs., I could earn plenty of $ and, by serving in a professional association like the AMA, could have a lot of influence. I know about these advantages because my two older bros. are Prof. Giordano and Dr. Giordano. I also know how hard they had to work for their degrees, so I think I'll stick with poli. sci. courses and look for a nice, safe govt. job after I get my B.A.

Note: See page 474 for an exercise involving abbreviations along with capitals and other mechanics.

ANSWERS: EXERCISE 1

1. On <u>Friday, October</u> 26, 1990, astronomers announced the discovery of the largest galaxy in the universe.
2. Measuring six million light <u>years</u> across, the galaxy is sixty times the size of the Milky Way.
3. A light <u>year</u>—<u>that is</u>, the distance that light can travel in one year in a vacuum—is 5.89 trillion <u>miles</u>.
4. Jeffrey R. Kuhn, Juan M. Uson, <u>and</u> Stephen P. Boughn studied the galaxy at the Kitt Peak <u>National</u> Observatory in <u>Arizona</u>.
5. Correct (or <u>USA</u> may be substituted for U.S.A.).

ANSWERS: EXERCISE 2

The advantages of a <u>graduate</u> degree are not lost on me. With a Ph.D. I might become a college <u>professor</u>, a job that would allow me to work only in the <u>afternoon</u>, so I wouldn't have to get up before 11:00 A.M., and only on <u>Tuesday, Wednesday,</u> and <u>Thursday,</u> my favorite days. Or I could get an M.D. and become a <u>doctor</u>. Though I might have to work long <u>hours,</u> I could earn plenty of <u>money</u> and, by serving in a professional association like the AMA, could have a lot of influence. I know about these advantages because my two older <u>brothers</u> are Prof. Giordano and Dr. Giordano. I also know how hard they had to work for their degrees, so I think I'll stick with <u>political science</u> courses and look for a nice, safe <u>government</u> job after I get my B.A.

ab
28f

HIGHLIGHTS

The representation of numbers in general writing is the subject of this chapter. The rules for when to use figures for numbers and when to write out numbers are few and easily memorized.

Chapter 29

 Numbers

Experienced writers vary in writing numbers out or using figures. In scientific and technical writing, all numbers are usually written as figures. In business writing, all numbers over ten are usually written as figures. In other academic and general writing—the subject of this chapter—numbers are more often spelled out.

 29a Use figures for numbers that require more than two words to spell out.

> The leap year has *366* days.
> The population of Minot, North Dakota, is about *32,800*.

Spell out numbers of one or two words. (See also 29b.)

> That hotel can accommodate no more than *seventy-five* people.
> The first writing we know of was done over *six thousand* years ago.
> The collection included almost *twelve hundred* drawings.

A hyphenated number between twenty-one and ninety-nine can be considered one word. (See 34d-2.)

> The ball game drew *forty-two thousand* people.

Exceptions: Round numbers over a million may be expressed in a combination of figures and words: *26 million, 2.45 billion.*

When you use several numbers together, they should be consistently spelled out or consistently expressed in figures.

Inconsistent	Only *ninety-nine* students attended the first lecture, but the audience increased to *126* for the second lecture and *two hundred* for the third.
Revised	Only *99* students attended the first lecture, but the audience increased to *126* for the second lecture and *200* for the third.

 Use figures instead of words according to standard practice.

Even when a number requires one or two words to spell out, we conventionally use figures for days and years; pages, chapters, volumes, acts, scenes, and lines; decimals, percentages, and fractions; addresses; scores and statistics; exact amounts of money; and the time of day.

Days and years

June 18, 1985   A.D. 12   456 B.C.   1999

Exception: The day of a month may be expressed in words when it is not followed by a year (*June fifth; October first*).

Pages, chapters, volumes, acts, scenes, lines

Chapter 9, page 123
Isaiah 28:1 in the Bible
Hamlet, Act 5 (*or* V), Scene 3
    (*or* iii), lines 35–40

Decimals, percentages, and fractions

22.5
48% (*or* 48 percent)
3½

Addresses

355 Clinton Avenue
419 Stonewall Street
Washington, D.C. 20036

Scores and statistics

21 to 7
a mean of 26
a ratio of 8 to 1

Exact amounts of money

$4.50
$3.5 million (*or* $3,500,000)
$2,763 (*or* $2763)

The time of day

9:00
3:45
2:30

Exceptions: Round dollar or cent amounts of only a few words may be expressed in words: *seventeen dollars; fifteen hundred dollars; sixty cents.* When the word *o'clock* is used for the time of day, also express the number in words: *two o'clock* (not *2 o'clock*).

num
29b

29c Always spell out numbers that begin sentences.

For clarity, spell out any number that begins a sentence. If the number requires more than two words, reword the sentence so that the number falls later and can be expressed as a figure.

Faulty   *103* visitors asked for refunds.

Awkward   *One hundred three* visitors asked for refunds.

Revised   Of the visitors, *103* asked for refunds.

ANSWERS: EXERCISE

1. The planet Saturn is 900 million miles, or 1.5 billion kilometers, from Earth.
2. Correct.
3. Thus, Saturn orbits the Sun only 2.4 times during the average human life span.
4. It travels in its orbit at about 21,600 miles per hour.
5. Fifteen to twenty times denser than Earth's core, Saturn's core measures seventeen thousand miles across.
6. The temperature at Saturn's cloud tops is −170 degrees Fahrenheit.
7. In 1933 astronomers found on Saturn's surface a huge white spot two times the size of Earth and seven times the size of Mercury.
8. Saturn's famous rings reflect almost 70% (or 70 percent) of the sunlight that approaches the planet.
9. The ring system is almost 40,000 miles wide, beginning 8,800 miles from the planet's visible surface and ending 47,000 miles from that surface.
10. Saturn generates about 130 trillion kilowatts of electricity.

num

29c

Exercise
Revising: Numbers

Revise the following sentences so that numbers are used appropriately for nontechnical writing. Circle the number preceding any sentence in which numbers are already used appropriately.

Example:

Carol paid two hundred five dollars for used scuba gear.
Carol paid $205 for used scuba gear.

1. The planet Saturn is nine hundred million miles, or nearly one billion five hundred million kilometers, from Earth.
2. Saturn revolves around the sun much more slowly than Earth does: a year on Saturn equals almost thirty of our years.
3. Thus, Saturn orbits the sun only two and four-tenths times during the average human life span.
4. It travels in its orbit at about twenty-one thousand six hundred miles per hour.
5. 15 to 20 times denser than Earth's core, Saturn's core measures 17,000 miles across.
6. The temperature at Saturn's cloud tops is minus one hundred seventy degrees Fahrenheit.
7. In nineteen hundred thirty-three astronomers found on Saturn's surface a huge white spot 2 times the size of Earth and 7 times the size of Mercury.
8. Saturn's famous rings reflect almost seventy % of the sunlight that approaches the planet.
9. The ring system is almost forty thousand miles wide, beginning 8,800 miles from the planet's visible surface and ending forty-seven thousand miles from that surface.
10. Saturn generates about one hundred thirty trillion kilowatts of electricity.

Note: See page 474 for an exercise involving numbers along with abbreviations and other mechanics.

Chapter 30

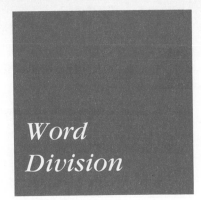

Word Division

HIGHLIGHTS

This chapter addresses one of the most frequent trouble spots in the mechanics of student writing—word division. Though errors in division are not more than misdemeanors, students can avoid the irritation and confusion that such errors afford readers by memorizing the few rules pertaining to word division.

As much as possible, avoid dividing words. If you must divide a word between the end of one line and the beginning of the next, follow these guidelines:

- Divide words only between syllables. (Consult a dictionary if necessary.)
- Put a hyphen at the end of the first line, never at the beginning of the second line.
- Try not to divide the last word on a page. In the act of turning the page, the reader may forget the beginning of the word.

Note that not all syllable breaks are appropriate for word division. Use the following rules to decide when and how to divide words.

 30a   **Any division should leave two or more letters at the end of a line and three or more letters at the beginning of a line.**

Faulty	A newspaper or television editorial for or *a-gainst* a candidate can sway an election.
Revised	A newspaper or television editorial for or *against* a candidate can sway an election.
Faulty	Counseling is required for every child *abus-er*.
Revised	Counseling is required for every child *abuser*.

30b One-syllable words should not be divided.

Since one-syllable words have no break in pronunciation, they should not be divided.

Faulty   The shiny, spinning space capsule *drop-ped* suddenly from the clouds.

Revised   The shiny, spinning space capsule *dropped* suddenly from the clouds.

30c Divide compound words only between the words that form them or at fixed hyphens.

Compound words are made up of two or more words (*drawback, homecoming*). Their component words may be separated by a hyphen (*well-paying, cross-reference*), in which case the hyphen is called **fixed.** Compound words should be divided only between their component words and at fixed hyphens.

Faulty   If you want to have friends, be *good-natured.*

Revised   If you want to have friends, be *good-natured.*

Faulty   Sherlock Holmes exemplifies the *mastermind.*

Revised   Sherlock Holmes exemplifies the *mastermind.*

(See 34d for guidelines on when to use hyphens in spelling compound words.)

div
30d

30d Make sure a word division will not confuse readers.

Some word divisions may momentarily confuse readers because the first or second part by itself forms a pronounceable (or unpronounceable) unit that does not fit with the whole. For example: *poi-gnant, read-dress, in-dict.* Avoid word divisions like these.

Confusing   Her walking out of class was an act of *heroism.*

Clear   Her walking out of class was an act of *heroism.*

Confusing   He claims that stealing never bothered his *con-
                  science.*

Clear   He claims that stealing never bothered his
                  conscience.

Exercise
Revising: Word division

Revise the following sentences to improve inappropriate word
divisions. Consult a dictionary if necessary. Circle the number
preceding any sentence in which word division is already appropriate.

Example:

I thought Harry's joke was sidesplit-
ting, but no one else even smiled.

I thought Harry's joke was *side-
splitting,* but no one else even smiled.

1. Samuel Johnson, British essayist and poet, com-
   piled the first real dictionary of the English language.
2. He followed a method used by dictionary makers ever since.
3. First, he read books about a wide range of subjects.
4. As a result he was probably the most well-edu-
   cated man in England.
5. When he discovered a new use for a word, he marked the passage for his secretary to copy on paper.
6. Since Johnson used a dark pencil to underline the passages, the books were damaged.
7. The books' owners were shocked when their well-thumb-
   ed and smudged volumes were returned.
8. The words were arranged alphabetically in large ledger books, with e-
   nough room between words for definitions.
9. For each word the definitions were organized with specialized uses last.
10. Finally, Johnson's secretaries recop-
    ied the entries onto clean paper for typeset-
    ting.

Note: See the next page for an exercise involving word division along with capitals and other mechanics.

ANSWERS: EXERCISE

1. Correct.
2. He followed a method used by dictionary
   makers <u>ever</u> since.
3. First, he read books about a wide range of
   <u>sub-jects</u>.
4. As a result, he was probably the most <u>well-
   educated</u> man in England.
5. When he discovered a new use for a word, he
   <u>marked</u> the passage for his secretary to copy
   on <u>paper</u> (or <u>pa-per</u>).
6. Correct.
7. The books' owners were shocked when
   their <u>well-thumbed</u> and smudged volumes
   were returned.
8. The words were arranged <u>alphabetically</u>
   in large ledger books, with <u>enough</u>
   room between words for definitions.
9. Correct.
10. Finally, Johnson's secretaries <u>recopied</u>
    the entries onto clean paper for <u>typesetting</u>
    (or <u>type-setting</u>).

div
30d

COLLABORATIVE LEARNING

ANSWERS: EXERCISE ON CHAPTERS 26–30

According to many sources—for example, the Cambridge Ancient History and Gardiner's Egypt of the Pharaohs—the ancient Egyptians devoted much attention to making life more convenient and pleasurable for themselves.

Our word pharaoh for the ancient Egyptian rulers comes from the Egyptian word pr'o, meaning "great house." Indeed, the Egyptians placed great emphasis on family residences, adding small bedrooms as early as 3500 B.C. By 3000 B.C., the Egyptians made ice through evaporation of water at night and then used it to cool their homes. About the same time they used fans made of palm fronds or papyrus to cool themselves in the day. To light their homes, the Egyptians abandoned the animal-fat lamps humans had used for fifty thousand years. Instead, around 1300 B.C. the people of Egypt devised the first oil lamps.

Egyptians found great pleasure in playing games. Around 4300 years ago they created one of the oldest board games known. The game involved racing ivory or stone pieces across a papyrus playing board. By 3000 B.C., Egyptian children played marbles with semiprecious stones, some of which have been found in gravesites at Nagada, Egypt. Around 1360 B.C., small children played with clay rattles covered (or cov-ered) in silk and shaped like animals.

To play the game of love, Egyptian men and women experimented with cosmetics applied to skin and eyelids. Kohl, history's first eyeliner, was used by both sexes to ward off evil. Five thousand years ago Egyptians wore wigs made of vegetable fibers or human hair. In 900 B.C., Queen Isimkheb wore a wig so heavy that she needed assistance in walking. To adjust their make-up and wigs, Egyptians (or Egyp-tians) adapted the simple metal mirrors devised by the Sumerians in the Bronze Age, ornamenting them with carved handles of ivory, gold, or wood. Feeling that only those who smelled sweet could be attractive, the Egyptians made deodorants from perfumed oils, for example, cinnamon and citrus.

mech

Exercise on Chapters 26–30
Revising: Mechanics

Revise the paragraphs below to correct any errors in the use of capital letters, underlining, abbreviations, numbers, and word division. (For abbreviations and numbers follow standard practice for nontechnical writing.) Consult a dictionary as needed.

According to many sources—e.g., the Cambridge Ancient History and Gardiner's Egypt of the Pharaohs—the ancient egyptians devoted much attention to making Life more convenient and pleasurable for themselves.

Our word pharaoh for the ancient egyptian rulers comes from the egyptian word pr'o, meaning "great house." Indeed, the egyptians placed great emphasis on family residences, adding small bedrms. as early as 3500 yrs. b.c. By 3000 b.c., the egyptians made ice through evaporation of water at night and then used it to cool their homes. About the same time they used fans made of palm fronds or papyrus to cool themselves in the day. To light their homes, the egyptians abandoned the animal-fat lamps Humans had used for 50 thousand yrs. Instead, around 1300 b.c. the people of Egt. devised the 1st oil lamps.

egyptians found great pleasure in playing games. Four thousand three hundred yrs. ago or so they created one of the oldest board games known. the game involved racing ivory or stone pieces across a papyrus playing board. By three thousand b.c., egyptian children played marbles with semiprecious stones, some of which have been found in gravesites at nagada, EG. Around one thousand three hundred sixty b.c., small children played with clay rattles cover-ed in silk and shaped like animals.

To play the game of love, egyptian men and women experimented with cosmetics applied to skin and eyelids. kohl, history's first eyeliner, was used by both sexes to ward off evil. 5000 yrs. ago egyptians wore wigs made of vegetable fibers or human hair. In 9 hundred b.c., queen Isimkheb wore a wig so heavy that she needed assistance in walking. To adjust their make-up and wigs, e-gyptians adapted the simple metal mirrors devised by the sumerians in the bronze age, ornamenting them with carved handles of ivory, gold, or wood. Feeling that only those who smelled sweet could be attractive, the egyptians made deodorants from perfumed oils, e.g., cinnamon and citrus.

Part VII

Effective Words

Chapter 31 deals with appropriate usage, exactness, and the avoidance of wordiness. Of course, no instructional short cut can substitute for experience in choosing the appropriate word, in knowing when slang or a colloquialism is actually more effective than a standard word or expression, or in deciding when a technical term is useful or requires definition. But students are often interested in such matters, and some class time may usefully be spent considering how alternative choices affect students' own sentences or paragraphs, in addition to the sample sentences provided by the exercises. Similarly, denotation and connotation, abstract and concrete words, and general and specific words are topics that often generate lively discussion. Because the effect and even the meaning of words may depend as much on the reader's perspective as on the writer's intention, class discussion and collaborative work can be excellent approaches to understanding diction.

Avoiding wordiness, the subject addressed in the final section of this chapter, often causes problems for students, who are likely to mistake brevity for conciseness and to confuse simple lack of development with economy. Some practice with the ways of simplifying sentences and word groups can be useful, as can attention to the empty words and phrases and to the unnecessary repetition that are more obvious sources of flabbiness in writing.

Chapter 31

Choosing and Using Words

Expressing yourself clearly and effectively depends greatly on what words you choose and how you employ them in sentences. English offers an uncommonly rich and extensive vocabulary from which to select the words that precisely suit your meaning and your writing situation (31a and 31b). And the language is uncommonly flexible when it comes to pruning unneeded words that make writing weak or inexact (31c).

31a Choosing the appropriate word

Appropriate words suit your writing situation—your subject, purpose, and audience. Like everyone, you vary your words depending on the context in which you are speaking and writing. Look, for example, at the differences in these two sentences.

> My sister decided to bag therapy because her shrink seemed even more strung out than she was.

> My sister decided to abandon therapy because her psychiatrist seemed even more disturbed than she was.

The first sentence might be addressed to friends in casual conversation. It uses colloquial or slang expressions such as *bag, shrink,* and *strung out* that friends would expect and understand. The second sentence, in contrast, is more suitable for a general audience, using more formal, widely understood words such as *abandon, psychiatrist,* and *disturbed.*

Appropriate and inappropriate words

Appropriate in all writing situations
Standard English (see below)

Appropriate in some writing situations
Slang (31a-1)
Colloquial language (31a-2)
Regional words and expressions (31a-3)

Neologisms (31a-5)
Technical language (31a-6)
Euphemisms (31a-7)

Rarely or never appropriate in writing or speech
Nonstandard language (31a-4)
Archaic and obsolete words (31a-5)
Double talk (31a-7)

Pretentious writing (31a-7)
Biased language: sexist, racist, ethnocentric, etc. (31a-8)

In most college and career writing you will explain, analyze, and sometimes defend your interpretation of facts, events, and ideas. To show your respect for your readers' intelligence and seriousness, and to win your readers' respect for yours, you will rely on the words of **standard** or **educated English**—that is, the English normally expected and used by educated readers and writers. The vocabulary of standard English is huge, allowing expression of an infinite range of ideas and feelings; but it does exclude words that only limited groups of people use, understand, or find inoffensive. Some of those more limited vocabularies should be avoided altogether; others should be used cautiously and in special situations, as when aiming for a special effect with an audience you know will appreciate it. Whenever you doubt a word's status, consult a dictionary (see 32b-2).

RESOURCES AND IDEAS

Mary Scott Simpson, "Teaching Writing: Beginning with the Word," *College English* 39 (1978): 934–39. The author describes class activities and readings designed to develop sensitivity to words and build vocabulary.

appr
31a

 1   Using slang only when appropriate

All groups of people—from musicians and computer scientists to vegetarians and golfers—create novel and colorful expressions called **slang.** The following quotation, for instance, is from an essay on the slang of "skaters" (skateboarders).

> Curtis slashed ultra-punk crunchers on his longboard, while the Rube-man flailed his usual Gumbyness on tweaked frontsides and lofty fakie ollies.
>
> —MILES ORKIN, "Mucho Slingage by the Pool"

"Slang," Orkin goes on to say, "is a convenient, creative, mildly poetic, cohesive agent in many subcultures." It reflects the experiences of a group and binds its members.

Some slang gives new meaning to old words, such as *bad* for "good." Some slang comes from other languages, such as *chow* (food) from the Chinese *chao,* "to stir or fry." The slang of a particular group may also spread to other groups, as *out to lunch, put on ice,* and *funky* have spread beyond their African-American origins.

Among those who understand it, slang may be vivid and forceful. It often occurs in dialogue, and an occasional slang expression can enliven an informal essay. Some slang, such as *dropout* (*she was a high school dropout*), has proved so useful that it has passed into the general vocabulary.

But most slang is too flippant and imprecise for effective communication, and it is generally inappropriate for college or business writing. Notice the gain in seriousness and precision achieved in the following revision.

Slang	Many students start out *pretty together* but then *get weird.*
General	Many students start out *with clear goals* but then *lose their direction.*

 2 Using colloquial language only when appropriate

Colloquial language designates the words and expressions appropriate to everyday spoken language. Regardless of our backgrounds and how we live, we all try to *get along with* each other. We sometimes *get together with* our neighbors. We play with *kids, go crazy* about one thing, *crab* about something else, and in our worst moments try to *get back at* someone who has made us do the *dirty work.* These expressions are not "wrong"; quite the contrary, more formal language might sound stilted and pompous in casual conversation and in some kinds of writing.

When you write informally, colloquial language may be appropriate to achieve the casual, relaxed effect of conversation. An occasional colloquial word dropped into otherwise more formal writing can also help you achieve a desired emphasis. But colloquial language does not provide the exactness needed in more formal college, business, and professional writing. In such writing you should generally avoid any words and expressions labeled "informal" or "colloquial" in your dictionary. Take special care to avoid **mixed diction,** a combination of standard and colloquial words.

| **Mixed diction** | According to a Native American myth, the Great Creator *had a dog hanging around with him* when he created the earth. |
| **Consistent** | According to a Native American myth, the Great Creator *was accompanied by a dog* when he created the earth. |

 Using regionalisms only when appropriate

Most national languages vary slightly from one geographical area to another. In American English regional differences are most marked in pronunciation: a Texan overhearing a conversation between a New Yorker and a Georgian will not mistake either for a fellow Texan. But regional vocabularies differ somewhat, too. Southerners may say they *reckon,* meaning "think" or "suppose." People in Maine invite their Boston friends to come *down* rather than *up* (north) to visit. New Yorkers stand *on* (rather than *in*) line for a movie. Regional expressions are appropriate in writing addressed to local readers and may lend realism to regional description, but they should be avoided in writing intended for a general audience.

| **Regional** | The house where I spent my childhood was *down the road a piece* from a federal maximum-security prison. |
| **General** | The house where I spent my childhood was *a short distance* from a federal maximum-security prison. |

 Revising nonstandard language

Words and grammatical forms called **nonstandard** are used by many intelligent people who speak dialects other than standard English. In spoken and written standard English, however, these nonstandard forms are considered unacceptable. Examples include *nowheres;* such pronoun forms as *hisn, hern, hisself,* and *theirselves; them* as an adjective, as in *them dishes, them courses;* the expressions *this here* and *that there,* as in *that there elevator;* verb forms such as *knowed, throwed, hadn't ought,* and *could of;* and double negatives such as *didn't never* and *haven't no.* Dictionaries label such expressions "nonstandard" or "substandard." Avoid or revise all nonstandard expressions in speaking and writing situations calling for standard English.

HUCK FINN

You may wish to make the following examples the subject of class discussion. Students usually find them quite interesting.

In his explanatory note at the beginning of *The Adventures of Huckleberry Finn,* Mark Twain explains one of the difficulties with using nonstandard language:

> In this book a number of dialects are used, to wit: the Missouri negro dialect; the extremist form of the backwoods Southwestern dialect; the ordinary "Pike County" dialect; and four modified varieties of this last. The shadings have not been done in a haphazard fashion, or by guesswork; but painstakingly, and with the trustworthy guidance and support of personal familiarity with these several forms of speech.
>
> I make this explanation for the reason that without it many readers would suppose that all these characters were trying to talk alike and not succeeding.
>
> —The Author

From the opening lines of *The Adventures of Huckleberry Finn:*

> You don't know about me without you have read a book by the name of *The Adventures of Tom Sawyer;* but that ain't no matter. That book was made by Mr. Mark Twain, and he told the truth, mainly. There was things which he stretched; but mainly he told the truth. That is nothing. I never seen anybody but lied one time or another, without it was Aunt Polly, or the widow, or maybe Mary. Aunt Polly—Tom's Aunt Polly, she is—and Mary, and the widow Douglas is all told about in that book, which is mostly a true book, with some stretchers, as I said before.

appr
31a

Revising obsolete or archaic words and neologisms

Since our surroundings and our lives are constantly changing, some words pass out of use and others appear to fill new needs. **Obsolete** and **archaic** are dictionary labels for words or meanings of words that we never or rarely use but that appear in older documents and literature still read today. Obsolete words or meanings are no longer used at all—for example, *enwheel* ("to encircle") and *cote* ("to pass"). Archaic words or meanings occur now only in special contexts such as poetry—for example, *fast* ("near," as in *fast by the road*) and *belike* ("perhaps"). Both obsolete and archaic words are inappropriate in nonfiction writing for a general audience.

Neologisms are words created (or coined) so recently that they have not come into established use. An example is *prequel* (made up of *pre-,* meaning "before," and the ending of *sequel*), which is a movie or book that takes the story of an existing movie or book back in time. Some neologisms do become accepted as part of our general vocabulary—*motel,* coined from *motor* and *hotel,* is an example. But most neologisms pass quickly from the language. Unless such words serve a special purpose in your writing and are sure to be understood by your readers, you should avoid them.

 Using technical words with care

All disciplines and professions rely on special words or give common words special meanings. Chemists speak of *esters* and *phosphatides,* geographers and mapmakers refer to *isobars* and *isotherms,* and literary critics write about *motifs* and *subtexts.* Such technical language allows specialists to communicate precisely and economically with other specialists who share their vocabulary. But without explanation these words are meaningless to the nonspecialist. When you are writing for a general audience, avoid unnecessary technical terms. If your subject requires words the reader may not understand, be careful to define them. (See also 31c-4 for a discussion of jargon.)

 Revising indirect or pretentious writing

In most writing, small, plain, and direct words are preferable to big, showy, or evasive words. Avoid euphemisms, double talk, and pretentious writing.

appr
31a

A **euphemism** is a presumably inoffensive word that a writer or speaker substitutes for a word deemed potentially offensive or too blunt. Government officials use euphemism when they describe an effort to cut waste in military spending as an *acquisitions-improvement program*. Because euphemisms conceal meaning instead of clarifying it, use them only when you know that blunt, truthful words would needlessly hurt or offend members of your audience.

A kind of euphemism that deliberately evades the truth is **double talk** (also called **doublespeak** or **weasel words**): language intended to confuse or to be misunderstood. Today double talk is unfortunately common in politics and advertising—the *revenue enhancement* that is really a tax, the *biodegradable* bags that last decades. Double talk has no place in honest writing. (See also 4c-4.)

Euphemism and sometimes double talk seem to keep company with fancy writing. Any writing that is more elaborate than its subject requires will sound **pretentious,** excessively showy. Choose your words for their exactness and economy. The big, ornate word may be tempting, but pass it up. Your readers will be grateful.

> **Pretentious**   Many institutions of higher education recognize the need for youth at the threshold of maturity to confront the choice of life's endeavor and thus require students to select a field of concentration.
>
> **Revised**   Many colleges and universities force students to make decisions about their careers by requiring them to select a major.

 Revising sexist and other biased language

Even when we do not mean it to, our language can reflect and perpetuate hurtful prejudices toward groups of people, especially racial, ethnic, religious, age, and sexual groups. (See 4c-1 for a discussion of the differences among prejudice, fact, opinion, and belief.) In any kind of speech or writing, a word such as *nigger, honky, mick, kike, fag, dyke,* or *broad*—with or without additionally insulting adjectives—reflects more poorly on the user than on the person or persons designated. Unbiased language does not submit to stereotypes. It refers to people as they would wish to be referred to.

Among the most subtle and persistent biased language is that expressing narrow ideas about men's and women's roles, posi-

**appr
31a**

tion, and value in society. This **sexist language** distinguishes needlessly between men and women in such matters as occupation, ability, behavior, temperament, and maturity. It can wound or irritate readers, and it indicates the writer's thoughtlessness or unfairness. The box below suggests some ways of eliminating sexist language.

appr
31a

Eliminating sexist language

- Avoid demeaning and patronizing language.

  Sexist   Pushy broads are entering almost every occupation.
  Revised   *Women* are entering almost every occupation.

  Sexist   President Reagan came to Nancy's defense.
  Revised   President Reagan came to *Mrs. Reagan's* defense.

- Avoid occupational or social stereotypes.

  Sexist   The caring doctor commends his nurse when she does a good job.
  Revised   Caring *doctors* commend *their nurses* on jobs well done.

  Sexist   The grocery shopper should save her coupons.
  Revised   *Grocery shoppers* should save *their* coupons.

- Avoid using *man* or words containing *man* to refer to all human beings.

  Sexist   Man has not reached the limits of social justice.
  Revised   *Humankind* (or *Humanity*) has not reached the limits of social justice.

  Sexist   The furniture consists of manmade materials.
  Revised   The furniture consists of *synthetic* materials.

- Avoid using the generic *he* to refer to both genders. (See also 8b-3, p. 257.)

  Sexist   The person who studies history knows his roots.
  Revised   The person who studies history knows *his or her* roots.
  Revised   *People* who study history know *their* roots.

Exercise 1
Revising: Appropriate words

Rewrite the following sentences as needed for standard written English. Consult a dictionary to determine whether particular words are appropriate and to find suitable substitutes.

Example:

If negotiators get hyper during contract discussions, they may mess up chances for a settlement.

If negotiators *become excited or upset* during contract discussions, they may *harm* chances for a settlement.

1. Acquired Immune Deficiency Syndrome (AIDS) is a major deal all over the world.
2. According to some estimates, millions of people haven't got a clue that they carry the bug.
3. A person who feels perfectly okay might be carrying the virus.
4. Such a carrier can transmit the virus to lots of unsuspecting folks.
5. The disease gets around primarily by sexual intercourse, exchange of bodily fluids, shared needles, and blood transfusions.
6. Those who think the disease is limited to homos and druggies are quite mistaken.
7. Stats suggest that one in every five hundred college kids carries the virus.
8. The number of babies born with the virus has shot way up.
9. Any nurse working with newborns has her own stories of babies with AIDS.
10. People with AIDS do not deserve to be subjected to exclusionary behavior or callousness on the part of their fellow citizens. Instead, they have the necessity for all the compassion, medical care, and financial assistance due those who are in the extremity of illness.

ANSWERS: EXERCISE 1
Possible Answers

1. Acquired Immune Deficiency Syndrome (AIDS) is a <u>serious threat</u> all over the world.
2. According to some estimates, millions of people are not <u>aware</u> that they carry the <u>virus</u>.
3. A person who feels perfectly <u>healthy</u> might be carrying the virus.
4. Such a carrier can transmit the virus to <u>many</u> unsuspecting <u>people</u>.
5. The disease <u>is transmitted</u> primarily by sexual intercourse, exchange of bodily fluids, shared needles, and blood transfusions.
6. Those who think the disease is limited to <u>homosexuals</u> and <u>drug users</u> are quite mistaken.
7. <u>Statistics</u> suggest that one in every five hundred college <u>students</u> carries the virus.
8. The number of babies born with the virus has <u>increased dramatically</u>.
9. Any nurse working with newborns <u>has stories</u> (or <u>has his or her own stories</u>) of babies with AIDS. *Or:* <u>Nurses</u> working with newborns <u>have their</u> own stories of babies with AIDS.
10. People with AIDS do not deserve <u>others' exclusion</u> or callousness. Instead, they <u>need</u> all the compassion, medical care, and financial assistance due the seriously ill.

31b   Choosing the exact word

To write clearly and effectively, you will want to find the words that fit your meaning exactly and convey your attitude precisely. If, like many people, you feel uncertain about words and their meanings, consult the next two chapters, on using a dictionary (32) and improving your vocabulary (33).

Don't worry too much about choosing exact words while you

are drafting an essay. If the right word doesn't come to you, leave a blank. Revision (2b) or editing (2c) is the stage to consider tone, specificity, and precision.

 Using the right word for your meaning

The precise expression of meaning requires understanding both the denotations and connotations of words. A word's **denotation** is the thing or idea it refers to, the meaning listed in the dictionary without reference to the emotional associations it may arouse in a reader. Using words according to their established denotations is essential if readers are to grasp your meaning. Here are a few guidelines:

- Become acquainted with a dictionary. Consult it whenever you are unsure of a word's meaning.
- Distinguish between similar-sounding words that have widely different denotations.

  Inexact   Older people often suffer *infirmaries* [places for the sick].

  Exact   Older people often suffer *infirmities* [disabilities].

  Some words, called **homonyms** (from the Greek meaning "same name"), sound exactly alike but differ in meaning: for example, *principal/principle* or *rain/reign/rein*. (See 34a-1 for a list of commonly confused homonyms.)

- Distinguish between words with related but distinct denotations.

  Inexact   Most spectators were amazed at the whale's *enormity* [abnormal wickedness].

  Exact   Most spectators were amazed at the whale's *enormousness* [huge size].

In addition to their emotion-free denotations, many words also carry associations with specific feelings. These **connotations** can shape readers' responses and are thus a powerful tool for writers. (At the same time they are a potential snare for readers. See 4c-4 on critical reading.) Some connotations are personal: the word *dog,* for instance, may have negative connotations for the letter carrier who has been bitten three times. Usually, though, people agree about connotations. The following word pairs have related denotations but very different connotations.

desire/lust	firm/stubborn	enthusiasm/mania
pride/vanity	lasting/endless	daring/reckless

exact

31b

Understanding connotation is especially important in choosing among **synonyms,** words with approximately, but often not exactly, the same meanings. *Cry* and *weep* are similar, both denoting the shedding of tears; but *cry* more than *weep* connotes a sobbing sound accompanying the tears. *Sob* itself connotes broken, gasping crying, with tears, whereas *wail* connotes sustained sound, perhaps without tears. Used in the blank in the sentence *We were disturbed by his _____ ing,* each of these words would evoke different sounds and images. Several resources can help you track down words with the exact connotations you want:

- A dictionary is essential. Many dictionaries list and distinguish among synonyms (see 33c-2 for an example).
- A dictionary of synonyms lists and defines synonyms in groups (see 32a-3 for titles).
- A thesaurus lists synonyms but does not distinguish among them (see 32a-3 for titles). Because it lacks definitions, a thesaurus can only suggest possibilities; you will still need a dictionary to discover the words' connotations.

Exercise 2
Revising: Denotation

Revise the following sentences to replace any underlined word that is not used according to its established denotation. If an underlined word is used correctly, circle it. Consult a dictionary if you are uncertain of a word's precise meaning.

Example:

Sam and Dave are going to Bermuda and Hauppauge, respectfully, for spring vacation.

Sam and Dave are going to Bermuda and Hauppauge, respectively, for spring vacation.

1. Maxine Hong Kingston was rewarded many prizes for her first two books, *The Woman Warrior* and *China Men.*
2. Kingston sites her mother's tales about ancestors and ancient Chinese customs as the sources of these memoirs.
3. Two of Kingston's progeny, her great-grandfathers, are focal points of *China Men.*
4. Both men led rebellions against suppressive employers: a sugar-cane farmer and a railroad-construction supervisor.
5. In her childhood Kingston was greatly effected by her mother's tale about a pregnant aunt who was ostracized by villagers.
6. The aunt gained avengeance by drowning herself in the village's water supply.
7. Kingston decided to make her nameless relative infamous by giving her immortality in *The Woman Warrior.*

PERSONAL RESPONSES

Give students a list of words and ask them to write out the personal connotations of each word. Asking students to share their responses with the class or a smaller group may further help them understand the potential richness of language.

ANSWERS: EXERCISE 2

1. Maxine Hong Kingston was awarded many prizes for her first two books, *The Woman Warrior* and *China Men.*
2. Kingston cites her mother's tales about ancestors and ancient Chinese customs as the sources of these memoirs.
3. Two of Kingston's progenitors (or ancestors), her great-grandfathers, are focal points of *China Men.*
4. Both men led rebellions against oppressive employers: a sugar-cane farmer and a railroad-construction supervisor.
5. In her childhood Kingston was greatly affected by her mother's tale about a pregnant aunt who was ostracized by villagers. [Ostracized correct.]
6. The aunt gained vengeance by drowning herself in the village's water supply.
7. Kingston decided to make her nameless relative famous by giving her immortality in *The Woman Warrior.* [Immortality correct.]

exact
31b

8. Kingston's novel *Tripmaster Monkey* has been called the <u>premier</u> novel about the 1960s.
9. Correct.
10. Kingston's innovative memoirs and novel <u>imply</u> her opposition to racism and sexism both in ancient China and in the modern United States.

ANSWERS: EXERCISE 3

1. <u>Slumbered</u>, <u>kissing</u>, and <u>bathes</u> all connote gentle slowness in the movement of the river. Related words such as <u>lies</u>, <u>smacking</u>, and <u>showers</u> would connote the opposite.
2. <u>Torn</u>, <u>whirling</u>, <u>intensely</u>, <u>rushing</u>, and <u>immense</u> all connote great violence and magnitude. Weaker synonyms such as <u>separated</u>, <u>turning</u>, <u>very</u>, <u>moving</u>, and <u>large</u> would not convey the same extremes.
3. <u>Bluster</u>, <u>bravado</u>, and <u>flashing</u> connote the swagger of boys. Synonyms such as <u>noise</u>, <u>bravery</u>, and <u>glimmering</u> would not convey the same strutting quality. <u>Meadows</u> connotes idyllic expanses in a way that <u>fields</u>, for instance, would not.
4. <u>Modified</u> connotes a lessening in the strength of principles—a meaning not specifically conveyed by the synonym <u>changed</u>. <u>Pulverized</u> connotes a more tangible sense of destruction than, say, <u>demolish</u>. <u>Center</u>—as opposed to say, <u>middle</u> or <u>core</u>—connotes a place around which competing forces might move.
5. <u>Swoop</u> connotes a bird's flight; a word like <u>drive</u> would not convey the same speed or ease of motion. <u>Streaked</u> connotes bright color, in contrast to the <u>dark</u> hills; words such as <u>covered</u> and <u>dim</u> would not convey the same contrast. <u>Wheatstubble</u> connotes a low, spiky landscape and intensifies the picture of harvested fields; even <u>wheat stalks</u> would not be so evocative.

8. Kingston's novel *Tripmaster Monkey* has been called the <u>premiere</u> novel about the 1960s.
9. Her characters <u>embody</u> the <u>principles</u> that led her to her own protest against the Vietnam War.
10. Kingston's innovative memoirs and novel <u>infer</u> her opposition to racism and sexism both in ancient China and in the modern United States.

Exercise 3
Analyzing connotations

Describe how the connotation of each italicized word in the following sentences contributes to the writer's meaning. Give at least one synonym or related word that the writer could have used instead of the italicized word, and describe how the new word would alter the meaning. Consult a dictionary as necessary.

1. [The river] *slumbers* between broad prairies, *kissing* the long meadow grass, and *bathes* the overhangmg boughs of elder bushes and willows or the roots of elms and ash trees and clumps of maples. —NATHANIEL HAWTHORNE
2. The new earth, freshly *torn* from its parent sun, was a ball of *whirling* gases, *intensely* hot, *rushing* through the black spaces of the universe on a path and a speed controlled by *immense* forces. —RACHEL CARSON
3. When the country loved it with a passion, baseball was boyhood eternal, all *bluster*, innocence, and *bravado flashing* across green *meadows* in the sunlight. —RUSSELL BAKER
4. I think all theories are suspect, that the finest principles may have to be *modified*, or may even be *pulverized* by the demands of life, and that one must find, therefore, one's own moral *center* and move through the world hoping that this center will guide one aright. —JAMES BALDWIN
5. After a long straight *swoop* across the pancakeflat prairies, hour after hour of harvested land *streaked* with the yellow *wheat-stubble* to the horizon, it's exciting to see hills ahead, *dark* hills under clouds against the west. —JOHN DOS PASSOS

 Balancing the abstract and concrete, the general and specific

To understand a subject as you understand it, your readers need ample guidance from your words. When you describe a building as beautiful and nothing more, you force readers to provide their own conceptions of the features that make a building beautiful. If readers bother (and they may not), they surely will not conjure up the image you had in mind. You'll be much more likely to achieve your purpose if you tell readers what you want them to know, that the beautiful building is *a sleek, silver sky-*

scraper with blue-tinted windows, for instance, or *a Victorian brick courthouse with tall, arched windows.*

Clear, exact writing balances abstract and general words, which outline ideas and objects, with concrete and specific words, which sharpen and solidify.

- **Abstract words** name qualities and ideas: *beauty, inflation, management, culture, liberal.* **Concrete words** name things we can know by our five senses of sight, hearing, touch, taste, and smell: *sleek, humming, brick, bitter, musty.*
- **General words** name classes or groups of things, such as *buildings, weather,* or *birds,* and include all the varieties of the class. **Specific words** limit a general class, such as *buildings,* by naming one of its varieties, such as *skyscraper, Victorian courthouse,* or *hut.*

Note that *general* and *specific* are relative terms. Here, for example, is a "ladder" with the most general words at the top and the most specific words at the bottom.

General

weather	bird
rain	parrot
downpour	cockatoo
sudden downpour	my pet cockatoo Moyshe

Specific

Abstract and general words are useful in the broad statements that set the course for your writing.

The wild horse in America has a *romantic* history.

We must be *free* from *government interference* in our *affairs.*

Relations between the sexes today are only a *little* more *relaxed* than they were in the past.

But such statements need development with concrete and specific detail. Writing seldom fails because it lacks abstraction and generality. It often fails because it lacks concrete and specific words to nail down meaning and make the writing vivid, real, and clear. When your meaning does call for an abstract or general word, make sure you define it, explain it, and narrow it. Look at how concrete and specific information turns vague sentences into exact ones in the examples below.

Vague	The size of his hands made his smallness real. [How big were his hands? How small was he?]
Exact	Not until I saw his white, doll-like hands did I realize that he stood a full head shorter than most other men.

exact
31b

Vague	The long flood caused a lot of awful destruction in the town. [How long did the flood last? What destruction did it cause? Why was the destruction awful?]
Exact	The flood waters, which rose swiftly and then stayed stubbornly high for days, killed at least six townspeople and made life a misery for the hundreds who had to evacuate their ruined homes and stores.

exact
31b

Exercise 4
Revising: Concrete and specific words

Make the following paragraph vivid by expanding the sentences with appropriate details of your own choosing. Concentrate especially on substituting concrete and specific words for the abstract and general ones in italics.

I remember *clearly* how *awful* I felt the first time I *attended* Mrs. Murphy's second-grade class. I had *recently* moved from a *small* town in Missouri to a *crowded* suburb of Chicago. My new school looked *big* from the outside and seemed *dark* inside as I *walked* down the *long* corridor toward the classroom. The class was *noisy* as I neared the door; but when I *entered, everyone* became *quiet* and *looked* at me. I felt *uncomfortable* and *wanted* a place to hide. However, in a *loud* voice Mrs. Murphy *directed* me to the front of the room to introduce myself.

Exercise 5
Using concrete and specific words

For each abstract or general word below, give at least two other words or phrases that illustrate increasing specificity or concreteness. Consult a dictionary as needed. Use the most specific or concrete word from each group in a sentence of your own.

> *Example:*
>
> tired, *sleepy, droopy-eyed*
>
> We stopped for the night when I became so *droopy-eyed* that the road blurred.

1. fabric	6. green	11. teacher
2. delicious	7. walk (*verb*)	12. nice
3. car	8. flower	13. virtue
4. narrow-minded	9. serious	14. angry
5. reach (*verb*)	10. pretty	15. crime

 Using idioms

Idioms are expressions in any language whose meanings cannot be determined simply from the words in them or whose component words cannot be predicted by any rule of grammar; often, they violate conventional grammar. Examples of English idioms include *put up with, plug away at,* and *make off with.*

Because they are not governed by rules, idioms usually cause particular difficulty for people learning to speak and write a new language. Those learning English as a second language often stumble over its prepositions, confusing them because of their similar meanings and uses (for instance, *in the afternoon* but *at night*), or omitting them with verbs that require them (*refer [to] a poem, look [in] the book*). A dictionary or a grammar book expressly for those learning English can be a helpful guide.

Even native speakers of English have problems with some combinations of verb and preposition or adjective and preposition. A number of these pairings are listed below.

Idioms with prepositions

abide *by* a rule
abide *in* a place or state

accords *with*
according *to*

accuse *of* a crime

adapt *from* a source
adapt *to* a situation

agree *on* a plan
agree *to* a proposal
agree *with* a person

angry *with*

capable *of*

charge *for* a purchase
charge *with* a crime

compare *to* something in a different class
compare *with* something in the same class

concur *in* an opinion
concur *with* a person

contend *for* a principle
contend *with* a person

differ *about* or *over* a question
differ *from* in appearance
differ *with* a person

identical *with* or *to*

impatient *at* her conduct
impatient *of* restraint
impatient *for* a raise
impatient *with* a person

independent *of*

infer *from*

inferior *to*

oblivious *of* or *to* one's surroundings
oblivious *of* something forgotten

occupied *by* a person
occupied *in* study
occupied *with* a thing

part *from* a person
part *with* a possession

prior *to*

rewarded *by* the judge
rewarded *for* something done
rewarded *with* a gift

superior *to*

wait *at* a place
wait *for* a train, a person
wait *on* a customer

6. green, dark green, bilious green
   The algae covered the surface with a <u>bilious green</u> scum.
7. walk, march, goose-step
   The soldiers <u>goose-stepped</u> menacingly.
8. flower, daisy, ox-eyed daisy
   Some people call the <u>ox-eyed daisy</u> a "brown-eyed Susan."
9. serious, solemn, grim
   His <u>grim</u> expression frightened us.
10. pretty; with small, regular features; with a button nose and a tiny, smiling mouth
    The infant, <u>with a button nose and a tiny, smiling mouth</u>, was a perfect model for baby products.
11. teacher, history teachers, American history teacher
    My <u>American history teacher</u> requires three research papers.
12. nice, considerate, sympathetic
    I need a <u>sympathetic</u> friend.
13. virtue, honesty, frankness
    His <u>frankness</u> was refreshing after I had heard so much flattery.
14. angry, furious, raging
    <u>Raging</u> uncontrollably, Andy insulted everyone around him.
15. crime, theft, armed robbery
    Drug addicts sometimes commit <u>armed robbery</u> to pay for their habits.

exact
31b

ANSWERS: EXERCISE 6

1. He had waited for years, growing impatient <u>with</u> her demands and <u>for</u> the money that she would leave to him.
2. The writer compared gorilla society <u>to</u> human society.
3. They agreed <u>on</u> most things, but they differed consistently <u>about</u> (or <u>over</u>) how to raise their child.
4. I was rewarded <u>for</u> my persistence <u>with</u> an opportunity to meet the senator.
5. He would sooner part <u>from</u> his friends than part <u>with</u> his Corvette.

Exercise 6
Using prepositions in idioms

Insert the preposition that correctly completes each idiom in the following sentences. Consult the preceding list or a dictionary as needed.

Example:

I disagree _____ many feminists who say women should not be homemakers.

I disagree *with* many feminists who say women should not be homemakers.

1. He had waited for years, growing impatient _____ her demands and _____ the money that she would leave to him.
2. The writer compared gorilla society _____ human society.
3. They agreed _____ most things, but they differed consistently _____ how to raise their child.
4. I was rewarded _____ my persistence _____ an opportunity to meet the senator.
5. He would sooner part _____ his friends than part _____ his Corvette.

RESOURCES AND IDEAS

Stephen Sossaman, "Detroit Designers: A Game to Teach Metaphors," *Exercise Exchange* 21 (1976): 2–3. Sossaman points out that car names provide good examples of metaphoric language.

 Using figurative language

Figurative language (or a **figure of speech**) departs from the literal meanings (the denotations) of words, usually by comparing very different ideas or objects. The sentence *As I try to write, I can think of nothing to say* is literal. The sentence *As I try to write, my mind is a blank slab of black slate* is figurative. The abstract concept of having nothing to say has become concrete, something that readers can understand with their senses as bare, hard, and unyielding.

Figurative language is commonplace in speech. Having *slept like a log,* you may get up to find it *raining cats and dogs* and to discover that the Yankees *shelled* the Royals last night. But the rapid exchange of speech leaves little time for inventiveness, and most figures of daily conversation, like those above, are worn and hackneyed. Writing gives you time to reject the tired figure and to search out fresh, concrete words and phrases.

The two most common figures of speech are the **simile** and the **metaphor.** Both compare two things of different classes, often one abstract and the other concrete. A simile makes the comparison explicit and usually begins with *like* or *as.*

We force their [children's] growth as if they were chicks in a poultry factory.

—ARNOLD TOYNBEE

exact
31b

> To hold America in one's thoughts is like holding a love letter in
> one's hand—it has so special a meaning.   —E. B. WHITE

Instead of stating a comparison, the metaphor implies it, omitting such words as *like* or *as*.

> I refuse to accept the notion that nation after nation must spiral
> down a militaristic stairway into the hell of nuclear war.
>   —MARTIN LUTHER KING, JR.

> A school is a hopper into which children are heaved while they
> are young and tender; therein they are pressed into certain stan-
> dard shapes and covered from head to heels with official rubber
> stamps.   —H. L. MENCKEN

Two other figures of speech are **personification** and **hyperbole.** Personification treats ideas and objects as if they were human.

> The economy consumes my money and gives me little in return.
> I could hear the whisper of snowflakes, nudging each other as
> they fell.

Hyperbole deliberately exaggerates.

> She appeared in a mile of billowing chiffon, flashing a rhinestone
> as big as an ostrich egg.
> I'm going to cut him up in small cubes and fry him in deep fat.

To be successful, figurative language must be fresh and unstrained, calling attention not to itself but to the writer's meaning. If readers reject your language as trite or overblown, they may reject your message. One kind of figurative language gone wrong is the **mixed metaphor,** in which the writer combines two or more incompatible figures. Since metaphors often generate visual images in the reader's mind, a mixed metaphor can be laughable.

> **Mixed**   Various thorny problems that we try to sweep un-
> der the rug continue to bob up all the same.

To revise a mixed metaphor, follow through consistently with just one image.

> **Improved**   Various thorny problems that we try to weed out
> continue to thrive all the same.

Exercise 7
Analyzing figurative language

Identify each figure of speech in the following sentences as a simile or a metaphor and analyze how it contributes to the writer's meaning.

**exact
31b**

1. All artists quiver under the lash of adverse criticism.
   —Catherine Drinker Bowen
2. Louisa spends the entire day in blue, limpid boredom. The caressing sting of it appears to be, for her, like the pleasure of lemon, or the coldness of salt water. —Elizabeth Hardwick
3. Every writer, in a roomful of writers, wants to be the best, and the judge, or umpire, or referee is soon overwhelmed and shouted down like a chickadee trying to take charge of a caucus of crows.
   —James Thurber
4. And meanwhile, like enormous, irresistible, gleaming and spinning toys, there are the missiles and their warheads, each one more destructive than one thousand Hiroshima bombs, loaded with magnificent navigational equipment more fun to play with than anything else on earth or in space.
   —Lewis Thomas
5. At best today it [the railroad in America] resembles a fabled ruin, a vast fallen empire. More commonly it suggests a stodgy and even dirtier-looking subway, a sprawling anachronism that conveys not ruin but mess, not age but senility, not something speeding across continents but stalled between stations.
   —Louis Kronenberger

Exercise 8
Using figurative language

Invent appropriate figurative language of your own (simile, metaphor, hyperbole, or personification) to describe each scene or quality below, and use the figure in a sentence.

> *Example:*
> The attraction of a lake on a hot day
> The small waves *like fingers beckoned* us irresistibly.

1. The sound of a kindergarten classroom
2. People waiting in line to buy tickets to a rock concert
3. The politeness of strangers meeting for the first time
4. A streetlight seen through dense fog
5. The effect of watching television for ten hours straight

5   **Avoiding trite expressions**

vocab

Trite expressions, or **clichés,** are phrases so old and so often repeated that they become stale. They include:

acid test	brought back to reality
add insult to injury	cool, calm, and collected
better late than never	crushing blow
beyond the shadow of a doubt	dyed in the wool

easier said than done	ripe old age
face the music	sadder but wiser
gentle as a lamb	shoulder the burden
hard as a rock	sneaking suspicion
heavy as lead	sober as a judge
hit the nail on the head	stand in awe
hour of need	strong as an ox
ladder of success	thin as a rail
moving experience	tired but happy
needle in a haystack	tried and true
point with pride	wise as an owl

Many of these expressions were once fresh and forceful, but constant use has dulled them. They, in turn, will dull your writing by suggesting that you have not thought about what you are saying and have resorted to the easiest phrase. To prevent clichés from sliding into your writing, be wary of any expression you have heard or used before. Substitute fresh words of your own or restate the idea in plain language.

Trite   A *motley crowd* of the singer's *ardent admirers* awaited her arrival *with bated breath.*

Revised   *Outfitted in wild, colorful costumes,* a crowd of the singer's *fans* awaited her arrival *in tense, eager silence.*

Exercise 9
Revising: Trite expressions

Revise the following sentences to eliminate trite expressions.

Example:

The basketball team had almost seized victory, but it faced the test of truth in the last quarter of the game.

The basketball team *seemed about to win,* but the *real test* came in the last quarter of the game.

1. The disastrous consequences of the war have shaken the small nation to its roots.
2. Prices for food have shot sky high, and citizens have sneaking suspicions that others are making a killing on the black market.
3. Medical supplies are so few and far between that even civilians who are as sick as dogs cannot get treatment.
4. With most men fighting or injured or killed, women have had to bite the bullet and bear the men's burden in farming and manufacturing.
5. Last but not least, the war's heavy drain on the nation's pocketbook has left the economy in a shambles.

ANSWERS: EXERCISE 9
Possible Answers

1. These <u>disasters</u> of the war have shaken the small nation <u>severely</u>.
2. Prices for food have <u>risen</u> markedly, and the citizens <u>suspect</u> that others are <u>profiting</u> on the black market.
3. Medical supplies are so <u>scarce</u> that even <u>very sick</u> civilians cannot get treatment.
4. With most of the men fighting or injured or killed, the women have had to <u>take the men's places</u> in farming and manufacturing.
5. <u>Finally</u>, the war's <u>high cost</u> has <u>destroyed the nation's economy</u>.

exact
31b

31c Writing concisely

Writing concisely means cutting whatever adds nothing to your meaning or the freshness of your writing. Don't worry about conciseness while drafting. But when editing your sentences, lo-

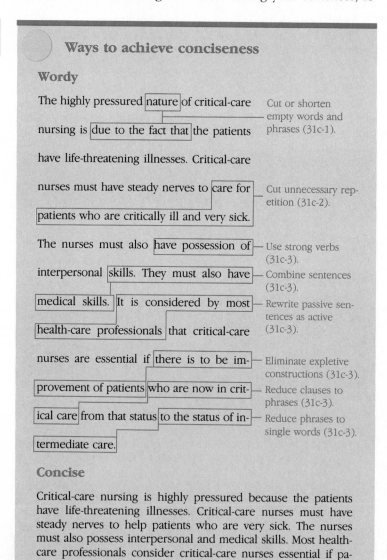

Ways to achieve conciseness

Wordy

The highly pressured nature of critical-care nursing is due to the fact that the patients have life-threatening illnesses. Critical-care nurses must have steady nerves to care for patients who are critically ill and very sick. The nurses must also have possession of interpersonal skills. They must also have medical skills. It is considered by most health-care professionals that critical-care nurses are essential if there is to be improvement of patients who are now in critical care from that status to the status of intermediate care.

— Cut or shorten empty words and phrases (31c-1).

— Cut unnecessary repetition (31c-2).

— Use strong verbs (31c-3).

— Combine sentences (31c-3).

— Rewrite passive sentences as active (31c-3).

— Eliminate expletive constructions (31c-3).

— Reduce clauses to phrases (31c-3).

— Reduce phrases to single words (31c-3).

Concise

Critical-care nursing is highly pressured because the patients have life-threatening illnesses. Critical-care nurses must have steady nerves to help patients who are very sick. The nurses must also possess interpersonal and medical skills. Most health-care professionals consider critical-care nurses essential if patients in critical care are to improve to intermediate care.

w
31c

cate the forceful and exact words that are essential to your meaning. Cross out all the empty words; cut out repetition that neither clarifies nor emphasizes your meaning; and be sure you have used the most direct grammatical form to express your ideas. Don't sacrifice necessary detail or original expression for mere brevity, however. Concise writing does not waste words but still includes the concrete and specific details that make meaning clear. In concise writing the length of an expression is appropriate to the thought.

 Cutting or shortening empty words and phrases

Empty words and phrases walk in place, gaining little or nothing in meaning. Shorten them to their essential meaning, or cut them entirely. Your writing will move faster and be easier to read, as this example shows.

> **Wordy** As far as I am concerned, because of the fact that a situation of discrimination continues to exist in the field of medicine, women have not yet achieved equality with men.
>
> **Concise** Because of continuing discrimination in medicine, women have not yet achieved equality with men.

The empty expressions cut from the second sentence are filler phrases, qualifying phrases, and all-purpose words.

Filler phrases say in several words what a single word can say as well.

For	Substitute
at all times	always
at the present time	now
at this point in time	now
in the nature of	like
for the purpose of	for
in order to	to
until such time as	until
for the reason that	because
due to the fact that	because
because of the fact that	because
by virtue of the fact that	because
in the event that	if
by means of	by
in the final analysis	finally

Many **qualifying phrases** can also be shortened or even deleted with no loss of clarity or meaning.

w
31c

all things considered	in a manner of speaking
as far as I'm concerned	in my opinion
for all intents and purposes	more or less
for the most part	

All-purpose words, as their name implies, could mean almost anything.

angle	element	nature
area	factor	situation
aspect	field	thing
case	kind	type
character	manner	

All-purpose words almost always clutter and complicate the sentences they appear in. Usually, they can be deleted altogether. Often their deletion exposes other wordiness that can also be eliminated.

Wordy   The *type* of large expenditures on advertising that manufacturers must make is a very important *aspect* of the cost of detergents.

Concise   Manufacturers' large advertising expenditures increase the cost of detergents.

EXERCISES: EXERCISE 10

Possible Answers

1. *Gerrymandering* <u>involves redrawing</u> the lines of a voting district to benefit a particular party or ethnic group.
2. The name <u>refers to</u> Elbridge Gerry, <u>who as</u> governor of Massachusetts in 1812 redrew voting districts in Essex County.
3. On the map one new district looked <u>like</u> a salamander.
4. Upon seeing the map, <u>a critic</u> of Governor Gerry's administration cried out, "Gerrymander!"
5. <u>Now</u> a dominant political group may try to <u>change a district's</u> voting pattern by gerrymandering to exclude rival groups' supporters.

w
31c

Exercise 10
Revising: Empty words and phrases

Revise the following sentences to achieve conciseness by cutting filler phrases, qualifying phrases, and all-purpose words.

   Example:

   I came to college because of many factors, but most of all because of the fact that I want a career in medicine.

   I came to college *mainly because* I want a career in medicine.

1. *Gerrymandering* refers to a situation in which the lines of a voting district are redrawn to benefit a particular party or ethnic group.
2. The name is explained by the fact that Elbridge Gerry, the governor of Massachusetts in 1812, redrew voting districts in Essex County.
3. On the map one new district looked in the nature of a salamander.
4. Upon seeing the map, a man who was for all intents and purposes a critic of Governor Gerry's administration cried out, "Gerrymander!"
5. At the present time, a dominant political group may try to change the character of a district's voting pattern by gerrymandering to exclude rival groups' supporters.

2   Cutting unnecessary repetition

Unnecessary repetition weakens sentences.

Wordy   Many unskilled workers *without training in a particular job* are unemployed *and do not have any work.*

Concise   Many unskilled workers are unemployed.

The use of one word two different ways within a sentence is confusing.

Confusing   Preschool instructors play a *role* in the child's understanding of male and female *roles.*

Clear   Preschool instructors contribute to the child's understanding of male and female roles.

The simplest kind of useless repetition is the **redundant phrase,** a phrase that says the same thing twice, such as *few in number* and *large in size.* Some common redundant phrases are listed below. (The unneeded words are italicized.)

biography *of his life*
circle *around*
consensus *of opinion*
cooperate *together*
final completion
frank and honest exchange
the future *to come*

habitual custom
important (*basic*) essentials
puzzling *in nature*
repeat *again*
return *again*
square (round) *in shape*
surrounding circumstances

descend down
revisit back

Exercise 11
Revising: Unnecessary repetition

Revise the following sentences to achieve conciseness. Concentrate on eliminating repetition and redundancy.

  Example:

  Because the circumstances surrounding the cancellation of classes were murky and unclear, the editor of the student newspaper assigned a staff reporter to investigate and file a report on the circumstances.

  Because the circumstances leading to the cancellation of classes were unclear, the editor of the student newspaper assigned a staffer to investigate and report the story.

1. Some Vietnam veterans coming back to the United States after their tours of duty in Vietnam had problems in readjusting again to life in America.

ANSWERS: EXERCISE 11
Possible Answers

1. After their tours of duty some Vietnam veterans had problems in readjusting to life in America.

2. Afflicted with Post-Traumatic Stress Disorder, <u>some veterans had</u> trouble holding jobs and maintaining relationships.
3. Some who <u>used drugs</u> in Vietnam could not break <u>their habits</u> after they <u>returned to</u> the United States.
4. The few veterans who committed crimes and violent acts gained so much <u>notoriety that</u> many Americans thought all veterans were <u>crazy.</u>
5. As a result of such <u>stereotyping,</u> Vietnam-era <u>veterans are protected by</u> antidiscrimination <u>laws.</u>

2. Afflicted with Post-Traumatic Stress Disorder, a psychological disorder that sometimes arises after a trauma, some of the veterans had psychological problems that caused them to have trouble holding jobs and maintaining relationships.
3. Some who used to use drugs in Vietnam could not break their drug habits after they returned back to the United States.
4. The few veterans who committed crimes and violent acts gained so much notoriety and fame that many Americans thought all veterans were crazy, insane maniacs.
5. As a result of such stereotyping of Vietnam-era veterans, veterans are included into the same antidiscrimination laws that protect other victims of discrimination.

 ### Simplifying word groups and sentences

Choose the simplest and most direct grammatical construction that fits your meaning. Combine sentences, reduce clauses to phrases and phrases to single words, use strong verbs, use the active voice, and delete expletive constructions.

REWRITE

Give students a particularly wordy sentence, and ask them to see who can rewrite it using the fewest words. This activity also works with whole paragraphs and can be used in small groups.

Combining sentences

Often the information in two or more sentences can be combined into one tight sentence.

Wordy   The French and British collaborated on building the Channel Tunnel. The tunnel links France and Britain. The French drilled from Sangatte. The British drilled from Dover.

Concise   The French and British collaborated on building the Channel Tunnel between their countries, the French drilling from Sangatte and the British from Dover.

Reducing clauses to phrases, phrases to single words

Modifiers—subordinate clauses, phrases, and single words—can be expanded or contracted depending on the emphasis you want to achieve. (See 5c on phrases and clauses and 16b on working with modifiers.) When editing your sentences, consider whether any modifiers can be reduced without loss of emphasis or clarity.

Wordy   The tunnel, *which was drilled for twenty-three miles, runs through a bed of solid chalk* under the English Channel.

Concise   The *twenty-three-mile* tunnel runs *through solid chalk* under the English Channel.

Using strong verbs

Weak verbs such as *is, has,* and *make* stall sentences. Strong verbs such as *slice* and *dispute* energize sentences, moving them along. Weak verbs usually carry extra baggage, too, such as unneeded prepositional phrases and long, abstract nouns or adjectives.

Wordy   The drillers *made slow advancement,* and costs *were over* $5 million a day. The slow progress *was worrisome for* some backers.

Concise   The drillers *advanced slowly,* and costs *topped* $5 million a day. The slow progress *worried* some backers.

Using the active voice

When a verb is in the **active voice,** the subject of the sentence names the *performer* of the verb's action. When a verb is in the **passive voice,** the subject names the *receiver* of the action.

Active   The *drillers used* huge rotary blades.

Passive   Huge rotary *blades were used* by the drillers.

The passive voice is usually wordier than the active voice, simply because it requires a helping verb (*were*) and a prepositional phrase to name the actor (*by the drillers*). Further, passive constructions are indirect, burying the actor or sometimes omitting it entirely (*Huge rotary blades are used*).

Revise a passive construction by changing the verb to the active voice and positioning the actor as the subject. (If you need help with this change, see pp. 243–44.)

Wordy   As many as *fifteen feet* of chalk an hour *could be chewed through* by the blades.

Concise   The *blades could chew through* as many as fifteen feet of chalk an hour.

Eliminating expletive constructions

Expletive constructions begin with *there is* or *it is* and postpone the sentence subject (see 5e-4). They are not only wordy but limp.

w
31c

Wordy   *There are more than half a million shareholders who* have invested in the tunnel. *It is they and the banks that* expect to profit when the tunnel opens to trains.

Concise   *More than half a million shareholders* have invested in the tunnel. *They and the banks* expect to profit when the tunnel opens to trains.

Exercise 12
Revising: Simplifying word groups and sentences

Rewrite each passage below into a single concise sentence. As necessary, combine sentences, reduce grammatical structures, replace weak verbs with strong ones, and eliminate passive and expletive constructions.

Example:

He was taking some exercise in the park. Then several thugs were suddenly ahead in his path.

He was *exercising* (or *jogging* or *strolling*) in the park *when* several thugs suddenly *loomed* in his path.

1. Chewing gum was originally introduced to the United States by Antonio López de Santa Anna. He was the Mexican general.
2. After he had been defeated by the Texans in 1845, the general, who was exiled, made the choice to settle in New York.
3. A piece of chicle had been stashed by the general in his baggage. Chicle is the dried milky sap of the Mexican sapodilla tree.
4. There was more of this resin brought into the country by Santa Anna's friend Thomas Adams. Adams had a plan to make rubber.
5. The plan failed. Then Adams had occasion to get a much more successful idea on the basis of the use to which the resin was put by General Santa Anna. That is, Adams decided to make a gum that could be chewed.

 4   Rewriting jargon

Jargon can refer to the special vocabulary of any discipline or profession (see 31a-6). But it has also come to describe vague, inflated language that is overcomplicated, even incomprehensible. When it comes from government or business, we call it *bureaucratese.* It sounds almost as if the writer deliberately ignored every suggestion for clear, concise writing.

You may find yourself writing jargon when you are unsure of your subject or when your thoughts are tangled. It's fine, even necessary, to stumble and grope while drafting. But you should straighten out your ideas and eliminate jargon during revision and editing.

Jargon	The necessity for individuals to become separate entities in their own right may impel children to engage in open rebelliousness against parental authority or against sibling influence, with resultant confusion of those being rebelled against.
Translation	Children's natural desire to become themselves may make them rebel against bewildered parents or siblings.
Jargon	The weekly social gatherings stimulate networking among members of management from various divisions, with the aim of developing contacts and maximizing the flow of creative information.
Translation	The weekly parties give managers from different divisions a chance to meet and to share ideas.

Exercise 13
Revising: Conciseness

Make the following passage as concise as possible. Cut unneeded or repeated words, and simplify words and grammatical structures. Consult a dictionary as needed. Be merciless.

Example:

The nursery school teacher education training sessions involve active interfacing with preschool children of the appropriate age as well as intensive peer interaction in the form of role plays.

Training for nursery school teachers involves *interaction* with *preschoolers* and *role playing with peers.*

At the end of a lengthy line of reasoning, he came to the conclusion that the situation with carcinogens [cancer-causing substances] should be regarded as similar to the situation with the automobile. Rather than giving in to an irrational fear of cancer, we should consider all aspects of the problem in a balanced and dispassionate frame of mind, making a total of the benefits received from potential carcinogens (plastics, pesticides, and other similar products) and measuring said total against the damage done by such products. This is the nature of most discussions about the automobile. Rather than responding irrationally to the visual, aural, and air pollution caused by automobiles, we have decided to live with them (while simultaneously working to improve on them) for the benefits brought to society as a whole.

ANSWERS: EXERCISE 13
Possible Answers

After much thought, he concluded that carcinogens could be treated like automobiles. Rather than giving in to a fear of cancer, we should balance the benefits we receive from potential carcinogens (such as plastic and pesticides) against the damage they do. Similarly, rather than responding irrationally to the pollution caused by automobiles, we have decided to live with them and enjoy their benefits while simultaneously working to improve them.

w
31c

Chapter 32

Using the Dictionary

A dictionary is a writer's essential aid. It can help you choose appropriate and exact words (Chapter 31); it can help you build your vocabulary (Chapter 33); and it can show you how to spell words (Chapter 34). It can answer most of the questions about words you may ask. This chapter will show you how to choose a dictionary that suits your purpose, how to read a dictionary without difficulty, and how to work with a dictionary as a flexible, compact, and thorough word reference.

 32a Choosing a dictionary

 1 Abridged dictionaries

Abridged dictionaries are the most practical for everyday use. Often called desk dictionaries because of their convenient size, they usually list 100,000 to 150,000 words and concentrate on fairly common words and meanings. Though you may sometimes need to consult an unabridged or a more specialized dictionary, a good abridged dictionary will serve most reference needs for writing and reading. All of the following abridged dictionaries, listed alphabetically, are dependable.

 The American Heritage Dictionary, 2nd college edition (1982). The definitions in this dictionary are arranged in clusters of related meanings, with the most common meaning generally first. Usage labels (*slang, informal,* and so on) are applied liberally. Many words are followed by usage notes, which reflect the consensus of a panel of writers, editors, and teachers. Additional material includes a brief writing guide and appendixes on abbreviations and geographical and biographical names.

The Random House Webster's College Dictionary (1991). Based on the unabridged *Random House Dictionary* (see below), this dictionary's list of words is particularly up to date. The dictionary avoids sexist language in definitions and explanations, and its usage notes indicate words or meanings considered offensive or disparaging to groups such as women and minorities. Appendixes include guidelines for avoiding sexist language.

Webster's New World Dictionary of the American Language, 3rd college edition (1988). This dictionary includes foreign words, abbreviations, and geographical and biographical names in the main alphabetical listing. The definitions of words are arranged in chronological order. Usage labels (*colloquial, slang,* and so on) are applied liberally, and words and phrases of American origin are starred. Appendixes on punctuation and mechanics and on manuscript form are included.

Webster's Ninth New Collegiate Dictionary (1987). This dictionary, based on the unabridged *Webster's Third New International Dictionary* (see below), concentrates on standard English and applies usage labels (such as *slang*) less frequently than do other dictionaries. Word definitions are listed in chronological order of their appearance in the language. The main alphabetical listing includes abbreviations. Geographical names and foreign words and phrases appear in appendixes, as does a manual of style.

2 Unabridged dictionaries

Unabridged dictionaries are the most scholarly and comprehensive of all dictionaries, sometimes consisting of many volumes. They emphasize the history of words and the variety of their uses. An unabridged dictionary is useful when you are studying a word in depth, reading or writing about the literature of another century, or looking for a quotation containing a particular word. The following unabridged dictionaries are available at most libraries.

The Oxford English Dictionary, 2nd edition, 20 volumes (1989). This is the greatest dictionary of our language, defining over half a million words. Its purpose is to show the histories and current meanings of all words. Its entries illustrate the changes in a word's spelling, pronunciation, and meaning with quotations from writers of every century, more than 2.4 million in all. Some

In our library

A BRIEF HISTORY OF DICTIONARIES

1721—Nathaniel Bailey's *Universal Etymological Dictionary of the English Language,* the first dictionary to resemble the dictionaries we have at present.

1755—Samuel Johnson's two-volume *Dictionary.*

1828—Noah Webster's *American Dictionary of the English Language.*

1857–1928—The compilation of the most comprehensive dictionary, the twelve-volume (now sixteen-volume) *Oxford English Dictionary.*

32a

entries span pages. The dictionary focuses on British words and meanings but includes American words and meanings. The first edition is still available in a compact, photographically reduced version of two volumes plus a supplement (1971, 1987).

The Random House Dictionary of the English Language, 2nd edition (1987). This dictionary is smaller (and less expensive) than many unabridged dictionaries (it has 315,000 entries compared with 450,000 in *Webster's Third New International*). Its entries and definitions are especially up to date, and it includes hundreds of usage notes. Among its appendixes are short dictionaries of French, Spanish, Italian, and German and a brief atlas with color maps.

Webster's Third New International Dictionary of the English Language (1986). This dictionary attempts to record our language more as it *is* used than as it *should be* used. Therefore, usage labels (such as *slang*) are minimal. Definitions are given in chronological order of their appearance in the language. Most acceptable spellings and pronunciations are provided. Plentiful illustrative quotations show variations in the uses of words. The dictionary is strong in new scientific and technical terms.

 3 **Special dictionaries**

Special dictionaries limit their attention to a single class of word (for example, slang, engineering terms, abbreviations), to a single kind of information (synonyms, usage, word origins), or to a specific subject (African-American culture, biography, history). (See 35c-1 for lists of subject dictionaries.) Special dictionaries provide more extensive and complete information about their topics than general dictionaries do.

Special dictionaries on slang or word origins not only can help you locate uncommon information but also can give you a sense of the great richness and variety of language. They often make entertaining reading.

For information on slang

Partridge's Concise Dictionary of Slang and Unconventional English. Edited by Paul Beale. 1990.
Wentworth, Harold, and Stuart Berg Flexner. *Dictionary of American Slang.* 2nd supplemented edition. 1975.

For the origins of words

Oxford Dictionary of English Etymology. Edited by Charles T. Onions et al. 1966.
Partridge, Eric. *Origins: A Short Etymological Dictionary of Modern English.* 4th edition. 1966.

ENGLISH AS A SECOND LANGUAGE

For ESL students, the most difficult part of learning English is learning idiomatic usage. The following sourcebooks may be particularly helpful to these students:

Freeman, William. *A Concise Dictionary of English Idioms.* Boston: Writer, 1976.

Whitford, Harold C., and Robert J. Dixson. *Handbook of American Idioms and Idiomatic Usage.* New York: Regents, 1973.

32a

Two kinds of special dictionaries—a usage dictionary and a guide to synonyms—are such useful references for everyday writing that you may want one of each on your own reference shelf. A dictionary of usage contains extensive entries for the words, phrases, and constructions that most frequently cause problems and controversy.

For guidance on English usage

Follett, Wilson. *Modern American Usage.* Edited by Jacques Barzun. 1966.

Fowler, H. W. *A Dictionary of Modern English Usage.* 2nd edition. Revised and edited by Sir Ernest Gowers. 1965.

Morris, William, and Mary Morris. *Harper Dictionary of Contemporary Usage.* 2nd edition. 1986.

A thesaurus provides lists of words with closely related meanings. The lists are much more extensive than the usage notes in a general dictionary. A dictionary of synonyms contains extended discussions and illustrations of various shades of meaning.

For information about synonyms

Lewis, Norman. *The New Roget's Thesaurus of the English Language in Dictionary Form.* 1964.

Webster's New Dictionary of Synonyms. 1973.

 Working with a dictionary's contents

 Finding general information

An abridged dictionary is a quick and accessible reference for all kinds of information. Most dictionaries will tell you the atomic weight of oxygen, Napoleon's birth and death dates, the location of Fort Knox, the population of Gambia, what the Conestoga wagon of the Old West looked like, the origin and nature of surrealism, or the number of cups in a quart. When an encyclopedia, textbook, or other reference book is unavailable or inconvenient to use, explore your desk dictionary.

 Answering specific questions

Dictionaries use abbreviations and symbols to squeeze a lot of information into a relatively small book. This system of condensed information may at first seem difficult to read. But all dictionaries

MISSPELLER'S DICTIONARY

Frequently, students complain that they cannot spell words correctly because they do not know how to find them in the dictionary without being able to spell them. Using a thesaurus is one solution to this problem. A second solution is to have students create a misspeller's dictionary based on the words incorrectly spelled in their papers. This dictionary would include all the variant spellings as well as the correct spellings for the misspelled words. The activity will use the efforts of both the good and the fair spellers and can be "published" for future use in classes that involve writing.

32b

include in their opening pages detailed information on the arrangement of entries, pronunciation symbols, and abbreviations. And the format is quite similar from one dictionary to another, so becoming familiar with the abbreviations and symbols in one dictionary makes reading any dictionary an easy routine.

Here is a fairly typical entry, from *Webster's Ninth New Collegiate Dictionary.* The labeled parts are discussed in the following sections.

Spelling and word division

The small initial letters for *reckon* indicate that it is not normally capitalized. (In contrast, *Franklin stove* is capitalized in *Webster's Collegiate* because *Franklin* is a proper noun.)

The centered period in **reck·on** shows the division into syllables. If you are writing or typing a word of more than one syllable and need to break it at the end of a line, follow the dictionary's division of the word into syllables. (See also Chapter 30 for general rules about word division.)

If a word is a hyphenated compound word, such as *cross-question,* a dictionary shows the hyphen as part of the spelling: **cross-ques·tion.** The treatment of foreign words such as *joie de vivre* or *ex post facto,* which are normally underlined (or italicized) in writing, is more varied. Some dictionaries use a special symbol to designate foreign terms; others label the terms *French, Latin,* and so on.

Dictionaries provide any variant spellings of a word at the beginning of an entry. Thus, for the word *dexterous, Webster's Collegiate* has "**dex·ter·ous** *or* **dex·trous,**" indicating that either spelling is acceptable.

ADDITIONAL SAMPLE ENTRY

From Webster's *New Universal Unabridged Dictionary,* 1983.

reck'ŏn, v.t.; reckoned, pt., pp.; reckoning, ppr. (ME. *rekenen, reknen,* from AS. *gerecenian,* to explain. A derivative verb allied to AS. *gereccan,* to rule, direct, order, explain, tell; D. *rekenen;* Ice. *reikna,* to reckon.)

1. to count; to figure up; to compute; to calculate. I *reckoned* above two hundred and fifty on the outside of the church.   —Addison
2. to consider as; to regard as being; to repute. He was *reckoned* among the transgressors.— Luke xxii. 37
3. to make account or reckoning of. (Obs.) Faith was *reckoned* to Abraham for righteousness.   — Rom. iv. 9
4. to judge; to consider; to estimate.
5. to suppose, think, or believe; as, I *reckon* it will rain. (Colloq. or Dial.)

reck'ŏn, v.i.,

1. to count up; to figure
2. to depend; to rely (with *on*)
3. to settle an account
4. to pay a penalty; to be answerable (Obs.)

If they fail in their bounden duty, they shall reckon for it one day.   —Sanderson

to reckon for; to be answerable or responsible for.

to reckon with; (a) to balance accounts and make a settlement with; (b) to take into consideration.

to reckon without one's host; to ignore, in a transaction, one whose cooperation is essential; hence, to reckon without considering some important factor or factors.

32b

Exercise 1
Seeking spellings and syllables

Check the spelling of the following words in a dictionary. Correct any incorrect spellings, and divide all the words into syllables.

1. England	5. inheritance	9. grievance
2. innoculate	6. over-estimate	10. secretery
3. reccommend	7. depreciation	11. trans-Atlantic
4. methodical	8. excruciating	12. crossreference

Pronunciation

In *Webster's Collegiate* the pronunciation appears in reversed slashes (\\\\). The stressed syllable is preceded by an accent mark ('rek-ən).

Dictionaries use symbols to indicate how to pronounce a word because the alphabet itself does not record all the sounds in the language. (Listen, for example, to the different sounds of *a* in only three words: *far, make,* and *answer.*) Most dictionaries provide a key to the pronunciation symbols at the foot of each page or every two facing pages. They also provide variant pronunciations, including regional differences.

Exercise 2
Seeking pronunciation

Consult a dictionary for the correct pronunciation of the following words. Write out the pronunciation as given, using the dictionary's symbols. (If more than one pronunciation is given, write them all out.)

1. crucifixion	5. bathos	9. polemic
2. mnemonics	6. epitome	10. yacht
3. timorous	7. miserable	11. promenade
4. utilitarian	8. obelisk	12. insouciance

Grammatical functions and forms

Dictionaries give helpful information about a word's functions and forms. The *Webster's Collegiate* entry for *reckon* shows the word to be a verb (*vb*), with the past tense and past participle *reckoned* and the present participle *reckoning,* and with both transitive (*vt*) and intransitive (*vi*) meanings.

Most dictionaries provide not only the principal forms of regular and irregular verbs but also the plural forms of irregular nouns and the comparative and superlative forms of adjectives and adverbs that commonly show degree with *-er* and *-est*. An adjective or adverb without *-er* and *-est* forms in the dictionary requires the addition of *more* and *most* to show the comparative and superlative.

The *Webster's Collegiate* entry for *reckon* ends with two uses of the word in idiomatic expressions (*reckon with* and *reckon*

32b

without). These phrases are defined because, as with all idioms, their meanings cannot be inferred simply from the words they consist of (see 31b-3).

Exercise 3
Seeking grammatical information

Consult a dictionary to determine the part of speech of each of the following words. If the word functions as more than one part of speech, list them all. If the word is a verb, list its principal parts; if a noun, its plural form; if an adjective or adverb, its comparative and superlative.

1. little
2. that
3. study
4. happen
5. machine
6. orient
7. roof
8. ring
9. upset
10. steal
11. manifest
12. firm

Etymology

Dictionaries provide the **etymology** of a word (its history) to indicate its origin and the evolution of its meanings and forms. The dictionary can compress much information about a word into a small space through symbols, abbreviations, and different type-faces. An explanation of these systems appears in the dictionary's opening pages. *Webster's Collegiate* traces *reckon* back to Old English (OE) by way of Middle English (ME). The notation "(13c)" at the end of the second line indicates that the first recorded use of *reckon* to mean "count" occurred in the thirteenth century. (See 33a for a brief history of the English language.)

Sometimes dictionaries do not give the etymology for a word. Their practices differ (and are explained in their opening pages), but in general they omit etymology when it is obvious, unknown, or available elsewhere in the dictionary.

Exercise 4
Seeking etymology

Consult a dictionary for the etymologies of the following words. Use the dictionary's own explanations of abbreviations and symbols to get the fullest history of the word, and write out that history in your own words.

1. grammar
2. engage
3. leaf
4. moon
5. penetrate
6. promote
7. retrieve
8. toxic
9. calico
10. chauvinism
11. assassin
12. water

32b

Meanings

Dictionaries divide the general meaning of a word into particular meanings on the basis of how the word is or has been actually used. They arrange a word's meanings differently, however, explaining the basis of their arrangement in their opening pages. *Webster's Collegiate* and *Webster's New World* list meanings in order of their appearance in the language, earliest first. The *American Heritage* and abridged *Random House,* in contrast, usually place the word's most basic or common meaning first and follow it with the other meanings. These different policies will result in roughly the same arrangement of meanings only when the oldest meaning of a word is also the most common. Thus you should be sure you know the system of any dictionary you are consulting. Then read through the entire entry before settling on the meaning that fits the context of what you're reading or writing.

Most dictionaries provide any special technical and scientific meanings of a word in separately numbered entries that are usually labeled. These labels are discussed below.

Exercise 5
Seeking meanings

Consult a dictionary for the meanings of the following words. How many distinct meanings does each word have? How does the dictionary list meanings, chronologically or in order of importance? If chronologically, is the oldest meaning also the most common? What changes have occurred in each word's use over time?

1. weight	5. order	9. prefer
2. recipe	6. apt	10. quit
3. color	7. astrology	11. spring
4. condition	8. offered	12. sue

Labels

Dictionaries apply labels to words or to particular meanings that have a special status or use. The labels are usually of four kinds: style, subject, region, and time.

Style labels restrict a word or one of its meanings to a particular level of usage.

- *Slang*: words or meanings inappropriate in writing except for a special effect, such as *crumb* for "a worthless or despicable person."
- *Informal* or *colloquial*: words or meanings appropriate for

REMINDER

For students: It is critical that you read the entire definition of a word before deciding its meaning for the context at hand. Careful reading of all the meanings of a word often reveals symbolism and intentions frequently missed by assumed understanding of a word's usage.

32b

ADDITIONAL EXAMPLES OF DICTIONARY LABELS

Slang—novel and colorful expressions that reflect a group's special experiences and set it off from others. Examples: *cool, into, funky, awesome.*

Colloquial—words and expressions appropriate to everyday spoken language and to informal writing. Example: Housework often takes a *bite* out of my weekend.

Regional—words and expressions used only in some geographical locations. For example, one kind of sandwich may be called a *hero,* a *hoagie,* a *submarine,* a *torpedo,* or a *grinder,* depending upon which region you are in.

Nonstandard—words and grammatical forms frequently used in speech but never acceptable in standard written English. Examples: *nowheres, hisself, throwed, could of,* and *hadn't ought.*

Obsolete or archaic—words or meanings of words that we never or rarely use but that appear in older documents and literature still read today. Examples: *enwheel* ("to encircle") and *belike* ("perhaps").

32b

informal writing but not formal writing, such as *great* to mean "very good," as in *a great movie.*

- *Nonstandard* or *substandard*: words or meanings inappropriate for standard speech and writing, such as *ain't.*
- *Vulgar* or *vulgar slang*: words or meanings considered offensive in speech and writing, as in profanity.
- *Poetic* or *literary*: words or meanings used only in poetry or the most formal writing, such as *eve* for *evening* and *o'er* for *over.*

Subject labels tell us that a word or one of its meanings has a special use in a field of knowledge or a profession. In its entry for *relaxation,* for instance, the *American Heritage* dictionary presents specialized meanings with the subject labels *physiology, physics,* and *mathematics.*

Region labels indicate that a particular spelling, pronunciation, or meaning of a word is not national but limited to some area. A regional difference may be indicated by the label *dialect. Webster's Collegiate* labels as dialect (*dial*) the uses of *reckon* to mean "suppose" or "think" (as in *I reckon I'll do that*). More specific region labels may designate areas of the United States or other countries. The word *bloke* (meaning "fellow") is labeled as British by most dictionaries. And *American Heritage* labels *arroyo,* "a deep gully" or "a dry gulch," as Southwestern U.S.

Time labels indicate words or their meanings that the language, in evolving, has discarded. These words and meanings are included in the dictionary primarily to help readers of some older texts that contain them. The label *obsolete* designates words or meanings that are no longer used; the label *archaic* designates words or meanings that are out of date but used occasionally.

See 31a for further discussion of levels of usage and their appropriateness in your writing.

Exercise 6
Seeking labels

Consult at least two dictionaries to determine the status of each of the following words or any one of their meanings according to subject, style, region, or time.

1. impulse	5. goof	9. mad
2. OK	6. goober	10. sing
3. irregardless	7. lift	11. brief (*n.*)
4. neath	8. potlatch	12. joint

Synonyms and antonyms

Synonyms are words whose meanings are approximately the same, such as *small* and *little.* **Antonyms** are words whose meanings are approximately opposite, such as *small* and *big*. *Webster's Collegiate* defines *reckon* with some words in small capital letters (COUNT, ESTIMATE, COMPUTE, and so on). These are both synonyms and cross-references, in that each word may be looked up in its alphabetical place. Some dictionaries devote separate paragraphs to words with many synonyms. Dictionaries specify antonyms less often than synonyms, usually with a boldface **ant** at the end of the entry.

Reading through the synonyms and antonyms for a word can help you locate its meaning in a given context more exactly. (See 33c-2 for a discussion of how to use the synonyms provided by a dictionary to increase your vocabulary.)

ADDITIONAL REFERENCE

For more synonyms and antonyms, students can consult Norman Lewis, *The New Roget's Thesaurus of the English Language in Dictionary Form* (New York: Putnam, 1978).

A DICTIONARY WITH PLENTY OF SYNONYMS

Of the many dictionaries that include synonyms with their definitions of words, the *Funk & Wagnall's New Standard College Dictionary* gives more extensive coverage than most. The *Funk & Wagnall's* includes paragraphs on synonyms that define the various shades of meaning.

Exercise 7
Seeking synonyms and antonyms

Consult a dictionary for the synonyms and antonyms of the following words. Use the word itself and each synonym and antonym appropriately in a sentence of your own.

1. suggest	4. discover	7. kind (*adj.*)
2. plain (*adj.*)	5. change (*v.*)	8. memory
3. high (*adj.*)	6. beautiful	9. serious

Illustrative quotations

Dictionaries are made by collecting quotations showing actual uses of words in all kinds of speech and writing. Some of these quotations, or others that the dictionary makers invent, may appear in the dictionary's entries as illustrations of how a word may be used. One such quotation illustrates a use of *reckon* in the *Webster's Collegiate* entry. Unabridged dictionaries usually provide many such examples, not only to illustrate a word's current uses but also to show the changes in its meanings over time. Abridged dictionaries use quotations more selectively: to illustrate an unusual meaning of the word, to help distinguish between two closely related meanings of the same word, or to show the differences between synonyms.

32b

Exercise 8
Seeking quotations

Consult a dictionary to find a quotation illustrating at least one meaning of each word below. Then write an illustrative sentence of your own for each word.

1. jolt	4. ceremonial	7. legitimate
2. articulate	5. sensuous	8. inquire
3. discreet	6. tremble	9. nether

HIGHLIGHTS

Most students can profit from systematic attention to improving their vocabulary; however, the course time available for such attention is often quite limited. Special workbooks are available, of course, for students with basic vocabulary problems. Chapter 33 provides a good introduction to vocabulary building for students who wish to enrich their vocabularies and suggests activities you may wish to assign. After glancing at the development of the English language and the variety of sources from which our rich vocabulary is drawn, the chapter looks at the roots, prefixes, and suffixes of words; it also looks at ways of learning new words from their context and the value of habitually consulting a dictionary—the best methods of gradually and continually expanding vocabulary while reading.

Chapter 33

*Improving
Your
Vocabulary*

RESOURCES AND IDEAS

Anne DiPardo, "Narrative Discourse in the Basic Writing Class: Meeting the Challenge of Cultural Pluralism," *Teaching English in the Two-Year College* 17 (1990): 45–53. DiPardo has found that student narratives are an excellent way for students to present their cultures, values, and linguistic styles.

A precise and versatile vocabulary will help you communicate effectively in speech and writing. To a great extent, you can improve your vocabulary by frequent and inquisitive reading, by troubling to notice and learn the interesting or unfamiliar words used by other writers.

This chapter has a twofold purpose: to provide a sense of the potential of English by acquainting you with its history and range of words; and to help you increase the range, versatility, and precision of your own vocabulary.

33a Understanding the sources of English

People change their language as they and their surroundings change. They revise spellings and pronunciations, alter meanings, and even add or drop words to keep the language fresh and useful. English changes continuously, but its subtle and complex character stays the same.

English has over 500,000 words, probably more than any other language. This exceptional vocabulary and the power and range of expression that accompany it derive from its special mix of word sources. Unlike many other languages, English has borrowed a large number of words.

How English drew on its several sources and acquired its large vocabulary is the story of historical changes. The ancestor of

English, Indo-European, was spoken (but not written) perhaps as far back as 5000 B.C., and it eventually spread to cover the area from India west to the British isles. In what is now England, an Indo-European offshoot called Celtic was spoken extensively until the fifth century A.D. But over the next few centuries, invaders from the European continent, speaking a dialect of another Indo-European language, Germanic, overran the native Britons. The Germanic dialect became the original source of English.

Old English, spoken from the eighth to the twelfth centuries, was a rugged, guttural language. It used a slightly different alphabet from ours (including the characters ð and þ for *th*), which has been transcribed in the sample below. The sample shows the opening lines of the Lord's Prayer: "Our Father, who art in heaven, hallowed be thy name. Thy kingdom come. Thy will be done on earth as it is in heaven."

> Fæder ure thu the eart on heofonum, si thin nama gehalgod. To-becume thin rice. Gewurthe thin willa on eorthan swa swa on heofonum.

Many of our nouns, such as *stone, word, gift,* and *foot,* come from Old English. So do most of our pronouns, prepositions, and conjunctions, some (such as *he, under,* and *to*) without any change in spelling. Other Germanic tribes, using a similar dialect but settling on the European continent instead of in England, fostered two other languages, Dutch and German. As a result, Dutch, German, and English are related languages with some similar traits.

In 1066 the Normans, under William the Conqueror, invaded England. The Normans were originally Vikings who had settled in northern France and had forsaken Old Norse for their own dialect of Old French. They made Norman French the language of law, literature, and the ruling class in England. As a result, English acquired many French words, including many military and governmental words such as *authority, mayor, crime, army,* and *guard.* The common English people kept English alive during the Norman occupation, but they adopted many French words intact (*air, point, place, age*). Eventually, the French influence caused the language to shift from Old to Middle English, which lasted from the twelfth through the fifteenth centuries. During this time a great many Latin words also entered English, for Latin formed the background of Norman French and was the language of the Church and of scholars. English words that entered Middle English directly from Latin or from Latin through French include *language, luminous, memory, liberal,* and *sober.*

Middle English, as the following passage from Geoffrey Chaucer's *Canterbury Tales* shows, was much closer to our own language than to Old English.

RESOURCES AND IDEAS

Journal of Basic Writing 2 (1979). This special issue on vocabulary includes general articles and notes on specific strategies.

example OE

33a

A clerk there was of Oxenford also,
That unto logyk hadde longe ygo.
As leene was his hors as is a rake,
And he nas nat right fat, I undertake,
But looked holwe, and therto sobrely.

HISTORY OF THE ENGLISH LANGUAGE

Prior to fifth century A.D.—Celtic-speaking peoples.

Fifth century—Anglo-Saxon invasion introduces Germanic dialects.

Eighth to twelfth century—In the Old English (OE) period the language combines Latin and Germanic dialects and contributes 183 of the 200 most frequently used words in Modern English. The Vikings arrive in A.D. 787 speaking Old Norse, which contributes hundreds of words to English.

A.D. 1066—The Normans invade and conquer England. Norman French, a dialect of Old French, replaces Old English as the official language of England, but English survives, continuing to evolve through the influence of French.

Twelfth century—English emerges in an altered form, Middle English (ME), which draws on both Old English and Norman French. Heavy borrowing of French words continues through the following centuries until the emergence of Modern English.

A.D. 1500 (approximately)—The language takes a form recognizable as Modern English.

Modern English evolved in the fourteenth and fifteenth centuries as the language's sound and spellings changed. This was the time of the Renaissance in Europe. Ancient Latin and Greek art, learning, and literature were revived, first in Italy and then throughout the continent. English vocabulary expanded rapidly, not only with more Latin and many Greek words (such as *democracy* and *physics*) but also with words from Italian and French. Advances in printing, beginning in the fifteenth century, made publications widely available to an increasingly literate audience. The Modern English of twentieth-century America is four centuries and an ocean removed from the Modern English of sixteenth-century England, but the two are fundamentally the same. The differences and the similarities are evident in this passage from the King James Bible, published in 1611:

And the Lord God commanded the man, saying, Of euery tree of the garden thou mayest freely eate. But of the tree of the knowledge of good and euill, thou shalt not eate of it: for in the day that thou eatest thereof, thou shalt surely die.

33b Learning the composition of words

Words can often be divided into meaningful parts. A *handbook,* for instance, is a book you keep at hand (for reference). A *shepherd* herds sheep (or other animals). Knowing what the parts of a word mean by themselves, as you do here, can often help you infer approximately what they mean when combined.

The following explanations of roots, prefixes, and suffixes provide information that can open up the meanings of words whose parts may not be familiar or easy to see. For more information, refer to a dictionary's etymologies, which provide the histories of words (see 32b).

1 Learning roots

A **root** is the unchanging component of words related in origin and usually in meaning. Both *illiterate* ("unable to read and write") and *literal* ("sticking to the facts or to the first and most obvious meaning of an idea") share the root *liter,* derived from

33b

littera, a Latin word meaning "letter." A person who cannot understand the letters that make up writing is illiterate. A person who wants to understand the primary meaning of the letters (the words) in a contract is seeking the *literal* meaning of that contract.

At least half our words come from Latin and Greek. The list below includes some common Latin and Greek roots, their meanings, and examples of English words containing them.

Root (source)	Meaning	English words
aster, astr (G)	star	astronomy, astrology
audi (L)	to hear	audible, audience
bene (L)	good, well	benefit, benevolent
bio (G)	life	biology, autobiography
dic, dict (L)	to speak	dictator, dictionary
fer (L)	to carry	transfer, referral
fix (L)	to fasten	fix, suffix, prefix
geo (G)	earth	geography, geology
graph (G)	to write	geography, photography
jur, jus (L)	law	jury, justice
log, logue (G)	word, thought, speech	astrology, biology, neologism
luc (L)	light	lucid, translucent
manu (L)	hand	manual, manuscript
meter, metr (G)	measure	metric, thermometer
op, oper (L)	work	operation, operator
path (G)	feeling	pathetic, sympathy
ped (G)	child	pediatrics
phil (G)	love	philosophy, Anglophile
phys (G)	body, nature	physical, physics
scrib, script (L)	to write	scribble, manuscript
tele (G)	far off	telephone, television
ter, terr (L)	earth	territory, extraterrestrial
vac (L)	empty	vacant, vacuum, evacuate
verb (L)	word	verbal, verbose
vid, vis (L)	to see	video, vision, television

[handwritten annotations: astronaut, audition, diction]

Exercise 1
Learning roots

Define the following italicized words, using the list of roots above and any clues given by the rest of the sentence. Check the accuracy of your meanings in a dictionary.

1. After guiding me through college, my *benefactor* will help me start a career.
2. Always afraid of leading a *vacuous* life, the heiress immersed herself in volunteer work.
3. The posters *affixed* to the construction wall advertised a pornographic movie.

ANSWERS: EXERCISE 1

1. benefactor: The root bene means "good," and so the benefactor is or does good. The rest of the sentence hints that the benefactor provides aid.
2. vacuous: The root vac means "empty," which makes sense in the sentence. The heiress takes up volunteer work to avoid an empty life.
3. affixed: The root fix means "to fasten," and so affixed means fastened.

33b

4. auditory: The root audi means "to hear." The auditory nerve is the nerve producing hearing.

5. empathized: The root path means "feeling," and the context completes the meaning. The child felt as his mother did.

4. After his *auditory* nerve was damaged, he had trouble catching people's words.
5. The child *empathized* so completely with his mother that he felt pain when she broke her arm.

 Learning prefixes

Prefixes are standard syllables fastened to the front of a word to modify its meaning. For example, the word *prehistory* is a combination of the word *history,* meaning "based on a written record explaining past events," and the prefix *pre-,* meaning "before." Together, prefix and word mean "before a written record explaining past events," or before events were recorded. Learning standard prefixes can help you improve vocabulary and spelling just as learning word roots can. The following lists group prefixes according to sense so that they are easier to remember. When two or more prefixes have very different spellings but the same meaning, they usually derive from different languages, most often Latin and Greek.

Prefixes showing quantity

Meaning	Prefixes in English words
half	*semi*annual; *hemi*sphere
one	*uni*cycle; *mon*arch, *mono*rail
two	*bi*nary, *bi*monthly; *di*lemma, *dicho*tomy
three	*tri*angle, *tri*logy
four	*quad*rangle, *quar*tet
five	*quin*tet; *penta*gon
six	*sex*tuplets; *hexa*meter
seven	*septu*agenarian; *hept*archy
eight	*oct*ave, *octo*pus
nine	*nona*genarian
ten	*deca*de, *deca*thlon
hundred	*cent*ury; *hecto*liter
thousand	*milli*meter; *kilo*cycle

Prefixes showing negation

Meaning	Prefixes in English words
without, no, not	*a*sexual; *il*legal, *im*moral, *in*valid, *ir*reverent; *un*skilled
not, absence of, opposing, against	*non*breakable; *ant*acid, *anti*pathy; *contra*dict

33b

Meaning	Prefixes in English words
opposite to, complement to	*counter*clockwise, *counter*weight
do the opposite of, remove, reduce	*de*horn, *de*vitalize, *de*value
do the opposite of, deprive of	*dis*establish, *dis*arm
wrongly, bad	*mis*judge, *mis*deed

Prefixes showing time

Meaning	Prefixes in English words
before	*ante*cedent; *fore*cast; *pre*cede; *pro*logue
after	*post*war
again	*re*write

Prefixes showing direction or position

Meaning	Prefixes in English words
above, over	*super*vise
across, over	*trans*port
below, under	*infra*sonic; *sub*terranean; *hypo*dermic
in front of	*pro*ceed; *pre*fix
behind	*re*cede
out of	*e*rupt, *ex*plicit; *ec*stasy
into	*in*jection, *im*merse; *en*courage, *em*power
around	*circum*ference; *peri*meter
with	*co*exist, *col*loquial, *com*municate, *con*sequence, *cor*respond; *sym*pathy, *syn*chronize

Exercise 2
Learning prefixes

Provide meanings for the following italicized words, using the lists of prefixes and any clues given by the rest of the sentence. Check the accuracy of your meanings in a dictionary.

1. In the twenty-first century some of our oldest cities will celebrate their *quadricentennials.*
2. Most poems called sonnets consist of fourteen lines divided into an *octave* and a *sestet.*
3. When the Congress seemed ready to cut Social Security benefits again, some representatives proposed the *countermeasure* of increasing Medicare payments.

ANSWERS: EXERCISE 2

1. Quadricentennial comes from quadri, meaning "four," cent, meaning "hundred," and annus, meaning "year." The cities will be celebrating their four-hundredth year.
2. Octave derives from oct, "eight"; sestet from sex, "six," The octave is eight lines, the sestet six.
3. The prefix counter means "opposite to"; a countermeasure is one opposed to another measure.

33b

4. The prefix *fore* means "before"; in trying to forestall the squeeze, the representatives are, in effect, trying to stall it before it happens.
5. The prefix *circum* means "around"; to circumnavigate means to navigate around.

4. By increasing Medicare payments, the representatives hoped to *forestall* the inevitable financial squeeze on the elderly.
5. Ferdinand Magellan, a Portuguese sailor, commanded the first expedition to *circumnavigate* the globe.

 Learning suffixes

Suffixes are standard syllables fastened to the end of a word to modify its meaning and usually its part of speech. The word *popular* is an adjective. With different suffixes, it becomes a different adjective, an adverb, a noun, and two different verbs.

Adjective	popular popul*ous*	**Noun**	popul*ation*
Adverb	popul*arly*	**Verb**	popul*ate* popul*arize*

Many words change suffixes in the same way. In fact, suffixes help us recognize what parts of speech many words are, as the following examples show.

Noun suffixes

mis*ery*	min*er*	intern*ship*	random*ness*
refer*ence*	bas*ement*	presid*ency*	brother*hood*
relev*ance*	national*ist*	discus*sion*	king*dom*
operat*or*	national*ism*	agit*ation*	

Verb suffixes

hard*en*	pur*ify*
national*ize*	agit*ate*

Adjective suffixes

miser*able*	presiden*tial*	wonder*ful*	use*less*
ed*ible*	gigan*tic*	fibr*ous*	self*ish*
nation*al*	friend*ly*	adopt*ive*	flatu*lent*

The only suffix regularly applied to adverbs is *-ly: openly, selfishly.*
Note: Inflectional endings—such as the plural *-s,* the possessive *-'s,* the past tense *-ed,* and the comparative *-er* or *-est*—appear at the ends of words but do not change a word's grammatical function.

RESOURCES AND IDEAS

Sandra Stotsky, "Teaching the Vocabulary of Academic Discourse, *Journal of Basic Writing* 2 (1979): 15–39. Stotsky examines the language of textbooks and suggests using reading, dictating, précis writing, and affix study to develop vocabulary for academic reading and writing.

33b

ANSWERS: EXERCISE 3
Possible Answers

1. magic, noun and adjective
   adjective: magical
   His success must be the result of magic. She performed magic tricks. Drawing everyone into a magical world, the movie charmed the audience.

Exercise 3
Learning suffixes

Identify the part of speech of each word below, and then change it to the part or parts of speech in parentheses by deleting, adding, or changing a suffix. Use the given word and each created word in a sentence. Check a dictionary, if necessary, to be sure suffixes and spellings are correct.

1. magic (*adjective*)
2. durable (*noun; adverb*)
3. refrigerator (*verb*)
4. self-critical (*noun*)
5. differ (*noun; adjective*)
6. equal (*noun; adverb*)
7. conversion (*verb; adjective*)
8. strictly (*adjective; noun*)
9. assist (*noun*)
10. qualification (*verb; adjective*)

 33c **Learning to use new words**

You can learn a new word not only by understanding its composition but also by examining the context in which it appears and by looking it up in a dictionary—both ways to increase your vocabulary by multiplying and varying your experience with language.

1 **Examining context**

Most people guess the meaning of an unfamiliar word by looking at familiar words around it. Parallelism shows you which ideas line up or go together and can often suggest the meaning of a new word. Watch for parallel ideas in the following sentence.

The kittens see their mother hunt and kill, and they in turn take up *predatory* behavior.

If you did not know the word *predatory,* you could put together clues from the context: parallel construction (*kittens see . . . and they . . . take up*); the tip-off phrase *in turn;* and the suggested idea of imitation (kittens watching their mother and taking up her behavior). These clues produce the correct assumption that predatory behavior consists of hunting and killing.

The phrase *is called* or the word *is* often signals a definition.

The point where the light rays come together is called the *focus* of the lens.

Sometimes definitions are enclosed in parentheses or set off by commas or dashes.

2. durable, adjective
noun: durability; adverb: durably
The durable chair withstood many years' wear. The durability of the old pitcher amazed the crowd. The pup tent was light but durably made.
3. refrigerator, noun
verb: refrigerate
Don't bother putting that in the refrigerator. I have already refrigerated it.
4. self-critical, adjective
noun: self-criticism
A self-critical stance is difficult to take. Her apparent self-criticism was really a plea for support.
5. differ, verb
noun: difference; adjective: different
We differ from each other. He was sure the campaign would not make any difference. The police found that she had committed a different crime.
6. equal, adjective
noun: equality; adverb: equally
Equal rights have not yet been achieved. Equality is the goal of a truly just society. The children were all punished, though all were not equally at fault.
7. conversion, noun
verb: convert; adjective: convertible
We expected her conversion to her new religion. To convert base metals into gold was the alchemists' dream. The convertible sofa comes in handy.
8. strictly, adverb
adjective: strict; noun: strictness
She was strictly raised. A strict parent need not be a tyrannical parent. The strictness of their morals makes the Victorians hard to understand today.
9. assist, verb
noun: assistance
Please assist us. Your assistance in this project will be greatly appreciated.
10. qualification, noun
verb: qualify; adjective: qualitative
The qualification he offered was important. To qualify for the Olympics, an athlete must be an amateur. The difference between the two tape decks is qualitative.

33c

RESOURCES AND IDEAS

Regina M. Hoover, "In the Beginning: The Word," *Journal of Basic Writing* 2 (1979): 82–87. Copying sentences containing unfamiliar words can help build vocabulary and improve writing.

In early childhood these tendencies lead to the development of *schemes* (organized patterns of behavior).

Many Chinese practice *Tai Chi,* an ancient method of self-defense performed as exercise in slow, graceful motions.

At *burnout*—the instant a rocket stops firing—the satellite's path is fixed.

Noticing examples can also help you infer the meaning of a word. The expressions *such as, for example, for instance, to illustrate,* and *including* often precede examples.

Society often has difficulty understanding *nonconformists* such as criminals, inventors, artists, saints, and political protesters.

The parallel examples help explain *nonconformist* because they all seem to be exceptions, people who go beyond the average or beyond the rules. Indeed, *nonconformists* are people who do not adapt themselves to the usual standards and customs of society.

Sometimes an example that reveals the meaning of an unfamiliar word is not announced by a phrase.

During the first weeks of *rehabilitation,* Smith exercised as best he could, took his medicine daily, and thought constantly about the physical condition he once possessed.

Guessing the meaning of *rehabilitation* requires considering what occurred during it: (1) exercising "as best he could," as if Smith had some kind of handicap; (2) taking medicine, as if Smith were ill; and (3) thinking about his past physical condition, as if Smith were wishing for the good shape he used to be in. Putting these examples together suggests that *rehabilitation* is returning to a healthy condition, which is one of its meanings. (The more precise definition, "restoring a former capacity," includes reviving a skill as well as recuperating from a sickness.)

33c

ANSWERS: EXERCISE 4

Individual response.

Exercise 4
Examining context

Use context to determine the meanings of the words italicized below (not including titles). Check the accuracy of your guess by consulting a dictionary.

1. Like America, Michael [Corleone, in *The Godfather*] began as a clean, brilliant young man *endowed* with incredible resources and believing in a humanistic idealism. Like America, Michael was an innocent who had tried to correct the ills and injustices of his *progenitors.* —Francis Ford Coppola
2. A photograph passes for *incontrovertible* proof that a given thing happened. The picture may distort; but there is always a *presumption* that something exists, or did exist, which is like what's in the picture. —Susan Sontag

3. It is not easy to describe or to account for our own culture's particular *predilection* for butter—a loyalty so fierce and so unreasoning that it is called, by those opposed to it, the "butter *mystique.*" —MARGARET VISSER

4. "And this, too, shall pass away." How much [this sentence] expresses! How *chastening* in the hour of pride! How *consoling* in the depths of *affliction!* —ABRAHAM LINCOLN

5. In a community where public services have failed to keep *abreast* of private consumption, . . . in an atmosphere of private *opulence* and public *squalor,* the private goods have full sway. —JOHN KENNETH GALBRAITH

2   Using the dictionary

The dictionary is a quick reference for the meaning of words (see 32b). It can give the precise meaning of a word whose general meaning you have guessed by examining the word's context. It can also help you fix the word in your memory by showing its spelling, pronunciation, synonyms and antonyms, and other features.

Although a dictionary of synonyms is the best source for the precise meanings of similar words (see 32a-3), an abridged dictionary will supply much information about synonyms (see 32a-1). Most abridged dictionaries list a word's common synonyms and either direct you to the entries for the synonyms or distinguish among them in one place. An example of the latter form is the paragraph below, which follows the main entry for the word *real* in *The American Heritage Dictionary.* By drawing on this information as you write, you can avoid overreliance on the word *real* when a more precise word is appropriate.

> **Synonyms:** *real, actual, true, authentic, concrete, existent, genuine, tangible, veritable. Real,* although frequently used interchangeably with the terms that follow, pertains basically to that which is not imaginary but is existent and identifiable as a thing, state, or quality. *Actual* connotes that which is demonstrable. *True* implies belief in that which conforms to fact. *Authentic* implies acceptance of historical or attributable reliability rather than visible proof. *Concrete* implies the reality of actual things. *Existent* applies to concepts or objects existing either in time or space: *existent tensions. Genuine* presupposes evidence or belief that a thing or object is what it is claimed to be. *Tangible* stresses the mind's acceptance of that which can be touched or seen. *Veritable,* which should be used sparingly, applies to persons and things having all the qualities claimed for them.

Exercise 5
Using the dictionary

Consulting the dictionary entry above (and another dictionary if necessary), write five sentences that make precise use of *real* and four of its synonyms.

ANSWERS: EXERCISE 5

Individual response.

33c

HIGHLIGHTS

No quick formula exists for turning poor spellers into good ones. Students with serious spelling problems may need systematic instruction in spelling, which, like systematic instruction in vocabulary, is rarely allowed by course time. You may want to refer such students to a skills center on campus or, if there are no such services, to a good spelling workbook. There are, however, activities and assignments that can help. Most students can improve their spelling markedly by learning and actually applying the limited number of standard rules, by maintaining a record of words that repeatedly cause them trouble, and by faithfully practicing brief groups of words from a spelling list. Such advice, though uninspired and unoriginal, does produce real improvement if a student can be persuaded to follow it, perhaps with the added reminder that lack of confidence in spelling distracts the student from more important matters in writing.

Chapter 34   *Spelling*

CHAPTER REFERENCE LIST

The following is an outline of the chapter for quick reference.

English spelling is difficult, even for some very experienced and competent writers. You can train yourself to spell better, and this chapter will tell you how. But you can also improve instantly by acquiring three habits:

- Carefully proofread your writing.
- Cultivate a healthy suspicion of your spellings.
- Compulsively check a dictionary whenever you doubt a spelling.

(See 34c for further discussion of these and some other tips.)

Caution: The spelling checkers for computerized word processors can help you find and track spelling errors in your papers. (See Appendix B4.) But their usefulness is limited, mainly because they can't spot the very common error of confusing words with similar spellings, such as *their/there/they're* or *to/too/two.* A spelling checker can supplement but can't substitute for your own care and attention.

34a   **Recognizing typical spelling problems**

Spelling well involves recognizing situations that commonly lead to misspelling: pronunciation can mislead you in several ways; different forms of the same word may have different spellings; and some words have more than one acceptable spelling.

Being wary of pronunciation

In English, unlike some languages, pronunciation of words is an unreliable guide to their spelling. The same letter or combination of letters may have different sounds in the pronunciation of different words. For an example, say aloud these different ways of pronouncing the letters *ough: tough, dough, cough, through, bough.* Another problem is that some words contain letters that are not pronounced clearly or at all, such as the *ed* in *asked,* the silent *e* in *swipe,* or the unpronounced *gh* in *tight.*

Pronunciation is a particularly unreliable guide to the spelling of **homonyms,** words pronounced the same though they have different spellings and meanings: for example, *great/grate, to/too/two, threw/through.* Some commonly confused homonyms and words with very similar pronunciations, such as *accept/except,* are listed below. (See 34c-4 for tips on how to use spelling lists.)

Words commonly confused

accept (to receive)
except (other than)

affect (to have an influence
    on)
effect (result)

all ready (prepared)
already (by this time)

allude (to refer to indirectly)
elude (to avoid)

allusion (indirect reference)
illusion (erroneous belief or
    perception)

ascent (a movement up)
assent (agreement)

bare (unclothed)
bear (to carry, or an animal)

board (a plane of wood)
bored (uninterested)

born (brought into life)
borne (carried)

brake (stop)
break (smash)

buy (purchase)
by (next to)

capital (the seat of a government)
    ment)
capitol (the building where a
    legislature meets)

cite (to quote an authority)
sight (the ability to see)
site (a place)

desert (to abandon)
dessert (after-dinner course)

discreet (reserved, respectful)
discrete (individual or distinct)
    tinct)

elicit (to bring out)
illicit (illegal)

fair (average, or lovely)
fare (a fee for transportation)

(continued)

**34d Using the hyphen to
form compound words**

1. Forming compound adjectives, p. 536
2. Writing fractions and compound numbers, p. 537
3. Forming coined compounds, p. 537
4. Attaching some prefixes and suffixes, p. 537
5. Eliminating confusion, p. 538

HOMONYM HOMEWORK

Sometimes the quickest way to learn distinctions in spelling between words that sound the same is to memorize the words and their definitions. Have students learn the correct spellings and definitions of these words by writing each word and its definition ten times.

sp
34a

RESOURCES AND IDEAS

Roger Clark and I. Y. Hashimoto, "A Spelling Program for College Students," *Teaching English in the Two-Year College* 11 (1984): 34–38. The authors present "a three-step program that emphasizes student participation in the diagnosis of spelling problems and practice in using an individualized reference dictionary created by students themselves from their own spelling errors."

Words commonly confused

(continued)

forth (forward)
fourth (after *third*)

gorilla (a large primate)
guerrilla (a kind of soldier)

hear (to perceive by ear)
here (in this place)

heard (past tense of *hear*)
herd (a group of animals)

hole (an opening)
whole (complete)

its (possessive of *it*)
it's (contraction of *it is*)

lead (heavy metal)
led (past tense of *lead*)

lessen (to make less)
lesson (something learned)

meat (flesh)
meet (encounter)

no (the opposite of *yes*)
know (to be certain)

passed (past tense of *pass*)
past (after, or a time gone by)

patience (forbearance)
patients (persons under medical care)

peace (the absence of war)
piece (a portion of something)

plain (clear)
plane (a carpenter's tool, or an airborne vehicle)

presence (the state of being at hand)
presents (gifts)

principal (most important, or the head of a school)
principle (a basic truth or law)

rain (precipitation)
reign (to rule)
rein (a strap for controlling an animal)

raise (to build up)
raze (to tear down)

right (correct)
rite (a religious ceremony)
write (to make letters)

road (a surface for driving)
rode (past tense of *ride*)

scene (where an action occurs)
seen (past participle of *see*)

stationary (unmoving)
stationery (writing paper)

straight (unbending)
strait (a water passageway)

their (possessive of *they*)
there (opposite of *here*)
they're (contraction of *they are*)

to (toward)
too (also)
two (following *one*)

waist (the middle of the body)
waste (discarded material)

weak (not strong)
week (Sunday through Saturday)

which (one of a group)
witch (a sorcerer)

who's (contraction of *who is*)
whose (possessive of *who*)

your (possessive of *you*)
you're (contraction of *you are*)

EXTRA EXAMPLES

In addition to the words listed here, words that can be expressed by different forms, depending on the intended meaning, might also give students trouble. For example, *a while* is almost always written *awhile*. The two most frequently miswritten expressions, however, are *a lot* (commonly written "alot") and *all right* (commonly written "alright").

2   **Distinguishing between different forms of the same word**

Other spelling problems occur when the noun form and the verb form of the same word are spelled differently. For example:

Verb	Noun	Verb	Noun
advise	advice	enter	entrance
describe	description	marry	marriage
speak	speech	omit	omission

Sometimes the noun and the adjective forms of the same word differ.

Noun	Adjective	Noun	Adjective
comedy	comic	height	high
courtesy	courteous	Britain	British
generosity	generous		

The principal parts of irregular verbs are usually spelled differently.

begin, began, begun   know, knew, known
break, broke, broken   ring, rang, rung

Irregular nouns change spelling from singular to plural.

child, children   shelf, shelves
goose, geese   tooth, teeth
mouse, mice   woman, women

Notice, too, that the stem of a word may change its spelling in different forms.

four, forty   thief, theft

3   **Using preferred spellings**

Many words have variant spellings as well as preferred spellings (see 32b-2). Often the variant spellings listed in an American dictionary are British spellings.

American	British
color, humor	colour, humour
theater, center	theatre, centre
canceled, traveled	cancelled, travelled
judgment	judgement
realize	realise

34b   **Following spelling rules**

Misspelling is often a matter of misspelling a syllable rather than the whole word. The following general rules focus on troublesome syllables, with notes for the occasional exceptions.

1   **Distinguishing between *ie* and *ei***

Words like *believe* and *receive* sound alike in the second syllable, but the syllable is spelled differently. How do you know which word should have *ie* and which one *ei?* Use the familiar jingle:

I before *e,* except after *c,* or when pronounced "ay" as in *neighbor* and *weigh.*

i* before *e	believe	bier	hygiene
	grief	thief	friend
	chief	fiend	
ei* after *c	ceiling	conceive	perceive
	receive	deceit	conceit
***ei* sounded as "ay"**	neighbor	freight	beige
	sleigh	eight	heinous
	weight	vein	

Exceptions: In some words an *ei* combination neither follows *c* nor is pronounced "ay." These words include *either, neither, foreign, forfeit, height, leisure, weird, seize,* and *seizure.* This sentence might help you remember some of them:

The weird foreigner neither seizes leisure nor forfeits height.

ANSWERS: EXERCISE 1

1. brief
2. deceive
3. receipt
4. seize
5. foreign
6. priest
7. grievance
8. fiend
9. leisurely
10. achieve
11. patience
12. pierce
13. height
14. freight
15. feint

Exercise 1
Distinguishing between *ie* and *ei*

Insert *ie* or *ei* in the words below. Check doubtful spellings in a dictionary.

1. br__f
2. dec__ve
3. rec__pt
4. s__ze
5. for__gn
6. pr__st
7. gr__vance
8. f__nd
9. l__surely
10. ach__ve
11. pat__nce
12. p__rce
13. h__ght
14. fr__ght
15. f__nt

2 Keeping or dropping a final *e*

Many words end with an unpronounced or silent *e:* for instance, *move, brave, late, rinse.* When adding endings such as *-ing* or *-ly* to these words, do you keep the final *e* or drop it? You drop it if the ending begins with a vowel.

    advise + able = advisable
    force + ible = forcible
    surprise + ing = surprising
    guide + ance = guidance

You keep the final, silent *e* if the ending begins with a consonant.

    advance + ment = advancement
    accurately + ly = accurately
    care + ful = careful
    like + ness = likeness

Exceptions: The silent *e* is sometimes retained before an ending beginning with a vowel. It is kept when *dye* becomes *dyeing,* to avoid confusion with *dying.* It is kept to prevent mispronunciation of words like *shoeing* (not *shoing*) and *mileage* (not *milage*). And the final *e* is often retained after a soft *c* or *g,* to keep the sound of the consonant soft rather than hard.

    courageous   changeable   noticeable
    outrageous   manageable   embraceable

The silent *e* is also sometimes *dropped* before an ending beginning with a consonant, when the *e* is preceded by another vowel.

    argue + ment = argument
    true + ly = truly
    due + ly = duly

Exercise 2
Keeping or dropping a final *e*

Combine the following words and endings, keeping or dropping final *e*'s as necessary to make correctly spelled words. Check doubtful spellings in a dictionary.

1. malice + ious
2. love + able
3. service + able
4. retire + ment
5. sue + ing
6. virtue + ous
7. note + able
8. battle + ing
9. suspense + ion

ANSWERS: EXERCISE 2

1. malicious
2. lovable *or* loveable
3. serviceable
4. retirement
5. suing
6. virtuous
7. notable
8. battling
9. suspension

sp
34b

Keeping or dropping a final _y_

Words ending in _y_ often change their spelling when an ending is added to them. The basic rule is to change the _y_ to _i_ when it follows a consonant.

beauty, beauties	worry, worried	supply, supplies
folly, follies	merry, merrier	deputy, deputize

But keep the _y_ when it follows a vowel, when the ending is -_ing,_ or when it ends a proper name.

day, days	cry, crying	May, Mays
obey, obeyed	study, studying	Minsky, Minskys

Exercise 3
Keeping or dropping a final _y_

Combine the following words and endings, changing or keeping final _y_'s as necessary to make correctly spelled words. Check doubtful spellings in a dictionary.

1. imply + s
2. messy + er
3. apply + ing
4. delay + ing
5. defy + ance
6. say + s
7. solidify + s
8. Murphy + s
9. supply + ed

 Doubling consonants

Words ending in a consonant sometimes double the consonant when an ending is added. Whether to double the final consonant depends first on the number of syllables in the word.

In one-syllable words, double the final consonant when a single vowel precedes the final consonant.

slap, slapping	flat, flatter
tip, tipped	pit, pitted

However, _don't_ double the final consonant when two vowels or a vowel and another consonant precede the final consonant.

pair, paired	park, parking
real, realize	rent, rented

sp
_34b_

In words of more than one syllable, double the final consonant when a single vowel precedes the final consonant and the stress falls on the last syllable of the stem once the ending is added.

submit, submitted   refer, referring
occur, occurred   begin, beginning

But *don't* double the final consonant when it is preceded by two vowels or by a vowel and another consonant, or when the stress falls on other than the stem's last syllable once the ending is added.

refer, reference   despair, despairing
relent, relented   beckon, beckoned
deal, dealer

Exercise 4
Doubling consonants

Combine the following words and endings, doubling final consonants as necessary to make correctly spelled words. Check doubtful spellings in a dictionary.

1. repair + ing
2. admit + ance
3. benefit + ed
4. shop + ed
5. conceal + ed
6. allot + ed
7. drip + ing
8. declaim + ed
9. parallel + ing

ANSWERS: EXERCISE 4

1. repairing
2. admittance
3. benefited
4. shopped
5. concealed
6. allotted
7. dripping
8. declaimed
9. paralleling

5   Attaching prefixes

Adding prefixes such as *dis-*, *mis-*, and *un-* does not change the spelling of a word. When adding a prefix, do not drop a letter from or add a letter to the original word.

uneasy   defuse
unnecessary   de-emphasize
antifreeze   misinform
anti-intellectual   misstate
disappoint   misspell
dissatisfied

(See also 34d-4 on when to use hyphens with prefixes.)

sp
34b

6 **Forming plurals**

Nouns

Most nouns form plurals by adding -*s* to the singular form.

boy, boys   table, tables
carnival, carnivals

Some nouns ending in *f* or *fe* form the plural by changing the ending to *ve* before adding -*s.*

leaf, leaves   wife, wives
life, lives   yourself, yourselves

Singular nouns ending in -*s, -sh, -ch,* or -*x* form the plural by adding -*es.*

kiss, kisses   church, churches
wish, wishes   fox, foxes

(Notice that verbs ending in -*s, -sh, -ch,* or -*x* form the third-person singular in the same way. *Taxes* and *lurches* are examples.)

Nouns ending in *o* preceded by a vowel usually form the plural by adding -*s.*

ratio, ratios   zoo, zoos

Nouns ending in *o* preceded by a consonant usually form the plural by adding -*es.*

hero, heroes   tomato, tomatoes

Some English nouns that were originally Italian, Greek, Latin, or French form the plural according to their original language: *piano, pianos; medium, media; datum, data; beau, beaux.*

Compound nouns

Compound nouns form plurals in two ways. An -*s* is added to the last word when the component words are roughly equal in importance, whether or not they are hyphenated.

city-states   bucket seats
painter-sculptors   booby traps
breakthroughs

When the parts of the compound word are not equal—especially when a noun is combined with other parts of speech—then -*s* is added to the noun.

fathers-in-law   passers<u>s</u>by

Note, however, that most modern dictionaries give the plural of *spoonful* as *spoonfuls*.

Exercise 5
Forming plurals

Make correct plurals of the following words. Check doubtful spellings in a dictionary.

1. pile
2. donkey
3. beach
4. summary
5. thief
6. box
7. switch
8. rodeo
9. criterion
10. cupful
11. libretto
12. sister-in-law
13. mile per hour
14. cargo
15. hiss

ANSWERS: EXERCISE 5

1. piles
2. donkeys
3. beaches
4. summaries
5. thieves
6. boxes
7. switches
8. rodeos
9. criteria
10. cupfuls
11. librettos *or* libretti
12. sisters-in-law
13. miles-per-hour
14. cargoes *or* cargos
15. hisses

34c Developing spelling skills

The essential steps in improving spelling skills were listed at the start of this chapter: proofread, be suspicious, and use a dictionary. These and a few additional aids are discussed below.

1 Editing and proofreading carefully

If spelling is a problem for you, give it high priority while editing your writing (see 2c) and again while proofreading, your last chance to catch misspelled words (see 2d). Reading a draft backward, word by word, can help you spot mistakes such as switched or omitted letters in words you know. Because the procedure forces you to consider each word in isolation, it can also highlight spellings you may be less sure of. A sense of uncertainty is crucial in spotting and correcting spelling errors, even for good spellers who make relatively few errors. Listen to your own uncertainty, and let it lead you to the dictionary.

CAREFUL PROOFREADING

Many of the errors made with spelling can be avoided through careful proofreading. Two proofreading techniques that force the writer to read more slowly and carefully are (1) reading the essay aloud and (2) reading the essay backward, from last to first paragraph.

sp
34c

2 Using a dictionary

How can you look up a word you can't spell? Start by guessing at the spelling and looking up your guess. If that doesn't work, pronounce the word aloud to come up with other possible spellings, and look them up. Unless the word is too specialized to be included in your dictionary, trial and error will eventually pay off.

Once you find the correct spelling, check the definition to be sure you have the word you want.

3 Pronouncing carefully

Careful pronunciation is not always a reliable guide to spelling (see 34a), but it can keep you from misspelling words that are often mispronounced. For example:

ath<u>l</u>etics (*not* atheletics)	nuc<u>l</u>ear (*not* nucular)
di<u>s</u>astrous (*not* di͞sasterous)	lib<u>r</u>ary (*not* libar͞y)
reco<u>g</u>nize (*not* reconi͞ze)	mischie<u>v</u>ous (*not* mischievious)
ligh<u>t</u>ning (*not* ligh͞tening)	strict<u>l</u>y (*not* stricly)
heigh<u>t</u> (*not* heighth͞)	govern<u>m</u>ent (*not* goverment)
irrel<u>e</u>vant (*not* irr͞evelant)	histo<u>r</u>y (*not* histry)
per<u>f</u>orm (*not* pre͞form͞)	represent<u>a</u>tive (*not* represe<u>n</u>tive)

4 Tracking and analyzing your errors

Keep a list of the words marked "misspelled" or "spelling" or "sp" in your papers. This list will contain hints about your particular spelling problems, such as that you tend to confuse *affect* and *effect* or to form plurals incorrectly. (If you need help analyzing the list, consult your writing instructor.) The list will also provide a personalized study guide, a focus for your efforts to spell better. As appropriate, use the suggestions in the next two sections (mnemonics and spellings lists) to master individual words.

5 Using mnemonics

Mnemonics (pronounced with an initial *n* sound) are techniques for assisting your memory. The *er* in *letter* and *paper* can

RESOURCES AND IDEAS

Muriel Harris, "The Big Five: Individualizing Improvement in Spelling," *Teaching the Basics—Really!* ed. Ouida H. Clapp (Urbana: NCTE, 1977) 104–07. Harris suggests making students aware of their habitual problems deriving from homophones, pronunciation, doubled consonants, word roots, and the schwa.

MEMORY AID

Separating the *-sedes*:

Students may learn to distinguish which *-sede* (*-ceed, -cede*) should be planted at the end of a word by memorizing the words *proceed, exceed, succeed,* and *supersede. Proceed, exceed,* and *succeed* are the only words ending in *-ceed. Supersede* is the only word ending in *-sede.* All the remaining *-cede* words end in *-cede.*

remind you that *stationery* (meaning "writing paper") has an *er* near the end; *stationary* with an *a* means "standing in place." Or the word *dome* with its long *o* sound can remind you that the building in which the legislature meets is spelled *capitol,* with an *o.* The *capital* city is spelled with *al* like *Albany,* the capital of New York. If you identify the words you have trouble spelling, you can take a few minutes to think of your own mnemonics, which may work better for you than someone else's.

6   Studying spelling lists

Learning to spell commonly misspelled words will reduce your spelling errors. For general improvement, work with the following list of commonly misspelled words. Study only six or seven words at a time. If you are unsure of the meaning of a word, look it up in a dictionary and try using it in a sentence. Pronounce the word out loud, syllable by syllable, and write the word out. (The list of similar-sounding words in 34a should be considered an extension of the one below.)

RESOURCES AND IDEAS

Jane McClellan, "A Clinic for Misspellers," *College English* 40 (1978): 324–29. McClellan suggests using several kinds of word lists and frequent drill to bring about improvement.

absence	altogether	bargain	chose
abundance	amateur	basically	climbed
acceptable	analysis	beginning	coarse
accessible	analyze	belief	column
accidentally	angel	believe	coming
accommodate	annual	beneficial	commercial
accuracy	answer	benefited	commitment
accustomed	apology	boundary	committed
achieve	apparent	breath	committee
acknowledge	appearance	Britain	competent
acquire	appetite	bureaucracy	competition
across	appreciate	business	complement
actually	appropriate		compliment
address	approximately	calculator	conceive
admission	argument	calendar	concentrate
adolescent	arrest	carrying	concert
advice	ascend	cede	condemn
advising	assassinate	cemetery	conquer
against	assistance	certain	conscience
aggravate	associate	changeable	conscious
aggressive	atheist	changing	consistency
all right	athlete	characteristic	consistent
all together	attendance	chief	continuous
almost	audience	chocolate	controlled
although	average	choose	controversial

sp
34c

convenience
convenient
coolly
course
courteous
criticism
criticize
crowd
cruelty
curiosity
curious

deceive
deception
decide
decision
definitely
degree
dependent
descend
descendant
describe
description
desirable
despair
desperate
destroy
determine
develop
device
devise
dictionary
difference
dining
disagree
disappear
disappoint
disapprove
disastrous
discipline
discriminate
discussion
disease
disgusted
dissatisfied
distinction
divide

divine
division
doctor
drawer

easily
ecstasy
efficiency
efficient
eighth
either
eligible
embarrass
emphasize
empty
enemy
entirely
environment
equipped
especially
essential
every
exaggerate
exceed
excellent
exercise
exhaust
existence
expense
experience
experiment
explanation
extremely

familiar
fascinate
favorite
February
finally
forcibly
foreign
foresee
forty
forward
friend
frightening
fulfill

gauge
generally
ghost
government
grammar
grief
guarantee
guard
guidance

happily
harass
height
heroes
hideous
humorous
hungry
hurriedly
hurrying
hypocrisy
hypocrite

ideally
illogical
imaginary
imagine
imitation
immediately
immigrant
incidentally
incredible
independence
independent
individually
inevitably
influential
initiate
innocuous
inoculate
insistent
integrate
intelligence
interest
interference
interpret
irrelevant
irresistible

irritable
island

jealousy
judgment

knowledge

laboratory
leisure
length
library
license
lightning
likelihood
literally
livelihood
loneliness
loose
lose
luxury
lying

magazine
maintenance
manageable
marriage
mathematics
meant
medicine
miniature
minor
minutes
mirror
mischievous
missile
misspelled
morale
morals
mournful
muscle
mysterious

naturally
necessary
neighbor
neither

nickel
niece
ninety
ninth
noticeable
nuclear
nuisance
numerous

obstacle
occasion
occasionally
occur
occurrence
official
omission
omit
omitted
opponent
opportunity
opposite
ordinary
originally

paid
panicky
paralleled
particularly
peaceable
peculiar
pedal
perceive
perception
performance
permanent
permissible
persistence
personnel
perspiration
persuade
persuasion
petal
physical
pitiful
planning
pleasant
poison

politician
pollute
possession
possibly
practically
practice
prairie
precede
preference
preferred
prejudice
preparation
prevalent
primitive
privilege
probably
procedure
proceed
process
professor
prominent
pronunciation
psychology
purpose
pursue
pursuit

quandary
quantity
quiet
quizzes

realistically
realize
really
rebel
rebelled
recede
receipt
receive
recognize
recommend
reference
referred
relief
relieve
religious

remembrance
reminisce
renown
repetition
representative
resemblance
resistance
restaurant
rhythm
ridiculous
roommate

sacrifice
sacrilegious
safety
satellite
scarcity
schedule
science
secretary
seize
separate
sergeant
several
sheriff
shining
shoulder
significance
similar
sincerely
sophomore
source
speak
speech
sponsor
stopping
strategy
strength
strenuous
stretch
strict
studying
succeed
successful
sufficient
summary
superintendent

supersede
suppress
surely
surprise
suspicious

teammate
technical
technique
temperature
tendency
than
then
thorough
though
throughout
together
tomorrow
tragedy
transferred
truly
twelfth
tyranny

unanimous
unconscious
undoubtedly
unnecessary
until
usually

vacuum
vegetable
vengeance
vicious
villain
visible

weather
Wednesday
weird
wherever
whether
wholly
woman
women
writing

RESOURCES AND IDEAS

Ann Ruggles Gere, "Alternatives to Tradition in Teaching Spelling," *Teaching the Basics— Really!* ed. Ouida H. Clapp (Urbana: NCTE, 1977) 100–03. Gere proposes the use of individualized word lists and classroom games and also the teaching of phoneme-grapheme correspondences and word division.

sp
34c

34d Using the hyphen to form compound words

The hyphen (-) is a mark of punctuation used either to divide a word or to form a compound word. Always use a hyphen to divide a word at the end of a line and continue it on the next line as explained in Chapter 30 on word division. Using a hyphen to form compound words is somewhat more complicated.

Compound words express a combination of ideas. They may be written as a single word, like the noun *breakthrough;* as two words, like the noun *decision making;* or as a hyphenated word, like the noun *cave-in.* Sometimes compound words that include the same element are spelled differently—for example, *cross-reference, cross section,* and *crosswalk.* Several reliable generalizations can be made about using the hyphen for compound words. But if you doubt the spelling of a compound word, consult a dictionary.

1 Forming compound adjectives

When two or more words serve together as a single modifier before a noun, a hyphen or hyphens form the modifying words clearly into a unit.

> She is a *well-known* actor.
> The conclusions are based on *out-of-date* statistics.
> No *English-speaking* people were in the room.

When the same compound adjectives follow the noun, hyphens are unnecessary and are usually left out.

> The actor is *well known.*
> The statistics were *out of date.*
> Those people are *English speaking.*

Hyphens are also unnecessary in compound modifiers containing an *-ly* adverb, even when these fall before the noun: *clearly defined terms; swiftly moving train.*

When part of a compound adjective appears only once in two or more parallel compound adjectives, hyphens indicate which words the reader should mentally join with the missing part.

> School-age children should have eight- or nine-o'clock bedtimes.

2   Writing fractions and compound numbers

Hyphens join the numerator and denominator of fractions.

three-fourths
one-half

The whole numbers twenty-one to ninety-nine are always hyphenated.

Eighteen girls and twenty-four boys took the bus.
The total is eighty-seven.

 3   Forming coined compounds

Writers sometimes create (coin) temporary compounds and join the words with hyphens.

Muhammad Ali gave his opponent a classic come-and-get-me look.

 4   Attaching some prefixes and suffixes

Prefixes are usually attached to word stems without hyphens: *predetermine, unnatural, disengage.* However, when the prefix precedes a capitalized word or when a capital letter is combined with a word, a hyphen usually separates the two: *un-American, non-European, A-frame.* And some prefixes, such as *self-, all-,* and *ex-* (meaning "formerly"), usually require hyphens no matter what follows: *self-control, all-inclusive, ex-student.* The only suffix that regularly requires a hyphen is *-elect,* as in *president-elect.*

A hyphen is sometimes necessary to prevent misreading, especially when a prefix and stem place the same two vowels together or when a stem and suffix place the same three consonants together.

deemphasize, de-emphasize
antiintellectual, anti-intellectual
trilllike, trill-like

Check a recent dictionary for the current form, particularly for words that join two *e*'s or *i*'s. If the word you seek does not appear in the dictionary, assume that it should be hyphenated.

hyph
34d

5 Eliminating confusion

If you wrote the sentence *Doonesbury is a comic strip character,* the reader might stumble briefly over your meaning. Is Doonesbury a character in a comic strip or a comic (funny) character who strips? Presumably you would mean the former, but a hyphen would prevent any possible confusion: *Doonesbury is a comic-strip character.*

Adding prefixes to words can sometimes create ambiguity. *Recreation* (*creation* with the prefix *re-*) could mean either "a new creation" or "diverting, pleasurable activity." Using a hyphen, *re-creation,* limits the word to the first meaning. Without a hyphen the word suggests the second meaning.

Exercise 6
Using hyphens in compound words

Insert hyphens as needed in the following compounds. Circle all compounds that are correct as given. Consult a dictionary as needed.

1. reimburse
2. deescalate
3. forty odd soldiers
4. little known bar
5. seven eighths
6. seventy eight
7. happy go lucky
8. preexisting
9. senator elect
10. postwar
11. two and six person cars
12. ex songwriter
13. V shaped
14. reeducate

Part VIII

Research Writing

The entire process of researching and writing—not simply the research paper itself—is the subject of this chapter and the three that follow (Chapters 35–38). Because working with sources can lead to several different kinds of writing—reporting, interpreting, or analyzing—these chapters provide two different examples of student papers-in-progress, one emphasizing interpretation, the other emphasizing analysis.

The present chapter looks at what are generally viewed as the earlier stages of the research/writing process. It acknowledges, however, that writing with sources, like writing in general, is often recursive and difficult to separate into discrete stages.

The chapter offers detailed and helpful advice about planning a research project and includes a planning form students may wish to adapt for their own projects. Following this, the chapter describes ways to find and limit a researchable topic as well as strategies for finding information and further refining a topic. Covered in detail are different research sources: reference books (and the library catalog), periodicals, general books, computerized data bases, and a writer's own sources (including interviews). The concluding section offers helpful advice on making a working bibliography and provides bibliographical models in accordance with the latest edition (3rd, 1988) of the *MLA Handbook.*

RESOURCES AND IDEAS

Christine Hult, "Expanded Roles for Computers in Writing Research Papers and Reports," *Teaching English in the Two-Year College* 17 (1990): 114–19. Hult describes how students can use the computer to find, organize, and store information as well as to compose, revise, and edit, thus illustrating that the computer can be well used throughout the process of writing the research paper.

Chapter 35

Beginning a Research Project

Like many students, you may dread research papers as tedious projects. It is true that responsible, honest research writing demands close attention to details. But tedium is entirely optional, a matter of your choice. You will probably be bored if your project seems a chore and fails to engage you. You will not be bored if you approach research writing as the exciting mental adventure it can be.

No doubt you've seen something of this excitement in the many television detectives, lawyers, and doctors who pursue investigations, digging through files, interviewing witnesses, peering through microscopes. One of your goals in research writing should be to experience such a concentrated and enthusiastic search, to become the detective locating a missing person or the scientist tracking an illness. In the end, you will know a topic in depth. You will also have acquired skills that will help you in school, in work, and in life outside work:

• Using the library
• Analyzing and evaluating others' work
• Drawing on others' work to form, support, and extend your own opinions
• Documenting your sources

Your investigation will be influenced by whether you are expected mainly to report, to interpret, or to analyze sources.

• In **reporting,** you survey, organize, and objectively present the available evidence about a topic.

- In **interpreting,** you examine a range of views on a topic in order to draw your own conclusions, or you search in varied sources for facts and opinions relevant to your thesis.
- In **analyzing,** you attempt to solve a problem or answer a question through critical evaluation (or analysis) of relevant scholarly sources or of texts such as literary works.

Reporting generally serves an explanatory purpose, while interpreting and analyzing may serve either an explanatory or a persuasive purpose (see 1c).

The three operations are not exclusive: for instance, a paper analyzing a repeated image in a poet's work would also involve a survey of poems and an interpretation of their meaning. Because the three operations overlap, the research and writing process described in this and the next three chapters can generally serve any one of them. Throughout these chapters we will follow the development of research papers by two students, Mark Shannon and Ann Weiss. Shannon's work, emphasizing interpretation, receives somewhat more attention; Weiss's work, emphasizing analysis, enters the discussion whenever her process differed significantly from Shannon's. Both students followed the same basic process, however.

35a Planning a research project

A thoughtful plan and systematic procedures will help you anticipate and follow through on the diverse and overlapping activities of research writing.

As soon as you receive an assignment for a research project, you can begin developing a strategy for completing it. The first step should be making a schedule that apportions the available time to the necessary work. A possible schedule appears on the next page. In it each item is a step in the process of research writing (discussed in the section given in parentheses). No general guide can tell you how long each step should take, but you can estimate that each segment marked off by a horizontal line will occupy *roughly* one-quarter of the total time—for example, a week in a four-week assignment or two weeks in an eight-week assignment. The most unpredictable segments are the first two, so it's wise to get started early enough to accommodate the unexpected.

The research-writing process outlined in the schedule corresponds to the general writing process discussed in Chapters 1–2: planning or developing (steps 1–8), drafting (step 9), and revising and editing (step 10), plus the additional important stage of documenting the sources you use (steps 11–12). Like any other essay, a

Dennis K. Renner, "Teaching the Research Assignment in the 1980's," *Clearing House* 54 (1980): 19–23. Mini–research assignments can be superior to traditional long research projects, which may be undermined because of problems in writing, reading, or the management of effort.

Robert A. Schwegler and Linda K. Shamoon, "The Aims and Process of the Research Paper," *College English* 44 (1982): 812–24. The authors suggest that the differences in how students and instructors view a research paper's aims and purposes are key in explaining why students' research papers often fail to meet requirements or expectations. They define the four basic patterns that research papers follow and provide an example of one pattern in use.

RESOURCES AND IDEAS

Michael Kleine, "What Is It We Do When We Write Papers Like This One—and How Can We Get Students to Join Us?" *The Writing Instructor* 6 (1987): 151–61. Kleine outlines a model of the research process based on his interviews with university scholars and suggests that instruction in the research paper (1) emphasize peers rather than teacher as audience and (2) encourage papers focusing on various areas of academic study.

Colleen Marshall, "A System for Teaching College Freshmen to Write a Research Paper," *College English* 40 (1978): 87–89. Marshall suggests first having students pose a thesis as a question in personal terms and then having them answer it in an undocumented opinion paper. Students are then asked to revise this paper, to list implicit questions, and to do research leading to a final paper.

35a

RESOURCES AND IDEAS

Patricia E. Connors, "The Research Paper: What Students Have to Say," *Teaching English in the Two-Year College* 17 (1990): 180–82. Connors describes a writing course requiring a research paper accompanied by letters from the students to the instructor analyzing the research and writing process. Students are mainly concerned with managing their time and topic, integrating their sources, and staying on target in terms of structure. She has found that peer interaction is especially helpful throughout the process.

Scheduling steps in research writing

Complete
by:

_____ 1. Planning a research project (35a)
_____ 2. Finding and limiting a researchable topic (35b)
_____ 3. Finding information and refining the topic (35c)
_____ 4. Making a working bibliography (35d)   *406*

_____ 5. Scanning and evaluating sources (36a)
_____ 6. Taking notes using summary, paraphrase, and direct quotation (36b) and avoiding plagiarism (36c)
_____ 7. Developing a thesis sentence (36d)

_____ 8. Creating a structure (36e)
_____ 9. Drafting the paper (36f) and using and introducing summaries, paraphrases, and quotations (36g)

_____ 10. Revising and editing the paper (36h)
_____ 11. Citing sources in your text (37a)
_____ 12. Preparing the list of works cited (37b)
_____ 13. Preparing and proofreading the final manuscript (36i)
_____ Final paper due

RESOURCES AND IDEAS

Ellen Strenski, "A Worksheet Approach to the Research Paper," *Freshman English Resource Notes* 3 (1978): 11–12. Strenski presents sample worksheets designed to help students develop research skills.

research paper evolves gradually, and the steps sometimes overlap and repeat. For instance, while you do research, your reading leads you to organize ideas; and while you organize ideas, you discover where you need to do more research.

Allowing for such inevitable shifts while continuing to work through the steps is one key to successful and rewarding research writing. Another is systematic procedures for locating, collecting, organizing, and using information—procedures that are the focus of this chapter and the next. These procedures will be easier to follow if you acquire some basic research equipment and carry it with you whenever you work on the project:

- A package of 3″ × 5″ index cards for source information (see 35d).
- Several packages of 4″ × 6″ index cards for notes from sources (see 36b).
- At least one pen plus a spare. Some researchers use several pens with different colors of ink to code their notes.
- Paper clips and rubber bands for organizing notes.
- Appropriate coins for operating the library's photocopiers.

35a

In addition, carry index cards or a notebook with you at all times to use as a **research journal,** a place to record your activities and ideas. (See 1e-1 on journal keeping.) In the journal's dated entries, you can keep a record of sources you consult, the leads you want to pursue, any dead ends you reach, and, most important, your thoughts about sources, leads, dead ends, new directions, relationships, and anything else that strikes you. Notes on what your sources actually say should be taken and organized separately—for instance, on the note cards discussed in 36b. The research journal is the place for tracking and developing your own ideas. You will probably find that the very act of writing in it opens your mind and clarifies your thinking, making your research increasingly productive and rewarding.

35b Finding and limiting a researchable topic

Before reading this section, you may want to review the suggestions given in 1b (p. 5) for finding and limiting an essay topic. Generally, the same procedure applies to writing any kind of research paper: take a subject assigned to you, or think of one that interests you, and narrow it to manageable dimensions by making it specific. However, selecting and limiting a topic for a research paper do present special opportunities and problems. If you have questions about your topic, consult your instructor.

A topic for a research paper has four primary requirements, each with corresponding pitfalls.

1. Ample published sources of information are available on the topic. Other researchers should have had a chance to produce evidence on the topic, weigh the evidence, and publish their conclusions. And the sources should be accessible.

   Avoid (*a*) very recent topics, such as the latest medical breakthrough, and (*b*) topics that are too removed geographically, such as a minor event in Australian history.

2. The topic encourages research in the kinds and number of sources required by the assignment.

   Avoid (*a*) topics that depend entirely on personal opinion and experience, such as the virtues of your hobby, and (*b*) topics that require research in only one source, such as a straight factual biography or a how-to like "Making Lenses for Eyeglasses." (The exception is a paper in which you analyze a single work such as a novel or painting. See 39b.)

3. The topic will lead you to an objective assessment of sources and to defensible conclusions. Even when a research paper is

RESOURCES AND IDEAS

Virginia Gunn Fick, "A History-Based Research Paper Course," *Teaching English in the Two-Year College* 17 (1990): 34–35. Fick describes a successful research paper course that focused on the popular culture of the 1930s.

Gwen Dungy et al., "Career Research: A Multi-Discipline Approach," *Community College Frontiers* 7 (1980): 15–19. The authors suggest teaching research skills by having students investigate possible careers in fields they find interesting.

Les Stanwood, "Careers Research: Out of the Term Paper Rut," *Media and Methods* 15 (1978): 41–42. Stanwood describes a ten-week unit that results in a book on careers created by students through interviews and research in the library.

Robert Armour, "The Teaching of Research Methods Through Models," *Exercise Exchange* 20 (1976): 5–6. Armour's assignments "prepare the students for their own research by having them study widely known research projects in order to broaden their definition of research. . . ." *All the President's Men* and *Men of Aran* are given as examples. Instructors can probably supply more up-to-date examples.

Bruce T. Peterson and Jill N. Burkland, "Investigative Reading and Writing: Responding to Reading with Research," *College Composition and Communication* 37 (1986): 236–40. The authors believe that research, rather than being limited to the research paper, should be viewed as "a way of thinking about reading, writing, and our experience of all texts." They offer a method for showing students how to approach research through their personal responses to the text.

35b

TRANSPARENCY MASTER
AVAILABLE

Checklist for a good research topic

1. Published sources are ample: the topic is neither too recent nor too removed.
2. Sources are diverse: the topic is neither wholly personal nor wholly factual.
3. Sources can be assessed objectively: the topic is not solely a matter of belief, dogma, or prejudice.
4. Sources can be examined thoroughly in the assigned time and length: the topic is not too broad.

intended to persuade, the success of the argument will depend on the balanced presentation of all significant points of view.

Beware controversial topics that rest on belief or prejudice, such as when human life begins or why women (or men) are superior. Though these topics may certainly be disputed, your own preconceptions could slant your research or conclusions. Further, your readers are unlikely to be swayed from their own beliefs.

4. The topic suits the length of paper assigned and the time given for research and writing.

Avoid broad topics that have too many sources to survey adequately, such as a major event in history or the collected works of a poet.

The students Mark Shannon and Ann Weiss took slightly different approaches to finding and limiting topics. For a composition course, Shannon's instructor assigned an interpretation with a persuasive purpose but left the selection of subject to the student. Since Shannon was currently enjoying a course in business management, he decided to take that broad subject as his starting point. Using clustering (see 1e-5), he pursued some implications of this subject as illustrated on the facing page. An awareness of sex-role stereotyping, developed during a psychology course in high school, encouraged Shannon to give the most thought to the issue of women in management. He posed questions and more questions until he arrived at the one that seemed potentially most interesting and fruitful: "How far do women still have to go in management, and why?"

In developing a topic for an analysis paper assigned in a composition course, Ann Weiss followed a somewhat different procedure. Instead of starting with a general subject, as Shannon did, Weiss began by looking for an unresolved question, interesting

35b

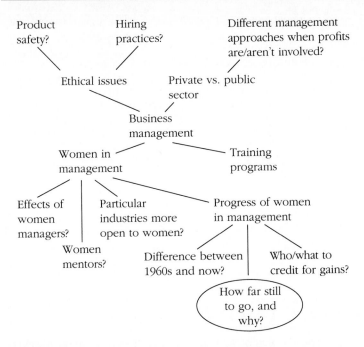

Product safety?

Hiring practices?

Different management approaches when profits are/aren't involved?

Ethical issues

Private vs. public sector

Business management

Women in management

Training programs

Effects of women managers?

Particular industries more open to women?

Progress of women in management

Women mentors?

Difference between 1960s and now?

Who/what to credit for gains?

How far still to go, and why?

problem, or disagreement among the experts in some field of study. She remembered from a discussion in history class that historians disagree about the sources of Thomas Jefferson's ideas in his draft of the Declaration of Independence. Weiss decided to pursue this dispute by consulting one of the recent books listed on the course syllabus. Scanning this book, she discovered an additional disagreement over whether or not Jefferson's draft of the Declaration was improved as it underwent extensive revision in the Continental Congress before it was signed. This issue was more interesting to Weiss than the one about Jefferson's sources, partly because it was narrower and partly because it gave her a chance to analyze the revisions of the Declaration in detail. Like Shannon, Weiss framed the issue as a question that would guide her research: "Was Jefferson's Declaration improved by the Continental Congress?"

Exercise 1
Finding and limiting a topic

Choose three of the following subjects and narrow each one to at least one topic suitable for beginning library work on a research paper. Or list and then limit three subjects of your own that you would enjoy investigating. (This exercise can be the first step in a research paper project that continues through Chapters 35–37.)

35b

1. Bilingual education
2. Training of teachers
3. Dance in America
4. The history of women's suffrage
5. Food additives
6. Immigrants in the United States
7. Exploration of outer space
8. The nuclear protest movement
9. The effect of television on professional sports
10. Child abuse
11. African-Americans and civil rights
12. Recent developments in cancer research
13. Computer piracy
14. Homelessness
15. The European exploration of North America before Columbus
16. Hazardous substances in the workplace
17. Television evangelism
18. Science fiction
19. Treatment or prevention of AIDS
20. Water pollution
21. Women writers
22. The history of child labor practices
23. Comic film actors
24. The best work of a prominent writer
25. Genetic engineering
26. Heroes and heroines in modern fiction
27. Computers and the privacy of the individual
28. Gothic or romance novels in the nineteenth and twentieth centuries
29. The social responsibility of business
30. Trends in popular music

RESOURCES AND IDEAS

Brenda Jo Brueggemann, "Signs and Numbers of the Times: 'Harper's Index' as an Essay Prompt," *College Composition and Communication* 41 (1990): 220–22. Basing their research writing on a column of statistical facts, Brueggemann's students produce insightful and sophisticated essays.

35c   Finding information and refining the topic

When you investigate a topic, you have access to a wide variety of sources, many of them discussed in this section. (See the index opposite.) These resources will be one of two kinds:

- **Primary sources** are firsthand accounts: historical documents (letters, speeches, and so on), eyewitness reports, works of literature, reports on experiments or surveys, or your own interviews, experiments, observations, or corre-

35c

A tip for researchers

If you are unsure of how to locate or use your library's resources, ask a reference librarian. A reference librarian is very familiar with all the library's resources and with general and specialized research techniques, and it is his or her job to help you and others with research. Even very experienced researchers often consult reference librarians.

spondence. Whenever possible, you should seek and rely on primary sources, drawing your own conclusions from them.

- **Secondary sources** report and analyze information drawn from other sources, often primary ones: a historian's account of a battle, a critic's reading of a poem, a physicist's evaluation of several studies, an encyclopedia or other standard reference book. Secondary sources may contain helpful summaries and interpretations that direct, support, and extend your thinking. However, most research-writing assignments expect your own ideas to go beyond those you find in such sources.

Index to research sources

Reference books: helpful for summaries of topics and information for further research

- General encyclopedias, 548
- Specialized encyclopedias, dictionaries, bibliographies, 548

Business and economics	Music and the visual arts
History	Philosophy and religion
Literature, theater, film, and television	Sciences
	Social sciences

- Unabridged dictionaries and special dictionaries on language, 551
- Biographical reference works, 551
- Atlases and gazetteers, 552
- Almanacs and yearbooks, 552

Periodicals: magazines, journals, and newspapers, containing detailed and current information

- Indexes to periodicals, 553

  General indexes
  Scholarly indexes

- Abstracts and citation indexes, 555
- Finding and using periodicals, 555

General books: literary works, nonfiction surveys, in-depth studies, and other materials, available for circulation

- The library catalog, 556
- References to books, 559

Computerized databases: indexes, bibliographies, and other sources, read on a computer monitor, 560

Your own sources: interviews, surveys, and other primary sources you create, 562

TAKING THE TOUR

Library tours, conducted by either the instructor or the librarian, are an effective way to introduce students to the library's research tools and materials. Have students, with topics in mind, take a library tour and then spend the remainder of the class time finding information that is pertinent to their topics.

RESOURCES AND IDEAS

Eleanor Blau, "The Forgotten Teacher," *The Independent School Bulletin* 31 (1972): 66–67. Blau argues that librarians can not only supervise a workshop but also provide instruction.

Richard L. Larson, "The 'Research Paper' in the Writing Course: A Non-Form of Writing," *College English* 44 (1982): 811–16. Larson argues that the research paper has no formal identity and that present methods of teaching it misrepresent and limit what research includes.

35c

1   Using reference books

Reference books available in the library include encyclopedias, dictionaries, digests, bibliographies, indexes, atlases, almanacs, and handbooks. Your research *must* go beyond these sources, but they can help you decide whether your topic really interests you and whether it meets the requirements for a research paper (pp. 543–44). Preliminary research in reference books will also direct you to more detailed sources on your topic. For an analysis paper, a specialized encyclopedia can identify the main debates in a field and the proponents of each side.

Mark Shannon's use of reference books illustrates how helpful such sources can be as a starting point. Shannon first consulted *Encyclopedia of Management,* which summarized women's advances since the Civil Rights Act of 1964. The encyclopedia also listed several books and articles for Shannon to pursue.

The following list gives the types of reference works and suggests when each may be profitable. Once you have a topic, you can scan this list for a reference book to start with. For a more comprehensive catalog and explanation of reference works, consult Eugene P. Sheehy, *Guide to Reference Books,* 10th ed. (1986).

General encyclopedias

General encyclopedias give brief overviews and brief bibliographies. Because they try to cover all fields, they are a convenient, but very limited, starting point. Be sure to consult the most recent edition.

> *Collier's Encyclopedia,* 24 vols.
> *Encyclopedia Americana,* 30 vols.
> *Encyclopedia International,* 20 vols.
> *The New Columbia Encyclopedia*
> *The New Encyclopaedia Britannica,* 30 vols.
> *Random House Encyclopedia*

Specialized encyclopedias, dictionaries, bibliographies

A specialized encyclopedia, dictionary, or bibliography generally covers an entire field or subject. These works will give you more detailed and more technical information than a general reference book will, and many of them (especially bibliographies) will direct you to particular books and articles on your subject. Note that some of these references are available on computerized databases as well as in print (see p. 560).

[handwritten margin notes: research goes beyond good starting points]

35c

One general reference work providing information on sources in many fields is the [*Essay and General Literature Index*] ✗ (published since 1900 and now updated semiannually). It lists tens of thousands of articles and essays that appear in books (rather than periodicals) and that might not be listed elsewhere.

Business and economics

Accountant's Handbook
Dictionary of Economics
Encyclopedia of Advertising
Encyclopedia of Banking and Finance
Encyclopedia of Management
Handbook of Modern Marketing
McGraw-Hill Dictionary of Modern Economics
The New Palgrave: A Dictionary of Economics

History

Bibliographical Guide to the History of Indian-White Relations in the United States
Cambridge Ancient History
Cambridge History of China
Cambridge Mediaeval History
Dictionary of American History
Encyclopedia of Latin-American History
Guide to Historical Literature
Harvard Guide to American History
The Negro in America: A Bibliography
New Cambridge Modern History
Oxford Classical Dictionary
The Study of the Middle East: Research and Scholarship in the Humanities and Social Sciences

Literature, theater, film, and television

Bibliographical Guide to the Study of the Literature of the U.S.A.
Cambridge Guide to English Literature
Cambridge History of English Literature
Film Research: A Critical Bibliography with Annotations and Essays
Handbook to Literature
International Television Almanac
Literary History of the United States: Bibliography
McGraw-Hill Encyclopedia of World Drama
MLA International Bibliography of Books and Articles on the Modern Languages and Literatures
Modern Drama: A Checklist of Critical Literature on Twentieth Century Plays

35c

New Cambridge Bibliography of English Literature
Oxford Companion to American Literature
Oxford Companion to the Theatre
Reference Sources in English and American Literature: An Annotated Bibliography

Music and the visual arts

Architecture: From Prehistory to Post-Modernism
Crowell's Handbook of World Opera
Dance Encyclopedia
Encyclopedia of Pop, Rock, and Soul
Encyclopedia of World Art
Harvard Dictionary of Music
International Cyclopedia of Music and Musicians
New Dictionary of Modern Sculpture

Philosophy and religion

Catholic Encyclopedia
Dictionary of the History of Ideas
Eastern Definitions: A Short Encyclopedia of Religions of the Orient
Encyclopedia of Philosophy
Encyclopedia of Religion
Interpreter's Dictionary of the Bible
New Standard Jewish Encyclopedia
Oxford Dictionary of the Christian Church

Sciences

Encyclopedia of Chemistry
Encyclopedia of Computer Science and Technology
Encyclopedia of Oceanography
Encyclopedia of the Biological Sciences
Encyclopaedic Dictionary of Physics
Introduction to the History of Science
Larousse Encyclopedia of Animal Life
McGraw-Hill Encyclopedia of Science and Technology
Outer Space: Myths, Name Meanings, Calendars from the Emergence of History to the Present Day
Van Nostrand's Scientific Encyclopedia

Social sciences

Dictionary of Anthropology
Encyclopedia of Educational Research
Encyclopedia of Psychology
Foreign Affairs Bibliography
Funk and Wagnalls Standard Dictionary of Folklore, Mythology and Legend

35c

International Bibliography of the Social Sciences
International Encyclopedia of the Social Sciences
Literature of Political Science
New Dictionary of the Social Sciences
Sources of Information in the Social Sciences: A Guide to the Literature

Unabridged dictionaries and special dictionaries on language

Unabridged dictionaries are more comprehensive than abridged or college dictionaries. Special dictionaries give authoritative information on individual aspects of language. (See Chapter 32 for more on the kinds of dictionaries and how to use them.)

Unabridged dictionaries

A Dictionary of American English on Historical Principles
The Oxford English Dictionary
The Random House Dictionary of the English Language
Webster's Third New International Dictionary of the English Language

[handwritten: college—abridged]

Special dictionaries

Follett, Wilson. *Modern American Usage.* Ed. Jacques Barzun.
Fowler, H. W. *Dictionary of Modern English Usage.* 2nd ed. Rev. and ed. Sir Ernest Gowers.
Lewis, Norman. *The New Roget's Thesaurus in Dictionary Form.*
Morris, William, and Mary Morris. *Harper Dictionary of Contemporary Usage.* 2nd ed.
Onions, Charles T., et al., eds. *The Oxford Dictionary of English Etymology.*
Partridge, Eric. *A Dictionary of Slang and Unconventional English.* 8th ed. Ed. Paul Beale.
Partridge, Eric. *Origins: A Short Etymological Dictionary of Modern English.*
Webster's New Dictionary of Synonyms.
Wentworth, Harold, and Stuart Berg Flexner. *Dictionary of American Slang.* 2nd supp. ed.

[handwritten: these provide authoritative info on individual aspects of lang.]

35c

Biographical reference works

If you want to learn about someone's life, achievements, credentials, or position, or if you want to learn the significance of a

name you've come across, consult one of the reference works below. Note, in addition, that more specialized biographical sources
are available in fields such as law, health care, and art.

American Men and Women of Science
Contemporary Authors
Current Biography
Dictionary of American Biography
Dictionary of American Negro Biography
Dictionary of Literary Biography
Dictionary of National Biography (British)
Dictionary of Scientific Biography
Notable American Women
Webster's Biographical Dictionary
Who's Who in America
World Authors

Atlases and gazetteers

Atlases are bound collections of maps; gazetteers are geographical dictionaries.

Cosmopolitan World Atlas
Encyclopaedia Britannica World Atlas International
National Geographic Atlas of the World
Times Atlas of the World
Webster's New Geographical Dictionary

Almanacs and yearbooks

Both almanacs and yearbooks are annual compilations of
facts. Yearbooks record information about the previous year in a
country, field, or other subject. Almanacs give facts and statistics
about a variety of fields.

Americana Annual
Britannica Book of the Year
Facts on File Yearbook
U.S. Bureau of the Census. *Statistical Abstract of the United States.*
World Almanac and Book of Facts

2 Using periodicals

Periodicals—journals, magazines, and newspapers—are in-
valuable sources of information in research. The difference be-

tween journals and magazines lies primarily in their content, readership, frequency of issue, and page numbering.⟩

√ • Magazines—such as *Psychology Today, Newsweek,* and *Esquire*—are nonspecialist publications intended for diverse readers. Most magazines appear weekly or monthly, and their pages are numbered anew with each issue.

√ • Journals often appear quarterly and contain specialized information intended for readers in a particular field. Examples include *American Anthropologist, Journal of Black Studies,* and *Journal of Chemical Education.* Many journals page each issue separately, but others do not. Instead, the issues for an entire year make up an annual volume, and the pages are numbered continuously throughout the volume, so that issue number 3 (the third issue of the year) may open on page 327. (The method of pagination determines how you cite a journal article in your list of works cited. See pp. 613–14.)

Using indexes to periodicals

√ Several guides provide information on the articles in journals, magazines, and newspapers. The contents, formats, and systems of abbreviation in these guides vary widely, and they can be intimidating at first glance. But each one includes in its opening pages an introduction and explanation to aid the inexperienced user. (Many of the indexes listed on the following pages have also been available on computerized databases since the early 1980s. See p. 560.)

√ A typical and general periodical guide is the *Readers' Guide to Periodical Literature.* It lists—by author, title, and subject—articles published each year in well over a hundred popular magazines. For a paper on a current topic you should consult at least several years' *Readers' Guide* volumes. Mark Shannon, checking a volume for 1990, found these possible sources:

WOMEN EXECUTIVES
    See also
   Clothing and dress—Businesswomen
   Daughter track
   Mommy track
   Women entrepreneurs
A bias in B-school—and in business [Harvard grads] L. Zinn. il *Business Week* p166–7 Je 18 '90
Dear Betty Harragan. B. L. Harragan. See issues of Working Woman through March 1990
How to work faster, smarter: the secret weapons of winners [cover story; special section] il *Working* Woman 15:77–86+ Ap '90
Power players [black women executives] A. R. Davis. il *Essence* 20:71–4+ Mr '90
Sex, lies and the business dinner. M. Dowd. il *Working Woman* 15:110 Je '90

RESOURCES AND IDEAS

James E. Ford, "The Research Loop: Helping Students Find Periodical Sources," *College Composition and Communication* 37 (1986): 223–27. Ford describes a "research loop" that leads students and their instructors through a systematic process for conducting research.

35c

Other general indexes to periodicals include the following:

The New York Times Index. This index to the most complete U.S. newspaper can serve as a guide to national and international events and can indicate what issues of unindexed newspapers to consult for local reactions to such events.

Poole's Index to Periodical Literature. An index by subject to British and American periodicals of the nineteenth century.

✓ *Popular Periodicals Index.* An index to about twenty-five contemporary, popular periodicals not listed in major indexes.

Wall Street Journal Index. An index to the leading business newspaper and to *Barron's.*

For scholarly journals, most libraries have a variety of specialized indexes. Shannon also consulted one of these, the *Social Sciences Index.* The listings below appeared in an index volume for 1990:

Women executives
The influence of legal mandates on the acceptance of women as professionals. R. D. Johnson. bibl *J Soc Psychol* 130:39–46 F '90
Women and minorities in management. A. M. Morrison and M. A. Von Glinow, Bibl *Am Psychol* 45:200–8 F '90

The following is a partial list of scholarly indexes:

America: History and Life

Applied Science and Technology Index. From 1913 to 1957 this work was combined with the *Business Periodicals Index* in the *Industrial Arts Index.*

Art Index

Biological and Agricultural Index. From 1916 to 1963 this work was called the *Agricultural Index.*

Business Periodicals Index. From 1913 to 1957 this work was combined with the *Applied Science and Technology Index* in the *Industrial Arts Index.*

The Education Index

ERIC (Education Resources Information Center). *Current Index to Journals in Education.*

General Sciences Index

Humanities Index. From 1965 to 1974 this author and subject index was combined with the *Social Sciences Index* in the *Social Sciences and Humanities Index.* From 1907 to 1965 the combined volume was called the *International Index.*

Index Medicus. From 1927 to 1959 this work was called *Quarterly Cumulative Index Medicus.* From 1899 to 1926 it was *Index Medicus.*

MLA International Bibliography of Books and Articles on the Modern Languages and Literatures

Music Index

35c

Philosopher's Index
Social Sciences Index. From 1965 to 1974 this author and subject
    index was combined with the *Humanities Index* in the *Social
    Sciences and Humanities Index.* From 1907 to 1965 the com-
    bined volume was called the *International Index.*

Using abstracts and citation indexes

Consulting a collection of article summaries—or **abstracts**—
can tell you in advance whether you want to pursue a particular
article further. Such collections are published in many academic
disciplines and are also frequently available on computerized
databases.

Abstracts of English Studies
America: History and Life (U.S. and Canadian history)
Biological Abstracts
Chemical Abstracts
Communications Abstracts
Dissertation Abstracts International (doctoral dissertations). Be-
    fore 1969, the title was *Dissertation Abstracts.*
Historical Abstracts (world history)
Psychological Abstracts
Sociological Abstracts

When you want to trace what has been written *about* an article or book you are consulting, use a **citation index.** This resource lists references to written works after they are published,
as when one scientific article comments on an earlier article. The
following is a partial list:

Arts and Humanities Citation Index
Science Citation Index
Social Science Citation Index

Finding and using periodicals ✓

Every library lists its complete periodical holdings either in
the main catalog (see below) or in a separate catalog. The listing
for each periodical tells how far back the issues go and where and
in what form the issues are stored. The recent issues of a periodical are usually held in the library's periodical room. Back issues
are usually stored elsewhere, in one of three forms: in bound volumes; on **microfilm,** a filmstrip showing pages side by side; or
on **microfiche,** a sheet of film with pages arranged in rows and
columns. Consulting periodicals stored on microfilm or microfiche requires using a special machine, or "reader," that locates

35c

and enlarges the page and projects it on a screen. (Some readers also make photocopies.) Any member of the library's staff will show you how to operate the reader.

If the periodical you seek is not available in your library, the librarian may be able to obtain a copy of the article you want through interlibrary loan. There may be a charge for the service, and it could take up to several weeks.

3 ✓ Using guides to books

The library catalog

The library's catalog lists books alphabetically by authors' names, titles of books, and subjects. (In some catalogs authors and titles are alphabetized together and subjects are alphabetized separately.) If you are starting research on a subject you don't know very well, begin by looking under subject headings. If you know of an expert in the field and you want to find his or her books, look under the author's name. If you know the title of a relevant book but not the author's name, look for the title.

The library's catalog may be the familiar card file, cabinets of drawers containing $3'' \times 5''$ cards. But to save space and time, many libraries have converted their catalogs to other forms. A printed catalog in bound volumes contains small reproductions of the cards traditionally found in drawers. A catalog on microfilm or microfiche (see above) shows the library's collection on film viewed with a special reader.

Increasingly, libraries are computerizing their catalogs. You gain access to the computer's memory by typing a code onto a keyboard along with the name of the author, the title of the work, or the subject heading, as described below. A screen then displays the requested information, along with further instructions.

At this point, most libraries have not yet computerized all their holdings, so older books are still listed only in another catalog—card, printed, microfilm, or microfiche. Find out whether your library is fully automated and, if not, what the dividing date is between nonautomated and automated listings. If you need books from before that date as well as after, you will have to consult both catalogs.

Seek help from a member of the library's staff if you are uncertain about the location, form, or use of the catalog. Library staffers can also help you obtain books not in your library by borrowing them from another library. Such interlibrary loans, though usually free or low-cost, can take a week or more from the time of your request, so plan accordingly.

35c

Though the storage systems vary, all book catalogs contain similar information and follow a similar organization. By far the most widely used catalog format is that of the Library of Congress card. Samples of author, title, and subject cards appear below, with notes on their features.

TRANSPARENCY MASTER
AVAILABLE

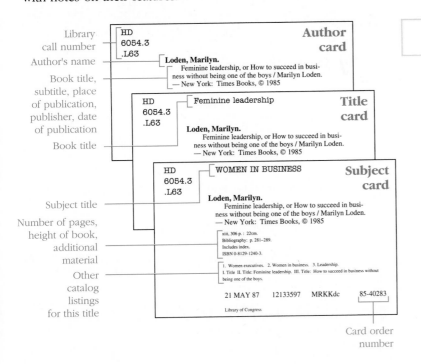

Search strategy

Unless you seek a specific author or title, your search in the library's catalog will be much more efficient and productive if you zero in on specific key words relating to your subject. You then use these key words to locate appropriate sources in any kind of catalog.

In searching the library's book catalog, you can find key words in *Library of Congress Subject Headings* (*LCSH*). This multivolume work lists headings under which the Library of Congress catalogs books. Consulting this source and following its system of cross-references and headings at different levels of specificity, you will be able to discover the headings most likely to lead to appropriate sources. Mark Shannon used *LCSH* to eliminate the heading of "Women—Employment," which was much too broad for his needs. He isolated the narrower "Women executives," with subcat-

35c

egories such as "Attitudes," "Employment," and "United States." He then used these words to search the library's computerized catalog, as illustrated on this and the facing page. (For more on selecting key words, see p. 561.)

Note that *LCSH* does not include most proper names of people, places, corporations, associations, government bodies, and the like.

Screen 1: Kind of search

What type of search do you wish to do?

    1. TIL – Title, journal title, series title, etc.

    2. AUT – Author, illustrator, editor, organization, etc.

    3. SUB – Subject heading assigned by library.

    4. NUM – Call number, ISBN, ISSN, etc.

    5. KEY – One word taken from a title, author or subject.

Enter number or code: 3   Then press SEND

Screen 2: Subject heading (key words)

Start at the beginning of the Library of Congress subject heading

and enter as many words of the subject heading as you know below.

Choose the most specific subject heading you can.

    Ex: Molecular biology (NOT biology)

    Ex: Bastille Day (NOT France—History)

Enter subject: WOMEN EXECUTIVES   Then press SEND

Screen 3: Partial listings under "Women Executives"

	No. of citations in entire catalog
1 Women executives—Recruiting.	1
2 Women executives—Sweden.	1
3 Women executives—United States.	26
4 Women executives—United States—Abstracts.	1
5 Women executives—United States—Addresses, essays>	4
6 Women executives—United States—Bibliography.	4
7 Women executives—United States—Biography.	5
8 Women executives—United States—Case studies.	3
9 Women executives—United States—Congresses.	1
10 Women executives—United States—Interviews.	1
11 Women executives—United States—Periodicals.	4
12 Women—Family relationships.	1
13 Women farmers—Africa—Congresses.	1

Enter number or code: 3   Then press SEND

35c

Screen 4: Partial listings under "Women Executives —United States"

```
This subject: Women executives--United St>          has 26 citations

Ref# Author                    Title                    Date
  12 Gallese, Liz Roman.      Women like us : what is happ>  1985
  13 Gilson, Edith.           Unnecessary choices : the hi> 1987
  14 Hardesty, Sarah.         Success and betrayal : the c> 1986
  15 Hardesty, Sarah.         Success and betrayal : the c> 1987
  16 Harlan, Anne.            Moving up: women in manager>  1981
  17 Harlan, Anne, 1947–      Sex differences in factors a> 1980
  18 Harragan, Betty Lehan.   Games mother never taught yo> 1977
  19 Harragan, Betty Lehan.   Games mother never taught yo> 1978
  20 Haynes, Karen S.         Woman managers in human serv> 1989
  21 Jensen, Marlene.         Women who want to be boss :>  1987
  22 Larwood, Laurie.         Women in management/          1977

Enter number or code: 13                       Then press SEND
```

Screen 5: Specific source

```
This subject: Women executives--United S>       Citation 13 of 26

   AUTHOR Gilson, Edith.
    TITLE Unnecessary choices: the hidden life of the executive
          woman
  EDITION 1st ed.
PUBLISHER New York: W. Morrow, c1987.

             Loan   Call              Cpy
Location     Type   Number            #    Status

MAIN         STACKS HD6054.4.U6G55 1987  1  Overdue
ANNEX        STACKS HD6054.4.U6G55 1987  1  On Loan
```

References to books

Two types of reference books can help you identify general books that have information about your topic: publishing bibliographies and digests. Publishing bibliographies tell whether a book is still in print, whether a paperback edition is available, what books were published on a certain topic in a certain year, and so on. Again, several of these are available both in print and on computer.

> *Books in Print.* Books indexed by author, title, and subject.
> *Cumulative Book Index*
> *Monthly Catalog of United States Government Publications*
> *Paperbound Books in Print*

You might, for example, want to know if the author of an encyclopedia article has published any relevant books since the date of the encyclopedia. You could look up the author's name in the latest *Books in Print* to find out.

35c

If you want to evaluate a book's relevance to your topic before you search for it, a review index such as the following will direct you to published reviews of the book:

Book Review Digest. Summarizes and indexes reviews of books.
Book Review Index
Index to Book Reviews in the Humanities
Recent Publications in the Social and Behavioral Sciences
Technical Book Review Index

 4   Using computerized databases

Kinds of databases

⌈Almost every college library is now automated to some degree with **databases,** electronic storehouses of information. Your library may have a computerized catalog of its holdings, at least the more recent ones.⌋ This database is discussed and illustrated on pages 556–59. Your library may also provide specialized indexes and other sources on compact disks. Just like music disks, these so-called CD-ROMs (Compact Disk—Read Only Memory) store data for "reading" but cannot record data. Indeed, CD-ROMs can store masses of data, as many as 200,000 text pages on a single disk. A general catalog of CD-ROMs is *CD-ROMs in Print.* Consult a librarian to find out which of the sources listed in it (or here in this book) are available in your library.

Most of the indexes listed on pages 553–55 are published in CD-ROM format as well as in print (though sometimes under different titles). And one huge index appears only in electronic form:

InfoTrac. Indexes more than one thousand business, technical, government, and general-interest periodicals.

A sample from *InfoTrac* appears on the facing page.

Besides providing CD-ROMs, many libraries also subscribe to commercial information services that provide bibliographic information, reports, and other materials from publishers and corporations. Obtaining data from these services involves calling into their systems, a task usually performed by a library staffer and usually costing a fee. The following are two widely used information services:

DIALOG *Information Services.* An immense inventory of more than 1.75 million records: bibliographic indexes, abstracts, even whole articles.
Bibliographic Retrieval Systems. Similar to DIALOG, but somewhat smaller.

35c

InfoTrac

General Periodicals Index—A

WOMEN EXECUTIVES
 —management

    Beyond macho: the power of womanly management. by
Sherry Suib Cohen il   v14   Working Woman   Feb   '89
p77(7)
    4803924   42X2127

    Breaking out: five entepreneurs lead the way for
women in business. (Jan Robinson, Trish Lane; Jalan
Inc.) by Karen Cook il   v9   Savvy   Nov   '88   p72(2)

    Engineering success. (Diane Graham, STRATCO Inc.)
by Mary Makarushka il   v9   Savvy   Nov   '88   p78(2)

    Should you manage like a man? (includes related
articles) by Nancy Arnott il   v11   Executive Female
March–April   '88   p20(5)

The illustration below shows only two of the eighty-one listings a librarian helped Mark Shannon find in the DIALOG
system under "Women and management—Sex role or stereotype."
Shannon decided to look up both articles, which he had not discovered in any other index.

DIALOG

 9/2/1
9393860   DIALOG Information Services, File 75: Management Contents
    Careers under glass. (barriers to advancement)
    Solomon, Charlene Marmer
    Personnel Journal   v69 April, 1990, p96(10)
    SOURCE FILE: MC File 75
    SPECIAL FEATURES: illustration; photograph
    COMPANY NAME: Corning Inc.—personnel management; Honey-
well Inc.—personnel management
    DESCRIPTORS: Women—Employment; Sex discrimination in
employment—analysis; Minorities—Employment; Discrimination in
employment—analysis

 9/2/2
0392431   DIALOG Information Services, File 75: Management Contents
    The value of androgynous management. (non-gender specific
management theories)
    Powell, Gary N.
    SAM Advanced Management Journal   v54 Spring, 1989, p10(4)
    SOURCE FILE: MC File 75
    DESCRIPTORS: Sex role in the work environment—analysis;
Management science—philosophy; Management—psychological aspect

Database searches

    To conduct a search through a computerized database, you
will need to devise key words (*descriptors* in computerese) that

35c

connect with the categories under which information has been indexed in the database. For most library catalogs, possible key words are listed in *Library of Congress Subject Headings* (see p. 557). Other databases also use this guide, but many have their own indexes of key words.

Here are a few guidelines for selecting key words:

- Key words should accurately encode your topic. If Mark Shannon had selected "Salaries" or "Executive stress," he probably would not have found the relevant sources he found under "Women executives."
- Key words should not be so narrow that they exclude possibly relevant information. For Shannon, "Women executives— Psychology" would have limited the search to only one facet of the topic.
- Key words should not be so broad that they call up many irrelevant sources. Either "Women" or "Executives" would have generated lengthy lists of sources for Shannon to examine. The more specific "Women executives" called up only those sources indexed under both terms.

Libraries vary in their policies and procedures for database searches. For a library-catalog search like that illustrated on pages 558–59, ample terminals, easy-to-follow instructions, and free use should encourage you to work independently (though of course you can ask questions). For other searches, you may opt or be required to obtain a librarian's assistance, and you may be charged a fee.

Many library computers are attached to printers, allowing you to print out particular records (such as an article listing), whole screens (several listings), or whole documents (entire articles). Printing information is quicker than copying it down and eliminates the risk of mistakes at your end. But there are also risks in accumulating (and losing) dozens of slips of paper in assorted sizes, with assorted information. Especially for source information, try to keep systematic, handy records by taping or transferring the print-out data to a file card (see 35d).

5   Generating your own sources

✓ Most of the sources you consult for a research project—and most of the resources of the library—are likely to be secondary sources whose authors draw their information from other authors. However, academic writing will also require you to consult pri-

35c

mary sources and to conduct primary research for information of your own. In many papers this primary research will be the sole basis for your writing, as when you analyze a poem or report on an experiment you conducted. In other papers you will be expected to use your research to support, extend, or refute the ideas of others.

Chapter 39 discusses the textual analyses, surveys, experiments, and other primary sources you may use in writing for various academic disciplines. One primary source not covered there is the personal interview with an expert in the topic you are researching. Because of the give-and-take of an interview, you can obtain answers to questions precisely geared to your topic, and you can follow up instantly on points of confusion and unexpected leads. In addition, quotations and paraphrases from an interview can give your paper added immediacy and authority. Mark Shannon used just such an interview in his paper on women executives (see pp. 650–52).

A few precautions will help you get the maximum information from an interview with the minimum disruption to the person you are interviewing.

1. If you do not already know whom to consult for an interview, ask a teacher in the field or do some telephone or library research. Likely sources, depending on your topic, are those who have written about your topic or something closely related, officials in government, businesspeople, even your own aunt, if she is an expert in your topic because of experience, scholarship, or both.

2. In-person interviews are often easier and more productive than telephone interviews. But use the phone rather than forgo a valuable source.

3. Call or write for an appointment. Tell the person exactly why you are calling, what you want to discuss, and how long you expect the interview to take. Be true to your word on all points.

4. Prepare a list of open-ended questions to ask—perhaps ten or twelve for a one-hour interview. Listen to your subject's answers so that you can ask appropriate follow-up questions and pick up on unexpected but worthwhile points.

5. Take careful notes; or, if you have the equipment and your subject agrees, tape-record the interview. Before you quote your subject in your paper, check with him or her that the quotations are accurate.

6. Send a thank-you note immediately after the interview. Promise your subject a copy of your finished paper, and send the paper promptly.

RESOURCES AND IDEAS

Thomas N. Tryzna, "Research Outside the Library: Learning a Field," *College Composition and Communication* 37 (1986): 217–23. The author suggests methods of finding sources outside the library and includes lists of organizations and their publications as possible sources.

TRANSPARENCY MASTER
AVAILABLE

35c

35d

ANSWERS: EXERCISE 2

Individual response.

Exercise 2
Using the library

To become familiar with its layout and resources, visit your library and find the answers to the following questions. (Ask a librarian for help whenever necessary.)

1. Where are reference books stored? How are they catalogued and arranged? Where are (*a*) *Contemporary Authors,* (*b*) *Encyclopaedia Britannica,* and (*c*) *MLA International Bibliography of Books and Articles on the Modern Languages and Literatures?*
2. Where is the catalog of the library's periodicals? Where and in what format(s) are the following periodicals stored: (*a*) the *New York Times,* (*b*) *Harper's* magazine, and (*c*) *Journal of Social Psychology?*
3. Where are the library's periodical indexes? Which, if any, are available on computer? If computerized indexes are available, what are the library's procedures for using them? Where (and in what formats) are (*a*) the *New York Times Index* and (*b*) the *Social Sciences Index?*
4. What is the format or formats of the library's catalog of books? If the catalog is in more than one format, are all formats complete? If any is incomplete, what is not included? If the catalog (or part of it) is computerized, where are the terminals, and how are they operated?
5. What are the library call numbers of the following books: (*a*) *The Power Broker,* by Robert Caro; (*b*) *Heart of Darkness,* by Joseph Conrad; and (*c*) *The Hero with a Thousand Faces,* by Joseph Campbell?

ANSWERS: EXERCISE 3

Individual response.

Exercise 3
Finding sources

List at least five sources you can consult for further leads on each of the three topics you produced in Exercise 1 (p. 545) or for three other topics. Use the information provided in the preceding section and additional information at your library.

35d Making a working bibliography

Trying to pursue every source lead as you came across it would prove inefficient and probably ineffective. Instead, you'll want to find out what is available before deciding which leads to follow, and that requires systematically keeping track of where information is and what it is. You can keep track of sources by making a **working bibliography,** a file of the books, articles, and other sources you believe will help you. When you have a substantial file, you can decide which sources seem most promising and look them up first.

A working bibliography is your opportunity to record all the information you need to find your sources. You can use whatever system you like to keep track of information, but many experienced researchers find a card file safer and more flexible than, say, self-stick notes or pages of lists. Writing each source on an individual 3″ × 5″ card will allow you to arrange your sources alphabetically by author, to discard irrelevant sources without disrupting your list, and later to transfer the information easily to your final list of sources. (If you print out source listings from a computer, you may want to copy or paste each one on a separate card.)

Make a bibliography card for each source you think may be useful, whether you find it in the book catalog, in a reference book, or in an index to periodicals. Include all the information listed in the box below. Getting all the information the first time will save you from having to retrace your steps later.

REMINDER FOR STUDENTS

Few things can be more frustrating than discovering, five pages into the writing of your paper, that you have forgotten to note key bibliographic information. Making detailed bibliography cards the first time you read your sources saves considerable time and footsteps. For detailed examples of bibliography cards and format, see the next page.

Information for a working bibliography

For a book

Library call number
Name(s) of author(s), editor(s), translator(s), or others listed
Title and subtitle
Place of publication
Publisher's name
Date of publication
Other important data, such as edition or volume number

For a periodical article

Name(s) of author(s)
Title and subtitle of article
Title of periodical
Volume number and issue number (if any) in which article appears
Date of issue
Page numbers on which article appears

For other sources

Name(s) of author(s) or others listed, such as a government department or a recording artist
Title of the work
Identifying numbers (if any)
Publisher's or producer's name
Date of publication, release, or production
Format, such as unpublished letter, computer service, or live performance

35d

Here are two samples from Mark Shannon's working bibliography, the first for a periodical and the second for a book.

Vincent Bozzi
"Assertiveness Breeds Contempt"
<u>Psychology Today</u>
September 1987
p. 15

HD
6054.3
.L63

Marilyn Loden
<u>Feminine Leadership, or, How</u>
<u>to Succeed in Business</u>
<u>Without Being One of the</u>
<u>Boys</u>
New York: Times Books
1988

When you turn in your paper, you will have to attach a list of the sources you have used (see 37b). So that readers can check or follow up on your sources, your list must include all the information needed to find the sources, in a format readers can understand. Most academic disciplines have special formats used by their practitioners. Several such systems are discussed and illustrated in this handbook: that of the Modern Language Association (MLA), used in many of the humanities, including English (see pp. 598–621); that of the American Psychological Association (APA), used in psychology and other social sciences (pp. 693–703); and that of the Council of Biology Editors (CBE), used in the biological and other sciences (pp. 713–15). You may want to consult one of these sections before compiling your working bibliography as a guide to what kind of information to include and how to arrange it.

35d

Exercise 4
Compiling a working bibliography

Prepare a working bibliography of at least ten sources for a research paper on one of the following people or on someone of your own choosing. Begin by limiting the subject to a manageable size, focusing on a particular characteristic or achievement of the person. Then consult reference books, periodical indexes, and the library's catalog of books. Record complete bibliographic information on note cards.

1. John Lennon, or another performer
2. Sandra Day O'Connor, or another Supreme Court justice
3. Emily Dickinson, or another writer
4. Kareem Abdul-Jabbar, or another sports figure
5. Isamu Noguchi, or another artist

Exercise 5
Compiling a working bibliography

Using one of the topics and the possible references for it from Exercise 3 (p. 564), or starting with a different topic and references, prepare a working bibliography of at least ten sources for your developing research paper. List on 3″ × 5″ cards the complete bibliographic information for each source.

ANSWERS: EXERCISE 4

Individual response.

ANSWERS: EXERCISE 5

Individual response.

35d

In this chapter, the discussion of the research/
writing process begun in Chapter 35 shifts focus
to what are generally considered the later stages
in the composition of a research paper: working
with sources, focusing and shaping ideas, and
drafting and revising a paper. Of particular interest is the emphasis on critical reading of sources
and its role in note taking and summarizing. The
links between critical reading as a part of the research process and Chapter 4's discussion of critical reading are made plain in the text through
cross references.

The essential but sometimes troublesome process of note taking (including paraphrasing and
direct quotation) is also covered in practical detail. Section 36c ("Avoiding Plagiarism") provides
a thorough treatment of this important matter.

Mark Shannon's and Amy Weiss's papers-in-
progress provide examples throughout the chapter, including Sections 36d–h, which cover the
actual writing and revising of research papers.
The advice in these sections presents strategies
for introducing summaries, paraphrases, and
quotations and for revising and editing. It concludes with advice about preparing the final
manuscript.

Chapter 36

Working with Sources and Writing the Paper

The previous chapter led you through laying the groundwork
for a research project. This chapter takes you into the most personal, most intensive, and most rewarding parts of research writing: reading, evaluating, and taking notes from sources; focusing
and shaping your ideas; and drafting and revising the paper. In
these stages you probe your topic deeply and make it your own.

As before, the work of Mark Shannon and Ann Weiss will illustrate the activity and thought that go into research writing.

36a   Scanning and evaluating sources

When to stop looking *for* sources and start looking *at* them
depends, of course, on the assigned length of the paper and on
the complexity of your subject. You are probably ready to begin
reading when your working bibliography suggests that you have
explored most aspects of your topic and have found at least some
sources that deal directly with your central concern. For a paper
of 1800 to 2300 words, ten to twenty promising titles should give
you a good base.

Once you have a satisfactory working bibliography, scan your
cards for the sources that are most likely to give you an overview
of your topic, and consult those sources first. Mark Shannon, for
instance, began investigating titles that indicated a focus on the
progress of women in upper corporate management. Ann Weiss,
in contrast, began reading about the editing of the Declaration of

Independence in some sources referred to in a recent book on the Declaration. For an analysis paper like Weiss's that examines a disagreement among experts in a field, a recent work by one of the experts often lays out the disagreement and cites the works of others involved in it.

As you glance through your sources, your purpose is to evaluate their usefulness and to shape your thinking, not to collect information. A source is potentially useful to you if it is relevant to your topic and if it is reliable. Both relevance and reliability can be determined in part by consulting works *about* the source you are considering—that is, the works listed in citation indexes (p. 555) or book review indexes (pp. 559–60). But unless you can dismiss the source on the basis of citations or reviews, you will also need to evaluate it yourself.

Scanning the introductions to books and articles and the tables of contents and indexes of books can help you determine whether a source is relevant. Reliability can be more difficult to judge. If you haven't already done so, study Chapter 4, especially pages 126–29 on analyzing and evaluating texts and pages 132–49 on reading an argument critically. When scanning potential sources, think critically, looking for assumptions, evidence, tone, fairness, and other features discussed in Chapter 4. In addition, look for information about the author's background to satisfy

RESOURCES AND IDEAS

Lawrence F. Laban, "One Model for Teaching Research Skills," *Exercise Exchange* 21 (1977): 16–19. Laban describes a program that includes, among other activities, an evaluation of a book, a comparison of two different articles on the same subject, a comparison of points of view in several articles, and a research paper. The program helps develop skills in evaluating and analyzing sources.

TRANSPARENCY MASTER
AVAILABLE

36a

Guidelines for evaluating sources

Determine **relevance:**
- Does the source devote some attention to your topic?
- Where in the source are you likely to find relevant information or ideas?
- How important is the source likely to be for your writing?

Judge **reliability:**
- How up to date is the source? Check the publication date.
- Is the author an expert in the field? Look for an author biography, or look up the author in a biographical reference (p. 551).
- Is the source appropriately specialized for your needs? Check the source's treatment of a topic you know something about, to ensure that it is neither too superficial nor too technical.
- What is the author's bias? Check biographical information or the author's own preface or introduction. Consider what others have written about the author or the source.
- Whatever his or her bias, does the author reason soundly, provide adequate evidence, and consider opposing views? (See 4c and 4d.)

yourself that the author has sufficient expertise in your subject. Then try to determine what his or her bias is. For instance, a book on parapsychology by someone identified as the president of the National Organization of Psychics may contain an authoritative explanation of psychic powers, but the author's view is likely to be biased. It should be balanced by research in other sources whose authors are more skeptical of psychic powers.

This balance or opposition is important. You probably will not find harmony among sources, for reasonable people often disagree in their opinions. Thus you must deal honestly with the gaps and conflicts in sources. Old sources, superficial ones, slanted ones—these should be offset in your research and your writing by sources that are newer, more thorough, or more objective.

Read each source quickly and selectively to obtain an overview of your topic. Don't allow yourself to get bogged down in taking very detailed notes at this stage. Without a sense of what information is pertinent, you may not leave time to cover all the potentially relevant sources.

However, do write down general ideas that seem fundamental to your topic. Be especially careful to record ideas of your own, such as a connection between statements by two different writers, because these may not occur to you later. Use your research journal (see 35a).

COLLABORATIVE LEARNING

ANSWERS: EXERCISE 1

Responses will vary. Packard's book is famously critical of advertising methods. Students should recognize Packard's bias while also valuing his expertise and evidence.

ANSWERS: EXERCISE 2

Individual response.

36a

Exercise 1
Evaluating a source

Imagine that you are researching a paper on the advertising techniques that are designed to persuade consumers to buy products. You have listed the following book in your working bibliography:

> Vance Packard, *The Hidden Persuaders,* revised edition, 1981

On your own or with your classmates (as your instructor wishes), obtain this book from the library and evaluate it as a source for your paper. Use the guidelines on page 569.

Exercise 2
Scanning and evaluating sources

Look up the sources in the working bibliography you made in Chapter 35, Exercise 5 (p. 567). Scan and evaluate the sources for their relevance and reliability. If the sources seem unreliable or don't seem to give you what you need, expand your working bibliography and evaluate the new sources.

36b   Taking notes using summary, paraphrase, and direct quotation

When you have decided which sources to pursue, you may be ready to gather information, or you may want to step back and get your bearings. Your choice will depend mainly on how familiar you are with the main issues of your topic and whether you have formed a central idea about it. If you feel fairly confident that you know what you're looking for in sources, then you might proceed with reading and note taking, as discussed below. But if you feel attracted to several different main ideas, or you don't see how the various areas of the topic relate, then you might try drafting a thesis sentence to focus your thoughts and making an outline to discover relationships. These steps are discussed in 36d and 36e, respectively.

1   Reading and note taking

The most efficient method of reading secondary sources during research is **skimming,** reading quickly to look for pertinent information. (Primary sources usually need to be read more carefully, especially when they are the focus of your paper.) When skimming:

- Read with a specific question in mind, not randomly in hopes of hitting something worthwhile.
- Consult the table of contents, index, or headings to find what you want.
- Concentrate on headings and main ideas, skipping material unrelated to the specific question you are researching.

When you find something relevant, read slowly and carefully to achieve a clear understanding of what the author is saying and to interpret and evaluate the material in the context of your own and others' opinions.

If it is effective, your final paper will show that you have digested and interpreted the information in your sources—work that can be performed most efficiently in note taking. Taking notes is not a mechanical process of copying from books and periodicals. Rather, as you read and take notes you assess and organize the information in your sources. Thus your notes both prompt and preserve your thoughts.

Using a system for taking notes helps simplify the process and later makes writing the paper easier. The most common method

36b

involves note cards: 4″ × 6″ cards allow more room than 3″ × 5″. (Using photocopies from sources is discussed on pp. 576–77.) Here are a few guidelines for taking notes on cards:

- Write only one fact or idea on a card so that you can easily rearrange information when you want to. (Such rearrangement is very difficult when notes are combined on sheets of paper.)
- If the same source gives you more than one idea or fact, make more than one card.
- Near the top of every card, write the author's last name and the page number(s) of the source so that you will always know where the note came from. (Write a shortened form of the title as well if you are using two or more sources by the same author.)
- Give the note a brief heading that will remind you of its content or what you intended to do with it. (If you have previously outlined your preliminary ideas, use outline headings for the cards.)

Several note cards on the next pages illustrate this format.

You can use four kinds of notes: summary, paraphrase, direct quotation, and a combination of these methods.

 2   **Summarizing**

When you **summarize,** you condense an extended idea or argument into a sentence or more in your own words. A full discussion of summary appears in 4b-4 (p. 124), and you should read that section if you have not already.

Mark Shannon summarized the following quotation from one of his sources, Ann Hughey and Eric Gelman, "Managing the Woman's Way," *Newsweek,* page 47:

> Generalizing about male and female styles of management is a tricky business, because stereotypes have traditionally been used to keep women down. Not too long ago it was a widely accepted truth that women were unstable, indecisive, temperamental and manipulative and weren't good team members because they'd never played football. In fighting off these prejudices many women simply tried to adopt masculine traits in the office.

Compare this passage with Shannon's one-sentence summary, in which he picks out the kernel of Hughey and Gelman's idea and expresses it in his own words:

36b

Masc. and fem. styles

Hughey and Gelman, p. 47

Rather than be labeled with the unflattering
stereotypes that prevented their promotions,
many women adopted masculine qualities.

Summary is most useful when you want to record the gist of
an author's idea without the background or supporting evidence.

3   Paraphrasing

When you **paraphrase,** you follow much more closely the
author's original presentation, but you still restate it in your own
words. Paraphrase is most useful when you want to reconstruct an
author's line of reasoning but don't feel the original words merit
direct quotation.

The note card below shows how Shannon might have paraphrased the passage by Hughey and Gelman given above.

Masc. and fem. styles

Hughey and Gelman, p. 47

Because of the risk of stereotyping, which
has served as a tool to keep women out of
management, it is difficult to characterize
a feminine management style. Women have
been cited for their emotionality, instability,
and lack of team spirit, among other
qualities. Many women have defended themselves at work by adopting the qualities of men.

**PARAPHRASING: GUIDELINES FOR
STUDENTS**

1. Read a source's material several times to be
   sure you understand what is being said.
   Avoid distorting the meaning of the material.
2. Restate the main ideas in your own words.
3. Do not change the emphasis or order of
   your source's material.
4. Write down all bibliographic information so
   that you may document your source.

36b

Notice how the paraphrase uses different sentence structures and different words to express Hughey and Gelman's idea:

Hughey and Gelman's words	Shannon's paraphrase
Generalizing about male and female styles of management is a <u>tricky business</u>, because stereotypes have traditionally been used to keep women down.	Because of the risk of stereotyping, which has served as a tool to keep women out of management, it is difficult to characterize a feminine management style.
Not too long ago it was a widely accepted truth that women were unstable, indecisive, temperamental and manipulative and weren't good team members because they'd never played football.	Women have been cited for their emotionality, instability, and lack of team spirit, among other qualities.
In fighting off these prejudices many women simply tried to adopt masculine traits in the office.	Many women have defended themselves at work by adopting the qualities of men.

As you summarize and paraphrase, be careful not to distort the author's meaning, but don't feel you have to put down in new words the whole passage or all the details. Select what is pertinent and restate only that. If complete sentences seem too detailed or cumbersome, use phrases. Just be sure not to omit connecting words, qualifiers, and other material whose absence will confuse you later or cause you to misrepresent the sources. (And be sure to cast your notes as full sentences in your final paper.)

Mark Shannon might have written this more telegraphic paraphrase of the quotation by Hughey and Gelman:

<u>Masc. and fem. styles</u>
Hughey and Gelman, p. 47

Difficulty of characterizing fem. mgmt. style — risk of stereotypes (emotionality, instability, etc.). Many women's defense: act like men.

36b

4   **Using direct quotation**

Use direct quotation from secondary sources only in special circumstances, such as when the author's wording is especially vivid. (See 36g for more on when to use quotations.) In a paper analyzing primary sources such as literary works, you will use direct quotation extensively to illustrate and support your analysis. (Ann Weiss used many quotations from her primary source, the Declaration of Independence; see her final paper, pp. 670–72.)

When taking a quotation from a source, copy the material *carefully.* Take down the author's exact wording, spelling, capitalization, and punctuation. Proofread every direct quotation *at least twice,* and be sure you have supplied big quotation marks so that later you won't confuse the direct quotation with a paraphrase or summary. If you want to add words for clarity, use brackets (see 25d). If you want to omit irrelevant words or sentences, use ellipsis marks, usually three spaced periods (see 25e).

The note card below shows how Shannon might have quoted Hughey and Gelman, using ellipses and brackets to make the quotation more concise and specific.

Masc. and fem. styles
Hughey and Gelman, p. 47

"Generalizing about male and female styles of management is a tricky business. . . . Not too long ago it was a widely accepted truth that women were unstable, indecisive, temperamental and manipulative and weren't good team members because they'd never played football. In fighting off these prejudices many women simply tried to adopt masculine traits [such as steadiness and sportsmanship] in the office."

---

 5   **Combining quotation, summary, and paraphrase**

Using quotation in combination with summary or paraphrase can help you shape the material to suit your purposes (although you must be careful not to distort the author's meaning). The card following shows how Shannon might have used a combination of quotation and paraphrase to record the statement by Hughey and

36b

DIRECT QUOTATIONS: GUIDELINES FOR STUDENTS

1. When to use direct quotations:
   a. When you feel an author's words give a special effect that you want to include.
   b. When you want to give impact to an expert's opinion.
   c. When you plan to use a graph, table, or diagram from a source.
   d. To illustrate and support your analysis.
2. Set off a quotation with quotation marks if the quotation is less than three typed lines. Use an indented paragraph if the quotation extends beyond three typed lines.
3. Use brackets to show additional words needed for understanding.
4. Use ellipsis marks (three spaced periods) to show omissions of irrelevant words or sentences.
5. Make sure to copy your source accurately. Proofread every direct quotation at least twice. Check for exact wording and for proper spelling, capitalization, and punctuation.
6. Document your sources.

See also pp. 590–93 on using and introducing borrowed material.

Gelman. Notice that the quotation marks are clearly visible and that the quotations are absolutely exact.

<u>Masc. and fem. styles</u>
Hughey and Gelman, p. 47

It is difficult to characterize a feminine style of management "because stereotypes have traditionally been used to keep women down." Women have been cited as "unstable, indecisive, temperamental and manipulative" and have been accused of not being "good team members." Many women defended themselves at work by adopting the qualities of men.

Caution: If the material you are quoting, summarizing, or paraphrasing runs from one page to the next in the source, make a mark (such as a check mark or a slash) at the exact spot where one page ends and the next begins. When writing your paper, you may want to use only a part of the material (say, the first or second half). The mark will save you from having to go back to your source to find which page the material actually appeared on.

 Photocopying from sources

To ensure accuracy of quotations and also to save time, researchers often photocopy sources. (All libraries provide one or more copying machines for this purpose.) But just running pages through a copier does not generate the creative, interpretive, and analytical thinking about sources that is so crucial in taking notes. If you do use a copier, turn to the photocopy soon after you make it, when you still have your hand on the original source and your thoughts about it are still fresh in your mind. At the top of the copy, write a heading from your outline, the author's name, the source title, and the page number as you would on a note card. Then circle or underline the relevant passages and make notes in the margin about their significance to your topic. To make it possible to integrate photocopied notes with your notes on cards, you might want to paste or tape the copy on a note card of the same size you are using for your handwritten notes. If the photocopy won't fit on one card, cut it apart and paste it on two or more

36b

cards. Be sure to write the appropriate source information at the top of each card so that you don't lose track of where the copy, or a part of it, came from.

Exercise 3
Summarizing and paraphrasing

Prepare two note cards, one containing a summary of the entire paragraph below and the other containing a paraphrase of the first four sentences (ending with the word *autonomy*). Use the format for a note card provided in the preceding section, omitting only the heading.

> Federal organization [of the United States] has made it possible for the different states to deal with the same problems in many different ways. One consequence of federalism, then, has been that people are treated differently, by law, from state to state. The great strength of this system is that differences from state to state in cultural preferences, moral standards, and levels of wealth can be accommodated. In contrast to a unitary system in which the central government makes all important decisions (as in France), federalism is a powerful arrangement for maximizing regional freedom and autonomy. The great weakness of our federal system, however, is that people in some states receive less than the best or the most advanced or the least expensive services and policies that government can offer. The federal dilemma does not invite easy solutions, for the costs and benefits of the arrangement have tended to balance out.
>
> —PETER K. EISINGER ET AL., *American Politics*, p. 44

Exercise 4
Combining summary, paraphrase, and direct quotation

Prepare a note card containing a combination of paraphrase or summary and direct quotation that states the major idea of the passage below. Use the format for a note card provided in the preceding section, omitting only the heading.

> Most speakers unconsciously duel even during seemingly casual conversations, as can often be observed at social gatherings where they show less concern for exchanging information with other guests than for asserting their own dominance. Their verbal dueling often employs very subtle weapons like mumbling, a hostile act which defeats the listener's desire to understand what the speaker claims he is trying to say (but is really not saying because he is mumbling!). Or the verbal dueler may keep talking after someone has passed out of hearing range—which is often an aggressive challenge to the listener to return and acknowledge the dominance of the speaker.
>
> —PETER K. FARB, *Word Play*, p. 107

COLLABORATIVE LEARNING

ANSWERS: EXERCISE 3
Possible Summary

Eisinger et al., American Politics, p. 44

Federalism, unlike a unitary system, allows the states autonomy. Its strength and its weakness—which are in balance—lie in the regional differences it permits.

Possible Paraphrase

Eisinger et al., American Politics, p. 44

Under federalism, each state can devise its own ways of handling problems and its own laws. The system's advantage is that a state can operate according to its people's culture, morals, and wealth. A unitary system like that in France does not permit such diversity.

COLLABORATIVE LEARNING

ANSWERS: EXERCISE 4
Possible Answers

Farb, Word Play, p. 107

Speakers at parties often "unconsciously duel" in conversations in order to assert "dominance" over others. A speaker may mumble, thus preventing a listener from understanding what is said. Or he or she may continue talking after the listener has moved away, a "challenge to the listener to return and acknowledge the dominance of the speaker."

36b

RESOURCES AND IDEAS

Alice Drum, "Responding to Plagiarism," *College Composition and Communication* 37 (1986): 241–43. Drum suggests that instructors place too much emphasis on the legal and moral implications of plagiarism rather than on its important pedagogical consequences.

Patricia C. Bjaaland and Arthur Lederman, "The Detection of Plagiarism," *Educational Forum* 37 (1973): 201–06. The authors classify and analyze the signs of plagiarism: changes in title, especially neat and well-typed manuscripts, and extensive bibliographies.

Dorothy S. Brown, "The Perils of Plagiarism," *College Composition and Communication* 26 (1975): 206–07. Brown recorded a taped conversation among students that highlights the different forms of plagiarism and indicates how hard it can be to explain plagiarism to students.

TRANSPARENCY MASTER
AVAILABLE

36c

36c   Avoiding plagiarism

Plagiarism (from a Latin word for "kidnapper") is the presentation of someone else's ideas or words as your own. Whether deliberate or accidental, plagiarism is a serious and often punishable offense.

- *Deliberate* plagiarism:

  Copying a phrase, a sentence, or a longer passage from a source and passing it off as your own.

  Summarizing or paraphrasing someone else's ideas without acknowledging your debt.

  Buying a term paper and handing it in as your own.

- *Accidental* plagiarism:

  Forgetting to place quotation marks around another writer's words.

  Omitting a source citation for another's idea because you are unaware of the need to acknowledge the idea.

You do not plagiarize, however, when you draw on other writers' material and acknowledge your sources. That procedure is a crucial part of honest research writing, as we have seen. This section shows you how to avoid plagiarism by acknowledging sources when necessary and by using them accurately and fairly.

Checklist for avoiding plagiarism

1. What type of source are you using: your own independent material, common knowledge, or someone else's independent material? You must acknowledge someone else's material.
2. If you are quoting someone else's material, is the quotation exact? Have you inserted quotation marks around quotations run into the text? Have you shown omissions with ellipses and additions with brackets?
3. If you are paraphrasing or summarizing someone else's material, have you used your own words and sentence structures? Does your paraphrase or summary employ quotation marks when you resort to the author's exact language? Have you represented the author's meaning without distortion?
4. Is each use of someone else's material acknowledged in your text? Are all your source citations complete and accurate? (See 37a.)
5. Does your list of works cited include all the sources you have drawn from in writing your paper? (See 37b.)

1   ### Knowing what to acknowledge

When you write a research paper, you coordinate information from three kinds of sources: (1) your independent thoughts and experiences; (2) common knowledge, the basic knowledge people share; and (3) other people's independent thoughts and experiences. Of the three, you *must* acknowledge the third, the work of others.

Your independent material

You need not acknowledge your own independent material— your thoughts, compilations of facts, or experimental results, expressed in your words or format—to avoid plagiarism. Such material includes observations from your experience (for example, a conclusion you draw about crowd behavior by watching crowds at concerts) as well as diagrams you construct from information you gather yourself. Though you generally should describe the basis for your conclusions so that readers can evaluate your thinking, you need not cite sources for them. However, someone else's ideas and facts are not yours; even when you express them entirely in your words and sentence structures, they require acknowledgment.

Common knowledge

Common knowledge consists of the standard information of a field of study as well as folk literature and commonsense observations. Standard information includes, for instance, the major facts of history. The dates of Charlemagne's rule as emperor of Rome (800–814) and the fact that his reign was accompanied by a revival of learning—both facts available in many reference books—do not need to be acknowledged, even if you have to look up the information. However, you must document independent knowledge: for instance, an interpretation of facts (a theory of how Charlemagne influenced Napoleon) or a specialist's observation (a historian's opinion that Charlemagne was sometimes needlessly cruel in extending his power).

Folk literature, which is popularly known and cannot be traced to particular writers, is considered common knowledge. Mother Goose nursery rhymes and fairy tales such as "Snow White" are examples. However, all literature traceable to a particular writer should be acknowledged. Even a familiar phrase like "miles to go before I sleep" (from Robert Frost's poem "Stopping

RESOURCES AND IDEAS

Frank McCormick, "The 'Plagiario' and the Professor in Our Peculiar Institution," *Journal of Teaching Writing* 8 (1989): 133–45. McCormick argues that students plagiarize not because they are immoral but because they need to be taught more carefully how to be responsible in their use of secondary materials.

MATERIAL THAT NEED NOT BE CITED

1. Standard information (such as major acts of history).
2. Folk literature.
3. Commonsense observations.
4. Information that comes up repeatedly, without acknowledgment, in the student's reading.

36c

by Woods on a Snowy Evening") is literature, not folk literature, and requires acknowledgment.

Commonsense observations, such as the idea that weather affects people's spirits or that inflation is most troublesome for people with low and fixed incomes, are considered common knowledge and do not require acknowledgment, even when they also appear in someone else's writing. But a scientist's findings about the effects of high humidity on people with high blood pressure, or an economist's argument about the effects of inflation on immigrants from China, will require acknowledgment.

You may treat common knowledge as your own, even if you have to look it up in a reference book. You may not know, for example, the dates of the French Revolution or the standard definition of *photosynthesis,* although these are considered common knowledge. If you do not know a subject well enough to determine whether a piece of information is common knowledge, make a record of the source as you would for any other quotation, paraphrase, or summary. As you read more about the subject, the information may come up repeatedly without acknowledgment, in which case it is probably common knowledge. But if you are still in doubt when you finish your research, always acknowledge the source.

Someone else's independent material

You must always acknowledge other people's independent material—that is, any facts or ideas that are not common knowledge or your own. The source may be anything, including a book, an article, a movie, an interview, a microfilmed document, or a computer program. You must acknowledge not only ideas or facts themselves but also the language and format in which the ideas or facts appear, if you use them. That is, the wording, sentence structures, arrangement of thoughts, and special graphic format (such as a table or diagram) created by another writer belong to that writer just as his or her ideas do. The following example baldly plagiarizes the original quotation from Jessica Mitford's *Kind and Usual Punishment,* page 9.

Original	The character and mentality of the keepers may be of more importance in understanding prisons than the character and mentality of the kept.
Plagiarism	But the character of prison officials (the keepers) is more important in understanding prisons than the character of prisoners (the kept).

Though the writer has made some changes in Mitford's original and even altered the meaning slightly (by changing *may be* to *is*),

36c

RESOURCES AND IDEAS

Michael T. O'Neill, "Plagiarism: (1) Writing Responsibility," *ABCA Bulletin* 43 (1980): 34–36. O'Neill argues that by clarifying the meaning of plagiarism, by teaching conventions, and by teaching paraphrasing that pays attention to ideas as well as words, instructors can help reduce unintentional plagiarism.

she has plagiarized on several counts. She has copied key words (*character, keepers, kept*), duplicated the entire sentence structure, and lifted the idea—all without acknowledging the source. As illustrated below and on the next page, the writer must either enclose the exact quotation in quotation marks or state the idea in her own words and in her own sentence. Whichever she does, she *must* acknowledge Mitford as the source.

You need to acknowledge another's material no matter how you use it, how much of it you use, or how often you use it. Whether you are quoting a single important word, paraphrasing a single sentence, or summarizing three paragraphs, and whether you are using the source only once or a dozen times, you must acknowledge the original author every time. See 37a for discussion and examples of how to acknowledge sources in your text.

If you read someone else's material during your research but do not include any of that material in your final draft, you need not acknowledge the source with a citation because you have not actually used the material. However, your instructor may ask you to include such sources in your list of works cited (see 37b).

 2   **Quoting, summarizing, and paraphrasing honestly**

When using direct quotation, be sure to copy the material from the source accurately and with clear quotation marks. Use the quotation marks in the running text of your paper even if you are only quoting a single word that the original author used in a special or central way. (See 24c for the style to use with poetry and long quotations, which are set off from the text and not enclosed in quotation marks.) Acknowledge the source in the manner appropriate for the documentation style you are using. (See p. 598 for the MLA citation style, p. 693 for the APA, and p. 713 for the CBE.)

To correct the plagiarism of Mitford's sentence opposite, the writer would place Mitford's exact words in quotation marks and cite the source properly (in this case, in MLA style).

> **Quotation**   According to one critic of the penal system, "The character and mentality of the keepers may be of more importance in understanding prisons than the character and mentality of the kept" (Mitford 9).

When you summarize or paraphrase, you do not use quotation marks, because the words are your own. However, you must acknowledge the author of the idea. Here is a paraphrase of the Mitford quotation above (with the source citation again in MLA style).

RESOURCES AND IDEAS

R. G. Martin, "Plagiarism and Originality: Some Remedies," *English Journal* 60 (1971): 621–28. Martin argues that requiring synthesis rather than regurgitation will forestall plagiarism.

36c

Paraphrase   One critic of the penal system maintains that we may be able to learn more about prisons from the psychology of the prison officials than from that of the prisoners (Mitford 9).

If you adopt the source's sentence pattern and simply substitute synonyms for key words, or if you use the original words and merely change the sentence pattern, you are not paraphrasing but plagiarizing, even if you acknowledge the source, because both methods use someone else's expression without quotation marks. The inadequate paraphrase below plagiarizes the original source, Frederick C. Crews's *The Tragedy of Manners: Moral Drama in the Later Novels of Henry James,* page 8.

Original   In each case I have tried to show that all the action in a "Jamesian novel" may be taken as a result of philosophical differences of opinion among the principal characters, and that these differences in turn are explainable by reference to the characters' differing social backgrounds.

Plagiarism   According to Crews, the action in a "Jamesian novel" comes from philosophical differences of opinion between characters, differences that can be explained by examining the characters' differing social backgrounds (8).

The plagiarized passage lifts several expressions verbatim from the source, without change and without quotation marks: *action in a "Jamesian novel"; philosophical differences of opinion; the characters' differing social backgrounds.* Thus, even though the writer acknowledges the author's work (by giving Crews's name and the parenthetical page number, 8), he plagiarizes because he does not also acknowledge the author's words with quotation marks. The paraphrase below both conveys and acknowledges the author's meaning without stealing his manner of expression.

Paraphrase   According to Crews, the characters in Henry James's novels live out philosophies acquired from their upbringing and their place in society (8).

In this paraphrase, although the writer retains Crews's essential meaning, he restates that meaning in a sentence that he himself has clearly constructed and designed to fit his larger purpose.

In paraphrasing or summarizing you must not only devise your own form of expression (or place quotation marks around the author's expressions) but also represent the author's meaning exactly, without distorting it. In the following inaccurate summary the writer has not plagiarized but has stated a meaning exactly op-

36c

posite that of the original. The original quotation, from the artist Henri Matisse, appears in Jack D. Flam, *Matisse on Art,* page 148.

Original	For the artist creation begins with vision. To see is itself a creative operation, requiring an effort. Everything that we see in our daily life is more or less distorted by acquired habits, and this is perhaps more evident in an age like ours when cinema posters and magazines present us every day with a flood of ready-made images which are to the eye what prejudices are to the mind.
Inaccurate summary	Matisse said that the artist can learn how to see by looking at posters and magazines (qtd. in Flam 148).

The revision below combines summary and quotation to represent the author's meaning exactly.

Improved summary	Matisse said that the artist must overcome visual "habits" and "prejudices," particularly those developed in response to popular cultural images (qtd. in Flam 148).

To be sure you acknowledge sources fairly and do not plagiarize, review the checklist on page 578 both before beginning to write your paper and again after you have completed your first draft.

Exercise 5
Recognizing plagiarism

The numbered items below show various attempts to quote or paraphrase the following passage. Carefully compare each attempt with the original passage. Which are plagiarized, inaccurate, or both, and which are acceptable? Why?

I would agree with the sociologists that psychiatric labeling is dangerous. Society can inflict terrible wounds by discrimination, and by confusing health with disease and disease with badness.
—GEORGE E. VAILLANT, *Adaptation to Life,* p. 361

1. According to George Vaillant, society often inflicts wounds by using psychiatric labeling, confusing health, disease, and badness (361).
2. According to George Vaillant, "psychiatric labeling [such as 'homosexual' or 'schizophrenic'] is dangerous. Society can inflict terrible wounds by . . . confusing health with disease and disease with badness" (361).
3. According to George Vaillant, when psychiatric labeling discriminates between health and disease or between disease and badness, it can inflict wounds on those labeled (361).

COLLABORATIVE LEARNING

ANSWERS: EXERCISE 5

1. Plagiarized. Takes phrases directly from the original without quotation marks.
2. Acceptable.
3. Inaccurate and plagiarized. The passage uses phrases from the original without quotation marks and distorts its meaning.

36c

4. Acceptable. Puts the original into the author's own words and correctly conveys its meaning.
5. Inaccurate and plagiarized. Fails to acknowledge the source and fails to convey accurately the concepts of "discrimination" and "confusing" outlined in the original.
6. Inaccurate. Ellipses are needed to indicate that material was omitted and brackets must be placed around lower case *s* to indicate revision.

ANSWERS: EXERCISE 6

Individual response.

4. Psychiatric labels can badly hurt those labeled, says George Vaillant, because they fail to distinguish among health, illness, and immorality (361).
5. Labels such as "homosexual" and "schizophrenic" can be hurtful when they fail to distinguish among health, illness, and immorality.
6. "I would agree with the sociologists that society can inflict terrible wounds by discrimination, and by confusing health with disease and disease with badness" (Vaillant 361).

Exercise 6
Taking notes from sources

Continuing from Exercise 2 (p. 570), as the next step in preparing a research paper, make notes of specific information from your sources. Use summary, paraphrase, direct quotation, or a combination as seems appropriate. Be careful to avoid plagiarism or inaccuracy. Mark each card (or photocopy) with the author's name, title, and page number as well as with a heading summarizing its content.

36d **Developing a thesis sentence**

Perhaps earlier in the research-writing process, but certainly once you have taken notes from your sources, you will want to express your central idea and perspective in a thesis sentence—or sentences, if you need more than one. (See 1f if you need guidance on developing a thesis sentence.) Drafting a thesis sentence will help you see the overall picture and organize your notes.

Mark Shannon's and Ann Weiss's work on their research papers illustrates how a thesis sentence evolves to become complete and specific. Before finishing his reading on women in management, Shannon wrote the following draft of a thesis sentence:

Tentative thesis sentence

Although women have come a long way in their journey up the corporate ladder, they still have a number of obstacles to overcome.

This thesis sentence stated Shannon's preliminary idea that women still have not overcome all obstacles to management. But Shannon's further reading led him to revise this idea: he discovered that women have broken most barriers into middle and upper management but still cannot penetrate a "glass ceiling" between themselves and the top jobs, corporate directorships. Many of his sources focused on the differences in managerial styles between men and women. Accordingly, Shannon altered his thesis to reflect his growing conviction that businesses create the glass ceiling for women by defining a successful management style as a masculine style. At the same time, a lack of space, time, and interest led Shannon to abandon an earlier plan to cover the progress of women in recent decades. This change is reflected in the opening of his revised thesis sentence.

Revised thesis sentence

If women are ever to break through the glass ceiling in significant numbers, business attitudes will have to change, particularly the definition of successful management styles.

For Ann Weiss, framing a thesis sentence for her paper on the Declaration of Independence meant first drawing a tentative conclusion about whether Jefferson's draft of the Declaration was improved by the Continental Congress. After skimming the works of the experts who disagreed on this question and closely reading the two versions of the Declaration, she came to believe that the Congress's version was generally more effective. Her tentative thesis sentence indicated that she disagreed with one of the experts:

Tentative thesis sentence

Despite one scholar's view that Jefferson's Declaration was damaged in revision, the changes made by the Congress actually improved the document.

This draft reflected Weiss's preference for the Congress's version but not her reasons. Expressing these concretely was the goal of her revision.

Revised thesis sentence

Despite one scholar's view that Jefferson's Declaration was damaged in revision, the changes made by the Congress improved the document in tone and strengthened it for the purposes it was intended to serve.

Exercise 7
Developing a thesis sentence

Draft and revise a thesis sentence for your research paper. Make sure the revised version states the topic specifically and implies your perspective on it. (If you need help, consult 1f.)

RESOURCES AND IDEAS

Robert M. Esch, "Research Paper Paranoia," *College Composition and Communication* 26 (1975): 42–43. Esch offers a humorous account of a student's nightmare about her teacher and her research paper, as a way of presenting the student's outlook.

ANSWERS: EXERCISE 7

Individual response.

36d

36e   Creating a structure

Before starting to draft your research paper, organize your ideas and information so that you know the main divisions of your paper, the order you'll cover them in, and the important supporting ideas for each division. The goal is to create a structure that presents your ideas in a sensible and persuasive sequence and that supports ideas at each level with enough explanation and evidence.

An outline can help you shape your research and also discover potential problems, such as inadequate support and overlapping or irrelevant ideas. As a prelude to outlining, arrange your note cards in groups of related ideas and information. (If you have written subject headings on the cards, they may help you make connections.) This is a good time to review your research journal. If you have kept it dutifully, it will undoubtedly contain connections between sources, ideas about sources, and other thoughts that can help you organize your paper.

As you move back and forth between specific notes and linking ideas, a structure will gradually evolve. If, however, you feel that you don't have enough information to complete an outline or that some of your ideas lack support, you may have to return to your sources for additional research. Consult your working bibliography for sources you skipped before, or read more deeply in the ones you took notes from.

For some research projects, you may find an **informal outline** sufficient to create a structure. As with the informal outline for an essay (see 1g-2), you list main points and supporting information in the order you expect to discuss them. Because of its informality, such an outline can help you try out different arrangements of material, even fairly early in the research process. Mark Shannon experimented with an informal outline while examining his sources, in order to see how his developing ideas might fit together.

How far women have come
  —Civil Rights Act of 1964
  —1970s workplace vs. present

Gains made since 1970s
  —Success: percentage of women in middle and upper management
  —Availability of mentors
  —Rise of high-tech and service industries

36e

Obstacles
 —Statistics on women at the top
 —Breaking the "glass ceiling"
   —Last bastion for males
   —Conservatism at the top
   —"Queen bees" and male clones
 —Masculine management style

This informal outline helped Shannon decide not to continue re-searching women's advances in business (the first two sections) and to concentrate on obstacles to advancement (last section).

Unlike an informal outline, a **formal outline** arranges ideas tightly and in considerable detail, with close attention to hierarchy and phrasing. The example below shows the formal outline's format and schematic content:

I. First main idea
  A. First subordinate idea   *1st sublevel*
     1. First evidence for subordinate idea   *2nd sublevel*
        a. First detail of evidence   *3rd sublevel*   *4th = (2)*
        b. Second detail of evidence
     2. Second evidence for subordinate idea
  B. Second subordinate idea
II. Second main idea

In this model main ideas are labeled with Roman numerals, the first sublevel with capital letters, the second with Arabic numerals, and the third with small letters. (A fourth sublevel, if needed, is labeled with Arabic numerals enclosed in parentheses.) Each level of the outline is indented farther than the one it supports.

To be an effective organizer for your thoughts, a formal outline should be detailed and should adhere to several principles of logical arrangement, clarity, balance, and completeness. These are discussed in detail and illustrated in Chapter 1, pages 38–40. Briefly:

- The outline should divide material into groups that indicate which ideas are primary and, under them, which are subordinate. A long, undivided list of parallel items probably needs to be subdivided.
- Parallel headings should represent ideas of equal importance and generality and should not overlap one another.
- Single sublevels should be avoided because they illogically imply that something is divided into only one part.

A formal outline is usually written either in phrases—a **topic outline**—or in sentences—a **sentence outline.** A complete

36e

topic outline is illustrated in Chapter 1, page 38. A complete sentence outline accompanies Mark Shannon's research paper on pages 634–35. Either is suitable for a research paper, though a sentence outline, because it requires complete statements, conveys more information.

ANSWERS: EXERCISE 8

Possible Answers

I. Processing, preserving, and improving the appearance of foods
   A. Processing
      1. Leavening
      2. Preventing foaming
      3. Binding ingredients together
   B. Preserving
      1. Protecting from internal destruction by enzymes
         a. Discoloration
         b. Overripening
      2. Protecting from external destruction
         a. Bacteria
         b. Fungi
         c. Heat
         d. Moisture
         e. Humidity
   C. Improving appearance
      1. Glazing
      2. Causing foaming in hot chocolate
      3. Firming canned fruits and vegetables
      4. Thickening texture
      5. Preventing discoloration

36e

Exercise 8
Analyzing a formal outline

Identify the flaws in the following partial outline for a research paper. Check especially for departures from formal outline form, including illogical subdivision of topics, inconsistent wording of items, and nonparallel placement of ideas of parallel importance.

Thesis sentence

Food additives, which aid in processing foods and in preserving them or improving their appearance, are more useful to us than they are dangerous.

Formal outline

I. Processing, preservation, appearance
   A. Processing
      1. Leavening agents
      2. Antifoaming agents
      3. Emulsifiers
         a. Bind ingredients together
   B. Preservation
      1. Protect from internal destruction
         a. Natural enzymes can cause discoloration or overripening
         b. Must remove or disable enzymes
      2. External destruction
         a. Bacteria
         b. Fungus
      3. Environment
         a. Heat, moisture, humidity
         b. Humectants protect foods from excess moisture
   C. Appearance
      1. Glazing agents
      2. Foaming agents cause bubbles to appear in hot chocolate
      3. Firming agents
         a. Keep fruits and vegetables firm in cans
         b. Thickeners
            1. Prevent ice crystal formation, as in ice cream
            2. Improve texture
         c. Sequestrants prevent discoloration

Exercise 9
Creating a structure

Continuing from Exercise 7 (p. 585), arrange your notes into a structure. As specified by your instructor, make an informal outline or a formal sentence or topic outline to guide the drafting of your paper.

36f Drafting the paper

Beginning a draft of what will be a relatively long and complicated paper can be difficult, so it may help to remember that you do not have to proceed methodically from beginning to end. To get your juices flowing and give yourself a sense of direction, try writing a quick two- or three-paragraph summary of what the paper will be about. (Pretend you're writing to a friend if that will help loosen you up.) Then, when you turn to the paper itself, skip any parts that scare you or give you undue trouble, even the introduction. Try starting with the section that you feel most confident about. Move from there to other sections of the paper, attempting to fit the sections together only after you begin to see the draft take shape.

In writing sections of your draft, remember that a primary reason for doing a research paper is learning how to evaluate and interpret the evidence in sources, draw your own conclusions from the evidence, and weave the two together in a convincing whole. The weaving will be easier if you view each principal idea in your outline as a unit. Depending on the importance of the idea to your scheme, on its complexity, and on the amount of evidence needed to support it, a unit may require a single paragraph or a block of two or three paragraphs.

Begin each unit by stating the idea, which should be a conclusion you have drawn from reading and taking notes. Follow the statement with specific support from your notes: facts and examples; summaries, paraphrases, or quotations of secondary sources;

Tips for drafting a research paper

1. As a warm-up, write a quick, brief summary of the paper.
2. Start wherever you like.
3. Work in chunks, one unit or principal idea at a time.
4. Insert source information (author's name and page number) into the draft as you quote, paraphrase, or summarize.

36f

quotations of passages from primary sources with your analysis; and so on. If your research focuses on or has uncovered a disagreement among experts, present the disagreement fairly and give the evidence that leads you to side with one expert or another. As much as possible, try to remain open to new interpretations or new arrangements of ideas that occur to you.

As you draft your paper, insert the source of each summary, paraphrase, and quotation in parentheses in the text—for instance, "(Hughey and Gelman 47)," referring to page 47 in a work by Hughey and Gelman. If you are conscientious about inserting these notes and carrying them through successive drafts, you will be less likely to plagiarize accidentally and you will have little difficulty citing your sources in the final paper. (Citing sources is discussed in Chapter 37.)

 36g | **Using and introducing summaries, paraphrases, and quotations**

 1 | **Using borrowed material**

One of your challenges in writing a research paper will be deciding when, where, and how to introduce summaries, paraphrases, and quotations from your sources into your text. You

---

Checklist for direct quotes

36g

 Tests for direct quotations

1. The author's original satisfies one of these requirements:
- The language is unusually vivid, bold, or inventive.
- The quotation cannot be paraphrased without distortion or loss of meaning.
- The words themselves are at issue in your interpretation.
- The quotation represents and emphasizes the view of an important expert.
- The quotation is a graph, diagram, or table.

2. The quotation is as short as possible.
- It includes only material relevant to your point.
- It is edited to eliminate unneeded examples and other material. (See 25e on the use of ellipsis marks for editing quotations.)

want to back up your conclusions with the evidence of others' information and opinions, to be sure, but you do not want to overwhelm your own point of view and voice. The point of research writing is to investigate and go beyond sources, to interpret them and convey your interpretations to readers.⌉

Most papers of six to ten pages should not need more than two to four quotations that are longer than a few lines each. Except when you are analyzing literature or other primary sources, favor paraphrases and summaries over quotations. For quotations from secondary sources, use the tests opposite.

 Introducing borrowed material

When using summaries, paraphrases, and quotations, integrate them smoothly into your own sentences. In the passage below, the writer has not meshed the structures of her own and her source's sentences.

Awkward	One editor disagrees with this view and "a good reporter does not fail to separate opinions from facts" (Lyman 52).
Revised	One editor disagrees with this view, maintaining that "a good reporter does not fail to separate opinions from facts" (Lyman 52).

Even when not conflicting with your own sentence structure, borrowed material will be ineffective if you merely dump it in readers' laps without explaining how you intend it to be understood.

Dumped	Many news editors and reporters maintain that it is impossible to keep personal opinions from influencing the selection and presentation of facts. "True, news reporters, like everyone else, form impressions of what they see and hear. However, a good reporter does not fail to separate opinions from facts" (Lyman 52).
Revised	Many news editors and reporters maintain that it is impossible to keep personal opinions from influencing the selection and presentation of facts. Yet not all authorities agree with this view. One editor grants that "news reporters, like everyone else, form impressions of what they see and hear." But, he insists, "a good reporter does not fail to separate opinions from facts" (Lyman 52).

36g

> ## Verbs for introducing summaries, paraphrases, and quotations
>
> Introduce borrowed material with a verb that conveys information about the source author's attitude or approach to what he or she is saying. In the sentence *King _____ that the flood might have been disastrous,* filling the blank with *observes, finds,* or *insists* would create different meanings.
>
> | Author is neutral | Author infers or suggests | Author argues | Author is uneasy or disparaging |
> |---|---|---|---|
> | comments | analyzes | alleges | belittles |
> | describes | asks | claims | bemoans |
> | explains | assesses | contends | complains |
> | illustrates | concludes | defends | condemns |
> | notes | considers | disagrees | deplores |
> | observes | finds | holds | deprecates |
> | points out | predicts | insists | derides |
> | records | proposes | maintains | laments |
> | relates | reveals | | warns |
> | reports | shows | **Author agrees** | |
> | says | speculates | | |
> | sees | suggests | admits | |
> | thinks | supposes | agrees | |
> | writes | | concedes | |
> | | | concurs | |
> | | | grants | |

In the first version, we must figure out for ourselves that the writer's opening sentence and the quotation represent opposite points of view. In the revised version, the writer's additions (underlined) tell us what to expect in the quotation. (A list of verbs for introducing borrowed material appears above.)

You can do even more to integrate a quotation into your text and inform readers why you are using it. If your readers will recognize it, you can provide the author's name in the text:

Author named   . . . Harold Lyman grants that "news reporters, like everyone else, form impressions of what they see and hear." But, Lyman insists, "a good reporter does not fail to separate opinions from facts" (52).

If the source title contributes information about the author or the context of the quotation, you can provide it in the text:

36g

**Title
given**
  . . . Harold Lyman, in his book *The Conscience of the Journalist,* grants that "news reporters, like everyone else, form impressions of what they see and hear." But, Lyman insists, "a good reporter does not fail to separate opinions from facts" (52).

Finally, if the quoted author's background and experience strengthen or clarify the quotation, you can provide these credentials in the text:

**Credentials
given**
  . . . Harold Lyman, a newspaper editor for more than forty years, grants that "news reporters, like everyone else, form impressions of what they see and hear." But, Lyman insists, "a good reporter does not fail to separate opinions from facts" (52).

You need not always name the author, source, or credentials in your text. In fact, such introductions may get in the way when you are simply establishing facts or weaving together facts and opinions from varied sources. In the following passage from Ann Weiss's paper, the information is more important than the source, so the name of the source is confined to a parenthetical acknowledgment:

To end the abuses of the British, many colonists were urging three actions: forming a united front, seceding from Britain, and taking control of their own international trade and diplomacy (Wills 325–36).

(See pp. 598–604 for an explanation of the parenthetical form of citation used in this passage and the ones above.)

In papers analyzing literature, historical documents, and other sources, quotations will often be both the target of your analysis and the chief support for your ideas. You may need to quote many brief passages, integrated into your sentences, and then comment on the quotations to clarify your analysis and win readers' agreement with it. An example of such extensive quotation can be seen in Ann Weiss's analysis of the Declaration of Independence (pp. 670–72) and in the two literary analyses in Chapter 39 (pp. 684–89).

If you need guidance in the mechanics of quotation, see 21h (punctuating explanatory words such as *he insists*), 24c (quoting poetry and long prose passages), 25d (using brackets for additions to quotations), and 25e (using ellipsis marks for deletions from quotations).

36g

ANSWERS: EXERCISE 10

Sample Paragraph

Why does a woman who is otherwise happy regularly suffer anxiety attacks at the first sign of spring? Why does a man who is otherwise a competent, relaxed driver feel panic whenever he approaches a traffic rotary? According to Willard Gaylin, a professor of psychiatry and a practicing psychoanalyst, such feelings of anxiety are attributable to the uniquely human capacities for remembering, imagining, and forming "symbolic and often unconscious representations" of experiences (23). The feeling of anxiety, Gaylin says, "is . . . compounded by its seemingly irrational quality," its appearance despite the absence of an immediate source of worry or pain (23). The anxious woman is not aware of it, but her father's death twenty years before in April has caused her to equate spring with death. Similarly, the man has forgotten that a terrible accident he witnessed as a child occurred at a rotary. For both people, the anxious feelings are not reduced but heightened because they seem to be unfounded.

Exercise 10
Using and introducing borrowed material

Drawing on the ideas in the following paragraph and using examples from your own observations and experiences, write a paragraph about anxiety. Integrate at least one direct quotation and one paraphrase from the following paragraph into your own sentences. In your paragraph identify the author by name and give his credentials: he is a professor of psychiatry and a practicing psychoanalyst.

There are so many ways in which man is unique from all the lower forms of animals, and almost all of them make us uniquely susceptible to feelings of anxiousness. Our imagination and reasoning powers facilitate anxiety; the anxious feeling is precipitated not by an absolute impending threat—such as the worry about an examination, a speech, travel—but rather by the symbolic and often unconscious representations. We do not have to be experiencing a potential danger. We can experience something related to it. We can recall, through our incredible memories, the original symbolic sense of vulnerability in childhood and suffer the feeling attached to that. We can even forget the original memory and still be stuck with the emotion—which is then compounded by its seemingly irrational quality at this time. It is not just the fear of death which pains us, but the anticipation of it; or the anniversary of a specific death; or a street, a hospital, a time of day, a color, a flower, a symbol associated with death.

—WILLARD GAYLIN, "Feeling Anxious," p. 23

36h   Revising and editing the paper

When you have written a first draft, take a break for at least a day so that you can gain some objectivity about your work and read the draft critically when you begin to revise. Then evaluate your first draft according to the advice and revision checklist in 2b (p. 53). Be especially attentive to the following:

- Ensure that your thesis sentence accurately describes your topic and your perspective as they emerged during drafting, so that the paper is unified and coherent.
- Be alert for major structural problems that may not have been apparent in your outline:
  —Illogical arrangements of ideas.
  —Inadequate emphasis of important points and overemphasis of minor points.
  —Imbalance between the views of others (support) and your own views (interpretation or analysis).

36h

- Hunt out irrelevant ideas and facts that crept in just because you had notes on them.
- Look for places where supporting evidence is weak.
- Examine your explanations to be sure your readers will understand them. Define terms and clarify concepts that readers may be unfamiliar with.

When you complete your revision, retype the new draft if possible so that you have a clean copy to edit. For editing, consult the advice and checklist in 2c (p. 59). Try to read the paper from the point of view of someone who has not spent hours planning and researching but instead has come fresh to the paper. Look for lapses in sense, awkward passages, poor transitions between ideas and evidence, unnecessary repetitions, wrong or misspelled words, errors in grammar, punctuation, or mechanics—in short, anything that is likely to interfere with a reader's understanding of your meaning.

Note: Before you prepare and proofread the final draft (next section), you must insert your source citations into the text and prepare your list of sources. For ease of reference, these steps are discussed fully in their own chapter (37), beginning on page 597.

Exercise 11
Drafting and revising your paper

Draft the research paper you have been preparing throughout Chapters 35 and 36. Before beginning the first draft, study your research journal and your notes. While drafting, follow your note cards, thesis sentence, and outline as closely as you need to, but stay open to new ideas, associations, and arrangements. Then revise and edit thoroughly and carefully, working to improve not only your presentation of ideas but also, if necessary, the ideas themselves.

36i   Preparing and proofreading the final manuscript

Prepare the final draft of your paper when you have edited the text (36h), added the source citations (37a), and written the list of works cited (37b). Most instructors expect research papers to be neatly typed with clear titling, double spacing, standard margins, and minimal handwritten corrections. For English courses the standard guide to manuscript format is the *MLA Handbook for Writers of Research Papers.* Its requirements are spelled out in Appendix A of this book and illustrated in the research papers of Mark Shannon and Ann Weiss, starting on page 632. The format is

36i

not difficult to follow, and it will make your paper professional looking and easy to read. (The MLA format is adaptable to other disciplines as well. See Chapter 39 for the special requirements of the American Psychological Association, p. 703, and the Council of Biology Editors, p. 715.)

Before you submit your paper, proofread it carefully for typographical errors, misspellings, and other slight errors. (See 2d for proofreading tips.) Unless the errors are very numerous (more than several on a page), you can correct them by whiting out or crossing out (neatly) and inserting the correction (neatly) in ink. (See Appendix A, p. 740, for an example.) Don't let the pressure of a deadline prevent you from proofreading, for even minor errors can impair clarity or annoy readers and thus negate some of the hard work you have put into your project.

ANSWERS: EXERCISE 12

Individual response.

Exercise 12
Preparing and proofreading your final manuscript

After adding source citations and a list of works cited (Chapter 37), prepare the final draft of your research paper. Unless your instructor specifies otherwise, follow the manuscript format recommended in Appendix A. Proofread and correct the final paper before handing it in.

Chapter 37

Documenting Sources

HIGHLIGHTS

Documenting sources according to the guidelines established by the Modern Language Association is the focus of this chapter. The chapter first discusses MLA style for citing sources within the text by using parenthetical citations. The "Index to MLA Parenthetical Citations" is given on page 599 for quick reference. The next section covers where to place citations in the text and how to use footnotes or endnotes in special circumstances. The next covers preparing the list of works cited after the MLA style and includes the helpful "Index to MLA Works-Cited Models" on page 606. Finally, the chapter describes using footnotes or endnotes to document sources and concludes with a list of common abbreviations found in source citations.

Every time you borrow the words, facts, or ideas of others, you must acknowledge the source so that readers know you borrowed the material and know where you borrowed it from. To cite sources is to **document** them, to supply references (documents) that legitimate your use of borrowed material and support your claims about its origins. You do not need to acknowledge your own ideas or ideas that are considered common knowledge when you express these in your own words. But you must acknowledge direct quotations, illustrations, and summaries or paraphrases of others' ideas, facts that aren't common knowledge, and associations between them—no matter what their length or how often you have already cited the source. (See 36c for a full discussion of what to acknowledge.)

Editors and teachers in most academic disciplines require special documentation formats (or styles) in their scholarly journals and in students' papers. This chapter concentrates on a style of in-text citation widely used in the arts and humanities: that of the Modern Language Association, published in the *MLA Handbook for Writers of Research Papers,* 3rd ed. (1988). Two other documentation styles are covered in Chapter 39: that of the American Psychological Association (APA), widely used in the social sciences (p. 693); and that of the Council of Biology Editors (CBE), widely used in the biological and other sciences (p. 713).

If your instructor does not assign a particular documentation style, you may opt to consult one of the following general guides:

The Chicago Manual of Style. 13th ed. 1982.

Turabian, Kate L. *A Manual for Writers of Term Papers, Theses, and Dissertations.* 5th ed. Rev. and exp. Bonnie Birtwistle Honigsblum. 1987.

Do follow some system for citing sources so that you provide all the necessary information in a consistent format.

37a   Citing sources in your text: MLA style

As you draft your paper, you should note source information for every quotation, summary, and paraphrase. These notes and the information in your working bibliography (35d) should give you everything you need to write source citations.

The documentation system of the *MLA Handbook* employs brief parenthetical citations within the text that direct readers to the list of works cited. For example:

```
Only one article mentions this discrepancy (Wolfe 62).
```

The name Wolfe directs readers to the article by Wolfe in the list of works cited, and the page number 62 specifies the page in the article on which the cited material appears.

The following pages describe this documentation system: what must be included in a citation (below), where to place citations (p. 603), and when to use footnotes or endnotes in addition to parenthetical citations (p. 604).

1   Writing parenthetical citations

The in-text citations of sources have two requirements:

1. They must include just enough information for the reader to locate the appropriate source in your list of works cited.
2. They must include just enough information for the reader to locate the place in the source where the borrowed material appears.

Usually, you can meet both these requirements by providing the author's last name and the page(s) in the source on which the material appears. The reader can find the source in your list of works

Index to MLA parenthetical citations

cited and find the borrowed material in the source itself. Refer to the index above to find the form of reference for the kind of source and citation you are using.

1. Author not named in the text

When you have not already named the author in your sentence, provide the author's last name and the page number(s), with no punctuation between them, in parentheses.

```
One researcher concludes that "women impose a distinctive

construction on moral problems, seeing moral dilemmas in

terms of conflicting responsibilities" (Gilligan 105).
```

2. Author named in the text

If the author's name is already given in your text, you need not repeat it in the parenthetical citation. The citation gives just the page number(s).

```
One researcher, Carol Gilligan, concludes that "women

impose a distinctive construction on moral problems,

seeing moral dilemmas in terms of conflicting responsi-

bilities" (105).
```

3. A work with two or three authors

If the source has two or three authors, give all their names in the text or in the citation:

MLA
37a

```
As Frieden and Sagalyn observe, "The poor and the minor-

ities were the leading victims of highway and renewal

programs" (29).
```

```
According to one study, "The poor and the minorities were

the leading victims of highway and renewal programs"

(Frieden and Sagalyn 29).
```

4. A work with more than three authors

If the source has more than three authors, you may list all their last names or use only the first author's name followed by "et al." (the abbreviation for the Latin "and others"). The choice depends on what you do in your list of works cited (see p. 608).

```
It took the combined forces of the Americans, Europeans,

and Japanese to break the rebel siege of Peking in 1900

(Lopez et al. 362).
```

```
It took the combined forces of the Americans, Europeans,

and Japanese to break the rebel siege of Peking in 1900

(Lopez, Blum, Cameron, and Barnes 362).
```

5. An entire work (no page numbers)

When you cite an entire work rather than a part of it, the reference will not include any page number. If the author's name appears in the text, no parenthetical reference is needed. But remember that the source must appear in the list of works cited.

```
Boyd deals with the need to acknowledge and come to terms

with our fear of nuclear technology.
```

6. A multivolume work

If you consulted only one volume of a multivolume work, your list of works cited will indicate as much (see p. 610), and you can treat the volume as any book.

```
After issuing the Emancipation Proclamation, Lincoln said,

"What I did, I did after very full deliberations, and
```

```
under a very heavy and solemn sense of responsibility"

(5: 438).
```

The number 5 indicates the volume from which the quotation was taken; the number 438 indicates the page number in that volume. If you are referring generally to an entire volume of a multivolume work and are not citing specific page numbers, add the abbreviation "vol." before the volume number, as in "(vol. 5)." Then readers will not misinterpret the volume number as a page number.

7. A work by an author of two or more works

If your list of works cited includes two or more works by the same author, then your citation must tell the reader which of the author's works you are referring to. Use the appropriate title or a shortened version of it in the parenthetical citation.

```
At about age seven, most children begin to use appropriate

gestures to reinforce their stories (Gardner, Arts 144-

45).
```

The title *Arts* is shortened from Gardner's full title, *The Arts and Human Development* (see the works-cited entry for this book on p. 608). Often, as here, the first main word in the title is enough to direct the reader to the appropriate source.

8. An unsigned work

Anonymous works are alphabetized by title in the list of works cited. In the text they are referred to by full or shortened title.

```
One article notes that a death-row inmate may demand his

own execution to achieve a fleeting notoriety ("Right").
```

This citation refers to an unsigned article titled "The Right to Die." A page number is unnecessary because the article is no longer than a page (see the entry for the article on p. 615).

9. A government document or a work with a corporate author

If the author of the work is listed as a government body or a corporation, cite the work by that organization's name. If the name is long, work it into the text to avoid an intrusive parenthetical citation.

MLA
37a

```
A 1983 report by the Hawaii Department of Education

predicts a gradual increase in enrollments (6).
```

10. An indirect source

When you quote or paraphrase one source's quotation of someone else, your citation must indicate as much. In the following citation "qtd. in" ("quoted in") says that Davino was quoted by Boyd.

```
George Davino maintains that "even small children have

vivid ideas about nuclear energy" (qtd. in Boyd 22).
```

The list of works cited then includes only Boyd (the work consulted), not Davino.

11. A literary work

Novels, plays, and poems are often available in many editions, so your instructor may ask you to provide information that will help readers find the passage you cite no matter what edition they consult. For novels, the page number comes first, followed by a semicolon and then information on the appropriate part or chapter of the work.

```
Toward the end of James's novel, Maggie suddenly feels

"the thick breath of the definite--which was the intimate,

the immediate, the familiar, as she hadn't had them for so

long" (535; pt. 6, ch. 41).
```

For verse plays and poems, you can omit the page number and instead cite the appropriate part or act (and scene, if any) plus the line number(s). Use Arabic numerals for acts and scenes ("3.4") unless your instructor specifies Roman numerals ("III.iv").

```
Later in King Lear Shakespeare has the disguised Edgar

say, "The prince of darkness is a gentleman" (3.4.147).
```

For prose plays, provide the page number followed by the act and scene, if any (see the reference to *Death of a Salesman* at the top of p. 604).

12. More than one work

If you use a parenthetical citation to refer to more than a single work, separate the references by a semicolon.

MLA
37a

```
Two recent articles point out that a computer badly used

can be less efficient than no computer at all (Richards

162; Gough and Hall 201).
```

Since long citations in the text can distract the reader, you may choose to cite several or more works in an endnote or foot-note rather than in the text. See the next page.

 2   **Placing parenthetical citations**

Generally, place a parenthetical citation at the end of the sentence in which you summarize, paraphrase, or quote a work. The citation should follow a closing quotation mark but precede the sentence punctuation. (See the examples in the previous section.) When a citation pertains to only part of a sentence, place the citation after the borrowed material and at the least intrusive point—usually at the end of a clause.

```
Though Spelling argues that American automobile manufac-

turers "have done the best that could be expected" in

meeting consumer needs (26), not everyone agrees with him.
```

When a citation appears after a quotation that ends in an ellipsis mark (. . .), place the citation between the closing quotation mark and the sentence period.

```
One observer maintains that "American manufacturers must

bear some blame for the current recession . . ." (Rosen-

baum 12).
```

When a citation appears at the end of a quotation set off from the text, place it two spaces *after* the punctuation ending the quotation.

```
In Arthur Miller's Death of a Salesman, the most poignant

defense of Willie Loman comes from his wife, Linda:

        He's not the finest character that ever lived.

        But he's a human being, and a terrible thing is

        happening to him.  So attention must be paid.
```

```
          He's not to be allowed to fall into his grave

          like an old dog.  Attention, attention must

          finally be paid to such a person.  (56; act 1)
```

(This citation of a play includes the act number as well as the page number. See model 11 on p. 602.)

See the two sample research papers starting on pages 632 and 664 for further examples of placing parenthetical references.

3   Using footnotes or endnotes in special circumstances

Occasionally, you may want to use footnotes or endnotes in place of parenthetical citations. If you need to refer to several sources at once, listing them in a long parenthetical citation could be intrusive. In that case, signal the citation with a numeral raised above the appropriate line of text and write a note with the same numeral to cite the sources:

Text   At least five subsequent studies have confirmed

Note   these results.[1]

    [1] Abbott and Winger 266-68; Casner 27;

Hoyenga 78-79; Marino 36; Tripp, Tripp, and Walk

179-83.

You may also use a footnote or endnote to comment on a source or provide information that does not fit easily in the text:

Text   So far, no one has succeeded in confirming these

Note   results.[2]

    [2] Manter reports spending nearly a year try-

ing to replicate the experiment, but he was never

able to produce the high temperatures reported by

the original experimenters (616).

In a note the raised numeral is indented five spaces and followed by a space. If the note appears as a footnote, place it at the bottom of the page on which the citation appears, set it off from the text with quadruple spacing, and single-space the note itself. If the note appears as an endnote, place it in numerical order with the other endnotes on a page between the text and the list of works cited; double-space all the endnotes. (See pp. 658–59 for examples of endnotes and the format to use in typing a page of endnotes.)

Exercise 1
Citing sources in your text

Using the preceding explanations and illustrations as a guide, prepare MLA-style text citations for your own research paper. (If you are instructed or given the option to do so, you may instead prepare citations in the style of the American Psychological Association, p. 693, or the Council of Biology Editors, p. 713.)

37b   Preparing the list of works cited: MLA style

In the documentation style of the *MLA Handbook,* your in-text parenthetical citations (discussed in 37a) refer the reader to complete information on your sources in a list you title "Works Cited" and place at the end of your paper. The list should include all the sources you quoted, paraphrased, or summarized in your paper. (If your instructor asks you to include sources you examined but did not cite, title the list "Works Consulted.")

Before typing the list of works cited, arrange your sources in alphabetical order by the last name of the author. If an author is not given in the source, alphabetize the source by the first main word of the title (excluding *A, An,* or *The*). Type the entire list double-spaced (both within and between entries). Indent the second and subsequent lines of each entry five spaces from the left. For examples of the works-cited format, see the papers by Mark Shannon (p. 660) and Ann Weiss (p. 674).

The index on the next page directs you to the MLA formats for specific kinds of sources you may use. The arrangement, spacing, and punctuation of information are precisely standardized to convey the most information in the least space.

Note: You may have to combine formats for particular sources. For example, to list a work by four authors appearing in a monthly periodical, you will have to draw on model 3 ("A book with more than three authors") and model 23 ("A signed article in a monthly or bimonthly magazine").

Index to MLA works-cited models

Listing books

The basic format for a book includes the following elements:

Gilligan, Carol. In a Different Voice: Psychological

Theory and Women's Development. Cambridge: Harvard

UP, 1982.

1. The author's full name: the last name first, followed by a comma, and then the first name and any middle name or initial. Omit any title or degree attached to the author's name on the source, such as Dr. or Ph.D. End the name with a period and two spaces.
2. The full title of the book, including any subtitle. Underline the complete title, capitalize all important words (see 26b), separate the main title and the subtitle with a colon and one space, and end the title with a period and two spaces.
3. The publication information:
    a. The city of publication, followed by a colon and one space.
    b. The name of the publisher, followed by a comma. Shorten most publishers' names—in many cases to a single word. For instance, use "Knopf" for Alfred A. Knopf and "Little" for Little, Brown. For university presses, use the abbreviation "UP," as in the example above.
    c. The date of publication, ending with a period.

All this information can be found on the title page of the book or on the page after the title page. When other information is required for a reference, it is generally placed either between the author's name and the title or between the title and the publication information, as specified in the models below.

1. A book with one author

Gilligan, Carol. In a Different Voice: Psychological

Theory and Women's Development. Cambridge: Harvard

UP, 1982.

2. A book with two or three authors

Frieden, Bernard J., and Lynne B. Sagalyn. Downtown, Inc.:

How America Rebuilds Cities. Cambridge: MIT, 1989.

MLA
37b

Give the authors' names in the order provided on the title page. Reverse the first and last names of the first author *only,* and separate the authors' names with a comma.

3. A book with more than three authors

Lopez, Robert S., et al. <u>Civilizations: Western and</u>

    <u>World</u>. Boston: Little, 1975.

You may, but need not, give all authors' names if the work has more than three authors. If you choose not to give all names, provide the name of the first author only, and follow the name with a comma and the abbreviation "et al." (for the Latin *et alii,* meaning "and others").

4. Two or more works by the same author

Gardner, Howard. <u>The Arts and Human Development</u>. New

    York: Wiley, 1973.

---. <u>The Quest for Mind: Piaget, Lévi-Strauss, and the</u>

    <u>Structuralist Movement</u>. New York: Knopf, 1973.

Give the author's name only in the first entry. For the second and any subsequent works by the same author, substitute three hyphens for the author's name, followed by a period and two spaces. Within the set of entries for the author, list the sources alphabetically by the first main word of the title. Note that the three hyphens stand for *exactly* the same name or names. If the second source above were by Gardner and somebody else, both names would have to be given in full.

5. A book with an editor

Ruitenbeek, Hendrick, ed. <u>Freud as We Knew Him</u>. Detroit:

    Wayne State UP, 1973

The abbreviation "ed.," separated from the name by a comma, identifies Ruitenbeek as the editor of the work.

6. A book with an author and an editor

Melville, Herman. <u>The Confidence Man: His Masquerade</u>.

    Ed. Hershel Parker. New York: Norton, 1971.

When citing the work of the author, give his or her name first, and give the editor's name after the title, preceded by "Ed." ("Edited by"). When citing the work of the editor, use the form above for a book with an editor, and give the author's name after the title preceded by "By": "Parker, Hershel, ed. The Confidence Man: His Masquerade. By Herman Melville."

7. A translation

Alighieri, Dante. The Inferno. Trans. John Ciardi. New

York: NAL, 1971.

When citing the work of the author, give his or her name first, and give the translator's name after the title, preceded by "Trans." ("Translated by"). When citing the work of the translator, give his or her name first, followed by a comma and "trans.," and after the title give the author's name preceded by "By": Ciardi, John, trans. The Inferno. By Dante Alighieri."

8. A book with a corporate author

Lorenz, Inc. Research in Social Studies Teaching. Balti-

more: Arrow, 1992.

List the name of the corporation, institution, or other body as author.

9. An anonymous book

Webster's Ninth New Collegiate Dictionary. Springfield:

Merriam, 1987.

List the book under its title. Do not use "anonymous" or "anon."

10. A later edition

Bollinger, Dwight L. Aspects of Language. 2nd ed. New

York: Harcourt, 1975.

For any edition after the first, place the edition number between the title and the publication information. Use the appropriate designation for editions that are named or dated rather than numbered—for instance, "Rev. ed." for "Revised edition."

11. A republished book

James, Henry. The Golden Bowl. 1904. London: Penguin,

1966.

MLA
37b

Place the original date of publication (but not the place of publication or the publisher's name) after the title, and then provide the full publication information for the source you are using.

12. A book with a title in its title

Eco, Umberto. <u>Postscript to</u> The Name of the Rose. Trans.

William Weaver. New York: Harcourt, 1983.

When a book's title contains another book title (as here: <u>The Name of the Rose</u>), do not underline the shorter title. When a book's title contains a quotation or the title of a work normally placed in quotation marks, keep the quotation marks and underline both titles: <u>Critical Response to Henry James's "Beast in the Jungle."</u> (Note that the underlining extends under the closing quotation mark.)

13. A work in more than one volume

Lincoln, Abraham. <u>The Collected Works of Abraham Lincoln.</u>

Ed. Roy P. Basler. 8 vols. New Brunswick: Rutgers

UP, 1953.

Lincoln, Abraham. <u>The Collected Works of Abraham Lincoln.</u>

Ed. Roy P. Basler. 8 vols. New Brunswick: Rutgers

UP, 1953. Vol. 5.

For a work published in more than one volume, give the total number of volumes regardless of how many you are using. Use an Arabic numeral and the abbreviation "vols.," and place the information after the title (see "8 vols." in both examples). If you use only one volume, add that information at the very end of the entry (see "Vol. 5" in the second example).

14. A work in a series

Bergman, Ingmar. <u>The Seventh Seal</u>. Modern Film Scripts

Series. New York: Simon, 1968.

Place the name of the series (no quotation marks or underlining) after the title.

15. Published proceedings of a conference

<u>Watching Our Language: A Conference Sponsored by the</u>

MLA
37b

Program in Architecture and Design Criticism. 6-8

May 1991. New York: Parsons School of Design, 1991.

Whether in or after the title of the conference, supply information about who sponsored the conference, when it was held, and who published the proceedings. If you are citing a particular presentation at the conference, treat it as a selection from an anthology or collection (model 16).

16. A selection from an anthology or collection

Auden, W. H. "A Healthy Spot." The Collected Poetry of

W. H. Auden. New York: Random, 1945. 134.

Give the author and the title of the selection you are citing, placing the title in quotation marks and ending it with a period. Then give the title of the anthology. If the anthology has an editor, add the name as in model 6. At the end of the entry give the inclusive page numbers for the entire selection, but do not include the abbreviation "pp."

17. Two or more selections from the same anthology

Brooks, Rosetta. "Streetwise." Martin 38-39.

Martin, Richard, ed. The New Urban Landscape. New York:

Rizzoli, 1990.

Plotkin, Mark J. "Tropical Forests and the Urban Land-

scape." Martin 50-51.

When citing more than one selection from the same source, avoid unnecessary repetition by giving the source in full (as in the Martin entry) and then simply cross-referencing it in entries for the works you used. Thus, instead of full information for the Brooks and Plotkin articles, give Martin's name and the appropriate pages in his book. Note that each entry appears in its proper alphabetical place among other works cited.

18. An article from a collection of reprinted articles

Gibian, George. "Traditional Symbolism in Crime and

Punishment." PMLA 70 (1955): 979-96. Rpt. in

Crime and Punishment. By Feodor Dostoevsky. Ed.

MLA
37b

```
George Gibian.  Norton Critical Editions.  New York:

      Norton, 1964.  575-92.
```

Some collections contain articles reprinted from other sources. For an article from such a collection, provide the author and title of the article, placing the title in quotation marks and ending it with a period. Then, unless your instructor specifies otherwise, provide the complete information for the earlier publication of the piece, followed by "Rpt. in" ("Reprinted in") and the information for the source in which you found the piece. If you are not required to provide the earlier publication information, use model 16.

19. An introduction, preface, foreword, or afterword

```
Donaldson, Norman.  Introduction.  The Claverings.  By

      Anthony Trollope.  New York: Dover, 1977.  vii-xv.
```

An introduction, foreword, or afterword is often written by someone other than the book's author. When citing such a work, give its name without quotation marks or underlining. Follow the title of the book with its author's name preceded by "By." Give the inclusive page numbers of the part you cite. (In the example above, the small Roman numerals indicate that the cited work is in the front matter of the book, before page 1.)

When the author of a preface or introduction is the same as the author of the book, give only the last name after the title:

```
Gould, Stephen Jay.  Prologue.  The Flamingo's Smile:

      Reflections in Natural History.  By Gould.  New York:

      Norton, 1985.  13-20.
```

20. An encyclopedia or almanac

```
"Mammoth."  The New Columbia Encyclopedia.  1975 ed.

Mark, Herman F.  "Polymers."  Encyclopaedia Britannica:

      Macropaedia.  1974.
```

Give the name of an author only when the article is signed; otherwise, give the title first. If the articles are alphabetized in the reference work, you needn't list the editors of the work itself or any page numbers. For familiar sources like those in the examples, provide only the edition number (if there is one) and the year of publication.

2 **Listing periodicals: Journals, magazines, and newspapers**

The basic format for an article from a periodical includes the following information:

① ②
Lever, Janet. "Sex Differences in the Games Children
③
Play." Social Problems 23 (1976): 478-87.
ⓐ   ⓑ ⓒ   ⓓ

1. The author's full name: last name first, followed by a comma, and then the first name and any middle name or initial. Omit any title or degree attached to the author's name on the source, such as Dr. or Ph.D. End the name with a period and two spaces.
2. The full title of the article, including any subtitle. Place the title in quotation marks, capitalize all important words in the title (see 26b), and end the title with a period (inside the final quotation mark) and two spaces.
3. The publication information:
    a. The underlined title of the periodical (minus any *A, An,* or *The* at the beginning).
    b. The volume or issue number (in Arabic numerals). See the note below.
    c. The date of publication, followed by a colon and a space. See the note below.
    d. The inclusive page numbers of the article (without the abbreviation "pp."). For the second number in inclusive page numbers over 100, provide only as many digits as needed for clarity (usually two): 100–01, 1026–36, 1190–206, 398–401.

Note: The treatment of volume and issue numbers and publication dates varies depending on the kind of periodical being cited, as the models indicate. For the distinction between journals and magazines, see page 553.

21. A signed article in a journal with continuous pagination throughout the annual volume

Lever, Janet. "Sex Differences in the Games Children

    Play." Social Problems 23 (1976): 478-87.

Some journals number the pages of issues consecutively through-out a year, so that each issue after the first in a year begins num-bering where the previous issue left off—say, at page 132 or 416. For this kind of journal, give the volume number after the title ("23" in the example above) and place the year of publication in parentheses. The page numbers will be enough to guide readers to the appropriate issue.

22. A signed article in a journal that pages issues separately or that numbers only issues, not volumes

```
Boyd, Sarah.   "Nuclear Terror."   Adaptation to Change 7.4

     (1981): 20-23.
```

Some journals page each issue separately (starting each issue at page 1). For these journals, use model 21, but give the volume number, a period, and the issue number (as in "7.4" in the Boyd entry). Then readers know which issue of the periodical to con-sult. When citing an article in a journal that numbers only issues, not annual volumes, treat the issue number as if it were a volume number, as in model 21.

23. A signed article in a monthly or bimonthly magazine

```
Stein, Harry.   "Living with Lies."   Esquire Dec. 1981: 23.
```

Follow the periodical title with the month (abbreviated) and the year of publication. Don't place the date in parentheses, and don't provide a volume or issue number.

24. A signed article in a weekly or biweekly magazine

```
Stevens, Mark.   "Low and Behold."   New Republic 24 Dec.

     1990: 27-33.
```

Follow the periodical title with the day, the month (abbreviated), and the year of publication. Don't place the date in parentheses, and don't provide a volume or issue number.

25. A signed article in a daily newspaper

```
Gargan, Edward A.   "Buffalo Concern Gives Pop Sound to

     Player Pianos."   New York Times 16 Feb. 1984: B1.
```

Give the name of the newspaper as it appears on the first page (but without *A, An,* or *The*). Then follow model 24, with one difference if the newspaper is divided into lettered or numbered sections, with each section paged separately. In that case, provide the section designation before the page number when the newspaper does the same (as in "B1" above), or provide the section designation before the colon when the newspaper does not combine the two in its numbering (as in "sec. 1: 1+" below).

26. An unsigned article

"The Right to Die." <u>Time</u> 11 Oct. 1976: 101.

"Protests Greet Pope in Holland." <u>Boston Sunday Globe</u> 12

    May 1985, sec. 1: 1+.

Begin the entry for an unsigned article with the title of the article. The page number "1+" indicates that the article does not run on consecutive pages but starts on page 1 and continues later in the issue.

27. An editorial or letter to the editor

"Bodily Intrusions." Editorial. <u>New York Times</u> 29 Aug.

    1990: A20.

Don't use quotation marks or underlining for the word "Editorial." For a signed editorial, give the author's name first.

Dowding, Michael. Letter. <u>Economist</u> 5-11 Jan. 1985: 4.

Don't use quotation marks or underlining for the word "Letter."

28. A review

Dunne, John Gregory. "The Secret of Danny Santiago."

    Rev. of <u>Famous All over Town</u>, by Danny Santiago. <u>New</u>

    <u>York Review of Books</u> 16 Aug. 1984: 17-27.

"Rev." is an abbreviation for "Review." The name of the author of the work being reviewed follows the title of the work, a comma, and "by." If the review has no title of its own, then "Rev. of . . ." (without quotation marks) immediately follows the name of the reviewer.

29. An abstract of a dissertation

Steciw, Steven K. "Alterations to the Pessac Project of

MLA
37b

```
Le Corbusier."  DAI 46 (1986): 565C.  Cambridge U,

England.
```

For an abstract appearing in *Dissertation Abstracts* (*DA*) or *Dissertation Abstracts International* (*DAI*), give the author's name and the title as for any article. Then give publication information for the source and the name of the institution granting the author's degree.

3 Listing other sources

30. A government document

```
Hawaii.  Dept. of Education.  Kauai District Schools,

      Profile 1983-84.  Honolulu: Hawaii Dept. of

      Education, 1983.

United States.  Cong.  House.  Committee on Ways and

      Means.  Medicare Payment for Outpatient Occupational

      Therapy Services.  102nd Cong., 1st sess.  Washing-

      ton: GPO, 1991.
```

Unless an author is listed for a government document, give the appropriate agency as author. Provide information in the order illustrated, separating elements with a period and two spaces: the name of the government, the name of the agency (which may be abbreviated), and the title and publication information. For a Congressional document (second example), the house and committee involved are given before the title, and the number and session of Congress are given after the title. In the second example, "GPO" stands for the U.S. Government Printing Office.

31. A pamphlet

```
Resource Notebook.  Washington: Project on Institutional

      Renewal Through the Improvement of Teaching, 1976.
```

Most pamphlets can be treated as books. In the example above, the pamphlet has no listed author, so the title comes first. If the pamphlet has an author, list his or her name first, followed by the title and publication information as given here.

32. An unpublished dissertation or thesis

```
Wilson, Stuart M.   "John Stuart Mill as a Literary

    Critic."  Diss.  U of Michigan, 1970.
```

The title is quoted rather than underlined. "Diss." stands for "Dissertation." "U of Michigan" is the institution that granted the author's degree.

33. A musical composition or work of art

```
Mozart, Wolfgang Amadeus.  Piano Concerto no. 20 in D

    Minor, K. 466.
```

Don't underline musical compositions identified only by form, number, and key. Do underline titled operas, ballets, and compositions (Carmen, Sleeping Beauty).

```
Sargent, John Singer.  Venetian Doorway.  Metropolitan

    Museum of Art, New York.
```

Underline the title of a work of art. Include the name and location of the institution housing the work.

34. A film or videotape

```
Allen, Woody, dir.  Manhattan.  With Allen, Diane Keaton,

    Michael Murphy, Meryl Streep, and Anne Byrne.  United

    Artists, 1979.
```

Start with the name of the individual whose work you are citing. (If you are citing the work as a whole, start with the title, as in the next model.) Give additional information (writer, lead actors, and so on) as seems appropriate. For a film, end with the film's distributor and date.

```
Serenade.  Videotape.  Chor. George Balanchine.  With San

    Francisco Ballet.  Dir. Hilary Bean.  San Francisco

    Ballet, 1987.  24 min.
```

For a videotape, filmstrip, or slide program, include the name of the medium after the title, without underlining or quotation marks. Add the running time to the end.

MLA
37b

35. A television or radio program

King of America. Writ. B. J. Merholz. Music Elizabeth

Swados. With Larry Atlas, Andreas Katsulas, Barry

Miller, and Michael Walden. American Playhouse.

PBS. WNET, New York. 19 Jan. 1982.

As in the models above, start with the title of the program or the name of the individual whose work you are citing, and provide other participants' names as seems appropriate. Also give the series title (if any), the broadcasting network (if any), and the local station, city, and date.

36. A performance

The English Only Restaurant. By Silvio Martinez Palau.

Dir. Susana Tubert. Puerto Rico Traveling Theater,

New York. 27 July 1990.

Ozawa, Seiji, cond. Boston Symphony Orch. Concert.

Symphony Hall, Boston. 25 Apr. 1991.

As with films and television programs, place the title first unless you are citing the work of an individual (second example). Provide additional information about participants after the title, as well as the theater, city, and date. Note that the orchestra concert in the second example is neither quoted nor underlined.

37. A recording

Mitchell, Joni. For the Roses. Asylum, SD 5057, 1972.

Brahms, Johannes. Concerto no. 2 in B-flat, op. 83.

Perf. Artur Rubinstein. Cond. Eugene Ormandy.

Philadelphia Orch. RCA, RK-1243, 1972.

Begin with the name of the individual whose work you are citing. Then provide the title of the recording (first example) or the title of the work recorded (second example), the names of any artists not already listed, the manufacturer of the recording, the catalog number, and the date.

38. A letter

Buttolph, Mrs. Laura E. Letter to Rev. and Mrs. C. C.

MLA
37b

> Jones. 20 June 1857. In <u>The Children of Pride: A</u>
>
> <u>True Story of Georgia and the Civil War</u>. Ed. Robert
>
> Manson Myers. New Haven: Yale UP, 1972. 334-35.

A published letter is listed under the writer's name. Specify that the source is a letter and to whom it was addressed, and give the date on which it was written. The remaining information is treated like that for an edited book. (See also model 27, p. 615, for the format of a letter to the editor of a periodical.)

> James, Jonathan E. Letter to his sister. 16 Apr. 1970.
>
> Jonathan E. James Papers. South Dakota State
>
> Archive, Pierre.

For a letter in the collection of a library or archive, specify the writer, recipient, and date, as above, and give the name and location of the archive as well.

> Packer, Ann E. Letter to the author. 15 June 1988.

For a letter you receive, give the name of the writer, note the fact that the letter was sent to you, and provide the date of the letter.

39. A lecture or address

> Carlone, Dennis J. "Urban Design in the 1990s." Sixth
>
> Symposium on Urban Issues. City of Cambridge.
>
> Cambridge, 16 Oct. 1988.

Give the speaker's name, the title if known (in quotation marks), the title of the meeting, the name of the sponsoring organization, the location of the lecture, and the date. If you do not know the title, replace it with "Lecture" or "Address" but *not* in quotation marks.

40. An interview

> Graaf, Vera. Personal interview. 19 Dec. 1990.
>
> Martin, William. Interview. "Give Me That Big Time
>
> Religion." <u>Frontline</u>. PBS. WGBH, Boston. 13 Feb.
>
> 1984.

Begin with the name of the person interviewed. Then specify "Personal interview" (if you conducted the interview in person), "Telephone interview" (if you conducted the interview over the phone), or "Interview" (if you did not conduct the interview)—without quotation marks or underlining. Finally, provide a date (first example) or provide other bibliographic information and then a date (second example).

41. A map or other illustration

Women in the Armed Forces. Map. Women in the World: An

   International Atlas. By Joni Seager and Ann Olson.

New York: Touchstone, 1986. 44-45.

List the illustration by its title (underlined). Provide a descriptive label ("Map," "Chart," "Table"), without underlining or quotation marks, and the publication information. If the creator of the illustration is credited in the source, put his or her name first in the entry, as with any author.

42. An information or computer service

Jolson, Maria K. Music Education for Preschoolers. ERIC,

   1981. ED 264 488.

Palfry, Andrew. "Choice of Mates in Identical Twins."

   Modern Psychology Jan. 1979: 16-27. DIALOG file

   261, item 5206341.

A source you get from an information or computer service should be treated like a book or a periodical article, as appropriate, with the author's name and then the title. If the source has not been published before, simply name the service (ERIC in the Jolson entry above), and give the year of release and the service's identifying number. If the source has been published before, give full publication information and then the name of the service and its identifying numbers, as in the Palfry entry.

43. Computer software

Project Scheduler 6000. Computer software. Scitor, 1991.

   MS-DOS, 256 KB, disk.

Include the title of the software, the name of the writer (if known), the name of the distributor, and the date. As in this example, you may also provide information about the computer or operating system for which the software is designed, the amount of computer memory it requires, and its format.

Exercise 2
Writing works-cited entries

Prepare works-cited entries from the following information. Follow the models of the *MLA Handbook* given above unless your instructor specifies a different style.

1. A book called *Black Voices: An Anthology of Afro-American Literature,* published in 1968 by the New American Library in New York, edited by Abraham Clapham.
2. An article in *Southern Folklore Quarterly,* volume 24, published in 1960. The article is "The New Orleans Voodoo Ritual Dance and Its Twentieth-Century Survivals," written by John Q. Anderson, on pages 135 through 143. The journal is paged continuously throughout the annual volume.
3. The fifth volume of the five-volume *The History of Technology,* published in 1958 in London by Oxford University Press, written by Charles Singer, E. J. Holmroyd, A. R. Hall, and Trevor I. Williams.
4. A pamphlet entitled *Italian Art, 1900–1945,* published in 1989 by Gruppo Editoriale in Milan, Italy.
5. A book by John Bartlett called *Familiar Quotations,* in its fifteenth edition, which was edited by Emily Morison Beck, published in 1980 by Little, Brown and Company in Boston, Massachusetts.

Exercise 3
Preparing your list of works cited

Prepare the final list of works cited for your research paper. Unless your instructor specifies otherwise, follow MLA style, using the models on the preceding pages.

ANSWERS: EXERCISE 2

The citations below are in MLA style:

1. Clapham, Abraham, ed. Black Voices: An Anthology of Afro-American Literature. New York: New American [*or* NAL], 1968.
2. Anderson, John Q. "The New Orleans Voodoo Ritual Dance and Its Twentieth-Century Survivals." Southern Folklore Quarterly 24 (1960): 135–43.
3. Singer, Charles, et al. The History of Technology. 5 vols. London: Oxford UP, 1958. Vol. 5.
4. Italian Art, 1900–1945. Milan: Gruppo Editoriale, 1989.
5. Bartlett, John. Familiar Quotations. 15th ed. Ed. Emily Morison Beck. Boston: Little, 1980.

ANSWERS: EXERCISE 3

Individual response.

37c Using footnotes or endnotes to document sources

Several disciplines in the arts and humanities use a system of footnotes or endnotes to cite sources. Until 1984, this was also the style recommended by the *MLA Handbook,* and the guide continues to explain and illustrate the formats for those who need to use them.

37c

When you document sources with notes (either footnotes or endnotes), you place a raised numeral (such as [1]) in the text at the end of the material you are acknowledging, and you number the citations consecutively throughout the paper. The notes themselves then fall in the same order. Footnotes are placed at the bottoms of appropriate pages; endnotes are collected on separate pages between the end of the paper and the list of works cited.

Here is a passage from Mark Shannon's paper showing the use of note numbers in the text.

> In a 1983 test of people's reactions to videotapes of male and female leaders, the psychologists Virginia Brown and Florence Geis found that "[a]lthough both leaders used the same script, the woman was faulted more than the man for being too dominating, cold, and insensitive."[6] Such results reveal that while sex-role stereotyping may not be as obvious as it was in a 1972 study,[7] it remains pervasive in our society.

For footnotes, begin the first entry four lines below the last line of text (two double spaces), single-space each footnote, and double-space between notes. For endnotes, double-space within and between notes, as in the following sample:

> [6] Virginia Brown and Florence Geis, "Turning Lead into Gold: Evaluations of Women and Men Leaders and the Alchemy of Social Consensus," Journal of Personality and Social Psychology 46 (1984): 822.
>
> [7] I. K. Broverman et al., "Sex-Role Stereotypes: A Current Appraisal," Journal of Social Issues 28.2 (1972): 59-78.

See pages 658–59 for the heading, spacing, and other elements of a page of endnotes.

The format for a note differs from that for an entry in the list of works cited.

37c

List of works cited

Gilligan, Carol. In a Different Voice: Psychological

    Theory and Women's Development. Cambridge: Harvard

    UP, 1982.

Note

    [1] Carol Gilligan, In a Different Voice: Psycho-

logical Theory and Women's Development (Cambridge:

Harvard UP, 1982) 27.

In the works-cited entry you start the first line at the left margin and indent the second and subsequent lines five spaces; but in the note you indent the first line and not the others. The note is intended to be read as a sentence, so a period appears only at the end while the body of the note is punctuated with commas and colons. In the note, unlike the works-cited entry, you enclose the publication information (place of publication, publisher, date of publication) in parentheses. Whereas you start the works-cited entry with the author's last name (to make it easier to find the name in an alphabetical listing), in the note you give the author's name in normal order. And in the note you include the specific page number(s) in the source from which the summary, paraphrase, or quotation is taken (but without "p." or "pp.").

The following note models are for first reference to a source. When you acknowledge the same source more than once in the same paper, you should use the shortened form of reference given on pages 628–29.

Note: For convenience, the raised number for each model below matches the number assigned the equivalent model in the works-cited discussion on pages 606–21. By tracing the note number back to the works-cited model, you can find an explanation of the information required for each kind of source.

Books

A book with one author

    [1] Carol Gilligan, In a Different Voice: Psycho-

logical Theory and Women's Development (Cambridge:

Harvard UP, 1982) 27.

37c

A book with two or three authors

[2] Bernard J. Frieden and Lynne B. Sagalyn, Downtown, Inc.: How America Rebuilds Cities (Cambridge: MIT, 1989) 16.

A book with more than three authors

[3] Robert S. Lopez et al., Civilizations: Western and World (Boston: Little, 1975) 281-82.

A book with an editor

[5] Hendrick Ruitenbeek, ed., Freud as We Knew Him (Detroit: Wayne State UP, 1973) 64.

A book with an author and an editor

[6] Herman Melville, The Confidence Man: His Masquerade, ed. Hershel Parker (New York: Norton, 1971) 49.

A translation

[7] Dante Alighieri, The Inferno, trans. John Ciardi (New York: NAL, 1971) 73-74.

An anonymous book

[9] Webster's Ninth New Collegiate Dictionary (Springfield: Merriam, 1987).

A later edition

[10] Dwight L. Bollinger, Aspects of Language, 2nd ed. (New York: Harcourt, 1975) 20.

A work in more than one volume

[13] Abraham Lincoln, The Collected Works of Abraham Lincoln, ed. Roy P. Basler, 8 vols. (New Brunswick: Rutgers UP, 1953) 5: 426-28.

37c

A selection from an anthology

[16] W. H. Auden, "A Healthy Spot," The Collected Poetry of W. H. Auden (New York: Random, 1945) 134.

An introduction, preface, foreword, or afterword

[19] Norman Donaldson, introduction, The Claverings, by Anthony Trollope (New York: Dover, 1977) viii.

An encyclopedia or almanac

[20] "Mammoth," The New Columbia Encyclopedia, 1975 ed.

Periodicals: journals, magazines, and newspapers

A signed article in a journal with continuous pagination throughout the annual volume

[21] Janet Lever, "Sex Differences in the Games Children Play," Social Problems 23 (1976): 482.

A signed article in a journal that pages issues separately or that numbers only issues, not volumes

[22] Sarah Boyd, "Nuclear Terror," Adaptation to Change 7.4 (1981): 20-21.

A signed article in a monthly or bimonthly magazine

[23] Harry Stein, "Living with Lies," Esquire Dec. 1981: 23.

A signed article in a weekly or biweekly magazine

[24] Mark Stevens, "Low and Behold," New Republic 24 Dec. 1990: 28.

A signed article in a daily newspaper

[25] Edward A. Gargan, "Buffalo Concern Gives Pop Sound to Player Pianos," New York Times 16 Feb. 1984: B1.

37c

An unsigned article

26 "The Right to Die," Time 11 Oct. 1976: 101.

An editorial or letter to the editor

27 "Bodily Intrusions," editorial, New York Times

29 Aug. 1990: A20.

A review

28 John Gregory Dunne, "The Secret of Danny

Santiago," rev. of Famous All over Town, by Danny

Santiago, New York Review of Books 16 Aug. 1984: 20.

An abstract of a dissertation

29 Steven K. Steciw, "Alterations to the Pessac

Project of Le Corbusier," DAI 46 (1986): 565C (Cambridge

U, England).

Other sources

A government document

30 United States, Cong., House, Committee on Ways and

Means, Medicare Payment for Outpatient Occupational

Therapy Services, 102nd Cong., 1st sess. (Washington:

GPO, 1991) 3.

A musical composition or work of art

33 Wolfgang Amadeus Mozart, Piano Concerto no. 21 in D

Minor, K. 466.

33 John Singer Sargent, Venetian Doorway, Metropolitan

Museum of Art, New York.

A film or videotape

34 Woody Allen, dir., Manhattan, with Allen, Diane

Keaton, Michael Murphy, Meryl Streep, and Anne Byrne,
United Artists, 1979.

[34] Serenade, videotape, chor. George Balanchine, with
San Francisco Ballet, dir. Hilary Bean, San Francisco
Ballet, 1987.

A television or radio program

[35] King of America, writ. B. J. Merholz, music
Elizabeth Swados, with Larry Atlas, Andreas Katsulas,
Barry Miller, and Michael Walden, American Playhouse, PBS,
WNET, New York, 19 Jan. 1982.

A performance

[36] The English Only Restaurant, by Silvio Martinez
Palau, dir. Susana Tubert, Puerto Rico Traveling Theater,
New York, 27 July 1990.

[36] Seiji Ozawa, cond., Boston Symphony Orch. Concert,
Symphony Hall, Boston, 25 Apr. 1991.

A recording

[37] Joni Mitchell, For the Roses, Asylum, SD 5057,
1972.

[37] Johannes Brahms, Concerto no. 2 in B-flat, op. 83,
perf. Artur Rubinstein, cond. Eugene Ormandy, Philadelphia
Orch., RCA, RK-1243, 1972.

A letter

[38] Mrs. Laura E. Buttolph, letter to Rev. and Mrs. C.
C. Jones, 20 June 1857, in The Children of Pride: A True
Story of Georgia and the Civil War, ed. Robert Manson
Myers (New Haven: Yale UP, 1972) 334.

[38] Ann E. Packer, letter to the author, 15 June 1988.

37c

An interview

⁴⁰ Vera Graaf, personal interview, 19 Dec. 1990.

An information or computer service

⁴² Maria K. Jolson, Music Education for Preschoolers (ERIC, 1981) 16 (ED 264 488).

⁴² Andrew Palfry, "Choice of Mates in Identical Twins," Modern Psychology Jan. 1979: 19 (DIALOG file 261, item 5206341).

Computer software

⁴³ Project Scheduler 6000, computer software, Scitor, 1991, MS-DOS, 256 KB, disk.

Subsequent references to the same source

To minimize clutter in notes and to give readers a quick sense of how often you acknowledge a source, you should use a shortened form for subsequent references to a source you have already cited fully. When you refer to only one source by the author cited (or only one source bearing the title cited if there is no author), the *MLA Handbook* recommends that subsequent references carry only the author's name (or a short form of the title) and the page reference appropriate for the later citation. Here are two examples, preceded by the full citations.

⁶ Herman Melville, The Confidence Man: His Masquerade, ed. Hershel Parker (New York: Norton, 1971) 49.

⁴⁴ Melville 62.

²⁶ "The Right to Die," Time 11 Oct. 1976: 101.

⁴⁵ "Right" 101.

However, if two of your sources are by the same author, give a shortened form of the appropriate title so there can be no confusion about which work you are citing. For example:

¹ Carol Gilligan, In a Different Voice: Psycho-

logical Theory and Women's Development (Cambridge:

Harvard UP, 1982) 27.

[46] Carol Gilligan, "Moral Development in the College

Years," The Modern American College, ed. A. Chickering

(San Francisco: Jossey-Bass, 1981) 286.

[47] Gilligan, "Moral" 288.

Note: The *MLA Handbook* discourages use of the Latin abbreviation "ibid." (in the same place) as a means of indicating that a citation refers to the source in the preceding note.

37d Understanding abbreviations

Most disciplines' documentation styles, including that of the MLA, use as few abbreviations as possible. However, they still use some, and you may encounter many more in your reading. The most common abbreviations found in source citations appear below.

anon.	anonymous
bk., bks.	book(s)
c., ca.	*circa* ("about"), used with approximate dates
cf.	*confer* ("compare")
ch., chs.	chapter(s)
col., cols.	column(s)
comp., comps.	compiled by, compiler(s)
diss.	dissertation
ed., eds.	edited by, edition(s), editor(s)
et al.	*et alii* ("and others")
ff.	and the following pages, as in pages 17 ff.
ibid.	*ibidem* ("in the same place")
illus.	illustrated by, illustrator, illustration(s)
l., ll.	line(s)
loc. cit.	*loco citato* ("in the place cited")
ms., mss.	manuscript(s)
n., nn.	note(s), as in p. 24, n. 2
n.d.	no date (of publication)
no., nos.	number(s)
n.p.	no place (of publication), no publisher
n. pag.	no pagination

37d

op. cit.	*opere citato* ("in the work cited")
P	Press (UP = University Press)
p., pp.	page(s)
passim	throughout
q.v.	*quod vide* ("which see")
rev.	revised, revision, revised by, review
rpt.	reprint, reprinted
sec.	section
supp., supps.	supplement(s)
trans.	translator, translated by
univ., U	university (UP = University Press)
vol., vols.	volume(s)

37d

Chapter 38

Two Sample Research Papers

HIGHLIGHTS

This chapter contains the finished research papers of Mark Shannon and Ann Weiss, presented as papers-in-progress throughout Chapters 35–36. Though the papers and the marginal comments on them are largely self-explanatory, you may wish to (1) discuss them at length in class or (2) use parts of them as examples to reinforce a lesson or to set a goal for your students' writing.

The following pages show the research papers of Mark Shannon and Ann Weiss, whose work we followed in Chapters 35 and 36. (Shannon's paper begins on the next page, Weiss's on p. 664.) Both students used the documentation style recommended by the *MLA Handbook,* and both typed their papers following the advice on manuscript format in Appendix A of this handbook. Facing each page of Shannon's paper are comments, keyed by number, that explain the format of his manuscript and some of the decisions he made in moving from research to writing. Comments in the margins of Weiss's paper note the distinctive features of her analysis.

Breaking the Glass Ceiling   1

By

Mark Shannon

English 101, Section B

Ms. C. Mahoney

May 28, 1991

MLA
38

1. **Title page format.** Provide a separate title page if your instructor requests it or if you are required to submit an outline with your paper. On his title page Shannon includes the title of his paper about a third of the way down the page, his own name (preceded by "By") about an inch below the title, and, starting about an inch below his name, some identifying information requested by his instructor (course number, section label, and instructor's name) and the date. He centers all lines in the width of the page and separates them from each other with at least one line of space. If your instructor does not require a title page for your paper, place your name, the identifying information, and the date on the first page of the paper. See Ann Weiss's paper (p. 664) for this alternative format.

Next two pages

2. **Outline format.** If your instructor asks you to include your final outline, place it between the title page and the text, as Shannon does on the following pages. Number the pages with small Roman numerals (i, ii), and place your name just before the page numbers in case the pages of your paper become separated. Place the heading "Outline" an inch from the top of the first page, and double-space under the heading.

3. **Outline content.** Shannon includes his final thesis sentence as part of his outline so that his instructor can see how the parts relate to the whole.

4. Shannon casts his final outline in full sentences. Some instructors request topic outlines, in which ideas appear in phrases instead of in sentences and do not end with periods.

5. Notice that each main division (numbered with Roman numerals) relates to the thesis sentence and that all the subdivisions relate to their main division.

MLA
38

Shannon i

Outline   2

Thesis sentence: If women are ever to break   3
through the glass ceiling in significant numbers,
business attitudes will have to change, particularly the definition of successful management
styles.

I. Women face resistance from both men and   4
    women in top management.

    A. Women are in a double bind: they are
        expected to act like men, but are
        criticized when they do.

    B. Women also face resistance from "queen
        bees," other women who are already
        executives.

        1. Queen bees feel that younger women
            should not have it any easier than
            they did.

        2. Queen bees interfere with working
            conditions, morale, and promotions.

II. Business favors a masculine management style   5
    over a feminine style.

    A. A masculine management style is charac-
        terized by a militaristic atmosphere
        that fosters competition.

Shannon ii

B.   Women are not given the option to exercise their own style.

C.   When women imitate men, they are subject to sex-role stereotyping and alienation.

    1.   Brown and Geis found stereotyping in their study.

    2.   Woman executives pass around a humorous list of characteristics of businessmen versus businesswomen.

    3.   Loden says that women are less effective when they imitate men.

III.   A feminine management style must be accommodated in business if women are to make it into top management.

A.   An interview with a female manager illustrates a feminine style of cooperation and participation.

B.   Powell emphasizes that an androgynous management style takes account of both tasks and emotions.

C.   An androgynous style of management will help not only women but business itself.

MLA
38

Shannon 1

Breaking the Glass Ceiling   **6**

"You've come a long way, baby." Most people   **7**
will recognize this slogan from popular cigarette
advertisements, but its meaning goes beyond
women's freedom to smoke in public. Nowhere are
women's gains more clear than in the business
world. The Civil Rights Act of 1964 made it   **8**
illegal to discriminate against women in employment. Twenty years later, women had established
themselves firmly in corporations on a number of
management levels. Their progress can be
measured by what is expected of companies with
regard to their treatment of women employees.
According to Business Week's Irene Pave,   **9**

> Back in 1966 the mark of a good company   **10**
> [for women to work in] was women in at   **11**
> least entry-level management and other
> non-clerical jobs. In 1976 it was
> women in middle management. Today a
> good company has women above that level
> or in jobs that have remained male turf
> in most companies. (75)   **12**

Clearly, women have come far in business.
But have they come far enough? The fact is,

6. **Title.** Shannon has chosen an intriguing title, just ambiguous enough to make his audience want to read further. A more descriptive title, such as "Why Women Are Still Rare in Top Corporate Management," would also have been appropriate but less interesting. **Paper format.** The margins of the paper are one inch all around. The title appears on the first page of the paper even if a title page is used. The title is typed an inch from the top of the page, with no quotation marks or underlining. The first line of text is typed two lines (double space) below the title. (See Ann Weiss's paper, p. 664, for the format of the first page when a title page is not required.)

7. **Introduction.** Shannon begins with a familiar sentence that calls to mind the strides women have made in the past century. He delays presenting his thesis (next page of paper) in order to establish some background: women have indeed made inroads into some levels of management (this paragraph), yet not into the highest levels (next paragraph). The question opening the second paragraph (bottom of this page) sets up the thesis at the end of the paragraph.

8. **Common knowledge.** Shannon did not know about the Civil Rights Act before he began his research, but he found it referred to without documentation in a number of sources. When he realized that it was considered common knowledge, he chose, correctly, not to document it. (See 36c for further discussion of common knowledge.)

9. **Introducing quotations.** Here and elsewhere, Shannon effectively introduces his quotations: he establishes the credentials of each source in an identifying phrase; and he summarizes each source's point of view. (For more examples, see p. 640. See 36g for a discussion of introducing quotations.)

10. **Format of long quotations.** The Pave quotation exceeds four typed lines, so Shannon sets it off from the text. Such a displayed quotation is set off by double-spacing above and below, is itself double-spaced, and is indented ten spaces from the left margin.

11. **Adding to quotations.** Shannon inserts a clarifying phrase so that readers will understand what Pave means by a "good company." The brackets tell the reader that the phrase is added (see 25d).

12. **Citation when the author is named in the text.** Shannon has already mentioned Pave's name in the text, so he does not repeat it in the citation. **Citation with displayed quotation.** The parenthetical citation after the quotation falls *outside* the sentence period and is separated from the period by two spaces.

MLA
38

women are still rare in the highest executive
positions, representing only about 2 percent of
the top executives in Fortune 500 companies in
1990 (Solomon 96). Pave notes that "no one cites   **13**
'equal numbers of men and women in top management   **14**
positions' as the mark of a good company for
women. No company would qualify" (76). Despite
women's persistence, a "glass ceiling," or invisible barrier, continues to separate women in
middle and upper management from positions in top
management.[1] If women are ever to break through   **15**
the glass ceiling in significant numbers, business attitudes will have to change, particularly
the definition of successful management styles.

    Most experts agree that the main reason   **16**
women have not broken through the glass ceiling
is, quite simply, that they are women. Often
these women find themselves in a double bind. On   **17**
the one hand, they face resistance from male
executives who want their successors to be just
like themselves and who therefore will not consider women for top-management positions (Pave
78). On the other hand, resistance sometimes

13. **Paraphrasing.** Shannon paraphrases Solomon because it is the statistic rather than the author's presentation of it that is important. For other instances of paraphrasing, see the bottom of this page and pages 6 and 7 of the paper. **Citation when the author is not named in the text.** Because Shannon has not used Solomon's name in the text, he provides it in the citation.

14. **Quotation within a quotation.** Since he must enclose Pave's words in double quotation marks, Shannon encloses her quotation in single quotation marks (see 24b).

15. **Using an endnote for supplementary information.** Here Shannon helps his readers by briefly defining a key term, "glass ceiling." He provides additional information about the term in a note at the end of the paper. (See p. 658.)

16. **Relation to outline.** This paragraph begins part I of Shannon's outline (see p. 634). Part II begins on page 5 of the paper and part III on page 8.

17. **Paraphrase.** Shannon paraphrases part of a quotation from Pave. His notecard follows.

> <u>Sexual stereotypes</u>
>
> Pave, p. 78
>
> "Male chauvinism is most crippling to women at the great divide between upper and top management. Senior managers who always pick men for top spots want clones... — so women always get locked out."

Citing a paraphrase. Shannon includes Pave's name in the citation (bottom of the page) because it is not used in the text. In contrast, the citation of Schwartz later in the paragraph does *not* include the name because the text *does*.

MLA
38

Shannon 3

comes from men who do not want to see women acting the role of executive. According to Felice
Schwartz, the founder and president of Catalyst,
a firm that conducts research on corporate women,
"It goes against the grain of most senior executives to encourage and welcome the women, so
unlike their wives, who put career before mar-
riage and rearing children" (185). Thus some   18
women are held back if they behave too much like
women, while others are held back because they
behave too much like men.

   As if these two problems were not enough,
women also encounter resistance from the few
women who have made it to the top. These successful women should be acting as mentors for
those coming up behind them, serving as role   19
models and providing guidance. Instead, many do
just the opposite. David Mathison, an associate
professor of business administration at Loyola
Marymount University, identifies the "queen bee
syndrome": a successful woman feels threatened
by the success of other women and resists them as
"intrusions" into her territory (qtd. in Bozzi).   20

18. **Interpreting sources.** In this summary sentence Shannon pulls together information from the two sources cited earlier in the paragraph and shows how the information relates to his point about the double bind women are in. Thus he does not force his readers to guess why he paraphrases and quotes sources, and he clears the way for the next point.

19. **Defining terms.** Shannon slips in a definition of "mentors" after the comma in this sentence. Since his audience would consist of his classmates as well as his instructor, he thought it likely that at least a few readers would not know the term. Yet he opted to abbreviate and downplay the definition in order not to offend any readers who already understood the term. Here is Shannon's edited draft of this passage:

These successful women should be acting as mentors. ~~A~~ *for* ~~those coming up behind them, serving as~~ *those coming up behind them, serving as* ~~mentor is usually an older and professionally more~~

~~advanced person who acts as a~~ role model*s* and provide~~s~~ *ing* ~~guidance.~~ *Instead, many do just the opposite.* ~~to a younger colleague who is usually younger and~~

~~subordinate. Yet often these successful women are the~~

~~opposite of mentors.~~

20. **Citation of indirect source.** With the use of "qtd. in," Shannon indicates correctly that he obtained the information on Mathison from the article by Bozzi. **Indirect sources.** The Mathison study is important for Shannon's paper, and the information in Bozzi's article clearly indicated that it had been published in a readily available journal. Instead of relying on a brief summary in a magazine, Shannon should have gone directly to Mathison's article. Use indirect sources (and "qtd. in") only when the original material is not available for you to consult. See, for example, page 7 of the paper and comment 32, page 649. **Citation of a one-page article.** Bozzi's article appears on only one page of the magazine it is in, and Shannon gives that page number in the list of works cited (see p. 660). Thus he does not need to repeat the page number in the citation.

MLA
38

Shannon 4

In a 1986 survey of executive women, Edith
Gilson, with Susan Kane, found that the "queen
bee" was thriving in American business: 68
percent of those responding to a questionnaire
felt that "their female colleagues were 'unnecessarily competitive' with one another." Some
of the respondents exhibited signs of the "queen
bee syndrome." One woman declared, "I managed
to climb to my position without any special
help. . . . It was tough, but if I did it, why
can't other women?" (184-86).

Gilson and Kane emphatically warn against
the dangers of this attitude among women:

> Women's undue competitiveness is a
> major stumbling block to their success.
> It keeps them awash in anger and fear
> when their energies could be used
> more constructively; sets a negative
> example for lower-level women; creates
> difficult working conditions for the
> women who are its targets; diminishes
> the effectiveness of teamwork; and, in
> some cases, <u>actively inhibits career
> progress</u>. (186-87; emphasis added)

21

22

23

24

21. **Citation of a book written with an assistant.** The word "with" appears before Kane's name on the cover and title page of the Gilson and Kane book. It indicates that Kane assisted Gilson, the researcher and principal author, probably by helping with the writing. Shannon makes this clear to his readers by using "with" as well. (See also the list of works cited, p. 13 of the paper, and comment 49, p. 661.) **Introducing and citing a discussion of one work.** By mentioning the names of Gilson and Kane at the beginning of the discussion, Shannon makes it clear that what follows is from their work. The page number at the very end of the paragraph announces that the citation covers all the intervening material. If, instead, Shannon had placed both parts of the citation together (the page number in the first sentence or the authors' names in the last sentence), readers might be unsure of how much material the citation covered. **Mixing summary, paraphrase, and quotation.** In the rest of this paragraph, Shannon summarizes, paraphrases, and quotes from several pages of Gilson and Kane's book to give the reader a good sense of one of Gilson's findings.

22. **Editing quotations.** Shannon uses an ellipsis mark to show that he has eliminated irrelevant material from the quotation (see 25e). The ellipsis itself consists of three spaced periods. It is preceded by a sentence period closed up to the last word in the sentence, and it is followed by two spaces.

23. **Placing and punctuating parenthetical citations.** The page reference for all the Gilson and Kane material in this paragraph falls at the end of the paragraph (see comment 21). Since the final quotation ends in a question mark, the citation is followed by a separate period.

24. **Adding emphasis to quotations.** Shannon underlines certain words in the quotation that reinforce his thesis especially clearly. He acknowledges this change inside the parenthetical citation, separated by a semicolon from the page number.

MLA
38

Shannon 5

Like the male executive's reluctance to promote   25
women, the "queen bee syndrome" must change
before women can make serious inroads into top
management.

Even more significant than the attitudes   26
described above, however, is the preference for a
masculine rather than feminine management style.
The feminine management styles seem to have succeeded quite well at the middle-management level.
But the continued prevalence of the masculine
style of management at top levels, along with the
apparent resistance of top managers to changing
that style, is the single most significant
obstacle to women seeking executive positions.

Characterizing the managerial style of most   27
American industrial corporations, Ann Hughey and
Eric Gelman of Newsweek refer to a "paramilitary
form of organization" enforced by "rigid, drill-
sergeant managers" (46). Marilyn Loden, the
author of Feminine Leadership, or, How to Succeed
in Business Without Being One of the Boys,
borrows a term from the feminist writer Betty
Friedan in noting the "masculinism" of the tra-

25. **Summary statement.** For three paragraphs Shannon has been discussing the single idea of how sex discrimination by both sexes holds women back. This concluding statement ties the paragraphs together in preparation for a new section of the paper.
26. **Relation to outline.** With this paragraph Shannon begins part II of his outline (see p. 634). **Transitional paragraph.** Shannon devotes a whole paragraph to the shift in direction, briefly summing up the preceding section and then introducing his most important point.
27. **Using sources effectively.** In this paragraph Shannon combines material from two sources to support a single point about corporate managerial style. The two sources reinforce each other and strengthen Shannon's conclusion at the end of the paragraph.

MLA
38

Shannon 6

ditional managerial style (23). Its basic

premise, Loden says, is competition: the suc-

cessful manager must conquer his corporate

enemies, just as he was trained for victory on

the football field or the battlefield; and stra-

tegic thinking must take precedence over emotion

(24-26). It is no wonder that women--who have   **28**

been reared to be emotional, cooperative, and

generous--encounter difficulties when attempting

to adapt to this style.

Despite the difficulties, women are encour-

aged to imitate men if they want to succeed.

Loden surveyed "how to" books written during the

1970s and discovered that virtually all of them

gave women exactly that advice (28). Yet women

who acquire more masculine traits are then sub-

ject to stereotyping. In a 1983 test of people's

reactions to videotapes of male and female lead-

ers, the psychologists Virginia Brown and

Florence Geis found that "[a]lthough both leaders   **29**

used the same script, the woman was faulted more

than the man for being too dominating, cold, and

insensitive" (822). Such results reveal that

while sex-role stereotyping may not be as obvious

28. **Drawing conclusions.** Shannon correctly places the page reference for Loden after the paraphrase but before the conclusion he draws from the evidence. His conclusion not only spells out the significance of the preceding paragraph but also prepares for the next paragraph. However, Shannon should have found and offered evidence for his understanding that women are "reared to be emotional, cooperative, and generous." The statement may seem self-evident, but many readers would justly criticize it as just the kind of stereotype that Shannon himself is criticizing.

29. **Altering capitalization in quotations.** In the source the word "although" began a sentence and was capitalized. To fit the quotation smoothly into his own sentence, Shannon wanted to use a small letter. The brackets indicate that he altered the capitalization. (See 26a.)

MLA

38

Shannon 7

as it was in a 1972 study (Broverman et al.), it   **30**

remains pervasive.

The dilemma of women is also illustrated in

a list comparing businessmen and businesswomen

that made the round of women executives several

years ago.

*A businessman is aggressive; a busi-   **31**

nesswoman is pushy.

*A businessman is good on details;

she's picky.

*He loses his temper at times because

he's so involved in his work; she's

temperamental.

*He knows how to follow through; she

doesn't know when to quit. (qtd. in   **32**

Loden 38)

The humor here underlines a serious problem.

Loden observes that if a woman tries to adapt to   **33**

male business culture without retaining any of

her feminine traits, she will end up feeling more

rather than less alienated (22). But this is

precisely what many women have been expected to

do--and in fact have done--in order to succeed.

Loden explains that "fraternity pledging"--the

30. **Citation of a work with more than three authors.** Here and in the list of works cited (see p. 13 of the paper), Shannon uses "et al." ("and others") to indicate that the work had at least three other authors besides the one named. Shannon could have given all authors' names, too. Either form is correct as long as the list of works cited and the text citation are consistent.

31. **Reproduction of list.** By indenting the list ten spaces like any other long quotation, Shannon indicates that it is indeed a quotation.

32. **Citation of an indirect source.** Shannon's use of "qtd. in" indicates that Loden herself quoted the list. In this case, unlike on page 3 of the paper, the use of an indirect source is appropriate because the list was available only in Loden's book, not also in another readily available source. (See comment 20, p. 641.)

33. **Selective quotation.** Throughout this paragraph, Shannon chooses quotations carefully. Since he is relying heavily on Loden in this section, he does not simply report what she says but rather uses her ideas and words selectively to support his thesis.

MLA

38

term she uses for the first stage of the adaptation process--"causes women to gradually deny
what they truly think and feel" (32). Thus rigid
insistence on a masculine managerial style is not
only detrimental in preventing many women from
making it to the top but also harmful in causing
those women who do make it to manage less effectively than they might.

It seems clear that if business is going to
benefit from women's talents, it must accommodate
a feminine managerial style. As Hughey and
Gelman observe, "the very qualities that men have
traditionally denigrated as feminine--sympathy,
sensitivity, a lack of the killer instinct--may
often be advantages when it comes to getting the
best out of people" (46).

A case in point is the story from a woman I
interviewed, Nora Crisi, who is a manager responsible for several departments in a retail organization. A subordinate of hers, Susan, refused
to use the guidelines in the company manual to
train her own subordinates. In debating how to
handle the situation, Crisi says,

> my only real role model was my own

34

35

34. **Relation to outline.** At this paragraph Shannon begins part III of his outline (see p. 635).

35. **Primary source: personal interview.** Shannon has tested his ideas by interviewing a woman in a management position. He weaves together paraphrases and quotations from the interview, which he tape-recorded after obtaining Crisi's permission. He does not use a parenthetical citation because all the necessary information (Crisi's name) appears in the text.

Shannon 9

boss, a man who kept everyone in line
like a drill instructor. He would have
called Susan in and given her a stern
lecture, complete with threats. I knew
I couldn't pull that off; it wasn't my
nature.

Instead, Crisi explained to Susan the necessity
for common training practices and encouraged the
young supervisor to offer suggestions for revising the manual if she found problems with it.
Then Crisi emphasized that she would not tolerate
any refusal to adhere to company policy. The result was surprising: "You know what? She thanked
me! I'd been expecting a fight, but I think
Susan saw that I respected her, and she appreciated not being treated like a schoolgirl."
Crisi's reliance on her sensitivity, coupled with   36
some of the firmness she had learned from her own
boss, served her well in a conflict that is
common between managers and subordinates.

Crisi's encouragement of feedback on the
company's policy illustrates another advantage of
a feminine management style: such "participative

36. **Drawing conclusions.** Again, Shannon does not force readers to figure out the significance of his evidence but states plainly what he got from the interview (and what he wants readers to get).

Shannon 10

management," as it is commonly called, permits   37

both emotional and rational assessments of and

responses to business situations.[2] Acknowledg-

ment of the importance of emotion has long been

absent from traditional management styles. But,   38

in the words of Antonia Shusta, an executive with

Citibank, "Business is all people and people in

large degree are very emotional. . . . If you

don't understand emotion, you're missing out on a

lot" (qtd. in Hughey and Gelman 47).

    Gary N. Powell, a professor of management at   39

the University of Connecticut, argues that nei-

ther a masculine nor a feminine style is more

effective for managers. The ideal, he says, is

what he and others call an "androgynous style":

both masculine and feminine, both "task-oriented

and people-oriented" (11). Powell cites a study

of 2000 managers in which the highest achievers

were concerned both with the work being done and

with the individuals who were doing it (11).

Powell cautions, however, that managers must have

the support of their organizations if they are to

shift to a more androgynous style (12-13).

37. **Using an endnote for supplementary information.** Shannon did not want to do more than mention the term "participative management," whose meaning he thought clear enough from the words themselves. For readers who might want more information, he provided an endnote with a source to consult.

38. **Selecting supporting evidence.** Shannon uses two separate sources here to develop his point, mixing the views of a practitioner and an expert.

39. **From note cards to paper.** Shannon wanted to use material from three different passages in Powell's article, which he had mainly quoted on his note cards (see below). In the paper, he opted to quote only Powell's concise definition of the androgynous style; for the rest Shannon used paraphrases because he could fit them together more smoothly. **Showing page breaks in notes.** On the last card below, Shannon inserted a check mark between "more" and "androgynous" to indicate the location of a page break in the original source.

Androgynous style
Powell, p. 11

"Androgynous management... a combination of task-oriented and people-oriented behavior."

Androgynous style
Powell, p. 11

Reports on study of 2000 managers by Susan Donald and Jay Hall: "High managerial achievers successfully integrated their concerns for task and people."

Androgynous style
Powell, pp. 12-13

"In many settings individual managers cannot become more ✓ androgynous on their own without taking considerable personal risk. They need organizational support to make the change successfully."

MLA
38

American business has been operating on a   40
masculine model since the industrial revolution.
But times have changed, and so has the business
population. Now women as well as men must be
encouraged to break through into top management.
In order for that to happen, the "old-boy network" must be penetrated, the "queen bee syndrome" must be cured, and old prejudices--women's
as well as men's--must be abandoned. Even more
important, for women and for business itself, is
the adaptation to a more flexible, androgynous
style of management. Only when these changes are
made will that glass ceiling finally be broken.

40. **Conclusion.** In his final paragraph Shannon summarizes the main points of his argument in a way that reminds readers of both what holds women back and what he thinks needs to change. The last sentence—by referring to the title and providing a vivid image—gives the paper a dramatic finish.

MLA

38

Shannon 12

Notes   **41**

[1] "Glass ceiling" is commonly used in   **42**
articles and books about women in management.
Although I was unable to find any information on
the origins of the term, it appears to have been
coined just to describe the situation of women
(not men). A related term, "glass wall,"
describes a barrier to lateral as well as upward
movement (Solomon 96).

[2] For further information on women and participative management, see "Special Talents."   **43**

41. **Format of notes.** The word "Notes" is centered one inch from the top of the page. (The heading would be singular— "Note"—if Shannon had only one note.) The notes begin two lines (one double space) below the heading. The notes themselves are double-spaced. The first line of each is indented five spaces and preceded by a raised number corresponding to the number used in the text. A space separates the number and the note.

42. **Endnotes for additional relevant information.** Shannon's first note provides readers with background information on a definition. His second note refers interested readers to an article on participative management.

43. **Citation of an unsigned article.** Since Shannon is citing an unsigned article, he uses a shortened form of the title for his citation. Since the article is only one page, he does not include the page number. See the entry for this work in the list of works cited, page 14 of the paper.

MLA
38

Shannon 13

Works Cited   44

Bozzi, Vincent. "Assertiveness Breeds Contempt."   45

Psychology Today Sept. 1987: 15.

Broverman, I. K., et al. "Sex-Role Stereotypes: 46

A Current Appraisal." Journal of Social

Issues 28.2 (1972): 59-78.

Brown, Virginia, and Florence Geis. "Turning   47

Lead into Gold: Evaluations of Women and

Men Leaders and the Alchemy of Social

Consensus." Journal of Personality and

Social Psychology 46 (1984): 811-24.

Crisi, Nora. Personal interview. 17 May 1990.   48

Gilson, Edith, with Susan Kane. Unnecessary   49

Choices: The Hidden Life of the Executive

Woman. New York: Morrow, 1987.

Hughey, Ann, and Eric Gelman. "Managing the   50

Woman's Way." Newsweek 17 Mar. 1986: 46-

47.

Loden, Marilyn. Feminine Leadership, or, How to   51

Succeed in Business Without Being One of the

Boys. New York: Times, 1985.

Pave, Irene. "A Woman's Place Is at GE, Federal

Express, P&G. . . ." Business Week 23 June

1986: 75+.   52

44. **Format of list of works cited.** The heading "Works Cited" is centered one inch from the top of the page. The first entry is typed two lines (one double space) below the heading, and the entire list is double-spaced. The first line of each entry begins at the left margin; subsequent lines of the same entry are indented five spaces. The entries are alphabetized.
45. Entry for a **signed article in a monthly periodical.**
46. Entry for an **article with more than three authors.** A source with more than three authors may be listed with all authors' names or just with the first author's name followed by "et al." ("and others"). In his working bibliography (see below), Shannon had all the names but opted not to use them. His text citation of the Broverman et al. article is consistent with this decision (see p. 7 of the paper).

Broverman, I. K., S. R. Vogel,
    D. M. Broverman, F. E. Clarkson, and
    P. S. Rosenkrantz
"Sex-Role Stereotypes: A Current Appraisal"
<u>Journal of Social Issues</u>
Vol. 28, no. 2, 1972
pp. 59-78

The Broverman entry also illustrates a **signed article in a journal that pages issues separately** (see p. 614).
47. Entry for a **signed article in a journal with continuous pagination throughout an annual volume** (see p. 613).
48. Entry for a **personal interview.**
49. Entry for a **book written with an assistant.** See the discussion of this source in comment 21, page 643. Note that this entry differs from one for a source with two authors, such as Hughey and Gelman, below.
50. Entry for a **signed article in a weekly periodical.**
51. Entry for a **book with one author.**
52. Entry for an **article in which pagination is not consecutive.** The "+" indicates that the article does not continue on page 76 but farther back in the issue.

Shannon 14

Powell, Gary N.   "The Value of Androgynous Man-

        agement."   SAM Advanced Management Journal

        54 (1989): 10-13.

Schwartz, Felice N.   "Don't Write Women Off as

        Leaders."   Fortune 8 June 1987: 185+.

Solomon, Charlene Marmer.   "Careers Under Glass."

        Personnel Journal 69 (1990): 96-105.

"The Special Talents Women Bring to Participative   53

        Management."   International Management Aug.

        1986: 60.

53. Entry for an **unsigned article.** The source is alphabetized in the list of works cited by the first main word of its title, "Special." Here is the card from Shannon's working bibliography.

"The Special Talents Women Bring to Participative Management"

<u>International Management</u>

Aug. 1986

p. 60

Weiss 1

Ann Weiss

History 164

Ms. Seaver

April 29, 1991

Format of
heading and
title when n(
title page is
required

                    The Editing of the

                 Declaration of Independence:

                      Better or Worse?

     The Declaration of Independence is so

widely regarded as a statement of American ideals

that its origins in practical politics tend to be

forgotten. The document drafted by Thomas Jeffer-

son was intensely debated in the Continental Con-

gress and then substantially revised before being

signed. Since then, most historians have agreed

that Jefferson's Declaration was improved in the

process. But Jefferson himself was disappointed

with the result (Boyd 37); and recently his view

has received scholarly support. Thus it is an

open question whether the Congress improved a

flawed document or damaged an inspired one. An

answer to the question requires understanding the

context in which the Declaration was conceived

and examining the document itself.

Statement of
topic

Focus on the
disagreemen(
to be resolve

Statement of
how the dis-
agreement w
be resolved

MLA
38

Weiss 2

The Continental Congress in 1776 was attended by representatives of all thirteen colonies. The colonies were ruled more or less separately by Great Britain and had suffered repeated abuses at the hands of King George III, the British parliament, and local appointed governors. To end the abuses of the British, many colonists were urging three actions: forming a united front, seceding from Britain, and taking control of their own international trade and diplomacy (Wills 325-26). They saw the three actions as dependent on each other, and all three were spelled out in a resolution that was proposed in the Congress on June 7, 1776 (Wills 326-27).

The Congress named a five-man committee to prepare a defense of this resolution in order to win the support of reluctant colonists and also to justify secession to potential foreign allies (Malone 219; Wills 330-31). Jefferson, the best writer on the committee, was assigned to draft the document. The other committee members made a few minor changes in his draft before submitting

Historical background: the context in which the Declaration was conceived (next two paragraphs)

MLA
38

Weiss 3

it to the Congress. The Congress made many small

and some quite large alterations before approving

the document on July 4 (Becker 171).

The most interesting major change, because   Isolation and

of the controversy it ultimately generated, was   summary of

the material

made in Jefferson's next-to-last paragraph. (See   be analyzed

Figure 1 on the next page for Jefferson's version

with the Congress's editing.) Jefferson made

several points in the paragraph: the colonists

had freely submitted to the British king but not

to the British parliament; they had tried repeat-

edly and unsuccessfully to gain the support of

the British people for their cause; yet the

British ("unfeeling brethren") had not only

ignored the colonists' pleas but also worsened

their difficulties by supporting the parliament.

These actions, Jefferson concluded, gave the

colonists no choice but to separate from England.

The Congress cut Jefferson's paragraph by almost

two-thirds, leaving only the points about the

colonists' appeals to the British, the refusal of

the British to listen, and the need for separa-

tion.

Weiss 4

Photocopy of
the material to
be analyzed (a
primary
source)

Nor have we been wanting in attentions to our British brethren. we have warned them from time to time of attempts by their legislature to extend ∧ [a] jurisdiction over ∧ [these our states.] we have reminded them of the circumstances of our emigration & settlement here, [no one of which could warrant so strange a pretension: that these were effected at the expence of our own blood & treasure, unassisted by the wealth or the strength of Great Britain: that in constituting indeed our several forms of government, we had adopted one common king, thereby laying a foundation for perpetual league & amity with them: but that submission to their parliament was no part of our constitution, nor ever in idea, if history may be credited: and,] we ∧ appealed to their native justice and magnanimity ∧ [as well as to] the ties of our common kindred to disavow these usurpations which ∧ [were likely to] interrupt our connection and correspondence. they too have been deaf to the voice of justice & of consanguinity, [and when occasions have been given them, by the regular course of their laws, of removing from their councils the disturbers of our harmony, they have, by their free election, re-established them in power. at this very time too they are permitting their chief magistrate to send over not only souldiers of our common blood, but Scotch & foreign mercenaries to invade & destroy us. these facts have given the last stab to agonizing affection, and manly spirit bids us to renounce for ever these unfeeling brethren. we must endeavor to forget our former love for them, and to hold them as we hold the rest of mankind enemies in war, in peace friends. we might have been a free and a great people together; but a communication of grandeur & of freedom it seems is below their dignity. be it so, since they will have it. the road to happiness & to glory is open to us too. we will tread[19] it apart from them, and] ∧ acquiesce in the necessity which denounces our [eternal] separation ∧ !

Margin annotations (left):
∧ an unwarrantable
∧ us
∧ have
∧ and we have conjured them
by
∧ would inevitably

Margin annotations (right):
∧ we must therefore
∧ and hold them as we hold the rest of mankind, enemies in war, in peace friends.

Fig. 1. Next-to-last paragraph of the Declaration of Independence, photocopied from Jefferson (318-19). The text is Jefferson's as submitted by the five-man committee to the Continental Congress. The Congress deleted the passages that are underlined and added the passages in the margin.

Figure caption
and source

MLA
38

Weiss 5

Until recently, most historians accepted all the Congress's changes in the Declaration as clear improvements. Dumas Malone, author of the most respected biography of Jefferson, expresses "little doubt that the critics strengthened" the Declaration, "primarily by deletion" (222). Julian Boyd, a historian of the period and the editor of Jefferson's papers, observes that "it is difficult to point out a passage in the Declaration, great as it was, that was not improved by their [the delegates'] attention" (36). Carl Becker, considered an expert on the evolution of the Declaration, agrees that "Congress left the Declaration better than it found it" (209). These scholars make few specific comments about the next-to-last paragraph. Becker, however, does say that Jefferson's emphasis on the British parliament is an allusion to a theory of government that is assumed in the rest of the document, so that the paragraph "leaves one with the feeling that the author, not quite aware that he is done, is beginning over again" (211-12).

Quotation and paraphrase of three important scholars on one side the disagreement

Weiss   6

The agreement in favor of the Congress's changes was broken in 1978 when the journalist and humanities scholar Garry Wills published a detailed defense of Jefferson's original, particularly his next-to-last paragraph. According to Wills, "Jefferson's declaration of independence is a renunciation of unfeeling brethren. His whole document was shaped to make that clear" (319). The British people had betrayed the colonists both politically (by supporting the intrusive parliament) and emotionally (by ignoring the colonists' appeals), and that dual betrayal was central to Jefferson's argument for secession (303). Wills contends that in drastically cutting the next-to-last paragraph, "Congress removed the heart of his argument, at its climax" (319).

As an explanation of Jefferson's intentions, Wills's presentation is convincing. However, a close examination of the original and edited versions of the next-to-last paragraph supports the opinions of earlier historians rather than Wills's argument that the Declaration was damaged

Quotation and paraphrase of the scholar on the other side of the disagreement

Weiss's resolution of the disagreement

MLA
38

Weiss 7

by the Congress. The paragraph may have expressed Jefferson's intentions, but it was
neither successful in its tone nor appropriate
for the purposes of the Congress as a whole.

> Thesis
> sentence

　　　　Part of Jefferson's assignment "was to
impart the proper tone and spirit" to the Declaration (Malone 221). He did this throughout
most of the document by expressing strong feelings in a solemn and reasonable manner. But in
the next-to-last paragraph Jefferson's tone is
sometimes overheated, as in the phrases "invade &
destroy us," "last stab to agonizing affection,"
and "road to happiness & to glory." At other
times Jefferson sounds as if he is pouting, as in
"we must endeavor to forget our former love for
them" and "a communication of grandeur & of freedom it seems is below their dignity." Wills
comments that critics have viewed this paragraph
as resembling "the recollections of a jilted
lover" (313). Wills himself does not agree with
this interpretation of the tone, but it seems
accurate. All the quoted passages were deleted
by the Congress.

> Supporting
> analysis of th
> Declaration,
> including qu
> tations and
> comment
> (next three
> paragraphs)
>
> Analysis of
> tone

Weiss 8

More important than the problem in tone is the paragraph's inappropriateness for the purposes of the Declaration as the Congress saw them. Specifically, the paragraph probably would not have convinced reluctant colonists and potential foreign allies of the justice and logical necessity of secession. The Congress needed the support of as many colonists as possible, but many colonists still felt strong ties to their friends and relatives in England (Becker 127-28; Boyd 31-32). They would probably have been unhappy with phrases such as "renounce forever" and "eternal separation" that threatened a permanent break in those ties. The Congress deleted those phrases, and it also gave greater stress to Jefferson's one hint of a possible reconciliation with the British: "We must . . . hold them as we hold the rest of mankind enemies in war, in peace friends." This thought was moved by the Congress from inside the paragraph to the very end, where it strikes a final note of hope.

The Congress also strengthened the appeal of the Declaration to potential allies, who would have needed assurance that the colonists

Analysis of appropriateness for purposes of Congress (next two paragraphs)

First purpose of Congress

Second purpose of Congress

MLA
38

Weiss 9

were acting reasonably and cautiously. Both Jefferson's and the Congress's versions note that
the colonists often "warned" and "reminded" the
British and "appealed to their native justice &
magnanimity," but that the British were "deaf to
the voice of justice & consanguinity" and left
the colonists no choice besides "separation."
However, Jefferson buried these statements in
lengthy charges against the British, while the
Congress stripped away the charges to emphasize
the colonists' patience in exploring all avenues
of redress and their reluctance in seceding. Instead of "beginning over again" as Becker says
Jefferson's version seems to do, the revised
paragraph clearly provides the final rational
justification for the action of the colonists.
At the same time, it keeps enough of Jefferson's
original to remind the audience that the colonists are feeling people, motivated by their
hearts as well as by their minds. They do not
secede enthusiastically but "acquiesce in the
necessity" of separation.

Though the Declaration has come to be a
statement of this nation's political philosophy,

Summary and
restatement of
thesis

Weiss 10

that was not its purpose in 1776. Jefferson's

intentions had to bow to the goals of the

Congress as a whole to forge unity among the

colonies and to win the support of foreign

nations. As Boyd observes, the Declaration of

Independence "was the result not just of

Jefferson's lonely struggle for the right phrase

and the telling point, but also of the focussing

of many minds--among them the best that America

ever produced" (38).

MLA
38

Weiss 11

Works Cited

Becker, Carl. The Declaration of Independence:

A Study in the History of Political Ideas.

New York: Knopf, 1956.

Boyd, Julian P. The Declaration of Independence:

The Evolution of a Text. Princeton: Prince-

ton UP, 1945.

Jefferson, Thomas. "Notes of the Proceedings in

the Continental Congress." The Papers of

Thomas Jefferson. Ed. Julian P. Boyd et

al. 21 vols. Princeton: Princeton UP,

1950-74. 1: 309-27.

Malone, Dumas. Jefferson the Virginian. Vol. 1

of Jefferson and His Time. 6 vols. Boston:

Little, 1948.

Wills, Garry. Inventing America: Jefferson's

Declaration of Independence. Garden City:

Doubleday, 1978.

Chapter 39

Writing in the Disciplines

Writing in the academic disciplines you study in college does much more than simply demonstrate your competence to your instructor. Writing is actually a way you learn concepts, focus ideas, analyze data, uncover assumptions, interpret patterns, and ask and answer questions.

This chapter builds on earlier material: Chapters 1–2 on the writing process, Chapter 4 on critical reading and writing, and Chapters 35–38 on research writing. Study those chapters, if you have not already, for the skills discussed there are fundamental to

---

● Guidelines for academic writers

1. For the discipline you are writing in, become familiar with the methodology and the kinds of evidence considered appropriate and valid.
2. Analyze the special demands of the assignment—the kind of research and sources you need. The questions you set out to answer, the assertions you wish to support, will govern how you choose your sources and evidence.
3. Become familiar with the specialized tools and language of the discipline.
4. Use the style of documentation and the manuscript format customarily used by writers in the discipline.

HIGHLIGHTS

Most composition instructors would agree that writing is an activity too important to be left to composition classes alone. Many colleges have recently developed writing-across-the-curriculum programs in recognition of the importance of writing (and the thinking that accompanies it) in all academic disciplines. Some of these programs consist of composition courses focusing on academic writing in general or on writing in a particular area, such as writing in the social sciences. Others consist of courses in a content area (such as biology or history) that are designed to be writing intensive.

This chapter provides both a reference guide for students in content area courses and a framework for a writing course focusing on the varieties of academic discourse. It looks in turn at the aims, methods, and forms of writing in the humanities, the social sciences, and the natural and applied sciences. Each section also reviews the preferred forms of documentation in the various disciplinary areas and provides sample student papers that can serve as both models and subjects for discussion.

TRANSPARENCY MASTER
AVAILABLE

675

RESOURCES AND IDEAS

David Bartholomae, "Inventing the University," *When a Writer Can't Write,* ed. Mike Rose (New York: Guilford, 1985) 134–65. For Bartholomae, mastering the various specialized discourses of the academic community is an essential part of being a college student but is also a gradual process that is likely to pass through several stages, each more closely approximating the work of thinking and writing that characterizes a discipline.

Art Young and Toby Fulwiler, eds., *Writing Across the Disciplines: Research into Practice* (Upper Montclair: Boynton/Cook, 1986). The essays in this collection describe and evaluate a universitywide writing-across-the-curriculum program. Included are essays on writing in the social sciences, the humanities, and the natural and applied sciences.

Mark A. Schlesinger, "The Road to Teaching Thinking," *JGE: The Journal of General Education* 36 (1984): 182–96. Schlesinger surveys four contemporary approaches to teaching students to think, including those that address global skills like analysis and synthesis; those that focus on strategies for problem solving; those that rely on developmental models like those of Piaget and Perry; and those that stress generic thinking skills such as selective attention or identifying components. He points out the overlapping among these approaches and identifies both their strengths and weaknesses.

academic writing. Here you will learn about academic writing in general (39a) and writing in the humanities (39b), the social sciences (39c), and the natural and applied sciences (39d). For each field, the chapter introduces the basic information you need to follow the guidelines on the preceding page.

39a Understanding the goals and requirements of the disciplines

1 Methods and evidence

The **methodology** of a discipline is the way its practitioners study their subjects—that is, how they proceed when investigating the answers to questions. Methodology relates to the framework used to analyze evidence and ideas (see 4b-5). For instance, a literary critic and a social historian would probably approach Shakespeare's *Hamlet* through quite different frameworks: the literary critic might study the play for its poetic images; the historian might examine the play's relation to Shakespeare's context, England at the turn of the seventeenth century.

Whatever their analytic framework, academic writers do not compose directly out of their personal experience. Rather, they collect and organize the kinds of evidence appropriate to the discipline, and they base any opinions on that evidence. The evidence comes from research like that described in the previous four chapters: from the researcher's own close observations and analysis of a text or experiment; or from sources, most likely those located in a library.

When you conduct original research, you generate your own evidence. You might analyze the images in a poem and then use examples as evidence for your interpretation of the poem. Or you might conduct a survey of fellow students and then use data from the survey to support your conclusions about students' attitudes. Either kind of evidence would be a **primary source,** a firsthand or original account that does not rely on others' sources. Additional examples of primary sources include historical documents such as letters and diaries, works of art such as plays or photographs, and reports on experiments that the writer has conducted. The research papers in the preceding chapter both use primary sources: Mark Shannon's paper includes the results of an interview he conducted (see p. 650), and Ann Weiss's includes her own analysis of changes made in the Declaration of Independence (see p. 670). The sample papers in this chapter also depend on primary sources.

Many primary sources can be found in the library. But more prevalent among a library's holdings are **secondary sources,** books and articles written *about* primary sources. Much academic writing requires that you use such sources to spark, extend, or support your own ideas, as when you review the published opinions and information on your subject before contributing conclusions from your original research.

Assignments

For most academic writing, your primary purpose will be either to explain something to your readers or to persuade them to accept your conclusions. (See 1c on purpose.) To achieve your purpose, you will adapt your writing process to the writing situation, particularly to the kinds of evidence required by the assignment and to the kinds of thinking you are expected to do. Most assignments will contain key words that tell you what these expectations are — words such as *compare, define, analyze,* and *illustrate* that express customary ways of thinking about and organizing a vast range of subjects. Sections 1e-8 and 3c-2 explore these so-called patterns of development. You should be aware of them and alert to the wording in assignments that directs you to use them.

Tools and language

When you write in an academic discipline, you use the scholarly tools of that discipline, including specialized references such as periodical indexes, abstracts, and computerized databases. (See 35c for helpful lists of references.) In addition, you may use the aids developed by practitioners of the discipline for efficiently and effectively approaching research, conducting it, and recording the findings. Many of these aids, such as a system of note cards for recording evidence from sources, are discussed in Chapters 35 and 36 and can be adapted to any discipline. Other aids are discussed in later sections of this chapter.

Pay close attention to the texts assigned in a course and any materials given out in class, for these items may introduce you to valuable references and other research aids, and they will use the specialized language of the discipline. This specialized language

RESOURCES AND IDEAS

Maria Burgar, "No Footnotes Necessary," *Bulletin of the Association for Business Communication* 52 (1989): 32–35. Burgar encourages English instructors to be familiar with and require the types of writing students may encounter in the core courses of their majors and in their professions. Burgar believes such a focus results in increased motivation and learning on the part of the students.

C. W. Griffin, ed., *New Directions for Teaching and Learning: Teaching Writing in All Disciplines* (San Francisco: Jossey-Bass, 1982). The essays in this collection look at ways to use writing as a tool for learning and at ways of helping students master the kinds of writing required by different disciplines.

39a

RESOURCES AND IDEAS

Worth Anderson et al., "Cross-Curricular Underlife: A Collaborative Report on Ways with Academic Words," *College Composition and Communication,* 41 (1990): 11–36. A research project by faculty and students revealed that the content of a typical freshman composition course had little in common with the type of writing expected in introductory courses within the disciplines.

allows practitioners to write to each other both efficiently and precisely. It also furthers certain concerns of the discipline, such as accuracy and objectivity. Scientists, for example, prefer the verb *indicate* rather than *prove* in discussing their conclusions, because all results are provisional. Some of the language conventions like this one are discussed in the following sections. As you gain experience in a particular discipline, keep alert for such conventions and train yourself to follow them.

 Documentation and format

Most disciplines publish journals that require authors to use a certain documentation style and manuscript format. In turn, most instructors in a discipline require the same of students writing papers for their courses.

When you document your sources, you tell readers which ideas and information you borrowed and where they can find your sources. Thus documentation indicates how much knowledge you have and how broad and deep your research was. It also helps you avoid **plagiarism,** the serious offense of presenting the words, ideas, and data of others as if they were your own. (See 36c on avoiding plagiarism.)

Manuscript format includes such features as margins and the placement of the title. But it also extends to special elements of the manuscript, such as tables or an abstract, that may be required by the discipline.

The following sections direct you to the style guides published by different disciplines and outline the basic requirements of the ones used most often. If your instructor does not require a particular style, consult one of the general guides listed on page 598, or use the style of the Modern Language Association, which is described and illustrated at length in Chapter 37 and Appendix A.

39b Writing in the humanities

The humanities, sometimes known as the reconstructive and speculative disciplines, include the arts, film, literature, history, and philosophy. The texts in these disciplines record and speculate about the growth, ideas, and emotions of human beings. Writing in the humanities explains, interprets, analyzes, and reconstructs, based on the evidence in both primary and secondary sources.

This section concentrates on writing about literature and

about history and concludes with two sample literary papers (see p. 684). The other disciplines mentioned have their own concerns, of course, but share many important goals and methods with literature and history.

 ## Methods and evidence in the humanities

Literature

As a reader and a student of literature, you read a work and interpret and analyze its implications. You make inferences or draw conclusions from the writer's written words (the text).

A literary analysis is often based only on the text or texts themselves, without recourse to secondary sources. Your assignment may, however, ask you to augment your own inferences with those of other critics who have written about the work(s). (See pp. 684 and 686 for examples of both kinds of literary analysis.)

When analyzing a literary work, you can use the list on the next page to track the elements of the work and ask questions about them.

History

History as a discipline attempts to reconstruct the past. In Greek the word for history means "to inquire": historians inquire into the past to understand the events of the past. Then they report, explain, analyze, and evaluate those events in their context, asking such questions as what happened before or after the events or how the events were related to the existing political and social structures.

Historians' reconstructions of the past—their conclusions about what happened and why—are always supported with reference to the written record. The evidence of history is mainly primary sources, such as eyewitness accounts and contemporary documents, letters, commercial records, and the like. For history papers, you might also be asked to support your conclusions with those in secondary sources.

In reading historical sources, you need to weigh and evaluate their evidence. If, for example, you find conflicting accounts of the same event, you need to consider the possible biases of the authors or their sources so that you can reject unreliable sources or balance opposing evidence. In general, the more a historian's conclusions are supported by public records such as deeds, marriage licenses, and newspaper accounts, the more reliable the conclusions are likely to be.

RESOURCES AND IDEAS

Dorothy McCoy, "Electrified Term Papers," *English Journal* 60 (1971): 107–10. McCoy argues for slides and movies with accompanying music growing out of the study of literature as an alternative to the traditional research projects.

Sylvan Barnet, *A Short Guide to Writing About Literature* 5th ed. (New York: HarperCollins, 1985). This text provides helpful advice about strategies for analytical reading and writing that students can use when preparing papers for a literature course or for a composition course built around literary texts.

39b

Questions for a literary analysis

Plot: The relationships and patterns of events in a short story, novel, or play.

> What actions happen?
> What conflicts occur?
> How do the events connect to each other and to the whole?

Characters: the people the author creates.

> Who are the principal people in the story, play, or poem?
> How do they interact?
> What do their actions, words, and thoughts reveal about themselves and others?
> How do they stay the same or change? Why?

Point of view: the perspective or attitude of the speaker in a poem or the voice who tells a story. The point of view may be **first person** (*I*) or **third person** (*he, she, it, they*). If third person, it may be **omniscient** (knows everything both inside and outside all characters), **limited** (knows only what the main character knows), or **objective** (knows only what is external to the characters—what they do and say).

> Who is the narrator? Is he or she identified?
> What are the significance and effect of the author's choice of narrator and point of view?
> Is the narrator subjective or objective? Is he or she trustworthy?

Tone: the feelings conveyed; the predominant attitude.

> Do the words sound sad? happy? something else?
> Does the narrator have an ironic tone, saying one thing and meaning another?
> What does the tone say about the author's intentions?

Images: word pictures or visual details.

> What images does the writer use? What pictures do they evoke?
> What is the significance of images to the author's meaning?

Form: the shape or structure of a story, play, or poem.

> How is the form noteworthy?
> What parts of the work does the form emphasize, and why?

Setting: the place where the action happens.

> What is the principal setting, and what does it contribute to the author's meaning?
> When the scene shifts, why does it?

Theme: the main idea or general meaning of the work.

> What do all the other elements point to as the author's intended meaning?

39b

Assignments in the humanities

Papers in the humanities generally perform one or more of the following operations:

- Using **explanation,** you might show how a film director created a particular sequence or clarify a general's role in a battle.
- Using **analysis,** you might examine the elements of a story or painting or break down the causes of a historical event.
- Using **interpretation,** you might infer the meaning of a poem from its images or the significance of a historical event from contemporary accounts of it.
- Using **synthesis,** you might find a pattern in a historical period or in a playwright's works.
- Using **evaluation,** you might judge the quality of an architect's design or a historian's conclusions.

Most likely, you will use these operations in combination—say, interpreting and explaining the meaning of a painting and then evaluating it. (All these operations except explanation are discussed in more detail in Chapter 4, pp. 126–29.)

 Tools and language in the humanities

Literature

Analyzing a work of literature (or any work of art) requires looking closely at its elements. As you read, pose questions about the text, such as why a character speaks with a lisp or why images of water recur in a poem. One helpful way of staying sharp and curious while reading is to make notes in a **reading journal,** a log of questions, reactions, and insights in any form you can reread and use later for writing. (It's a good idea to note page numbers of the text in your journal so that you can always find the appropriate passages.) If you own your copy of the text, you can also underline key passages and use the margins for comments and questions. The point is to interact with the text—talk back to it, ask questions of it, analyze it.

When you write about a literary work, you explicate or unfold its meaning or the meaning of devices employed by the author. Your evidence is mainly direct quotations from the work, although you will occasionally use paraphrase and summary as well (see 36b). When using quotations, keep the following guidelines in mind.

39b

Guidelines for using quotations in literary analysis

1. Choose quotations that clearly support your assertions. Don't use your own words merely to explain quotations, and don't use quotations just to use quotations. Instead, make quotations serve your ideas.
2. When you use a quotation, specify how it relates to your idea. Introduce it, and draw a conclusion from it.
3. Work quotations into your own prose. Avoid dumping quotations in readers' laps. (See 36g.)
4. Reproduce spelling, punctuation, capitalization, and all other features exactly as they appear in the source. (See 25d for the use of brackets when you need to add something to a quotation; and see 25e for the use of an ellipsis mark when you need to omit something from a quotation.)
5. Document your sources. (See opposite.)

Generally, literary analysts avoid claiming absolute certainty about an author's meaning, saying that the author *suggests* or *implies* (rather than *means* or *intends*) to convey that they are making inferences. Note also that it is conventional in writing about literature to use the present tense of verbs in describing both the author's work and the action in the work. For example:

> On the surface, the poet *addresses* a young child, Margaret, who *mourns* the falling of the gold-colored leaves in a grove.

History

The historian's tools are those of any thorough and efficient researcher, as discussed in Chapters 35 and 36: a system for finding and tracking sources (35c, 35d); methodical examination of sources, including evaluation of their biases (36a); a system for taking notes from sources (36b); and a separate system, such as a research journal, for tracking one's own evolving thoughts (35a).

When writing about history, it's important to remain as objective as possible. Historians strive for precision and logic; they do not guess about what happened or speculate about "what if." They avoid trying to influence readers' opinions with words having strongly negative or positive connotations, such as *stupid* or *brilliant* (see 31b-1). Instead, they show the evidence and draw conclusions from that. Generally, they avoid using *I:* it tends to draw attention away from the evidence and toward the writer and it may imply a bias even when there is none.

Writing about history demands some attention to the tenses of verbs to maintain consistency. (See also 13b.) Generally, historians use the past tense to refer to events that occurred in the past. They reserve the present tense only for statements about the present or statements of general truths (see 7e-1). For example:

> Franklin Delano Roosevelt *died* in 1945. Many of Roosevelt's economic reforms *persist* in programs such as Social Security, unemployment compensation, and farm subsidies.

4 Documentation and format

Most writers in the humanities follow the guidelines for documentation and manuscript format established by the Modern Language Association (MLA) and set forth in the *MLA Handbook for Writers of Research Papers,* 3rd ed. (1988). In the MLA documentation style, parenthetical citations in the text of a paper refer to a list of works cited at the end. The system is thoroughly explained and illustrated in Chapter 37.

You should be aware that some literature instructors and practitioners of other disciplines in the humanities prefer an earlier MLA style of endnotes or footnotes rather than parenthetical citations. This earlier style is explained and illustrated in 37c. Some historians and philosophers may prefer a different style of endnotes or footnotes or a different style of parenthetical citations (such as that of the American Psychological Association; see p. 693). Clearly, your first move in deciding what documentation style to use is to ask your instructor.

The MLA guidelines for manuscript format are given in Appendix A of this book (p. 734). Consult this appendix if you are in doubt about matters of format, and ask your instructor if he or she has any special requirements not mentioned there.

5 Two sample literary papers

The following sample papers illustrate two kinds of literary analysis, one based solely on the literary work itself, and one drawing as well on secondary sources. The poem each student writes about precedes each paper.

39b

A literary analysis (no secondary sources)

Gerard Manley Hopkins

Spring and Fall

To a Young Child

Margaret, are you grieving   1
Over Goldengrove unleaving?
Leaves, like the things of man, you
With your fresh thoughts care for, can you?
Ah! as the heart grows older   5
It will come to such sights colder
By and by, nor spare a sigh
Though worlds of wanwood leafmeal lie;
And yet you will weep and know why.
Now no matter, child, the name: 10
Sorrow's springs are the same.
Nor mouth had, no nor mind, expressed
What heart heard of, ghost guessed:
It is the blight man was born for,
It is Margaret you mourn for.   15

John D. Teehan

Professor Roche

English 203

October 29, 1991

Death and Resurrection in Hopkins's

"Spring and Fall"

In Gerard Manley Hopkins's poem "Spring and Fall: To a Young Child," a duality presents itself through the poet's address to a young child: namely, death and resurrection.

On the surface, the poet addresses a young child, Margaret, who mourns the falling of the gold-colored leaves in a grove. As a child, the poet implies, Margaret may not yet understand that mortal things such as leaves

39b

or "things of man" (line 3) all eventually come to an end.
They are born, they live, and they die. The poet then
goes on to explain that as one grows older, one becomes
accustomed to such routine cycles as the falling of
leaves or decaying trees and even comes "to such sights
colder / By and by" (6-7). This cycle of death,
decomposition, rebirth, life, and back to death is
inevitable.

Humans, too, as part of this natural process, are
born to die. Margaret has no conception of this fact, but
the poet, being older and less innocent, recognizes that
she mourns the leaves in anticipation of her own death:
"It [death] is the blight man was born for, / It is
Margaret you mourn for" (14-15). Eventually she "will
weep and know why" (9). She can escape neither her own
death nor an awareness of it. And that awareness will
always form "Sorrow's springs" (11).

But death may also lead to resurrection. For Hopkins
as a Christian and more especially as a priest, all humans
and human-born Christ inevitably come to death, just as
the leaves on a tree must inevitably fall; but then they
are reborn. Hopkins omits any explicit reference to
resurrection in this rather bleak poem. Yet it permeates
the whole because of the person to whom this bleakness is
addressed: the innocent Margaret. It may be, as Hopkins
says, that the aging heart grows increasingly cold to
death and does not "spare a sigh / Though worlds of
wanwood leafmeal lie" (7-8). In Margaret, however, with

39b

her "fresh thoughts" (4), Hopkins demonstrates that
innocence is constantly being reborn. The poet implies
that even as Margaret comes to the realization of the
inevitability of death and her part in it, other innocents
will take her place to prove the equal inevitability of
new life.

Thus this poem about death also seems to be about
life. The young child heads unaware to her own end, but
briefly, at least, she signifies immortality.

[New page.]

Work Cited

Hopkins, Gerard Manley. "Spring and Fall: To a Young

Child." The Poems of Gerard Manley Hopkins. Ed.

W. H. Gardner and N. H. Mackenzie. 4th ed. London:

Oxford UP, 1967.

A literary analysis with secondary sources

Gwendolyn Brooks

The Bean Eaters

They eat beans mostly, this old yellow pair.
Dinner is a casual affair.
Plain chipware on a plain and creaking wood,
Tin flatware.

Two who are Mostly Good.   5
Two who have lived their day,
But keep on putting on their clothes
And putting things away.

And remembering . . .
Remembering, with tinklings and twinges,   10
As they lean over the beans in their rented back room that is
    full of beads and receipts and dolls and cloths, tobacco
    crumbs, vases and fringes.

39b

Kenneth Scheff

Professor MacGregor

English 101A

February 7, 1991

                    Marking Time Versus Enduring in

              Gwendolyn Brooks's "The Bean Eaters"

     "The Bean Eaters," by Gwendolyn Brooks, is a poem of

only eleven lines. It is written in plain language about

very plain people. Yet its meaning is ambiguous. One

critic, George E. Kent, says the old couple who eat beans

"have had their day and exist now as time-markers" (141).

However, another reader, D. H. Melhem, perceives not so

much time marking as "endurance" in the old couple (123).

Is this poem a despairing picture of old age or a more

positive portrait?

     "The Bean Eaters" describes an "old yellow pair" who

"eat beans mostly" (line 1) off "Plain chipware" (3) with

"Tin flatware" (4) in "their rented back room" (11).

Clearly, they are poor. Their existence is accompanied

not by friends or relatives--children or grandchildren are

not mentioned--but by memories and a few possessions (9-

11). They are "Mostly Good" (5), words Brooks capitalizes

at the end of a line, perhaps to stress the old people's

adherence to traditional values as well as their lack of

saintliness. They are unexceptional, whatever message

they have for readers.

     The isolated routine of the couple's life is some-

thing Brooks draws attention to with a separate stanza:

39b

Two who are Mostly Good.

Two who have lived their day,

But keep on putting on their clothes

And putting things away. (5-8)

Brooks emphasizes how isolated the couple is by repeating "Two who." Then she emphasizes how routine their life is by repeating "putting."

A pessimistic reading of this poem seems justified. The critic Harry B. Shaw reads the lines just quoted as perhaps despairing: "they are putting things away as if winding down an operation and readying for withdrawal from activity" (80). However, Shaw observes, the word "But" also indicates the couple's "determination to go on living, a refusal to give up and let things go" (80). This dual meaning is at the heart of Brooks's poem: the old people live a meager existence, yes, but their will, their self-control, and their connection with another person--their essential humanity--are unharmed.

The truly positive nature of the poem is revealed in the last stanza. In Brooks's words, the old couple remember with some "twinges" perhaps, but also with "tinklings" (10). As Melhem says, these people are "strong in mutual affection and shared memories" (123). And the final line, which is much longer than all the rest and which catalogs the evidence of the couple's long life together, is almost musically affirmative: "As they lean over the beans in their rented back room that is full of beads and receipts and dolls and cloths, tobacco crumbs, vases and fringes" (11).

39b

What these people have is not much, but it is

something.

[New page.]

Works Cited

Brooks, Gwendolyn. "The Bean Eaters." The Bean Eaters.

New York: Harper, 1960.

Kent, George E. A Life of Gwendolyn Brooks. Lexington:

UP of Kentucky, 1990.

Melhem, D. H. Gwendolyn Brooks: Poetry and the Heroic

Voice. Lexington: UP of Kentucky, 1987.

Shaw, Harry B. Gwendolyn Brooks. Boston: Twayne, 1980.

39c Writing in the social sciences

The social sciences—including anthropology, economics, education, management, political science, psychology, and sociology—focus on the study of human behavior. As the name implies, the social sciences examine the way human beings relate to themselves, to their environment, and to each other.

1 Methods and evidence in the social sciences

Researchers in the social sciences systematically pose a question, formulate a **hypothesis** (a generalization that can be tested), collect data, analyze those data, and draw conclusions to support or disprove their hypothesis. This is the scientific method developed in the natural sciences (see p. 711). Social scientists gather data in several ways. They make firsthand observations of human behavior and record the observations in writing or on audio- or videotape. They interview subjects about their attitudes and behavior, recording responses in writing or on tape. (See p. 563 for guidelines on conducting an interview.) They conduct broader surveys using questionnaires that ask people about their attitudes and behavior. (See the box on the next page.) And they conduct controlled experiments, structuring an environment in which to encourage and measure a specific behavior. In their writing, social

RESOURCES AND IDEAS

Linda K. Shamoon and Robert A. Schwegler, "Sociologists Reading Student Texts: Expectations and Perceptions," *The Writing Instructor* 7 (1988): 71–81. The authors argue that the way sociologists perceive the features of a student paper differ considerably from the way composition instructors often perceive the features. Sociologists look first of all for a line of sociological reasoning carried throughout a paper, supported by evidence acceptable to sociologists and made clear by indicators such as topic sentences.

39c

Conducting a survey

1. Decide what you want to find out—what your hypothesis is. The questions you ask should be dictated by your purpose.
2. Define your population. Think about the kinds of people your hypothesis is about—for instance, college men, or five-year-old children. Plan to sample this population so that your findings will be representative.
3. Write your questions. Surveys may contain closed questions that direct the respondent's answers (check lists and multiple-choice, true/false, or yes/no questions) or open-ended questions allowing brief, descriptive answers. Avoid loaded questions that reveal your own biases or make assumptions about subjects' answers, such as "Do you want the United States to support democracy in El Salvador?" or "How much more money does your father make than your mother?"
4. Test your questions on a few respondents with whom you can discuss the answers. Eliminate or recast questions that respondents find unclear, discomforting, or unanswerable.
5. Tally the results in actual numbers of answers, including any nonanswers.
6. Seek patterns in the raw data that conform or conflict with your hypothesis. Revise the hypothesis or conduct additional research if necessary.

scientists explain their own research or analyze and evaluate others' research.

The research methods of social science generate two kinds of data, quantitative and qualitative. **Quantitative data** are numerical, such as statistical evidence based on surveys, polls, tests, and experiments. When public-opinion pollsters announce that 47 percent of Americans polled approve of the President's leadership, they are offering quantitative data gained from a survey. Social science writers present quantitative data in graphs, charts, and other illustrations that accompany their text. (See p. 704.)

Qualitative data are not numerical but more subjective: they are based on interviews, firsthand observations, and inferences, taking into account the subjective nature of human experience. An example is the work of the anthropologist Margaret Mead, whose experiences among the people of Samoa led to an important description of how adolescent Samoans become aware of adult concerns and rituals. Mead's book, *Coming of Age in Samoa,* contains few numbers; the data are qualitative.

2   Assignments in the social sciences

Depending on what social science courses you take, you may be asked to complete a variety of assignments.

- A **summary or review of research** reports on the available research literature on a subject, such as infant perception of color.
- A **case analysis** explains the components of a phenomenon, such as a factory closing.
- A **problem-solving analysis** explains the components of a problem, such as unreported child abuse, and suggests ways to solve it. A problem-solving analysis begins on page 705.
- A **research paper** interprets and sometimes analyzes and evaluates the writings of other social scientists about a subject, such as the effect of national appeals in advertising. An example appears in Chapter 38, page 632.
- A **research report** explains the author's own original research or attempt to replicate someone else's research.

Many social science disciplines have special requirements for the content and organization of each kind of paper. The requirements appear in the style guides of the disciplines, such as the *Publication Manual of the American Psychological Association* (APA). (Guides for other disciplines are listed on p. 693.) The APA manual specifies the following outline for the text of a research report.

1. *Abstract:* a summary (about 100 words) of the subject, the research method, the findings, and the conclusions.
2. *Introduction:* a presentation of the problem researched, the research method used, the background (such as other relevant studies), the purpose of the research, and the hypothesis tested.
3. *Method:* a detailed discussion of how the research was conducted, including a description of the research subjects, any materials or tools used (such as questionnaires), and the procedure followed.
4. *Results:* a summary of the data collected and how they were statistically analyzed, along with a detailed presentation of the data, often in tables, graphs, or charts.
5. *Discussion:* an interpretation of the data and presentation of conclusions, related to the original hypothesis. (When the discussion is brief, it may be combined with the previous section under the heading "Results and Discussion.")

39c

To this basic text are added a title page and a list of references (the latter described on pp. 696–98).

Because of the differences among disciplines and even among different kinds of papers in the same discipline, you should always ask your instructor what he or she requires for an assignment.

 Tools and language in the social sciences

Although a **research journal** or **log** may not be required in your courses, such a notebook can be very helpful. Use it to pose preliminary questions as you begin formulating a hypothesis. Then in the field (that is, when conducting research), use the journal to react to the evidence you are collecting, to record changes in your perceptions and ideas, and to assess your progress. To avoid confusing your reflections on the evidence with the evidence itself, keep records of actual data—notes from interviews, observations, surveys, and experiments—separately from the field journal.

Each social science discipline has specialized terminology for concepts basic to the discipline. In sociology, for example, the words *mechanism, identity,* and *deviance* have specific meanings different from those of everyday usage. And *identity* means something different in sociology, where it applies to groups of people, than in psychology, where it applies to the individual. Social scientists also use precise terms to describe or interpret research. For instance, they say *The subject expressed a feeling of* rather than *The subject felt* because human feelings and intentions are not knowable for certain; or they say *These studies indicate* rather than *These studies prove* because conclusions are only tentative.

Just as social scientists strive for objectivity in their research, so they strive to demonstrate their objectivity through language in their writing. They avoid expressions such as *I think* in order to focus attention on what the evidence shows rather than on the researcher's opinions. (However, many social scientists prefer *I* to the artificial *the researcher* when they refer to their own actions, as in *I then interviewed the subjects.* Ask your instructor for his or her preferences.) Social scientists also avoid direct or indirect expression of their personal biases or emotions, either in discussions of other researchers' work or in descriptions of research subjects. Thus, one social scientist does not call another's work *sloppy* or *immaculate* and does not refer to his or her own subjects as *drunks* or *innocent victims.* Instead, the writer uses neutral language and ties conclusions strictly to the data.

39c

Documentation and format

As mentioned earlier, some of the social sciences publish style guides that advise practitioners how to organize, document, and type papers. The following is a partial list:

American Psychological Association. *Publication Manual of the American Psychological Association.* 3rd ed. 1983.
American Sociological Association. "Editorial Guidelines." Inside front cover of each issue of *American Sociological Review.*
American Anthropological Association. "Style Guide and Information for Authors." *American Anthropologist* (1977): 774–79.

Disciplines that do not have their own style guides may rely on one of those above or may recommend any of several guides. In business, for example, teachers and practitioners often use the *Publication Manual of the American Psychological Association* (APA), listed above; the *MLA Handbook for Writers of Research Papers* (p. 597), or the *Chicago Manual of Style* or Turabian's *Manual for Writers of Term Papers, Theses, and Dissertations* (see p. 598).

Always ask your instructor in any discipline what style you should use. The APA style and manuscript format are explained and illustrated below because they are by far the most often used in the social sciences and are similar to the styles in sociology, economics, and other disciplines.

APA parenthetical citations

The APA documentation style is like that of the Modern Language Association in that parenthetical citations within the text refer the reader to a list of sources at the end of the text. The APA style (like the MLA) thus uses footnotes or endnotes only for information that does not fit easily into the text.

APA parenthetical citations contain the author's last name, the date of publication (a key difference from MLA style), and often the page number from which material is borrowed. See the next page for an index to the models for various kinds of services.

1. Author not named in the text

One critic of Milgram's experiments insisted that the

subjects should have been fully informed of the possible

effects on them (Baumrind, 1968, p. 34).

Index to APA parenthetical citations

When you do not name the author in your text, place in parentheses the author's name, the date of the source, and the page number(s) preceded by "p." or "pp." Separate the elements with commas. Position the reference so that it is clear what material is being documented *and* so that the reference fits as smoothly as possible into your sentence structure. The following would also be correct:

```
In the view of one critic of Milgram's experiments

(Baumrind, 1968, p. 34), the subjects should have been

fully informed of the possible effects on them.
```

2. Author named in the text

```
Baumrind (1968, p. 34) insisted that the subjects in

Milgram's study should have been fully informed of the

possible effects on them.
```

When you use the author's name in the text, do not repeat it in the reference. Position the reference next to the author's name. If you cite the same source again in the paragraph, you need not repeat the reference as long as the page number (if any) is the same and it is clear that you are using the same source. Here is a later sentence from the paragraph containing the preceding example.

```
Baumrind also criticized the experimenters' rationale.
```

3. A work with two authors

```
Pepinsky and DeStefano (1977) demonstrate that a teacher's

language often reveals hidden biases.
```

APA
39c

One study (Pepinsky & DeStefano, 1977) demonstrated the

hidden biases often revealed in a teacher's language.

When given in the text, two authors' names are connected by "and." In a parenthetical citation, they are connected by an ampersand, "&."

4. A work with three to six authors

Pepinsky, Dunn, Rentl, and Corson (1973) further

demonstrated the biases evident in gestures.

In the first citation of a work with three to six authors, name all the authors, as in the example above. In the second and subsequent references to a work with three to six authors, give only the first author's name, followed by "et al." (Latin for "and others"):

In the work of Pepinsky et al. (1973), the loaded gestures

included head shakes and eye contact.

5. A work with more than six authors

One study (Rutter et al., 1976) attempts to explain these

geographical differences in adolescent experience.

For more than six authors, even in the first citation of the work, give only the first author's name, followed by "et al."

6. A work with a corporate author

An earlier prediction was even more somber (Lorenz, Inc.,

1970).

For a work with a corporate or group author, treat the name of the corporation or group as if it were an individual's name.

7. An anonymous work

One article ("Right to Die," 1976) noted that a death-row

inmate may crave notoriety.

For an anonymous or unsigned work, use the first two or three words of the title in place of an author's name, excluding an initial *The, A,* or *An.* Underline book and journal titles. Place quotation marks around article titles. (In the list of references, however, do not use quotation marks for article titles. See pp. 700–01.) Capitalize the significant words in all titles cited in the text. (But in the reference list, treat only journal titles this way. See pp. 700–01.)

8. One of two or more works by the same author(s)

At about age seven, most children begin to use appropriate

gestures to reinforce their stories (Gardner, 1973a, pp.

144-145).

When you cite one of two or more works by the same author(s), the date will tell readers which source you mean—as long as your reference list includes only one source published by the author(s) in that year. If your reference list includes two or more works published by the same author(s) *in the same year,* the works should be lettered in the reference list (see p. 699). Then your parenthetical citation should include the appropriate letter, as in the example above.

9. Two or more works by different authors

Two studies (Herskowitz, 1974; Marconi & Hamblen, 1980)

found that periodic safety instruction can dramatically

reduce employees' accidents.

List the sources in alphabetical order by the first author's name. Insert a semicolon between sources.

10. An indirect source

Supporting data appear in a study by Wong (cited in

Marconi & Hamblen, 1980).

The phrase "cited in" indicates that the reference to Wong's study was found in Marconi and Hamblen. You are obliged to acknowledge that you did not consult the original source (Wong) yourself. In the list of references, give only Marconi and Hamblen.

APA reference list

APA
39c

In APA style, the in-text parenthetical citations refer to the list of sources at the end of the text. This list, titled "References," includes full publication information on every source cited in the paper.

Caution: The APA style is quite different from that of the *MLA Handbook* (p. 605). Don't confuse the two styles.

Index to APA references

In the APA "References" the sources are arranged alphabetically by the author's last name or, if there is no author, by the first main word of the title. In the models that follow for various sources, observe these features:

- Double-space all entries. Type the first line of each entry at the left margin, and indent all subsequent lines three spaces.
- List all authors last-name first, separating names and parts of names with commas. Use initials for first and middle names. Use an ampersand (&) rather than "and" before the last author's name.
- In titles of books and articles, capitalize only the first word of the title, the first word of the subtitle, and proper names; all other words begin with small letters. In titles of journals, capitalize all significant words. Underline the titles of books and journals. Do not underline or use quotation marks around the titles of articles.
- Give full names of publishers, excluding "Co.," "Inc.," and the like.
- Use the abbreviation "p." or "pp." before page numbers in books, magazines, and newspapers, but *not* for scholarly jour-

TRANSPARENCY MASTER
AVAILABLE

APA
39c

nals. For inclusive page numbers, include all figures: "667–668."

- Separate the parts of the reference (author, date, title, and publication information) with a period and two spaces.

Note: You may have to combine models to provide the necessary information on a source—for instance, combining "A book with one author" (1) and "A book with an editor" (3) for a book with only one editor.

1. A book with one author

Rodriguez, R. (1982). <u>A hunger of memory: The education</u>

<u>of Richard Rodriguez</u>. Boston: David R. Godine.

The initial "R" appears instead of the author's first name, even though the author's full first name appears on the source. In the title, only the first words of title and subtitle and the proper name are capitalized.

2. A book with two or more authors

Nesselroade, J. R., & Baltes, P. B. (1979). <u>Longitudinal</u>

<u>research in the study of behavioral development</u>. New

York: Academic Press.

An ampersand (&) separates the authors' names.

3. A book with an editor

Dohrenwend, B. S., & Dohrenwend, B. P. (Eds.). (1974).

<u>Stressful life events: Their nature and effects</u>.

New York: John Wiley.

List the editors' names as if they were authors, but follow the last name with "(Eds.)."—or "(Ed.)." with only one editor. Note the periods inside and outside the final parenthesis.

4. A book with a translator

Trajan, P. D. (1927). <u>Psychology of animals</u>. (H. Simone,

Trans.). Washington, DC: Halperin & Bros.

The name of the translator appears in parentheses after the title, followed by a comma, "Trans.," a closing parenthesis, and a final period. Note also the absence of periods in "DC."

5. A book with a corporate author

Lorenz, Inc.   (1992).   <u>Research in social studies</u>

   <u>teaching</u>.   Baltimore: Arrow Books.

For a work with a corporate or group author, begin the entry with the corporate or group name. In the references list, alphabetize the work as if the first main word (excluding *The, A,* and *An*) were an author's last name.

6. An anonymous book

<u>Webster's seventh new collegiate dictionary</u>.   (1963).

   Springfield: G. & C. Merriam.

When no author is named, list the work under its title, and alphabetize it by the first main word (excluding *The, A, An*).

7. Two or more works by the same author(s)

Gardner, H.   (1973a).   <u>The arts and human development</u>.

   New York: John Wiley.

Gardner, H.   (1973b).   <u>The quest for mind: Piaget, Lévi-</u>

   <u>Strauss, and the structuralist movement</u>.   New York:

   Alfred A. Knopf.

When citing two or more works by exactly the same author(s), arrange the sources in order of their publication dates, earliest first. When citing two or more works by exactly the same author(s), published in the same year—as in the examples above—arrange them alphabetically by the first main word of the title and distinguish the sources by adding a letter to the date. Both the date *and* the letter are used in citing the source in the text (see p. 696).

8. A later edition

Bollinger, D. L.   (1975).   <u>Aspects of language</u> (2nd ed.).

   New York: Harcourt Brace Jovanovich.

The edition number in parentheses follows the title and is followed by a period.

9. A work in more than one volume

Lincoln, A.   (1953).   <u>The collected works of Abraham</u>

APA
39c

```
        Lincoln (R. P. Basler, Ed.). (Vol. 5). New

    Brunswick: Rutgers University Press.

Lincoln, A. (1953). The collected works of Abraham

    Lincoln (R. P. Basler, Ed.). (Vols. 1-8). New

    Brunswick: Rutgers University Press.
```

The first entry cites a single volume (5) in the eight-volume set. The second cites all eight volumes. Use the abbreviation "Vol." or "Vols." in parentheses, and follow the closing parenthesis with a period. In the absence of an editor's name, the description of volumes would follow the title directly: The collected works of Abraham Lincoln (Vol. 5).

10. An article or chapter in an edited book

```
Paykel, E. S. (1974). Life stress and psychiatric dis-

    order: Applications of the clinical approach. In

    B. S. Dohrenwend & B. P. Dohrenwend (Eds.), Stress-

    ful life events: Their nature and effects (pp. 239-

    264). New York: John Wiley.
```

The publication date of the collection (1974) is given as the publication date of the article or chapter. Following the article or chapter title and a period, information on the collection begins with "In," then the editors' names (in normal order), then "(Eds.)" and a comma, and then the title of the collection and the page numbers of the article in parentheses.

11. An article in a journal with continuous pagination throughout the annual volume

```
Emery, R. E. (1982). Marital turmoil: Interpersonal

    conflict and the children of discord and divorce.

    Psychological Bulletin, 92, 310-330.
```

See page 553 for an explanation of journal pagination. Note that the article title is not placed in quotation marks and that only the first words of the title and subtitle are capitalized. The journal title, in contrast, is underlined, and all significant words are capitalized. The volume number is separated from the title by a comma and is underlined. No "pp." precedes the page numbers.

12. An article in a journal that pages issues separately

```
Boyd, S.  (1981).  Nuclear terror.  Adaptation to Change,

    7(4), 20-23.
```

Again, consult page 553 for an explanation of journal pagination. In this case, the issue number in parentheses follows the volume number without intervening space. The issue number is *not* underlined.

13. An article in a magazine

```
Van Gelder, L.  (1986, December).  Countdown to mother-

    hood: When should you have a baby?  Ms., pp. 37-39,

    74.
```

In the absence of a volume number, give the month of publication after the year, separating them with a comma. Give all page numbers even when the article appears on discontinuous pages. Use "pp." before the page numbers.

14. An article in a newspaper

```
Herbers, J.  (1988, March 6).  A different Dixie: Few

    but sturdy threads tie new South to old.  The New

    York Times, sec. 4, p. 1.
```

Give month *and* date along with year of publication. Use The in the newspaper name if the paper itself does.

15. An unsigned article

```
The right to die.  (1976, October 11).  Time, p. 101.
```

List and alphabetize the article under its title, as you would an anonymous book (model 6, p. 699).

16. A review

```
Dinnage, R.  (1987, November 29).  Against the master and

    his men.  [Review of A mind of her own: The life of

    Karen Horney].  The New York Times Book Review, pp.

    10-11.
```

If the review is not titled, use the bracketed information as the title, keeping the brackets.

APA
39c

17. A report

Gerald, K. (1958). <u>Medico-moral problems in obstetric</u>

<u>care</u> (Report No. NP-71). St. Louis: Catholic

Hospital Association.

Treat the report like a book, but provide any report number in parentheses immediately after the title, with no punctuation between them.

18. An information service

Jolson, Maria K. (1981). <u>Music education for preschool-</u>

<u>ers</u>. New York: Teachers College, Columbia Univer-

sity. (ERIC Document Reproduction Service No. ED 264

488)

Place the name of the service and the document number in parentheses after the original publisher and a period. No period follows the number.

19. A government document

United States Commission on Civil Rights. (1983).

<u>Greater Baltimore commitment</u>. Washington DC:

Author.

If no individual is listed as author, list the document under the name of the sponsoring agency. When the agency is both the author and the publisher, use "Author" in place of the publisher's name.

20. An interview

William C. Brisick. (1988, July 1). [Interview with

Ishmael Reed]. <u>Publisher's Weekly</u>, pp. 41-42.

List a published interview under the interviewer's name. Provide the publication information appropriate for the kind of source the interview appears in (here, a magazine). Immediately after the title, in brackets, specify that the piece is an interview and, if necessary, provide other identifying information. If the interview has its own title, insert it after the date, as with a review (model 16).

Note that interviews you conduct yourself are not included in the list of references. Instead, use an in-text parenthetical citation: if the subject is already named, "(personal communication, July 7, 1991)"; if not, "(L. Kogod, personal communication, July 7, 1991)."

21. A videotape or other nonprint source

Heeley, D. (Director), & Kramer, J. (Producer). (1988).

Bacall on Bogart [Videotape]. New York: WNET Films.

The names of major contributors are followed by parenthetical designation of their function. The medium is specified in brackets after the title, with no intervening punctuation. Other nonprint sources include films, slides, art works, and musical performances.

22. Computer software

Project scheduler 6000. (1991). [Computer program].

Orlando: Scitor.

If no individual is given as author, list the software under its title. Identify the entry as a "Computer program" in brackets, add a period, and provide the name of the producer. If there is a catalog or other reference number, give it in parentheses at the end of the entry, as in model 18.

APA manuscript format

In general, the guidelines of the APA for manuscript format coincide with those of the MLA, explained in Appendix A of this book. There are, however, some important differences and additions:

- Use a 1½-inch margin on the left and 1-inch margins on the other three sides.
- Number pages consecutively, starting with the title page. Identify each page (including the title page) with a shortened version of the title as well as a page number. For instance:

Dating Violence

5

66 males) at a large state university in the northeast

United States. The sample consisted of students enrolled

APA
39c

- Put the abstract (if there is one) on a page by itself immediately after the title page, with the heading "Abstract" centered at the top of the page.
- Run into your text all quotations of fewer than forty words, and enclose them in quotation marks. For quotations of more than forty words, set them off from your text by indenting all lines five spaces, double-spacing above and below, and double-spacing the quotation itself. Do not use quotation marks around a quotation displayed in this way.
- Do not label the introduction with a heading. For other main sections of your paper, such as "Method" and "Results," center the heading, type it in capital and small letters, do not underline it, and double-space above and below it. (Do not start new pages for these sections.) If you use another level of heading below the main level, begin at the left margin, use capital and small letters, and underline the heading. See page 706 for examples of both headings.
- Present data in tables and figures (graphs or charts), as appropriate. (See the sample on p. 708 for a clear format to follow.) Begin each illustration on a separate page. Number each kind of illustration consecutively and separately from the other (Table 1, Table 2, etc., and Figure 1, Figure 2, etc.). Refer to all illustrations in your text—for instance, "(See Figure 3.)." Either place illustrations immediately after the text references to them, or, if there are many illustrations, collect them at the end of the paper, after the reference list. (See pp. 715–16 for more information on illustrations.)
- The reference list starts a new page after the last page of the text, with the heading "References" centered at the top of the page and the entire list typed double-space. (See p. 709.) The references themselves follow the models on pages 698–703.

Because many departments and instructors have their own preferences for manuscript format, you should ask your instructor for his or her wishes before preparing your final draft.

RESOURCES AND IDEAS

Carol Berkenkotter, "Writing and Problem Solving," *Journal of Basic Writing* 5 (1988).

APA
39c

 5   **A sample social science paper**

On the following pages are excerpts from a sociology paper. The student followed the organization described on page 691 both in establishing the background for her study and in explaining her own research. She also followed the APA style of documentation and manuscript format, although page borders are omitted and only the required page breaks are indicated.

Excerpts from a problem-solving analysis (sociology)

[Title page: center vertically and horizontally.]

An Assessment of

Dating Violence on Campus

Karen M. Tarczyk

Sociology 213

Mr. Durkan

May 6, 1990

[New page.]

Abstract

Little research has examined the patterns of abuse
and violence occurring within couples during courtship.
With a questionnaire administered to a sample of college
students, the extent and nature of such abuse and violence
were investigated. The results, some interpretations, and
implications for further research are discussed.

[New page.]

An Assessment of

Dating Violence on Campus

In recent years, a great deal of attention has been
devoted to family violence. Numerous studies have been
done on spouse and child abuse. However, violent behavior
occurs in dating relationships as well. The problem of
dating violence has been relatively ignored by sociological research. It should be examined further since the premarital relationship is one context in which individuals
learn and adopt behaviors that surface later in marriage.

The sociologist James Makepeace (1979) contends that

APA
39c

courtship violence is a "potential mediating link" between violence in one's family of orientation and violence in one's later family of procreation. His provocative study examining dating behaviors at Bemidji State University in Minnesota caused a controversy. Makepeace reported that one-fifth of the respondents had had at least one encounter with dating violence. He concluded by extending these percentages to students nationwide, suggesting the existence of a major hidden social problem.

[The introduction continues.]

All these studies indicate a problem that is being neglected. The present study's objective was to gather information on the extent and nature of premarital violence and to discuss some possible interpretations.

Method

Sample

I conducted a survey of 200 students (134 females, 66 males) at a large state university in the northeast United States. The sample consisted of students enrolled in an introductory sociology course. The mean age of the respondents was 19.35 years, ranging from 18 to 31. Most students (87.8%) resided in campus dormitories, not at home or in their own apartments. Moreover, the majority of the sample (93.5%) were single and not self-supporting.

The Questionnaire

A questionnaire exploring the personal dynamics of relationships was distributed during regularly scheduled class. Questions were answered anonymously in a 30-minute

time period. The survey consisted of three sections:
section 1 and section 2 were filled out by all respondents; section 3 was filled out only by students currently
dating someone (123 of 200 students).

[The explanation of method continues.]

Section 3 required participants to provide information about their current dating relationships. Levels of
stress and frustration, communication between partners,
and patterns of decision making were examined. These
variables were expected to influence the amount of
violence in a relationship. The next part of the survey
was adopted from Murray Strauss's Conflict Tactics Scales
(1982). These scales contain 19 items designed to measure
conflict and the means of conflict resolution, including
reasoning, verbal aggression, and actual violence. The
final page of the questionnaire contained general questions on the couple's use of alcohol, sexual activity, and
overall satisfaction with the relationship.

Results

The incidence of verbal aggression and threatened and
actual dating violence was examined. A high number of
students, 50% (62 of 123 subjects), reported that they had
been the victim of verbal abuse, either being insulted or
sworn at. In addition, 14% (17 of 123) of respondents
admitted being threatened with some type of violence. Low
percentages were reported for the various types of actual
physical violence. (See Table 1.)

[The explanation of results continues.]

APA
39c

[Table on a page by itself.]

Table 1

Incidence of Courtship Violence

Type of violence	Number of students reporting	Percentage of sample
Insulted or swore	62	50.4
Threatened to hit or throw something	17	13.8
Threw something	8	6.6
Pushed, grabbed, or shoved	18	14.9
Slapped	8	6.6
Kicked, bit, or hit with fist	7	6.0
Hit or tried to hit with something	2	1.6
Threatened with a knife or gun	1	0.8
Used a knife or gun	1	0.8

Discussion

Violence within premarital relationships has been relatively ignored. The results of the present study indicate that abuse and force do occur in dating relationships. Although the percentages are small, so was the sample. Extending them to the entire campus population would mean significant numbers. For example, if the 6% incidence of being kicked, bitten, or hit with a fist is typical, then 300 students of a 5,000-member student body might have experienced this type of violence.

[The discussion continues.]

If the courtship period is characterized by abuse and violence, what accounts for it? The other sections of the survey examined some variables that appear to influence the relationship. Level of stress and frustra-

39c

tion, both within the relationship and in the respondent's life, was one such variable. The communication level between partners, both the frequency of discussion and the frequency of agreement, was also seen to have an influence on the nature of the relationship.

[The discussion continues.]

   The method of analyzing the data in this study, utilizing frequency distributions, provided a clear overview. However, more tests of significance and correlation need to be done. A closer look at the social and individual variables affecting the relationship is warranted. The courtship period may set the stage for patterns of married life. It merits more attention.

[New page.]

                          References

Cates, R. L., Rutter, C. H., Karl, J., Linton, M., &
    Smith, K. (1982). Premarital abuse: A social
    psychological perspective. Journal of Family Issues
    3(1), 79-90.

Glaser, R., and Rutter, C. H. (Eds.). (1984). Familial
    violence [Special issue]. Family Relations, 33(3).

Laner, M. (1983). Recent increases in dating violence.
    Social Problems, 22, 152-166.

Makepeace, J. M. (1981). Courtship violence among col-
    lege students. Family Relations, 30, 97-102.

Socko performance on campus. (1981, June 7). Time, pp.
    66-67.

Strauss, M. L. (1982). Conflict tactics scales. New
    York: Sociological Tests.

APA
39c

39d Writing in the natural and applied sciences

The natural and applied sciences include biology, chemistry, physics, mathematics, engineering, computer science, and their branches. Their purpose is to understand natural and technological phenomena. (A *phenomenon* is a fact or event that can be known by the senses.) Scientists conduct experiments and write to explain the step-by-step processes in their methods of inquiry and discovery.

1 Methods and evidence in the sciences

Scientists investigate phenomena by the **scientific method,** a process of continual testing and refinement. (See the box opposite.) Scientific evidence is almost always quantitative—that is, it consists of numerical data obtained from the measurement of phenomena. These data are called **empirical** (from a Greek word for "experience"): they result from observation and experience, generally in a controlled laboratory setting but also (as sometimes in astronomy or biology) in the natural world. Often the empirical evidence for scientific writing comes from library research into other people's reports of their investigations. Surveys of known data or existing literature are common in scientific writing.

2 Assignments in the sciences

No matter what your assignment, you will be expected to document and explain your evidence carefully so that anyone reading can check your sources and replicate your research. It is important for your reader to know the context of your research—both the previous experimentation and research on your particular subject (acknowledged in the survey of the literature) and the physical conditions and other variables surrounding your own work.

Assignments in the natural and applied sciences include the following:

- A **summary** distills a research article to its essence in brief, concise form. (Summary is discussed in detail in 4b-4.)
- A **critique** summarizes and critically evaluates a scientific report.

39d

The scientific method

1. Observe carefully. Accurately note all details of the phenomenon being researched.
2. Ask questions about the observations.
3. Formulate a **hypothesis,** or preliminary generalization, that explains the observed facts.
4. Test the hypothesis with additional observation or controlled experiments.
5. If the hypothesis proves accurate, formulate a **theory,** or unified model, that explains *why.* If the hypothesis is disproved, revise it or start anew.

- A **laboratory report** explains the procedure and results of an experiment conducted by the writer. (An example begins on p. 716.)
- A **research report** reports on the experimental research of other scientists and the writer's own methods, findings, and conclusions.
- A **research proposal** reviews the relevant literature and explains a plan for further research.

A laboratory report has four or five major sections:

1. *Abstract:* a summary of the report. (See p. 716.)
2. *Introduction* or *Objective:* a review of why the study was undertaken, a summary of the background of the study, and a statement of the problem being studied.
3. *Method* or *Procedure:* a detailed explanation of how the study was conducted, including any statistical analysis.
4. *Results:* an explanation of the major findings (including unexpected results) and a summary of the data presented in graphs and tables.
5. *Discussion:* an interpretation of the results and an explanation of how they relate to the goals of the experiment. This section also describes new hypotheses that might be tested as a result of the experiment. If the section is brief, it may be combined with the previous section in a single section labeled *Conclusions.*

In addition, laboratory or research reports may include a list of references (if other sources were consulted). They almost always include tables and figures (graphs and charts) containing the data from the research (see pp. 715–16).

39d

RESOURCES AND IDEAS

John Olmsted III, "Teaching Varied Technical Writing Styles in the Upper Division Laboratory," *Journal of Chemical Education* 61 (1984): 798–800. Olmsted describes a course that asks students to prepare reports in a variety of styles on experiments they have conducted. He describes in detail the twelve different kinds of reports students must submit during the course.

RESOURCES AND IDEAS

W. Daniel Goodman and John C. Bean, "A Chemistry Laboratory Project to Develop Thinking and Writing Skills," *Journal of Chemistry Education* 60 (1983): 483–84. The authors outline "a method for conducting an undergraduate chemistry laboratory, in this case sophomore organic chemistry, that integrates a project laboratory with a writing task involving peer group interaction." The method requires "students to carry out an independent investigation of the synthesis of one or more aliphatic esters and to present their research in the form of professional papers."

39d

Tools and language in the sciences

Keeping a journal or notebook can help you reflect on and rethink your ideas for writing, pose and answer questions, or explore your changing attitudes about a subject. In the sciences, a **lab notebook** or **scientific journal** is almost indispensable for accurately recording the empirical data from observations and experiments. Use such a notebook or journal for these purposes:

- Record observations from reading, from class, or from the lab.
- Ask questions and refine hypotheses.
- Record procedures.
- Record results.
- Keep an ongoing record of ideas and findings and how they change as data accumulate.
- Sequence and organize your material as you compile your findings and write your report.

When writing in your notebook, try to observe as well the special conventions of language in the sciences. The main convention is the use of objective language that removes the writer as a character in the situation and events being explained, except as the impersonal agent of change, the experimenter. Accordingly, scientists rarely use *I* in their reports and evaluations, and they often resort to the passive voice of verbs, as in *The mixture was then subjected to centrifugal force.* This conscious objectivity focuses attention (including the writer's) on the empirical data and what they show. It discourages the writer from, say, ascribing motives and will to animals and plants. For instance, instead of asserting that the sea tortoise *evolved* its hard shell *to protect* its body, a scientist would write only what could be observed: that the hard shell *covers and thus protects* the tortoise's body.

As in the social sciences, each discipline in the natural and applied sciences has a specialized vocabulary that permits precise, accurate, and efficient communication. Some of these terms, such as *pressure* in physics, have different meanings in the common language and must be handled carefully in science writing. Others, such as *enthalpy* in chemistry, have no meanings in the common language and must simply be learned and used correctly.

Documentation and format in the sciences

Within the natural and applied sciences, the practitioners of each discipline use a slightly different style of documentation and manuscript format. Following are some of the style guides most often consulted:

American Chemical Society. *Handbook for Authors of Papers in American Chemical Society Publications.* 1978.

American Institute of Physics. *Style Manual for Guidance in the Preparation of Papers.* 3rd ed. 1978.

American Mathematical Society. *A Manual for Authors of Mathematical Papers.* 8th ed. 1980.

American Medical Association. *Style Book: Editorial Manual.* 6th ed. 1976.

Council of Biology Editors. *CBE Style Manual: A Guide for Authors, Editors, and Publishers in the Biological Sciences.* 5th ed. 1983.

As in any discipline, always ask your instructor what style and format he or she prefers before you prepare your final draft.

Documentation

Some documentation styles in the sciences closely resemble other styles discussed in this chapter and Chapter 37: the APA system of in-text parenthetical citations and a separate reference list (see p. 693) or a system of in-text raised numerals referring to separate footnotes or endnotes (see p. 621).

A third style is common in the biological sciences, physics, mathematics, the health sciences, and other disciplines: source citations consist of in-text numbers that refer to a list of correspondingly numbered references. A version of this style, appearing in the *CBE Style Manual* for the biological sciences, is outlined below.

CBE numbered citations

Two standard references (1, 2) use this term. . . .

These forms of immunity have been extensively researched

(3). . . .

According to one report (3, p. 160), research into some

forms of viral immunity is almost nonexistent. . . .

Hepburn and Tatin (1) do not discuss this project. . . .

- Within the text, use a number or numbers in parentheses to refer to numbered sources in the reference list at the end of the text.

TRANSPARENCY MASTER
AVAILABLE

CBE
39d

- The number for each source is based on the order in which you cite the source in the text: the first cited source is 1, the second is 2, and so on.
- When you cite a source you have already cited and numbered, use the original number again (see the last two examples above).
- When you cite two or more sources at once, arrange their numbers in sequence and separate them with a comma: "(1, 2)."
- When you need to cite a page number, separate it from the source number with a comma and precede it with "p." (or "pp."). (See the third example above.)

CBE reference list

Begin the numbered list of sources on a new page at the end of the text, and title it "References." Double-space the entries. Arrange them in numerical order—that is, in order of their citation in the text, *not* alphabetically. The following examples, keyed to the text citations above, illustrate standard entries for a book with two authors (1), a book with an editor (2), and a journal article with three authors (3).

1. Hepburn, P. X.; Tatin, J. M. Human physiology. New
   York: Columbia University Press; 1975.

2. Jonson, P., editor. Anatomy yearbook. Los Angeles:
   Anatco; 1987.

3. Ancino, R.; Carter, K. V.; Elwin, D. J. Factors
   contributing to viral immunity: a review of the
   research. Developmental Biology 30:156-169; 1983.

- Each entry begins a new line and is numbered. The number is followed by a period and a space. Subsequent lines of each entry then begin directly under the first word of the first line.
- Authors' first and middle names are represented by initials.
- Authors' names are separated by semicolons (1 and 3).
- No titles are underlined or placed in quotation marks.
- Only in journal titles (3) is any but the first word of a title capitalized. In book and article titles and subtitles, all words after the first word begin with small letters (1–3).
- The name of the publisher is separated from the date of publication by a semicolon (1 and 2).
- No punctuation falls between a journal's title and volume

TRANSPARENCY MASTER
AVAILABLE

CBE
39d

number (3). Page numbers are connected to the volume number with an unspaced colon. The date of publication then follows a semicolon and a space.

(Though somewhat similar, CBE forms and those of the APA differ in important features such as punctuation and the handling of titles. Compare pp. 696–703.)

Manuscript format

Each science discipline has its own preferred manuscript format. The CBE format closely resembles that of the APA (see p. 703). Again, ask your instructor for his or her preferences.

The most troublesome aspects of manuscript preparation in the sciences are equations or formulas and illustrations (tables and figures). When typing equations or formulas, be careful to reproduce alignments, indentions, underlining, and characters accurately. If your typewriter or word processor lacks special characters, write them in by hand. (Stationery and art-supply stores also have sheets of transfer type with special characters in different sizes that can be applied to your manuscript by rubbing.)

Because you will be expected to share your data with your readers, most of your writing for the sciences is likely to require illustrations to present the data in concise, readable form. Tables usually summarize raw data (see p. 718 for an example), whereas figures (mainly charts and graphs) recast the data to show noteworthy comparisons or changes. Follow these guidelines in preparing and positioning illustrations:

- Give each illustration a clear label. Number tables and figures separately (Table 1, Table 2, etc.; Figure 1, Figure 2, etc.).
- Give each illustration a clear title so that readers know what to look for in it. (Generally, a table's label and title are placed above the illustration, whereas a figure's label and title are placed under the illustration.)
- Provide clear labels for all the parts of illustrations, such as columns in a table and bars in a bar graph. Unless your instructor specifically requests abbreviations, avoid them in the interest of clarity.
- If you borrow the data or the whole illustration from another source, provide a source note under the illustration. For instance:

```
Source:  Ann Menaker.  Spectroscopy of plasmas.  New York:

Van Nostrand; 1981.
```

CBE

39d

- Refer to each illustration ("See Figure 6") at the point(s) in the text where readers will benefit by consulting it.
- If your paper includes many illustrations, collect them at the end of the paper, after the reference list. If it includes only a few illustrations, place each one on a page by itself immediately after the page that refers to it.

 A sample science paper

The following excerpts from a laboratory report in genetics, a branch of biology, illustrate many of the features described in the preceding pages. Some elements, such as page borders and identifiers, have been omitted, but otherwise the format illustrates that recommended by the Council of Biology Editors (CBE). (The paper is based entirely on the student's own laboratory experiment and thus does not include text citations or a reference list.)

Excerpts from a laboratory report (biology)

[Title page: center title vertically and horizontally.]

Demonstration:

Genetic Engineering

Lynn Treacy
Genetics
Dr. Smith
March 29, 1991

[New page.]

Abstract

The transfer of the conjugative plasmid for chloramphenicol resistance from the donor, E. coli HT-99, to a suitable recipient, E. coli J-53R, was demonstrated using in vitro techniques.

[New page.]

CBE
39d

Demonstration: Genetic Engineering

Objective

The purpose of this experiment was to illustrate the
basic goal of genetic engineering through a demonstration/
experiment. In this experiment, a donor, E. coli
HT-99, which is resistant to chloramphenicol and sensitive
to rifampicin, and a host cell, E. coli J-53R, which is
resistant to rifampicin and sensitive to chloramphenicol,
were mated. The donor cell contained a chimera, a plasmid
of the E. coli donor that had the gene for resistance to
the antibiotic chloramphenicol, which would serve as a
marker for the detection of a successful conjugation.

Procedure

The results of the experiment were gathered from the
observance of growth or lack of growth of the donor, host,
and suspected exconjugant on nutrient agar plates containing (1) rifampicin, (2) chloramphenicol, and (3) both
rifampicin and chloramphenicol.

[The explanation of procedure continues.]

Conclusions

The HT-99 cells will grow in the presence of chloramphenicol, because they contain the genes to make them
resistant to chloramphenicol, whereas they will not grow
in the presence of rifampicin (either alone or with
chloramphenicol). After successful conjugation the exconjugant cells should grow on both plates since the cells
possess the genes coding for resistance to rifampicin, and
they also have the genes for resistance to chloramphenicol

CBE
39d

contained in a plasmid. The first test for exconjugants was negative because the constant agitation of the shaker did not allow conjugation to occur (interrupted the mating between the cells). After the mixture sat overnight, the exconjugant cells were found, since successful conjugation had occurred.

[Table on a page by itself.]

Table 1. Growth (+) or nongrowth (-) of donor, host, and exconjugant

| | Growth on plates containing | | |
Organism	Rifampicin	Chloramphenicol	Rifampicin and chloramphenicol
Donor	-	+	-
Host	+	-	-
Exconjugant, 4 hrs	NA	NA	-
Exconjugant, 18 hrs	NA	NA	+

NA = not applicable because not tested for.

[The conclusions continue.]

Successful conjugation is easily detected by the use of nutrient agar plates containing the antibiotics chloramphenicol and rifampicin; the simple observation of growth and of no growth is all that is needed to signal a successful or unsuccessful mating.

Part IX

Practical Writing

Though they have written essay exams before coming to college, most students have not mastered this form of expression and are probably quite uncomfortable with it. This chapter provides helpful advice on the various processes involved in writing an exam essay, from preparing for the exam and planning an answer to rereading a completed essay.

Chapter 40

Essay Examinations

In writing an essay for an examination, you summarize or analyze a topic, usually in several paragraphs or more and usually within a time limit. An essay question not only tests your knowledge of a subject (as short-answer and objective questions do) but also tests your control and synthesis of that knowledge and helps you see it in a new way (as the other questions usually cannot do).

40a Preparing for an essay examination

To do well on an essay exam, you will need to understand the course content, not only the facts but the interpretation of them, not only the relations pointed out to you but others you discover on your own.

- Take careful lecture notes.
- Thoughtfully, critically read the assigned texts or articles. (See 4b on critical reading.)
- Review regularly so the material has time to sink in and stimulate your thinking.
- Create summaries that recast others' ideas in your own words and extract the meaning from notes and texts. (See 4b-4 for instructions on summarizing.)
- Prepare notes or outlines that reorganize the course material around key topics or issues: in a business course, the advantages and disadvantages of several approaches to manage-

ment; in a short-story course, a theme running through all the stories you have read by a certain author or from a certain period; in a psychology course, various theorists' views of what causes a disorder such as schizophrenia. Any one of these is a likely topic for an essay question. Thinking of such categories can help you anticipate the kinds of questions you may be asked and increase your mastery of the material.

40b   Planning your time and your answer

When you first receive an examination, take a few minutes to get your bearings and plan an approach. The time spent will not be wasted.

1. Always read an exam all the way through at least once before you start answering any questions.
2. As you scan the exam, determine which questions seem most important, which ones are going to be most difficult for you, and approximately how much time you'll need for each question. (Your instructor may help by assigning a point value to each question as a guide to its importance or by suggesting an amount of time for you to spend on each question.)

Planning continues when you turn to an individual essay question. This stage is like the planning of an essay or a research paper, but much quicker. Resist the temptation to rush right into an answer without some planning, for a few minutes can save you time later and help you produce a stronger essay.

1. Read the question at least twice. You will be more likely to stick to the question and answer it fully.
2. Examine the words in the question and consider their implications. Look especially for words such as *describe, define, explain, summarize, analyze, evaluate,* and *interpret,* each of which requires a different kind of response. See the box on the next page and consult earlier discussions of such terms in 3c-2 and 4b.
3. After you are sure you understand the question, make a brief outline of the main ideas you want to include in your essay. Use the back of the exam sheet or booklet for scratch paper.
4. Write a brief thesis sentence for your essay that responds directly to the question and represents your view of the topic. (If you are unsure of how to write a thesis sentence, see 1f.) Include key phrases that you can expand with supporting evidence for your view.

40b

40c

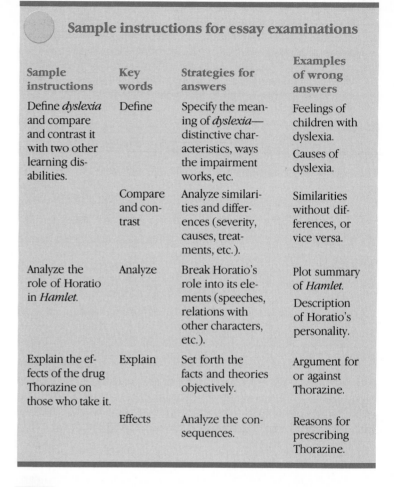

Sample instructions for essay examinations

Sample instructions	Key words	Strategies for answers	Examples of wrong answers
Define *dyslexia* and compare and contrast it with two other learning disabilities.	Define	Specify the meaning of *dyslexia*—distinctive characteristics, ways the impairment works, etc.	Feelings of children with dyslexia. Causes of dyslexia.
	Compare and contrast	Analyze similarities and differences (severity, causes, treatments, etc.).	Similarities without differences, or vice versa.
Analyze the role of Horatio in *Hamlet*.	Analyze	Break Horatio's role into its elements (speeches, relations with other characters, etc.).	Plot summary of *Hamlet*. Description of Horatio's personality.
Explain the effects of the drug Thorazine on those who take it.	Explain	Set forth the facts and theories objectively.	Argument for or against Thorazine.
	Effects	Analyze the consequences.	Reasons for prescribing Thorazine.

40c **Starting the essay**

Drawing on the brief thesis you devised during planning, you can begin your essay effectively by stating your thesis immediately and including in it an overview of the rest of your essay. Such a capsule version of your answer tells your reader (and grader) generally how much command you have and also how you plan to develop your answer. It also gets you off to a good start.

The opening statement should address the question directly and exactly. The following thesis sentence, in response to the question below, does *not* meet these criteria.

Question

Given humans' natural and historical curiosity about themselves, why did a scientific discipline of anthropology not arise until the twentieth century? Explain, citing specific details.

Tentative thesis sentence

The discipline of anthropology, the study of humans, actually began in the early nineteenth century and was strengthened by the Darwinian revolution, but the discipline did not begin to take shape until people like Franz Boas and Alfred Kroeber began doing scientific research among nonindustrialized cultures.

This tentative thesis sentence says nothing about *why* anthropology did not arise as a scientific discipline until the twentieth century. Instead, it supplies an unspecific (and unrequested) definition of anthropology, vaguely reasserts the truth implied by the question, and adds irrelevant details about the history of anthropology. The following thesis sentence—revised to address the question directly, to state the writer's view, and to preview the essay—begins the answer more effectively.

Revised thesis sentence

Anthropology did not emerge as a scientific discipline until the twentieth century because nineteenth-century Westerners' limited contact with remote peoples and the corresponding failure to see those other people as human combined to overcome natural curiosity and to prevent objective study of different cultures.

This thesis sentence specifies the writer's view of the two main causes of the slow emergence of anthropology—limited contact with remote peoples and, related to that, a narrow definition of humanity—that she will analyze in her essay.

40d Developing the essay

Develop your essay as you would develop any piece of sound academic writing:

- Observe the methods, terms, or other special requirements of the discipline you are writing in (see Chapter 39).
- Support your thesis sentence with solid generalizations (each one perhaps the topic sentence of a paragraph).
- Support each generalization with *specific, relevant* evidence (see 4f-2).

40e

If you observe a few *don't*'s as well, your essay will have more substance:

- Avoid filling out the essay by repeating yourself.
- Avoid other kinds of wordiness that pad and confuse, whether intentionally or not. (See 31c.)
- Avoid substituting purely subjective feelings for real definition, analysis, or whatever is asked of you. (It may help to abolish the word *I* from the essay.)

The student answering the anthropology question must show that contact between Western and non-Western cultures was limited and must specify how the limitations dulled curiosity, prevented objective study, and hampered the development of anthropology. She also needs to demonstrate how a consequently narrow definition of humanity had the same results. And she *must* support her assertions with concrete evidence. For instance, she might cite nineteenth-century writings that illustrate feelings of superiority toward distant peoples.

The student would not be providing effective evidence if she introduced unsupported generalizations or substituted her subjective feelings for an objective analysis of the problem. For instance, a blanket statement that all nineteenth-century Westerners were narrow-minded or a paragraph condemning their narrowness would only weaken the essay.

 40e **Rereading the essay**

The time limit on an essay examination does not allow for the careful rethinking and revision you would give an essay or research paper. You need to write clearly and concisely the first time. But try to leave yourself a few minutes after finishing the entire exam for rereading the essay (or essays) and doing touchups.

- Correct illegible passages, misspellings, grammatical mistakes, and accidental omissions.
- Verify that your thesis is accurate—that it does, in fact, introduce what you ended up writing about.
- Check to ensure that you have supported all your generalizations. Cross out irrelevant ideas and details, and add any information that now seems important. (Write on another page, if necessary, keying the addition to the page on which it belongs.)

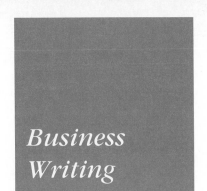

Chapter 41

Business Writing

HIGHLIGHTS

Chapter 41 is more than a reference guide students can consult when writing one of the kinds of documents covered in the discussion: business letters, letters of request or complaint, job applications and résumés, and business memos. It offers instructors an opportunity to design writing assignments that incorporate these forms of writing, knowing that they will not have to spend valuable class time on matters of format and can direct attention to more substantive issues.

When you write a letter to request information, to complain about a product or bill, or to apply for a job, or when you write a memo or report to someone you work with, you are addressing busy people who want to see quickly why you are writing and how they should respond to you. A wordy, incoherent letter or memo full of errors in grammar and spelling may prevent you from getting what you want, either because the reader cannot understand your wish or because you present yourself poorly. In business writing, state your purpose at the very start. Be straightforward, clear, objective, and courteous, and don't hesitate to be insistent if the situation warrants it. Observe conventions of grammar and usage, for these not only make your writing clear but also impress a reader with your care.

 41a   **Writing business letters and job applications**

1   **Using a standard form**

Business correspondence customarily adheres to one of several acceptable forms. Use either unlined white paper measuring 8½″ × 11″ or what is called letterhead stationery with your address printed at the top of the sheet. Type the letter single-spaced (with double space between elements) on only one side of a

41a

sheet. Follow a standard form for each of the letter's elements. The two most common forms for business letters—the full block and the modified block—are illustrated and described on the following pages.

The letter

The **return-address heading** of the letter gives your address (but not your name) and the date. If you are using letterhead, you need add only the date. Place your heading at least an inch from the top of the page, or two lines below the letterhead if there is one. Align all lines of the heading on the left. In the block style, the return-address heading falls at the left margin (see opposite). In the modified block style, it falls to the right of the center of the paper (see p. 730).

The **inside address** shows the name, title, and complete address of the person you are writing to, just as this information will appear on the envelope. Place the address at least two lines below the return-address heading. In both block and modified block styles, the address falls at the left margin of the page.

The **salutation** greets the addressee. In both styles it falls at the left margin, two lines below the inside address and two lines above the body of the letter. It is followed by a colon. If you are not addressing someone whose name you know, use a job title (*Dear Personnel Manager, Dear Customer Service Manager*) or use a general salutation (*Dear Sir or Madam, Dear Smythe Shoes*). Use *Ms.* as the title for a woman when she has no other title, when you don't know how she prefers to be addressed, or when you know that she prefers to be addressed as *Ms.* If you know a woman prefers to be addressed as *Mrs.* or *Miss,* use the appropriate title.

The **body** of the letter, containing its substance, begins at the left margin in both letter styles. Instead of indenting the first line of each paragraph, place an extra line of space between paragraphs so that they are readily visible.

The letter's **close** begins two lines below the last line of the body and aligns with the return-address heading. That is, in the block style the close falls at the left margin (see opposite), whereas in the modified block style it falls to the right of the center of the page (p. 730). The close should reflect the level of formality in the salutation. For formal letters, *Respectfully, Cordially, Yours truly,* and *Sincerely* are common closes. For less formal letters, you may choose to use *Warmest regards, Regards, Best wishes,* or the like. Only the first word of the close is capitalized, and the close is followed by a comma.

Business letter in block style

```
17A Revere Street  ⌐
Boston, MA 02106   |————— Return-address
January 1, 1992    �epsilon        heading

Ms. Ann Herzog          ⌐
Circulation Supervisor  |
Sporting Life           |————— Inside address
25 W. 43rd Street       |
New York, NY 10036      ⌐

Dear Ms. Herzog: ⌐————————— Salutation

Thank you for your letter of December 20, which    ⌐
notifies me that Sporting Life will resume my      |
subscription after stopping it in error after I    |
had received the July issue.  Since I missed at    |
least five months' issues because of the maga-     |
zine's error, I expected my subscription to be     |
extended for five months after it would have       |
lapsed--that is, through June 1992.  Instead, you  |
tell me that the magazine will send me the back    |
issues that it failed to send and that the Jan-    |
uary issue (which I have not received) will        |
complete my current subscription.                  |
                                                   |—— Body
I have no interest in receiving the back issues    |
of Sporting Life because the magazine is not use-  |
ful or interesting unless it is current.  Since    |
Sporting Life erred in stopping my subscription    |
prematurely, I still expect it to make up the      |
difference on the other end of my subscription.    |

Unless I hear otherwise from you, I will count on  |
your extending my subscription at least through    |
June 1992.  If Sporting Life cannot compensate     |
for its error in this way, I will cancel my sub-   |
scription and request a refund.                    ⌐

Sincerely, ⌐————————————— Close

Janet M. Marley       ⌐
                      |————— Signature
Janet M. Marley       ⌐
```

41a

The **signature** of a business letter falls below the close and has two parts. One is your name typed on the fourth line below the close. The other is your handwritten signature, which fills the space between the close and your typed name. The signature should consist only of your name, as you sign checks and other documents.

Below the signature at the left margin, you may want to include additional information such as *Enc. 3* (indicating, in this case, that there are three enclosures with the letter); *cc: Margaret Newton* (indicating that a copy is being sent to the person named); or *CHC/enp* (the initials of the author/the initials of the typist).

The envelope

The envelope of the letter (see below) should show your name and address in the upper-left corner and the addressee's name, title, and address in the center. Use an envelope that will adequately accommodate the letter once it is folded horizontally in thirds.

```
Janet M. Marley
17A Revere Street
Boston, MA 02106


                         Ms. Ann Herzog
                         Circulation Supervisor
                         Sporting Life
                         25 W. 43rd Street
                         New York, NY 10036
```

RESOURCES AND IDEAS

Robert Mehaffy and Constance Warloe, "Corporate Communications: Next Step for the Community Colleges?" *Technical Writing Teacher* 16 (1989): 1–11. Mehaffy and Warloe show the curriculum design for a professional writing course taking into account adult learning styles, computer-assisted composition, reader-centered writing, interviewing for information, project management, and team design.

 2   Writing requests and complaints

Letters requesting something—for instance, a pamphlet, information about a product, a T-shirt advertised in a magazine—must be specific and accurate about the item you are requesting. The letter should describe the item completely and, if applicable, include a copy or description of the advertisement or other source that prompted your request.

Letters complaining about a product or a service (such as a wrong billing from the telephone company) should be written in a reasonable but firm tone. (See the sample letter on p. 727.) Assume that the addressee is willing to resolve the problem when he or she has the relevant information. In the first sentence of the letter, say what you are writing about. Then provide as much background as needed, including any relevant details from past correspondence (as in the sample letter). Describe exactly what you see as the problem, sticking to facts and avoiding discourses on the company's social responsibility or your low opinion of its management. In the clearest and fewest possible words and sentences, proceed directly from one point to the next without repeating yourself. Always include your opinion of how the problem can be solved. Many companies are required by law to establish a specific procedure for complaints about products and services. If you know of such a procedure, be sure to follow it.

3   Writing a job application and résumé

In applying for a job or requesting a job interview, send both a résumé and a letter. Both should be on high-quality 8½″ × 11″ paper. For the letter use the block or modified block style (pp. 727, 730). In the body announce at the outset what job you desire and how you heard about it. (See the sample on the next page.) Then summarize your qualifications for the job, including facts about your education and employment history. Include only the relevant facts, mentioning that additional information appears in an accompanying résumé. Include any special reason you have for applying, such as a specific career goal. At the end of the letter, mention that you are available for an interview at the convenience of the addressee, or specify when you will be available (for instance, when your current job or classes leave you free, or when you could travel to the employer's city).

The résumé that you enclose with your letter of application should contain, in table form, your name and address, career objective, and education and employment history, along with information about how to obtain your references. (See the sample on p. 731.) Use headings to mark the various sections of the résumé, spacing around them and within sections so that important information stands out. Try to limit your résumé to one page so that it can be quickly scanned. However, if your experience and education are extensive, a two-page résumé is preferable to a single cramped, unreadable page. In preparing your résumé, you may wish to consult one of the many books devoted to application letters, résumés, and other elements of a job search. Two helpful guides are Richard N. Bolles, *What Color Is Your Parachute? A Practical Manual for Job-Hunters and Career Changers,* and Tom Jackson, *The Perfect Résumé.*

SOME SUGGESTIONS FOR ASSIGNMENTS

Students who have chosen business or public administration as a field may sense the usefulness of an assignment like "Prepare a résumé for yourself." For other students (and for some business students as well) the best approach is to design an assignment in which a memo or letter grows out of a specific situation. Providing students with the details of a social situation in which the writing meets a specific need and within which they as writers have a number of rhetorical and value judgments to make (sometimes called a *case approach* to writing instruction) often leads to better writing and thinking.

41a

Job-application letter in modified block style

3712 Swiss Avenue
Dallas, TX 75204
March 2, 1992

Personnel Manager
<u>Dallas News</u>
Communications Center
Dallas, TX 75222

Dear Personnel Manager:

In response to your posting in the English Department of Southern Methodist University, I am
applying for the summer job of part-time editorial assistant for the <u>Dallas News</u>.

I am now enrolled at Southern Methodist University as a sophomore, with a dual major in English
literature and journalism. As the enclosed
résumé shows, I have worked on the university
newspaper for nearly two years, and I worked a
summer on my hometown newspaper as a copy aid.
My goal is a career in journalism. I believe my
educational background and my work experience
qualify me for the opening you have.

I am available for an interview at any time and
would be happy to show samples of my newspaper
work. My telephone number is 744-3816.

                         Sincerely,

                         Ian M. Irvine

                         Ian M. Irvine

Enc.

Résumé

Ian M. Irvine
3712 Swiss Avenue
Dallas, Texas 75204
Telephone: 214-744-3816

Position desired
Part-time editorial assistant.

Education
Southern Methodist University, 1990 to present.
Current standing: sophomore.
Major: English literature and journalism.

Abilene (Texas) Senior High School, 1986-1990.
Graduated with academic, college-preparatory
degree.

Employment history
Daily Campus, student newspaper of Southern
Methodist University, 1990 to present.
Responsibilities include writing feature stories
and sports coverage.

Longhorn Painters, summer 1991.
Responsibilities included exterior and interior
house painting.

Abilene Reporter-News, summer 1990.
Responsibilities as a copy aid included routing
copy, monitoring teleprinter, running errands,
and assisting reporters.

References
Academic: Placement Office
               Southern Methodist University
               Dallas, TX 75275

Employment: Ms. Millie Stevens
             Abilene Reporter-News
             Abilene, TX 79604

Personal: Ms. Sheryl Gipstein
             26 Overland Drive
             Abilene, TX 79604

41b Writing business memos

Unlike business letters, which address people in other organizations, business memorandums (memos, for short) address people within the same organization. A memo can be quite long, but more often it reports briefly and directly on a very specific topic: an answer to a question, a progress report, an evaluation. Both the form and the structure of a memo are designed to get to the point and dispose of it quickly.

The memo has no return address, inside address, salutation, or close. Instead, as shown in the sample memo on the facing page, the heading typically consists of the company name, the addressee's name, the writer's name, the date, and a subject description or title. Type the body of the memo as you would the body of a business letter: single-spaced, double-spaced between paragraphs, and no paragraph indentions. Never sign a business memo, though you may initial your name in the heading. If copies of the memo need to be sent to people not listed in the "To" line, add a notation two spaces below the last line, and list the persons to whom copies are being sent.

Immerse your reader in your subject at the very beginning of the memo. State your reason for writing in the first sentence, but do not waste words with expressions like "The purpose of this memo is. . . ." Devote the first paragraph to a succinct presentation of your answer, conclusion, or evaluation. In the rest of the memo explain how you arrived at your answer, the facts on which you base your conclusion, and your method of evaluation. The paragraphs may be numbered so that the main divisions of your message are easy to see.

A business memo can be more informal in tone than a business letter, particularly if you know the addressee; but it should not be wordy. Use technical terms if your reader will understand them, but otherwise keep language simple and use short sentences. Provide only the information that your reader needs to know.

The sample memo opposite illustrates these guidelines. Notice especially the form of the memo, the writer's immediate statement of her purpose, the clear structure provided by the three numbered paragraphs, and the direct tone of the whole.

Bigelow Wax Company

TO: Aileen Rosen, Director of Sales
FROM: Patricia Phillips, Territory 12
DATE: March 15, 1992
SUBJECT: 1991 sales of Quick Wax in Territory 12

Since it was introduced in January of 1991, Quick
Wax has been unsuccessful in Territory 12 and has
not affected the sales of our Easy Shine. Discussions with customers and my own analysis of
Quick Wax suggest three reasons for its failure
to compete with our product.

1. Quick Wax has not received the promotion
    necessary for a new product. Advertising--
    primarily on radio--has been sporadic and has
    not developed a clear, consistent image for
    the product. In addition, the Quick Wax
    sales representative in Territory 12 is new
    and inexperienced; he is not known to cus-
    tomers, and his sales pitch (which I once
    overheard) is weak. As far as I can tell,
    his efforts are not supported by phone calls
    or mailings from his home office.

2. When Quick Wax does make it to the store
    shelves, buyers do not choose it over our
    product. Though priced competitively with
    our product, Quick Wax is poorly packaged.
    The container seems smaller than ours, though
    in fact it holds the same eight ounces. The
    lettering on the Quick Wax package (red on
    blue) is difficult to read, in contrast to
    the white-on-green lettering on the Easy
    Shine package.

3. Our special purchase offers and my increased
    efforts to serve existing customers have had
    the intended effect of keeping customers
    satisfied with our product and reducing their
    inclination to stock something new.

Copies: L. Goldberger, Director of Marketing
         L. MacGregor, Customer Service Manager

Appendix A

Preparing a Manuscript

A legible, consistent, and attractive manuscript is a service to readers because it makes reading easier. This appendix discusses the materials necessary for manuscript preparation and some conventions of format adapted from the *MLA Handbook,* 3rd ed. (Most of these guidelines are standard, but your instructor may request that you follow different conventions in some matters.)

 A1 Choosing the appropriate materials

 a Handwritten papers

For handwritten papers, you can use regular white paper, 8½″ × 11″, with horizontal lines spaced between one-quarter and three-eighths of an inch apart. Don't use paper torn from a notebook, unlined paper, paper with narrow lines, colored paper, or paper other than 8½″ × 11″ (such as legal or stenographer's pads). Use the same type of paper throughout a project. Write on only one side of a sheet.

Use black or blue ink, not pencil. If possible, use an ink eraser or eradicator to correct mistakes. If you must cross out material, draw a single line through it. Don't scribble over or black out a mistake, and don't write corrections on top of mistakes.

Typewritten papers

For typewritten papers, use 8½″ × 11″ white bond paper of sixteen- or twenty-pound weight. Some instructors also accept the same size surface-coated bond paper (called "erasable" or "corrasable"), but ink smears easily on such paper. Onionskin sheets, paper torn from notebooks, colored paper, and paper smaller or larger than 8½″ × 11″ are unacceptable. Use the same type of paper throughout a project. Type on only one side of a sheet.

Use a black typewriter ribbon that is fresh enough to make a dark impression, and make sure the keys of the typewriter are clean. To avoid smudging the page when correcting mistakes, use a liquid correction fluid or a correction tape. Don't use hyphens or *x*'s to cross out mistakes, and don't type corrections (strike-overs) on top of mistakes.

 Papers produced on a word processor

Two kinds of printers are used with most computerized word processors. Letter-quality printers (including daisywheel and laser printers), like a regular typewriter, produce characters with solid lines. Dot-matrix printers form characters out of tiny dots, and the legibility of their type varies considerably. If you use a word processor with a dot-matrix printer, make sure the dots are close enough together to produce legible characters. In addition, make sure the tails on letters such as *j, p,* and *y* descend below the line of type, as they do in the typeface used here. Resist the temptation to use any of the unusual type sizes or styles that your printer may be capable of producing—including *italic* rather than <u>underlined</u> type. Such embellishments can clutter your manuscript and distract readers from what you are saying. Before you submit a paper printed on a dot-matrix printer, show your instructor a sample of the type to be sure it is acceptable.

Be sure the printer ribbon or cartridge produces a dark impression. Use standard-sized (8½″ × 11″) white bond paper of sixteen- or twenty-pound weight, not the lightweight green-striped paper associated with computer print-outs. If you use continuous paper folded like a fan at perforations, it will also come with a row of holes along each side for feeding the paper into the printer. Before submitting your paper, remove these strips of holes along the perforations and separate the pages at the folds.

ms
A1

ms
A2

A2 Following a standard format

A consistent physical format makes the script, margins, paging, title, and identification visually effective and avoids the illegibility and the confusion of inconsistencies. The samples below show most of the features discussed here. For the special formats of source citations and a list of works cited, see Chapter 37 and the sample research papers in Chapter 38.

TRANSPARENCY MASTER
AVAILABLE

First page of paper with no title page

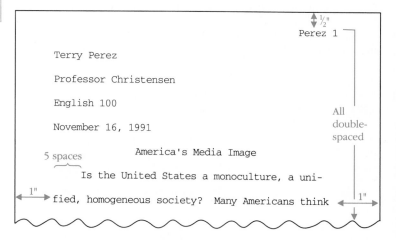

A later page of the paper

ms
A2

 Script

Handwritten script should be reasonably uniform and clear. Be sure letters are easily distinguishable. Cross all *t*'s; dot all *i*'s with dots, not circles; form the loops of letters carefully. Make capital letters and small letters clearly different. Space consistently between words and between sentences. If your handwriting is difficult to read, submit a typed paper if possible. If you don't have access to a typewriter and your handwriting is illegible or unusual in size, decoration, or slant, make it more legible or conventional when writing the final manuscript. Indent the first line of every paragraph about an inch. Write on every line or every other line as specified by your instructor.

In script produced on a typewriter or word processor, indent the first line of every paragraph five spaces and double-space throughout. Leave one space between words. Type punctuation as indicated in the box on the next page. Use handwriting to make any symbols that are not on your keyboard, leaving three or four spaces and then inserting the symbol in ink.

For both typed and handwritten script, try to avoid breaking words at the ends of lines. If you must break a word, follow the guidelines in Chapter 30. Don't start a line with any mark of punctuation other than a dash, an opening parenthesis, an opening quotation mark, or an ellipsis mark when one of these is called for.

Set off quotations of more than four lines of prose or three lines of poetry; two- or three-line poetry quotations may be set off or placed in the text (see 24c). In handwritten copy, indent all lines of a displayed quotation an inch from the left margin. In typewritten copy, indent all lines ten spaces. Double-space above and below each quotation, and double-space the quotation itself. (See p. 636 for a sample.)

b Margins

Use one-inch margins on all sides of each page. The top margin will contain the page numbers (see p. 739). If the right margin is uneven, it should be no narrower than an inch. If you have a word processor or electronic typewriter that produces an even (or justified) right margin, use the feature only if it does not leave wide spaces between words and thus interfere with readability. When using a word processor, be sure to instruct the computer to set appropriate margins. Don't let the lines of type run across the perforations on continuous fanfold paper.

ms
A2

Forming and spacing punctuation

One space after

Comma	`dog, and`
Semicolon	`dog; and`
Colon	`dog: its`
Apostrophe ending word	`dogs' toys`
Closing quotation mark	
Double	`"dog" and`
Single	`'dog' and` (use apostrophe)
Closing parenthesis	`(dog) and`
Closing bracket	`[dog] and` (or leave space and handwrite: `[ dog ]`)

Two spaces after

Sentence period	`dog. The`
Question mark	`dog? The`
Exclamation point	`dog! The` (or type an apostrophe over a period)

No space either side

Dash (two hyphens)	`dog--its`
Hyphen	`one-half`
Apostrophe within word	`dog's`

One space before and after

Ellipsis mark within sentence	`dog . . . in`

Exceptions

Two spaces after closing quotation mark, parenthesis, or bracket after the end of a sentence:

`dog." The          dog.) The          dog.] The`

When an ellipsis mark ends a sentence, one space after the sentence period and two spaces after the ellipsis mark:

`dog. . . . The`

No space between two or more adjacent punctuation marks:

```
"Who knows the word 'anoxia'?"
(The dog finally came home.)
```

c   Paging

Whether or not you provide a separate title page, begin numbering your paper on the first text page, and number consecutively through the end. Use Arabic numerals (1, 2, 3), and do not add periods, parentheses, hyphens, or the abbreviation "p." However, place your last name before the page number in case the pages become separated after you submit your paper. Align the page number with the right margin, and position it about half an inch from the top of the page, at least two lines above the first line of text.

d   Title and identification

If you do not use a separate title page for an essay, provide your name and the date, plus any other information requested by your instructor, on the first text page. Place this identification an inch from the top of the page, aligned with the left margin and double-spaced. Double-space again, and center the title. Don't underline the title or place quotation marks around it, and capitalize the words in the title according to guidelines in 26b. Double-space between the title and the first line of text.

For a research paper, your instructor may ask you to provide a separate title page. If so, follow the guidelines and example on pages 632–33. On page 1 of the paper repeat the title, centered an inch from the top of the page, and double-space between the title and the first line of text. (See p. 636 for an example.)

A3   Proofreading, correcting, and submitting the final manuscript

Proofread each page of your paper carefully, concentrating on spelling, punctuation, mechanics, grammar, and manuscript format. (See 2d for proofreading tips and a proofreading exercise.) If a page has several errors, retype or rewrite the page. If it has one or two errors and you can't eradicate them, correct them in ink. Draw a single line through a word you want to delete. Don't try to correct a misspelled word without crossing out and rewriting the whole word. To replace a word or mark of punctuation, draw a line through the item, place a caret (∧) underneath it, and write the new word or mark in the space above the old one. To add

ms
A3

words or marks of punctuation, place a caret underneath the line at the point where you wish to insert the word or mark; then center the word or mark over the caret in the space above the line.

An ecosystem is a community of ⟨*organisms*⟩ ~~arganisms~~ interacting with each other and with ⟨*the*⟩ environment.

If you have to add more words than will fit between the lines of text, rewrite or retype the page.

When you submit your final paper, be sure the pages will stay together when the paper is shuffled in with others. Depending on the wishes of your instructor, you may fold the paper in half lengthwise, paper-clip or staple the pages in the upper-left corner, or place the paper in a special binder.

Appendix B

Writing with a Word Processor

SOFTWARE AVAILABLE

HarperCollins publishes *The 53rd Street Writer*, a custom word processor with an on-line handbook drawn from *The Little, Brown Handbook*. Word-processing features include a spelling checker, a split screen which enables two documents to be open at once, and easy-to-use menus.

The 53rd Street Writer was developed for HarperCollins by Daedalus, Inc.—a company formed by composition experts who specialize in developing software for the composition classroom. They designed this program with an emphasis on ease of use. Students don't spend a lot of time learning to use the software, so they have more time to spend improving their writing.

The on-line handbook allows students to answer routine queries without leaving the computer. Then they can return to the document and instantly apply the grammatical rule or documentation style they just reviewed on the screen. *The 53rd Street Writer* is available to students at a nominal price.

Writing with a word processor can save time and make writing easier. The advantage of word processing is that you can perform such operations as adding to notes, rearranging outlines, and rewriting first drafts without having to cut pages apart or retype entire pages. The machine will not think for you, but it may leave you more time for the important work of thinking, exploring ideas, focusing and organizing material, and improving content and clarity. This appendix explains how you can incorporate a word processor into your writing process, following the stages of development, drafting, and revising discussed in Chapters 1 and 2.

Using a word processor does not require an understanding of computers or expert typing skills. All it takes is a little perseverance and a few hours of practice. If you do not have your own word processor, find out what's available at your school, for many colleges have computers available for student use. When you begin using a word processor, carefully read the system's **documentation**—the materials that explain the system, such as a user's manual or tutorial. Study the keyboard, and make a list of the basic keystrokes you need to perform important commands, such as inserting, deleting, saving, and printing text. Be adventurous: experiment with commands, and learn by trial and error. Your play will not hurt the machine, and it will help you.

You may have heard of writers losing all their work because their word processor somehow failed or "crashed." It is possible to lose text accidentally, but a few precautions will prevent permanent loss of your work. These are spelled out in the box on the next page.

B1

Tips for successful word processing

1. Save your work frequently by using the **save** or **file** command. Then your text will be permanently stored—usually on a magnetic disk that is either part of the computer (a "hard disk") or removable from it (a "floppy disk").
2. Think of each computer disk as a separate file drawer containing electronic copies of your papers. Label each paper with its own **file** or **document name** for easy retrieval.
3. Make a **back-up** or duplicate disk of your work at the end of each word-processing session as insurance against the loss or damage of your working disk.
4. Keep your disks in dust covers, and store them safely away from heat, cold, or sources of magnetism such as the computer itself or a stereo or television.
5. Regularly print paper copies of your work. They serve as second back-up copies, and, more important, they give you something to work on when you revise and edit.

 B1   Using a word processor for development

All word processors can aid the initial steps of the writing process (see Chapter 1). You can generate ideas on the computer, expand and reorganize them, and then transfer usable material directly into your draft or revision.

 Finding a topic and generating ideas

A word processor is an excellent medium for freewriting (see 1e-3). Most computer monitors, or screens, have a dial that controls the brightness of the images on the screen. While freewriting, you can turn the brightness all the way down so that the screen appears blank. The computer will record what you write but keep it from you and thus prevent you from tinkering with your prose. This **invisible writing** can free the mind for very creative results. When you're finished freewriting, simply turn up the brightness control to read what you've written and then save or revise it as you see fit. Later, you can transfer some or all of your freewriting into your draft.

The computer is also useful for listing ideas or brainstorming (see 1e-4). You may actually find that you can generate more ideas faster with a computer than with a pen or a typewriter. When you're finished, delete weak ideas and expand strong ones. As you exhaust your topic, save your list and print it for further consideration. Later, you can develop it further by adding, deleting, and rearranging. You can also freewrite from the list, exploring items that seem promising.

Making notes

Keeping an electronic journal is a good way to build a file of ideas. Write and save regular entries, just as you would in a paper journal (see 1e-1). Then you can move blocks of it into another discovery exercise or a draft.

The computer can also help you take notes from your reading or create notes according to your own structure. For example, you can type passages underlined or marked in your reading into the computer—as long as you are careful to protect against plagiarism by using quotation marks and keeping a record of the author, source, and page number(s) (see 36b–36c). When you are ready to do so, you can transfer the best quotations (and the citations for them) into your draft.

To develop your own notes, try using the journalist's questions (see 1e-7) or the questions derived from the patterns of development (1e-8). Type either list of questions into the computer and save it. Then for each writing project, duplicate the list in a new file and insert possible answers. Print out your notes so that you can select material from them for future drafts.

Considering audience and organizing ideas

You can create a standard file of questions for considering audience by typing the "Questions About Audience" from page 13 into your computer and saving them. For each assignment, duplicate the file and insert appropriate answers between the questions. Save the answers under a new file name, and print a copy for future reference.

The ease of adding, deleting, and rearranging on a word processor makes it the ideal tool for shaping and organizing material (see 1g). Beginning with just a list of ideas, you can isolate the more general points and then use the computer's tab settings to indent the more specific material. Unusable ideas can be deleted; redundant ideas can be merged. Print out each version of your outline to work on or use as a guide to planning, drafting, or re-

B2

vising. The outline in memory can be called up and revised as needed to reflect changes in your thinking and writing.

Many word processors can display separate files on the screen at the same time, in slots sometimes called **windows.** To organize notes with this feature, start with a blank screen, retrieve a file of notes, and transfer selected copy (such as a thesis statement and general ideas) to the blank slot. Or convert an informal outline to a formal one by transferring details from notes in one slot to an informal outline in another one, inserting appropriate indentions, numbers, and letters for different levels of generality.

B2   Using a word processor for drafting

Many writers find that a word processor eases the transition from developing ideas to drafting. You can retrieve notes to the screen and rewrite, delete, or insert as needed. You can expand your outline into a draft by composing paragraphs directly under headings, deleting the remnants of the outline and adding transitions as you go along. Or you can freewrite a first draft, starting with a blank screen and letting the words flow until you're ready to consult your notes or outline for new material. If you're borrowing material from other writers, be sure to transfer source information as well as quotations from your notes to your draft so that you don't plagiarize, even accidentally. (The split-screen capability—windows—can help with documentation if you write your draft on one part and retrieve quotations and source citations from notes on the other part.)

Whatever your drafting style, take advantage of the word processor's speed and flexibility. Don't stop to correct errors or rewrite—both of which the computer will help you handle easily in a later draft. Put alternative ideas or phrasings in brackets so that you can consider them later without getting sidetracked now. Use an asterisk (*) or some other symbol to mark places where you feel blocked or very uncertain. Later, you can find these places quickly by instructing the computer to search for the symbol. If it helps, use invisible writing just to keep moving through a draft (see p. 742).

Frequently save or file the text you're drafting—at least once every twenty minutes or every few pages and every time you take a break or leave the computer for any reason. When you finish a drafting session, save your work, make a back-up copy on a separate disk, and print a paper copy in case anything happens to your disks. You will need the paper copy for revising and editing.

B3   Using a word processor for revising and editing

The convenience of extensive revision and editing is the greatest advantage of word processing. The machine eliminates the tedious, often messy labor of typing or writing out successive drafts or pieces of drafts. Instead, working on a copy of the most recent draft stored in the computer, you can add, delete, and move words, lines, and whole passages with a few keystrokes. If you want to compare, say, two different organizations or ways of explaining an important point, you can work on two duplicates of the latest draft, print both, and read them side by side. (A split-screen word processor allows this function on the screen as long as the passages are fairly short.)

Like most writers, you may find that you revise and edit more on a word processor than you do on a typewriter or in handwriting. It's important, though, that you not let the ease of revision lure you into obsessive rewriting—a kind of wheel-spinning in which changes cease to have a marked effect on meaning or clarity and may in fact sap the writing of energy. In addition, you need to think beyond the confines of the screen so that larger issues of meaning and structure are not lost to superficial matters such as word choice and sentence arrangement.

Here are some guidelines for using a word processor as an effective revision tool.

- Deal with major revisions first: see the revision checklist on page 53. Save editing, formatting the manuscript, and proofreading for later drafts.
- Use commands for deleting and moving blocks of copy as you would cut and paste a handwritten draft.
- Save earlier drafts under their own file names in case you need to consult them for ideas or phrasings. Make a duplicate of any draft you want to revise, and work on the duplicate.
- If you tend to rewrite excessively when working on the computer or have trouble finding your focus or organizing your paper, print a copy of your draft and work on it. Many writers prefer to work on paper copy (also called **hard copy**) because it is easier to read and allows a view of the whole not permitted on the computer screen. It is an easy matter to transfer changes from printed copy to computer.

The word processor is also an excellent tool for editing and proofreading—tightening, clarifying, refining, and correcting. (See the editing checklist on p. 59.) The following guidelines will help you make the most of the machine.

B4

- Save your drafts on the computer, print your work, and do your editing on a paper copy. Almost everyone finds it much harder to spot errors on the computer screen than on paper. And paper copy may discourage you from overediting to the point where you say less with less life. You can easily transfer the editing changes from paper to the computer.
- After editing, return to the draft in the computer. Either work through the draft line by line or use the **search command** to find the places you want to change. The search command directs the computer to locate any words or phrases you specify.
- Use the search command as well to find misused words or stylistic problems that tend to crop up in your writing. Such problems might include *there are, it is,* and other expletive constructions; *the fact that* and other wordy phrases; and *is, are,* and other forms of *be,* which often occur in wordy constructions and passive sentences. (All of these problems are discussed in 31c.)
- Make sure that you neither omit needed words nor leave in unneeded words when deleting or inserting text on the computer.
- Resist the temptation to view the final draft coming out of the printer as perfect simply because the copy is clean. Always proofread your final draft *carefully.* (See 2d for proofreading tips.)

A note on manuscript format

Most word processors provide automatic settings for margins, tabs, indentions, and other features of manuscript format. Use these settings to produce a manuscript that coincides with the format described in Appendix A or any format requested by your instructor. Appendix A also contains advice about print styles, paper, and other aspects of word processing. See especially A1-c and A2-b.

B4 Using optional programs on a word processor

Many word processors either come with optional programs such as spelling checkers or are compatible with optional programs. These programs cannot think for you, and sometimes (as noted below) their usefulness is limited. But they can support and speed your efforts. The following are the kinds of programs you are most likely to see.

- *Invention or discovery programs* help you develop a topic by prompting you with a structured set of questions or by providing creative analogies that help you think imaginatively. These programs can help you get started and develop new insights.
- *Outlining programs* help you organize your work by providing automatic indentions, easy resequencing, and other features.
- *Style-checking programs* help you find and correct wordy and awkward phrases and faulty grammar and punctuation. These programs are usually limited because they cannot identify the context of a possible flaw or error. Consult this book whenever you are unsure of a style checker's advice.
- *Thesaurus programs* help with word choices by responding to your word with a display of several synonyms (words with similar meanings) and sometimes antonyms (words with opposite meanings). A single keystroke allows you to replace your word with a displayed word. (However, you should always consult a dictionary for the meaning of any word you are not sure of.)
- *Spell-checking programs* help you find typographical errors and misspelled words, and they display correct spellings on the screen. They can be valuable proofreading aids. However, they are limited because they cannot store every possible word and thus may identify a word you use as misspelled even though it is correct. In addition, they are unreliable because they cannot identify errors such as a confusion among *there, their,* and *they're.* Maintain a file of your frequent misspellings and use the search command to check them yourself.

B4

Glossary of
Usage

This glossary provides notes on words or phrases that often cause problems for writers. The recommendations for standard written English are based on current dictionaries and usage guides such as the ones listed in 32a. Items labeled **nonstandard** should be avoided in speech and especially in writing. Those labeled **colloquial** and **slang** occur in speech and in some informal writing but are best avoided in the more formal writing usually expected in college and business. (Words and phrases labeled *colloquial* include those labeled by many dictionaries with the equivalent term *informal.*) See Chapter 31 for further discussion of word choice and for exercises in usage. See 32b-2 for a description of dictionary labels. Also see 34a-1 for a list of commonly confused words that are pronounced the same or similarly. The words and definitions provided there supplement this glossary.

The glossary is necessarily brief. Keep a dictionary handy for all your writing, and make a habit of referring to it whenever you doubt the appropriateness of a word or phrase.

a, an   Use *a* before words beginning with consonant sounds, including those spelled with an initial pronounced *h* and those spelled with vowels that are sounded as consonants: *a historian, a one-o'clock class, a university.* Use *an* before words that begin with vowel sounds, including those spelled with an initial silent *h: an orgy, an L, an honor.*

When you use an abbreviation or acronym in writing (see 28b), the article that precedes it depends on how the abbreviation is to be read: *She was once an HEW undersecretary (HEW* is to be read as three separate letters, and *h* is pronounced "aitch"). *Many Americans opposed a SALT treaty (SALT is to be read as one word, salt).*

See also *article* in the Glossary of Terms (p. 768).

accept, except   *Accept* is a verb meaning "receive." *Except* is usually a preposition or conjunction meaning "but for" or "other than"; when it is used as a verb, it means "leave out." *I can accept all your suggestions except the last one. I'm sorry you excepted my last suggestion from your list.*

adverse, averse   *Adverse* and *averse* are both adjectives, and both mean "opposed" or "hostile." But *averse* describes the subject's opposition to something, whereas *adverse* describes something opposed to the subject: *The President was averse to adverse criticism.*

advice, advise   *Advice* is a noun, and *advise* is a verb: *Take my advice; do as I advise you.*

affect, effect   Usually *affect* is a verb, meaning "to influence," and *effect* is a noun, meaning "result": *The drug did not affect his driving; in fact, it seemed to have no effect at all.* But *effect* occasionally is used as a verb meaning "to bring about": *Her efforts effected a change.* And *affect* is used in psychology as a noun meaning "feeling or emotion": *One can infer much about affect from behavior.*

aggravate   *Aggravate* should not be used in its colloquial meaning of "irritate" or "exasperate" (for example, *We were aggravated by her constant arguing*). *Aggravate* means "make worse": *The President was irritated by the Senate's stubbornness because he feared any delay might aggravate the unrest in the Middle East.*

agree to, agree with   *Agree to* means "consent to," and *agree with* means "be in accord with": *How can they agree to a treaty when they don't agree with each other about the terms?*

ain't   Nonstandard for *am not, isn't,* or *aren't.*

all, all of   Usually *all* is sufficient to modify a noun: *all my loving, all the things you are.* Before a pronoun or proper noun, *all of* is usually appropriate: *all of me, in all of France.*

all ready, already   *All ready* means "completely prepared," and *already* means "by now" or "before now": *We were all ready to go to the movie, but it had already started.*

all right   *All right* is always two words. *Alright* is a common misspelling.

all together, altogether   *All together* means "in unison," or "gathered in one place." *Altogether* means "entirely." *It's not altogether true that our family never spends vacations all together.*

allusion, illusion   An *allusion* is an indirect reference, and an *illusion* is a deceptive appearance: *Paul's constant allusions to Shakespeare created the illusion that he was an intellectual.*

almost, most   *Almost* is an adverb meaning "nearly"; *most* is an adjective meaning "the greater number (or part) of." In formal writing, *most* should not be used as a substitute for *almost: We see each other almost* (not *most*) *every day.*

a lot   *A lot* is always two words, used informally to mean "many." *Alot* is a common misspelling.

among, between   In general, *among* is used for relationships involving more than two people or things. *Between* is used for relationships involving only two or for comparing one thing to a group to which it belongs. *The four of them agreed among themselves that the choice was between New York and Los Angeles.*

amongst   Although common in British English, in American English *amongst* is an overrefined substitute for *among.*

amount, number   *Amount* refers to a quantity of something (a singular noun) that cannot be counted. *Number* refers to countable items (a plural noun). *The amount of tax depends on the number of deductions.*

an, and   *An* is an article (see *a, an*). *And* is a coordinating conjunction. Do not carelessly omit the *d* from *and.*

and etc.   *Et cetera* (*etc.*) means "and the rest"; *and etc.* therefore is redundant. See also *et al., etc.*

and/or   *And/or* is awkward and often confusing. A sentence such as *The decision is made by the mayor and/or the council* implies that one or the other or both make the decision. If you mean both, use *and;* if you mean either, use *or.* Use *and/or* only when you mean three options.

and which, and who   When *which* or *who* is used to introduce a relative clause, *and* is superfluous: *WCAS is my favorite AM radio station, which* (not *and which*) *I listen to every morning.* And *which* or *and who* is correct only when used to introduce a second clause beginning with the same relative pronoun: *Jill is my cousin who goes to school here and who calls me constantly.*

ante-, anti-   The prefix *ante-* means "before" (*antedate, antebellum*); *anti-* means "against" (*antiwar, antinuclear*). Before a capital letter or *i, anti-* takes a hyphen: *anti-Freudian, anti-isolationist.*

anxious, eager   *Anxious* means "nervous" or "worried" and is usually followed by *about. Eager* means "looking forward" and is usually followed by *to. I've been anxious about getting blisters. I'm eager* (not *anxious*) *to get new running shoes.*

anybody, any body; anyone, any one   *Anybody* and *anyone* are indefinite pronouns; *any body* is a noun modified by an adjective; *any one* is a pronoun or adjective modified by *any. How can anybody communicate with any body of government? Can anyone help Amy? She has more work than any one person can handle.*

any more, anymore   *Any more* is used in negative constructions to mean "no more." *Anymore,* an adverb meaning "now," is also used in negative constructions. *He doesn't want any more. She doesn't live here anymore.*

anyplace   Colloquial for *anywhere.*

anyways, anywheres Nonstandard for *anyway* and *anywhere*.

apt, liable, likely *Apt* and *likely* are interchangeable. Strictly speaking, though, *apt* means "having a tendency to": *Horace is apt to forget his lunch in the morning. Likely* means "probably going to": *Horace is leaving so early today that he's likely to catch the first bus.*

    Liable normally means "in danger of" and should be confined to situations with undesirable consequences: *Horace is liable to trip over that hose.* Strictly, *liable* means "responsible" or "exposed to": *The owner will be liable for Horace's injuries.*

as Substituting for *because, since,* or *while, as* may be vague or ambiguous: *As we were stopping to rest, we decided to eat lunch.* (Does *as* mean "while" or "because"?) Usually a more precise word is preferable. See also 16c.

    As never should be used as a substitute for *whether* or *who. I'm not sure whether* (not *as*) *we can make it. That's the man who* (not *as*) *gave me directions.*

as, like In formal speech and writing, *as* may be either a preposition or a conjunction; *like* functions as a preposition only. Thus, if the construction being introduced is a full clause rather than a word or phrase, the preferred choice is *as* or *as if* (see 16c): *The plan succeeded as* (not *like*) *we hoped. It seemed as if* (not *like*) *it might fail. Other plans like it have failed.*

    When *as* serves as a preposition, the distinction between *as* and *like* depends on meaning. *As* suggests that the subject is equivalent or identical to the description: *She was hired as an engineer. Like* suggests resemblance but not identity: *People like her do well in such jobs.* See also *like, such as.*

as, than In comparisons, *as* and *than* may be followed by either subjective- or objective-case pronouns: *You are as tall as he* (subjective). *They treated you better than him* (objective). The case depends on whether the pronoun is the subject or object of a verb: *I love you more than he* (*loves you*). *I love you more than* (*I love*) *him.* See also 6e.

assure, ensure, insure *Assure* means "to promise": *He assured us that we would miss the traffic. Ensure* and *insure* often are used interchangeably to mean "make certain," but some reserve *insure* for matters of legal and financial protection and use *ensure* for more general meanings: *We left early to ensure that we would miss the traffic. It's expensive to insure yourself against floods.*

as to A stuffy substitute for *about: The suspect was questioned about* (not *as to*) *her actions.*

at The use of *at* after *where* is wordy and should be avoided: *Where are you meeting him?* is preferable to *Where are you meeting him at?*

at this point in time Wordy for *now, at this point,* or *at this time.*

averse, adverse See *adverse, averse.*

awful, awfully Strictly speaking, *awful* means "awe-inspiring." As intensifiers meaning "very" or "extremely" (*He tried awfully* *hard*), *awful* and *awfully* should be avoided in formal speech or writing.

a while, awhile   *Awhile* is an adverb; *a while* is an article and a noun. Thus *awhile* can modify a verb but cannot serve as the object of a preposition, and *a while* is just the opposite: *I will be gone awhile* (not *a while*). *I will be gone for a while* (not *awhile*).

bad, badly   In formal speech and writing, *bad* should be used only as an adjective; the adverb is *badly*. *He felt bad because his tooth ached badly*. In *He felt bad,* the verb *felt* is a linking verb and the adjective *bad* is a subject complement. See also 9b.

being as, being that   Colloquial for *because,* the preferable word in formal speech or writing: *Because* (not *Being as*) *the world is round, Columbus never did fall off the edge*.

beside, besides   *Beside* is a preposition meaning "next to." *Besides* is a preposition meaning "except" or "in addition to" as well as an adverb meaning "in addition." *Besides, several other people besides you want to sit beside Dr. Christensen*.

better, had better   *Had better* (meaning "ought to") is a verb modified by an adverb. The verb is necessary and should not be omitted: *You had better* (not *better*) *go*.

between, among   See *among, between*.

bring, take   Use *bring* only for movement from a farther place to a nearer one and *take* for any other movement. *First, take these books to the library for renewal, then take them to Mr. Daniels. Bring them back to me when he's finished*.

bunch   In formal speech and writing, *bunch* (as a noun) should be used only to refer to clusters of things growing or fastened together, such as bananas and grapes. Its use to mean a group of items or people is colloquial; *crowd* or *group* is preferable.

burst, bursted; bust, busted   *Burst* is a standard verb form meaning "to fly apart suddenly" (principal parts *burst, burst, burst*). The past-tense form *bursted* is nonstandard. The verb *bust* (*busted*) is slang.

but, hardly, scarcely   These words are negative in their own right; using *not* with any of them produces a double negative (see 9f). *We have but an hour* (not *We haven't got but an hour*) *before our plane leaves. I could hardly* (not *couldn't hardly*) *make out her face*.

but, however, yet   Each of these words is adequate to express contrast. Don't combine them. *He said he had finished, yet* (not *but yet*) *he continued*.

but that, but what   These wordy substitutes for *that* and *what* should be avoided: *I don't doubt that* (not *but that*) *you are right*.

calculate, figure, reckon   As substitutes for *expect* or *imagine* (*I figure I'll go*), these words are colloquial.

can, may   Strictly, *can* indicates capacity or ability, and *may* indicates permission: *If I may talk with you a moment, I believe I can solve your problem.*

can't help but This idiom is common but redundant. Either *I can't help wishing* or the more formal *I cannot but wish* is preferable to *I can't help but wish.*

case, instance, line Expressions such as *in the case of, in the instance of,* and *along the lines of* are usually unnecessary padding in a sentence and should be avoided.

censor, censure To *censor* is to edit or remove from public view on moral or some other grounds; to *censure* is to give a formal scolding. *The lieutenant was censured by Major Taylor for censoring the letters his soldiers wrote home from boot camp.*

center around *Center on* is more logical than, and preferable to, *center around.*

climatic, climactic *Climatic* comes from *climate* and refers to weather: *Last winter's temperatures may indicate a climatic change. Climactic* comes from *climax* and refers to a dramatic high point: *During the climactic duel between Hamlet and Laertes, Gertrude drinks poisoned wine.*

complement, compliment To *complement* something is to add to, complete, or reinforce it: *Her yellow blouse complemented her black hair.* To *compliment* something is to make a flattering remark about it: *He complimented her on her hair. Complimentary* can also mean "free": *complimentary tickets.*

conscience, conscious *Conscience* is a noun meaning "a sense of right and wrong"; *conscious* is an adjective meaning "aware" or "awake." *Though I was barely conscious, my conscience nagged me.*

contact Often used imprecisely as a verb instead of a more exact word such as *consult, talk with, telephone,* or *write to.*

continual, continuous *Continual* means "constantly recurring": *Most movies on television are continually interrupted by commercials. Continuous* means "unceasing": *Cable television often presents movies continuously without commercials.*

convince, persuade In the strictest sense, to *convince* someone means to change his or her opinion; to *persuade* someone means to move him or her to action. *Convince* thus is properly followed by *of* or *that,* whereas *persuade* is followed by *to: Once he convinced Othello of Desdemona's infidelity, Iago easily persuaded him to kill her.*

could of See *have, of.*

couple of Used colloquially to mean "a few" or "several."

credible, creditable, credulous *Credible* means "believable": *It's a strange story, but it seems credible to me. Creditable* means "deserving of credit" or "worthy": *Steve gave a creditable performance. Credulous* means "gullible": *The credulous Claire believed Tim's lies.* See also *incredible, incredulous.*

criteria The plural of *criterion* (meaning "standard for judgment"):

gl / us

gl / us

Of all our criteria for picking a roommate, the most important criterion is a sense of humor.

data   The plural of *datum* (meaning "fact"): *Out of all the data generated by these experiments, not one datum supports our hypothesis.* Usually, a more common term such as *fact, result,* or *figure* is preferred to *datum.* Though *data* is often used as a singular noun, most careful writers still treat it as plural: *The data fail* (not *fails*) *to support the hypothesis.*

device, devise   *Device* is the noun, and *devise* is the verb: *Can you devise some device for getting his attention?*

differ from, differ with   To *differ from* is to be unlike: *The twins differ from each other only in their hair styles.* To *differ with* is to disagree with: *I have to differ with you on that point.*

different from, different than   *Different from* is preferred: *His purpose is different from mine.* But *different than* is widely accepted when a construction using *from* would be wordy: *I'm a different person now than I used to be* is preferable to *I'm a different person now from the person I used to be.*

discreet, discrete   *Discreet* (noun form *discretion*) means "tactful": *What's a discreet way of telling Maud to be quiet? Discrete* (noun form *discreteness*) means "separate and distinct": *Within a computer's memory are millions of discrete bits of information.*

disinterested, uninterested   *Disinterested* means "impartial": *We chose Pete, as a disinterested third party, to decide who was right. Uninterested* means "bored" or "lacking interest": *Unfortunately, Pete was completely uninterested in the question.*

don't   *Don't* is the contraction for *do not,* not for *does not: I don't care, you don't care,* but *he doesn't* (not *don't*) *care.*

due to   *Due* is an adjective or noun; thus *due to* is always acceptable as a subject complement: *His gray hairs were due to age.* Many object to *due to* as a preposition meaning "because of" (*Due to the holiday, class was canceled*). A rule of thumb is that *due to* is always correct after a form of the verb *be* but questionable otherwise.

due to the fact that   Wordy for *because.*

each and every   Wordy for *each* or *every.* Write *each one of us* or *every one of us,* not *each and every one of us.*

eager, anxious   See *anxious, eager.*

effect   See *affect, effect.*

elicit, illicit   *Elicit* is a verb meaning "bring out" or "call forth." *Illicit* is an adjective meaning "unlawful." *The crime elicited an outcry against illicit drugs.*

ensure   See *assure, ensure, insure.*

enthused   Used colloquially as an adjective meaning "showing enthusiasm." The preferred adjective is *enthusiastic: The coach was enthusiastic* (not *enthused*) *about the team's victory.*

especially, specially   *Especially* means "particularly" or "more than other things"; *specially* means "for a specific reason." *I especially treasure my boots. They were made specially for me.*

et al., etc. *Et al.,* the Latin abbreviation for "and other people," is often used in source references for works with more than three authors: *Jones et al.* (see 37a–b). *Etc.,* the Latin abbreviation for "and other things," should be avoided in formal writing and should not be used to refer to people. When used, it should not substitute for precision, as in *The government provides health care, etc.* See also *and etc.*

everybody, every body; everyone, every one *Everybody* and *everyone* are indefinite pronouns: *Everybody (everyone) knows Tom steals. Every one* is a pronoun modified by *every,* and *every body* a noun modified by *every.* Both refer to each thing or person of a specific group and are typically followed by *of: The game commissioner has stocked every body of fresh water in the state with fish, and now every one of our rivers is a potential trout stream.*

everyday, every day *Everyday* is an adjective meaning "used daily" or "common"; *every day* is a noun modified by *every: Everyday problems tend to arise every day.*

everywheres Nonstandard for *everywhere.*

except See *accept, except.*

except for the fact that Wordy for *except that.*

explicit, implicit *Explicit* means "stated outright": *I left explicit instructions. The movie contains explicit sex. Implicit* means "implied, unstated": *We had an implicit understanding. I trust Marcia implicitly.*

farther, further *Farther* refers to additional distance (*How much farther is it to the beach?*), and *further* refers to additional time, amount, or other abstract matters (*I don't want to discuss this any further*).

fewer, less *Fewer* refers to individual countable items (a plural noun), *less* to general amounts (a singular noun): *Skim milk has fewer calories than whole milk. We have less milk left than I thought.*

field The phrase *the field of* is wordy and generally unnecessary: *Margaret plans to specialize in* (not *in the field of*) *family medicine.*

figure See *calculate, figure, reckon.*

fixing to Avoid this colloquial substitute for "intend to": *The school intends* (not *is fixing*) *to build a new library.*

flaunt, flout *Flaunt* means "show off": *If you have style, flaunt it. Flout* means "scorn" or "defy": *Hester Prynne flouted convention and paid the price.*

flunk A colloquial substitute for *fail.*

former, latter *Former* refers to the first-named of two things, *latter* to the second-named: *I like both skiing and swimming, the former in the winter and the latter all year round.* To refer to the first- or last-named of three or more things, say *first* or *last: I like jogging, swimming, and hang gliding, but the last is inconvenient in the city.*

gl / us

fun   As an adjective, *fun* is colloquial and should be avoided in most writing: *It was a pleasurable* (not *fun*) *evening.*

further   See *farther, further.*

get   This common verb is used in many slang and colloquial expressions: *get lost, that really gets me, getting on. Get* is easy to overuse; watch out for it in expressions such as *it's getting better* (substitute *it's improving*) and *we got done* (substitute *we finished*).

good, well   *Good* is an adjective, and *well* is nearly always an adverb: *Larry's a good dancer. He and Linda dance well together. Well* is properly used as an adjective only to refer to health: *You don't look well. Aren't you feeling well?* (*You look good,* in contrast, means "Your appearance is pleasing.")

good and   Colloquial for "very": *I was very* (not *good and*) *tired.*

had better   See *better, had better.*

had ought   The *had* is unnecessary and should be omitted: *He ought* (not *had ought*) *to listen to his mother.*

half   Either *half a* or *a half* is appropriate usage, but *a half a* is redundant: *Half a loaf* (not *A half a loaf*) *is better than none. I'd like a half-gallon* (not *a half a gallon*) *of mineral water, please.*

hanged, hung   Though both are past-tense forms of *hang, hanged* is used to refer to executions and *hung* is used for all other meanings: *Tom Dooley was hanged* (not *hung*) *from a white oak tree. I hung* (not *hanged*) *the picture you gave me.*

hardly   See *but, hardly, scarcely.*

have, of   Use *have,* not *of,* after helping verbs such as *could, should, would, may,* and *might: You should have* (not *should of*) *told me.*

he, she; he/she   Convention has allowed the use of *he* to mean "he or she": *After the infant learns to creep, he progresses to crawling.* However, many people today object to this use of *he* because readers tend to think of *he* as male, whether or not that is the writer's intention. The construction *he/she,* one substitute for *he,* is awkward and objectionable to most readers. The better choice is to use *he or she,* to make the pronoun plural, or to rephrase. For instance: *After the infant learns to creep, he or she progresses to crawling. After infants learn to creep, they progress to crawling. After learning to creep, the infant progresses to crawling.* See also 8b-3 and 31a-8.

herself, himself   See *myself, herself, himself, yourself.*

hisself   Nonstandard for *himself.*

hopefully   *Hopefully* means "with hope": *Freddy waited hopefully for a glimpse of Eliza.* The use of *hopefully* to mean "it is to be hoped," "I hope," or "let's hope" is now very common; but since many readers continue to object strongly to the usage, you should avoid it. *I hope* (not *Hopefully*) *Eliza will be here soon.*

idea, ideal   An *idea* is a thought or conception. An *ideal* (noun) is a model of perfection or a goal. *Ideal* should not be used in place of *idea: The idea* (not *ideal*) *of the play is that our ideals often sustain us.*

if, whether   For clarity, begin a subordinate clause with *whether* rather than *if* when the clause expresses an alternative: *If I laugh hard, people can't tell whether I'm crying.*

illicit   See *elicit, illicit.*

illusion   See *allusion, illusion.*

impact   Careful writers use both the noun and the verb *impact* to connote forceful or even violent collision. Avoid the increasingly common diluted meanings of *impact:* "an effect" (noun) or "to have an effect on" (verb). The diluted verb (*The budget cuts impacted social science research*) is bureaucratic jargon.

implicit   See *explicit, implicit.*

imply, infer   Writers or speakers *imply,* meaning "suggest": *Jim's letter implies he's having a good time.* Readers or listeners *infer,* meaning "conclude": *From Jim's letter I infer he's having a good time.*

in, into   *In* indicates location or condition: *He was in the garage. She was in a coma. Into* indicates movement or a change in condition: *He went into the garage. She fell into a coma. Into* is also slang for "interested in" or "involved in": *I am into Zen.*

in . . .   A number of phrases beginning with *in* are unnecessarily wordy and should be avoided: *in the event that* (for *if*); *in the neighborhood of* (for *approximately* or *about*); *in this day and age* (for *now* or *nowadays*); *in spite of the fact that* (for *although* or *even though*); and *in view of the fact that* (for *because* or *considering that*). Certain other *in* phrases are nothing but padding and can be omitted entirely: *in nature, in number, in reality,* and *in a very real sense.* See also 31c.

incredible, incredulous   *Incredible* means "unbelievable"; *incredulous* means "unbelieving": *When Nancy heard Dennis's incredible story, she was frankly incredulous.* See also *credible, creditable, credulous.*

individual, person, party   *Individual* should refer to a single human being in contrast to a group or should stress uniqueness: *The U.S. Constitution places strong emphasis on the rights of the individual.* For other meanings *person* is preferable: *What person* (not *individual*) *wouldn't want the security promised in that advertisement? Party* means "group" (*Can you seat a party of four for dinner?*) and should not be used to refer to an individual except in legal documents.

infer   See *imply, infer.*

in regards to   Nonstandard for *in regard to* (or *as regards* or *regarding*). See also *regarding.*

inside of, outside of   The *of* is unnecessary when *inside* and *outside* are used as prepositions: *Stay inside* (not *inside of*) *the house. The decision is outside* (not *outside of*) *my authority. Inside of* may refer colloquially to time, though in formal English *within* is preferred: *The law was passed within* (not *inside of*) *a year.*

instance   See *case, instance, line.*

gl / us

gl / us

insure   See *assure, ensure, insure.*

irregardless   Nonstandard for *regardless.*

is because   See *reason is because.*

is when, is where   These are mixed constructions (faulty predication; see 15b) in sentences that define: *Adolescence is a stage* (not *is when a person is*) *between childhood and adulthood. Socialism is a system in which* (not *is where*) *government owns the means of production.*

its, it's   *Its* is a possessive pronoun: *That plant is losing its leaves. It's* is a contraction for *it is: It's likely to die if you don't water it.* Many people confuse *it's* and *its* because possessives are most often formed with *-'s;* but the possessive *its,* like *his* and *hers,* never takes an apostrophe.

-ize, -wise   The suffix *-ize* changes a noun or adjective into a verb: *revolutionize, immunize.* The suffix *-wise* changes a noun or adjective into an adverb: *clockwise, otherwise, likewise.* Avoid the two suffixes except in established words: *The two nations are ready to settle on* (not *finalize*) *an agreement. I'm highly sensitive* (not *sensitized*) *to that kind of criticism. Financially* (not *Moneywise*), *it's a good time to buy real estate.*

kind of, sort of, type of   In formal speech and writing, avoid using *kind of* or *sort of* to mean "somewhat": *He was rather* (not *kind of*) *tall.*

Kind, sort, and type are singular and take singular modifiers and verbs: *This kind of dog is easily trained.* Agreement errors often occur when these singular nouns are combined with the plural demonstrative adjectives *these* and *those: These kinds* (not *kind*) *of dogs are easily trained. Kind, sort,* and *type* should be followed by *of* but not by *a: I don't know what type of* (not *type* or *type of a*) *dog that is.*

Use *kind of, sort of,* or *type of* only when the word *kind, sort,* or *type* is important: *That was a strange* (not *strange sort of*) *statement. He's a funny* (not *funny kind of*) *guy.*

later, latter   *Later* refers to time; *latter* refers to the second-named of two items. See also *former, latter.*

lay, lie   *Lay* is a transitive verb (principal parts *lay, laid, laid*) that means "put" or "place" and takes a direct object. *If we lay this tablecloth in the sun next to the shirt Sandy laid out there this morning, it should dry quickly. Lie* is an intransitive verb (principal parts *lie, lay, lain*) that means "recline" or "be situated": *I lay awake last night, just as I had lain the night before. The town lies east of the river.* See also 7b.

leave, let   *Leave* and *let* are interchangeable only when followed by *alone; leave me alone* is the same as *let me alone.* Otherwise, *leave* means "depart" and *let* means "allow": *Julia would not let Susan leave.*

less   See *fewer, less.*

let   See *leave, let.*

liable   See *apt, liable, likely.*

lie, lay   See *lay, lie.*

like, as   See *as, like.*

like, such as   When you are giving an example of something, use *such as* to indicate that the example is a representative of the thing mentioned, and use *like* to compare the example to the thing mentioned: *Steve has recordings of many great saxophonists such as Ben Webster and Lee Konitz. Steve wants to be a great jazz saxophonist like Ben Webster and Lee Konitz.*

Most writers prefer to keep *such* and *as* together: *Steve admires saxophonists such as . . .* rather than *Steve admires such saxophonists as. . . .*

likely   See *apt, liable, likely.*

line   See *case, instance, line.*

literally   This adverb means "actually" or "just as the words say," and it should not be used to qualify or intensify expressions whose words are not to be taken at face value. The sentence *He was literally climbing the walls* describes a person behaving like an insect, not a person who is restless or anxious. For the latter meaning, *literally* should be omitted.

lose, loose   *Lose* is a verb meaning "mislay": *Did you lose a brown glove? Loose* is an adjective meaning "unrestrained" or "not tight": *Ann's canary got loose. Loose* also can function as a verb meaning "let loose": *They loose the dogs as soon as they spot the bear.*

lots, lots of   Colloquial substitutes for *very many, a great many,* or *much.* Avoid *lots* and *lots of* in college or business writing. When you use either one informally, be careful to maintain subject-verb agreement: *There are* (not *is*) *lots of fish in the pond.*

may, can   See *can, may.*

may be, maybe   *May be* is a verb, and *maybe* is an adverb meaning "perhaps": *Tuesday may be a legal holiday. Maybe we won't have classes.*

may of   See *have, of.*

media   *Media* is the plural of *medium* and takes a plural verb: *All the news media are increasingly visual.*

might of   See *have, of.*

moral, morale   As a noun, *moral* means "ethical conclusion" or "lesson": *The moral of the story escapes me. Morale* means "spirit" or "state of mind": *Victory improved the team's morale.*

most, almost   See *almost, most.*

must of   See *have, of.*

myself, herself, himself, yourself   The *-self* pronouns are reflexive or intensive, which means they refer to or intensify an antecedent (see 5a-2): *Paul and I did it ourselves; Jill herself said so.* The *-self* pronouns are often used colloquially in place of personal pronouns, but that use should be avoided in formal speech and writing: *No one except me* (not *myself*) *saw the accident. Our delegates will be Susan and you* (not *yourself*).

nohow   Nonstandard for *in no way* or *in any way.*

gl / us

nothing like, nowhere near These colloquial substitutes for *not nearly* are best avoided in formal speech and writing: *That program is not nearly* (not *nowhere near*) *as expensive.*

nowheres Nonstandard for *nowhere.*

number See *amount, number.*

of, have See *have, of.*

off of *Of* is unnecessary. Use *off* or *from* rather than *off of: He jumped off* (or *from,* not *off of*) *the roof.*

OK, O.K., okay All three spellings are acceptable, but avoid this colloquial term in formal speech and writing.

on, upon In modern English, *upon* is usually just a stuffy way of saying *on.* Unless you need a formal effect, use *on: We decided on* (not *upon*) *a location for our next meeting.*

on account of Wordy for *because of.*

on the other hand This transitional expression of contrast should be preceded by its mate, *on the one hand: On the one hand, we hoped for snow. On the other hand, we feared that it would harm the animals.* However, the two combined can be unwieldy, and a simple *but, however, yet,* or *in contrast* often suffices: *We hoped for snow. Yet we feared that it would harm the animals.*

outside of See *inside of, outside of.*

owing to the fact that Wordy for *because.*

party See *individual, person, party.*

people, persons In formal usage, *people* refers to a general group: *We the people of the United States. . . . Persons* refers to a collection of individuals: *Will the person or persons who saw the accident please notify. . . .* Except when emphasizing individuals, prefer *people* to *persons.*

per Except in technical writing, an English equivalent is usually preferable to the Latin *per: $10 an* (not *per*) *hour; sent by* (not *per*) *parcel post; requested in* (not *per* or *as per*) *your letter.*

percent (per cent), percentage Both these terms refer to fractions of one hundred and should be avoided except when specifying actual statistics. Use an expression such as *part of, a number of,* or *a large* (or *small*) *proportion of* when you mean simply "part."

    Percent always follows a numeral (*40 percent of the voters*), and the word should be used instead of the symbol (%) in general writing. *Percentage* usually follows an adjective (*a high percentage*).

person See *individual, person, party.*

persons See *people, persons.*

persuade See *convince, persuade.*

phenomena The plural of *phenomenon* (meaning "perceivable fact" or "unusual occurrence"): *The Center for Short-Lived Phenomena judged that the phenomenon we had witnessed was not a flying saucer.*

plenty A colloquial substitute for *very: He was going very* (not *plenty*) *fast when he hit that tree.*

plus *Plus* is standard as a preposition meaning *in addition to: His income plus mine is sufficient.* But *plus* is colloquial as a conjunctive adverb: *Our organization is larger than theirs; moreover* (not *plus*), *we have more money.*

practicable, practical *Practicable* means "capable of being put into practice"; *practical* means "useful" or "sensible": *We figured out a practical new design for our kitchen, but it was too expensive to be praticable.*

precede, proceed The verb *precede* means "come before": *My name precedes yours in the alphabet.* The verb *proceed* means "move on": *We were told to proceed to the waiting room.*

prejudice, prejudiced *Prejudice* is a noun; *prejudiced* is an adjective. Do not drop the *-d* from *prejudiced: I was fortunate that my parents were not prejudiced* (not *prejudice*).

pretty Overworked as an adverb meaning "rather" or "somewhat": *He was somewhat* (not *pretty*) *irked at the suggestion.*

previous to, prior to Wordy for *before.*

principal, principle *Principal* is a noun meaning "chief official" or, in finance, "capital sum." As an adjective, *principal* means "foremost" or "major." *Principle* is a noun only, meaning "rule" or "axiom." *Her principal reasons for confessing were her principles of right and wrong.*

proceed, precede See *precede, proceed.*

provided, providing *Provided* may serve as a subordinating conjunction meaning "on the condition (that)"; *providing* may not. *The grocer will begin providing food for the soup kitchen provided* (not *providing*) *we find a suitable space.*

question of whether, question as to whether Wordy substitutes for *whether.*

raise, rise *Raise* is a transitive verb that takes a direct object, and *rise* is an intransitive verb that does not take an object: *The Kirks have to rise at dawn because they raise cows.*

real, really In formal speech and writing, *real* should not be used as an adverb; *really* is the adverb and *real* an adjective. *Popular reaction to the announcement was really* (not *real*) *enthusiastic.*

reason is because A mixed construction (faulty predication; see 15b). Although the expression is colloquially common, formal speech and writing require a *that* clause after *reason is: The reason he is absent is that* (not *is because*) *he is sick.* Or: *He is absent because he is sick.*

reckon See *calculate, figure, reckon.*

regarding, in regard to, with regard to, relating to, relative to, with respect to, respecting Stuffy substitutes for *on, about,* or *concerning: Mr. McGee spoke about* (not *with regard to*) *the plans for the merger.*

respectful, respective *Respectful* means "full of (or showing) respect": *Be respectful of other people. Respective* means "separate": *The French and the Germans occupied their respective trenches.*

rise, raise See *raise, rise.*

gl / us

scarcely   See *but, hardly, scarcely.*

sensual, sensuous   *Sensual* suggests sexuality; *sensuous* means "pleasing to the senses." *Stirred by the sensuous scent of meadow grass and flowers, Cheryl and Paul found their thoughts growing increasingly sensual.*

set, sit   *Set* is a transitive verb (principal parts, *set, set, set*) that describes something a person does to an object: *He set the pitcher down. Sit* is an intransitive verb (principal parts *sit, sat, sat*) that describes something done by a person who is tired of standing: *She sits on the sofa.* See also 7b.

shall, will   *Will* is the future-tense helping verb for all persons: *I will go, you will go, they will go.* The main use of *shall* is for first-person questions requesting an opinion or consent: *Shall I order a pizza? Shall we dance?* (Questions that merely inquire about the future use *will: When will I see you again?*) *Shall* can also be used for the first person when a formal effect is desired (I *shall expect you around three*), and it is occasionally used with the second or third person to express the speaker's determination (*You shall do as I say*).

should, would   *Should* expresses obligation for first, second, and third persons: *I should fix dinner. You should set the table. Jack should wash the dishes. Would* expresses a wish or hypothetical condition for all three persons: *I would do it. Wouldn't you? Wouldn't anybody?* When the context is formal, however, *should* is sometimes used instead of *would* in the first person: *We should be delighted to accept.*

should of   See *have, of.*

since   *Since* is often used to mean "because": *Since you ask, I'll tell you.* Its primary meaning, however, relates to time: *I've been waiting since noon.* To avoid confusion, some writers prefer to use *since* only in contexts involving time. If you do use *since* in both senses, watch out for ambiguous constructions, such as *Since you left, my life is empty,* where *since* could mean either "because" or "ever since."

sit, set   See *set, sit.*

situation   Often unnecessary, as in *The situation is that we have to get some help* (revise to *We have to get some help*) or *The team was faced with a punting situation* (revise to *The team was faced with punting* or *The team had to punt*).

so   Avoid using *so* alone as a vague intensifier: *He was so late. So* needs to be followed by *that* and a clause that states a result: *He was so late that I left without him.*

some   *Some* is colloquial as an adverb meaning "somewhat" or "to some extent" and as an adjective meaning "remarkable": *We'll have to hurry somewhat* (not *some*) *to get there in time. Those are remarkable* (not *some*) *photographs.*

somebody, some body; someone, some one   *Somebody* and *someone* are indefinite pronouns; *some body* is a noun modified by an adjective; and *some one* is a pronoun or an adjective modified by *some. Somebody ought to invent a shampoo that will give hair some body. Someone told Janine she should choose some one plan and stick with it.*

someplace   Informal for *somewhere.*

sometime, sometimes, some time   *Sometime* means "at an indefinite time in the future": *Why don't you come up and see me sometime? Sometimes* means "now and then": *I still see my old friend Joe sometimes. Some time* means "span of time": *I need some time to make the payments.*

somewheres   Nonstandard for *somewhere.*

sort of, sort of a   See *kind of, sort of, type of.*

specially   See *especially, specially.*

such   Avoid using *such* as a vague intensifier: *It was such a cold winter. Such* should be followed by *that* and a clause that states a result: *It was such a cold winter that Napoleon's troops had to turn back.*

such as   See *like, such as.*

supposed to, used to   In both these expressions, the *-d* is essential: *I used to* (not *use to*) *think so. He's supposed to* (not *suppose to*) *meet us.*

sure   Colloquial when used as an adverb meaning *surely: James Madison sure was right about the need for the Bill of Rights.* If you merely want to be emphatic, use *certainly: Madison certainly was right.* If your goal is to convince a possibly reluctant reader, use *surely: Madison surely was right. Surely Madison was right.*

sure and, sure to; try and, try to   *Sure to* and *try to* are the preferred forms: *Be sure to* (not *sure and*) *buy milk. Try to* (not *Try and*) *find some decent tomatoes.*

take, bring   See *bring, take.*

than, as   See *as, than.*

than, then   *Than* is a conjunction used in comparisons, *then* an adverb indicating time: *Holmes knew then that Moriarty was wilier than he had thought.*

that, which   *That* always introduces restrictive clauses: *We should use the lettuce that Susan bought* (*that Susan bought* identifies the specific lettuce being referred to). *Which* can introduce both restrictive and nonrestrictive clauses, but many writers reserve *which* only for nonrestrictive clauses: *The leftover lettuce, which is in the refrigerator, would make a good salad* (*which is in the refrigerator* simply provides more information about the lettuce). See also 21c.

their, there, they're   *Their* is the possessive form of *they: Give them their money. There* indicates place (*I saw her standing there*) or functions as an expletive (*There is a hole behind you*). *They're* is a contraction for *they are: They're going fast.*

theirselves   Nonstandard for *themselves.*

then, than   See *than, then.*

these kind, these sort, these type, those kind   See *kind of, sort of, type of.*

gl / us

this here, these here, that there, them there Nonstandard for *this, these, that,* or *those.*

thru A colloquial spelling of *through* that should be avoided in all academic and business writing.

thusly A mistaken form of *thus.*

till, until, 'til *Till* and *until* have the same meaning; both are acceptable. *'Til,* a contraction of *until,* is an old form that has been replaced by *till.*

time period Since a *period* is an interval of time, this expression is redundant: *They did not see each other for a long time* (not *time period*). *Six accidents occurred in a three-week period* (not *time period*).

to, too, two *To* is a preposition; *too* is an adverb meaning "also" or "excessively"; and *two* is a number. *I too have been to Europe two times.*

too Avoid using *too* as an intensifier meaning "very": *Monkeys are too mean.* If you do use *too,* explain the consequences of the excessive quality: *Monkeys are too mean to make good pets.*

toward, towards Both are acceptable, though *toward* is preferred. Use one or the other consistently.

try and, try to See *sure and, sure to; try and, try to.*

type of See *kind of, sort of, type of.* Don't use *type* without *of: It was a family type of* (not *type*) *restaurant.* Or, better: *It was a family restaurant.*

uninterested See *disinterested, uninterested.*

unique As an absolute adjective (see 9e-5), *unique* cannot sensibly be modified with words such as *very* or *most: That was a unique* (not *a very unique* or *the most unique*) *movie.*

until See *till, until, 'til.*

upon, on See *on, upon.*

usage, use *Usage* refers to conventions, most often those of a language: *Is "hadn't ought" proper usage? Usage* is often misused in place of the noun *use: Wise use* (not *usage*) *of insulation can save fuel.*

use, utilize *Utilize* means "make use of": *We should utilize John's talent for mimicry in our play.* In most contexts, *use* is equally or more acceptable and less stuffy.

used to See *supposed to, used to.*

wait for, wait on In formal speech and writing, *wait for* means "await" (*I'm waiting for Paul*), and *wait on* means "serve" (*The owner of the store herself waited on us*).

ways Colloquial as a substitute for *way: We have only a little way* (not *ways*) *to go.*

well See *good, well.*

whether, if See *if, whether.*

which See *that, which.*

which, who *Which* never refers to people. Use *who* or sometimes *that* for a person or persons and *which* or *that* for a thing or things: *The baby, who was left behind, opened the door, which we had closed.* See also 12f.

who's, whose   *Who's* is the contraction of *who is: Who's at the door? Whose* is the possessive form of *who: Whose book is that?*

will, shall   See *shall, will.*

-wise   See *-ize, -wise.*

with regard to, with respect to   See *regarding.*

would   See *should, would.*

would have   Avoid this construction in place of *had* in clauses that begin *if* and state a condition contrary to fact: *if the tree had* (not *would have*) *withstood the fire, it would have been the oldest in town.* (See also 7g-2.)

would of   See *have, of.*

you   In all but very formal writing, *you* is generally appropriate as long as it means "you, the reader." In all writing, avoid indefinite uses of *you,* such as *You can see the resemblance between me and my brother* or *In one ancient tribe your first loyalty was to your parents.* See 12d.

your, you're   *Your* is the possessive form of *you: Your dinner is ready. You're* is the contraction of *you are: You're bound to be late.*

yourself   See *myself, herself, himself, yourself.*

gl / us

Glossary of Terms

absolute phrase   A phrase that consists of a noun or pronoun and a participle, modifies a whole clause or sentence (rather than a single word), and is not joined to the rest of the sentence by a connector: *Our accommodations arranged, we set out on our trip. They will hire a local person, other things being equal.* See 5c-3.

abstract and concrete   Two kinds of language. **Abstract** words refer to ideas, qualities, attitudes, and conditions that can't be perceived with the senses: *beauty, guilty, victory.* **Concrete** words refer to objects, persons, places, or conditions that can be perceived with the senses: *Abilene, scratchy, toolbox.* See 31b-2. See also *general and specific.*

acronym   A pronounceable word formed from the initial letter or letters of each word in an organization's title: NATO (North Atlantic Treaty Organization). See 20b and 28b.

active voice   See *voice.*

adjectival   A term sometimes used to describe any word or word group, other than an adjective, that is used to modify a noun. Common adjectivals include nouns (*wagon train, railroad ties*), phrases (*fool on the hill*), and clauses (*the man that I used to be*). See *clause* and *phrase.* See 5c.

adjective   A word used to modify a noun or a word or word group used as a noun.

- A **descriptive adjective** names some quality of the noun: *beautiful morning, dark horse.*
- A **limiting adjective** narrows the scope of a noun. It may be a **possessive** (*my, their*); a **demonstrative adjective** (*this train,*

these days); an **interrogative adjective** (*what time? whose body?*); or a **number** (*two boys*).

- A **proper adjective** is derived from a proper noun: *French language, Machiavellian scheme.*

Adjectives also can be classified according to position.

- An **attributive adjective** appears next to the noun it modifies: *full moon.*
- A **predicate adjective** is connected to its noun by a linking verb: *The moon is full.* See also *complement.*

See Chapter 9.

adjective clause   See *clause.*

adjective phrase   See *phrase.*

adverb   A word used to modify a verb, an adjective, another adverb, or a whole sentence: *If you go south you'll hit a more heavily traveled road* (*south* modifies the verb *go; heavily* modifies the adjective *traveled;* and *more* modifies the adverb *heavily*). See Chapter 9.

adverb clause   See *clause.*

adverbial   A term sometimes used to describe any word or word group, other than an adverb, that is used to modify a verb, an adjective, another adverb, or a whole sentence. Common adverbials include nouns (*This little piggy stayed home*), phrases (*This little piggy went to market*), and clauses (*This little piggy went wherever he wanted*). See 5c. See also *clause* and *phrase.*

adverbial conjunction   See *conjunctive adverb.*

adverb phrase   See *phrase.*

agreement   The correspondence of one word to another in person, number, or gender. A verb must agree with its subject; a pronoun must agree with its antecedent; and a demonstrative adjective must agree with its noun. *Every week the commander orders these kinds of sandwiches for his troops* (the verb *orders* and the pronoun *his* both agree with the noun *commander;* the demonstrative adjective *these* agrees with the noun *kinds*). See Chapter 8.

   Logical agreement requires consistency in number between other related words, usually nouns: *The students brought their books* (not *book*). See 13a.

analogy   A comparison between members of different classes, such as a nursery school and a barnyard or a molecule and a pair of dancers. Usually, the purpose is to explain something unfamiliar to readers through something familiar. See 1e-8 and 3c-2.

analysis (division)   The separation of a subject into its elements. Analysis is fundamental to critical thinking, reading, and writing. See 1e-8, 3c-2, and especially 4b-5.

antecedent   The noun, or word or word group acting as a noun, to which a pronoun refers: *Jonah, who is not yet ten, has already chosen the college he will attend* (*Jonah* is the antecedent of the pronouns *who* and *he*). See 8b.

gl / tm

gl / tm

APA style The style of documentation recommended by the American Psychological Association and used in many of the social sciences. For discussion and examples, see 39c-4.

appeals Attempts to engage and persuade readers. An **emotional appeal** touches readers' feelings, beliefs, and values. An **ethical appeal** presents the writer as competent, sincere, and fair. A **rational appeal** engages readers' powers of reasoning. See 4g-1.

appositive A word or phrase appearing next to a noun or pronoun, or to a word or word group acting as a noun, that explains or identifies it and is equivalent to it: *My brother Michael, the best horn player in town, won the state competition* (*Michael* is a restrictive appositive that identifies which brother is being referred to; *the best horn player in town* is a nonrestrictive appositive that adds information about *My brother Michael*). See 5c-5 and 21c-2.

argument Writing whose primary purpose is to convince readers of an idea or persuade them to act. See 4c-4.

article The word *a, an,* or *the.* Articles are usually classed as adjectives; they are sometimes called **determiners** because they always signal that a noun follows. See the Glossary of Usage (p. 748) for when to use *a* or *an* before a noun or abbreviation.

Articles often present problems for those whose native language is not English, because many languages use articles differently or less frequently than English does. The main conventions for using articles in English can be summarized as follows:

TRANSPARENCY MASTER
AVAILABLE

- *The* is a **definite article:** it precedes a noun when the thing named is already known to the reader (*Visitors may tour the house*). *A* and *an* are **indefinite articles:** they precede a noun when the thing named is not already known to the reader (*They share a house*).
- Use *a, an,* or *the* with a singular count noun—that is, a singular noun that names something countable: *a glass, an apple, the mirror.* Count nouns can form plurals with the addition of *-s* or *-es* (*glass, glasses*) or in some irregular way (*child, children*).
- Do not use *a* or *an* with a plural noun: *apples* (not *an apples*). And do not use *a* or *an* with a mass noun—that is, a singular noun that names something not normally countable: *mail* (not *a mail*), *supervision* (not *a supervision*). Unlike count nouns, mass nouns do not form plurals. Note, however, that many nouns are sometimes count nouns and sometimes mass nouns: in *We have a room for you, room* is a count noun meaning "walled area"; in *We have room for you, room* is a mass noun meaning "space."
- Do not use *the* with a plural noun or a mass noun when the noun refers generally to all representatives of what it names: *Men* (not *The men*) *and women* (not *the women*) *are different. Democracy* (not *The democracy*) *fosters freedom* (not *the freedom*) *of expression* (not *the expression*). Use *the* when referring to one or more specific representatives of what the noun names: *The women came and went.*

This summary omits many special uses of articles. Fuller discussions can be found in many composition textbooks designed for students using English as a second language.

assertion   A positive statement that requires support. Assertions are the backbone of any argument. See 4c-1.

assumption   A stated or unstated belief or opinion that underlies an argument, connecting assertions and evidence. See 4c-3.

audience   The intended readers of a piece of writing. Knowledge of the audience's needs and expectations helps a writer shape writing so that it is clear, interesting, and convincing. A **general audience** consists of people of diverse backgrounds and interests. See 1d.

auxiliary verb   See *helping verb*.

balanced sentence   A sentence consisting of two clauses with parallel constructions: *Do as I say, not as I do. Befriend all animals; exploit none.* Their balance makes such sentences highly emphatic. See 18a-2.

belief   A conviction based on morality, values, or faith. Statements of belief often serve as assumptions and sometimes as evidence, but they are not arguable and so cannot serve as the thesis in an argument. See 4c-1.

body   In a piece of writing, the large central part where ideas supporting the thesis are presented and developed. See also *conclusion* and *introduction*.

brainstorming   A technique for generating ideas about a topic: concentrating on the topic for a fixed time (say, fifteen minutes), you list every idea and detail that comes to mind. See 1e-4.

cardinal number   The type of number that shows amount: *two, sixty, ninety-seven*. Contrast *ordinal number* (such as *second, ninety-seventh*).

case   The form of a noun or pronoun that indicates its function in the sentence. Nouns have two cases: the **plain case** (*John, ambassador*), for all uses except to show possession; and the **possessive** (or **genitive**) **case** (*John's, ambassador's*). Pronouns have three cases: the **subjective** (or **nominative**) **case** (*I, she*), denoting the subject of a verb or a subject complement; the **possessive case,** for use as either an adjective (*my, her*) or a noun (*mine, hers*); and the **objective case** (*me, her*), denoting the object of a verb, verbal, or preposition. See page 213 for a list of the forms of personal and relative pronouns.

cause-and-effect analysis   The determination of why something happened or what its consequences were or will be. See 1e-8 and 3c-2.

CBE style   A style of documenting sources recommended by the Council of Biology Editors and frequently used in the natural and applied sciences. For explanation and examples, see 39d-4.

chronological organization   The arrangement of events as they occurred in time, usually from first to last. See 1g-3 and 3b-1.

gl / tm

citation   In research writing, the way of acknowledging material borrowed from sources. Most systems of citation discussed in this handbook are basically similar: a brief parenthetical reference in the text indicates that particular material is borrowed and directs the reader to a detailed list of sources at the end of the work. The systems do differ, however. See 37a–37b (MLA style), 39c-4 (APA style), and 39d-4 (CBE style).

classification   The sorting of many things, people, or other elements into groups based on their similarities. See 1e-8 and 3c-2.

clause   A group of related words containing a subject and predicate. **A main (independent) clause** can stand by itself as a sentence; a **subordinate (dependent) clause** cannot.

Main clause	*We can go to the movies.*
Subordinate clause	We can go *if Julie gets back on time.*

Subordinate clauses may function as adjectives, adverbs, or nouns.

- **Adjective clauses** modify nouns or pronouns: *The car that hit Fred was running a red light* (clause modifies *car*).
- **Adverb clauses** modify verbs, adjectives, other adverbs, or whole clauses or sentences: *The car hit Fred when it ran a red light* (clause modifies *The car hit Fred*).
- **Noun clauses,** like nouns, function as subjects, objects, or complements: *Whoever was driving should be arrested* (clause is sentence subject).

See 5c-4.

clichés   See *trite expressions.*

climactic organization   The arrangement of material in order of increasing drama or interest, leading to a climax. See 3b-1.

clustering   A technique for generating ideas about a topic: drawing and writing, you branch outward from a center point (the topic) to pursue the implications of ideas. See 1e-5.

coherence   The quality of an effective essay or paragraph that helps readers see relations among ideas and move easily from one idea to the next. See 1g-4 and 3b.

collaborative learning   In a writing course, students working together in groups to help each other become better writers and readers. See 2e.

collective noun   See *noun.*

colloquial language   The words and expressions of everyday speech. Colloquial language can enliven informal writing but is generally inappropriate in formal academic or business writing. See 31a-2. See also *formal and informal.*

comma splice   A sentence error in which two main clauses are separated by a comma with no coordinating conjunction. See 11a and 11b.

Comma splice	The book was long, it contained useful information.
Revised	The book was long; it contained useful information.
Revised	The book was long, *but* it contained useful information.

common noun   See *noun.*

comparative   See *comparison.*

comparison   The inflection of an adverb or adjective that shows its relative intensity. The **positive degree** is the simple, uncompared form: *gross, clumsily.* The **comparative degree** compares the thing modified to at least one other thing: *grosser, more clumsily.* The **superlative degree** indicates that the thing modified exceeds all other things to which it is being compared: *grossest, most clumsily.* The comparative and superlative degrees are formed either by adding the endings *-er* and *-est* or by preceding the modifier with the words *more* and *most, less* and *least.* See 9e.

comparison and contrast   The identification of similarities (comparison) and differences (contrast) between two or more subjects. See 1e-8 and 3c-2.

complement   A word or word group that completes the sense of a subject, an object, or a verb.

- A **subject complement** follows a linking verb and modifies or refers to the subject. It may be an adjective, noun or pronoun, or word or word group acting as an adjective or noun: *I am a lion tamer, but I am not yet experienced* (the noun *lion tamer* and the adjective *experienced* complement the subject *I*). Adjective complements are also called **predicate adjectives.** Noun complements are also called **predicate nouns** or **predicate nominatives.**

- An **object complement** follows and modifies or refers to a direct object. The complement can be an adjective, a noun, or a word or word group acting as an adjective or noun: *If you elect me president, I'll keep the students satisfied* (the noun *president* complements the direct object *me,* and the adjective *satisfied* complements the direct object *students*).

- A **verb complement** is a direct or indirect object of a verb. It may be a noun, pronoun, or word or word group acting as a noun: *Don't give the chimp that peanut* (*chimp* is the indirect object and *peanut* is the direct object of the verb *give;* both objects are verb complements).

See 5a-3.

complete predicate   See *predicate.*

complete subject   See *subject.*

complex sentence   See *sentence.*

gl / tm

compound   Consisting of two or more words that function as a unit. **Compound words** include **compound nouns** (*milestone, featherbrain*); **compound adjectives** (*two-year-old, downtrodden*); and **compound prepositions** (*in addition to, on account of*). **Compound constructions** include **compound subjects** (*Harriet and Peter poled their barge down the river*); **compound predicates** (*The scout watched and waited*) or parts of predicates (*He grew tired and hungry*); and **compound sentences** (*He smiled, and I laughed*). See 5d.

compound-complex sentence   See *sentence*.

compound predicate   See *compound*.

compound sentence   See *sentence*.

compound subject   See *compound*.

conciseness   Use of the fewest and freshest words to express meaning clearly and achieve the desired effect with readers. See 31c.

conclusion   The closing of an essay, tying off the writer's thoughts and leaving readers with a sense of completion. See 3d-2 for suggestions.

A *conclusion* is also the result of deductive reasoning. See *deductive reasoning* and *syllogism*.

concrete   See *abstract and concrete*.

conditional statement   A statement expressing a condition contrary to fact and using the subjunctive mood of the verb: *If she were mayor, the unions would cooperate.* See also *mood*.

conjugation   A list of the forms of a verb showing tense, voice, mood, person, and number. The conjugation of the verb *know* in present tense, active voice, indicative mood is *I know, you know, he/she/it knows, we know, you know, they know*. See Chapter 7, pages 233–34.

conjunction   A word that links and relates parts of a sentence. **Coordinating conjunctions** (*and, but, or, nor, for, so, yet*) connect words or word groups of equal grammatical rank: *The lights went out, but the doctors and nurses continued caring for their patients.* See 5d-1. **Correlative conjunctions** or **correlatives** (such as *either . . . or, not only . . . but also*) are pairs of coordinating conjunctions that work together: *He was certain that either his parents or his brother would help him.* See 5d-1. **Subordinating conjunctions** (*after, although, as if, because, if, when, while,* and so on) begin a subordinate clause and link it to a main clause: *The seven dwarfs whistle while they work.* See 5c-4.

conjunctive adverb (adverbial conjunction)   An adverb (such as *besides, consequently, however, indeed,* and *therefore*) that relates two main clauses in a sentence: *We had hoped to own a house by now; however, housing costs have risen too fast.* See 5d-2.

connector (connective)   Any word or phrase that links words, phrases, clauses, or sentences. Common connectors include coordinating, correlative, and subordinating conjunctions; conjunctive adverbs; and prepositions.

connotation An association called up by a word, beyond its dictionary definition. See 31b-1. Contrast *denotation*.

construction Any group of grammatically related words, such as a phrase, a clause, or a sentence.

contraction A condensation of an expression, with an apostrophe replacing the missing letters: for example, *doesn't* (for *does not*), *we'll* (for *we will*). See 23c.

contrast See *comparison and contrast*.

coordinate adjectives Two or more adjectives modifying the same noun or pronoun: *The camera panned the vast, empty desert.* See 21f-2.

coordinating conjunction See *conjunction*.

coordination The linking of words, phrases, or clauses that are of equal importance, usually with a coordinating conjunction: *He and I laughed, but she was not amused.* See 16a. Contrast *subordination*.

correlative conjunction (correlative) See *conjunction*.

count noun See *noun*.

critical thinking, reading, and writing Looking beneath the surface of words and images to understand, analyze, and evaluate meaning and intentions.

cumulative (loose) sentence A sentence in which modifiers follow the subject and verb: *Ducks waddled by, their tails swaying and their quacks rising to heaven.* See 18a-1. Contrast *periodic sentence*.

dangling modifier A word or phrase modifying a term that has been omitted or to which it cannot easily be linked. See 14f.

> **Dangling** *Having arrived late,* the concert had already begun.
>
> **Revised** Having arrived late, *we* found that the concert had already begun.

declension A list of the forms of a noun or pronoun, showing inflections for person (for pronouns), number, and case. See Chapter 6, page 213, for a declension of the personal and relative pronouns.

deductive reasoning Applying a generalization to specific circumstances in order to reach a conclusion. See 4f-1. See also *syllogism*. Contrast *inductive reasoning*.

definition Specifying the characteristics of something to establish what it is and is not. See 1e-8 and 3c-2.

degree See *comparison*.

demonstrative adjective See *adjective*.

demonstrative pronoun See *pronoun*.

denotation The main or dictionary definition of a word. See 31b-1. Contrast *connotation*.

gl / tm

dependent clause   See *clause*.

derivational suffix   See *suffix*.

description   Detailing the sensory qualities of a thing, person, place, or feeling. See 1e-8 and 3c-2.

descriptive adjective   See *adjective*.

determiner   A word such as *a, an, the, my,* and *your* which indicates that a noun follows. See also *article*.

developing (planning)   The stage of the writing process when one finds a topic, explores ideas, gathers information, focuses on a central theme, and organizes material. See Chapter 1. Compare *drafting* and *revising*.

dialect   A variety of a language used by a specific group or in a specific region. A dialect may be distinguished by its pronunciation, vocabulary, and grammar.

diction   The choice and use of words. See Chapter 31.

dictionary form   See *plain form*.

direct address   A construction in which a word or phrase indicates the person or group spoken to: *Have you finished, John? Farmers, unite*.

direct object   See *object*.

direct question   A sentence asking a question and concluding with a question mark: *Do they know we are watching?* Contrast *indirect question*.

direct quotation (direct discourse)   See *quotation*.

division (analysis)   See *analysis (division)*.

documentation   In research writing, supplying citations that legitimate the use of borrowed material and support claims about its origins. See Chapter 37. Contrast *plagiarism*.

double negative   A nonstandard form consisting of two negative words used in the same construction so that they effectively cancel each other: *I don't have no money.* Rephrase as *I have no money* or *I don't have any money.* See 9f.

double possessive   A possessive using both the ending *-'s* and the preposition *of: That is a favorite expression of Mark's*.

double talk (doublespeak)   Language intended to confuse or to be misunderstood. See 31a-7.

drafting   The stage of the writing process when ideas are expressed in connected sentences and paragraphs. See 2a. Compare *developing (planning)* and *revising*.

editing   A distinct step in revising a written work, focusing on clarity, tone, and correctness. See 2c. Compare *revising*.

ellipsis   The omission of a word or words from a quotation, indicated by the three spaced periods of an **ellipsis mark:** *"that all . . . are created equal."* See 25e.

elliptical clause   A clause omitting a word or words whose meaning is understood from the rest of the clause: *David likes Minneapolis better than (he likes) Chicago.* See 5c-4.

emotional appeal   See *appeals*.

emphasis   The manipulation of words, sentences, and paragraphs to stress important ideas. See Chapter 18.

essay   A nonfiction composition on a single subject and with a central idea or thesis.

ethical appeal   See *appeals.*

etymology   The history of a word's meanings and forms.

euphemism   A presumably inoffensive word that a writer or speaker substitutes for a word deemed possibly offensive or too blunt—for example, *passed beyond* for "died." See 31a-7.

evaluation   A judgment of the quality, value, currency, bias, or other aspects of a work. See 4b-6 and 36a.

evidence   The facts, examples, expert opinions, and other information that support assertions. See 4c-2 and 4f-2.

expletive   A sentence construction that postpones the subject by beginning with *there* or *it* followed by a form of the verb *be: It is impossible to get a ticket; I don't know why there aren't more seats available* (*to get a ticket* is the subject of *is; seats* is the subject of *aren't*). See 5e-4.

exposition   Writing whose primary purpose is to explain something about a topic.

fallacies   See *logical fallacies.*

faulty predication   A sentence error in which the meanings of subject and predicate conflict, so that the subject is said to be or do something illogical: *The installation of an air bag occupies considerable space in a car.* See 15b.

figurative language (figures of speech)   Expressions that suggest meanings different from their literal meanings in order to achieve special effects. Some common figures:

- **Hyperbole,** deliberate exaggeration: *The bag weighed a ton.*
- **Metaphor,** an implied comparison between two unlike things: *The wind stabbed through our clothes.*
- **Personification,** the attribution of human qualities to a thing or idea: *The water beckoned seductively.*
- **Simile,** an explicit comparison, using *like* or *as,* between two unlike things: *The sky glowered like an angry parent.*

    A **mixed metaphor** is a confusing or ludicrous combination of incompatible figures: *The wind stabbed through our clothes and shook our bones.* See 31b-4.

finite verb   A term used to describe any verb that makes an assertion or expresses a state of being and can stand as the main verb of a sentence or clause: *The moose eats the leaves.* See also 5c-2. Contrast *verbal (nonfinite verb),* which is formed from a finite verb but is unable to stand alone as the main verb of a sentence: *I saw the moose eating the leaves.*

first person   See *person.*

formal and informal   Levels of usage achieved through word choice and sentence structures. More informal writing, as in a let-

gl / tm

ter to an acquaintance or a personal essay, resembles some speech in its colloquial language, contractions, and short, fairly simple sentences. More formal writing, as in academic papers and business reports, avoids these attributes of speech and tends to rely on longer and more complicated sentences.

format   In a manuscript such as an essay or research paper, the arrangement and spacing of elements on the page. See Appendix A.

fragment   See *sentence fragment.*

freewriting   A technique for generating ideas: in a fixed amount of time (say, fifteen minutes), you write continuously without stopping to reread. See 1e-3.

function word   A word, such as an article, conjunction, or preposition, that serves primarily to clarify the roles of and relations between other words in a sentence: *We chased the goat for an hour but finally caught it.* Contrast *lexical word.*

fused sentence (run-on sentence)   A sentence error in which two main clauses are joined with no punctuation or connecting word between them. See 11c.

> **Fused**   I heard his lecture it was dull.
>
> **Revised**   I heard his lecture; it was dull.

future perfect tense   See *tense.*

future tense   See *tense.*

gender   The classification of nouns or pronouns as masculine (*he, boy, handyman*), feminine (*she, woman, actress*), or neuter (*it, typewriter, dog*).

general and specific   Terms designating the relative number of instances or objects included in a group signified by a word. The following list moves from most **general** (including the most objects) to most **specific** (including the fewest objects): *vehicle, four-wheeled vehicle, automobile, sedan, Ford Taurus, blue Ford Taurus, my sister's blue Ford Taurus named Hank.* See 1g-1 and 31b-2. See also *abstract and concrete.*

general audience   See *audience.*

generalization   An assertion inferred from evidence. See 4f-1. See also *inductive reasoning.*

genitive case   Another term for possessive case. See *case.*

gerund   A verbal that ends in *-ing* and functions as a noun. Gerunds may have subjects, objects, complements, and modifiers: *Working is all right for killing time* (*working* is the subject of the verb *is; killing* is the object of the preposition *for* and takes the object *time*). See 5c-2. See also *phrase* and *verbal.*

grammar   A description of how a language works so that it is meaningful to those who speak and write it.

helping verb (or auxiliary verb)   A verb used with a main verb in a verb phrase: *will give, has been seeing, could depend.* Helping verbs indicate tense and sometimes also indicate voice, person, number, or mood. **Modal auxiliaries** include *can, could,* *may, might, must, ought, shall, should, will,* and *would.* They indicate a necessity, possibility, capability, willingness, or the like: *He can lift 250 pounds. You should write to your grandmother.* See Chapter 7, pages 225–26.

homonyms   Words that are pronounced the same but have different spellings and meanings, such as *heard/herd* and *to/too/two.* See 34a-1.

hyperbole   See *figurative language.*

idiom   An expression that is peculiar to a language and that may not make sense if taken literally: for example, *dark horse, bide your time,* and *by and large.* See 31b-3 for a list of idioms involving prepositions, such as *agree with them* and *agree to the contract.*

illustration or support   Supplying examples or reasons to develop an idea. See 1e-8 and 3c-2.

imperative   See *mood.*

indefinite pronoun   See *pronoun.*

independent clause   See *clause.*

indicative   See *mood.*

indirect object   See *object.*

indirect question   A sentence reporting a question, usually in a subordinate clause, and ending with a period: *Writers wonder if their work must be lonely.* Contrast *direct question.*

indirect quotation (indirect discourse)   See *quotation.*

inductive reasoning   Inferring a generalization from specific evidence. See 4f-1. Compare *deductive reasoning.*

infinitive   A verbal formed from the plain form of the verb plus the **infinitive marker** *to: to swim, to write.* Infinitives and infinitive phrases may function as nouns, adjectives, or adverbs. See 5c-2. See also *phrase* and *verbal.*

infinitive marker   See *infinitive.*

infinitive phrase   See *phrase.*

inflection   The variation in the form of a word that indicates its function in a particular context. See *declension,* the inflection of nouns and pronouns; *conjugation,* the inflection of verbs; and *comparison,* the inflection of adjectives and adverbs.

inflectional suffix   See *suffix.*

informal   See *formal and informal.*

intensifier   A modifier that adds emphasis to the word(s) it modifies: for example, *very slow, so angry.*

intensive pronoun   See *pronoun.*

interjection   A word standing by itself or inserted in a construction to exclaim or command attention: *Hey! Ouch! What the heck did you do that for?*

interpretation   The determination of meaning or significance—for instance, in a work such as a poem or in the literature on some issue such as job discrimination. See 4b-5 and Chapter 35, page 541.

interrogative   Functioning as or involving a question.

interrogative adjective   See *adjective.*

gl / tm

interrogative pronoun   See *pronoun.*

intransitive verb   See *verb.*

introduction   The opening of an essay, a transition for readers between their world and the writer's. The introduction often contains a statement of the writer's thesis. See 3d-1 for suggestions. See also *thesis sentence.*

invention   The discovery and exploration of ideas, usually occurring most intensively in the early stages of the writing process. See 1e for invention techniques.

inversion   A reversal of usual word order in a sentence, as when a verb precedes its subject or an object precedes its verb: *Down swooped the hawk. Our aims we stated clearly.*

irony   The use of words to suggest a meaning different from what the words say literally: *What a happy face!* (said to someone scowling miserably); *With that kind of planning, prices are sure to go down* (written with the expectation that prices will rise). See 4c-4.

irregular verb   A verb that forms its past tense and past participle in some other way than by the addition of *-d* or *-ed* to the plain form: for example, *go, went, gone; give, gave, given.* See 7a for a list of irregular verbs. Contrast *regular verb.*

jargon   In one sense, the specialized language of any group, such as doctors or baseball players. In another sense, jargon is vague, pretentious, wordy, and ultimately unclear writing such as that found in some academic, business, and government publications. See 31c-4.

journal   A personal record of observations, reactions, ideas, and other thoughts. Besides providing a private place to think in writing, a journal can be useful for discovering ideas for essays (1e-1), making notes about reading (4b-1), and keeping track of a research project (35a).

journalist's questions   A set of questions useful for probing a topic to discover ideas about it. See 1e-7.

lexical word   A word, such as a noun, verb, or modifier, that carries part of the meaning of language. Contrast *function word.*

linking verb   A verb that relates a subject to its complement: *Julie is a Democrat. He looks harmless. The boy became a man.* Common linking verbs are the forms of *be;* the verbs relating to the senses, such as *look* and *smell;* and the verbs *become, appear,* and *seem.* See 5a-3.

logical agreement   See *agreement.*

logical fallacies   Errors in reasoning. Some evade the issue of the argument; others oversimplify the argument. See 4d for a checklist and discussion of fallacies.

main clause   See *clause.*

main verb   The part of a verb phrase that carries the principal meaning: *had been walking, could happen, was chilled.* See also *phrase.*

mass noun   See *noun*.

mechanics   The use of capital letters, underlining (italics), abbreviations, numbers, and divided words. See Chapters 26–30.

metaphor   See *figurative language*.

misplaced modifier   A modifier so far from the term it modifies or so close to another term it could modify that its relation to the rest of the sentence is unclear.

> **Misplaced**   The boys played with firecrackers that they bought illegally *in the field.*
>
> **Revised**   The boys played *in the field* with firecrackers that they bought illegally.

A **squinting modifier** could modify the words on either side of it: *The plan we considered seriously worries me.* See 14a–14e.

mixed construction   A sentence containing two or more parts that do not fit together in grammar or in meaning. See 15a and 15b.

mixed metaphor   See *figurative language*.

MLA style   The style of documenting sources recommended by the Modern Language Association and used in many of the arts and humanities, including English. For explanation and examples, see Chapter 37.

modal auxiliary   See *helping verb*.

modifier   Any word or word group that limits or qualifies the meaning of another word or word group. Modifiers include adjectives and adverbs as well as words, phrases, and clauses that act as adjectives and adverbs. See 5c and Chapter 9.

mood   The form of a verb that shows how the speaker views the action. The **indicative mood,** the most common, is used to make statements or ask questions: *The play will be performed Saturday. Did you get us tickets?* The **imperative mood** gives a command: *Please get good seats. Avoid the top balcony.* The **subjunctive mood** expresses a wish, a condition contrary to fact, a recommendation, or a request: *I wish George were coming with us. Did you suggest that he join us?* See 7g.

narration   Recounting a sequence of events, usually in the order of their occurrence. See 1e-8 and 3c-2.

neologism   A word coined recently and not in established use. See 31a-5.

nominal   A noun, a pronoun, or a word or word group used as a noun: *Joan and I talked. The rich owe a debt to the poor* (adjectives acting as subject and object). *Baby-sitting can be exhausting* (gerund acting as subject). *I like to play with children* (infinitive phrase acting as object).

nominative   See *case*.

nonfinite verb   See *verbal*.

nonrestrictive element   A word, phrase, or clause that does not limit the term or construction it refers to and that is not essential

gl / tm

gl / tm

to the meaning of the sentence's main clause. Nonrestrictive elements are usually set off by commas: *The new apartment building, in shades of tan and gray, will house fifty people* (nonrestrictive adjective phrase). *Sleep, which we all need, occupies a third of our lives* (nonrestrictive adjective clause). *His wife, Patricia, is a chemist* (nonrestrictive appositive). See 21c. Contrast *restrictive element.*

nonstandard   Words and grammatical forms not conforming to standard English. See 31a-4.

noun   A word that names a person, place, thing, quality, or idea: *Maggie, Alabama, clarinet, satisfaction, socialism.* Nouns normally form the possessive case by adding *-'s* (*Maggie's*) and the plural by adding *-s* or *-es* (*clarinets, messes*), although there are exceptions (*men, women, children*). **Common nouns** refer to general classes: *book, government, music.* **Proper nouns** name specific people or places: *Susan, Athens, Candlestick Park.* **Collective nouns** name groups: *team, class, family.* **Count nouns** name things that can be counted: *ounce, camera, person.* **Mass nouns** name things that are not normally counted: *milk, music, information.* See 5a-2.

noun clause   See *clause.*

number   The form of a noun, pronoun, demonstrative adjective, or verb that indicates whether it is singular or plural: *woman, women; I, we; this, these; runs, run.* See Chapter 8.

object   A noun, a pronoun, or a word or word group acting as a noun that receives the action of or is influenced by a transitive verb, a verbal, or a preposition.

- A **direct object** receives the action of a verb or verbal and frequently follows it in a sentence: *We sat watching the stars. Emily caught whatever it was you had.*
- An **indirect object** tells for or to whom or what something is done: *I lent Stan my car. Reiner bought us all champagne.*
- An **object of a preposition** usually follows a preposition and is linked by it to the rest of the sentence: *They are going to New Orleans for the jazz festival.*

See 5a-3 and 5c-1.

object complement   See *complement.*

objective   See *case.*

opinion   A conclusion based on facts; an arguable, potentially changeable assertion. Assertions of opinion form the backbone of any argument. See 4c-1.

ordinal number   The type of number that shows order: *first, eleventh, twenty-fifth.* Contrast *cardinal number* (such as *one, twenty-five*).

paragraph   Generally, a group of sentences set off by a beginning indention and developing a single idea. That idea is often stated in a **topic sentence.** See Chapter 3.

parallelism Similarity of grammatical form between two or more coordinated elements: *Rising prices and declining incomes left many people in bad debt and worse despair.* See Chapter 17.

paraphrase The restatement of source material in one's own words and sentence structures, useful for borrowing the original author's line of reasoning but not his or her exact words. Paraphrases must always be acknowledged in source citations. See 36b-3 and 36c.

parenthetical citation In the text of a paper, a brief reference, enclosed in parentheses, indicating that material is borrowed and directing the reader to the source of the material. See 37a. See also *citation.*

parenthetical element A word or construction that interrupts a sentence and is not part of its main structure, called *parenthetical* because it could (or does) appear in parentheses: *Childe Hassam (1859–1935) was an American painter and etcher. The book, incidentally, is terrible.* See 21c-3.

participial phrase See *phrase.*

participle A verbal showing continuing or completed action, used as an adjective or part of a verb phrase but never as the main verb of a sentence or clause.

- A **present participle** ends in -*ing: My heart is breaking* (participle as part of verb phrase). *I like to watch the rolling waves* (participle as adjective).

- A **past participle** most commonly ends in -*d, -ed, -n,* or -*en* (*wished, shown, given*) but sometimes changes the spelling of the verb (*sung, done, slept*): *Jeff has broken his own record* (participle as part of verb phrase). *The meeting occurred behind a closed door* (participle as adjective).

See 5c-2. See also *phrase* and *verbal.*

parts of speech The classes into which words are commonly grouped according to their form, function, and meaning: nouns, pronouns, verbs, adjectives, adverbs, conjunctions, prepositions, and interjections. See separate entries for each part of speech. See also 5a to 5d.

passive voice See *voice.*

past participle See *participle.*

past perfect tense See *tense.*

past tense See *tense.*

patterns of development Ways of thinking that can help develop and organize ideas in essays and paragraphs. See 1e-8 and 3c-2.

perfect tenses See *tense.*

periodic sentence A suspenseful sentence in which modifiers precede the main clause, which falls at the end: *Postponing decisions about family while striving to establish themselves in careers, many young adults are falsely accused of shallowness or greed.* See 18a-1. Contrast *cumulative sentence.*

gl / tm

person   The form of a verb or pronoun that indicates whether the subject is speaking, spoken to, or spoken about. In English only personal pronouns and verbs change form to indicate difference in person. In the **first person,** the subject is speaking: *I am* (or *We are*) *planning a party.* In the **second person,** the subject is being spoken to: *Are you coming?* In the **third person,** the subject is being spoken about: *She was* (or *They were*) *going.* See Chapter 8.

personal pronoun   See *pronoun.*

personification   See *figurative language.*

phrase   A group of related words that lacks a subject or a predicate or both and that acts as a single part of speech. There are several common types of phrases:

- An **absolute phrase** consists of a noun or pronoun and usually a participle. It modifies a whole clause or sentence: *Our seats being reserved, we probably should stay.* See 5c-3.
- A **prepositional phrase** consists of a preposition and its object, plus any modifiers. It functions as an adjective, an adverb, or occasionally a noun: *We could come back for the second show* (adverb). See 5c-1.
- A **verb phrase** is a verb form of more than one word that serves as the predicate of a sentence or clause: *He says the movie has started.* See Chapter 7, page 225.
- A **verbal phrase** is formed from a verbal. An **infinitive phrase** consists of an infinitive and its object, plus any modifiers, and it sometimes also includes a subject. It functions as a noun, adjective, or adverb: *I'd hate to go all the way home* (noun). A **participial phrase** consists of a participle and its object, plus any modifiers. It functions as an adjective: *The man collecting tickets says we may not be too late.* A **gerund phrase** consists of a gerund (the *-ing* form of a verb used as a noun) and its object, plus any modifiers, and it sometimes also includes a subject. It functions as a noun. *Missing the beginning is no good, though.* See 5c-2.

plagiarism   The presentation of someone else's ideas or words as if they were one's own. Whether accidental or deliberate, plagiarism is a serious and often punishable offense. See 36c.

plain case   See *case.*

plain form   The dictionary form of a verb: *make, run, swivel.* See also *principal parts.*

planning   See *developing (planning).*

plural   More than one. See *number.*

positive degree   See *comparison.*

possessive   See *case.*

predicate   The part of a sentence other than the subject and its modifiers. A predicate must contain a finite verb and may contain modifiers, objects of the verb, and complements. The **simple**

predicate consists of the verb and its helping verbs: *A wiser person would have made a different decision.* The **complete predicate** includes the simple predicate and any modifiers, objects, and complements: *A wiser person would have made a different decision.* See 5a and 5b.

predicate adjective   See *complement.*

predicate noun (predicate nominative)   See *complement.*

prefix   A letter or group of letters (such as *sub-, in-, dis-, pre-*) that can be added at the beginning of a root or word to create a new word: *sub- + marine = submarine; dis- + grace = disgrace.* See 33b-2. Contrast *suffix.*

premise   Generally, an assertion or assumption basic to an argument. In a deductive syllogism, one premise applied to another leads logically to a conclusion. See 4f-1. See also *syllogism.*

preposition   A word that links a noun, a pronoun, or a word or word group acting as a noun (the object of the preposition) to the rest of a sentence: *If Tim doesn't hear from that plumber by four, he'll call someone else before dinner.* Common prepositions include those in the preceding example as well as *about, after, beside, between, for, in,* and *to.* See 5c-1 for a fuller list. See also *object* and *phrase.*

prepositional phrase   See *phrase.*

present participle   See *participle.*

present perfect tense   See *tense.*

present tense   See *tense.*

pretentious writing   Writing that is more elaborate than the writing situation requires, usually full of fancy phrases and showy words. See 31a-7.

primary source   Firsthand information, such as an eyewitness account of events; a diary, speech, or other historical document; a work of literature or art; a report of a survey or experiment; and one's own interview, observation, or correspondence. See 35c. Contrast *secondary source.*

principal clause   A main or independent clause. See *clause.*

principal parts   The three forms of a verb from which its various tenses are formed: the **plain form** (*stop, go*); the **past tense** (*stopped, went*); and the **past participle** (*stopped, gone*). See Chapter 7. See also *participle* and *tense.*

process analysis   The explanation of how something works or how to do something. See 1e-8 and 3c-2.

progressive tense   See *tense.*

pronoun   A word used in place of a noun or noun phrase (its antecedent). There are eight types of pronouns: **Personal pronouns** (*I, you, he, she, it, we, they*): *They want you to come with us.* **Reflexive pronouns** (*myself, themselves*): *Can't you help yourselves?* **Intensive pronouns** (*myself, themselves*): *She herself said so.* **Interrogative pronouns** (*who, which, what*): *What was that?* **Relative pronouns** (*who, which, that*): *The noise that* *scared you was made by the boy who lives next door.* **Demonstrative pronouns** (*this, that, these, those*): *These are fresher than those.* **Indefinite pronouns** (*each, one, anybody, all*): *One would think somebody must have seen it.* **Reciprocal pronouns** (*each other, one another*): *I hope we'll see each other again.* See 5a-2 and Chapter 6.

proofreading   Reading and correcting a final draft for misspellings, typographical errors, and other mistakes. See 2d.

proper adjective   See *adjective.*

proper noun   See *noun.*

purpose   For a writer, the chief reason for communicating something about a topic to a particular audience. See 1c.

quotation   Repetition of what someone has written or spoken. In **direct quotation (direct discourse),** the person's words are duplicated exactly and enclosed in quotation marks: *Polonius told his son, Laertes, "Neither a borrower nor a lender be."* An **indirect quotation (indirect discourse)** reports what someone said or wrote but not in the exact words and not in quotation marks: *Polonius advised his son, Laertes, not to borrow or lend.* See Chapter 24.

rational appeal   See *appeals.*

reciprocal pronoun   See *pronoun.*

reflexive pronoun   See *pronoun.*

regional language   Expressions common to the people in a particular geographical area. See 31a-3.

regular verb   A verb that forms its past tense and past participle by adding *-d* or *-ed* to the plain form: *love, loved, loved; open, opened, opened.* See 7a. Contrast *irregular verb.*

relative clause   A subordinate clause beginning with a relative pronoun such as *who* or *that* and functioning as an adjective. See *clause.*

relative pronoun   See *pronoun.*

restrictive element   A word, phrase, or clause that is essential to the meaning of a sentence because it limits the thing it refers to. Restrictive elements are not set off by commas: *The keys to the car are on the table. That man who called about the apartment said he'd try again tonight.* See 21c. Contrast *nonrestrictive element.*

revising   The stage of the writing process in which one considers and improves the meaning and underlying structure of a draft. See 2b. Compare *developing (planning)* and *drafting.*

rhetoric   The principles for finding and arranging ideas and for using language in speech or writing so as to achieve the writer's purpose in addressing his or her audience.

rhetorical question   A question asked for effect, with no answer expected. The person asking the question either intends to provide the answer or assumes it is obvious: *If we let one factory pollute the river, what does that say to other factories that want to dump wastes there?*

run-on sentence   See *fused sentence.*

secondary source   A source reporting or analyzing information in other sources, such as a critic's view of a work of art or a sociologist's summary of others' studies. See 35c. Contrast *primary source.*

second person   See *person.*

sentence   A complete unit of thought, consisting of at least a subject and a predicate that are not introduced by a subordinating word. Sentences can be classed on the basis of their structure in one of four ways. A **simple sentence** contains one main clause: *I'm leaving.* A **compound sentence** contains at least two main clauses: *I'd like to stay, but I'm leaving.* A **complex sentence** contains one main clause and at least one subordinate clause: *If you let me go now, you'll be sorry.* A **compound-complex sentence** contains at least two main clauses and at least one subordinate clause: *I'm leaving because you want me to, but I'd rather stay.* See *clause* and 5f.

sentence fragment   A sentence error in which a group of words is set off as a sentence even though it begins with a subordinating word or lacks a subject or a predicate or both. See Chapter 10.

Fragment	She wasn't in shape for the race. *Which she had hoped to win.* [*Which,* a relative pronoun, makes the italicized clause subordinate.]
Revised	She wasn't in shape for the race, which she had hoped to win.
Fragment	He could not light a fire. *And thus could not warm the room.* [The italicized word group lacks a subject.]
Revised	He could not light a fire. Thus *he* could not warm the room.

sentence modifier   An adverb or a word or word group acting as an adverb that modifies the idea of the whole sentence in which it appears rather than any specific word: *In fact, people will always complain.* See 21b.

sexist language   Language expressing narrow ideas about men's and women's roles, positions, capabilities, or value. See 31a-8.

simile   See *figurative language.*

simple predicate   See *predicate.*

simple sentence   See *sentence.*

simple subject   See *subject.*

simple tense   See *tense.*

singular   One. See *number.*

slang   Expressions used by the members of a group to create bonds and sometimes exclude others. Most slang is too vague, short-lived, and narrowly understood to be used in any but very informal writing. See 31a-1.

gl / tm

source A place where information or ideas may be found: book, article, work of art, television program, and so on.

spatial organization In a description of a person, place, or thing, the arrangement of details as they would be scanned by a viewer—for instance, from top to bottom or near to far. See 1g-3 and 3b-1.

specific See *general and specific*.

split infinitive The often awkward interruption of an infinitive and its marker *to* by an adverb: *Management decided to immediately introduce the new product.* See 14e. See also *infinitive*.

squinting modifier See *misplaced modifier*.

standard English The English used and expected by educated writers and readers in colleges and universities, businesses, and professions. See 31a.

subject In grammar, the noun, or word or word group acting as a noun, that performs the action expressed in the predicate of a sentence or clause. The **simple subject** consists of the noun alone: *The quick brown fox jumps over the lazy dog.* The **complete subject** includes the simple subject and its modifiers: *The quick brown fox jumps over the lazy dog.* See 5a.

subject complement See *complement*.

subjective See *case*.

subjunctive See *mood*.

subordinate clause See *clause*.

subordinating conjunction (subordinator) See *conjunction*.

subordination The use of grammatical constructions to make one element in a sentence dependent on rather than equal to another and thus to convey the writer's sense that the dependent element is less important to the whole: *Although I left six messages for him, the doctor failed to call me back.* See 16b. Contrast *coordination*.

substantive A word or word group used as a noun.

suffix A **derivational suffix** is a letter or group of letters that can be added to the end of a root word to make a new word, often a different part of speech: *child, childish; shrewd, shrewdly; visual, visualize.* See also 33b-3. **Inflectional suffixes** adapt words to different grammatical relations: *boy, boys; fast, faster; tack, tacked.* See also 5a and 5b.

summary A condensation and restatement of source material in one's own words and sentence structures, useful for presenting the gist of the original author's idea but not his or her line of reasoning or evidence. Summaries must always be acknowledged in source citations. See 36b-2 and 36c. Summarizing material can also help one understand it. See 4b-4.

superlative See *comparison*.

syllogism A form of deductive reasoning in which two premises stating generalizations or assumptions together lead to a conclusion. *Premise:* Hot stoves can burn me. *Premise:* This stove is hot.

Conclusion: This stove can burn me. See 4f-1. See also *deductive reasoning.*

synonyms Words with approximately but not exactly the same meanings, such as *snicker, giggle,* and *chortle.* See 31b-1.

syntax In sentences, the grammatical relations among words and the ways those relations are indicated.

synthesis Drawing connections among the elements within a work (such as the images in a poem) or among entire works (entire poems). See 4b-5.

tag question A question attached to the end of a statement and consisting of a pronoun, a helping verb, and sometimes the word *not: It isn't raining, is it? It is sunny, isn't it?*

tense The form of a verb that expresses the time of its action, usually indicated by the verb's inflection and by helping verbs.

- The **simple tenses** are the **present** (*I race, you go*); the **past** (*I raced, you went*); and the **future,** formed with the helping verb *will* (*I will race, you will go*).
- The **perfect tenses,** formed with the helping verbs *have* and *had,* indicate completed action. They are the **present perfect** (*I have raced, you have gone*); the **past perfect** (*I had raced, you had gone*); and the **future perfect** (*I will have raced, you will have gone*).
- The **progressive tenses,** formed with the helping verb *be* plus the present participle, indicate continuing action. They include the **present progressive** (*I am racing, you are going*); the **past progressive** (*I was racing, you were going*); and the **future progressive** (*I will be racing, you will be going*).

See Chapter 7, pages 232–35.

thesis The central, controlling idea of an essay, to which all assertions and details relate. See 1f.

thesis sentence A sentence that asserts the central, controlling idea of an essay, conveying the writer's purpose and attitude and perhaps previewing the essay's organization. See 1f.

third person See *person.*

tone The sense of a writer's attitudes toward self, subject, and readers revealed by words and sentence structures as well as by content. See 1d-3 and 4c-4.

topic The subject of an essay, narrowed so that it is appropriately specific for the prescribed purpose, length, and deadline. See 1b-3.

topic sentence See *paragraph.*

transitional expression A word or phrase, such as *thus* or *similarly,* that links sentences and shows the relations between them. See 3b-6, page 89, for a list.

transitive verb See *verb.*

trite expressions (clichés) Stale expressions that dull writing and suggest that the writer is careless or lazy. See 31b-5.

gl / tm

gl / tm

unity   The quality of an effective essay or paragraph in which all parts relate to the central idea and to each other. See 1g-4 and 3a.

variety   Among connected sentences, changes in length, structure, and word order that help readers see the importance and complexity of ideas. See Chapter 19.

verb   A word or group of words indicating the action or state of being of a subject. A **transitive verb** conveys action that has an object: *He shot the sheriff.* An **intransitive verb** does not have an object: *The sheriff died.* A **linking verb** connects the subject and a complement that describes or renames the subject: *The sheriff was brave.* Some verbs may be transitive, intransitive, or linking, depending on their use in a sentence: *The dog smelled the bone* (transitive). *The dog smelled* (intransitive). *The dog smelled bad* (linking).

The inflection of a verb and the use of helping verbs with it indicate its tense, mood, voice, number, and sometimes person. See separate listings for each aspect. See also Chapter 7.

verbal (nonfinite verb)   A verb form used as a noun (*Swimming is good exercise*), an adjective (*Blocked passes don't make touchdowns*), or an adverb (*We were prepared to run*). A verbal can never function as the main verb in a sentence (contrast *finite verb*). Verbals may have subjects, objects, complements, and modifiers (see *phrase*). See 5c-2. See also specific kinds of verbals: *participle, gerund,* and *infinitive.*

verbal phrase   See *phrase.*

verb phrase   See *phrase.*

voice   The active or passive aspect of a transitive verb. In the **active voice** the subject is the agent of the verb's action: *We all made the decision.* In the **passive voice** the subject receives the verb's action: *The decision was made by all of us.* See Chapter 7, pages 242–44.

word order   The arrangement of the words in a sentence, which plays a large part in determining the grammatical relation among words in English.

writing process   The mental and physical activities that go into producing a finished piece of writing. The overlapping stages of the process—developing or planning, drafting, and revising—differ for different writers and even for the same writer in different writing situations. See Chapters 1–2.

writing situation   The unique combination of writer, subject, and audience that defines an assignment and helps direct the writer's choices. See 1a.

(continued from page iv)

Arthur L. Campa. From "Anglo vs. Chicano: Why?" *Western Review,* 1972. Reprinted by permission of Mrs. Arthur L. Campa.

Bruce Catton. From "Grant and Lee: A Study in Contrasts." Copyright © 1956 United States Capitol Historical Society. All rights reserved. Reprinted with permission.

David L. Chandler. From "Air Bags—Life-Saving and Unavailable," *The Boston Globe,* 20 March 1988. Reprinted courtesy of The Boston Globe.

Arthur C. Clarke. Excerpt from *The Star of the Magi,* copyright © 1972 by Arthur C. Clarke. Reprinted by permission of the author and the author's agent, Scott Meredith Literary Agency, Inc., 845 Third Avenue, New York, NY 10022.

Rosalind Coward. Excerpt from "Our Song." From *Female Desires* by Rosalind Coward. Copyright © 1985 by Rosalind Coward. Reprinted by permission of Grove Weidenfeld.

Emily Dickinson. Poem #781. Reprinted by permission of the publishers and the Trustees of Amherst College from *The Poems of Emily Dickinson,* Thomas H. Johnson, ed., Cambridge, Mass.: The Belknap Press of Harvard University Press, Copyright © 1951, 1955, 1979, 1983 by the President and Fellows of Harvard College.

Joan Didion. Excerpt from "Los Angeles Notebook" from *Slouching Towards Bethlehem* by Joan Didion. Copyright © 1967, 1968 by Joan Didion. Reprinted by permission of Farrar, Straus and Giroux, Inc., and The Wallace Agency.

Annie Dillard. Excerpt from "Sojourner" from *Teaching a Stone to Talk* by Annie Dillard. Copyright © 1982 by Annie Dillard. Reprinted by permission of HarperCollins Publishers and Blanche C. Gregory, Inc.

Peter F. Drucker. From "How Best to Protect the Environment," *Harper's* Magazine, January 1972. Copyright © 1971 by Minneapolis Star and Tribune Co., Inc. Reprinted by permission of the author.

Freeman J. Dyson. Excerpt from *Disturbing the Universe* by Freeman J. Dyson. Copyright © 1979 by Freeman J. Dyson. Reprinted by permission of HarperCollins Publishers.

Peter Eisinger et al. From *American Politics: The People and the Polity.* Copyright © 1978 by Little, Brown and Company. Reprinted by permission.

Ralph Ellison. From "Harlem Is Nowhere" in *Shadow and Act.* Copyright © 1953, 1964 by Ralph Ellison. Reprinted by permission of Random House, Inc.

Joseph Epstein. From *Ambition: The Secret Passion.* Copyright © 1980 by Joseph Epstein. Used by permission of the publisher, Dutton, an imprint of New American Library, a division of Penguin Books USA Inc. and Georges Borchardt, Inc., for the author.

Peter Farb. From *Word Play: What Happens When People Talk.* Copyright © 1973 by Peter Farb. Reprinted by permission of Alfred A. Knopf, Inc., and Brandt & Brandt.

James Fenton. Excerpt from "The Philippine Election," *Granta,* 18, 1986. Reprinted by permission of Sterling Lord Literistic, Inc. Copyright © 1986 by James Fenton.

Robert Frost. Two lines from "The Death of the Hired Man" (Copyright 1930, 1939, © 1969 by Holt, Rinehart and Winston. Copyright © 1958 by Robert Frost. Copyright © 1967 by Lesley Frost Ballentine) and two lines from "Stopping by Woods on a Snowy Evening" (Copyright 1923, © 1969 by Holt, Rinehart and Winston. Copyright 1951 by Robert Frost). From *The Poetry of Robert Frost* edited by Edward Connery Lathem. Reprinted by permission of Henry Holt and Company, Inc., the estate of Robert Frost, and Jonathan Cape Ltd.

Willard Gaylin. Excerpt from *Feelings: Our Vital Signs* by Willard Gaylin. Copyright © 1979 by Willard Gaylin. Reprinted by permission of HarperCollins Publishers and Georges Borchardt, Inc., for the author.

Donald Hall. From *String Too Short to Be Saved.* Copyright © 1979, 1961, 1960 by Donald Hall. Reprinted by permission of David R. Godine, Publisher, Boston.

E. T. Hall. Excerpt from *The Hidden Dimension.* Copyright © 1966 by Edward T. Hall. Reprinted by permission of Doubleday, a division of Bantam Doubleday Dell, Inc., and Blassingame, McCauley & Wood.

Gilbert Highet. From *Poets in a Landscape* by Gilbert Highet. Reprinted by permission of Curtis Brown, Ltd. Copyright © 1957 Gilbert Highet.

Emmet John Hughes. From "The Presidency vs. Jimmy Carter," *Fortune,* 4 December 1978. Reprinted by permission.

Mac Jeffery. From "Does Rx Spell Rip-off?" *The New York Times,* 7 August 1978. Copyright © 1978 by The New York Times Company. Reprinted by permission.

Pauline Kael. Excerpt from "Silliness." From *State of the Art* by Pauline Kael. Copyright © 1983, 1984, 1985 by Pauline Kael. Originally published in *The New Yorker.* Used by permission of the publisher, Dutton, an imprint of New American Library, a division of Penguin Books USA Inc.

Charles Kuralt. From *Dateline America*. Text copyright © 1979 by CBS, Inc. Reprinted by permission of Harcourt Brace Jovanovich, Inc.

Lawrence A. Mayer. From "The Confounding Enemy of Sleep," *Fortune,* June 1974. Reprinted by permission.

Jan Morris. From *Destinations: Essays from Rolling Stone* by Jan Morris. Copyright © 1980 by Rolling Stone Press and Jan Morris. Reprinted by permission of Oxford University Press, Inc.

Herbert Muschamp. Excerpt from *Man About Town,* copyright © 1988. Reprinted by permission of The MIT Press.

Gloria Naylor. Excerpt from "Sexual Equality in a TV Fantasy," *The New York Times,* 30 January 1986. Reprinted by permission of Sterling Lord Literistic, Inc. Copyright © 1986 by Gloria Naylor.

Newsweek. From "The New Immigrants," 7 July 1980. Copyright © 1980, by Newsweek, Inc. All rights reserved. Reprinted by permission.

Susan Orlean. Excerpt from *Saturday Night in America.* Copyright © 1990 by Susan Orlean. Reprinted by permission of Alfred A. Knopf, Inc.

Robert Ornstein. Excerpt from "A Letter from the Director," *Human Nature,* August 1978. Copyright © 1978 by Human Nature, Inc. Reprinted by permission of the publisher.

William G. Ouchi. Excerpt from *Theory Z: How American Business Can Meet the Japanese Challenge,* copyright © 1981 by Addison-Wesley Publishing Company, Inc.

Francine Prose. From "Therapy Clichés," *The New York Times,* 9 May 1985. Copyright © 1985 by The New York Times Company. Reprinted by permission.

Readers' Guide to Periodical Literature. Listings under "Women Executives" from Vol. 90, #8, August 1990. Copyright © 1990 by The H. W. Wilson Company. Reprinted by permission.

Phyllis Rose. Excerpt from "On Shopping." From *Never Say Goodbye* by Phyllis Rose. Copyright © 1991 by Phyllis Rose. Reprinted by permission of Doubleday, a division of Bantam Doubleday Dell Publishing Group, Inc.

Ruth Rosen. Excerpt from "Search for Yesterday." From *Watching Television* edited by Todd Gitlin. Copyright © 1986 by Ruth Rosen. Reprinted by permission of Pantheon Books, a division of Random House, Inc.

Social Sciences Index. Listings under "Women Executives" from Vol. 17, #2, September 1990. Copyright © 1990 by The H. W. Wilson Company. Reprinted by permission.

Susan Tallman. Excerpt from "Money," *Arts,* January 1990. Reprinted by permission of the publisher and the author.

Barbara Tuchman. From "The Decline of Quality," *The New York Times,* 2 November 1980. Copyright © 1980 The New York Times Company. Reprinted by permission.

Stewart L. Udall. From *The Quiet Crisis.* Copyright © 1963 by Stewart L. Udall. Reprinted by permission of Holt, Rinehart and Winston, Publishers.

Michael Walzer. From "The Community," *The New Republic,* 1 March 1982. Reprinted by permission of The New Republic. © 1982 The New Republic, Inc.

Judith Wax. From *Starting in the Middle.* Copyright © 1979 by Judith Wax. Reprinted by permission of Henry Holt and Company.

Bayard Webster. From "Should Vivisection Be Abolished?" *The New York Times,* 27 September 1983. Copyright © 1983 by The New York Times Company. Reprinted by permission.

Webster's Ninth New Collegiate Dictionary. Entry for *reckon.* By permission. From *Webster's Ninth New Collegiate Dictionary,* © 1990 by Merriam-Webster Inc., publisher of the Merriam Webster Dictionaries.

Diane White. Excerpt from "At Large" column, *The Boston Globe,* 27 January 1979. Reprinted courtesy of The Boston Globe.

E. B. White. From *The Wild Flag* (Houghton Mifflin). Copyright © 1943, 1971 by E. B. White. Originally in *The New Yorker.* Reprinted by permission.

Kenneth Woodward. From "Life After Death?" *Newsweek,* 12 July 1976. Copyright © 1976 by Newsweek, Inc. All rights reserved. Reprinted by permission.

Richard Wright. Excerpt from *Black Boy* by Richard Wright. Copyright © 1937, 1942, 1944, 1945 by Richard Wright. Reprinted by permission of HarperCollins Publishers and the author's estate.

William Zinsser. From *The Lunacy Boom* by William Zinsser. Copyright © 1966, 1968, 1969, 1970 by William Zinsser. Reprinted by permission.

Index

A

a, an
  capitalization in titles, 453
  uses of, 173, 748–49, 768
Abbreviations, 463–67
  a vs. *an* with, 748–49
  for academic degrees, 463
  common Latin, 465
  for courses of instruction, 466
  for dates and numbers, 464–65
  for days, months, and holidays, 466
  for frequently used terms, 464
  for geographical names, 466
  Inc., Bros., Co., and *&,* 465–67
  misused, 466
  for names of people, 464, 466
  in nontechnical writing, 463–67
  for organizations, 377, 464
  for parts of books, 466
  periods with, 377, 464
  in source citations, 629–30
  for titles with names, 463
  for units of measurement, 466
Absolute phrases
  defined, 192, 766
  punctuation of, 192, 393–94
  subordination with, 335
Absolute statement, 147
Abstract and concrete words
  in argument, 135–36

defined, 487, 766
and exactness, 486–88
Abstracts
  in academic papers, 691, 711
  on computerized databases, 560
  footnotes or endnotes for, 626
  list of, 555
  MLA works-cited form for, 615–16
  as research sources, 555
Academic terms or years, capitalization
  of, 457
Academic writing, 675–717
  appropriate role and tone for,
    15–16
  audience for, 17
  goals and requirements of, 676–78
  in humanities, 678–89
  in natural and applied sciences,
    710–17
  in social sciences, 689–709
accept, except, 523, 749
accordingly, as conjunctive adverb,
    203
according to, accords with, 489
accuse of, 489
Acknowledgment of sources
  necessity for, 578–83
  using APA style, 697–703
  using CBE style, 713–15
  using footnotes or endnotes, 621–29
  using MLA style, 598–621

Index

Index

Index

Index

Index